INDIAN FINANCIAL SYSTEM

(Useful for MBA (Finance), M.Com., MFA, MFC, PGDFM, PGDBM, CFA and Civil Services)

Dr. G. Ramesh Babu
Lecturer in Commerce,
S.S.R. Jyoti College,
Khammam 507 002,
Andhra Pradesh.
E-mail: ramesh_238712@Rediffmail.com

Himalaya Publishing House
ISO 9001:2015 CERTIFIED

First Edition : 2005
Reprint : 2010, 2012
Reprint : 2013, 2021
Reprint : 2025

Published by : Mrs. Meena Pandey
for **HIMALAYA PUBLISHING HOUSE PVT. LTD.,**
"Ramdoot", Dr. Bhalerao Marg, Girgaon, Mumbai - 400 004.
Phone: 022-23860170, 23863863; **Fax:** 022-23877178
E-mail: himpub@bharatmail.co.in; **Website:** www.himpub.com

Branch Offices :

New Delhi : "Pooja Apartments", 4-B, Murari Lal Street, Ansari Road, Darya Ganj, New Delhi - 110 002. Phone: 011-23270392, 23278631; Fax: 011-23256286

Nagpur : Kundanlal Chandak Industrial Estate, Ghat Road, Nagpur - 440 018. Phone: 0712-2721215, 2721216

Bengaluru : Plot No. 91-33, 2nd Main Road, Seshadripuram, Behind Nataraja Theatre, Bengaluru - 560 020. Phone: 080-41138821; Mobile: 09379847017, 09379847005

Hyderabad : No. 3-4-184, Lingampally, Besides Raghavendra Swamy Matham, Kachiguda, Hyderabad - 500 027. Phone: 040-27560041, 27550139

Chennai : No. 34/44, Motilal Street, T. Nagar, Chennai - 600 017. Mobile: 09380460419

Pune : "Laksha" Apartment, First Floor, No. 527, Mehunpura, Shaniwarpeth (Near Prabhat Theatre), Pune - 411 030. Phone: 020-24496323, 24496333; Mobile: 09370579333

Cuttack : Plot No 5F-755/4, Sector-9, CDA Market Nagar, Cuttack - 753 014, Odisha. Mobile: 09338746007

Kolkata : 3, S.M. Bose Road, Near Gate No. 5, Agarpara Railway Station, North 24 Parganas, West Bengal - 700109. Mobile: 09674536325

Printed by : M/s. Charita Impressions, Hyderabad on behalf of HPH.

Dedicated to

"Lord Balaji"

The Most Powerful Man in the Universe

My Wife Vani, Son Harish and Daughter Gowthami

PREFACE

Indian Financial System is a subject of growing importance and interest. In this book an attempt is made to give a comprehensive coverage of the Indian Financial System. This book has been written as per the Syllabus prescribed for the MBA (Finance), M.Com., CS, CA, MFA, MFM, MFC, PGDBF, CFA and PGDBM etc. I am confident that this book will greatly help the students, faculty members, Executives in Finance area, Stock brokers and Fund managers of mutual funds as well as those individuals who desire to update their knowledge on Finance area.

Since the book is a synthesis, I am indebted to all the authors who have contributed to the world of Finance Area. I hope that I have interpreted their views correctly. I am also indebted to my seniors and professionals and to countless students — would be impossible to list them all. Anyhow for evincing personal interest, undertaking a project of this magnitude and making invaluable suggestions from time to time, I would like to thank all those who had directly and indirectly encouraged and helped in completion of this book. I received invaluable suggestions from many luminaries. Though it is difficult to thank all of them individually, it is my pleasure to express grateful thanks to Shri K. Ram Mohan, President, Jyothi Education Society, Dr. D. Ramachandra Bose, Principal, SSR Jyothi College and Shri P. Raghurama Rao, Treasurer, Jyothi Education Society, Khammam. I am also thankful to my Prof. P. Madhusadana Rao, Prof. A. Shankaraiah, Prof. V. Gangadhar, Prof. G. Narasimha Murthy, Prof. Sudarshan, Prof. S. Raviprakash, Prof. Rajeshwar Rao, Prof. Krishna Reddy, whose elderly advice has been of immense use to me. I must also place on record my sincere thanks to my teachers, who taught alphabets in Commerce, Shri P.V. Anjaneyulu, Shri G. Satyanarayana, Shri K.V. Kameswar Rao and Dr. K. Srinivas Rao. I also record my gratitude to Prof. Sethu, Dean, UTI Institute of Capital Market, Navi Mumbai, for his help and encouragement.

I owe my gratitude to Shri D.P. Pandey of Himalaya Publishing House for giving his personal attention in expediting printing of this book.

Dr. G. RAMESH BABU

E-mail: ramesh_238712@Rediff.mail.com

CONTENTS

INDEX UNIT-I

INDIAN FINANCIAL SYSTEM

Introduction – An Overview of Indian Financial System – First Phase – Second Phase – Financial Development – Equity Culture – Secondary Markets – Major Reforms – Policy Reforms – Banking Reforms – Capital Market Reforms – Primary Market Reforms – Secondary Market Reforms – Government securities market reforms – Global Financial Market Reforms – Monetary policy 2002-03. Monetary Measures – CRR – Bank Rate – SLR – RRB Interest Rate Policy. – Interest Rate Flexibility Prime Lending Rate and Spreads – Interest Rate on Export Credit – Deemed Exports – Abolition of minimum lending rates for cooperative banks. Liberalization of Investment norms under FCNR (B) Deposits – Credit Delivery Mechanism – Priority Sector Lending – Credit Facilities for SSIs – Housing Finance – Kisan Credit Cards – Rural Infrastructure Development Fund – Micro Credit – Money Market – Reliance on Call Money – Collateral Lending Facility – Certificate of Deposits – Government Securities – Review of Recent Developments – Uniform Price Auction – Negotiable Dealing System – Government Securities Act – Retaining Govt. Securities Through Non-Competitive Bidding. Treasury Bills – Government Stocks – Floating Rate Bonds – Calendar for Dated Securities – Separate Trading for Registered and Interest and Principle of Securities – Satellite Dealer System – Issue of Long-Term bonds for Insurance companies – Automatic debit mechanism – Urban Cooperative Banks – New Apex Supervisory Body – Working Group on Asset Liability Management – Supervisory Rating System for Urban Co-op. Banks – Supervision and Monitoring –Present status of prudential measures – Technology Upgradation – Net Working Branches – Extension of Electronic Fund Transfer – Real Time Gross Settlement System – Indian Financial System – Privatization – Reorganization – Investor Protection.

Introduction

The financial system is concerned about money, credit and finance. Money is used as a medium of exchange and as a standard of value. The economic development became possible with the help of money. ***Credit*** is a sum of money and it should return with interest *Finance* is the basic foundation to all kinds of economic activities. The business needs money to make more money. Finance is the provision of money at the time it is wanted. It is a monetary resource. It comprises debt and ownership funds of the state, company or person. Therefore money credit and finance are the lifeblood of the economic system. The importance of finance depends upon the desired nature of development. There are *three* different schools of thoughts regarding finance. According to one thought, the finance is not important at all. The second view regarding finance is that, it is the most important factor in economic development. The third argument takes a cautionary view that men, material and money are important inputs in production aspects. A well developed financial system can influence the economic development. The economic development can be accelerated through three factors, (a) Technical progress (b) Capital formation (c) Time. It has been argued by economists that the development of a nation depends upon the Technical knowledge and not on labour and capital. The technology makes more perfect to go ahead in the process of economic development. The technology is the barometer to measure the efficiency of a country. Capital formation is the second component of the economic development. The development depends upon the rate of capital formation, the relationship between capital and output is very strong. The capital formation depends upon the quantum of amount of finance available at that time the numerical history of India's progression is presented below.[1]

THE INDIAN ECONOMY 1950-2001

Sl.No.	*Particulars*	*1950-51*	*1960-61*	*1970-71*	*1980-81*	*1990-91*	*2000*
1.	Gross Capital formation	8.7%	14.4%	15.4%	20.3%	26.3%	23%
2.	Gross domestic savings	8.9%	11.6%	14.6%	18.9%	23.1%	22%
3.	Forex Reserves ($ millions)	2161	637	975	6823	5834	350%

Nature and Role of Financial System

Savings and investment processes influence the economic development. The financial system has the scale and structure effect on savings and investment. Savings are the excess of income over expenditure for economic unit. They are obtaining from present consumption for a future use. They may also come from households. The savings will be made by the people for future needs, precautionary measures, leading to a rise in the standard of living. The savings and investments have interrelations to the financial system. Growth is the important aspect to a nation. The economic performance is reflected in the growth of income. Growth leads to a rise in output and incomes. If the economy develops, the production of goods and services may increase. This situation may lead to a rise in the consumption and the standard of living of people. Development means a rise in income levels and qualitative improvement in the standard of the living of the people. Development also includes growth plus socio-economic changes. The development of any nation will depend upon the ***financial architecture***. The increase in investment in capital goods leads to capital formation. The rise in capital formation results in a rise in output. In India the savings come mainly from household sector. The savings from middle class families dominate, the total savings of the country. The foreign sector contributes to net savings due to a larger inflow of funds.

The savings rate depends on the structure of the economy. The economy is dominated by the agriculture sector. It generates more employment opportunities with lower levels of income. The savings potential of this sector is very low. The growth process leads to shifts in the structure of the economy.

The role of the financial system is to promote savings and investment in the economy. It has an vital role to play in the productive process and in the mobilization of savings and their distribution among the various productive activities.

Savings are the excess of current expenditure over income. The domestic savings has been categorised into three sectors, ***households, Government and private sector.***

The savings from household sector dominates the domestic savings component. The savings will be in the form of currency, bank deposits, non bank deposits, life insurance funds, provident funds pension funds, shares, debentures, bonds, Units and trade debt. All of these ***currency and deposits*** are voluntary transactions and precautionary measures. The savings in the household sector are mobilised directly in the form of units, premium, provident fund, and pension fund. These are the contractual forms of savings.

1. Business India, Anniversary Issue, 2002, p. 27.

Financial Activity deals with the production, distribution and consumption of goods and services. The financial system will provide inputs to productive activity. Financial sector provides inputs in the form of cash credit and assets in financial for production activities.

The function of a financial system is to establish a bridge between the savers and investors. It helps in mobilization of savings to materialise investment ideas into realities. It helps to increase the output towards the existing production frontier. The growth of banking habit helps to activise saving and undertake fresh saving. The financial system encourages investment activity by reducing the cost of finance and risk.

It helps to make investment decisions regarding projects by sponsoring, encouraging, export project appraisal, feasibility studies, monitoring and execution of the projects.

The society for Capital Market Research and Development[2] conducted its 3rd household investors survey in 1997. The survey results are presented below.

PERCENTAGE OF HOUSEHOLD SECTORS GROSS FINANCIAL SAVING, ACCOUNTED FOR BY VARIOUS INVESTMENT TYPES 1990-91 TO 1998-99

(a) Shares and Debenture of Private Corporate Sector

Year	*% of financial savings*
1990-91	4.1
1991-92	6.0
1992-93	8.4
1993-94	7.5
1994-95	8.0
1995-96	6.7
1996-97	3.6
1997-98	1.6
1998-99	1.5

(b) UTI and Other Mutual Fund Units

Year	*% of financial savings*
1990-91	9.1
1991-92	16.4
1992-93	8.6
1993-94	5.5
1994-95	3.8
1995-96	0.5
1996-97	2.7
1997-98	0.6
1998-99	1

(c) Small Savings Scheme

Year	*% of financial savings*
1990-91	13.2
1991-92	7.6
1992-93	4.9
1993-94	5.9
1994-95	9.0
1995-96	7.4
1996-97	7.0
1997-98	10.6
1998-99	10.6

(d) Deposits with Commercial Banks

Year	*% of financial savings*
1990-91	27.2
1991-92	21.3
1992-93	33.6
1993-94	27.9
1994-95	35.3
1995-96	26.5
1996-97	25.6
1997-98	38.3
1998-99	30.8

2. "Household Investment Preferences. The Third All India Investor Survey", L.C. Gupta, ***Society for Capital Market Research and Development,*** Delhi Jan. 2002, P.No. 128.

(e) Life Insurance

Year	% of financial saving
1990-91	8.5
1991-92	9.4
1992-93	8.0
1993-94	8.0
1994-95	7.2
1995-96	10.5
1996-97	9.5
1997-98	9.9
1998-99	10

(f) Provident and Pension Fund

Year	% of financial saving
1990-91	18.9
1991-92	18.3
1992-93	18.4
1993-94	16.7
1994-95	14.7
1995-96	18.1
1996-97	19.1
1997-98	20.5
1998-99	22.7

Shareholding Population in India

Year	Shareholders
1980	24,00,000
1985	60,00,000
1990	90,00,000
1997	2,00,00,000

Sources: Households Investment Preference, L.C. Gupta, Society for Capital Market Research and Development Delhi, 2001, P. 121.

The financial system encourages the saving based investments. There are two schools of thoughts in this regard. The first theory was submitted by ***Kalecki and Schumpeter***. They reveal that the financial system plays a positive and catalytic role by creating and providing finance in anticipation of savings. The savings will be invested in a given period of time with independent decision. The investment financed through created credit generate the appropriate level of income. This theory was applied in the first five year plan in India to play in the process of economic development. The investment out of created credit results in prompt income generation. The second school of thought was presented by ***Keynes.*** He argues that the investment and not saving, is the constraint on growth. He further reveals that the investment determines savings. The monetary expansion results in a number of saving and growth promoting forces. The following factors will influence the level of savings.

(a) If the financial resources are deployed, they generate inflation.

(b) If the financial resources are there they influence the demand output and savings.

(c) There will be changes in levels of income due to inflation.

(d) Inflation transfers resources to the government through the taxation.

An Overview of Indian Financial System

The evaluation of Indian financial system has been briefly review over 70 years. The Indian financial system can be studied through ***Three phases.***

(1)	First phase	(prior to 1950)
(2)	Second phase	(1951 to 1990)
(3)	Third phase	(1991 to ....)

First Phase Prior to 1950

The evolution of the various Constituents of the system such as currency and money supply banking system, small savings Insurance funds, stock markets, fixed public deposits, government securities, treasury bill markets and Interest rates. All these aspects have been discussed prior to 1950 presented below.

Currency and Money is the most important element in Indian financial system. The Indian currency had not been standardised during this phase. After silver standard the gold exchange came into the picture. The gold system did not fulfil the other requirements of the method. The gold coins were not much in circulation. The gold system was abolished by England in September 1931. Then paper currency has been introduced in India since the beginning of the ***19th century***. The currency notes were issued by the commercial banks. The use of the currency notes was extremely limited. The government had taken the responsibility of issuing currency notes. The currency circulation have been increased tremendously from ***11 crore*** in 1874 to ***Rs. 1199 crore*** in 1948. Currency dominated the money supply.

Banking System is the another important factor in Indian Financial system. Earlier the indigenous banks dominated the financial system. They financed to trade, industry and commerce. They offered financial services such as fund transfer, collected revenue on behalf of the government and as money changers. The modern banking became effective in 1910. The modern banking business in India was negligible till 1910. The modern banking era was commenced after the establishment of three presidency banks. They are: ***Bank of Bengal 1806, Bank of Bombay 1840 and The Bank of Madras 1846.*** During this period some exchange banks and Indian joint stock banks were set up. The banking sector had not been quite encouraging due to the following reason.

(a) Failure of banks.

(b) Stagnant economic conditions during that period.

(c) Introduction of currency act 1861.

(d) A decline in prices.

The banking system has increased tremendously in the first half of this century. The deposits have increased exponentially. The world wars contributed to raising the level of economic activity. The three presidency banks have been amalgamated to establish the Imperial Bank of India in 1921. It functioned as a quasi-central bank. The money market was not developed until 1935. The RBI was "established in 1935. The Imperial Bank of India had been appointed as an agent to the RBI, where the RBI did not present. The Imperial bank continued to act as an agent for other banks. It involved in discounting. The government bills were taken as collateral security and granted the demand loans. All of these functions have been undertaken by the SBI. The banking system in India in 1950 comprised RBI, IBI, cooperative banks, exchange banks and joint stock banks. Therefore the joint stock banks were further categorised into four kinds according the amount of paid up capital and reserves held by them. They are classified as A-class, B-class, C-class and D-class. But the RBI categorised them as ***Scheduled and Non–scheduled banks.*** The following conclusions emerged with reference to the banking system in India during the first phase.

(a) There was high degree of concentration in the banking business.

(b) The degree of concentration declined after 1935.

(c) The smaller banks have emerged for providing banking facilities in the country.

(d) The big banks have failed to tap the deposits.

The banking sector was unorganised during this phase comparable data on the liabilities and assets of the various groups were not available. There is no organised system in this sector during this phase. The various banks invested in different financial assets and there was no similarity in the portfolio of banks. Therefore the credit deposit ratio was not balanced properly in the banking sector. The portfolio behaviour of the banks have been discussed below.

(1) Deposits are the ***oxygen*** to the commercial banks. But the deposits ratio have been declined significantly during this phase.

(2) Before the first world war, the deposits were high but after the war, the deposits declined significantly.

(3) The major factors for declining the deposits were:

(a) Competition from other investment channels.

(b) Inflation during that period.

(c) Growth of securities market.

(d) Decline in rate of interest on FDRs.

(4) The credit deposit ratio was low.

(5) The raising of cash credit, overdraft and loans during this phase.

(6) The bill financing activities declined sharply during this period.

(7) The call money market was inactive during this period (except at the end of second world war).

(8) Their imbalance in supply and demand of money market.

(9) The interest rates were different in various regions in the country.

(10) The commercial banks did not invest in government securities.

(11) The compulsion of war finance have forced them to invest heavily in government securities.

(12) The banks did not invest in industrial securities to any significant extent during this phase.

(13) The major part of advances to commercial sector were given to the wholesale trade.

(14) The growth of commercial banking was an indicator of the progress of the banking habit, volume of business transactions.

(15) The volume of cheques cleared at the clearing houses increased substantially.

The commercial banks involved in providing the short term credit to the industrial sector. The working capital of the corporate sector have been fulfilled by the commercial banks. The banks provided credits mainly to the large scale units. There were two important gaps arised in the field of industrial finance. The commercial banks have been failed to supply long term funds to SSIs and industrial units. The New industrial units have been established in the private sector to fill the gap for long term finance. The supply of long term funds to the industrial sector have been commenced from the planning period.

Cooperative Banks plays an important role in the Indian financial system. The inadequate supply of short term and long term funds to the agriculture sector led to the emerging of the cooperative sector. The money lenders and unorganised players efforts dominated the Indian financial system during this phase. The cooperative banks played a little role in the system during this period. The cooperative sector failed to provide the financial assistance to the agriculture sector. The RBI made efforts in 1935, to channelise more funds to this sector and help the cooperative sector. There had been a significant change in the size of flow of funds to the agriculture sector.

Small Savings are one of the traditional media for community savings in India. India has the largest population and varying low income levels of different groups of people. The importance of small savings is noticed by the government and corporate sector. The government encouraged the wage earners, small and medium farmers and the middle class people to save through government saving scheme. The post office savings bank took over the savings business from the treasury operations in 1886. The postal department offered various schemes at different periods of time. The Central Government introduced the post office defence savings deposits in between April 1941 and 1947. The post office savings bank deposits have been increased substantially during this phase.

Insurance is one of the savings scheme which is popular among the public. The insurance business began on the enactment of the LIC act 1912. It was carried on by LIC and Foreign companies, Provident fund societies, Post and Telegraph department. They also started such as *fire, marine* insurance business. The volume of general insurance business declined relatively to that of life insurance. The life insurance business is concerned, the foreign companies share is declined significantly and Indian companies share increased. The volume of business of provident societies and post and Telegraph department has been negligible. The Insurance companies have been providing mortgage loans substantially.

Stock Market is the barometer of the industrial sector of a nation. It plays an important role in the economic development of a country. The private and public sector raises large amount of funds from the stock market. The first stock exchange was established in Mumbai in 1877. The BSE had provided adequate funds to the private and public sector during the 1st half of the 20th century. The peace of industrialisation, the two world wars, protection to domestic industries led to the growth of the active stock markets. The private sector has grown substantially during this phase. There is no organised data available on the actual capital issues by the corporate sector in this phase. The equity issues were also well recognised by the public during this phase. The debentures were not accepted by the public in 1950. The following were the reasons for rejecting the debt instruments by the public.

(a) Dislike in the form of investment by the public.

(b) The rich community preferred towards the speculative scrips.

(c) High stamp duty on purchase and transfer of debentures.

(d) The avoidance of debentures by insurance and financial institutions.

Government Securities markets also expanded phenomenally during this phase. The gross issues of central and provincial government securities have been increased during this period. The gilt edged market had become wide and active. During the IInd world war many issues were made on a tap basis. Treasury bills were first issued in India in Oct. 1917. The bills were of different maturities of three six, nine and twelve months. The bills of maturity were also issued for four and eight months. Treasury bills were used to be sold by tender method. This method was adopted for the purpose of provincial governments, semi government institutions and foreign holders. The RBI provided the discounting facility for the treasury bills to banks. They did not have a wide appeal among banks and other institutions. The RBI was the main supporter of the bill market. The bills were also issued by the provincial governments. But these bills were not preferred by the RBI and other financial institutions in this period. The discount rate on provincial treasury bills was higher than that of the treasury bills of the union government. The ad hoc bill system was started from this period.

Interest is the most important factor in the capital formation of a nation. The interest rates during this period were different from bank to bank. The Imperial bank of India did not pay any interest on current deposits. The Indian joint stock banks and exchange banks offered interest on them. The average rate of interest on current deposits by leading commercial banks in India was *2.56%* in 1921, *1.29%* in 1935 and *0.26%* in 1943. The interest rate on FDRs, and SB A/cs were different from bank to bank. They charged different interest rates on loans granted by them. There was a wide variation in interest rates in different regions. The interest rates were high in Madras, South India and also in Indus and gangetic plains. In industrially developed cities such as Bombay, Calcutta and Ahmedabad the rates were relatively low. These places involved in manufacturing the goods. The interest rates were different in different regions due to the following reasons:

(1) The closeness of the Central bank to the particular region.

(2) The access of the transferability of the funds.

(3) The size of capital demanded and supply of region.

(4) The measure activities involved in agriculture, manufacturing and commencing the progress towards consolidation of the banking system, the growth of branch banking increase in the offices of the RBI improvement in the fund transfer facilities, growth in transport and communication facilities etc., due to the interest rates had greatly diminished since 1950. The rate of interest was quite higher in the organised sector during this phase.

Second Phase 1950-91

The second phase starts from 1950 and the background of the financial system has been determined by the mixed economy system. The growth, sectoral priorities, distribution have influenced the development of the Indian financial system. All sectors of the economy have undergone significant changes during this phase. India has witnessed all types of financial innovations in respect of the financial institutions, instruments and services. During this phase a large number of new institutions have been set up to cater the needs of the society. Therefore we have a highly diversified structure of the financial institutions. A large number of new financial instruments have been introduced. Therefore we have diversified portfolio of financial claims. The financial system has been greatly effected by the changes in ownership, consolidation and members of financial institutions, deregulation, computerisation, globalization and reorganization.

Financial Development

The financial system is a weapon to counter the poverty. It is a tool to construct a good and strong economy. The financial system can make dreams to realities. The wealth of a nation can only be constructed through a better financial system. It directly helps to increase the savings by offering better returns to the savers. It will convert the savers into investors successfully. It enhances the efficiency of business concern which is reflected in the economic development. Their relationship between economic development and financial development is mutually reinforcing. The financial development is a part of the economic development. Development creates and nourishes the economy. The financial system is complex and it is closely connected with various aspects i.e. ***financial instruments, financial institutions, financial markets*** and ***financial services.*** Financial system occupies a crucial role in the functioning of the economy. It includes all those activities that deal in finance and are organised into a system. The growth of the Indian financial system is accompanied by the diversification and financial innovation. India has witnessed all types of financial innovations. Financial innovation can be defined as "the introduction of financial instrument or service or practice or introducing new uses of funds or finding out new sources of funds or introducing new process or techniques to handle the day to day operations or carrying out a new organisation".[3]

At present the Indian economy has a highly diversified structure of financial institutions. Similarly a large number of new financial instruments have to be introduced to fulfil the needs of the dynamic corporate sector. The innovative instruments can leverage the corporate financial muscle. The financial development of a nation can be observed through the following powerful indicators.

(1) Finance Ratio.

(2) Financial Interrelation Ratio.

(3) New Issue Ratio.

(4) Intermediation Ratio.

1. **Finance Ratio** is a macro analysis of an economy. It measures the total analysis of primary and secondary claims of the ***National Income.*** National Income is an important component of the economy. The National income influences the purchasing capacity of the citizens. An increase in national income

3. L.M. Bhole, Financial Institutions and Markets, 1998, P.No. 13.

leads to higher purchasing capacity. The per capita income will be raised and the standard of living will be more qualitative.

2. **Financial Interrelation Ratio** is the relationship between financial assets and physical assets. It measures the ratio between financial structure and real assets structure of the economy. It is the ratio of financial assets to physical assets.

3. **New Issue Ratio** means the shares that are offered by the newly promoted companies to the public for the first time. The new issues are called public issues. Public issues consist of the following methods.

(a) *Initial issues:* The first time issue of shares to the public by a new company.

(b) *Further issues:* Shares are issued by the existing companies.

(c) *New money issues:* Newly created securities which are issued to the first time.

(d) *Non-economy issues:* The shares are sold in the market by underwriters.

(e) *Bonus issues :* Shares are offered to the existing shareholders freely.

(f) *Exchange issue :* The process of exchanging securities between the companies.

The contribution of new issues reflects the industrial growth of a country. New issues facilitate the transfer of funds from the savers to the entrepreneurs. New issue ratio indicates the relationship between primary and physical capital formation in the country.

4. **Intermediation Ratio** is the relationship between primary and secondary issues. Primary issues means the shares will be sold to the public in the open market. Secondary issues means the trading of securities which are already issued. The secondary market did not form any additional capital to the market. But the secondary market creates liquidity to the stock market. The primary issues response will be depended upon the activeness of the secondary market. If the secondary market was inactive, prices would decline. Then there would be no room for primary issues. The ratio reveals the importance of middle men as mobilisation of funds relative to real sectors. The Intermediaries are more important persons in the mobilisation of savings. They mobilise the funds of savings made by the households towards the industrialisation of a nation.

Equity Culture

Equity shares have much less importance in India. The investors prefer debt securities than equity. There is not much demand for *risk* securities. The equity culture has not much developed in India during this phase. There is a strong need to develop the equity culture in India to achieve the economic growth of the nation. The Individual savers are widely scattered and there is no good means of communication. Therefore the equities are bound to remain unimportant and unexposed. But the foreign share markets are connected by the latest electronic network and exposed globally. The equity is unlikely to become popular due to the rural sector in India. The equity culture has not really developed in India due to various reasons. At the first instance, there is an increase in household investments in units, bank deposits increase in security holdings by banks, the increase in risk of financial markets. There is a change in spending pattern among the savers all these factors can cause instability. The second fact is the deployment of funds in large scale in equities decreases the availability of finance to non corporate sectors. The equity market is a ***barometer*** of the health of the economy. The financial policies in India should be quite encouraging to the growth of bank deposits. The government should not be shown any discriminatory policies against banks. During the years 1996 and 1997, the Indian investors preferred debt instruments. The Government allowed the financial institutions to set up *100%. Debt* funds to invest in government securities and corporate bonds. The *premier exchange* the NSE has set up a separate segment to develop the whole sale debt market in India. The Bombay Stock Exchange has also introduced a separate segment to develop a separate section for corporate debt instruments. The RBI has also introduced the primary dealers to improve the liquidity in Government securities market.

The Indian financial system has undergone many changes over the years. The banking sector dominates the Indian financial system. It now become an important part of the Indian financial system. The bank deposits have the largest share in the total financial resources of the country. The NBFCs participation cannot be ignored in the Indian financial system. The policy makers should take into consideration the role of NBFCs without ignorance of their presence.

Secondary Markets

The growth in the volume of financial assets is low. The markets in most of these assets are under developed and inactive. The second markets have not been developed due to the official efforts. There is no encouragement, no concessions, schemes to this sector. The commercial bill market, treasury bills market, mortgages and debentures are not highly developed. The secondary market in Government securities does exist. The participants in this segment are very few. The government securities market and treasury bills market are confined to a few financial institutions. The institutional investors are buying corporate securities and units of mutual funds substantially. Their operations on the stock exchanges have been increased significantly.

There has been considerable transformation of the sector and the roles of different financial institutions have been changed. The commercial banks are only confined to self liquidating, short term credits. The loan business of the banking sector have been grown substantially. The UTI and LIC institutions were also allowed to enter the call market. The statutory financial institutions now provide a wide range of financing schemes. They provide long term funds to the private sector, medium and large sized concerns and working capital funds to the SSIs. The PSUs are allowed into the capital market and they can raise large amounts of funds directly through bonds and deposits.

The financial institutions have to fulfil the requirement of *Social Justice* and sectoral balance of the community. Therefore the institutions opened rural branches to provide adequate finance to the agricultural sector, financial assistance to SSIs, loans to individuals, financial assistance to backward areas, provision for sick units providing financial assistance at different rate of interests. Now the financial institutions extended their cooperation to the capital market related activities. The commercial banks and financial institution are entering into the areas of home finance, banking, merchant banking and mutual funds. The financial institutions have been transformed into ***Universal banking*** and ***Mega banking*** taking place in India.

The financial system has become much more integrated. It has been categorised as organised and unorganised sectors. The following factors have been greater integration:

(a) The government entry in a very big way in trading of commodities.

(b) Expansion of network of rural bank branches.

(c) Financial institutions have been transformed.

(d) Introduction of innovative financial instruments.

(e) Evolution of financial institutions.

(f) Increasing the activities of financial intermediaries.

(g) The refinance and rediscounting schemes of financial institutions like IDBI, NABARD.

The Money market, government securities markets and foreign exchange market have facilitated liquidity in recent years. The expansion of the network of the rural branches also contributed to greater integration. The banks and term lending financial institution become more integrated.

The Indian financial system needs serious attention to be devoted with a view to improve the better functioning of the system. There is a strong need to propose the credit discipline in lending financial institutions. These institutions are intervened by political parties and government to patronise their community.

The people have controlling interests in many companies without having adequate equity. The functioning of the public financial institutions have to be improved. The capital market become like a *casino finance.* The people want to make quick money through the middlemen's margin's commissions advisory and consultancy fee. The Dutt committee recommended in late 1960 for the control of private sector by some people with public money in public financial institutions.

The Investors in India have not been satisfied in respect of the risk, return and liquidity of their commitments. The return on investment has not been really adequate the tax payer savers have been in a position to earn more than the savers with low income. There is no liquidity position for small investors investment. The ordinary shares possess liquidity to a limited extent due to the following reasons.

(a) The small size of floating stock.

(b) A limited number of active market.

(c) Limited number of trading hours.

(d) The insensivity of brokers.

(e) The frequent closure of stock exchanges.

The primary and secondary markets are dominated by a few large companies and financial institution. The markets are highly speculative, volatile, imperfect and lacks free entry. The risk of financial asset is high due to many factors such as dishonest practices, frauds committed and unethical investment culture. The Indian investors are in helplessness position. They feel insecurity regarding the safety of the principal amount. Therefore the investors do not have confidence in financial markets. The investment in debts instruments is quite risky. The central government conducted loan melas and loan waivers in earlier years. This lead to bad debts, low profitability and low capital base. The bank deposits also became risky. The failure of commercial credit bank, Indian bank and CRB capitals made to deep sickness in the financial system. The banking system has failed due to the following factors.

(1) The politicisation of the financial system.

(2) Patronising the vote banks through ***"Runa Melas"***.

(3) Psychological impact generated by the political parties.

(4) Wilful defaulters.

(5) Delays in sanctions and disbursement of loans.

(6) Failed to ensure proper project appraisal.

(7) Effective follow up of projects.

(8) Tight repayment schedules.

(9) Inflexible procedures.

(10) Shorter loan maturities.

Third Phase (1991 to ......)

The evolution of Indian financial system enters into third phase. It starts from 1991 onwards. The New Economic Policy has been announced by the central government in June 1991. The NEP has received special attention as a part of this policy. After the announcement of the NEP the central government had appointed a high level committee on the financial system. The committee has been appointed for examining all the aspects relating to the structure, organisation functions and procedures of the system. The committee submitted its report in November 1991. Then the authorities have introduced a number of reforms in the Indian financial sector with reference to this report. The position of the financial institutions and Markets led to the financial reforms. Financial markets and institutions were in a bad shape. The banking sector was running either at a loss or low profits. They were unable to provide adequately for loan defaults and their capital. The banking sector has been facing the following problems.

(1) Organisational inadequacies among the banks.
(2) Lack of control functions.
(3) Weak management.
(4) The erosion of work culture.
(5) Growth restrictive practices.
(6) Imposition of high Cash Reserve Ratio & SLR.
(7) Providing loans on subsidised interest rates.
(8) Depressed rate of interest on deposits.
(9) Higher interest rates on loans to the Industries.
(10) Recovery process of debt become politicised.
(11) Finance to Non-viable sick units.
(12) Lack of transparency in preparation of accounts.
(13) Customer services were poor.
(14) Use of outdated technology.
(15) High transaction costs.
(16) Lack of delegation of authority, inadequate internal control and poor house keeping.
(17) Over staffing.
(18) Massive branch expansion.
(19) No freedom to the staff.

The Government of India introduced the financial reforms in 1991 and the main objectives of these reforms have been presented.

- To develop a transparent, autonomous, world standards, competitive and market oriented financial system.
- To increase the effective utilisation of available savings and to promote accelerated growth of real sector.
- To bring accountability, viability, profitability, balanced growth professionalism and depoliticisation in the financial sector.
- To dismantle the administered system of interest rates.
- To encourage competition by free entry and exit for institutions and market players.
- To build an excellent financial infrastructure relating to audit, technology and legal matters.

Major Reforms (1991–97)

The reforms objective is to correct and eliminate financial repressions and to transform the system as hurdle free. The financial sector reforms have been operating for economic stability and growth of the country. The reforms have had a wide operational matters such as banking capital markets, external sector policies. Some others have categorised these reforms in three areas (a) Resident banking system, (b) Development of Institutions, (c) Monetary policy. The major reforms are listed below:

(1) Policy reforms.
(2) Banking reforms.

(3) Capital market reforms.
(4) Global financial market reforms.

(1) Policy Reforms

(1) The Interest rates in the economy were deregulated.
(2) The reduction of SLR from 38.5% to 25%.
(3) The incremental CRR was removed upto 10%.
(4) The average CRR were reduced from 15% in 1991-92 to 10% in 1995-96.
(5) The CRR of FCNR (B) and NRNR deposit accounts removed.
(6) The CRR on NRE deposits outstanding as on 27.10.1995 were reduced from 14% to 10%. The CRR on an increase in NRE deposits removed.
(7) Capital adequacy norms for banks, FIs and all market intermediaries was introduced.
(8) The Basle Committee framework were adopted for capital adequacy.
(9) A separate division was established in RBI for financial supervision with an advisory council. This division would supervise banks, All India FIs, NBFCs from April-July 1995. The supervisory division will focus on critical areas such as capital adequacy asset quality. management, earnings and liquidity.
(10) Banks and financial institutions act, 1993 was passed for recovery of debts and set up special Recovery Tribunals to facilitate quicker recovery.
(11) The system of ad hoc Treasury bills was abolished and it was replaced by the system of ways and means advances w.e.f. 1-4-1997.
(12) The private sector was allowed to set up banks, mutual funds, MMMF, Insurance companies.
(13) PSUs Banks permitted diversified ownership by law subject to 51% holding of government.
(14) RBI, SBI, IFCI and IRBI were converted into public limited companies.
(15) IDBI act has amended to raise capital upto 49% of its paid up capital from the public.
(16) The foreign banks are permitted to open branches.
(17) The office of the CCI was abolished.
(18) SEBI was made as statutory body in Feb. 1992.
(19) Floating interest rate on financial assistance was introduced by all India development banks.
(20) All NBFCs with net owned funds of Rs. 25 lakhs and more must be registered with the RBI.
(21) OTC and NSE was established and made operational.

(2) Banking Reforms

(1) Interest rates on deposits and advances of banks including urban cooperative banks were deregulated.
(2) Nationalised and SBI are allowed to enter the capital market.
(3) Prudential norms for banks, and financial institutions introduced.
(4) The performance, obligations and commitments should be fulfilled and submitted to the RBI.
(5) Introduction of International Accounts standards for banks to make their balance sheets fully transparent.
(6) Banks gave greater freedom to open, shift and swap branches.
(7) The rules has been liberalised in respect of project finance.
(8) The budgetary support was extended for recapitalisation of weak public sector banks.
(9) The recommendations of Goiporia committee were adopted to resolve customer's grievances.

(10) Banks set free to fix their own foreign exchange position limit subject to the RBI approval.

(11) Loan system was introduced for delivery of bank credit.

(3) Capital Market Reforms

The capital Market reforms were further simplified into the following areas:

(a) Primary market reforms.

(b) Secondary market reforms.

(c) Government securities market reforms.

(d) Global financial market reforms.

(e) Monetary policy 2002-2003. (RBI)

(a) Primary Market Reforms

(1) Mutual funds permitted to underwrite public issues.

(2) A norm of five shareholders for every Rs. 1 lakh of fresh issues of capital and 10 shareholders for every Rs. 1 lakh of offer for sale were prescribed as an initial and continuing listing requirement.

(3) The companies have been directed to pay interest to the investors from the **30th** day of the closure of public issue.

(4) Debt issues permitted to be sold entirely by the book building process.

(5) The payment of any kind of discount or commission to persons receiving firm allotment was prohibited.

(6) Housing finance companies considered to be registered for issue purposes, if they are getting refinance facility from the NHB.

(7) Issuers were allowed to list debt securities on stock exchanges.

(b) Secondary Market Reforms

(1) The stock exchanges required to disclose, carry forward position, scrip wise and broken wise at the beginning of carry forward session.

(2) Stock lending scheme was introduced without attracting capital gains.

(3) Depositories act 1996 was passed to provide a legal framework for the establishment of depositories.

(4) Banks, Mutual funds and IDBI are allowed to dematerialise their scrips.

(5) The stock exchanges are being modernised and electronic trading system is introduced.

(6) All stock exchanges are required to institute the buy in or action process.

(7) The BSE is allowed to expand its trading terminals.

(8) Large and short sales are to be regulated through the imposition of margins.

(9) Stock exchanges are asked to collect 100% daily margins on the notional loss of a broker for every scrip.

(c) Government Securities Market Reforms

(1) A 364 day treasury bill had replaced the 182 day bill in 92-93 and was being sold by fortnightly auction since April 1992.

(2) Auction of 91 day bills was commenced from January 1993.

(3) Maturity period for new issue of central government securities were shortened from 20 to 10 years and for state government securities from 15 to 10 years.

(4) The state governments and PFs were allowed to participate 91 day TB auctions on a non-competitive basis from August 1994.

(5) Reverse repo-facility with RBI in government dated securities was extended to DFHI and Securities Trading Corporation of India.

(6) The guidelines for the primary dealers in the government securities market was issued in March 1995.

(7) The following six new instruments were introduced.

 (a) Zero coupon bonds.

 (b) Tap stock.

 (c) Partly paid government stock.

 (d) Tap and partly paid stock.

 (e) Floating rate bonds.

 (f) Capital Indexed bonds.

(8) A system of delivery versus payment in subsidiary General ledger transactions was introduced in Bombay in July 1995.

(9) Funding of auction of treasury bills into fixed coupon dated securities at the option of the holders has been introduced since 19-4-1993.

(d) Global Financial Market Reforms

(1) Flexible exchange rate system was introduced.

(2) Exchange controls are largely dismantled.

(3) FIIs are allowed to enter the capital market on registration with SEBI.

(4) FIIs are permitted to invest upto 10% in equity of any company.

(5) FIIs are permitted to invest in unlisted companies upto 10% of equity of the company.

(6) FIIs permitted to set up 100% debt funds.

(7) University Funds, charitable trusts, societies Foreign endowment funds are allowed to register as FII.

(8) Indian companies are allowed to raise funds from global markets through various instruments.

(9) FERA was replaced by FEMA to attract more capital inflows.

(10) Introduced capital account convertibility.

(11) The long term capital gain tax on portfolio investment by NRIs are reduced from 20% to 10%.

(12) FIIs, NRIs, OCBs are permitted to invest upto 24% in equities of Indian companies engaged in all activities except Agriculture and plantation.

(13) All corporates institutions railways, telecommunications are permitted to use the foreign currency proceeds upto US$ 3 millions.

(14) RBI made a single window agency for overseas investments by the Indian companies.

(15) Foreign Investments promotion council is set up to promote foreign direct investment in India.

(e) RBI Monetary and Credit Policy: 2002-03

Reserve Bank of India on Monetary and Credit Policy for the year 2002-03 is presented as follows:

I. Review of Macro Economic and Monetary Developments (2001-02).

II. Stance of Monetary Policy for 2002-03.

III Financial Sector Reforms.

Monetary Policy: 2002-03

The overall stance of monetary policy in 2001-02 as outlined in last years annual policy statement was as follows:

Provision of adequate liquidity to meet credit growth and support revival of investment demand while continuing a vigil on movements in the price level. Within the overall framework of imparting greater flexibility to the interest rate regime in the medium term to continue the present stable interest rate environment with a preference for softening to the extent the evolving situation warrants.

The Monetary Management in 2001-02 was largely in conformity with the monetary policy stance announced in annual policy statement of April 2001 and reiterated in the mid term review of Oct. 2001. However, the monetary management in 2001-02 was fought with several challenges like overhang of liquidity global slowdown, external developments the overall stance of monetary policy for 2002-03 will be.

(a) Provision of adequate liquidity to meet credit growth and support investment demand in the economy while continuing a vigil on movements in the price level.

(b) In line with the above to continue the present stance on interest rates including preference for soft interest rates.

(c) To impart greater flexibility to the interest rate structure in the medium term.

Financial Sector Reforms

The annual policy statements as well as mid term reviews have been focussing on the structural and regulatory measures to strengthen the financial system and improve the functioning of various segment of the financial market. These measures, introduced after extensive consultations with experts and market participants have been directed towards increasing operational effectiveness of monetary policy, redefining the regulatory role of the Reserve bank, strengthening the prudential and supervisory norms, improving the credit delivery system and developing technological and institutional infrastructure of the financial sector. It is proposed to speed up the process further to enable the Indian financial sector to be better equipped to meet the global competition. The financial reforms consists of the following tools to take up measures.

(1) Monetary Measures.

(2) Credit Delivery Mechanism.

(3) Money Market.

(4) Government Securities.

(5) Non-Banking Financial Companies.

1. MONETARY MEASURES

In this monetary measures, the RBI takes the following steps to control the economy.

(a) Rationalisation and Reduction in Cash Reserve Ratio.

(b) Bank Rate.

(c) Statutory Liquidity Ratio-Regional Rural Banks.

(d) Interest Rate Policy.

(a) Cash Reserve Ratio: The RBI has been pursuing its medium term objectives of reduction in CRR to the statutory minimum level of 3%. In this direction, RBI gradually reduced the CRR from **11%** in August 1998 to 7.5% by May 2001. In the mid term review of Oct. 2001, CRR of scheduled commercial banks (excluding RRBs) was reduced by 200 basis points to the present level of 5.5% of their net demand and time liabilities. Rationalisation of CRR was also initiated by withdrawing various exceptions given to the banks on certain specific categories of liabilities for the CRR requirements. Subsequently all categories of banks including cooperative banks were subjected to the CRR prescription as applicable to the scheduled commercial banks. These measures were designed to facilitate the development of short term yield curve, develop money market, enhance availability of lendable resources with banks and improve the efficacy of indirect instruments in the conduct of monetary policy. Further RBI announced its intention to move away from sector specific refinance. As a further step in the direction of moving towards the medium term objectives of reducing the CRR while strengthening the LAF and introducing better prudential standard it its proposed to

(i) reduce CRR further from *5.5%* to 5% effective fortnight beginning June 15, 2002.

The proposed reduction in CRR is being made effective from fortnight beginning June 15, 2002 in view of the prevailing excess liquidity with the banking system as can be seen by larger turnover in the call money market and the higher average recourse to RBI repos. However, in case there is an unexpected change in the liquidity conditions in the market, RBI may advance the effective date of reduction before the above announced date.

(b) Bank Rate: At present there is substantial excess liquidity in the system which is reflected in the repo amounts received by the RBI during the past six weeks. On April 4, 2002, the total amount tendered by the way of repo was as high as Rs. 30,005 crore on the average amounts tendered by banks in one or three day repos have ranged from *Rs. 1565 crore to Rs. 16024 crore* in the part six weeks. The repos rate is currently *6%*. which is below the bank rate of 6.5% and call money rates on several days have also been lower than the bank rate. In response to the easy liquidity situation, some banks have also recently reduced their deposit rates as well as lending rates. Further, yields on fixed income securities have also come down substantially. Under these circumstances, on balance, it is considered desirable to leave the bank rate unchanged. The matter, however will be kept under constant review. In case the overall liquidity and credit situation warrants and inflation rate continue to remain low, a reduction in the bank rate upto half a percentage point 50 basis points will be considered by RBI as and when necessary.

(c) SLR-RRB: RRBs are required to maintain SLR at 25% of their NDTL in cash or gold or in unencumbered government and other approved securities. Unlike in the case of scheduled commercial banks balances maintained in call or fixed deposits by Regional Rural banks with their sponsor banks are treated as cash and hence reckoned towards their maintenance of SLR. As a prudential measure, it is desirable on the part of all RRBS to maintain their entire SLR portfolio in government and other approved securities which many of them are already doing.

Accordingly all RRBs may maintain their entire SCR holdings in government and other approved securities. In order to allow sufficient time to RRBs to convert existing deposits with sponsor banks into government securities, this provision may be complied with by March, 31, 2003.

(d) Interest Rate Policy: The RBI has the interest policy according to the following steps.

(a) Interest rate flexibility.

(b) Prime lending rate and spreads.

(c) Interest rate on savings A/c.

(d) Interest rate on export credit.

(e) Deemed exports.

(f) Abolition of minimum lending rate for co-op. banks.

(g) FCNR (B) deposits.

(h) Interest rate on FCNR (B) deposits.

(i) Overseas market.

(j) External commercial borrowings.

(a) Interest Rate Flexibility: The year 2001-02 witnessed one of the steepest declines in interest rates on long term government securities. The yield on 10 year government securities declined by as much as 287 basis points. The secondary market yield on 10 year paper is currently 7.27%. The bank rate, the repo rate and the overnight call money rates have also been very low in recent months ranging between 6% and 7%. The bank rate and short term rates are now fairly reasonable.

However the sharp reduction in nominal and real interest rates is not yet fully reflected in the interest rates generally charged by the banks on advances. There is also some evidence that the spread between the interest rates charged by banks to different borrowers has also tended to widen. The relatively lesser reduction in the rates of interest that most borrowers have to pay is despite the action taken by the government in the last 3 years to lower administered interest rates on Relief Bonds and small savings etc, as well as the sharp reduction by RBI in the CRR of banks (along with an increase in the interest rate paid by RBI on eligible cash balances maintained by banks with RBI). The reasons for the relative downward inflexibility in the commercial interest rate structure seems to be primarily due to the following factors;

The average cost of deposits for major banks continue to be relatively high ***(6.25 to 7.25%)***. Further a substantial portion of deposits is in the form of long term deposits at fixed interest rates. Thus flexibility is available to banks to reduce interest rates in the short run without adversely affecting their return on assets. The relatively high overhang of non performing assets (NPAs) further pushes up the average cost of funds for banks, particularly public sector banks.

The non interest operating expenses of banks are worked out to 2.5 to 3% of total assets putting pressure on the required spread over the cost of funds.

In view of legal constraints and procedural bottlenecks in recovery of dues by banks the risk premium tends to be higher resulting in wider spread between deposit rates and lending rates.

The large borrowing programme of the Government over and above SLR requirements provides significant prospects for deployment of funds by banks in sovereign paper.

From the medium term prospective it is necessary to initiate measures to make the interest rate structure in India more flexible and reflective of the underlying inflationary situation so far as reduction in spreads is concerned, it is no doubt necessary to improve the manpower productivity and also to reduce the establishment costs. Some progress in this area has been made in the last two years, but there is still a long way to go. However, it has to be recognised that given various constraints especially poor debt recovery systems, actual progress in reducing average spreads is likely to be slow.

Without prejudice to further progress in reduction in spreads and other measures to reduce delays in recovery, in order to impart flexibility to interest rate structure, following measures to be considered as early as possible.

Encourage introduction of flexible interest rate system for all new deposits with reset at six monthly intervals. At the same time the fixed rate option should also be made available to the depositors illustratively the banks may offer longer term deposits with six monthly reset conditions and at the same time offer a fixed rate for a similar maturity. The interest rate on which may be higher or lower. It depends on the period of deposits and banks perception regarding inflation as well as interest rate outlook over the longer period. All banks are advised to put such flexible rate system in practice as early as possible.

Banks are also urged to devise schemes for encouraging depositors to convert their existing long term fixed rate past deposits into variable rate deposits. Banks may consider paying the depositors at the contracted rate for the period of deposit already run and waive the penalty for premature withdrawal if the same deposit is renewed at the variable rate.

(b) Prime Lending Rate and Spreads: In the mid term review at Oct. in 1996, it was stated that a number of banks are charging lending rates for higher then CLR on a significant position of bank credit to borrowers with credit limits of over ***Rs. 2,00,000***. It has been decided that banks along with the announcement of PLR, should also announce the maximum spread over of the prime lending rate for all advances other than consumer credit. Banks should attain the approval of their respective boards for the fixation of maximum spread over the prime lending rate.

As per the latest available information spreads above PLR of the some banks are substantial. In the present interest rate environment, it is not reasonable to keep very high spreads over PLR. Banks are urged to review the present maximum spread over PLR, and reduce them wherever they are unreasonably high so that credit may be available to the borrowers at reasonable interest rates. Further, banks should also announce the maximum spread over PLR to the public along with the announcement of PLR. The Reserve bank will review the matter again in Oct. 2002 after further consultations with select banks with very high spread over PLR.

In the Interest of Customer protection and also meaningful competition, it is necessary to have a greater degree of transparency in actual interest rates for depositors as well as borrowers. In this direction the following measures are proposed.

* Banks should provide information on maximum and minimum interest rates charged to their borrowers. RBI will put this information also in public domain.
* Banks are urged to switch over to all cost concept for borrowers by explicitly charging the processing charges to the borrowers. Such bank charges may also be publicly announced.

(c) Interest Rate on Savings Account: No change in the recent year, banks have been given freedom in fixing interest rate on various deposit liabilities and flexibility in offering interest rates depending upon turnover and size of deposits with the approval of their boards. The only interest rate on deposits side which is regulated by RBI is on "savings Account" with cheque facility. This rate is at present ***4% P.A.***

However although the nominal interest rate is ***4% P.A.***, The yield on such deposits work out to ***3.4% P.A.*** only as interest is payable on the minimum balance between ***10th*** and last day of each month. ***Nearly four fifths of such saving deposits are held by households.***

In view of this present deregulated interest rate environment and the reduction in interest rates on governments small savings schemes in the recent period. There is an apparent case for deregulation of interest rates on saving account also. However considering the fact that bulk of such savings deposits are held by households, including households in rural and semi urban areas on balance is not considered as opportune time to deregulate the interest rate on savings account for the present. In any case, the present effective yield of ***3.4%*** is quite reasonable in relation to others prevailing interest rates on even short term instruments.

(d) Interest Rate on Export Credit: Exporters have option to avail the pre-shipment and post shipment credit in foreign currency from banks in India. This type of credit is currently available at ***LIBOR*** plus a maximum spread of ***1%*** point making this rate Internationally competitive for Indian exporters. In order to make this interest rate even move competitive in the present low interest rate environment, it is desirable to further low the ceiling rate on foreign currency loans for Indian exports by banks accordingly.

The ceiling rate on export credit in foreign currency is reduced to ***LIBOR plus 0.75%*** point from the present ***LIBOR plus 1% point.***

Considering this competitive interest rate on foreign currency loans and to migrate any possible exchange risk exporters are encouraged of make maximum use of foreign currency loans in one or more currencies of their choice depending on the currency of their export receipts (e.g: US dollars Euro, Pound, Sterling) Indian banks located in areas with concentration of exporters are being advised to give this important facility due publicity and make it easily accessible to all exporters including small exporters.

In the Annual policy statement of April 2001, interest rates on export credit in rupee terms were rationalised and ceilings were prescribed for both ***pre-shipment*** and ***post shipment*** credit linked to PLR. This prescription of ceiling of 1.5% points below PLR has facilitated exporters to avail the credit at substantially lower rates than the PLR of the banks considering the universal international development, effective September, 26, 2001. The ceilings on export credit interest rates were further reduced to ***2.5%*** points below PLR for a period of 6 months (i.e., upto March 31, 2002). From April 7, 2002, the ceiling rates were to revert to 1.5% points below PLR. However, keeping in view the continued international uncertainties the period during which interest rate of 2.5% points below PLR will be applicable, has been extended upto September 30, 2002, with this concession, the ceiling rate on pre-shipment rupee export credit upto 180 days works out to ***7.5% to 8.5%*** for most public sector banks. As exporters are eligible to sell their export earnings in the forward market premia, the effective interest cost to exporters becomes only **2 to 3%** which is Internationally highly competitive.

In view of the need to ensure transparency and also encourage banks to continue to provide finance at competitive rates, there is a need for putting in place a reporting system by which the commercial banks provide information on Interest rates charged on pre-shipments and post shipments credit. This will facilitate exporters in choosing the most competitive rates accordingly.

With effect from fortnight beginning from 15-6-2000, banks will report to the RBI, the minimum and maximum lending rates to exporters. This information will be placed in public domain.

In view of the above proposals (i.e. a reduction in Interest rates for foreign currency loans to exporters and maximum lending rates charged by banks to exporters) a further proposal which requires consideration is to deregulate the interest rate on export credit in domestic currency. Linking of domestic Interest rates on export credit to ***PLR*** has become redundant in the present circumstances, when the effective Interest rates are in any case substantially lower than the ***PLR*** for exporter. Deregulation of the present ceiling on interest rate for domestic currency may in fact encourage greater competition among banks and may have the effect of further lowering interest rates for exporters with a good credit record. This proposal will be considered by the RBI after further consultations as necessary.

(e) Deemed Exports: As per the extent guidelines, banks are permitted to extend rupee preshipment and post shipment supply rupee credit at concessional rate of interest to parties against orders for supplies in respect of deemed exports such as rupee export credits both at pre and post shipment supply stages are eligible for refinance from the RBI. However it has been represented that some exporters still do not get the advantage of the concession rate of interest in the case of deemed exports. Banks are therefore urged to widely publicise the concessionality in the interest rates for deemed exports and make these available to eligible exporter.

(f) Abolition of Minimum Lending Rates for Co-operative Banks: The state and central cooperative banks were given freedom to determine their lending rates subject to the prescription of minimum lending rate (MLR) of ***12% P.A.*** By the RBI since Oct. 18, 1994. Similarly, the Urban cooperative banks were subject to the prescription of MLR at ***13% P.A.*** effective from 21-6-1995 which was reduced to ***12%*** effective from 2-3-2002. Since 26-8-96 The RRBs were given freedom to determine their lending rate. At present, commercial banks other than the RRBs have this freedom in directing their ***PLRs*** with the approval of their boards. In the annual policy statement of April 2001, PLR was made a reference bench mark rate, so that commercial banks are free to lend at PLR rates to credit worthy borrowers. In order to provide greater flexibility to cooperative banks in a competitive market, it is proposed.

(1) To withdraw the stipulation of MLR for all Co-op. banks with immediate effect. co-op. banks will now be free to determine their lending rates taking up into account their cost of funds transaction cost etc with approval of their managing committee. This will help the cooperative banks in attracting good/prime borrowers.

(2) It should be ensured that the interest rates charged by the co-op. banks are transparent and known to all their customers. Banks are requested to publish the Min. and Max interest rates charged by them and display information in branches.

(g) Liberalisation of Investment Forms of Funds Mobilised under FCNR (B) Deposits: At present banks are allowed to accept FCNR (B) deposits for a period of ***1-3 years.*** However on the asset side there are certain restrictions on deploying funds. Presently banks can lend funds to Indian Residents for their foreign exchange requirements for financing of Joint Ventures or wholly owned subsidiaries set up by resident corporates. Besides, Banks can also invest such funds in certain Money Market Instruments which satisfy prescribed rating. In view of restrictions on the deployment of funds, the assets side could be shorter in tenor than the liabilities side resulting in asset liability mismatches. Further, there exists interest rate risk in view of charges in LIBOR rates, if matching investment opportunities are not available to Banks. In this regard the RBI has received a number of representations from the banks for reviewing the investment norms.

In order to avoid asset liability mismatches, and also consistent with the risk management guidelines put in place by the RBI, banks are now permitted:

To invest their FCNR (B) deposits in longer term fixed income instruments, subject to the condition that these instrument should have an appropriate rating fixed for the money market instruments. Moreover, banks have to obtain prior approval from their Boards with regard to type/tenure tenor of instruments along with relevant rating and likely cap on such investment within the Asset Liability Management (ALM) guidelines in force.

(h) Interest Rate on FCNR (B) Deposits: Currently, banks are free to accept FCNR (B) deposits for a maturity period of 1-3 years and to offer fixed and floating rates, subject to the ceiling of LIBOR/SWAP rates. In view of the prevailing international environment of low interest rates, and to reduce the cost of FCNR (B) deposits, it is decided:

⇒ To revise the above ceiling rate downward to LIBOR/SWAP rates for the corresponding maturities minus 25 basis points.

(i) Relaxation on Borrowing from and Investment in Overseas Market by Banks: At present, Banks in India are allowed to borrow from and invest in Overseas banks upto 15% of their unimpaired tier I capital or US $ 10 M, whichever is higher. In order to enable banks to have greater operational flexibility and also to align the domestic interest rate with overseas market, it is decided:

(1) To allow banks to borrow upto 25% of unimpaired Tier I Capital from overseas market. The borrowings should be within the banks' Open Position Limit and maturity mismatch limits. (Gap Limits) for which detailed guidelines will be issued.

(2) On the same lines, the existing limit of 15% of unimpaired Tier I Capital for investment in Overseas market is being raised to 25% of Unimpaired Tier I capital. The investment in money market instruments will be within the existing Open Position Limit and maturity mismatch limits. (Gap Limits). This will ensure uniformity in Overseas borrowing and investment portfolio of banks.

The increased borrowing limit would enable banks to get cheaper funds and help them to have adequate rupee resources and thus reduce the cost of funds for banks. While it will enhance the process of integration of Indian financial market, different segments of the domestic market will also get further integrated.

(j) Crystallisation of External Commercial Borrowings: It is compulsory for the overseas branches of the ADs in foreign exchange to extend external commercial borrowings (ECBs) to Indian Corporates against guarantees/letters of comfort issued by their branches in India. A suggestion was made by the banks that they should have the freedom to crystallise the foreign exchange liability in rupees in select cases. Where circumstances warrant, keeping in view the status of account of the corporates and their impact on liabilities of overseas branches. In order to provide greater freedom and flexibility to banks in their fund management, it is proposed to:

⇒ Grant permission with appropriate safeguards for crystallisation of ECBs into rupee loans where it is considered necessary by banks to do so.

2. CREDIT DELIVERY MECHANISM

A. Priority Sector Lending: In order to improve credit delivery mechanism for the priority sector, the Reserve Bank has taken various measures to reduce procedural delays and provide greater flexibility to banks. In order to further improve credit delivery to the priority sector, and in particular to agriculture, the following measures are proposed:

(1) The limits for financing of distribution of inputs for allied activities such as cattle feed, poultry feed, etc. Under priority sector is being increased to Rs. 25 lakhs from the present limit to Rs. 15 lakhs.

(2) In order to help the farmers in marketing their products, credit limits for marketing of crops (pledge financing) is being increased from Rs. 1 lakh to Rs. 5 lakhs. Further, the repayment schedules of such credit has been enhanced to 12 months from 6 months at present. With this liberalization, farmers can have maximum benefit in marketing their agricultural products.

(3) To avoid any double counting, sponsor banks while meeting the priority sector targets, should exclude funds provided to RRBs for on-lending to priority sector.

B. Credit Facilities for Small Scale Industries: Recognising the requirement of providing collateral securities as a bottle-neck in the flow of bank credit to every small units, RBI in its annual policy statement of April 2000, announced dispensation of collateral requirement for loans upto Rs. 5 lakhs for tiny sector. This dispensation was extended subsequently to all small scale industrial (SSI) units. In order to further improve the flow of credit to SSIs.

Banks may, on the basis of good track record of the units and the financial position of the units, increase the limit of dispensation of collateral requirement for loans from the existing rupees 5 lakhs to Rs. 15 lakhs.

Banks are also advised to take a pro-active stance in providing timely assistance for rehabilitation of small scale units which are affected by the Industrial downturn, and delays in payments against supplies made by them to large scale and other units. In January 2002, following the report of a high level working Group, the RBI issued detailed guidelines to scheduled commercial banks for providing timely assistance to potentially viable small scale units. These guidelines, inter alia, provide for waiving of penal rate of interest to such units, and for extension of working capital at 1.5% points below the prevailing fixed/prime lending rates. Provision has also been made in these guidelines for extension of term loans at reduced rate of interest. Banks are requested to implement these guidelines fully and to submit a report to their Boards by the end of the current calendar year on the progress made in assisting small scale units under the new guidelines.

C. Security Session and Risk Weights for Housing Finance: Banks have been playing an important role in providing credit to the housing sector in consonants with the goals of National Housing and Habitat Policy recognising the growing importance of the construction sector including its forward and backward linkages with other sectors of the economy. The RBI has encouraged banks to increase the flow of credit to this sector and has advised banks to allocate a minimum of 3.0% of incremental deposits for Housing for the year 2001-02. In order to increase the flow of credit, term loans extended by the banks to the Intermediaries against the loans sanctioned by them were allowed to be reckoned as the part of housing finance. Also, investment in bonds issued by ***HUDCO and NHB*** exclusively for financing of housing is being reckoned for priority sector targets.

At present, bank loans and advances secured by mortgage on residential property and also commercial property are assigned a risk weight of **100%** for capital Adequacy. So far, no explicit risk weights have been prescribed for banks investment in securitised papers. The Basiel capital accord of 1988 and also the New capital adequacy framework which is at the consultative stage, envisage risk weight of ***50%*** and ***100%*** for claims secured by residential property and commercial real estate respectively.

With a view to further improve the flow of credit to housing sector it is proposed to liberalise the prudential requirements for housing finance by banks and encourage investments by banks in securitised debt instruments of Housing Finance Companies accordingly:

Banks extending loans against ***Residential Housing Properties*** would be required to assign risk weight of ***50%*** instead of present ***100%*** Loans against the security of commercial real estate would continue to attract 100% risk weight as hitherto.

Investments made by banks in ***Mortgage backed securities*** of residential assessed by HFCS which are recognised and surprised by NHB would also be assigned a risk weight of 50% for the purpose of capital Adequacy. However investment made by banks in MBS of Housing Assets which include commercial properties would attract 100% risk weight.

Investments by banks in MBS issued by HFCs supervised by NHB will be reckoned for inclusion in the prescribed Housing Finance Allocation of 3.0%.

Working group would be set up to suggest Modalities for widening the investors base, improving the quality of assets, creating liquidity for trading in such assets and other related issues.

D. Kisan Credit Cards: Kisan Credit Cards (KCC) scheme formulated in 1998 has helped the farmers considerably and has been very successful. The Reserve Bank has advised all banks pursuant to the budget 2002-03 announcement, to make concerted efforts to reach the annual target of 33 lakhs KCCs by March 2002. Further, banks are advised to ensure that all the existing and prospective KCC holders are covered under the personal Accident Insurance Policy. In addition, banks are urged to make suitable plans for covering all eligible borrowers in Agricultural sector under the KCCs by March 2004. It is proposed that a survey may be conducted for assessing the impact of the scheme on the beneficiaries. This survey may be entrusted to an outside agency.

E. Rural Infrastructure Development Fund: Pursuant to the announcement made in the Budget 2002-03, funds for RIDF VIII will be enhanced to Rs. 5,500 crores and the rate of interest on loans to the state government will be reduced from 10.5% to 8.5% i.e. Bank rate plus 2.0% age points. Henceforth, interest rate on loans to states from RIDF are linked to the Bank Rate.

F. Micro-Credit: Micro-Credit institutions and Self Help Groups (SHGs) are important vehicles for the generation of income and delivery of credit to self-employed persons. Special emphasis was also placed on the promotion of micro enterprises in rural areas set up by vulnerable sectors including women SC/ST and other backward classes. Banks were also advised to provide maximum support to SHGs in this regard. As the scheme of Micro credit through SHGs is progressing well, the target for the same has been raised to 1.25 lakhs for 2002-03. Accordingly, schedule commercial banks and NABARD may take immediate steps in forming such linkages across the country so as to achieve the aforesaid target.

3. MONEY MARKET

A. Moving further towards Pure Interbank Call Money Market: It may be recalled that in the annual policy statement of April 2001, the intention to move towards a pure inter bank call/notice money market, by gradually phasing out non-bank participation, was highlighted. Accordingly, a time-frame was outlined in 4 stages for implementation. In stage-1 non-bank participants are allowed to lend, on average upto 85% of their average lending during 2000-01 in a reporting fortnight. These limits are strictly monitored by the RBI. However, in case a particular financial institution has excess liquidity at some point of time but could not explore proper avenues for investment, the RBI permits the institution to lend more than the prescribed limit for a specific period with suitable limits. A review of progress revealed that phasing out non-banks has not caused any strain on the market the volatility in the call money rate has reduced and average daily turnover in the call money market has gone up. Simultaneously, net lending through repo transactions by non-banking financial institutions and mutual funds have also increased. In view of these encouraging developments, and with the operationalisation of NDs and CCIL, it is felt necessary to accelerate the progress of moving towards a pure inter-bank call/notice money market and facilitate further deepening of the repo market. Accordingly it has been decided:

To move towards stage-II, wherein non-bank participants would be allowed to lend, on average, in a reporting fortnight upto 75% of their average lending in call market during 2000-01 with effect from a date to be announced later. RBI will announce the date of effectiveness of stage-II depending on the date when NDS/CCIL becomes fully operational and widely accessed.

B. Reliance on Call/Notice Money Market: Narasimham committee II had recommended that there must be clearly defined prudent limits beyond which banks should not be allowed to rely on call/notice money market, and that access to this market should essentially be for meeting unforeseen mismatches and not as a regular means of financing banks' lending operations. This was also recognised in the guidelines on Asset Liability Management System issue by RBI in February 1999 which required inter alia, that mismatches during the first 2 time buckets viz., 1-14 days 15-28 days should not, in any case, exceed 20% of the cash outflows in each time bucket. Further, in order to reduce excessive reliance on short term funding, banks were also advised to set a cap on inter-bank borrowings, especially call borrowings.

Some banks, however, continue to depend overwhelmingly on call money market for carrying out their banking operations. It needs to be appreciated that call money borrowings, being uncolateralised in nature, have the potential to create serious instability in the financial market because of unethical or imprudent behaviour of some participants. In view of such an observed phenomenon in early part of the last year, a ceiling on access to call money market was imposed in respect of a select segment. At present, except for UCBs, which are subject to a ceiling on borrowing of 2.0% of their aggregate deposits of previous financial year, other entities are not under any explicit limit.

An internal working Group has examined the need to place prudential limits on exposure to call/notice money market in a symmetric way so as to preserve the integrity of the financial system.

The group felt that building up of substantial exposure relative to balance sheet size by some participants on a continuous basis has the potential not only for default and the consequent systematic instability, but also impedes the development of other segments of money market, particularly the term money market. The Technical Advisory Committee on money and Government Securities Market (TAC) also suggested linking of borrowing and lending in call/notice money market to the size of the balance sheet accordingly:

(1) Lendings of scheduled commercial banks in the call/notice money market, on a daily basis, should not exceed 25% of their owned funds (paid up capital plus reserves) as at the end of March of the previous financial year.

(2) Borrowings by scheduled commercial banks in the call/notice money market on a daily basis, should not exceed 100% of their owned funds or 2% of aggregate deposits as at the end of March of the previous financial year, whichever is higher.

(3) In order to ensure that scheduled commercial banks do not face any disruption in their ALM in adjusting to this stipulation, the existing borrowers and lenders should unwind their positions in excess of the prudential limits by the end of August 2002.

(4) The borrowings of State Co-operative Banks (SCBs) and District Central Cooperative Banks (DCCBs) in the call/notice money market on a daily basis should not exceed 2.0% of their aggregate deposits as at the end of March of the previous financial year.

(5) In case any bank has, for a temporary period, some mismatches in their liquidity positions, RBI, on request, may consider allowing them further access to call/notice market. Similarly, if any bank has put in place a fully functional ALM system to the satisfaction of RBI, an increased access over the stipulated norm may be permitted by RBI for a longer period.

(6) A working Group is being constituted with representatives from eligible entities to recommend by June 30, 2002, the criteria for fixing the limits for Primary Dealers (PDs) in call/notice money market and suggest a road map for phasing them out from the call money market. In the meanwhile, all PDs are urged to keep their call money lending/borrowing within a prudent limit in relation to their net-owned funds.

The limits so prescribed for call/notice money market are prudential in nature, and are sufficiently high for most of the participants in the market, and it is expected that all legitimate liquidity needs of bank would be met.

C. Collateralised Lending Facility: At present, RBI is providing standing liquidity facilities comprising:

(1) Export Credit Refinance (ECR) and Collateralised Lending Facility (CLF) to banks and

(2) Liquidity support to PDs.

These are in addition to facilities operated through LAF as also outright sales/purchases of government securities as part of open market operation (OMO). With the inherent superiority of the LAF in moderating liquidity in the financial system, both banks and PDs have tended to rely to a predominant extent on LAF.

Scheduled Commercial banks are provided CLF against the collateral of excess holdings of Government of India dated Securities/Treasury Bills over their SLR requirement. The extent of liquidity support available to each bank has been stipulated at equivalent to 0.125% of its fortnightly average outstanding aggregate deposits in 1997-98. Accordingly, the overall limit for the system stands at Rs. 656.61 crores as of now; however the average utilisation of this facility in 2001-02 upto the fortnight ended March 22, 2002 was Rs. 124 crores. With the development of inter bank repo market and operationalisation of CCIL, the standing facilities could be phased out accordingly.

(1) CLF may be phased out with effect from the fortnight beginning October 5, 2002. RBI, however, will have the option to reintroduce CLF for a temporary period in future, should it be considered necessary to do so in the light of changes in monetary conditions.

(2) The apportionment of liquidity facilities to PDs between normal and back-stop will be reviewed by the working group.

D. Certificates of Deposit: Several developments in financial market have so far been undertaken by RBI, which include issuing of guidelines for Commercial Paper (CP) in consultation with the market players. Subsequently, Fixed Income Money Market and Derivatives Association (FIMMADA) was requested to prepare the necessary standard procedures and documentation to be followed by the participants in the CP market. Such guidelines were issued by FIMMADA in June 2001. Instructions were issued to banks and FIs that they should make investments and hold CPs only in the dematerialised form and convert existing outstandings also into demat form by October 31, 2001. It was felt that on similar lines standard procedures and guidelines for issuing Certificates of Deposits (CDs) may also be prepared for the benefit of issuers of CDs. Accordingly FIMMADA has prepared the guidelines and documentation procedures in consultation with market participants, depositories and RBI. Pending release of final guidelines and as a further step towards transparency, it has been decided that :

With effect from June 30, 2002, banks and FIs should issue CDs only in the dematerialised form. The existing outstandings of CDs shall be converted into the demat form by October 2002.

4. GOVERNMENT SECURITIES — REVIEW OF RECENT DEVELOPMENT

The Reserve Bank has been continuously making attempts in deepening and widening the government securities market both in primary and secondary segments. Some significant steps which RBI has taken include: elongation of the maturity profile of outstanding issuance including issuances of bonds of 25 years maturity, development of new bench-mark government securities by consolidating new issuances in key maturities, enhancing fungibility, and liquidity through consolidation by reissuances of existing loans, promoting retailing of government securities and introduction of floating rate bonds.

Important development in infrastructure facilitating trading and settlement in money and government securities markets are the operationalisation of the NDS and CCIL. The market has also become more diversified with the entry of new participants such as high networth individuals, co-operative banks, large corporates, mutual funds and insurance companies. The uniform valuation basis, as announced by FIMMADA, provides transparency to the market and facilitates active management of portfolios. The regulatory and supervisory framework for the PDs has been strengthened in accordance with the risks perceived in the market, in line with international practices.

A. Uniform Price Auction: With the experience of uniform price auction in the issuance of 91-day Treasury Bills (since Nov. 6, 98) the annual policy statement of April 2001 proposed to extend uniform price auction format to the auctions of Government of India dated securities on selective and experimental basis. In line with this policy, the uniform price auction was extended to the auctions of floating rate Bonds (FRBs) on Nov. 21 and Dec. 5, 2001. The government securities auction held on April 4, 2002 was also based on uniform price auction, on an experimental basis. RBI will continue to take recourse to uniform price auctions on an experimental and selective basis during this calendar year also as considered necessary.

B. Negotiated Dealing System: The Negotiated Dealing system (Phase-1) has been operationalised effective from Feb. 15, 2002. The NDS provides on line electronic bidding facility in the primary auctions of central /state government securities, OMO/LAF auctions, screen-based electronic dealing and reporting of transaction in money market instruments including repo. Secondary market transactions in government securities and dissemination of information on trades with the least time lag. In addition, the NDS facilitates "paperless" settlement of transactions in government securities with connectivity to CCIL and the DVP settlement system at the Public Debt Office. So far, 80 market participants including 31 non-bank participants are members of NDS. All entities have SGL Accounts with RBI have been advised to become members of NDS by May 31, 2002.

C. Government Securities Act: The Reserve Bank made a proposal to replace the existing Public Debt Act, 1944 by government securities Act to simplify the procedures for transactions in government securities, allow lien marking/pledging of securities as also electronic transfer in dematerialised form. This proposal was approved by the government of India. The state governments have completed the process of passing the requisite resolutions under Article 252 of the constitution of India empowering the parliament to enact the Government Securities Bill. With the concurrence of all state legislatures also having been obtained, the Finance Minister in his Budget Speech for 2002-03 proposal to introduce the Bill in the present Parliament Session.

D. Retailing of Government Securities Through Non-competitive Bidding: In the Mid-term Review of Oct. 2001, RBI had announced finalisation of a scheme to encourage retail participation, in particular by mid-segment investors like UCBs, non-banking financial companies (NBFCs), trusts etc in the primary market of government dated securities. Accordingly, the scheme of non-competitive bidding facility with a provision for allocation upto 5% of the notified amount to retail investors at the weighted rate that evolves in the case of competitive bidding was announced on Dec. 7, 2001.

The scheme was operationalised on Jan. 14, 2002, when auction of 15 year government stock was held. In this auction, 36 non-competitive bids from 273 applicants were received through PDs and banks amounting to Rs. 148.3 crores against the allocation of Rs. 250 crores. In the turn auctions held on April 4, 2002, for 7-year and 10-year government stocks, 46 non-competitive bids from 304 applicants amounting to Rs. 238.5 crores were received as against the reserved amount of Rs. 350 crores. While 2.97% of the notified amount was allotted on Jan. 14, 2002 auction, on April 4, 2002, it was 3.41%. The scheme was continued in the auction of a new 15-year government stock for Rs. 6,000 crores held on April 15, 2002, wherein 19 bids from 137 applicants for an amount of 95.49 crores (1.59% of the notified amount) have been received and fully allotted.

It is advisable for banks to provide schemes for sale / purchase of government securities over their counters to retail investors through demat accounts with depositories or with CSGL account holders. A few banks and PDs have taken useful initiatives to promote retail investment in government securities by offering these securities for sale at retail outlets coupled with facility of holding investments and servicing thereof through existing demat account with depositories or in CSGL accounts. The proposed Government Securities Act specifically recognises the rights of ownership of such investors. In formulating such schemes, PDs and banks may also provide both sale and purchase facility to ensure that the retail investors one assured of liquidity of such investments. Banks could also promote retail sale of government securities along with schemes for availing of automatic finance against such investment at attractive rates, thereby providing ready liquidity.

E. Treasury Bills: The auctions of 14-day and 182-day treasury Bills were discontinued since May 14, 2001. The notified amount of 91-day treasury Bills was increased to Rs. 250 crores from May 16, 2001. The notified amount of 364-day treasury Bills was enhanced from Rs. 750 crores to Rs. 1,000 crores with effect from April 3, 2002.

F. Consolidation of the Government Stocks: The Consolidation of the Government stocks by improving fungibility impacts liquidity to the existing stocks, limits the number of floating stocks and helps in building benchmark securities. However, flexibility in active consolidation is limited because of large market borrowing programme of the Government year after year. Since April 1999. RBI has been attempting passive consolidation" by reissuing the existing stocks through price based auctions which resulted in limiting the number of outstanding stocks. As at the end of Mar. 2002, there were 111, government securities with outstanding amount of Rs. 5,36,325 crores, of which 23 securities, each with minimum outstanding amount of Rs. 10,000 crores, accounted for more than 50%.

G. Floating Rate Bonds: In order to cater to the diverse needs of investors in government securities, several innovative instruments, like Zero Coupon Bonds, Floating Rate Bonds (FRBs), Index Linked Bonds, etc. were issued in the past. Currently, except for one Capital Indeed Bond, which will mature this year, all outstanding government market loans are in the form of plain vanilla fixed rate bonds. In view of ALM and risk weight needs of the major investors such as banks, 2 FRBs of 5-year and 8-year maturity were issued for a total amount of Rs.5,000 crores in November / December 2001 which were fully subscribed. FRBs serve as a diversifying instrument in debt management as it takes advantage of the term premium while minimizing refinancing risk. However FRBs are vulnerable to interest rate risks. Considering both the advantages and risks, issue of further FRBs in the current year would be examined.

H. Calendar for Dated Securities: In order to enable both institutional and retail investors to plan their investments better, the government announced issuance of calendar for dated securities for 2002-03. Such an advance calendar imparts transparency to the government's borrowing programme and is expected to bring stability in the government securities market. Out of the total expected borrowing for first 6 months, a calendar for an amount of Rs. 68,000 crores was announced. The remaining market borrowing programme for the first half of the year, as in the past, will be announced from time to time depending on the emerging requirement of the government and market conditions.

I. Separate Trading for Registered Interest and Principal of Securities: A road map for developing "STRIPS" has prepared and put on RBI web-site for comments and suggestions from the market participants. The government was requested to issue necessary clarification on tax treatment of zero coupon Bonds. In order to operationalise the scheme of STRIPS, it has been decided:

To constitute a working group comprising banks and market participants to suggest operational and prudential guidelines in respect of STRIPS.

J. Satellite Dealer System: In the Mid-term Review Oct. 2001, RIB announced its decision to undertake a review of Satellite Dealer (SD) system in consultation with market participants. After obtaining the views of the Primary Dealers Association of India (PDAI) and after further discussions in TAC and considering their role in the present conditions, it has been decided to discontinue the system Accordingly:

(1) No new SDs will be licensed.

(2) Existing SDs will be required to make action plans, satisfactory to RBI for termination of their operations as SDs by May 31, 2002.

K. Issue of Long-term Bonds for Insurance Companies and Others: RBI has been consciously elongating the maturity profile of government debt having regard to its implications for the government's annual borrowing requirements and debt redemption pattern, need for establishing benchmark for long term financing for infrastructure and catering to the needs of long term investors such as insurance companies provident funds and pension funds. During 2001-02 a 25-year bond was issued for Rs. 8,000 crores after a span of 17 years. RBI proposes to continued its policy of issuing long-term bonds to meet the requirements of such investors.

L. Automatic Debit Mechanism: In some cases, State Governments have given instructions to RBI to debit their accounts on specified dates either as a matter of course to meet certain obligations or in case of specified events. Such automatic debits carry an over-riding priority over other payments. After examining the past experience with automatic debts, a Technical committee of State Finance Secretaries on State Government Guarantees had observed that pre-emption through automatic debit mechanism runs the risk of resulting in insufficient funds for financing critical minimum obligatory payments such as salaries, pensions, amortisation and interest payments. In view of the recommendation of the committee, and keeping in view the need to maintain integrity of the public debt segment of debt markets, it is proposed that:

(1) In future, as a general policy, with prospective effect, to dispense with such automatic debits where there are no legal or other compulsions.

(2) Where there is a legal compulsion for creation of such mechanism, to such amendments to such provisions.

(3) To review all the existing automatic debits in consultation with state governments and others concerned, with a view to dispensing with such mechanisms wherever feasible.

Urban Co-operative Banks

A. New Apex Supervisory Body: The annual policy statement of April 2001 had announced a proposal to set up a New Apex supervisory Body to take over the entire inspection / supervisory functions relating to scheduled and non-scheduled UCBs in consultation with the central government. In the Mid-term Review of Oct. 2001, it was mentioned that RBI has submitted a draft bill on setting up of a separate supervisory Authority. The matter is under consideration of the government.

The events of the last 2 years have made it abundantly clear that the present system of dual/triple regulatory and supervisory control (involving centre, states and RBI) is not conducive to efficient functioning of the cooperative banks in the interest of their depositors. Several committees in the past have also recommended elimination of multiple layers of supervision and regulation of this sector. In view of the local interest involved, it is also clear that there is no consensus at present in favour of removing regulatory and supervisory responsibilities at central/state government levels, and for entrusting it exclusively to RBI. As a result, the managements and boards of several cooperative institutions continue to reflect political interests rather than genuine cooperative spirit, and are not always amenable to normal banking discipline in their operations. In view of this, it would be best, in the interest of the public depositors, if the situation is faced squarely and a separate supervisory authority is set up, with representatives of centre, state and other interested elements. Such a body can then be exclusively made responsible for efficient functioning of the cooperative institutions and also take responsibility for ensuring the safety of public deposits.

B. Working Group on Asset-liability Management: It was indicated in the Mid-term Review of Oct. 2001 that RBI has circulated the report of the working Group on ALM guidelines for UCBs to select UCBs for their comments. Only 6 banks responded, however, their responses were positive. It was felt that the guidelines need simplification and towards smooth implementation, a few workshops may be held to explain these guidelines for obtaining feedback from the officials | CEOs of UCBs in their implementation. The first workshop held on Jan. 14-15, 2002 at College of Agricultural Banking, Pune was attended by 37 executives from 17 UCBs. The second workshop was conducted at Bankers training college Mumbai. After taking into account the suggestions received from the participating banks in the 2 workshops, the guidelines have since been issued.

C. Supervisory Rating System for UCBs: The Reserve Bank, based on its onsite inspection, had put in place a supervisory rating "CAMELS" model for Indian commercial banks and 'CACS' model for foreign banks so as to assess their performance. In 1999, onsite inspection based on "CAMELS" model was extended to UCBs as an additional tool for supervision. Since UCBs are members of the payment system and also beneficiaries of deposit insurance scheme, in the light of recent experience, it is felt that there is a need to further strengthen the supervisory regime for UCBs. Towards this end, RBI constituted a working group in Oct. 2001 to evolve a suitable rating model for UCBs taking into account their operational characteristics. The working group in consultation with CEOs of large UCBs, submitted its report on March 23, 2002. The recommendations of the group are being examined and necessary guidelines would be issued in due course.

Supervision and Monitoring

Progress made in respect of certain announcements made in the annual policy statement of Apr. 2001 is reviewed below:

A. Offsite Monitoring and Surveillance: The Reserve Bank had rationalized off-site returns to monitor liquidity and interest rate risks on quarterly basis in 1999. With the intention to finally more over to a fortnightly reporting system, in consultation with the banks, a revised system was put in place in June 2000. The reporting schedule for the reports on:

1. Interest rate sensitivity.
2. Structural liquidity, both for rupee and forex transaction.
3. Assets, liabilities and exposures.
4. Exposure to sensitive sectors and
5. Indian subsidiaries, was made monthly effect from Oct. 2001.

B. Risk based Supervision: The Project Implementation Group formed for the smooth switch over to risk Based supervision (RBS) process by 2003, has initiated certain management processes which include preparation of dicision paper, risk profiling, manual writing, training and legal requirements. The responses from banks on the discussion paper were analysed and in order to assess their progress and needs in this regard, a consultation process has started. The group has prepared a draft risk assessment template for risk profiling of banks under the RBS approach. The template is being tested with a few banks for further customisation and refinement. An internal group was constituted for drafting of manuals.

C. Prompt Corrective Action: As indicated in the Mid-term Review of Oct. 2001, the scheme of prompt corrective action (PCA) with various trigger points for prompt responses by the supervisors was developed and sent to the government for their views before implementation. The government has since cleared the scheme which will be put in place shortly.

D. Macro-prudential Indicators: It was indicated in the annual policy statement of Apr. 2001 that pilot reviews using macro-prudential indicators (MPIs) for the half-year ended Mar. 2000 and Sept. 2000 were prepared for internal circulation. Subsequently, the reviews for the half-year ended in Mar. 2001 and Sept. 2001 were also prepared. While the earlier reviews were largely compilation of MPIs, scope and coverage of the subsequent reviews are enhanced by including data on capital market, forex market and other segments of the financial system.

E. Consolidated Accounting and Supervision: As mentioned in the annual policy statement of April 2001, the Board for Financial Supervision (BFS) has evolved an approach for consolidated supervision as appropriate in the Indian context. A multi-disciplinary working group was set up to look into the introduction of consolidated accounting and quantitative techniques for consolidated supervision, in line with international best practices. The groups report was placed before BFS on Jan. 29, 2002. The report was also put in public domain for comments / suggestions. Based on the comments, necessary guidelines would be issued by RBI.

Present Status of Prudential Measures

Increasing globalization and blurring of distinction among different segments of financial intermediaries have proposed a special challenge for banking sector. Being the mainstay of financial intermediation, developing a sound and healthy banking system through motion of prudent financial practices has become essential to sustain financial stability. It has been recognised that Indian banking system should be in the tune with well laid down international standards of capital adequacy and prudential norms.

RBI initiated the banking sector reforms as per the recommendations of committed on the financial system to improve the financial health and enhance the efficiency, productivity and profitability of the Indian banking system over time. Keeping in view the changes in pace and pattern of developments in the financial sector and with the objective of achieving convergence between Indian standards and international best practices, a number of measures were announced in earlier policy statements. The progress made in the implementation of these measures along with further measures considered necessary are indicated below:

A. Adoption of 90 Days Norm for Recognition of Loan Impairment: As indicated in the annual policy statement of Apr. 2001, banks were advised to adopt 90 days norm to classify their assets from the year ending Mar. 31, 2004. They are asked to chalk out an appropriate transaction path for smoothly moving over to the 90 days norm and submit their action plans with the approval of their Boards to RBI. As a facilitating measure, they were advised to move over to charging of interest at monthly rests by Apr. 1, 2002. In this connection, some banks sought clarifications on application of interest for longer rests, etc. In consultation with IBA, detailed guidelines were issued clarifying with effect from Apr. 1, 2002, banks may move over to charging of interest on loans/advances at monthly rests except for agricultural advances.

B. New Basel Capital Accord: In the Mid-term Review of Oct. 2001, it was mentioned that RBI had forwarded its comments on the second consultative people on the New Capital Accord issued by the Basel Committee of Banking, supervision, (BCBS). The committee received over 200 responses from national supervisors, banks, international institutions and others which can be accessed at WWW.bis.org. Such wide variety of comments indicate the fact that achieving global consensus on the methodology of capital regulation is not on easy task. Many respondents have expressed their concerns at the difficulties that would be experienced in implementing the proposals on account of their complexity and costs. Several respondents have also pointed out that capital requirements could increase across the board in most jurisdictions on account of the new proposals.

In view of these, the consultation process has been extended and some modifications to the proposals are currently being discussed by BCBS which could mitigate more than the anticipated upward impact on capital requirements. Another Quantitative Impact Study (QIS) will be conducted in the coming months with wider participation and the Reserve Bank will also be participating in this impact assessment. At the some time, an interval group in RBI is also engaged in developing a suitably modified approach. Within the philosophical framework of the Basel proposals which could be adapted to the Indian situation and simpler to implement and supervise. For this purpose, the internal group will invite representatives from select banks to provide inputs into the development of the modified approach as well as the upcoming (QIS). Further, assigning risk weights for bank assets should largely be a matter for the banks or their supervisors. Banks are expected to constitute an expert internal team to study the methodology of the new proposals and its likely impact.

C. Counterparty and Country Risks: The Reserve Bank is committed to the implementation of the "core Principles for effective banking Supervision", drawn up by BCBS. It is a matter of satisfaction that the banking system in India is largely complacent with most of the core principles.

In Oct. 1999, RBI had issued risk management guidelines which, inter alia, advised banks to use the country ratings of international rating agencies and classify the countries into low risk, mode rate risk and high risk categories and endeavour to develop an internal matrix and reckons the counterparty and the country risks. With a view to moving further in complying with the core principles, RBI would be shortly issuing draft guidelines on country risk management and provisioning therefore in consultation with Banks, IBA and other market participants.

D. Capital for Market Risk: It was announced in the Mid-term Review of Oct. 1998, that the government and other approved securities which would have to be provided for a risk weight of 2.5% towards market risk by Mar. 31, 2000. Guidelines on categorisation and valuation of banks investments, in consonance with international practices, were also announced in the Mid-term Review of Oct. 2000 and were effective from the half-year ended Sept. 30, 2000. Accordingly, banks were required to provide for 2.5% risk weight on SLR and non-SLR securities, with effect from Mar. 31, 2000 and 2001, respectively, as an interim arrangement, till such time as banks move over to the framework suggested by the Basel committee.

The Basel norms provide for assigning capital for market risk on a standardised or on internally developed value at risk (VAR) methods. As the valuation norms on banks' investment portfolio have already been put in place and aligned with the international best practices, it is appropriate to adopt the Basel norms on capital for market risk. In view of this, banks are advised to study the Basel framework on capital for market risk as envisaged in amendment to the Capital Accord to incorporate market risks published in Jan. 1996 by BCRS and prepare themselves to follow the international practices in this regard at a suitable date to be announced by RBI.

E. Prevention of Money Laundering: India has been sharing the increasing international concern on the use of the financial system for money laundering and financing of terrorism. The challenges faced by the international community in combating financial crimes require sustained and coordinated action among the various agencies concerned with regulation and enforcement responsibilities, both in India and abroad. RBI and the Government have initiated various steps from time to time to check any misuse of the financial system for laundering proceeds of criminal activities.

As part of these initiatives, RBI is in the process of issuing a Master Circular setting out the policy, procedures and controls required to be introduced by banks. These include strict adherence to know your customer (KYC) procedures for prevention of misuse of banking system for money laundering and financing of terrorist activity. The recommendations of the working group on anti-Money laundering set up by IBA would also be taken into account while framing the guidelines.

F. Reduction in Transition Period of a Sub-standard Asset to Doubtful Category: Narasimhan Committee II had recommended that an asset should be classified as doubtful, it is in the substandard category for 18 months in the first instance and for 12 months subsequently. Accordingly RBI had announced in the Mid-term Review of Oct. 1998 and with effect from Mar. 31, 2001, an asset should be classified as doubtful if it has remained in the sub-standard category for 18 months.

Consistent with the recommendations of Narasimhan committee II and with a view to moving closer to international best practices, it is proposed that:

With effect from Mar. 31, 2005, an assets would be classified as doubtful if it remained in the sub-standard category for 12 months. Banks are permitted to phase the consequent additional provisioning over a four-year period, with a minimum of 20% each year.

G. Recovery of Non-performing Assets: It was indicated in the mid-term Review of Oct. 2001, that the broad framework provided for compromise settlements of NPAs issued by RBI in 1995 will continue to be in place and banks are free to design and implement their own policies for recovery and write off incorporating compromise and negotiated settlements with the approval of their Boards. The Finance Minister in his meeting with the CMDs of banks held on Nov. 12, 2001 at New Delhi had indicated that a suitable scheme be evolved for small borrowers by banks for recovery of dues upto Rs. 25,000. Accordingly, banks have been advised to formulate a policy for recovery of dues, principal amount (excluding the interest element) in all sectors irrespective of the nature of business or purpose, which have become NPAs and on Mar. 31, 1998. As announced in the Budget 2002-03, a special one-time settlement (OTS) scheme for small and marginal farmers to cover loans upto Rs. 50,000 has been issued : At the request of government of India, RBI also conducted a review of the functioning of the Debt recovery tribunals (DRTs) subsequent to various amendments carried out in the Recovery of Debts dues to Banks and FIs (Amendment) Act, 2000, with reference to their position as on Mar. 31, 2001.

H. Corporate Debt Restructuring: It may be recalled that in August 2001, RBI had issued guidelines on corporate Debt Restructuring (CDR) for implementation by banks and FIs to put in place a framework outside the purview of BIFR, DRT and other legal procedures to ensure timely and transparent mechanism for restructuring debts of viable corporate entities facing financial problems. As proposed in the Budget 2002-03, RBI constituted a high level group (chairman) : Shri Vepa Kamesam, Deputy Governor) to review the operations of the CDR scheme to identify the operational difficulties, if any, in smooth implementation of the scheme and to suggest measures to make the scheme even more effective. As an interim measure, it has been decided that permission for debt restructuring will be made available by RBI on the basis of specific recommendations of CDR "core-group", if a minimum of 75% (by value) of the lenders constituting banks and FIs consent for CDR, irrespective of differences in classification of the assets by banks/financial institutions.

I. Non-SLR Investments by Banks and Financial Institutions: A mention was made in the Mid-term Review of Oct. 2001 that further prudence should be observed by banks and FIs in order to contain the risk arising out of non-SLR investment portfolio of banks and FIs, in particular through the private placement routine. The draft prudential guidelines on management of non-SLR investment portfolio were issued to banks for their comments/view. On the basis of feedback, guidelines are being finalized and would be issued in due course.

J. Investment Fluctuation Reserve: The Reserve bank, with a view to building up adequate reserves to guard against, any possible reversal of interest rate environment in future due to unexpected developments, advised banks in Jan. 2002, to build up an IFR of a minimum 5.0% of the investment portfolio within a period of 5 years. However, banks have been given the freedom to build up IFR to a maximum of 10.0% of the portfolio depending on the size and composition of their portfolio, with the approval of their board. On the basis of feedback received from the banks on the above proposals, it has been decided that IFR should be computed with reference to investments in 2 categories, viz. "Held for trading and "Available for sale". Thus it will not be necessary to include the investment under "Held to maturity" category, which is not meant to be traded for purposes of computation of IFR.

Technology Upgradation

The RBI has been playing a pivotal role upgrading the payment and settlement system in the country. The progress achieved so far in consolidating the existing payment systems developing new technologically advanced modes of payment and moving towards the ultimate objective of linking various payment and settlement into an efficient and integrated system that will function in real time environment has been substantial.

The Mid term Review of October 2000 mentioned the preparation of a ***"payment system visitor document"***. After examining the comments the final version of the vision document was published in ***Dec. 2001.*** It provides a road map of important developments in the payment system projects. This would facilitate banks in getting fully prepared to participate effectively in the new products aimed at better payment and settlement services.

(A) Networking of branches of banks for information dissemation.

(B) Extension of electronic fund transfer facilities.

(C) Real time gross settlement system.

A. Networking of Branches: The process of reforms in the payment and settlement system has gained momentum with the implementation of projects such as *NDS,* Centralized fund management system for better funds management by banks and structured financial messaging solutions for secure message transfer to be routed electronically across banks using the modem of the ***Indian financial network (INFINET).*** To reap the full benefits of such electronic message transfer it is necessary that banks below sufficient attention on the computerization and networking of the branches situated at commercially networking would facilitate in addressing the last mile problem which would in turn result quick and efficient.

B. Extension of Electronic Funds Transfer Facilities: Recognizing that the key to quick, safe and efficient funds transfers lies in the use of electronic modes of funds transfers, the Reserve Bank has improved the existing facilities under electronic funds transfer (EFT). The EFT is now available for the transfer of funds across banks and 13 different centres with one settlement a day and an enhanced per transaction limit of Rs. 2.0 crore which would make EFT attractive even for corporate funds movement. In the case of four metropolitan cities, the settlement is being effected at three time slots, every day which will shortly be extended to all the other centres so as to enable transfers "T + O basis". Adequate security features are also being incorporated in the EFT scheme, apart from providing for Integration of the RBI's EFT scheme with various schemes already in vogue within some banks. Once all banks start using the EFT on a large scale, the dependence on conventional funds transfer modes would diminish thus bringing about greater efficiency in the movement of funds, better funds management capabilities for constituents of banks and reductions in risks associated with funds transfers which take time.

C. Real Time Gross Settlement System-Status: In earlier policy statements, RBI had announced its intention of putting in place a RTGs system, which will enable a real time movement of funds. The preparatory work for RTGS system has been completed and a suitable vendor for designing and development of the system has been selected. The work on design specifications is in progress. These specifications would take into account the international best practices as suitable to requirements of Indians banking. The system in scheduled to be ready for testing in about a year.

Ownership Functions of Reserve Bank of India

It was indicated in the annual policy statement of April 2001 that RBI should not own the institutions it regulates. Towards this end, in the case of Discount and Finance House of India (DFHI) and Securities Trading Corporation of India. (STCI), The process of disinvestment has already been completed.

The Finance Minister in his budget speech for 2002-03 announced that the Deposit Insurance and Credit Guarantee Corporation (DICGC) will be converted into the Bank Deposits Insurance Corporation (BDIC) to make it an effective instrument for dealing with depositor's risks and distressed banks. Appropriate legislative changes will be proposed for this purpose. In the case of transfer of ownership of RBI in State Bank of India, National Bank for Agriculture and Rural Development and National Housing Bank, an internal Working Group was constituted to recommend the modalities, viz., valuation, payment adjustments etc. and the legislative measures required consequent to transfer of shareholding. The Working Group has submitted its report in Nov. 2001 which was forwarded to the Government for their comments.

5. NON-BANKING FINANCIAL COMPANIES

The Reserve Bank has received applications for Certificate of Registration (CoR) from 36,414 Non-Banking Financial Companies (NBFCs), of which, 14,079 applications were approved and 19,058 were rejected as at the end of Mar. 2002. Out of 14,079 Companies, only 780 NBFCs have been allowed to accept/hold deposits from the public. Applications of 3,277 companies are still pending for various legal/procedural reasons. Out of these, 2,916 applications are held in obeyance pending enactment of the Financial Companies Regulation Bill, 2002.

Certain NBFCs were granting demand/call loans with an open period or without any stipulation regarding the rate of interest and servicing. Difficulty was experienced in ensuring compliance with prudential norms on income recognition, asset classification and provisioning in respect of such loans. In order to obviate these difficulties and to ensure that all such loans are appropriately classified and the position of NPAs is truly reflected in the financial statements of NBFCs, it was decided that all NBFCs granting/intending to grant demand/call loans should lay down a policy duly approved by their Board. The policy should cover aspects such as stipulation of cut-off date within which the repayment of the loan will be demanded/called up, stipulation of the rate of interest and the periodic rests for payment of interest, stipulation of cut off date not exceeding 6 months for review of the performance of loan, criteria for renewal. Directions covering NPA classification and provisioning requirements have also been issued.

With a view to further strengthening the regulatory/supervisory framework for NBFCs, the following measures are proposed.

A. Formation of SRO for NBFC Sector: The Reserve Bank has taken a number of steps to speed up the reform process in the functioning of NBFC sector along prudent lines. For further development of this sector, emphasis has been placed on formation of a Self Regulatory Organisation (SRO), particularly for the benefit of smaller NBFCs. Towards this end, as mentioned in the Mid-term Review of Oct. 2001, RBI has been on an ongoing basis discussing with the Informal Advisory Group of NBFCs and also with various NBFC Associations. In the meeting of the Informal Advisory Group held on Mar. 11, 2002, the matter was discussed and the representatives of NBFC Associations have informed that SRO would be constituted at the earliest.

B. Submission of Returns by NBFCs: NBFCs are required to submit periodic control returns to RBI. However, as laxity has been observed in this regard, in order to inculcate a sense of discipline in this sector, it has been decided to take action against NBFCs for non-submission of returns. Accordingly, in the first instance :

RBI would impose penalties as provided for in the Reserve Bank of India Act, 1934 as also launch Court proceedings, besides considering rejection/cancellation of the CoR of NBFCs having public deposits of Rs. 50 crores and above, in case of default in the submission of returns.

The above stipulation in respect of the size of NBFCs (i.e. Rs. 50 crores and above) will be progressively reduced over time to ensure that as far as possible, all NBFCs submit periodic returns on a timely basis.

Rationalisation of Current Account Facility with the Reserve Bank

As indicated in the Mid-term Review of October 2001, an Internal Group was set up to rationalise the present policy of access to current account facility provided by RBI in view of phasing out of non-banks from call/notice money market, upgradation of payment system infrastructure such as operationalisation of CCIL and NDS and operations of DMO/LAF only through Banks and PDs. These would obviate the need of non-bank entities to have access to Current account with RBI. In this Context, a group of Senior Executives of RBI was constituted to examine the recommendations of the report, suggest modifications and take such other follow-up actions as necessary. In order to ensure that current account facility with the Reserve Bank Serves its core objectives, it has been decided that current account facility may be extended only to scheduled commercial banks, scheduled co-operative banks, and PDs. Current account facility for entities other than those indicated above would be phased out in due course. A programme for phasing out current account facility in respect of all India Financial Institutions will be chalked out concurrently. At a later stage, depositories like NSDL, CDSL and other custodians like SHCIL will also be phased out and they can then operate through banks.

International Financial Standards and Codes: The mid-term review of October 2001 mentioned the progress made by the Advisory Groups on International Financial Standards and codes. All the ten advisory groups constituted by the Standing Committee have submitted their reports to the chairman of the Standing Committee and these reports were placed on RBI website for wider dissemination. It was also mentioned that the Standing Committee will prepare its own report indicating the course of follow-up/reforms required and the regulatory agencies involved in such follow-up actions. The Standing Committee is synthesizing the views and comments of all the advisory groups and the final report will be placed shortly in the public domain for wider dissemination and appropriate follow-up action.

Short-term Liquidity Assessment Model: Considering the importance of guiding monetary policy operations on a sound basis, the annual policy statement of April 1999 mentioned the need for developing a short-term operational model which takes into account the behavioural relationships among different segments of the financial system. Under the guidance of a group of eminent academic exports, an operational model was developed and is being tested. The draft model will also be put on RBI's website for wider public debate. Once the model is made operational, it may be feasible to constitute a technical committee in order to assist in monetary policy strategy. It is felt that in future, a technical monetary policy committee would act as a back office projecting various alternate policy strategies as is the practice in some other Central Banks.

Mid-term Review: A review of credit and monetary developments in the first half of the current year will be undertaken in October 2002. The Mid-term Review will be confined to a review of monetary developments and to such changes as may be necessary in monetary policy and projections for the second-half of the year. Mumbai, April 29, 2002.

Annexure

RBI WORKING GROUPS – PROGRESS REPORT EXPERT COMMITTEE ON BANK FRAUDS

The export committee on Bank Frauds (chairman Dr. Numitra) submitted its report to the RBI in September 2001. The report was examined as per the directions of the BFs and the report along with the comments of the RBI was forwarded to the high level group on Frauds in banking sector constituted by Central Vigilance Commission (CVC) for its examination and comments.

Consultative Group for Strengthening the Internal Supervisory Role of Boards of Banks

A Consultative group of Directors of Banks and FIs was constituted under the chairmanship of Dr. A. S. Ganguly, Director Central Board, RBI to suggest, for consideration of the Government/RBI, measures that could be taken in respect of strengthening the internal supervisory role of Boards of banks/FIs in view of the on-going financial sector reforms which has entrusted greater autonomy and powers to the banks Boards. The group submitted its report recently which is under examination.

Transparency and Accounting Standards

A working group was constituted under the chairmanship of Shri N. D. Gupta, president, ICAI along with representatives from RBI and commercial banks to put in place appropriate arrangements to identify the compliance and also gaps in Compliance with the accounting standards issued by ICAI and to recommend steps to eliminate/reduce such gaps. The working group will, inter alia, analyse the difficulties faced by the banks in adoption of the accounting standards and evolve suitable guidelines in this regard. Result is awaited.

Defaulter's List — Widening the Coverage

A working group was constituted under the chairmanship of Shri S. R. Iyer, Chairman, Credit Information Bureau (India) Ltd. (CIBIL), with representatives from RBI, commercial banks and FIs, to examine the possibility of the CIBIL, performing RC role of collecting and disseminating information on the list of suit field accounts and list of defaulter's including, wilful defaulters, which is presently handled by RBI. The group submitted its report which is under examination.

Indian Financial System during the IIIrd phase is briefly outlines as follows :

(A) Privatisation, (Financial Institutions).

(B) Re-organisation.

(C) Investor Protection.

(A) PRIVATISATION

The financial system was under the control of the central government. Gradually the GOI wanted to privatise the ***PSUs*** in a phased manner. The privatisation is a part of the strategy. The government wants to reduce its liability from the public sector because of mismanagement. Privatisation of the Financial Institutions is a part of the New Industrial Policy. Therefore the government has taken the steps to privatise the important financial institutions. The government converted the ***IFCI*** into a public company. The IFCI and IDBI have offered their equity to the investors. The SEBI has permitted the private mutual funds under its guidelines. A number of private mutual funds came into existence under the control of the RBI. The R. N. Malhotra committee recommended the scheme of reorganisation of the structure of the insurance industry. The enactment of ***Insurance Regulatory and Development Authority Act, 1999*** leads to the rapid development in the insurance business. According to the act the private companies can enter into the insurance sector for the benefit of the public. Foreign promoters are also allowed in the sector. Thus the monopoly of LIC, GIC has been dismantled in a phased manner. The PFIs are also permitted to sell. The equity, bonds and debentures to the public sector enterprises. Hence radical changes have been arose in the Indian Economy due to introduction of privatisation.

(B) RE-ORGANISATION

The Indian Financial System is undergoing an outstanding transformation and it can create wonders in the capital market if it sticks on to a strong policy. Now the entire economy is market based and the strong presence in the market can only make it sensitive. Therefore every enterprise should be in a competent manner highly skilled and talented people with a proper strategy. All these factors can boost the profitability of the commercial enterprises drastic change have occurred in the financial sector with reference to the competitive markets. The sponsorship of the DFIs made the re-organisation of the institutional structure. The development banks, lending institutions, banks, MFs have entered into the capital market in an innovative way. The reorganisation of the institutional structure are made in the following areas.

(A) Commercial banks.

(B) NBFC.

(C) Mutual Funds.

(D) Public Financial Institutions.

(E) Capital Market.

The commercial banks has undergone a major transformation with the introduction of the ***liberalisation, privatisation and globalisation.*** The radical changes have been rising in the structure operating policies and accounting norms. The present environment has created the banking sector in the expansion process and in the development of the branch banking system. The branches are also opened in rural and semi urban areas and the share of the priority sector in the total bank credit. But the branch banking has an adverse effect on the profitability and efficiency of the business. The RBI controls the banks through ***SLR and CRR***. The prudential banking is required to run the business very smoothly. The Narasimhan committee made recommendations to the better functioning of the commercial banks. The prudential norms relating to this income asset and capital adequacy are applicable to the PSBs. The bank also expedite to the recovery of overdues through the Debt Recovery Tribunals. The RBI has also published the names of the defaulters who filed in the courts for the recovery of loans. The banks are also facing the problems of NPAs. The Non-performing Assets of the PSB shot upto ***Rs. 56,608*** crores in Sept. 2001. This staggering number not only reduces the yield on advances but also has an adverse impact on the profitability of banks. The huge NPAs of the banks are mostly because of the debt or friendly for closure and bankruptcy laws which allows the customers to default with impurity. The particulars of the NPAs are presented below.[4]

Year	*Gross NPA (Rs in crore)*	*Gross NPA as % of Gross Advance*	*Net NPA*	*Net NPA as % of Net Advance*
1993	39,253	23.2%	NA	NA
1994	41,041	24.8%	NA	NA
1995	38,385	19.5%	17,567	10.7%
1996	41,661	18%	18,297	8.9%
1997	47,300	15.7%	22,340	8.1%
1998	50,815	14.4%	23,761	7.3%
1999	58,722	14.7%	28,020	7.6%

4. Sources : The Problem of NPA, BT, P. 88, AI 2000.

Statement showing the Combined Assets of the Public Sector Banks (27 Banks) Rs in crores

1996-97	5,05,698.40
1997-98	5,56,296.00
1998-99	6,49,503.94
1999-2000	7,70,144.92
2000-2001	8,90,951.73

STATEMENT SHOWING THE PROFITABILITY OF THE BANKS

Year	*PSU Banks*	*New Private Banks*	*Foreign Banks*
1995-96	— 0.07%	1.85%	1.58%
1996-97	0.57%	1.73%	1.19%
1997-98	0.77%	1.55%	0.97%
1998-99	0.42%	1.03%	0.69%
1999-2000	0.57%	0.97%	1.17%
Net profit as a percentage of total assets			

STATEMENT SHOWING THE MARKET SHARE IN DEPOSITS BY

	Deposits	*1995*	*1996*	*1997*	*1998*	*1999*	*2000*
1.	PSBs	82.12%	82.85%	81.49%	80.51%	78.23%	77.34%
2.	Nationalised	55.44%	55.26%	54.94%	53.73%	52.94%	52.02%

	Advançes	*1995*	*1996*	*1997*	*1998*	*1999*	*2000*
1.	27 PSBs	76.66%	75.16%	73.70%	73.90%	75.26%	73.55%
2.	19 Nationalised banks	48.26%	45.91%	44.93%	45.65%	47.39%	46.40%

Emergence of New Private Banks

The eight new private banks that have emerged on the Indian financial topography since 1994 clear out the performers in troubled sector. In 7 years these banks have grown to account 6% of the total assets and 10% of the total profits of the banking industry ***(2000-2001)***. It was the Narasimhan committee report dated 1991 that envisaged a large role for the private sector banks. The RBI agreed in an effort to make the sector more efficient and competitive, it issued in Jan 1993, the guidelines governing the entry of the new private banks a minimum paid up capital of ***Rs. 100 crore*** among others. This was the first time after the nationalisation of banks in 1969 the RBI issued fresh banking license to private sector.

The NPBs have not grown just organically, but also through the mergers and acquisition. The HDFC bank merged with the Times Bank in the all stock deal valued at ***Rs. 200 crore*** in Nov. 1999. The ICICI bank acquired, the bank of Madura in a stock swap deal in ***Dec. 2000*** to become the largest among the NPBs.

History of Banking

July 1 and 3, 1991, the RBI had devalued the rupee in a two step downward adjustment of 17.38. July 3, 1991, the bank rate which was dormant since July 1981, is hiked from ***10%*** to ***11%*** and further to ***12%*** on Oct 8, 1991.

Nov. 1991 Narasimhan Committee on reforming the financial system presented its report. Among other things it suggests the phased reduction of the SCR to ***25%*** in 3 years and then CRR to 10% in 4 years. April 1982 : the RBI introduces the risk asset ratio system for the banks as a capital adequacy measure. March 1, 1992 : Dual exchange rate system is instituted under the liberalised exchange rate management enabling orderly transition from a managed floating regime to market determined on January 8, 1993 : The FERA amended and subsequently repealed and replaced by the FERA amendment act 1993 Jan. 1993 : Guidelines for setting up the private banks by March 93: Rupee is made convertible Sept. 93 : New bank of India emerged with the Punjab National Bank. March 94 : With the receipt of a license the UTI bank becomes the first private sector bank to start operating. June 13, 1994 : The RBI issues guidelines on the prudential norms banks to achieve the minimum capital adequacy ratio 6% in their risk weighted assets and off balance sheet exposure by 31-3-95 and 8% by March 1996.

July 15, 1994 : With an amendment to the banking companies act, 1970 nationalised banks are allowed to strengthen their capital base by tapping the capital market to public contribution if their capital upto 49%. August 1994 : Second step towards the full convertibility is taken by making rupee convertible on the current account.

Oct 1994 : Oriental Bank of Commerce becomes the first nationalised bank to access the capital market to raise Rs. 387.24 crores. Oct 1, 1995 : Banks are allowed to fix own interest rates on domestic term deposits with maturity of 2 years. July 1996 : The IRDA is set up to privatise insurance sector. May 9, 1997: The RBI issues the new norms for the NBFCs. December 7, 1997: The RBI constituted SH Khan Committee to study about the developments of FIs and banks April 24, 1998 : The Khan committee submits recommendations to introduce universal banking. Aug 9, 2000 : Banks with a minimum of Rs. 500 crore can enter the insurance business through a joint venture. Nov. 10, 2002 : Banks are allowed to invest upto 5% of its total outstanding domestic credit in the capital market. Jan 3, 2001 : RBI issued new required guidelines for licensing the new banks in the private sector. These stipulate a minimum initial paid up capital of Rs. 200 crore (to be raised to Rs. 300 crores within 3 years of commencement of business) with a minimum of 40% as a contribution from the promoter. March 15, 2001 : The government reduces the interest rate payable on the relief bonds issued under the 9% 1999 scheme to 8.5%. The fixed deposit schemes specially for senior citizens offering higher fixed rate of interest. April 28, 2001 : The RBI clarifies to approach the Universal banking term lending and refinancing institutions.

The Future of the Banking

The global environment has been changing. The increased competition will squeeze the profitability across the globe. Mostly they hit the small banks. The larger banks will be able to mobilise sufficient capital to the back asset expansion and fund investments technology. Mergers and Acquisitions are not new to the Indian Banking Sector. The government has used them in the past to bailout weaker banks, through their mergers with other public sector banks. The new private banks has created a new environment in the history of market driven mergers and acquisitions in India. The amalgamation of the HDFC bank with the times bank and the acquisition of Bank of Madura by the ICICI bank herald a trend driven by the commercial considerations.

MERGERS IN BANKING SECTOR 1984-2001

Sl. No.	*Bank*	*Year*	*Merged with*
1.	Lakshmi Commercial Bank	1984	Canara Bank
2.	Bank of Cochin	1984	SBI
3.	Miraj State Bank	1984	UBI
4.	Hindustan Commercial Bank	1985	PNB
5.	Trades Bank	1987	Bank of Baroda
6.	United Industrial Bank	1988-89	Allahabad Bank
7.	Bank of Tamilnadu	1988-89	IOB
8.	Bank of Tanjavur	1988-89	Indian Bank
9.	Porur Central Bank	1988-89	Bank of Baroda
10.	Purbachal Bank	1990	CBI
11.	New Bank of India	1993	PNB
12.	BCCI	1993	SBI
13.	Bank of Karad	1994	Bank of India
14.	Kashinath Seth Bank	1995	SBI
15.	Baridoab Bank and Punjab Co-operative Bank	1997	OBC
16.	Bareilly Corporation Bank	1999	Bank of Baroda
17.	Sikkim Bank	1999	UBI
18.	Times Bank	1999	HDFC
19.	Bank of Madura	2000	ICICI Bank

Mobile banking became very popular at present. Mobile banking will always add on to the traditional banking channels. The number of consumers using it will increase with the corresponding rise in the number of cellular subscribers in the country. Several banks have mobile banking services already. Today we can make a balance enquiry, request for a cheque book, get a mini statement of transactions or pay utility bills through the mobile. Still, Indian banks have much to learn from Europe and Japan. In France, for instance, most phones comes with a built in credit card slot, something that addresses several thorny payment issues. In Japan the users of the mobile service i-Mode can carry out banking transactions online i-Mode has partnership with 280 banks and several securities brokers. In Mumbai, it carries 19000 transactions a day : and BPL 25,000.

The following policy matters have been taken to improve the efficiency and profitability of banks.

(1) Closing of Unprofitable branches.

(2) Mergers of banks.

(3) Deregulation of interest rates on lending.

(4) The reduction in SLR and CRR.

(5) Greater operational flexibility.

(6) The permissions to the banks to directly undertake leasing, factoring and hire purchase business (upto a maximum 10% of total advances).

Non-Banking Financial Institutions

The Non-Banking Financial Companies play an important role in the Indian Financial System. Recently they recorded marked growth in terms of deposits. They expanded their activities in financial services sector. They involve in both fee based and fund based activities. They actively involve in equipment leasing, hire purchase finance, venture capital, housing finance, factoring, bill discounting etc. All these activities are fund based. They also involve in fee based or advisory services which are presented below:

(a) Mergers and Acquisitions.

(b) Loan Syndication.

(c) Leasing.

(d) Corporate Counselling.

(e) Portfolio Management.

(f) Issue Management.

The regulatory framework has been done on the basis of recommendations of the ***Khanna and Vasudev Committee***. The RBI has set up a separate department of Non-banking to superwise and monitor the activities of the NBFCs. The element of regulations presented below :

(1) Prudential norms RBI directions 1998

(2) RBI Act-Chapter III-B 1998

(3) RBI acceptance of deposits regulations 1998

(4) RBI directions audit report 1998.

Mutual Funds

The mutual funds have been very popular in the Indian Financial System. They have been playing an important role in the stock market. They have been emerging as the backbone of the capital market. It is the vehicle for institutionalisation of the security investments. The following factors influence the investment decisions of the small investors.

(1) Tax exemptions to the unit holders.

(2) Firm allotment to the mutual funds.

(3) Proportionate allotment in case of over-subscription.

(4) The adjustment for capital gains tax.

(5) The minimum limit in the primary market is raised to Rs. 5,000.

(6) Full monitoring activities of the funds by SEBI.

Mutual funds in India began in 1964.[5] The UTI was launched in 1964. The scheme ***US 64*** was established in 1964. It was only in 1987 that banks and Insurance Companies got into with the initiative of the SEBI. 40% of mutual funds were promoted by the banks and Insurance Companies. The first private mutual fund ***Kothari pioneer*** was launched in 1993. More mutual funds joined the party and the total assets under them grew to ***Rs. 61,301*** crore in March 1994. With the fall of the **sensex** the investor's preference shifted to the fixed instruments in 1996. Many of the new entrants found it difficult to compete with the UTI which had assured return on debt products. The period 1996-98 was the worst period in the history of the mutual funds. But several AMCs used this opportunity to restructure their portfolios and got ready for the 1999 boom in equities. In 1999-2000 the value of assets under the management

5. The mutual funds boom, Business Today Anniversary Issue, 2002, P. 69.

swelled to ***Rs. 1,07,946*** crores. Today there are 34 MFs managing ***614 schemes*** and ***Rs. 94,571*** crores in assets. Not all of them will survive, but performance and transparency tell in the long-run.

STATEMENT SHOWING MUTUAL FUNDS BOOM

(Rs. in crore)

Year	*Corpus Funds.*
1964-69	65
1969-74	172
1974-79	402
1979-84	1,261
1986-87	4,563.68
1987-88	6,738.81
1988-89	13,455.65
1989-90	19,110.92
1990-91	23,060.45
1991-92	37,480.20
1992-93	46,988.02
1993-94	61,301.21
1994-95	75,050.21
1995-96	81,026.52
1996-97	80,539.00
1997-98	68,984.00
1998-99	68,472.00
1999-2000	1,07,946.10
2000-2001	90,587.00
2001	94,571.00

Public Financial Institutions

The public financial institutions occupy an important role in the financial system. They act as a substitute for the capital market and cater the needs of the growing industrial sector. But recently they are gearing up to play the traditional role to supplement the capital market. They constitute the backbone of the financial system. They still play a dominant role but the shift in the corporate financing leads to decline its role. The corporate sector depends upon non-institutional sources of finance. They provide term loans, project finance, underwriting, direct subscription, lease financing, etc. and also working capital to the Industry. They also provide financial services such as ***merchant banking, project counselling, portfolio management services, credit syndication, new issue management M and A, corporate advisory services, registrars, STAs debenture trusteeship and sponsoring mutual funds.*** The financing of the ***PFI*** from the government, RBI and now geared to access the capital market through the issue of capital to the public and other bonds.

The ***PFIs*** assumed the character of financial supermarket in addition to the term lending. They are changes in tune with the capital market. The focus is on the development finance and the major objective is to promote the entrepreneurship. Three credit rating agencies have been funded by them. The other institutions sponsored by them are stockholding corporation of India, investor services of India and IFCI Custodial Services Ltd. They also established two stock exchanges namely the NSE and OTC.

Capital Market

The capital market is an important segment of the Indian Financial System. It emerged as mechanism allocating the resources in the economy. The structure of the capital market has witnessed significant changes. It can be categorized into primary market and secondary market. Another classification can also be made as money market and securities market. It is regulated by the SEBI.

The capital market deals with the long term funds. It deals with shares, stocks debentures and bonds. The funds which flow into the capital market comes from the savers. It diverts the resources from wasteful and unproductive channels to productive way. The growth of capital market indicates the growth of joint stock companies. In 1951 there were ***28,500 Companies*** with a paid up capital of nearly ***Rs. 775 crores*** and as on 31-3-98 there were more than 2,00,000 companies with a paid up capital of nearly ***Rs. 1,37,959 crores***. The growth of investments has been quite phenomenal in recent years in accordance with the accelerated tempo of development in the Indian economy. Capital Market consists of gilt edged market and the industrial securities market, the growth of the capital market is determined by the following factors:

(1) Rapid Industrialisation.
(2) Economic development.
(3) Technology advances.
(4) Corporate performance.
(5) Regulatory framework.
(6) Participation of FIIs in the capital market.
(7) Financial innovation.
(8) Economic and financial sector reforms.
(9) Globalisation.
(10) Political stability.
(11) NRI investment.
(12) International developments.
(13) Liquidity factors.
(14) Agency costs.
(15) Financial intermediaries.
(16) Information and access.

Money market is a market for short term funds. It provides the funds for less than a period of one year. It is dominated by the central bank. The RBI is the watch dog of the monetary system. Money market includes money, capital and bills markets. In money market the fund is being sold and purchased at a certain price. It is like the commodity market it refers to lending and borrowing activities of banking, financial institutions and individuals.

A number of instruments are introduced in the money market.

(a) 14 day Treasury bills.
(b) 28 day T-bills.
(c) 182 days T-bills.
(d) 364 days T-bills.
(e) Commercial paper.
(f) Certificate of deposits.
(g) Money Market Mutual Funds.

(C) INVESTORS PROTECTION

Today the investors face several problems in the capital market. The corporate sector has come to rely on the securities markets increasingly to finance its long term requirements of funds. The companies indulging malpractices. The innocent investors are exploited. The companies indulges in malpractices in the following ways.

(a) Wrong disclosure material in prospectus.

(b) Manipulated financial information.

(c) Financial window dressing.

(d) Price rigging.

(e) Insider trading.

(f) Private placement.

(g) Promoters quota.

The financial intermediaries indulge in irregularity like non disclosure to the client regarding the sale and purchase of shares and debentures, non-delivery of share certificates against payments, bad deliveries, excess commission charged, excess brokerage for badla transactions.

In earlier phase, a fairly comprehensive legislature measures are taken. The regulatory frameworks are formed by the government. The capital issue act is administered by the CCI in the Ministry of finance. According to the rules, every company should get prior consent for the issue of capital to the public. The pricing and the debt equity ratio were controlled by the government. The government also controls through the *securities contract Regulations act*. It is administered by the ***Directorate of stock exchange*** and the *Ministry of finance*. The acts aim is to prevent the malpractices in the market.

The securities market has to develop more and more. It focuses the regulatory framework and its development by autonomous body. It is achieved by the establishment of the *securities and exchange Board of India*. It was set up in 1998 and commenced its operation in April 1992. It has become a statutory autonomous body. It is established for the purpose of protecting the investors rights. It registers, regulates and monitor various intermediaries in the Capital market the SEBI issued the certain guidelines with reference to the investor's protection.

(1) Publishing data a regarding the price.

(2) Inspecting the books of the brokers.

(3) Receiving and redressing the investors grievances promptly.

(4) Enforcing the capital adequacy norms.

(5) Amendment to the bye laws of the stock exchanges.

(6) Redressal of the investor's grievances.

(7) Enforcing the margin requirement strictly.

The SEBI has introduced the prudential norms of capital adequacy for the brokers and the norms for broker client relationship. It has undertaken the inspection of the stock exchanges. It also made attempts to develop a strong liquid market for the benefit of the investors. It encourages the transparency and fairness in the transactions. It handles individual investor complaints the organisational structure of all the components of financial markets. Financial institutions and financial assets will be discussed at preceding chapters of this book.

The role of the financial system is to accelerate the growth rate of the economic development. The standard of living and social welfare of the public depends upon the state of the economy. The objective can be achieved through the mobilisation of savings. The savings may be diverted towards the productive way. The Indian Financial System is presented in the following diagram.

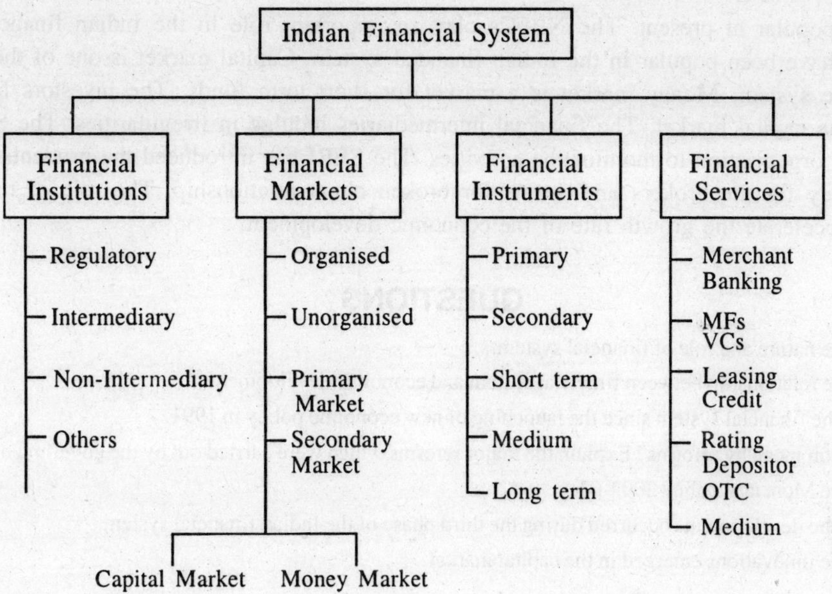

Source: LM Bhole, Financial Institutions and Markets TMH, P. 4, 1988.

The financial system is concerned about ***Money credit and finance.*** Money is used as a medium of exchange and as a stand of value credit is a sum of money and it should be returned with interest. Finance is the provision of money at the time it is wanted. A well developed financial system can influence the economic development. Savings and investment processes influence the economic development. The savings rate depends upon the structure of the economy. Financial activity deals with the production, distribution and consumption of goods and services. The financial system encourages the saving based investments. The investment determines savings. *currency and Money* is the most important element in Indian financial system. ***Banking*** System is another important aspect in our economy. The banking system has increased tremendously in the first half of this century. The banking sector was unorganised during the first phase. The commercial banks involved in providing the short term credit to the industrial sector. Small savings are one of the tradition media for community savings in India. Insurance is one of the savings scheme which is popular among the public. Stock market is the barometer of the performance of industrial sector of a nation. Government securities markets also expanded phenomenal during the first phase. Interest is the most important factor in the capital formation of a nation. The second phase starts from 1950 and the background of the financial system has been determined by the mixed economy system. The financial system is a weapon to counter the poverty. The financial development of a nation can be observed through the powerful indicators such as finance ratio. Financial interrelation ratio, new issue ratio, Intermediation ratio. Equity shares have much less importance in India. The Indian financial system has undergone many changes over the years. The financial institutions have to fulfil the requirement of social justice and sectoral balance of the community. The money market, government securities market and forex market have facilitated liquidity in recent years. The investors in India have not been satisfied in respect of risk, return and liquidity of their commitments. The third phase starts from 1991 onwards. The new economic policy has been announced by the government in June 1991. The government introduced the financial reforms in 1991. The major reforms are policy reforms, banking reforms, capital market reforms, global financial market reforms. The RBI announced its monetary policy for the year 2002-03. The policy contains the review of macro economic and monetary developments Monetary policy 2002-03 and financial sector reforms. The Indian financial system during the third phase consists of privatization, reorganisation and investor protection. The global environment has been changing the increased competition will squeeze the profitability across the globe mobile banking become very popular at present. The NBFCs play an important role in the Indian financial system. Mutual funds have been popular in the Indian financial system. Capital market is one of the important segment of the system. Money market is a market for short term funds. The investors face several problems in the capital market. The financial intermediaries indulge in irregularities. The SEBI is the most powerful organisation to monitor the activities. The SEBI has introduced the prudential norms of capital adequacy for the brokers and norms for broken client relationship. The role of the financial system is to accelerate the growth rate of the economic development.

QUESTIONS

(1) Explain the nature and role of financial system.

(2) What is the relationship between financial system and economic development.

(3) Evaluate the financial system since the launching of new economic policy in 1991.

(4) What do you mean by reforms? Explain the major reforms which were carried out by the government?

(5) Explain the Monetary policy 2002-03.

(6) What are the developments occurred during the third phase of the Indian financial system.

(7) Explain the innovations emerged in the capital market.

❑ ❑ ❑

INDEX UNIT – II

FINANCIAL INSTITUTIONS

Financial Institutions - Introduction - (A) Reserve Bank of India - Introduction - Definition - Functions - Authorities - Monetary Policy of the RBI - Techniques of Monetary Control - Balance Sheet of RBI - (B) Commercial Banks - Introduction - Characteristics of the Bankers - Functions of Banks - Banks and Development - The Balance Sheet of a Bank - Commercial Banking in India - Ist Phase - IInd Phase - IIIrd Phase - Social Control - Nationalisation - Priority Sectors - Narasimhan Committee I and II - Kinds of Banks - Commercial Banks - Industrial Banks - Central Bank - Scheduled Banks - World Bank - Agricultural Banks - Savings Banks - Public Sector Banks - Private Sector Banks - Co-operative Sector Banks - Domestic Banks - Foreign Banks - Exchange Banks - Non-scheduled Banks - Credit Cards - (C) Insurance - UTI.

Introduction

Financial Institutions are the active players in the capital Market. These organisations provide long term loans on easy instalments to the corporate sector. They help in promoting new business enterprises expansion and diversification of existing companies. In under-developed countries, there is a strong need for the establishment of the financial institutions because of a large number of organisations exists in the market. A number of ***FIs*** have been set up at all India and regional levels for accelerating the growth of Industries.

They involve in the mobilisation of funds and in channalising the savings towards the productive way. They provide credit to the commercial enterprises. They provide a wide range of services to the public. They deal with the financial assets like ***deposits, loans and securities.*** They mobilise the savings either directly or indirectly from the financial markets. They deal with the financial market. The ***FIs*** are a part of the financial market. They rotate always in a business environment. The peace of the industrialisation of a country depends upon the disbursements of loans by these institutions. They play an important role in the development of a nation for the following reasons.

(1) Lack of Organised Capital Market.

(2) Low rate of savings.

(3) Low capital formation.

(4) Lack of entrepreneurial spirit.

(5) Low rate of GDP.

(6) Attitude of the investors.

(7) Lack of financial facilities to ***Mega projects***.

The financial institutions do not directly add to the volume of the real capital formation. They are only intermediaries between the savers and users. They encourage savings. They are classified into the following categories.

(A) Regulatory.

(B) Intermediaries.

(C) Non-Intermediaries.

(D) Others.

The FIs may be categorised as Banking and Non-banking. They completely involve in Money and Financial aspects of the entire nation. Banking institutions are based on services basis. They create the money or finance. They are the creators of wonderful sculptor of a *new economy.* They create wealth of the nation. They comprise of the commercial and cooperative banks. The Non banking institutions involve in the Indirect finance of the corporate sector. They actively participate in the capital market. However the non banking institutions have a financial muscle and vast resources at their disposal. They will fulfil the needs of socio economic and political objectives of the mixed economy. The examples for NBIs are ***LIC, UTI, IDBI*** etc. All the companies of Insurance were nationalised and renamed as ***LIC*** in 1956. The Unit Trust of India was started in 1964. The IDBI was established in 1964 as a subsidiary to the RBI.

The financial institutions are further classified as *Intermediaries and Non-Intermediaries.* Intermediaries involve in the mobilisation of the deposits from the customers to dispose the funds at interest for various purposes. They provide deposits, grant loans to the needy sector. They disburse the loans in the form of *short, medium and long-term* loans. All banking institutions belong to the Intermediaries. The Non-Intermediary Institutions lend the money from their own resources. All the Non-banking institutions act as the Non-banking financial intermediaries. ***IDBI, IFCI*** are the best examples. These institutions are established to provide the financial assistance for the specified purposes sectors and regions. They have been established by the Government of India by introducing an act in the parliament. The structure of the Intermediaries are presented below.

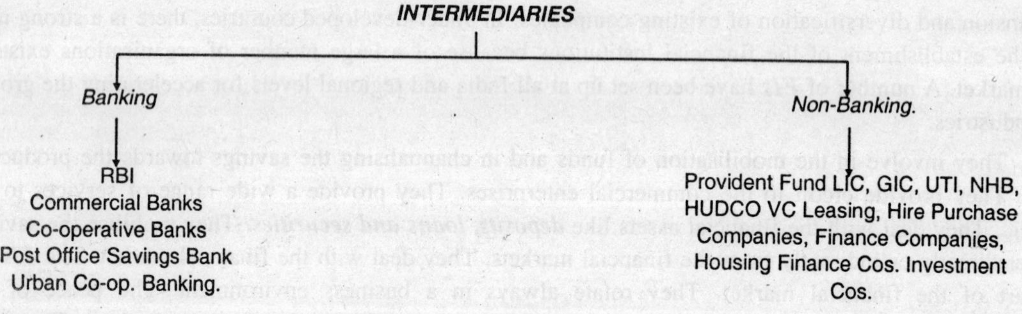

A. RESERVE BANK OF INDIA

Introduction

The Central Bank plays an important role in the monetary and banking structure of a nation. It supervises controls and regulates the activities of the banking sector. It has been assigned to handle and control the currency and credit of a country. It has been traced in olden days. In most of the nations, the Central Banks were empowered to issue the currency notes and bankers to the Union governments. The first Central Bank in the world was the *Risks Bank of Sweden*. It was established in *1656.* The Bank of England was established in *1694* for advancing money to the government. It leds to the development of the Central Banks in other parts of the world. ***The Bank of France*** was established in *1800.* The Bank of Netherland was established in 1814. The National Bank of Austria was instituted in 1817. The Bank of Norway was established in 1817. The National Bank of Denmark was set up in 1818, The National Bank of Belgium was formed in 1850, the Bank of Spain was set up in 1829. All these affairs were the landmarks in the history of Central banking. The Bank of Russia was established in 1860, The Reichs Bank of Germany was formed in 1875, The bank of Japan was formed in 1882.

Definition

The Central bank has the responsibility of managing all the economic and monetary affairs of the nation. The Central bank has been defined by *RP Kent* as an institution charged with the responsibility of managing the expansion and contraction of the volume of money in the interest of the "general public welfare"[1]

According to *Decock* the Central bank has defined. A Central bank being generally recognised as a bank which constitutes the apex of the monetary and banking structure of its country and which performs as best as it can; in the national economic interest. It performs the following functions.

(1) The regulation of currency in accordance with the requirements of business and the general public for the purpose of which it is granted either the sole right of note issue or at least a partial monopoly thereof.

(2) The performance of general banking and agency services for the state.

(3) The custody of the cash resources of the banks.

(4) The custody and management of the nations reserves of international currency.

(5) The granting of accommodation in the form of rediscounts or collateral advances, to commercial bank, bill brokers and dealers or other financial institutions and the general accept once of the responsibility as the last resort.

(6) The settlement of clearance balances among banks.

(7) The control of credit in accordance with the needs of business and with a view to carry out the broad monetary policy adopted by the state.

A further requisite of a central bank is that it should not to any extent, perform such banking transactions as accepting deposits from the general public and accommodating regular commercial customers with discounts or advances.

The Central banks are not profit making enterprises. But they earn much profits through its function. The Central bank monitors the operations of Commercial banks, Industrial banks Agricultural banks and Investment banks. The Central bank is controlled by the Central government. It has certain relationship with the banks. An independent act is formulated to regulate the activities of the Central bank. The Central bank has no authority to accept the deposits from the public. It has been playing an important role in the economy. It plays a more positive role in the development of a national. It plays a dynamic role in the development of the nation. The financial muscle of a nation depends upon the soundness of the policies of the Central banking. The objectives of the Central banking system are presented below.

(1) It should work with the national interest of the country.

(2) It must aim at the stabilisation of the mixed economy.

(3) It aims at the stabilisation of the price level at average price.

(4) The stabilisation of the exchange rates is essential.

(5) It should aim at the promotion of economic activities.

It is the nucleus of Indian financial system. It is the apex institution since the inception of the economy it has been guiding, regulating, controlling, monitoring the financial system. It is the oldest among the other developed banks. The functions of the Central bank as mentioned by *Decork*[2] as Bank

1. R. P. Kent, Money and Banking, p. 551.
2. Money Banking and International Trade and Public Finance M. N. Mishra. S. Chand & Sons 1987, p. 512.

of Issue, banker to the government, banker's bank, lender of the last resort, controller of credit. The regulatory framework of the financial sector in India was controlled by the Ministry of Finance and the Government of India. The ministry of Finance administers the *Companies act, 1956. The securities Regulations act 1956, RBI, SEBI, The IRDA stock exchanges and a few financial institutions.* The RBI and the SEBI have a special role and responsibility at first let us discuss about the RBI.

The Reserve Bank of India is the Central bank of the Country. It has been occupying an important role in the Indian financial system. It started the functioning from April 1, 1935. It was set up under the RBI act, 1934. The RBI till January 1949 was under the management of the private shareholder's. The private institution because a state owned institution under the RBI act 1948. The act empowers the Central government to issue the directions in the interest of the public. The Central government has full authority to guide, regulate monitor the activities of the RBI. It has the authority to appoint *Governor and Deputy Governor* of the RBI. The RBI is managed by a Board of directors. The board of directors constitute the Governor, Four deputy governors, 15 directors nominated by the Central government. The Central board of directors consists of 4 local boards of directors and a committee. The Local boards are set up for giving advices to the central board on specific matters and are also required to perform the duties delegated to them. The Central board of directors have the supreme authority to control the activities of the bank. The internal Organisation of the bank structure may change from time to time depending upon the volume of work. It has been working on the basis of the *functional specialisation* with adequate co-ordination. For smooth functioning of the RBI. It has been divided into ***20 departments*** and ***03 training establishments*** besides banking and issue departments.

Functions

The RBI functions are based on the mixed economy. It should maintain a close and continuous relationship with the Union government while implementing the policies if any differences arise the government's decision will be final. The main functions of the RBI are presented below.

- To Welfare of the state.
- To maintain the financial stability of the country.
- To execute the financial transaction safely.
- To develop the financial infrastructure of the country.
- To allocate the funds efficiently.
- To regulate the overall credit column for price stability.

Authorities

The RBI has full authority in the following aspects:

(1) Currency Issuing Authority.

(2) Monitoring Authority.

(3) Banker to the Central Government.

(4) Foreign Exchange Control Authority.

(5) Promoting Authority.

(1) Currency Issuing Authority: The RBI has the sole authority in issuing the Currency notes and coins. It is the fundamental right of the RBI. The coins and rupee notes are issued by the government, but they are circulated through the RBI. The notes issued by the RBI has the legal entity every where in India. The RBI issues notes in the denominations of *Rs. 1000, 500, 100, 50, 20 and 10.* It has the authority to circulate and withdraw the currency from circulation. It has also the authority to exchange notes and coins from one denomination to the other denominations as per the requirement of the public.

The Note issues and exchange of denominations are handled by the *Issue dept.* The Currency notes may be distributed throughout the country by its 15 full pledged offices, 2 branch offices and more than 4000 currency chests. The Currency chests are maintained by different banks in various locations. The RBI issues currency notes based on the availability of balance of gold bullion, foreign securities, rupee coins GOI securities and permitted bills. The RBI notes are backed by ***100%*** asset security. At present it is following a minimum value of gold coin, bullion and foreign securities as a part of the total approved assets.

(2) Monitoring Authority: The RBI has full authority to control all the aspects of the banking system in India. It is known as banker's bank. The banking system in India works according to the guidelines issued by the RBI. It is the premier banking institute among the banks. All banks, in India should obey the rules which are issued by it from time to time. It controls the deposits of the banks through various techniques. Every bank should deposits a certain amount in the RBI. The banks have the power to borrow the money from the RBI when they are in need of finance. Hence it is known as the *lender of the last resort*. The RBI has the authority to control the credit supply in the economy or monetary systems of the nation. The RBI has the following powers with regard to the banking system.

(1) It has the power to grant the licenses for the establishment of new banks in India.

(2) It has the power to issue the licenses for the branch expansion of the banks.

(3) It has the authority to fix the norms regarding paid up capital, Reserves, transfer of reserve fund maintenance of cash reserves and other liquid assets.

(4) It has the authority to inspect the banks of its branches in India and abroad.

(5) It can check the banks Organisational set up, branch expansion, mobilisation of funds, credit portfolio management, Regionwise performance, profit planning, training, credit appraisal etc.

(6) It has the authority to conduct the equity investigations against complaints, irregularities and frauds in the banks.

(7) It has the authority to ***Mergers and Acquisitions*** among banks.

(8) It has the authority to appoint the *CEOS* of the private banks. Reappointment, termination of chairman also lies with it.

(9) It also controls the methods of operations of the banks.

The Narasimhan Committee (1991) recommended that, for supervision of banks, a separate department should be created. On the basis of recommendations, The GOI created a separate department of supervision from 22-11-93. The RBI has set up a particular department on the eve of securities scam for monitoring the activities of the financial sector. The Board of Financial supervision was formed on *16-11-1994*. The department of supervision took the responsibility of conducting the inspection of commercial banks. From 1995, it also supervises All India financial institutions and *NBFCs*. The board of Financial supervision has a full time vice chairman and *6* other members. The RBI Governor is the chairman. The wing has the powers to supervise and inspect banks, financial institutions, NBFCs. A five member advisory council has been formed for rendering the services. The department of supervision assists the board. However all these bodies failed to curb the rising number of frauds irregularities in the financial sector. Therefore the department of supervision should have the full powers in detecting the frauds and irregularities in the banking sector.

(3) Banker to the Government: All over the world the Central bank dominates the banking sector and able to give advises to the government on monetary policies. The RBI is a banker to the government and also to the state governments in the country. It provides a wider range of banking services to the government. It works as a bank with reference to the government context. The RBI accepts the deposits, withdrawal of funds by cheques made by the government. It also transfers the funds, collect the receipts and makes payment on behalf of the government. It also manages the public debt. The government will not pay any remuneration or brokerage to the RBI for rendering the financial services. Any deficit or surplus in the Central government account with the RBI is adjusted by creation or cancellation of treasury bills. The treasury bills are known *as "Ad hoc Treasury bills"* The RBI has the authority to maintain ways and means advances to both the central government and state governments. The ways and means is a device to the governments for borrowing the money from the RBI. The RBI will make temporary advances in order to bridge the gap between the receipts and payments of the state and central government affairs. The maximum maturity period of these advances is *3 months.* The Central government will issue the *Ad hoc treasury* bills for adjusting the deficit in the ways and means account. The ways and means to the state governments are subjected to some conditions. These advances may be categorised as *clean, secured and special* advances. ***The clean advances*** are made by the RBI to various state governments without any collateral security. *The secured advances* will be made by the RBI to the states against the pledge of the central government securities. ***The special advances*** is a facility granted by the RBI to its discretion for states. All these advances will be offered by the RBI to various states on the Interest basis. The Interest rates will change from time to time.

The RBI sanction not only WMAs but also overdrafts to various states. The ODs are the excel limits of WMAs. On OD the RBI may charge interest above the bank rate. Almost all the states are utilising the facility of the OD. The major functions of the RBI is to issue, the management and administration of the public debt for rendering these services the RBI charges a commission from the both governments.

(4) FERA: The RBI's another major function is to control the foreign exchange reserves position from time to time. It maintains the stability of the external value of the rupee. It controls the external value of the rupee through its ***domestic polices*** and ***Forex market.*** The RBI has the full authority to regulate the market as presented below:

- To monitor the foreign exchange control.
- To prescribe the exchange rate system.
- To maintain the relation between rupee and other currencies.
- To interact with the foreign counterparts.
- To manage the foreign exchange reserves.

It administers the *FERA 1973.* It is replaced by the *FEMA (Foreign Exchange Management Act),* which would be consistent with full capital account Convertability with policies of the central government. The RBI is the Custodian of the country's foreign exchange reserves. The foreign exchange is precious and it takes the responsibility to better utilisation.

(5) Promoting Authority: The RBI Function is to look after the welfare of the financial system. It renders the promotion services to strengthen the banking and financial structure. It helps in mobilising the savings and diverting them towards the productive channel. Thus the economic development can be achieved. After the nationalisation of the banks, the RBI has taken a number of series of action to develop the economy such as ***Agriculture sector, Industrial sector, Lead bank Scheme and Co-op. sector.*** The agriculture sector has been facing the finance problems. It occupies important role in the economy. The RBI is rendering the services to the agriculture sector by providing credit flow. The act also emphasises the need to support the agriculture sector for the better output of the commodities. It appointed a deputy governor especially for providing the rural credit. It conducts an indepth analysis on the problems of the rural credit and conducted an ***All India Rural Credit*** survey in 1954. It was followed by studies of the All India Rural Credit Review Committee in 1968. In 1978 another Committee was formed to review the arrangements for institutional credit for agriculture and rural development. As a part of its efforts, the Committee was formed in ***1986.*** The RBI fully involves in providing short term finance at a concessional rate for seasonal agricultural operations and marketing of crops. It contributes to the debentures of land development banks. It helps the agriculture sector through the Cooperative institutions for long and short term finances in the form of National Agricultural credit (long term) fund and the National agriculture credit stabilisation fund. It established especially for agriculture sector in July 1963, a separate entity known as *NABARD* for providing medium and long term finance for agriculture. The Agriculture finance corporation was established by the RBI to look after the welfare of the farmers.

The RBI has been playing an important role in the industrial sector. The RBI has established all the special development institutions to undertake the welfare of the industrial sector at national level. It rendered services for promoting several financial institutions the RBI took initiative steps for the establishment of the UTI. A number of institutions are established only because of the efforts of RBI.

The lead bank scheme was proposed and implemented by the RBI. It has been acting as a leader in sponsoring the scheme. The RBI has the statutory authority to grant the licenses. Therefore it has been expanding branches with an appropriate geographical distribution of bank branches. The RBI has taken a step in 1962 to ensure the security of deposits with the banks. Hence it took initiative in setting up of the *Deposit Insurance Corpn.*

Monetary Policy of the RBI

Every nations's government objective is to stabilise the economy by framing the policy matters. The RBI treats the monetary policy as a weapon. The aim of the planning is growth, social justice and stability. Stability is the most important factor in a planned economy. The objective of the monetary policy is to accelerate the economic development of the country. It is concerned with the control of credit and money supply with reference to seasonal requirements for credit. The credit expansion process will be undertaken by the light of price variations without considering the industrial output. It is able to avoid the waste resources and it creates an environment for better employment opportunities. The policy also helps to eradicate poverty, regional imbalance growth. It strives for the self efficiency. It is also aims at to boost the exports. The policy was done a programme of food procurement operations. The steps have been taken to deregulate the interest rates. It is concentrated for introducing flexibility, encouraging diversification promoting more competitive environment and imparting greater indiscipline.

Techniques of Monetary Control

The Monetary policy is basically concerned with the regulation of money supply and interest rates. The policy describes various control techniques to stabilise the economy. The techniques are presented below:

(1) Open market operations.

(2) Refinance and Rediscounting.

(3) Bank rate.

(4) Cash Reserve Ratio (CRR).

(5) Statutory Liquidity Ratio (SLR).

(6) Credit planning.

(7) Regulation of Interest rates.

(8) Credit norms.

(9) Credit authorisation scheme.

(10) Selective credit controls.

(11) Credit rationing.

The above techniques were not used equally and actively in the past. Some of the important techniques are evaluated below.

(1) Open Market Operations: Open market operations are actively used in USA, UK and many countries. It deals with the purchase and sale of government securities. The RBI has the authority to monitor the reserve positions of the banks, yields on government securities and cost of bank credit. It is a powerful weapon in the hands of the RBI. The RBI may not restrict the quantity or maturity of the government securities in buying and selling or to hold it. The bank has the authority to conduct the open market operations in treasury bills, central government securities and state securities. But actually the transactions are carried out in the name of central government securities. It does not purchase them as against cash. It purchases and sells the government securities from time to time with surplus funds of the *IDBI, NABARD and EXIM* bank. The operations are performed according to the objectives of monetary and fiscal policy. The objectives of the policy are presented below.

(a) To control the reserves base of the banks.

(b) To maintain stability in the government securities market

(c) To make bank rate more effective.

(d) To facilitate the government borrowing programme.

(e) To provide smooth flow of credit in seasonal requirement basis.

The operations are carried out by the RBI for the purpose of debt management. But the govt. securities market is not well organised. The RBI has recognised the OMO as one of the important monetary policy tools in stabilising the economy. The RBI has taken a large no. of measures to develop OMOs. Therefore the coupon rates of the govt. securities have been raised and thus made the market more competitive. The OMO have helped in regulating the flow of bank credit to the private sector more effectively.

(2) & (3) Refinance and the Bank Rate: The RBI is the premier bank in India and it provides the financial accommodation to the banking sector, Industrial and co-op. sector. It provides the finance provision in the form of ***Rediscounting promissory notes, loans and advances etc.*** The bank rate is the most important factor in financing and rediscounting the facilities. It is defined by the RBI act, section 49 "as the standard rate at which the bank is prepared to buy or rediscount bills of exchange or other commercial paper." In the past, the financial accommodation was made by the RBI to the banking sector at the bank rate the bank rate is charged by the RBI for various sectors at different rates. The bank rate and cost of refinance are used to regulate the volume of resources of the banks and other financial institutions. The *Refinance policy* has to be kept in mind about the seasonal requirement of funds for various sectors. The major changes will arise the refinance policy of the RBI from time to time.

(4) Cash Reserve Ratio: The Commercial banks should follow the guidelines issued by the RBI from time to time on various aspects. As per the norms every bank should keep a fraction of their deposit liabilities in the form of liquid cash this system is known as "Functional Reserve Banking System". The RBI utilises the CRR as a weapon to ensure the safety and liquidity of deposits of the banking sector. The CRR has become an important tool for regulating the lending capacity of the banks. The RBI uses the two important financial weapons for controlling the credit in the country. The two financial weapons are known as ***Cash Reserve Ratio*** and ***Statutory liquidity Ratio.*** The CRR means the cash which banks have to maintain with the RBI as a certain percentage of their demand and time liabilities. The RBI has the authority to change the CRR from time to time according to the market situations. The CRR is also applicable to various NRI deposits accounts. It has the power to impose penalty interest rates. If any bank fails to the requirement of the prescribed CRR. The RBI disallows the refinance and rediscount of bills for the defaulted banks in the CRR.

(5) Statutory Liquidity Ratio: Another financial weapon to control the credit flow in an economy is *SLR* in the hands of the RBI. The RBI frequently uses this ratio to monitor and control the banks. The SLR is the ratio that every bank keeps cash in hand, balance in current account with the SBI, the balances with other counterparts and the RBI. It also includes gold and approved securities. The SLR is the most important ratio in the banking sector. The SLR is also applicable to Co-op banks, non scheduled banks and Regional Rural banks. The norms are applicable to ***Foreign Currency accounts (Non-Resident) and Non-Resident Rupee account (external) deposits.*** The RBI has the authority to change the SLR according to the market movements. An increase in the SLR is possible only through the expenditure of the private sector. The SLR involves in the distribution of the bank resources in favour of the government sector.

(6) Credit Planning: The credit plan was introduced by the RBI in 67-68. It is an innovative tool for the credit management. It is made as a product of economic planning. It is aimed to work as a tool in the macro credit management of the economy. It works in a specified environment. It is a unique tool of credit management. The objectives of the credit planning are presented below:

(a) To facilitate the flow of the funds to a desired level.

(b) To facilitate the flow of funds to desired sectors, areas, purposes.

(c) The quantum and qualitative aspects of funds flow.

The credit plan is an input for the national monetary plan, fiscal and economic plan. The credit plan will be prepared at national level and district level. The process of credit plan involves at the bank level. Every bank is required to prepare the realistic annual credit budget incorporating the estimates of volume and growth of deposits and demands for credit. The budgets are revised in the light of change in the credit policy and banking trends. All the banks their budgets are submitted to the RBI makes continuous monitoring.

(7) Regulation of Interest Rates: The RBI has the authority to directly regulate the interest rates on bank deposits and credit. The bank rate to technique has been very weak till 1999. Basically a change in the bank rate is reflected in all market rates of interest. It has lost its significance. It used to solve the situation by regulating the market rates of interest directly. The RBI has been fixing all the deposits rates of the Commercial banks and their lending rates. The co-op. banks deposits rates have come under the regulation in 1974. The 1991 policy has changed the entire picture of the market with the introduction of the deregulation of interest rates.

(8) Credit Norms: The RBI has undertaken the responsibility for the direct administration of the interest rates in the economy when the bank rate technique weakened. The monetary policy's objective is to quantify the control of credit or credit ceiling. The credit technique was introduced in *Nov. 1973* by the RBI. The RBI has been stipulating certain targets for the credit distribution to various sectors.

(9) Credit Authorisation Scheme: The RBI has introduced credit authorisation scheme in *Nov. 1965.* The scheme was promoted to regulate the heavy amount of borrowers. The scheme is aimed to sanction the financial assistance for the short term needs of the corporate sector. The objectives of the schemes have been presented below.

(a) To regulate the credit to control the inflation.

(b) To impose the financial discipline on commercial borrowers.

(c) To provide the credit for the productive ways.

(d) To ensure that the credit is supplied in accordance with the planning.

(e) To curb the monopolistic ways for the credit sanctions.

The scheme is applicable to the commercial banks, PSBs, Co-op. banks and private banks. It is also applied to the long and short term loans. It operates for more than 20 years and the RBI decided to withdraw after the review of its working. It is replaced by a new scheme known as Credit Monitory Arrangement. According to this scheme a credit proposal for *Rs 5 crores* and above as its working capital which should be submitted to the RBI. More than Rs. 2 crores should also be submitted to the RBI for term loans as credit proposal.

(10) Selective Credit Control: The selective credit control a popular technique. It is environment and the inflation pressure have made it useful in our context. It changes the composition of the credit. It is used to reduce the supply of credit and prevent the speculative holding in sensitive commodities. The commodities such as *paddy, pulses, oilseeds, vanaspathi, cotton and sugar* influence the speculation motives. They are applied to credit given for trading in shares. They are now applied both to commercial and co-op. banks. They are applied to the private sector trading. But the public sector trading is not covered by these control techniques. The RBI applies these controls in three forms.

(A) Fixation of Margin's requirements.

(B) Fixation of separate minimum lending rates.

(C) The fixation of ceiling on flow of credit.

THE ASSETS AND LIABILITIES OF THE RBI *(Rs. in crores)*

	Assets and Liabilities	*1990-91*	*1999-00*	*2000-01*	*2001-02*
(1)	Issue department	53,807	1,92,534	2,12,937	2,37,515
(2)	Banking Dept.	66,884	1,60,654	1,72,028	1,72,956
		1,20,691	3,53,188	3,84,965	4,10,461

The break up values of other particulars are presented in the next page.

ASSETS AND LIABILITIES OF THE RBI

(Issues dept.) 1990-91, 99-00, 2000-2001

Liabilities *(Rs. in crores)*

	Liabilities	*1990-91*	*1999-2000*	*2000-2001*	*2001-2002*
(1)	Notes in Circulation	53,784	1,92,483	2,12,858	2,37,484
(2)	Notes held in Banking department	23	51	79	31
	Total liabilities	53,807	1,92,534	2,12,937	2,37,515

Assets *(Rs. in crores)*

	Assets	*1990-91*	*1999-2000*	*2000-2001*	*2001-02*
(1)	Gold coin and bullion	6,654	10,598	10,324	11,242
(2)	Foreign securities	200	72,700	91,700	1,23,700
(3)	Rupee coin (1)	29	102	78	107
(4)	Government of India Rupee securities	46,924	1,09,134	1,10,835	1,02,466
		53,807	1,92,534	2,12,937	2,37,515

ASSETS AND LIABILITIES OF THE RBI

(Banking Dept.) 1990-91, 1999-00, 2000-2001, 2001-02 *(Rs. in crores)*

	Liabilities	*1990-91*	*1999-2000*	*2000-2001*	*2001-02*
(1)	Deposits	38,542	86,551	87,828	70,618
(2)	Central government	61	500	100	101
(3)	State governments	33	41	41	41
(4)	Scheduled banks	33,484	77,781	76,939	60,854
(5)	Scheduled state co-op. banks	244	816	978	1099
(6)	Non scheduled Co-operative banks	13	45	61	42
(7)	Other banks	88	246	918	1,276
(8)	Others	4,619	7,122	8,791	7,206
(9)	Other liabilities	28,342	74,102	84,199	1,02,338
		66,884	1,60,654	1,72,028	1,72,956

	Assets	1990-91	1999-2000	2000-2001	2001-02
(1)	Notes and coins	23	52	80	31
(2)	Balances held abroad	4,008	52,313	92,600	99,161
(3)	**Loans and advances:**				
	(a) Central government	—	982	—	9,221
	(b) State governments	916	7,519	4,395	8,035
	(c) Scheduled commercial banks	8,169	9,513	5,980	1,927
	(d) Scheduled state Co-op. banks	38	15	27	25
	(e) IDBI	3,705	1,740	1,440	1,110
	(f) NABAR	3,328	5,884	6,580	5,855
	(g) EXIM Bank	745	697	617	532
	(h) Others	1,616	11,541	9,104	4,201
(4)	**Bills Purchased and Discount:**				
	(a) Govt. treasury bills.	1,384	—	—	—
	(b) Investments	40,286	62,660	43,127	36,682
(5)	**Other assets**	2,666	7,738	8,078	6176
		66,884	1,60,654	1,72,028	1,72,956

Sources: RBI Bulletin, Feb. 2002, pp. 5-108.

B. COMMERCIAL BANKS

Introduction

Commercial banks are the fastest growing financial intermediaries in India. They provide various types of financial services to the customers. The banking system in India works under the rigorous rules and regulations. It has no freedom in discharging of its functions. Its objective is to make profits. Banks must pay much more attention towards liquidity and profitability.

The Commercial banks are the oldest institutions having a wide network of branches. They were established as corporate bodies with share holdings by private individuals. Banks have been defined differently by several authors. According to ***"Prof. Hart"*** A banker is one, who in the ordinary course of his business receives money which he repays by honouring cheques of persons from whom or on whose account he receives it".[3]

According to *sec. 5 (b)* of Indian Banking Act, 1949" Banking means, the accepting, for the purpose of lending or investments, of deposits of money from the public repayable on demand or otherwise and withdrawable by cheque draft order or otherwise".

Characteristic of Bankers

The main characteristic of bankers are given below:

(1) Bank accepts deposits of the public.

(2) The deposited amount will be advanced in the form of loan to the customer.

(3) The banks perform the functions of agency services.

(4) The banks should have a particular place of business.

The functions of banks are divided into three kinds:

3. M. N. Mishra, Money, Banking and International Trade, S. Chand & Co. 1987, p. 245.

(A) Primary functions.

(B) Agency functions.

(C) Misalliance functions.

(A) Primary Function

The Primary functions of banks can be divided into two kinds.

(1) Accepting of deposits.

(2) Advancing of loans.

(1) Accepting of Deposits: Accepting of deposits is the basic function of a banks. They collect surplus money from the public. They pay different interest amounts according to the deposit scheme. The depositors are benefited into two ways. At first their amount is **100%** safe and they will get interest also. On the other hand the banks can earn a sum of money on the amount mobilised from the public. The higher the amount of deposits, the higher the capacity to create credits. The banks have different types of deposits which are briefly discussed below:

(A) Fixed Deposit Account.

(B) Current Account.

(C) Savings Bank Account.

(D) Recurring Deposit Account.

(E) Long Term Fixed Deposit.

(F) Other Accounts.

Fixed Deposits are the main source of funds for the banks. The quantum of advancing loans will depend upon the amount of deposit mobilisation. The fixed deposits are accepted by the banks from *90 days to 3 years* The banks may get a higher rate of interest on these deposits. Therefore the banks are permitted to use the deposits for a certain period of time. The form of fixed deposits benefits the small customers because they are unable to make investments in stock market. They do not want to take the risk of their capital. A large number of investors prefer this form of investment. The form of deposit has come more lucrative. An investor can combine the fixed deposit with the recurring deposit by transferring the monthly rate of interest to the RD A/c. The rate of interest depends upon the length of the period and the amount of deposits. The deposited amount cannot be withdrawn before the expiry period of deposits. But the banks may grant the loan on the basis of fixed deposit made by the borrower. The Receipts are issued at the time of the fixed deposits. The receipts are not negotiable instruments. It cannot be transferred to any one.

Current Accounts are beneficial to the business community. Current Account is one type of flexible account because the account holder may withdraw the amount by several times from his account of deposits. This account is more useful to the businessmen as an evidence of revenue for the purpose filling income tax rebate. The issuing of cheques is useful to the businessmen for all their payments and collection. No interest is paid on this account. Traditionally nominal charges will be charged for meeting the expenses of maintaining such account.

Saving Bank Account is useful to the savers. It is ideal to middle income and low income group people. They do not require money to be withdrawn from the bank. In this account the depositors is all owned to withdraw the money thrice in a week. But the customer is allowed to deposit the money at any time. The Interest will be paid on this type of account. But the rate of interest is lower than the fixed deposit. Interest will be calculated on the basis of balance maintained in the account. At present some banks have now provided the facility of withdrawing the money by way of cheques. It is becoming more popular in all the commercial banks.

Recurring Deposit Account provides a higher rate of interest than the savings bank a/c. It is a combination of fixed account and saving account. This account is becoming popular in India. It suits the requirements like education, marriage etc. A fixed amount is periodically deposited in this account which is accumulated at compound rate of interest. The accumulated will be returned to the depositor after the fixed period.

Long term Fixed Deposits are mobilised by the bank to build a strong portfolio of different schemes. The bank will not pay interest to the customer. The amount of interest is also redeposited, the rate of interest is the highest on this deposit. The depositor can encash the money after the fixed period of time. This type of account is most suitable for old age provision. The banks are encouraging the savers to deposit their money in this account.

Other Accounts are prevalent in India. There are various savings accounts available to the depositors. The other saving account popular in the banking sector are home safe account, private saving accounts and special savings account.

(2) Advancing of Loans: The advances are the most important element in the bank portfolio. The banks are mobilising the deposits through various types of accounts, may deploy the funds for disbursal of advances to the borrowers. The bank can make advances in the form of *loans*. The loans are sanctioned to the borrowers in different kinds: They are usually overdrafts, cash credits, discounting bills of exchange. Bank does not lend its own money. Bank deals other's money. The capital of the bank is blocked in assets form. The banks loan more than the amount of deposits. The banks usually sanction the loan in the following methods.

(a) Loans.

(b) Cash credits.

(c) Discounting of bills.

(a) Loans are the main profitable avenue for the bank. Loans are sanctioned to the borrower by the banker with specific conditions. Loans are made by debiting the customers loan account and by crediting his current account. The borrower is allowed to withdraw the amount of loans in several statements. The banks will take proper care in exercising to select the customers. Personal security and collateral security is required for advancing the loans. The interest is charges on the full amount. Loans and advances involve lower operating cost. The loans are given usually against securing of movable and immovable asset.

(b) Cash Credit are the another form of sanctioning of the loan. The banker allows his customer to borrow money upto a sanctioned limit against the security of certain bonds promissory notes, shares, jutes, rice, seeds etc. The borrower is required to pay interest on the amount of advance. The banks can disburse the large amount. Cash credits granted through this account. Cash credits are more useful to the business community. It provides adequate amount for meeting essential expenditures of business. This type of credit is usually a short term loan.

Bank Overdraft is the important component is loans segment of the banking sector. It is allowed on the current account with interest. This facility is allowed to the business community. There is no collateral security is required for this kind of credit. It is more advantageous to the customers because interest is charged only on the amount withdrawn. It can be used at anytime. It may be used for long term purposes. It is the most important useful form of credit to the industrial and commercial units. The bank will decide the overdraft facility period for a particular time with the agreement made by the customer.

(c) Discounting of Bills will be made by the banks. The banks discount only clear and reputed bills. The business involves buying and selling of the goods. The goods are sold on the basis of exchange which is drawn by the seller of goods and is accepted by the purchaser, whereby the purchaser accepts the credit terms and pays the amount of dues after due days. Meanwhile if the seller is willing to discount the bill he can do so from his banks and obtain the amount of discount. The bills of exchange can also be followed by the *Railway Receipt* bill of lading etc. The banks can rediscount these bills of exchange from the central bank. The rediscounting facility is benefit to the buyer, seller and discounting bank. The buyer can get goods on credit and the seller can get cash from the bank after discounting the bills of exchange. The bill is a legal document of debt. The debtor cannot deny the debt. The bills of exchange can be transferred from one party to another and from one bank to another. The bill of exchange do not require any collateral security. The bill market in India is gradually increasing.

(B) Agency Function

The banks provide so many facilities by discharging their agency functions. The banks act as agents of their customers. They act as trustees, administrators, attorneys of their customers. The banks purchase and sell on behalf of their customers. The banks will provide the following services.

(a) Buying and selling of shares on behalf of customers.

(b) They collect and pay dues.

(c) They act as trustees and attorneys.

(d) They act as underwriter.

(e) They supply the information and statistic of the country.

(C) Miscellaneous Functions

The Misl. functions will be performed by the banks to provide facilities to the customers. They will undertake the safe custody of valuable articles such as jewels, gold, diamond of the customers. The bank will provide *safe lockers* to the customers on rental basis. The bank issue letters of credit of various kind for different purposes. The banks act as referee for the business community regarding the financial aspects of a particular party. The banks can supply the credit worthiness of the various parties. The banks collect various information and statistic of the country. The banks have a separate statistic department to present the data to the central government or RBI. The banks also involve in foreign exchange transactions. Therefore the transactions in this segment become easier. The customers have nothing to worry about the foreign trade and payment. The banks issue traveller's cheque to help the customers. The banks also issues ***credit cards.*** The credit cards are more convenient to the salaried people and business community. The present trend in banking is to provide ***ATMs, Internet banking****, mobile banking, Debit cards, smart cards,* ***Factoring,*** etc.

Banks and Development

In the digital economy the banks are to be considered not only as money lenders but also the leaders in development. They are the wealth creators of the country. They are stored powerhouse. The banks command excellent financial resources at their disposal. The banks are the ***financial architecture*** of the Asia's lion. They can make or brake the wealth of a nation. The economic progress depends upon the growth of sound banking system. The banks taking active part in the development of the country.

(a) Industrialisation.

(b) Money Creators.

(c) Encouragement to savers.

(d) Encourages trade and industry.

(e) Regional balanced development.

(f) Development of Agriculture sector.

Industrialisation of a country depends upon the availability of financial resources in the economy. The banks have excellent financial resources at their command and they can divert that huge amount of resources towards the establishment of new industries. Therefore the banks are playing an important role in the capital formation of the country. Capital formation is the most important determinant of economic development. The capital formation will depend upon three factors. They are ***savings habits of the society, mobilisation of savings canalisation of savings.*** The banks can do excellent task to influence these factors. The banks will create an environment for small savings. The savers are offered with incentives by the banks in order to encourage them.

Banks are the money creators and they allow money to play an active role in the economy. They sanction the loan to the borrower and the amount will be credited to his account. Therefore the sanction of the loan amount may also become as deposit.

The banks encourages directly by a reduction in the interest rate which makes the investment more profitable and stimulates the economic activity. An increase in the rate of interest discourages investment and economic activity. The bankers can influence economic activity by the availability of credit. The bank cheque, bills of exchange bank draft have revolutionised the internal and international trade. The use of these instruments accelerated the peace of industrialisation. The expansion of the trade and industrialisation could not have been made possible without the development of the banking system.

Bank can play an important role in achieving balanced development in different regions of the economy. They transfer the financial resources from surplus location to shortage location. Therefore it balances the development factor of the economy. The realisation of funds between two regions will promote the economic development.

The underdeveloped nations will depend upon mainly on agriculture and the population live in rural areas. Therefore the economic development of the nation depends upon the development of agriculture sector. Therefore the banks in underdeveloped countries have been concentrating to trade and commerce sector and neglected the agriculture sector.

The Balance Sheet of a Bank

The balance sheet of a bank consist of Assets and liabilities. Assets refer to all credit items containing the banks claims on others. In balance sheet the liabilities are shown on the left side and the assets on the right side of the balance sheet. The total amounts on both sides are equal.

(1) Assets.

(2) Liabilities.

(1) Assets: The assets side of the balance sheet shows the manner in which the funds of the bank are utilised. The following items will appear in the balance sheet in an ascending order of profitability.

(a) Cash.

(b) Call money.

(c) Discounted bills.

(d) Investments.

(e) Loans and advances.

(f) Endorsements.

(g) Fixed assets.

(a) Cash is the most important item in the financial institutions. It is also known as liquid assets. But the cash is non generating income asset. Each and every bank should keep certain levels of amount of cash in order to meet the cash requirements of the depositors. The cash item includes three items currency in hand, cash kept with the central bank and cash kept with other banks.

(b) Call Money is also known as short notice money. It refers to loans which are receivables by the bank on demand or at a very short notice. The loan facility will be sanctioned by the banks to the borrowers for a period of 15 days only. These loans are earning as well as high liquid assets. The call money will be provided to the share brokers, to other banks and deployment in treasury bills.

(c) Discounted Bills play an important role in the banks asset. The bank deploy the funds trade bills and Treasury bills. The specified amount of the bill is collected by the bank on maturity. The commercial banks will prefer the bills because of the following reasons.

(1) They are negotiable.

(2) They are liquid assets.

(3) They are eligible for rediscounting with the RBI.

(4) High income.

(d) Investment the banks invest funds in profit yielding assets like government securities. Government securities are more safe because they are backed by the Union Government. The banks can borrow the money from the Central bank against these securities. They also invest in fixed income bearing securities such as debentures or bonds of well established industrial concerns. The investment in bonds or debentures involves risk.

(e) Loans and Advances are one of the profitable avenues for the banking sector. The loans granted to the customers are least liquid assets of the bank. They provide loans and advances to the business community through any kind of credit. There is a lot of difference between loans and advance, Loan means relatively for long period, advance refers to short term credit. Loans and advances facilitates the bank with a higher rate of interest income and carry risk. They generate more revenues through loans and advances and they are mostly preferred by banks. But the Loans and Advances are not liked by the banks in view of their liquidity and safety.

(f) Endorsement the banks generally involve in bill market for more revenues. The banks accept the bills for its customers and they rediscount with the central bank. When a bank accepts bills the amount of the bill becomes customer's liability and banker's asset.

(g) Fixed Assets: The banks invest in movable and immovable properties. They invest in *fixed assets* such as *office buildings, furniture.* These assets do not generate any revenues to the banks. The assets constitute very small proportion of the assets of the bank.

(2) Liabilities: The liabilities of the balance sheet is very simple and it consists of the following items.

(a) Share capital.

(b) Reserve fund.

(c) Deposits.

(d) Borrowings.

(e) Acceptance/Endorsement.

(f) Other liabilities.

(a) Share Capital is initially raised by all banks. Share capital constitutes the liability of the bank. It is the contribution of shareholders. It consist (a)authorised capital (b) issued capital (c) subscribed capital (d) paid up capital. The authorised capital is the maximum amount of capital which the bank is allowed to raise in the form of shares. Issued capital is the part of authorised capital in the form of share capital for subscription. Subscribed capital is the part of the issued capital and actually subscribed by the public.

(b) Reserve Fund is the part of the profits. They are accumulated over the years out of undistributed profits. Reserve fund is the financial strength to the banks. It commands financial soundness of the bank.

Generally the entire profit is not distributed by the banks. The Certain portion of the profit will be diverted to reserve fund account.

(c) Deposits are the main components of the liabilities. They constitute the major portion of the banks. The banks accepts various kinds of deposits. They are demand deposits. Time deposits, savings deposits. Demand deposits can be withdrawn at any time and no interest will be paid. Time deposits can be withdrawn only after the stipulated period of the time and they are required to pay a high rate of interest. Savings deposits can be withdrawn to the limited extent in a given period of time and on which some interest is paid. Deposits are the liabilities of a bank. They are also assets of the banks.

(d) Borrowings are necessary in the banking sector to meet the increased demand for money. The banks borrow money from other banks on a temporary basis. Central bank is the lender of the last resort. They provide loan facilities to banks in special circumstances. The surplus amount of bank money can be parked in another bank for some interest.

(e) Accepting & Endorsing the banks create liabilities by accepting or endorsing the bills of exchange on behalf of its customers.

(f) Other Liabilities the banks faces some other liabilities such as acting as agent makes collection on behalf of its customers.

Management of Assets and Liabilities

The bank has to manage its assets and liabilities properly. It has to maximise the profit and minimise the risk without compromising in any aspect. Therefore it requires a suitable portfolio management service. The bank should not ignore the liquidity and solvency position of the financial status portfolio management aims at satisfying the needs of the bank without any risk. The needs of the banks must be on competitive basis in order to get more profitability. The management of assets and liabilities objectives are presented below.

(A) Liquidity.

(B) Solvency.

(C) Profitability.

(A) Liquidity is the most important aspect of the balance sheet item. It refers the ability of the bank to provide cash on demand. The business of the financial institutions depends upon the credibility of the organisation. Therefore the credibility will be reflected in the form of liquidity. Liquidity is the oxygen to the banking institutions. The depositors feel confident when they have confidence that they can demand their money back at any time. Therefore the bank must keep adequate amount of cash balance with them to meet the demand of the depositors without fail. The Liquid assets are assets either in the form of cash or that can be easily turned into cash. The liquid assets of the banks are cash in hand, call money, Treasury bills and bills of exchange. Liquidity is necessary for maintaining public confidence. If bank does not maintain liquidity it will lose depositors confidence and damages to its own business. The following factors will affect the liquidity position of the financial institution

(1) Cash reserve.

(2) Money market.

(3) Seasonal demand.

(4) Business conditions.

(5) Economy status.

(6) Clearing house arrangements.

(7) Banking system.

Cash Reserve is the most important factor in the portfolio management. Every bank should maintain a minimum cash balance as stipulated by banking act. The Central bank has the authority to give instructions in this regard to maintain the ratio from time to time. If the minimum reserve ratio is high the banks have to keep greater liquidity. If the minimum reserve is low they will have lesser liquidity. Therefore the banks have to follow the rules according to the Central bank.

Money Market is a short term market. It facilitates supply and demand of funds for short term basis. The situation of the money market determines the requirements of cash from the banks. Generally the banks will deploy the surplus funds in the money market in order to keep the funds for more proper utilisation.

Seasonal Demand is one of the most important element in the portfolio management. The banks have to keep more money in order to meet the increasing demand from the customer during the festival season, sowing and harvesting season.

Business Conditions determined the level of liquidity position. Business consists of inflation and depression. During inflation the banks require a small amount of proportion of cash in order to support large deposits. During the depression the banks have to maintain a larger amount of funds.

The Nature of the Economy leads to a greater liquidity position of the bank. In developed economy the banks need less cash resources because all the transactions will be settled through the check system. But in underdeveloped economy the major transactions will be settled in the form of cash therefore there is a greater need of liquidity.

Clearing House plays an important role in liquid position of the banks. If a country has the better clearing facilities, the bank claims can be easily settled and banks need not keep large cash balances. If there are no clearing facilities in the country the transactions will not be settled immediately therefore the banks require a large amount of cash balance with them the bank should think about the proper utilisation of money. Heavy amount of cash balances with the bank reduces the profitability and shortage of cash leads to a damage for the goodwill of the bank.

(B) Solvency: Solvency is the most important factor in the portfolio management. Solvency depends upon the relation between assets and liabilities. According to solvency condition the assets must always equal to the liabilities solvency is different from liquidity.

Liquidity is the ability to pay cash without delay to the depositors. Solvency means assets of the bank which is equal to liabilities. A financial institution or bank may be solvent but not liquid. An insolvent bank may exist to operate without any liquidity problem. If the insolvency position exposes to the public immediately there will be rush for refund of their deposits. The following factors are responsible for insolvency.

(1) Risk of default.

(2) Internal risk.

(3) Changes in interest rates.

The bank should always keep in mind about minimising profit and maximising loss due to its business functions. The banking activities fully involved in the mobilisation of funds and disbursal of funds to the borrowers. Therefore the risk may give all crises from the defaulters. The failure of the repayment by the borrower leads to a reduction in assets value. The assets that are below its liabilities lead to insolvency of the bank. If the bank wants to reduce its risk, the following points should be kept in mind:

(a) The loans should disburse to large number of people.

(b) The loans should be sanctioned to few persons with higher amounts.

(c) The reputation and financial position of the buyer should be enquired before granting of the loans.

(d) Proper care should be taken about the securities which are shown by the borrowers.

(e) Banks should prefer for advancing the short term loan.

Internal risk means a threat from the employees. The employees nature and functions are the most important aspects in the financial institutions and banks. The bank funds may be misappropriated by the dishonest or inefficient employees. The employees may involve in cheating or fraud cases. The misappropriation of assets may lead down the value of assets and endangers the solvency of the bank.

Changes in interest rate may show an impact as the long term investments. There is an inverse relationship between interest rate and the market value of securities. If the interest rates are increased there is risk of prospective fall in the market value of the long term securities.

(C) Profitability: The basic objective of the bank is to maximise the return and minimise the risk. The bank must earn sufficient revenue in order to meet the expenses. The banks have been compelled to invest high yield investments. Income of a bank depends upon the factors such as the income generated from an asset during a particular period. The cost of acquiring the cost and the variable cost in owning the asset. Therefore all the three objectives are not equally important. The basic objective is liquidity and solvency and the secondary objective is profitability. The profitability should not be achieved at the cost of the primary objectives.

COMMERCIAL BANKING IN INDIA

Commercial banks are simple business which involve in mobilisation and disbursal of funds. Their objective is to make profits. Banks deal others money. They have a special role·in India. The structure and working of the banking system are integral to a country's financial stability. The nature and significance of the emerging trends in Indian banking since the early fifties. The evolution of Indian banking can be studied in three phases.

(A) Ist phase (1951-64)

(B) IInd phase (1964-90)

(C) IIIrd phase (1991 onwards)

Ist phase 1951-64

The first phase starts from 1951 to 1964. The banking sector was undeveloped and in unorganised form during this phase. The banking industry faced many problems during this period. This period was marked by a large number of unsound and uneconomic banks, banking frauds and malpractices. The banking system did not get public confidence during this phase. There are a lot of malpractices in the banking industry during this period. There was a strong need for the promotion of sound banking. The important factors in evolution of the Indian banking during this period were presented below.

(1) Banking structure.

(2) Public confidence.

(3) Banking policies and practices.

The banking structure during this period was not strong. The banking companies act was replaced by Banking regulation act 1949 for the promotion of sound banking system. The amendments have been made from time to time. The amendment was made to weed out non-viable banking units, to check the malpractices and tone up the administration by eradicating unsound practices. The RBI has the highest authority with mandatory powers to weed out small banks, non-viable and financially weak units by absorbing them with the stronger ones.

The banking structure should restore the public confidence in order to increase the business volume of this sector. Therefore the government established deposit insurance corporation in 1962. It was established under the deposit insurance corporation act 1961. The corporation was established for the purpose of protecting the depositors. The insurance cover was changed from time to time and currently it stands at Rs. 1,00,000.

There are so many changes in banking policies and practices in the banking sector. The changes have been made in regard to the following factors.

(1) Credit Supply.

(2) Functional Coverage.

The banking sector faced a remarkable changes during the first phase. The banking operations have been modified to suit the needs of the five year plans. It has been designed to the priorities of the planning commission. The RBI also modified its monetary policies and credit policies in the form of selective credit control, moral suasion, and other such macro type controls, to encourage the banks to orient their operational policies to the finance for industry, prior to the Ist phase, the commercial banks have neglected all the sectors except for trade and commerce. The banks are engaged to serve the needs of trade and commerce only. The second five year plan has concentrated as rapid industrialisation, there was an upsurge in the bank financing of the industry. This was reflected in the total advances made by the banks. The commercial banks in India were officially encouraged to enter new forms of financing in two kinds.

(a) Term Lending.

(b) Underwriting.

The term loans have been introduced by commercial banks in India. The term loans were not short term, but they were involved in long period of time. There was also need for expanding institutional credit facilities for the small scale and medium-sized industries. Therefore the government encouraged the banks to provide more long term finance to industry. The government also formulated a specific scheme for this purpose in 1958. Under this scheme the commercial banks were provided refinancing facility for their approved term loans. The amount of finance which were disbursed to the term loans segment, the amount was refinanced through the ***Refinance Corporation of India***. The RCI was especially created for this purpose. But the RCI was merged with the IDBI on ***1-9-64.*** The banks also actively participated in the activities of underwriting of new corporate issues. The central banking enquiry committee suggested the banks to enter into the field of underwriting business. ***The Shroff*** committee also recommended to enter this segment. It recommended the formation of Joint Underwriting consortium of banks and insurance companies. But the idea of forming the consortium was finally dropped. Some banks have started participating in underwriting activity during this period.

Functional Coverage means that the banks further directed to provide finance to SSIs, exports and agriculture sectors. These sectors have been neglected by the Indian economy. These sectors received very little credit from the banking sector. This credit provision must operate within that sphere of the planning priorities. The policy may stimulate these sectors.

(A) SSI.

(B) Agriculture.

(C) Exports.

Small industries was completely ignored by the banks during the period. Therefore the government has taken remedial changes in the channelisation of bank funds to the small industries. They have taken measure to streamline. The process (A) Systematic Study of Problems, (B) Involving Credit Guarantee Scheme, (C) RBI Credit Policy.

At the first instance the Central Government made a systematic study on the problems involved in financing the small scale industries. The bankers were trained up towards financing this sector. The study group recommended some suggestions to provide more finance to this sector.

Secondly the government formulated a scheme on the basis of the recommendations made by study group. The scheme was known as ***Credit Guarantee Scheme***. It was prepared by the government in consultation with the RBI in July 1960 to guarantee the major part of the advances given by banks to the SSIs. The Credit Guarantee Scheme was administered by the RBI. The guarantee was given by the Central Government on the payment of a small fee related to the amount of advance. In 1969 the RBI set up a working committee to examine the provisions of the Credit Guarantee Scheme in detail. The committee after thoroughly examined the scheme suggested some modifications in this regard. The modifications were incorporated in a scheme that came into effect from 1-2-1970. The recommendations stated that the guarantee was made available to all eligible advances on an automatic basis subject to entering into contract with the Credit Guarantee Corporation. The Credit Guarantee Corporation was required to submit all the particulars about all eligible loans and advances made available on charging a guarantee fee from them. The CGO covered all credit facilities and allowed SSIs and the guarantee cover was upto 75% of the amount defaulted or the amount guaranteed whichever was lower. However the maximum assistance was made available to a ceiling amount of ***Rs. 7.5 lakh*** in respect of working capital advance from the CGO. The ceiling limit was for ***Rs. 2.5 lakhs*** in respect of the term loans per borrower. The CGS had taken more responsibilities in financing the small scale enterprises.

At last the RBI incorporated some devices in its credit policy to stimulate bank credit to this sector. The RBI evolved a scheme in 1962 for granting additional rights to the banks to borrow funds at concessional rates if they provide a higher amount of finance to SSIs segment. These concessions were provided to the banks in different aspects. Therefore there was a rapid rise in the amount of finance to the SSIs by the banks.

The Agriculture Sector was completely ignored prior to this phase. The government has taken a step for establishing the Agricultural Refinance Corporation. The RBI had taken initiative and set up the ARC Ltd., as a subsidiary in 1963. It was promoted for providing medium and long term finance to all eligible financial institutions by way of refinance. The banks should not get refinance other than ARC for the purpose of agriculture sector.

The Credit Authorisation Scheme was introduced in Nov. 1965 to regulate the bank credit to the large borrowers. According to the scheme, the banks should get prior approval from the RBI for granting any cash credit exceeding of rupee one crore to any individual party the CAS objective was to control the big borrowers as well as to coordinate the credit activities of the banks with the planning priorities. The scheme was further modified to ensure a better control over the end use of credit. The CAS was discontinued in 1975 and replaced by Credit Monitoring Arrangement.

Exports sector also neglected by the banking sector prior to Ist phase. Some measures have been taken up by the central government to facilitate credit for exports. Therefore the Export Risk Insurance Corporation was set up in 1957. It was established for the purpose of offering insurance to exporters against exchange controls or multiple currency practices. The Corporation was renamed in 1964 as the ***Export Credit and Guarantee Corporation Ltd.*** The corporation extended guarantees to the banks for various types of finance for export segment. The corporation also provided insurance facility to the exporters. The Government of India provided the banks at concessional rate of interest of the funds towards financing the export segment.

IInd Phase (1964-90)

The second phase starts from 1964 to 1990. It was known as revolutionary phase. During the period of second phase the banking sector has been changed significantly due to various reasons particularly the rapid changes in political scenario have been shown an impact on functioning of the banking sector. The problem of concentration of economic power in few hands was exposed. Several official reports investigated these problems by the following committees:

(a) Mahalanobi Committee 1964.

(b) The Monopolies Inquiry Commissions 1965.

(c) R. K. Hazari Committee 1966.

(d) Patel Committee 1966.

(e) R. K. Hazari Committee 1967.

(f) Dutt Committee 1969.

These committees formed the basis of significant policy changes in Indian Banking Sector. There was a strong need to spread the credit flow equally to among the various classes of borrowers. There was a strong feeling that the entire credit facilities from the banking sector was enjoyed by the large industrial houses. At the same time the banks totally neglected the priorities sectors such as SSIs, agriculture exports and other sectors etc. These feelings provided a broad satting for the revolutionary changes in the structure, operations policies and practices of banks during this phase. The main features of this phase was influenced by the following factors.

(a) Social Control.

(b) Nationalisation.

(c) Priority Sectors.

(A) Social Control: The RBI made rigorous rules and regulations in the Ist phase of the banking sector. But even then the banking system suffered in terms of coverage and credit gaps. The network of branches covered only the geographical locations like populated cities and excluded the rural and smaller towns. But the agriculture, export, SSIs sectors was entirely neglected by the banking sector. Therefore the government had concentrated to provide the credit flow to agriculture, exports, SSIs, artisans, retail traders self employed persons and so on. All these sectors did not enjoy the credit facility. The control of banking sector was in the hands of leading industrial houses. Therefore the government introduced the scheme of social control at the end of 1967. The bank credit was an instrument for the attainment of the socioeconomic objectives. The government made its efforts to remove the control of the bu iness houses over banks without removing the private ownership of banks. The social control was strongly influenced by the following factors.

(a) Credit flow to all segments of the society.

(b) National Credit Council.

The scheme of social control requires the reorganisation of the board of directors of the banks. The board of directors of the bank had been revamped and introduced the persons who had specialised knowledge in agriculture rural economy, small scale industries, cooperation and banking etc. The chairman of the bank who are industrialists were replaced by professional managers. The professional managers were highly skilled, knowledge and talented with expertism. They were related to banking, finance, economic and business administration.

The next important step was the establishment of National Credit Council in Feb. 68. The council was created for the purpose of assessing credit priorities on an all India basis. The basic functions of the councils were presented below.

(a) To predict the future demand to the bank credit from all sectors of the economy.

(b) To proper utilisation of available resources towards granting of loans to priority sectors.

(c) To coordinate the lending and investment activities of the banking sector.

The NCC appointed two study groups in Oct. 1968 for examining the problems regarding the equitable allocation of bank credit to all the sectors. The first group was headed by Prof. D. R. Gadgil to enquire into the question of credit gaps. The second group was appointed under the supervision of Shri V. T. Dehejia, which look into the matters like concentration of economic power in few hands.

As per the recommendations of the first group, the government revamped its banking activities and followed the urban orientation of the banking system. The banking sector also drew its attention to the problems of small farmers. The committee reported that the bank credit should be available to priorities sector without fail. The committee also found that the bank credit was unevenly distributed among different states. The banking sector prepared its new agricultural strategy in order to reduce the disparities in various sectors. The New agriculture strategy suggested for the creation of Agriculture Finance Corporation to fulfil the needs of the agriculture sector. The Agriculture Finance Corporation was established as a Joint sector entity. The corporation helped the banks to participate actively in developing the agriculture sector.

The Committee also suggested that the banks should follow the area approach. Area approach refers to branch expansion. The individual banks may devote for intensive development of special geographical areas under the network process. The network process expand their efforts at deposit mobilisation and finance to agriculture and small scale industries. Every bank was appointed as a lead bank which undertake the responsibility for intensively developing chosen areas with regard to their network in that area. The designated lead bank had to make a detailed survey of the area of their operations.

The study group suggested another recommendations for the formulation of a better coordinating facilities. There is a strong need of coordination between the banks. The cooperative institutions, financial institutions and the government organs. The committee also felt the integration of the credit and banking business with their activities. The lead banks were involved in financing the agriculture and small scale industries to improve their efficiency. The lead bank at distinct level plays an important role in providing finance to priority sectors. The branch expansion led to better coordination between banks and cooperative institutions. The RBI appointed a committee of bankers in 1969. Under the chairmanship of ***FKF Nariman***. The Committee adopted the area approach and encouraged the lead bank scheme. The lead banks were allotted specific districts for taking up credit survey and business opportunities. Prof. Gadgil Committee recommended the lead bank scheme and it was endorsed by the Nariman committee. Therefore the RBI finalised the scheme at the end of 1969. According to this scheme, all the 336 districts in the country were distributed among the major schedule banks. But the Metros and Union Territories, Delhi and Goa were excluded from this scheme. The criterial for allotment of lead bank in a particular district was the size of the bank located in that district, size of its resources, the regional orientation of the bank and the desirability of the state government. The lead bank scheme enabled the banks to fully involve in the developmental activities of the society.

The second committee was headed by Shri Dehejia, submitted its report in September 1969. The group was appointed to look into the matter regarding the credit flow exceeds its limits to the industry sector. The industry enjoyed the bank credit and ignored the remaining portfolios of the economy. The group further recommended that the need for minimising the inventory holdings by industry in order to reduce the demand for bank finance. The committee recommended the credit flow to the priority sector. The RBI appointed the All India Rural Credit Review Committee for reviewing the agricultural programmes. The committee was appointed in 1969 and found that there was more demand for rural credit to expand rapidly to develop the agriculture sector more fruitfully.

(B) Nationalisation: There was a radical change emerged during the second phase of banking sector history. To satisfy the ideology 14 major banks with individual deposits exceeding Rs. 50 crore were nationalised on July 19, 1969. The aim of the nationalisation was to control the heights of the economy and meet progressively and serve better the needs of the development of the economy in confirmity with national policy and objectives. Nationalisation gives a new orientation to the banking system.

The post nationalisation period yielded significant changes in the operational policies and practices of the banks. The following developments occurred after the nationalisation of the banks. The developments were:

(a) Deheji Committee.

(b) Tandon Committee.

(c) Chare Committee.

(d) Marathe Committee.

(a) Deheji Committee: The Deheji Committee recommended the introduction of New bill market scheme. The committee had found that the bank credit to industry provided more than its output the industry. It was found that additional amount of finance was diversified by the industry to acquire the fixed assets. But actually the provision of bank credit was meant for the purpose of short term needs. Therefore this method of acquisition of fixed assets was not a healthy trend for the industry. The findings and recommendations led to the introduction of new methods like new bill market scheme. The Narasimham group was appointed by the RBI in Feb. 1970 to study the use of bill exchange as an instrument for providing credit and the creation of new bill market in India. The Committee found that the cash credit system has been misused by the industry. The call money activities involved in problems. Therefore the RBI introduced New bill market system in 1970.

(b) Tandon Committee: The Tandon Committee was appointed in 1974 to frame the guidelines for follow up of bank credit. It was a revolutionary development in the banking sector. The Committee studied about the scientific evolution of bank credit. The committee suggested about the strong need of bank credit that should be in safe limits to avoid inflationary pressure on the economy. Bank credit portion has been rationed to the industrial sector and increased the contribution to the priority sector. There is a maximum scope for misuse on the part of the credit users. The Tandon committee had been concentrated to solve this problem.

(c) Chare Committee: had been appointed to study the implementation of the Tandon's Committee framework. The committee also reviewed about the notable development in the sphere of working capital. The committee further enquired about the functioning of the ***cash credit system***.

(d) Marathe Committee: was appointed to study about the credit functioning of the banking sector. The committee recommended the credit Monitoring Arrangement. According to this scheme the bank can grant the loan to the industrial houses without the approval of the RBI. The RBI will stipulate the post sanction monitoring activities.

IIIrd Phase 1991 (onwards Prudential Banking)

The government introduced the liberalisation, deregulation, globalisation of economy. They have thrown a challenge to the banking sector. The era of 1991, Indian banking is essentially a phase of profitable banking, viable and prudential banking. The Union Government appointed a committee to study about the functioning of the financial sector 1991. The committee was headed by Narasimhan. The other Committee was appointed to study about the Banking sector Reforms in 1998. This committee was also headed by Mr. Narasimhan. The following were the important committees appointed during the third phase.

(1) Narasimhan Committee (1991)

(2) Narasimhan Committee (1998)

Narasimhan Committee (1991): The committee on financial sector had been appointed in 1991 to study about the Indian banking sectors transformation. The banking system had grown in this phase exponentially. The committee reviewed banking system in conformity with the expanding and emerging needs of the Indian economy. The post nationalisation era (1969-91) saw the rise of banking sector in India. The following recommendations were made by the Narasimhan committee.

(1) The committee was appointed to suggest the measures to enhance efficiency, productivity and profitability of the banking sector.

(2) The SLR should be brought down to 25% over a period of five years.

(3) The RBI should have the flexibility to operate CRR to serve its monetary policy objectives.

(4) The directed credit programme should be phased out.

(5) The priority sector should consists of small and marginal farmers SSIS, tiny sector small business and transport operators, village and khadi industries rural artisans and other weaker sections.

(6) The interest rates should be regulated.

(7) The banks should achieve minimum capital adequacy ratios.

(8) Good banks can be permitted to enter the capital market.

(9) The assets of each bank should be evaluated on the basis of their realisable value to arrive the capital adequacy ratio.

(10) All banks should follow the accounting policies with regard to income and asset valuations uniformly.

(11) No income should be recognised in accounts in respect of non performing assets.

(12) The assets should be classified into four categories.

  (a) Standard.

  (b) Substandard assets. (provision 10% of the total outstanding)

  (c) Doubtful (100% of security shortfall)

  (d) Loss (100% or fully written off)

  The above norms should be implemented in a phased manner over a period of four years.

(13) The balance sheet of the banks must be prepared in compliance with the international Accounting Standard in phased manner.

(14) Special tribunals should be set up to speedy recovery of the debts.

(15) An Assets Reconstruction Fund should be established with a special powers of recovery.

(16) The banking sector should be encouraged for mergers and acquisitions.

(17) There should not be any further nationalisation of banks

(18) Branch licensing should be abolished.

(19) Expansion of branches depends upon the market forces.

(20) Opening of foreign bank branches should be encouraged.

(21) The foreign operations of the Indian banks to be rationalised.

(22) Internal management of the banks should be left for individual banks.

(23) The medium and large banks should have a three tier structure (a) head office (b) Zonal office (c) branch office.

(24) The large banks should have four structure organisation (a) Head office (b) Zonal office (c) Regional office (d) Branch office

(25) Computerisation of banking activities should be encouraged.

(26) Banks should be provided internal autonomy.

(27) Recruitment should be dispensed with the BSRBs.

(28) There is a strong need in a work technology and culture.

(29) The personnel policies by management should create satisfying work environment.

(30) The Indian banking system is presently overregulated and over administered. This situation must be avoided.

(31) The appointment of top level management should be done on the basis of professionalism.

(2) Narasimhan Committee 1998: The committee had been appointed to suggest the remedial measures for banking sector reforms. It was set up in 1998 and submitted the following recommendations.

(1) The capital adequacy requirements should take into account of market and credit risk.

(2) The minimum capital to risk assets ratio should be increased to 10% from its present level of 8% in a phased manner.

(3) The additional capital requirements of the public sector banks should mobilise from capital market or from the central government

(4) An asset should be classified as doubtful if it is in the sub-standard category for 18 months in the first instance and 12 months eventually (against two years now) and loss when identified though not written off.

(5) The advanced amount covered by the government guarantee but have turned sticky and it has been classified as nonperforming asset, should be treated as NPA.

(6) No further recapitalisation of banks should be undertaken from the government budget.

(7) The committee targeted the average level of NPAs for all banks, below 5% by the year 2000 and 3% by 2002.

(8) Financial restructuring in the form of living off the NPA portfolio from the books of the banks.

(9) The current practice of earmarking 10% of bank credit to priority sector may continue

(10) The international norm of 90 days for income recognition should be followed.

(11) A general provision should be made at 1% on standard assets in a phase manner.

(12) The income recognition, asset classification, and provisioning norms should apply for future government guaranteed advances.

(13) Full disclosure should be made available to the public.

(14) The banks should be encouraged to adopt statistical risk management techniques like value at risk in respect of balance sheet items.

(15) For reduction of transaction cost, the banks should adopt new technology

(16) The banks should bring out revised operational Manuals and up date them regularly.

(17) The computer credit would require close scrutiny.

(18) Statutory auditors should be appointed by individual bank auditors.

(19) The recruiting powers should be given to the individual banks and it should not continue the process with the BSRB.

(20) Surplus staff should be redeployed on new business and activities.

(21) Flexibility should be provided in determining the managerial remuneration.

(22) The tenure for CMDs should be five years and performance based remuneration.

(23) Banks should explore the avenues for training programmes in the financial services industry.

(24) Redefinition of the scope of external vigilance and investigate agencies with regard to banking business.

(25) The banks should adopt the latest IT technology

(26) The development financial institutions should over a period of time convert themselves into banks.

(27) Mergers between banks must make sound commercial sense.

(28) The policy of licensing of new private sector banks may continue.

(29) Foreign banks may be allowed to set up subsidiaries, joint ventures in India.

(30) There is a strong need for reform of the deposit insurance scheme.

(31) The inter bank call and notice market and inter bank term money market should be strictly restricted to banks.

(32) The banking system should equip itself to identify the government sponsored programme such as the IRDP.

(33) The expanded flow of credit to the economically weaken segments and other sub sectors of priority sector lending has resulted in higher NPAs.

(34) There is a need to review thė present institutional set up of state level financial/industrial development institutions.

(35) To improve the soundness and stability of the Indian banking system.

(36) The regulatory authorities should take note of the recent developments all over the globe and incorporate in India for the benefit of the nation

(37) Banks should be required to publish the half yearly disclosure requirements in two parts.

(38) As integrated system of regulation and sub-envision has to be put in place to regulate and supervise the activities of the banks.

(39) Debt recovery machinery should be established.

Types of Banks

Banks can be categorised into various types on the basis of their ownership, functions domiciles etc. The following are the various kinds of banks:

(a) Commercial banks.

(b) Industrial banks.

(c) Central bank.

(d) Scheduled banks.

(e) World bank.

(f) Agricultural banks.

(g) Saving banks.

(h) Public sector banks.

(i) Private sector banks.

(j) Cooperative sector banks.

(k) Domestic banks.

(l) Foreign banks.

(m) Exchange banks.

(n) Non scheduled banks.

(a) Commercial banks: The banks which provide all kinds of banking activities are known as commercial banks. They usually finance trade and commerce and render the services to customers. Generally the banks mobilise deposits from the public and lend the same amount to the borrowers at high rate of interest. The banks pay less amount of interest on deposits mobilised by them. The payment of interest and receipt of interest is main source of income of the commercial banks. The commercial banks generally lend the money on short term basis because their deposits lies with them for the some period. Generally the banks avoid long term financing. The commercial banks are also known as joint stock banks. Majority of the commercial banks are in the public sector.

The commercial banking in India began in 1770 with the establishment of the first joint stock bank called as ***Bank of Hindustan*** in Calcutta. But it failed in 1832. The Bank of Bengal was established in 1806, and started the modern commercial banking in India. The bank of Bombay and the bank of Madras were set up in 1840 and 1843 respectively. All these banks were known as ***presidency banks.*** They were financed by East India Company. The first Indian bank was started in 1881 Oudh Commercial Bank. The Punjab National Bank was established in 1894 and the people's banking 1901. The Swadeshi movement encouraged the growth of commercial banks in India. The State Bank of India was established in 1955. The SBI has seven subsidiary banks. On July 19, 1969 14 major Commercial Banks were nationalised. Again on April 15, 1980, six more Commercial Banks were nationalised. The Commercial banks in India can be divided into two kinds.

(A) Public Sector Banks.

(B) Private Sector Banks.

The Public Sector Banks can be divided into 4 kinds. They are:

(1) State Bank of India

(2) SBI Associates

(3) Nationalised Banks.

(4) Regional Rural banks.

The private sector banks can be divided into two kinds. They are:

(1) Scheduled banks

(2) Non scheduled banks.

The Commercial Banks in India are joint stock banks. They are registered under the Indian companies act. The operations of these banks are controlled and regulated by the RBI. The Commercial Banks are eligible for their rediscounting facilities. The Commercial Banks perform the following functions.

(1) The Commercial Banks accept various kinds of deposits.

(2) They provide loans to traders, producers for short periods.

(3) They provide services to the customers

(4) They provide general utility services.

THE FOLLOWING STATISTICS WILL REVEAL ABOUT THE FINANCIAL STATUS OF THE NATIONALISED BANKS 1996-2001

(in percentage)

	Name of the Bank	*Capital Adequacy Ratio*		*ROA*		*Net NPA*		*Total Assets*	
		1996-97	*2000-01*	*1996-97*	*2000-01*	*1996-97*	*2000-01*	*96-97*	*2000-01*
(1)	Allahabad Bank	10.57	10.50	0.51	0.18	14.84	11.23	3.05	3.0
(2)	Andhra bank	12.05	13.40	0.01	0.59	4.10	2.95	2.98	2.45
(3)	Bank of Baroda	11.80	12.80	0.73	0.45	7.53	6.77	3.21	3.06
(4)	Bank of India	10.25	12.23	1.01	0.44	6.93	6.72	3.00	2.78
(5)	Bank of Maharashtra	9.07	10.64	0.57	0.24	9.66	7.41	3.67	2.93
(6)	Canara bank	10.17	9.84	0.44	0.43	9.32	4.84	3.19	2.83
(7)	CBI	9.41	10.02	0.65	0.10	14.40	9.72	3.17	3.07
(8)	Corporation bank	11.27	13.30	1.66	1.55	3.63	1.98	3.87	2.95

(9)	Dena bank	10.81	7.73	0.81	0.00	9.38	18.37	3.85	2.51
(10)	Indian bank	18.81	—	—	—	25.24	10.06	0.71	1.84
(11)	IOB	10.07	10.24	0.58	0.38	7.64	7.01	2.38	2.91
(12)	OBC	17.50	11.81	1.60	0.80	5.64	3.60	3.89	2.91
(13)	Punjab & Sind	9.22	11.42	0.29	0.10	12.04	12.27	2.60	2.50
(14)	PNB	9.15	10.24	0.71	0.73	10.38	6.69	3.47	3.21
(15)	Syndicate bank	8.80	11.72	0.43	0.91	7.53	4.05	3.17	3.87
(16)	UCO bank	3.16	9.05	–1.46	0.14	13.73	6.35	1.93	2.42
(17)	UBI	10.53	10.86	1.01	0.40	6.98	6.87	3.41	3.13
(18)	United bank of India	8.20	10.40	—	0.10	19.20	10.50	1.54	2.39
(19)	Vijaya bank	11.50	11.50	0.30	0.53	9.56	6.23	2.91	3.23

Sources: EPW, June 8, 2002, p. 2253.

STATEMENT SHOWING FINANCIAL STATUS OF THE COMMERCIAL BANKING IN INDIA (1994-95 to 2000-01)

(percentage)

Banks	*Deposits*		*Advances*		*Net Profit*		*Assets*	
	1994-95	*2000-01*	*1994-95*	*2000-01*	*1994-95*	*2000-01*	*1994-95*	*2000-01*
I. Public Sector Banks								
(a) Nationalised banks	57.60	51.86	54.60	50.26	12.68	32.61	56.14	48.41
(b) State bank group	**28.20**	29.58	30.00	28.62	39.86	34.59	31.06	31.11
II. Private Sector Banks:								
(a) Old pvt. sector banks	6.90	6.99	7.30	7.22	14.61	8.14	5.27	6.53
(b) New private sector	—	5.96	—	5.72	0.00	9.95	0.00	6.08
III. Foreign banks	7.30	5.61	8.10	8.18	32.85	14.71	7.54	7.87
Total	**100**	**100**	**100**	**100**	**100**	**100**	**100**	**100**

STATEMENT SHOWING THE RETURN ON TOTAL ASSETS ON BANKS (GROUPWISE) *(per cent)*

Sr. No.	*Bank group*	*1997-98*	*1998-99*	*1999-2000*	*2000-01*
I	**Public Sector Banks:**	0.77	0.42	0.57	0.42
	(a) Nationalised bank group	0.62	0.37	0.44	0.33
	(b) State bank group	1.06	0.51	0.80	0.55
II	**All Private Banks:**	1.04	0.68	0.88	0.71
	(a) Old private sector	0.81	0.48	0.81	0.62
	(b) New Private sector	1.55	1.03	0.97	0.81
III	**Foreign Banks**	0.97	0.69	1.17	0,93
	All banks	0.82	0.49	0.66	0.50

Sources: EPW, June 2002, p. 2250.

STATEMENT SHOWING THE DIVIDEND PAID BY THE NATIONALISED BANKS TO GOVERNMENT OF INDIA

Sr. No.	*Dividend for the Year*	*No. of Banks Out of the 19*	*Amount (Rs. in crores)*
(1)	1995-96	07	210
(2)	1996-97	08	315
(3)	1997-98	10	400
(4)	1998-99	14	399
(5)	1999-2000	15	465
(6)	2000-2001	14	505
Total			2294.

Source: *Public Sector Banks in India, B2 Mathew, EPW, June 8, 2000, p. 22.*

STATEMENT SHOWING DEPOSITS AND ADVANCES OF THE COMMERCIAL BANKS (1994-95, 2000-2001)

(percentage)

Bank/Groupwise	*Assets*		*Deposits*		*Advances*		*Net profit*	
	1994-95	*2000-01*	*1994-95*	*2000-01*	*1994-95*	*2000-01*	*1994-95*	*2000-01*
(1) Nationalised bank	56	48	58	52	55	50	13	33
(2) SBI group	31	31	28	30	30	29	40	35
(3) Old private sector banks	5	7	7	7	7	7	15	8
(4) New private sector banks	0	6	0	6	0	6	0	10
(5) Foreign banks	8	8	7	6	8	8	33	15

STATEMENT SHOWING THE FINANCIAL CONTOURS OF BANKING (1990-91, 2000-01)

Particulars	*All Scheduled Commercial Banks*	*Public Sector Banks*	*SBI Group*	*Nationalised Banks*	*Private Indian Banks*	*Foreign Banks*
(1) Net Interest	8,553	7,647	3,388	4,259	333	573
(2) Profit after tax	743	476	150	326	35	232
(3) Total assets	2,84,162	2,59,308	93,012	1,66,296	8,869	15,985
(4) Share of total assets (%)	—	91.3	32.7	58.5	3.1	5.6
(5) Share of profits (%)	—	64.1	20.2	43.9	4.7	31.2
(6) Profit after tax (%)	0.26	0.18	0.16	0.20	0.39	1.45
						(2000-2001)
(1) Net Interest	36,799	29,291	11,114	18,178	3,805	3,703
(2) PAT	6,424	4,317	2,222	2,095	1,162	945
(3) Total Assets	12,94,974	10,29,770	4,02,878	6,26,892	1,63,383	1,01,824
(4) Share of total assets(%)	—	79.5	31.1	48.4	12.6	7.9
(5) Share of profits (%)	—	67.2	34.6	32.6	18.1	14.7
(6) PAT(%)	0.50	0.42	0.55	0.33	1.43	0.93

Sources: Sumithra Chaudhary, *Some Issues in Indian Public Sector Banks, EPW, June, 2002, p. 2155.*

STATEMENT SHOWING THE CAPITAL TO RISK WEIGHTED ASSETS RATIO OF THE COMMERCIAL BANKS

Bank	*Tier I*	*Tier II*	*Total*
I. Nationalised Banks:			
(a) Allahabad bank	6.70	3.80	10.50
(b) Andhra bank	9.76	3.64	13.40
(c) Bank of Baroda	8.49	4.31	–2.80
(d) Bank of India	7.62	4.61	12.23
(e) Bank of Maharashtra	6.39	4.25	10.64
(f) Canara bank	7.31	2.53	9.84
(g) Central bank of India	5.74	4.28	10.02
(h) Corporation bank	13.00	0.30	13.30
(i) Dena bank	4.38	3.35	7.73
(j) Indian bank	(–)	Nil	(–)
(k) Indian overseas bank	5.81	4.43	10.24
(l) Oriental bank of commerce	11.45	0.36	11.81
(m) Punjab & Sind bank	6.87	4.55	11.42
(n) Punjab National bank	6.84	3.40	10.24
(o) Syndicate bank	7.88	3.84	11.72
(p) UCO bank	5.36	3.69	9.05
(q) Union bank of India	6.19	4.67	10.86
(r) United Bank of India	7.00	3.40	10.40
(s) Vijaya bank	8.04	3.46	11.50
II. State Bank of Group			
(a) SBI	8.58	4.21	12.79
(b) State bank of Bikaner	11.62	0.77	12.39
(c) SBH	9.56	2.72	12.28
(d) SBI	9.12	3.61	12.73
(e) State bank of Mysore	6.76	4.40	11.16
(f) State bank of Patiala	10.69	1.68	12.37
(g) State bank of Saurashtra	13.65	0.24	13.89
(h) State bank of Travancore	7.73	4.06	11.79
III. New Private Banks			
(a) Bank of Punjab	8.52	2.50	11.02
(b) Centurion bank	6.88	9.61	16.49
(c) Global Trust bank	8.79	3.92	12.71
(d) HDFC bank	8.69	2.40	11.09
(e) ICICI bank	10.42	1.15	11.57
(f) IDBI bank	7.89	3.83	11.72
(g) Indus Ind bank	12.56	2.44	15.00
(h) UTI bank	5.84	3.16	9.00
			(%)

STATEMENT SHOWING IPOS AND CURRENT PRICES OF VARIOUS BANKS

	Bank	*IPO Date*	*IPO price*	*Current price*
(1)	Andhra bank	Feb. 01	10	8.40
(2)	Bank of Baroda	Dec. 96	85	39.10
(3)	Bank of India	Feb. 97	45	16.70
(4)	Corporation bank	Oct. 97	80	129.00
(5)	Dena bank	Oct. 96	30	6.50
(6)	Indian overseas bank	Sep. 00	10	7.70
(7)	Oriental bank	Oct. 94	60	33.35
(8)	Syndicate bank	Oct. 99	10	9.25
(9)	Vijaya bank	Dec. 00	10	7.70
(10)	State bank of India	Dec. 93	100	207.00
(11)	State bank of Bikaner	Nov. 97	540	315.00
(12)	State bank of Travarcore	Dec. 97	600	—
(13)	Bank of Punjab	May 95	—	12.30
(14)	Centurion bank	Sept. 99	10	11.00
(15)	GTB	Aug. 94	10	26.00
(16)	HDFC bank	Oct. 94	10	225.00
(17)	ICICI bank	Aug. 97	35	102.00
(18)	IDBI bank	Feb. 99	18	19.05
(19)	Indus Ind bank	Nov. 97	45	12.25
(20)	UTI bank	Sept. 98	21	29.00

Sources: Mayur Shetty, *Insearch of Deep Pockets, Economic Times Dt: 21/11/2002, p. 9.*

Statement showing the Net Interest Income a Percentage of Total Assets

	Name of the bank	*Net interest 97-98*	*Income 98-99*	*as % of 99-00*	*Total 00-01*
I.	**Public Sector Banks**				
(1)	Allahabad bank	2.88	2.82	2.86	3.09
(2)	Andhra bank	3.37	2.91	2.68	2.45
(3)	Bank of Baroda	2.91	3.01	2.85	3.06
(4)	Bank of India	2.77	2.61	2.33	2.78
(5)	Bank of Maharashtra	3.50	3.29	3.07	2.93
(6)	Canara bank	2.49	3.17	2.64	2.83
(7)	Central bank of India	3.11	2.97	2.96	3.07
(8)	Corporation bank	3.46	2.49	2.73	2.95
(9)	Dena bank	3.48	2.97	2.46	2.51
(10)	Indian bank	0.57	0,92	1.61	1.84
(11)	I.O.B.	2.31	2.31	2.46	2.91
(12)	Oriental bank of commerce	3.38	3.10	2.90	2.92
(13)	Punjab Sind bank	2.68	2.38	2.35	2.51

(14)	Punjab National bank	3.25	3.57	2.99	3.21
(15)	Syndicate bank	2.85	2.94	3.04	3.87
(16)	UCO bank	1.89	2.15	2.35	2.42
(17)	Union bank of India	3.17	2.66	2.73	3.13
(18)	United bank of India	2.74	2.00	2.10	2.39
(19)	Vijaya bank	2.76	2.86	2.03	3.23
(20)	SBI	3.01	2.72	2.65	2.61
(21)	State bank of Bikaner	3.68	3.23	3.00	3.29
(22)	SBH	3.61	3.53	3.35	3.33
(23)	State bank of Indore	3.86	3.92	2.99	2.84
(24)	State bank of Mysore	3.94	3.58	3.39	3.33
(25)	State bank of Patiala	3.64	3.53	3.78	4.22
(26)	State bank of Saurashtra	3.63	3.49	3.20	2.93
(27)	State bank of Travancore	2.94	2.20	2.27	2.73
II.	**Old Private Sector Banks:**				
(1)	The Bank of Rajasthan	2.38	1.76	2.35	3.06
(2)	The Benares state bank	2.50	1.49	1.26	0.90
(3)	Barath overseas bank	2.56	2.05	2.15	2.75
(4)	The Catholic Syrian bank	2.47	1.97	2.34	2.72
(5)	City Union bank	2.09	1.87	3.03	2.95
(6)	Development credit bank	1.99	2.05	1.81	2.19
(7)	Dhanalakshmi bank	2.72	2.16	2.49	2.34
(8)	The Federal bank	1.89	1.09	2.37	2.69
(9)	Ganesh bank of Kurundwad	2.60	2.06	2.40	2.09
(10)	J & K bank	3.60	3.49	2.71	2.81
(11)	The Karnataka bank	3.58	2.38	1.99	2.28
(12)	The Karur Vyshya bank	3.28	2.91	3.66	3.67
(13)	The Lakshmi Vilas bank	2.53	2.31	2.59	2.55
(14)	Lord Krishna bank	2.14	1.66	1.41	1.44
(15)	The Nainital bank	3.90	4.11	3.83	3.80
(16)	The Nedugadi bank	3.23	2.54	2.14	1.04
(17)	The Ratnakar bank	3.21	3.12	2.82	3.07
(18)	The Sangli bank	3.37	2.75	2.57	3.14
(19)	SBI Commercial & Int.	1.15	1.38	1.98	1.19
(20)	The South Indian bank	2.52	2.46	2.66	2.87
(21)	Tamilnadu Mercantile bank	3.68	2.96	2.88	3.29
(22)	United Western bank	2.38	2.30	2.38	1.91
(23)	Vyshya bank	1.57	1.25	1.24	1.71
III.	**New Private Sector Banks:**				
(1)	Bank of Punjab	2.58	1.95	2.31	3.04

(2)	Centurion bank	2.93	3.17	1.54	1.74
(3)	Global Trust bank	2.02	1.02	2.50	2.11
(4)	HDFC bank	3.65	3.38	2.60	3.24
(5)	ICICI bank	2.23	1.70	1.54	2.05
(6)	IDBI bank	2.03	1.87	2.02	2.07
(7)	Indus Ind bank	2.43	1.86	1.70	1.84
(8)	UTI bank	1.05	1.86	1.36	0.91
IV.	**Foreign Bank:**				
(1)	ABN Amro bank NV	3.23	3.30	3.22	3.93
(2)	Abudabhi comml. bank	2.23	1.92	2.10	0.9
(3)	American express bank	3.29	2.77	3.91	2.61
(4)	Arab Bangladesh bank	3.62	5.49	5.82	6.6
(5)	Bank International Indonesia	5.43	2.75	2.77	2.81
(6)	Bank Muscat SAOG	0.00	2.78	2.14	3.06
(7)	Bank of America NA	3.98	4.41	4.65	3.28
(8)	Bank of Bahrain and Kuwait	0.92	1.11	1.55	1.62
(9)	Bank of Ceylon	4.70	6.54	4.99	3.86
(10)	The bank of Nova Scotia	2.85	3.24	2.60	2.21
(11)	Bank of Tokyo – Mitsubhishi	4.04	3.64	6.34	6.23
(12)	Banclays bank PLC	2.78	3.58	2.37	1.54
(13)	BNP Paribas	3.24	3.14	2.70	2.61
(14)	Chinatrust comml. bank	7.50	3.27	3.94	4.22
(15)	Cho Hung bank	11.34	7.19	7.88	8.21
(16)	Citi bank	4.40	5.44	4.56	3.97
(17)	Commerz bank	4.32	3.11	3.02	1.82
(18)	Credit Agricole Indosuez	–0.63	2.83	2.48	1.46
(19)	Credit lyonnais	3.89	3.63	3.52	3.10
(20)	Deustche bank AG	6.70	4.93	5.01	5.14
(21)	Devt. bank of Singapore	1.95	3.01	3.32	2.89
(22)	Drender bank AG	2.66	4.15	5.58	6.29
(23)	HSBC	3.38	2.69	2.75	3.03
(24)	ING bank NV	1.80	3.57	6.22	1.50
(25)	KBC bank NV	0.00	0.99	2.97	3.21
(26)	Krung Thai bank	7.21	7.48	7.79	8.28
(27)	Mashreq bank PSC	5.18	2.35	2.23	1.10
(28)	Morgan Guarantee trust	0.00	0.60	2.01	1.87
(29)	Oman Intnl. bank SAOG	1.35	–0.56	–0.46	0.51
(30)	Overseas Chinese banking	6.05	7.23	7.18	8.60
(31)	The Sanwa bank	6.37	5.63	4.24	3.89
(32)	Staur commercial bank	6.59	6.34	5.62	1.77

(33)	Societe Generale	2.47	2.78	1.09	1.29
(34)	Sonali bank	1.60	3.18	0.94	2.29
(35)	Standard Chartered bank	3.57	3.57	4.24	3.73
(36)	SC Grindlays bank	4.56	3.67	4.87	5.11
(37)	State bank of Mauritius	6.46	2.78	3.12	3.08
(38)	The Sumitomo bank	2.19	4.35	3.96	2.54
(39)	Chase Manhattan bank	0.39	0.93	0.77	2.79
(40)	The Fuji bank	4.94	4.75	1.75	2.99
(41)	The Sakura bank	7.46	6.81	6.37	4.25
(42)	Tornto Daminon bank	5.37	11.49	7.60	11.52

Sources: Trends, ET, 17-4-2002, p. 12.

The commercial banks in India are under stress, while the lack of new industrial investment is affecting their credit off take adversely increasing interest liabilities are putting pressure on their margins. The net result is a deteriorating profitability ratio.

The growth of bank credit to industry declared to 10.5% in 2000-01 against 12.9% in the previous year. The declaration was even sharpen in case of credit to wholesale trade aggregate credit offtake by the wholesale traders increased by just about 6.1% in 2000-2001 as compared to 20.4% in 1999-00.

A segment wise analysis shows that once the multinations were the biggest losers. They suffered the maximum fall in spread during the period.

STATEMENT SHOWING THE PROGRESS OF COMMERCIAL BANKING IN INDIA

	Particulars	*1951 (at the end)*	*1969 (Dec.)*	*1987 (June)*	*1999 (Dec.)*
(1)	Number of banks	566	89	279	298
(2)	Number of offices	4,151	8,262	53,840	65,408
(3)	Total deposits of scheduled banks	908	4,646	1,07,345	7,65,790
(4)	Total credit of scheduled banks	547	3,599	63,753	4,27,436

Source: S.N. Maheswari, *Banking and Financial Services,* Kalyani Publishers, 2001, p. 79.

The post independence, the emergence of planning has given a direction and guidance to the commercial banks. Radical changes have been taken place in structure and functioning of the banking system in India the number of banks has declined considerably. The decline in the number of banks is mainly the result of RBI policy regarding merger and amalgamation of small and nonviable banks with big banks. There had been a rapid branch expansion of commercial banks in India. There has been considerable growth in branch expansion in rural areas. The commercial banks have played an excellent role in deposit mobilization from the public. The credit of Indian commercial banks has been increasing significantly over the years, Nationalisation of commercial banks is the significant development in the banking sector. The government of India on July 19, 1969, nationalised the banks through an ordinance. Fourteen commercial banks in the country with deposits exceeding 50 crores each. Again on April 15, 1980.

Six more commercial banks were nationalised. The following were the arguments in favour of nationalisation.

(1) The banks will under the control of the government to serve the public more and more.

(2) Nationalisation process reduced the concentration of wealth and power.

(3) It reduced the diversion of funds.

(4) It was favoured in order to extend financial help to the small business units.

(5) It was hoped to contribute to the development of neglected agriculture system.

(6) The banks will help to the government for financing the economic plans of the economy.

(7) Nationalisation will provide 100% safety to the depositors.

(8) It eliminates wasteful competition and raises the efficiency of the banks.

(9) It is necessary for achieving socialism.

The following were the arguments against nationalisation:

(1) Nationalisation leads to political interference in the functioning of banks.

(2) Monopoly would be reduced by changing and reforming of the economic system and not the nationalisation of banks.

(3) Malpractices in the banking system can be checked by the RBI there is no need of nationalisation of the banks.

(4) Lending to agriculture sector is very risk and unremunerative therefore profitability will be reduced.

(5) There is no need of 100% security to the depositors because the existence of deposit insurance and credit guarantee corporation is functioning.

(6) Nationalisation will not bring much money to the government.

The commercial banks, has improved and showed better performance after nationalisation of the banks. The banks have been achieved various objectives in post nationalisation period. They are (a) the rapid development of banking industry (b) financing to priority sectors (c) Innovative banking.

The development of banking industry leads to the better credit facilities to the public. After nationalisation, the public sector banks have adopted the development role in the interest of the country. The RBI introduced ***lead back scheme in 1969*** to provide bank credit to all the districts of the country. The objective of the lead bank scheme was to coordinate the operations of commercial banks, cooperative banks, and other financial institutions for the purpose of intensive development of the country.

After nationalisation of commercial banks, there has been a spectacular expansion of the bank branches. The thrust of branch expansion is to provide banking facilities to the rural areas. There had been a significant increase in the rural branches of banks since 1969. Branch expansion reduced the regional imbalance in the country. The branch expansion policy aims at providing a bank office within ***10 kms*** each village after nationalisation of banks, there has been a significant growth in deposits of the commercial banks. Post nationalisation leads to expansion of the bank credit substantially. In the post nationalisation the share of agriculture, small industries and other priority sectors, food procurement agencies, exports increased. The main objective of the nationalisation of banks was to extend the credit facilities to the neglected sector of the borrowers. To achieve this objective the banks formulated various schemes to provide credit facilities to the small borrowers in the priority sectors. The post nationalisation of the banks, provided better credit facilities to the ***small scale industries.*** Special cells have been set up in the banks to provide guidance to the borrowers from small scale sector.

The nationalisation of banks in 1969, is a story of various developments and innovations introduced in the functioning of banks to meet the needs of the ***digital economy.*** The following are the innovations in banking which have been introduced recently:

(a) Consortium approach.

(b) Credit card facilities

(c) Social banking

(d) Mutual funds

(e) Merchant banking

(f) Factoring services
(g) Offshore banking
(h) Service area approach
(i) Customer service
(j) Venture capital
(k) Hire purchase
(l) New technology

The RBI introduced ***consortium approach*** in 1974 for lending activities of the banks. The RBI directed all the commercial banks that a larger amount of finance should be arranged by a group of banks. It is also known as financial Syndicate. This approach enables banks to spread risk of lending. It breaks the monopoly of big banks. It evolves the banks to pool their resources and enables them to shares the experience and expertism.

Another innovention in commercial banking is the introduction of credit cards. The ***credit card facility*** was introduced in early 1980. This facility has become increasingly popular among banks as well as in public. The card minimises the use of hard cash in routine life. It is a document that shows the credit worthiness of card holder. These cards are issued to people who have a certain minimum level of income. It is a most convenient medium of exchange to buy goods and services without cash. These cards are mostly used by elite corporate executives, businessmen and middle income groups. The banking sector now introduced the latest cards such as; ***ATM cards, phone cards, smart cards, pre-paid mobile sim card.*** The Issuing bank bears the risk of default on the part of cardholder.

Social banking is the new policy of the banking sector to meet the socio-economic obligations of the country. It requires greater financial assistance to the priority sector. The policy is implicated by expansion of bank offices in the rural areas. Lead bank scheme was introduced in December 1969 to develop on the basis of area approach. The lead banks are expected to formulate district wise plans for branch expansion and deposit mobilisation.

Mutual funds are financial intermediaries, they obtain resources by selling units or shares. They offer the Units to the investors. They enable small investors to obtain high returns and low risk from their indirect holding of equities and other assets. The units which are offered to the investor are either open ended or close ended. They are either income oriented or growth oriented. Mutual funds are specialist in stock market. They appoint highly skilled, talented and professionals as fund managers. UTI has a monopoly to mutual fund business is India. In the banking sector, a number of banks has entered into this segment through their subsidiaries. The public sector banks entered in this segment such as ***SBI, Canara bank, Punjab National bank, Andhra bank, Indian bank.*** The following statement contains different mutual funds which are existing in the market. The private sector mutual funds are also existing in the market.

(1) Public Sector Mutual Funds.
(2) Private Sector Mutual Funds.

(1) Public Sector Mutual Funds

(a) UTI Mutual fund
(b) SBI Mutual fund
(c) BOB Mutual fund
(d) GIC Mutual fund
(e) IDBI MF
(f) ILFS MF
(g) Prudential ICICI

(h) LIC MF

(i) HDFC MF

(j) PNB MF

(k) Canara bank MF

(2) Private Sector Mutual Funds

(1) Alliance Mutual fund

(2) Birla Mutual fund

(3) Kothari Pioneer MF

(4) Zurich MF

(5) Cholamandalam MF

(6) DSP Merrilynch MF

(7) JM MF

(8) Kotak Mahindra MF

(9) Reliance MF

(10) Sun F & C MF

(11) Sundaram MF

(12) Tata MF

(13) Taras MF

(14) Templeton MF

(15) Dundee MF

(16) Escorts MF

Statement showing the Financial Performance of Various Mutual Funds as on 31-3-2002[4]: The fund rating takes both risk and return into account. The analysis reveals the historical performance of a fund relative to a risk free investment. The schemes have been categorised as best in various categories.

(A) Equity funds.

(B) Hybrid funds.

(C) Debt funds.

(A) BEST IN CLASS
EQUITY FUNDS (DIVERSIFIED, TAX PLANNING)

Sl No.	*MF*	*Risk*	*NAV*	*Return since launch*	*Return 1 year*	*Return upto 31/03/02*	*Assets (Rs. crores)*
(1)	Zurich India tax saver	Low	19.86	36.66	24.34	18.71	40.96
(2)	Alliance Capital Tax Relief 96	Average	55.65	41.18	15.22	15.46	18.18
(3)	JM Basic	Low	15.83	33.94	65.76	86.89	0.5
(4)	Pioneer ITI blue chip	below average	22.84	22.51	12.79	21.42	336.30
(5)	Pioneer ITI tax shield	below average	24.96	35.99	13.76	14.60	97.41
(6)	Zurich India Equity	Low	22.31	11.67	35.71	21.58	108.57
(7)	Pioneer ITI prima plus	below average	23.80	12.24	25.00	20.02	127.62

4. Navjit Gill, *Smart Investing,* Business World, 15-4-2002, p. 40.

(8)	Tata Tax saving fund	above average	11.18	16.73	16.24	21.41	27.85
(9)	Pioneer ITI prima	average	26.21	12.25	44.41	31.38	52.03
(10)	Birla advantage	average	26.00	17.55	6.21	11.11	368.22
(11)	Pioneer ITI Infotech	above average	14.57	34.50	0.69	4.67	213.14
(12)	Alliance Equity	above average	26.66	31.36	6.98	11.59	400.6
(13)	Reliance growth	below average	24.11	14.53	24.02	22.08	11.92
(14)	IDBI principal Tax saving fund	average	13.76	10.90	8.39	24.53	43.5
(15)	Birla Equity plan	above average	11.67	10.92	9.04	13.02	26.9
(16)	Tata pure Equity	average	10.14	22.72	1.95	12.09	32.74
(17)	Reliance vision	below avg.	19.30	10.67	38.75	25.49	10.42
(18)	Prudential ICICI growth plan	average	19.98	20.07	13.07	13.27	357.55
(19)	Magnum Tax again	High	13.10	5.50	–4.03	9.81	43.51
(20)	Prudential ICICI power	average	11.94	2.37	16.83	11.28	29.57
(21)	Libra Leap	above avg.	10.14	5.18	–10.20	5.93	12.32
(22)	Can expo	average	11.43	3.02	–8.78	5.54	17.21
(23)	Templeton India growth	below average	13.11	6.84	15.61	14.30	158.16
(24)	Zurich India Top 200 fund	below average	16.26	13.24	18.25	19.03	37.95
(25)	Magnum Equity	high	8.79	9.58	–1.12	9.06	113.20
(26)	DSP ML Equity	average	13.82	11.74	1.99	10.38	30.42
(27)	Zurich India capital builder	Low	11.03	1.21	8.03	19.37	31.03
(28)	Sundaram Growth fund		12.31	10.93	11.91	12.63	26.40
(29)	UTI Index select equity		13.55	10.88	6.15	8.81	25.97
(30)	Can equity Tax ever		10.66	7.51	–10.72	5.23	7.23

HYBRID FUNDS (BALANCED FUNDS AND DEBT WITH MARGINAL EQUITY)

Sl No.	*MF*	*Risk*	*NAV*	*Return since launch*	*Return 1 year*	*Return upto 31/03/02*	*Assets (Rs. crores)*
(1)	Alliance 95	Above average	47.24	25.04	11.36	9.00	305.26
(2)	Zurich India Prudence	Average	22.10	14.20	26.94	14.81	98.78
(3)	Can premium	below avg.	12.53	19.01	33.81	4.02	6.70
(4)	Unit scheme 95	average	18.00	17.08	10.88	6.45	214.26
(5)	JM balance – a	average	16.04	12.00	53.64	8.23	10.86
(6)	Pioneer ITI cap Gift plan	Low	16.37	13.76	16.60	4.40	1.94
(7)	Tata Income Dlt	Low	10.28	13.63	11.70	2.33	203.70
(8)	Tata Income G	Low	18.31	13.04	12.71	2.99	209.65
(9)	Escort Income plan	Low	16.09	13.11	14.11	3.04	47.80
(10)	Pioneer ITI pension plan	Low	18.43	13.00	12.65	5.68	27.04
(11)	Magnum balanced	High	9.87	9.72	0.82	2.60	102.71
(12)	Tata young citizens	Average	10.22	11.43	7.11	8.58	66.0
(13)	Tata balanced	Above avg.	13.42	8.60	8.16	10.47	104.25

(14)	Dhanaraksha 89	below avg.	10.98	7.61	11.56	0.53	74.19
(15)	UTI Retirement benefit Unit plan	average	16.51	9.16	1.06	2.23	279.18
(16)	Grihalaxmi Unit plan 94	average	10.07	5.78	–8.79	2.03	72.58
(17)	Cantriple +	above avg.	19.33	6.59	12.32	6.56	207.38
(18)	JM balance fund	above average	9.15	8.21	5.29	7.90	—
(19)	Canganga	above average	8.46	–0.98	4.06	7.63	38.26
(20)	GIC balanced	average	9.80	2.94	8.17	10.11	44.81

DEBT FUNDS (MEDIUM & LARGE)

Sl No.	*MF*	*Risk*	*NAV*	*Return since launch*	*Return 1 year*	*Return upto 31/03/02*	*Assets (Rs. crores)*
(1)	Zurich India sovereign cult pro.	average	14.01	17.55	26.52	5.08	11.80
(2)	JM Income fund G.	below avg.	21.63	11.18	18.59	4.19	601.0
(3)	DSPML GSE longer duration	above average	16.17	21.02	28.97	5.84	99.49
(4)	DSPML bond.	below avg.	18.78	13.54	17.45	3.76	1362
(5)	K.Bond wholesale	below avg.	13.97	14.91	17.60	3.84	—
(6)	PNB Debt	average	15.77	17.86	21.96	4.58	79
(7)	K bond deposit	below avg	13.75	14.16	17.07	3.73	870.6
(8)	Prudential ICICI income plan	below avg.	16.18	13.56	16.82	3.72	2780.6
(9)	Dundee bond Corporate	Low	12.36	9.46	9.20	1.55	1.49
(10)	Templet on India Income	below average	19.49	14.02	16.64	3.67	1910.17
(11)	UTI bond	below average	15.80	12.84	13.67	3.27	1380.43
(12)	Birla Income plus	below average	22.84	13.67	16.95	3.82	2075.32
(13)	Zurich India High Interest	below average	18.75	13.48	17.04	3.53	1008.28
(14)	Pioneer ITI Income builder	below average	18.92	14.29	17.88	4.24	1333.50
(15)	Alliance Income fund	below average	18.81	13.25	16.90	4.21	1085.72
(16)	Magnum income.	below average	15.29	13.29	16.63	4.30	960.61

DEBT FUNDS SHORT-TERM (CASH FUNDS, GILT SHORT-TERM AND MM)

Sl No.	*MF*	*Risk*	*NAV*	*Return since launch*	*Return 1 year*	*Return upto 31/03/02*	*Assets (Rs. crores)*
(1)	Zurich India Liquidity investment	below average	12.30	9.12	8.49	1.82	23.93
(2)	Zurich India	below average	10.80	8.87	7.94	1.78	14.56
(3)	Pioneer ITITMA	below average	1405.60	9.07	8.20	1.76	391.22
(4)	Zurich India liquidity saving	below average	11.71	8.94	8.10	1.72	478.48
(5)	JM High liquidity-G	below average	15.66	11.11	7.96	1.79	411.58
(6)	Birla cash plus	below average	15.26	9.22	8.00	1.74	744.90
(7)	Prudential ICICI liquid plan	below average	13.93	9.16	7.83	1.68	1712.20
(8)	Templet on India Liquid	below average	14.02	9.33	7.76	1.64	444.83
(9)	Sundaram Money	below average	11.87	8.65	7.64	1.65	43.56
(10)	UTI MMF	below average	15.88	9.82	8.33	1.71	103.28

(11)	Alliance cash Manager	below average	1389.03	8.83	7.92	1.70	469.53
(12)	Reliance Liquid Treasury plan.	below average	13.69	8.09	7.79	1.70	617.13
(13)	Magnum Inst a cash (cash)	below average	12.72	8.74	7.49	1.72	53.46
(14)	Sun F & C Money value liquid Normal	below average	13.22	8.57	7.60	1.57	29.50
(15)	DSPML Liquidity	below average	13.79	8.24	7.59	1.73	193.65

Smart Investing

The investor before making investment decision. The following principles shall be followed in order to get maximum return with minimum risk.[5]

(A) Diversity with funds.

(B) Give fancy funds a miss.

(C) Beat the budget.

(D) Avoid Index huggers.

(E) Set sell targets.

Diversity with funds is the basic fundamental principle. First time investor should get start with an investment in a corefund. The corefund should ideally be a well diversified equity fund or an index fund. After some time, the investor should start diversifying among mutual funds by constructing a portfolio of funds around the core. The investor can diversify across asset like debt and equity. Equity fund investors can also diversify across the two major growth and value styles. The investor should make diversification properly. Two funds with a similar portfolio or even with similar sector weightages could add more to risk than to the total returns.

Give fancy funds a miss is the another principle in understanding the investment activities according to this principle don't invest fund you don't understand do well. Most of the basic products are already available in India. If you want to invest in equities for the long term, there are so many ways of doing it. An index fund or a well diversified equity fund is the best option for the low risk retail investors.

There are several reasons for sector fund not such a hot idea, especially in India. The main reason is that the investor who puts his money in a sector fund effectively tells the fund manager how to invest that money. Asset allocation funds that are completely into one kind of asset stock, debt, cash at any time are not a great idea either. Imagine the prohibitive costs of moving completely from a 100% equity position to debt and back again.

Beat the budget is another smart investing technique in mutual funds. The dividend tax on debt funds can be avoided by opting the growth option. Therefore the investor liable only for the long term capital gains tax, which remains rock steady at *10%*. If the investor need a regular income from the fund, he must go for an automatic encashment plan or a *systematic withdrawal plan.* These plans allow the investor to decide the amount he wants to withdraw at regular intervals. A large percentage of what the investor will withdraw each time is the capital invested and after the first year, he will be liable only for long term capital gains tax on the income portion. Using a SWP turns out to be a more tax efficient strategy than using a dividend plan.

Avoid Index Huggers is one of the investment principle. In 2000, many diversified funds has heavily concentrated portfolios. The high exposure to the *technology, communication and entertainment sectors* was responsible for the steep drop in these funds when the market crashed. That was then. It has markets shadowing the index too closely is a classic play safe strategy some money managers adopt. If your fund manager is tracking the benchmark index too closely dump the fund. A well diversified

5. *Smart Investing,* Business World, 15 April 2002, p. 38.

equity fund should have a sectoral allocations that are broadly similar to the one in the benchmark. At the same time the whole idea behind active management is that fund manager spots winners that are yet to find their way into the indices.

When markets are in a bear hug there is a huge temptation to avoid taking risks. But a fund that starts looking and behaving too much like the index is a loser. Not only if the fund doing the Job of a passive index fund, it is also charging you higher management fee for the pleasure. If the investor wants an index fund invest in it directly the costs are way lower.

Set Sell targets is the financial principle in making investment decisions. Some financial planners will tell that there is no such thing as a mutual fund peaking. So fixing sell targets could set the investor adrift from a fund just before it goes ballistics. Bull, the whole idea of setting sell targets is to realise your investments and meet financial goals. For ex: If you want Rs. 5.00 lakh in 15 years for your child's college education and your Rs. 1 lakh investment bloats to Rs. 5.00 lakh in 10 years, sell. In any case, you should start withdrawing money out of an equity fund a couple of years before you actually need the funds, and put it into a money market mutual fund. The investor should follow this strategy even if you believe that stocks are entering the mother of all bull markets.

MERCHANT BANKING

Introduction

Merchant banks occupies an important role in the financial services sector. It is an advisory financial service. The Merchant banks are also known as Accepting and issuing houses in the U.K. In USA They are called as ***Investment banks.*** The merchant banks are specialised in accepting bills of exchange. They possess special knowledge of the financial requirements of the business community. The Merchant bankers shall have a highly specialised professional staff with talents and good contacts in the market.

The commercial banks have entered into this segment by setting up their separate subsidiaries and offer a wide range of services. In 1991 they have started their equipment leasing and merchant banking subsidiaries. The first merchant banking activities were started by the ***Grindlays Bank*** in 1969. It had undertaken the management of public issues and financial consultancy followed by other foreign banks. The banking commission recommended in 1972 to enter into this area by the commercial banks. Therefore the SBI started its merchant banking services in 1973. The ICICI was also started in 1974. The time span of mid seventies witnessed a boom in the country which were sponsored by banks, financial institutions, NBFCs, brokers. The formation of SEBI in 1992 led the evolution of merchant banking as a professional service in the country. Merchant banking organisations have to be mandatorily registered with the SEBI.

According to SEBI,[6] "A merchant banker is a person who is engaged in the business of issue management either by making arrangement regarding selling, buying or subscribing to securities as manager, consultant, advisor or rendering corporate advisory service in relation to such issue management."

The Merchant banks provide financial advice and services on a fixed fee basis. They deal with selective large industrial units. Their activities are primarily non-fund based. They undertake a wide range activities. They handle all aspects of the sale of industrial securities. They guarantee the success of issues by underwriting them. Merchant banking services are provided by the following organisations in India.

(a) SBI Capital Market Ltd.

(b) Canfina.

(c) BOB Fiscal.

---

6. M.Y. Khan, *Financial Services*, TMH, 2000, p. 12-39.

(d) ICICI, IDBI, IFCI.

(e) DSP Financial consultants.

(f) JM Financial and Investment services Ltd.

(g) Credit Capital Finance Corpo.

(h) Technical consultancy organisation.

The merchant bankers must compulsorily register with the SEBI to carry out their activities. They are categorised into four categories.

(a) Category I Merchant bankers.

(b) Category II Merchant bankers

(c) Category III Merchant bankers.

(d) Category IV Merchant bankers.

Category I merchant bankers carry on any activity relate to issue management. They can also act as advisor, consultant, manager, Underwriter or portfolio manager. Category II merchant bankers can act as advisor, consultant, Co-manager, underwriter portfolio manager. Category III merchant bankers can act as an underwriter, advisor and consultant to an issue. The category I merchant bankers can act as ***lead managers*** to an issue. SEBI is the licensing authority to grant the license to the merchant bankers. SEBI may grant the status of the merchant banker based on the capital adequacy norms. The ***minimum networth*** requirement for each category is presented below.

(a) Category I (Rs. 5 crore)

(b) Category II (Rs. 0.5 crore)

(c) Category III (Rs. 0.2 crore)

(d) Category IV Nil.

A merchant banker has to pay a fee at the time of original registration as well as renewal.

	Category	*Registration Fee*	*Renewal Fee*
(a)	Category I	Rs. 2.5 lakhs annually for the first two years and Rs. 1.00 for the third year.	First two years Rs. 1.00 lakh and the 3rd year Rs. 20,000
(b)	Category II	Rs. 1.50 lakh annually for the first two years and Rs. 50,000 for the Third year.	First two year Rs. 75,000 and 3rd year Rs. 10,000.
(c)	Category III	Rs. 1.00 lakh annually for the first two years and Rs. 25,000 for the Third year	For the first two years Rs. 50,000 and in 3rd year Rs. 5,000.
(d)	Category IV	Rs. 5,000 annually for the first two years and Rs. 1,000 for the third year	For the first two years Rs. 5,000 and 3rd year Rs. 2,000.

SEBI has the full authority to grant the license or suspend the registration. It has also the right to cancel the registration of the merchant banker. The SEBI can undertake the inspection of the books of accounts records and documents of a merchant banker. The merchant banker has an obligation to furnish all information called by the SEBI. The SEBI imposes penalties for non-compliance of conditions for registration and contravention of the rules. The defaults are categorised into 4 kinds.

(a) general.

(b) minor.

(c) major.

(d) serious.

The merchant bankers in India provide the following services.

(a) Underwriting of public issues.

(b) Project promotion services and project finance.

(c) Syndication of credit.

(d) Leasing.

(e) Corporate advisory services.

(f) Investment management.

(g) Services to NRIs.

Factoring is a highly specialised financial service. It provides resources to finance receivables as well as facilitates the collection of debt. Credit sales generate the factoring business in usual course of business dealings. The realisation of credit sales is the basic function of factoring services. If a credit sales transaction is completed, the factor steps realise the sales. The factors provide various services at a charge. It implies the advances payment of credit by the banks to the customer factor is a financial institution which manages the collection of debt of the business community. The first factoring service in India has been started by the SBI. Canara bank also setup separate subsidiaries for entering the factoring service.

Offshore banking is known as overseas banking. At present many banks have a global dimension in the offshore banking. The Commercial banks involve in international business which are spread over 25 countries and specialise in various areas of international banking. Nine commercial banks were operating in foreign countries.

Service area approach has been introduced by the RBI in 1988. The aim of the scheme is to provide better credit facilities to rural areas. It refers to a system of designating special areas to each bank branch. Therefore the banks can concentrate towards productive lending which leads to the development of that area.

Customer service is the most important aspect to any business, particularly the banking sector requires a special attention towards better services to customers. A number of steps have been taken to improve the quality of customer services. The commercial banks have been permitted to computerise their branches. Therefore the computerisation facilitates not only quick service but also it is cost effective. The RBI Introduce the ***Electronic clearing service*** in April 1995 at Mumbai and Chennai. This system reduces the time period of clearing instruments. The RBI has also started electronic fund transfer between Mumbai and Chennai for retail customers. Banks are making an attempt to redress customer complaints.

Venture capital is an innovative financial intermediary. It has emerged in India in 1980s. Venture capital provides risk capital, management and marketing expertise to highly risky and new private businesses. They involve in technology oriented businesses. It is a high risk return business. Grindlay's banks have set up India's first private sector venture capital fund. The fund has been known as *India Investment fund.* The Indian commercial banks such as SBI and Canara bank have been floated venture capital funds. The following VCFs are operating in India.

(1) Technology Development and Information Company of India Ltd., (TDICI)

(2) Risk Capital and Technology Finance Corporation Ltd., (RCTFC)

(3) Credit Capital Venture Fund Ltd.,

Hire purchase credit facilitates purchase of goods on the basis of instalments. It refers to term loans provided for the purchase of consumer goods. The amount of loans are repayed in instalments during the specified period. In India the hire purchase business is run by financial institutions, retail and wholesale traders, specialised hire purchase finance companies etc.,

New technology plays an important role in input cost. It reduces the cost substantially. It introduces mechanisation, computerisation in the operations of the banking activities. It enhances the productivity.

INDUSTRIAL BANKS

Financial is described as the life blood of industry. It is a pre-requisite to mobilise real resources for higher productivity. In a underdeveloped economy finance is the main factor to influence the capital formation. If the finance is available other important factors will influence the economic development. The corporate sector requires short term, medium term and long term finance. Short term finance refers to funds required for a period of less than one year. It is usually required to meet variable, seasonal and working capital requirements the short term finance can be met by the corporate sector by borrowing from the commercial banks. The sources of the short term finance are *trade credit, customer advances, and instalment credit* ***Medium term finance*** is usually regarded for a period of 5 years. It is usually required for permanent working capital, small expansion, replacements, modifications. Medium term finance may be raised by equity, debt, borrowings and retaining profits. ***Long term finance*** is exceed 5 years periods of long term. It is required for procuring and establishing fixed assets for commencing new businesses and substantial expansion of existing business. The sources of the long term finance are issue of shares, debt, retained earnings and loans from financial institutions.

Industrial banks are also known as *Development banks* development bank is a multi purpose institution. It shares entrepreneurial risk, encourages new industrial projects in tune with the changes in industrial climate. The industrial banks render the services such as discovery of new projects, undertaking the preparation of projects provision of technical advise and managerial services, the following institutions are fully involved in promotion of industries.

(A) Industrial Development Bank of India (IDBI)

(B) Industrial Credit and Investment Corporation of India (ICICI)

(C) Industrial Finance Corporation of India (IFCI)

INDUSTRIAL DEVELOPMENT BANK OF INDIA

Introduction

The Industrial Development Bank of India was established in 1964. It has been empowered to finance all types of industrial concerns. It provides direct and indirect finance to the corporate sector. As direct financier. It renders assistance to the corporate sector in the following ways.

(a) Sanctioning term loans and advances.

(b) Underwriting the issue of shares or debentures

(c) Sanctioning third party loans to business sector.

The Direct financial assistance is usually granted for purchase of fixed assets for expansion and modernisation of existing units. The Direct financial assistance is the most useful to the large scale manufacturing units. As an indirect financier, it assists in the following ways.

(1) Refinancing of Industrial loans provided by banks and SFCS.

(2) Providing financial assistance to the financial institutions by subscribing the shares and debentures of them.

(3) Rediscounting of bills.

(4) Refinancing of export credit sanctioned by the banks to exporters.

(5) Renders consultancy services to the corporate sector.

The bank provides loans which are normally repayable over a period of 10 years. The authorised capital of the IDBI was ***Rs. 2,000 crores.*** It can be further increased to Rs. 5000 crores. The sources of funds are:

(1) Borrowing from central government and RBI

(2) Issue of shares and bonds

(3) Grants and loans from world bank

Management: The IDBI is managed by the board of directors. The board of directors consists of 22 persons including Chairman and Managing Director the Chairman and Managing director is appointed by the Central government. The other members of the board comprise of a representative of the RBI, a representative each of the All India Financial Institutions, two officials of the Central government, 3 representatives from each PSBs and SFCs, 5 members having special knowledge and experience of Industry. The board of directors has constitutes an Executive committee which consist of 10 members.

Role: In was set up as the principal financial institution for the industrial development in the country. Now it is playing an important role in the capital market. The role of the IDBI for the purpose of exposure can be categorised into three phases.

(a) Ist phase

(b) IInd phase

(c) IIIrd phase

Ist Phase (1964-75): It was set up as a statutory corporation in July 1964. It was a wholly owned subsidiary of the RBI. The ownership was transferred to the government. In 1955, the IDBI act was amended to provide greater operational flexibility. The amendment of the act was made during the dynamic phase of the bank. The life cycle of the IDBI started from 1964 to 1975, as first phase. The transformation of the IDBI took more than 35 years. The first phase was the most important stage in the life of the IDBI. The first phase had been concentrated towards Industrialisation of the nation. The bank had focussed on establishing the core industries such as textiles, fertilisers chemical products, basic metals and machinery. The Industrialisation strategy was also required to encourage the small ancillary industries to create more employment opportunities in the country. At this point of time SFCs, ***SIDCs*** where already in place to promote and encourage these segments of the industry. The ***IDBI*** took over the activities of the Refinance Corporation in 1964. Therefore it started providing financial support to the SFCs and other primary lending institutions in the country by Refinancing facility. The IDBI had introduced the Rediscounting of the machinery bills scheme and encouraged the capital goods industry. Hence the IDBI fully involved in the direct project loans, Refinance and bill rediscounting scheme to the industries.

The IDBI played an important role for the development of exports sector balance regional development and coordination between financial institutions. The IDBI started scheme during this phase for financing exports and export of capital goods and deferred payment basis. It actively participated in the formation of export and import bank of India. It played an important role in achieving the balanced regional development strategy. It initiated steps to conduct surveys for identifying industrial potential in backward areas and other specific locations. It played an important role in setting up of technical consultancy organisations in collaboration with other financial institutions. The central government provided long term loans to the IDBI at concessional rate of interest. The RBI created a separate industrial credit fund to meet the long term operations of the corporate sector. It received loans from this fund. The government had exempted from income tax. It also focussed on developing linkages with other financial institutions.

IInd Phase (1976-85): The second phase started from 1976 to 1985. Because the IDBI was linked from the RBI on 16-02-76. It was accorded as principal financial institution, wholly owned by the government. This period was the most important in the life of the IDBI. The RBI had transmitted its all responsibilities to the IDBI. It also transferred the initial capital of the ***IFCI and the UTI***. The share capital of the SFCs was also transferred to the IDBI by the RBI. It become an autonomous institution during this period, it activity involved in the process of Industrialisation. It focussed on the widening of the entrepreneurial base in the country. It had achieved a certain degree of maturity during the second phase. It introduced a soft loan scheme involving loans at concessional rate of interest during this phase. The scheme was designed to meet the modernisation programme in industries such as Jute, Cotton, textile, sugar, cement and Engineering goods a revised modernisation package was introduced for all industries. The central government created a special technical development fund for modernisation of industries to boost the process of technology upgradation. According to this scheme, the IDBI provided concessional assistance for the import of balancing equipment, acquiring technical know how and consultancy services for upgrading existing technology of the approved units. It also actively participated to provide assistance to sick units. It had taken various measures during this period to meet the requirement of small village and cottage industry. It initiated package of refinance to small and medium sectors towards meeting the modernisation requirements. The technology upgradation required a higher amount of foreign currency. It diversified its resources base and borrowed the foreign currency from the global markets.

The term lending is an important aspect of industrial financing system. It is the oxygen for promoting the industrial growth. The term lending widens the entrepreneurial base and the related infrastructure, services etc., the industrial activities will be increased only when the entrepreneurial base widens. Therefore the IDBI took initiative to educate the entrepreneurs by setting up a number of institutions for EDPs in association with other financial institutions. It encouraged the entrepreneurs by introducing. Scheme which is known as seed capital scheme.

IIIrd Phase (1986...): The third phase was one of the tremendous growth in activities of the IDBI. It provided several new challenges due to economic restructuring programme initiated by the government. During this period, the IDBI introduced new products to meet the growing needs of entrepreneurs. It also focussed on balanced regional development of the country, sectoral growth of the industries and capital market in India. The central government announced the technology upgradation scheme in 1987 to upgrade the technology of select capital goods industries. It was assigned to formulate the system for this scheme. It also established in 1986 a textile modernisation fund to provide a point for modernisation efforts in the industry. The world bank helped it in the modernisation of cement industry.

It introduced an export incentive scheme in 1986. It encouraged the export units by providing incentives in the form of rebate of interest on rupee loans. It established a venture capital fund in 1986 to provide financial assistance for industries concerns. It was also giving top priority to energy conservation sector and environmental audit aspects. The world bank provided a special assistance to pollution control projects. It played a major role in the development of the capital market. It took initiative steps to set up several subsidiaries and associate concerns. These concerns offered a wide range of products and services. It set up the ***Stock Holding Corporation of India (SHCIL)*** in 1987.

It provided depository services to the financial institutions the central government had also assigned the responsibility of setting up the SEBI. The NSE was also established by the IDBI with the instructions from the central government. The NSE provides nationwide screen based trading system. It became the India's premier stock exchange. It had thrown a challenge to the BSE. The BSE was the competitor of the NSE. It promoted the following institutions with the directions from govt.

(a) National Securities Depository Ltd.

(b) Credit Analysis and Research Ltd.,

(c) IDBI Capital Market Securities Ltd.,

(d) IDBI Investment Management Company Ltd.,

(e) IDBI Bank Ltd.,

(f) North Eastern Development Finance Corpn. Ltd.,

(g) Infrastructure development Finance Co. Ltd.,

(h) Over the counter exchange of India (with others)

(i) Tourism Finance Corporation of India (with others)

(j) Shipping Credit and Investment Corporn. (with others)

(k) Biotech consortium of India Ltd.,

It decentralized its offices and processing of projects to meet the competition from the market. It devised a host of new products to meet the needs of the modern corporate sector. It also empowered to manage its own foreign currency.

INDUSTRIAL CREDIT AND INVESTMENT CORPORATION OF INDIA

Introduction

The Industrial credit and investment corporation was incorporated on 5-1-1955. It was formed by the government of India, world bank and others. It was promoted as a public company. It has been established for the purpose of assisting industries in the private sector. The aim of setting up of the ICICI was to provide foreign currency finance to industrial projects and promote industries in private sector. It provides financial packages for *RED*, *Commercialization of technology, Venture capital*, pollution control and environment protection. It had diversified into a number of other activities. It had also been managing United States Agency for international development and world bank funds through its technological financing programmes.

The ICICIs principal business was to provide medium and long term project financing, underwriting to shares, guarantees to suppliers of equipment and foreign lenders. It has entered into new areas of business like commercial banking, investment banking, Non-banking finance, broking, investor financing, venture capital financing and infrastructure financing. It operated in general in accordance with the guidelines of *RBI/SEBI*. It had the status of public financial institution. This status is useful in getting the benefits of taxation. Its bonds were treated as public securities for investment by trusts.

Financial Resources: The resources of the ICICI comprised two kinds

(A) Foreign currency resources

(B) Rupee resources.

The resources of the ICICI consisted with interest free loan from the GOI and an advance in foreign currency from the world bank. The rupee resources of the ICICI comprise the following components.

(a) Share capital

(b) Reserves

(c) Borrowings

(d) Public deposits

(a) Share capital: The bank started with the initial resources of about Rs. 17.5 crores. At the end of March 1996 the paid up capital amounted to Rs. 376.3 crore and reserves and surplus amounted to Rs. 2059.4 crores. A large part of the capital is held by PSBS, CIC, GIC, IDBI, UTI, etc., It issued **ADRs and GDRs** and a significant change was resulted in its share ownership patterns.

(b) Resources: It has been consistently building up a large chunk of reserves. Reserves are the most important element for the financial companies. The higher amount of reserves is the financial strength of the company. The reserves consists of capital reserves, capital redemption reserve, share premium account general reserve and special reserve.

(c) Borrowings: It mobilises the funds from domestic and foreign markets. The domestic borrowings by the ICICI. are from.

(a) The government of India.

(b) Institutional borrowings.

(c) Government backed bonds.

(d) Public issue of bonds.

(e) Misl.

The foreign currency resources consist of the following borrowings.

(A) Multilateral borrowings.

(B) Commercial borrowings.

The multilateral borrowings have been from the multilateral institutions. The world bank played an important role in setting up of the bank. It had been providing financial assistance on regular lines of credit. It also received financial assistance from Asian Bank development commonwealth the development corporation UK. It was also getting assistance from the govt. export credit agencies. All these lines of credit were guaranteed by the GOI. It had received assistance from the overseas development Administration of the *UK* through the government of India. It had been receiving financial assistance from various foreign agencies.

Commercial borrowings played an important role of the financial *architecture* of the bank. It had diversified its resources as base with a view to establish in the global market. It raised a public issue of SF 8 million bonds in the Swiss markets in 1973. It depended upon the increase of the borrowing. The borrowings from various countries made them financial stability to survive in the global market. It borrowed the commercial borrowings in the following ways.

(A) Euro credits and other loans.

(B) Bond issues in Switzerland.

(C) Private placements in Japan.

(D) Euro convertible debt market.

It received strong support from the international banking and financial community. It also achieved its objectives of interest and currency diversification by borrowing in various markets in dollar, Swiss francs, yen, pound, sterling. It had been constantly searching for financial assistance in the global markets. It launched a global medium term note programme in 96-97 to facilitate borrowings in small amounts at competitive rates.

(d) Public Deposits: It started accepting public deposits from 1979. It is only a marginal source of funds. It also invited public deposits from the public by offering competitive rates of interest.

Business Operations

The business operations of the ICICI can be categorised into five kinds.

(a) Lending market operations.

(b) Capital market operations.

(c) Sponsorship.

(d) Subsidiaries.

(e) Advisory services.

(A) Lending Market Operations: Lending is the basic operations of any financial institution. This activity refer to the provision of funds for asset creation to the business concerns. The lending operations generate income to the bank. The lending operations of the ICICI consist the following activities.

(A) Project finance.

(B) Technology finance.

(C) Non-project finance.

Project finance is the most important activity of the bank. It grants the loan to business concerns in the form of rupee and foreign currency, underwriting, and direct subscription to issue of shares and debentures. It also provides financial assistance for the modernisation expansion of manufacturing and processing units. The rupee projects loans are involved in financing the purchase of equipment and machinery. It also finances under this scheme towards cost of land, construction of factory and preliminary expenses etc. The rupee currency loans dominated the portfolio of loans disbursed by ICICI the share of rupee loans in the total financial assistance is provided by the bank increased substantially. Foreign currency project loans are provided to finance the purchase of imported capital goods. The world bank channelise foreign currency resources for the private industry through ICICI. It did not sanction any foreign loans during the commencement of its operations. It started financing the foreign currency loans from 1958 with the emergence of foreign exchange crisis. After 1971 the component of foreign currency loan declined substantially. This was due to the recessionary state of the economy. At present the Indian companies directly accessing International capital markets through the issue of GDPs.

It started guaranteeing loans from the private investment sources. It charges 1% PA on the outstanding balances of guarantee issued in rupees and *1.8%* in case of foreign currencies. It also offers assistance to corporate sector by underwriting the issue of shares and debentures. Now it has been following the policy of direct subscription of shares to the extent of Rs. 1 crore.

Technology financing has emerged as one of the sources to finance. It is the largest financiers of technology in India. This source of finance runs with the help of US agency of International development and world bank. They are providing funds for various schemes of financing. It offers a wide varies of financial packages for RED, commercialization of technology. It also offers package relating to pollution control and environmental protection. The schemes are offered by the ICICI such as ***SPREAD, ACE, TEST PACT, PACER.*** Sponsored research and development programme is one of the schemes which are offered by the ICICI. It encourages Indian corporate sector to set up their RED activities. It links up the technology and industry. The package offers for the projects which are involved in development of new product or process. The Product modification will also be considered by this package. The package allows activities like preparation of feasibility studies, laboratory trials and pilot plant operations. The project under this scheme should have feasible and quantifiable objectives. The project should not take longer than two years to be completed. The company should bear 50% of the total cost of the project. The remaining amount will be granted as eligible project specific expenses which are included equipment, facilities materials, payment to consultant, fee payable to technology institutions, project related travel and overhead expenses. The financial assistance provided by the ICICI will be charged with an interest rate of 6% during the implementation period of the ***R&D project.*** The repayment period is up to 10 years. At the final stage of the project, the rate of interest will be ***15%.***

The Agricultural commercialisation enterprises act is another programme which is funded by the ICICI. It is formulated for the development of agribusiness in India. It provides financial assistance for setting up innovative projects in Horticulture, floriculture, Mushrooms, fruits, essential oils, herbal products, and enzymes. This project activities involve loans to private sector, providing technical assistance and conducting travels. It conducts field trips to members of industry for observing and knowing the technical aspects. It is conducting another research based programme which relates to commercialization of energy. It provide funds for the development of the technology toward energy sector. The financial assistance is provided for the technology development of energy such as renewable sources of energy conservation, fossils etc.,

The ICICI is also financing Indo US joint ventures in R&D for the development of technology process in specified areas. The scheme is applicable to agriculture, health and other areas. It aims at improving the availability of quality products and services in the segments of child health, AIDS, and reproductive health. It also finances for the technology development of the environmental and pollution control.

It provides non project finance to the industry with medium and long term maturity period. It provides short term loans to the corporate sector to meet working capital needs.

(b) Capital Market Operation: The ICICI mobilised funds through debt and equity. It actively involves in capital market operations. It encourages entrepreneurs by making investments in their companies by direct subscription to public issue. It participates in the CMOs by taking up rights issue of the companies, conversion option of loan assisted companies, participating in private placement of the corporate sector and provide rehabilitation package for the sick industries. It does not acquire securities in the secondary market. Its investment operations has been increasing. It also offers fee based services. These activities are advisory in nature. It provide consultancy services. It has been offering project advisory services since 1991 to PSUs and private sector companies. It acts as a trustee for the holders of convertible and NCDs issues. These financial instruments are issued by the companies to the public in the form of rights issue, private placement. It offers comprehensive custodial services since 1992. Its clients included ***FIIs*** overseas depository banks.

The ICICI has been actively involving in promoting a no. of institutions which are strengthening the institution structure of the money and capital market. ***The Credit Rating Information Services of India Ltd.,*** had been established in association with UTI in 1987. It provides a variety of consultancy services to the corporate sector. It involves in rating various types of financial instruments that are offered to the investing public. It is also instrumental in promoting the institutions such as, *technology Development and Information company of India Ltd., over the counter exchange, DFHI, Management development institute.*

After the liberalization, privatization and a globalisation, It entered new areas of business like investment banking, asset management, commercial banking etc. It has set up specialised subsidiaries which are presented below.

(1) ISEC Ltd.,
(2) ICICI brokerage
(3) ICICI banking
(4) ICICI Infotech
(5) ICICI personal financial Services Ltd.,
(6) ICICI Capital Services Ltd.,
(7) ICICI Venture Ltd.,
(8) ICICI International
(9) ICICI Properties

Mergers of ICICI with ICICI Bank: The ICICI has merged with ICICI bank on 28-3-2002. The Universal bank plans major thrusts on the retail and international fronts. The ICICI and ICICI banks have been moving towards a merger for over two years now. The formal announcement was made on 25-10-2001. There has been frentic activity in the ***ICICI group*** to confirm to the statutory obligations to turn into a universal bank. The merger process required the bank to show *Rs. 23,000 crore* by the way of SLR for the combined activity. The bank already has ***Rs. 5,000 crore*** in its SLR portfolio an additional Rs. 18,000 crore was required from ICICI. Then the ICICI was mobilised the fund through a combination of retail deposits and asset swaps. The remaining Rs, 10,000 crore was brought in by way of retail deposits. The merger regulations didn't allow merged entity to have any subsidiary that was involved in non-banking activities. The swap ratio has been fixed at one share of the ICICI bank for every two shares of the ICICI. Therefore the final **2:1** ratio falls within the ambit of all the valuation norms. The aim of the post merger was aggressive capital management optimal size technology intensive, multi channel delivery architecture world class skill bases, and enduring customer relationship. The post merger will bring several advantages. ICICI itself gets access to cheaper retail funds. The merged entity is focussing on the new avenues, they are fee income, trade finance for *ex:* Remittances, Cash management service, dividend management, Agri business, small and medium enterprises, consumer finance auto loans, credit and debit cards, housing finance, personal loans, Internet banking retail banking, third party products, mutual funds, Insurance, pension products smart cards and fund transfer.

Recently it introduced *"e cheque"* system in fund transfer process. According to this scheme, the customer can transfer money to any account in any bank in any of ***14 cities***. Another service has been launched in *Delhi* any cell phone owner can tap up with the ICICI ATM. It also focussing on cross selling instead of individual marketing. The major advantage of cross selling is that the customer acquisition cost comes down massively. Customer loyalty and satisfaction is reflected in cross selling. The other major thrust area is the international division. The international business is to provide 10-15% of ICICI banks turnover and profits in the forthcoming 5 years but zero today. It identified four geographies setting up representative offices in the ***US, UK, Dubai, Singapore, and London.*** The International division will be setting up a consultancy to provide services to banks and other financial sector players globally.

The Indian economy requires large banks to cater its requirements. The ICICI merger will create a significant player the merger is clearly a reflection of the overdue consolidation of the banking industry needs.

The expressions by the analysts and experts are that the new merged entity may be sitting on mountain of NPAs that may come home to roost. Their conclusion is that its loan portfolio cannot be too different from that of IDBI or IFCI. All of them were lending to the same sectors and companies with similar profiles. ICICI comes with net NPAs at a rounds Rs. 3,000 crore or 5.3%. The bank has net NPAs at **1.36%**

INDUSTRIAL FINANCE CORPORATION OF INDIA

Introduction

The Industrial Finance Corporation of India was set up in *July 1948* by the Government of India. It was established under the IFCI act, 1948 with the basic objective of providing finance to the industries in private sector. At present it is also providing financial assistance to Co-op. Joint, Public Sector Units. It provides loans for expansion, diversification and modernisation of existing units. It also underwrites and directly subscribes to industrial securities, merchant banking services and lease finance. It renders financial assistance both in rupees and foreign currencies to the corporate sector.

The SSIs, proprietory and partnership concerns were not eligible for financial assistance from the IFCI. It did not grant assistance for the purpose of working capital. It did not provide assistance for the acquisition of capital goods for commercial or trading purposes. It did not grant loans in foreign currencies for purchasing of raw materials, imports or payments of royalties, interest and dividends. Its act was amended in 1986. The authorised business was presented below.

(a) It acts as agent to world bank.

(b) It provides technical, administrative, marketing assistance to corporate sector

(c) It is appointed as administrator.[7]

7. *The Big Picture,* Business India, April 1-4-2002, p. 51.

Financial Resources: The sources of the funds are share capital, Retained Earnings, issue of bonds, borrowings from the government, repayment of past loans and sale of Investments borrowings from IDBI, borrowings from foreign lending institutions, foreign capital markets and public deposits. The *paid up* Capital of the IFCI was held directly by the central government and the RBI. The holdings of the two concerns were transferred to the IDBI. The balance of the paid up capital was contributed by the commercial banks, Insurance organisations and cooperative banks. It made a first public issue of equity shares in *Dec. 1993*. The authorised capital now increased in ***Rs. 339.1 crores.*** It had consistently increased and built up sizeable reserves. The reserves of the IFCI consists of the following elements.

(A) General Reserves.

(B) Reserve fund.

(C) Benevolent Reserve.

(D) Special Reserve.

(E) Specific grant from the GOI.

(F) Share premium accounts.

It mobilised the funds from the sale of bonds. It grants ***Rupee currency and foreign currency loans.*** The Rupee currency loans are met from the domestic market and foreign market respectively. Its policy is to reduce its dependence on the government. It focussed on market borrowings by issue of bonds. The bonds are guaranteed by the government and Redeemable at par at coupon rates ranging from *8.75%* and *13.5%*. It depends on bonds which are privately placed and issued to public. The bonds carry a maturity of ***7 to 30 years.*** The privately placed bonds have a notoriety of one to 27 years. It offered a variety of innovative bonds targeting different segments. It also issued deep discount bonds, education bonds, gift bonds, retirement bonds floating millionaire bonds etc.

It was authorised in 1952 to borrow in foreign currency. It had been borrowing from foreign agencies. It was allowed to borrow from global markets. It obtained financial assistance from USA, Germany, France and UK, The borrowings from the International capital markets are from ***Euro currency market, Germany markets, and Japanese capital markets.*** It diversified its resources base by raising short term funds through certificate of deposits and commercial papers. It reduced its dependance on GOI and RBI. Its main funding source is market borrowings through a variety of Innovative family bonds.

Business Activities: It actively participated in Industrialisation of the country. It provided financial assistance to corporate sector through different schemes. The industrial financing activities consists of two segments ***project finance and financial services.*** Project finance covers the entire funding new projects expansion, diversification and modernisation in the form of foreign currency and rupee term loans. The project finance is the main activity of the IFCI. The projects will be financed through the term loans. The IDBI directly subscribes to equity of smaller new companies to encourage the new breed of entrepreneurs.

It also involves in capital market operations. Its investment portfolio consists of acquisitions of shares for underwriting obligations, direct subscription to shares, bonus issues, subscription to rights shares, convertion of convertible debentures proportion, conversion of dues into shares or debentures. It also guarantees to finance the industry. It also provide indirect finance for leasing companies. It has started providing short-term loans to corporates for meeting the working capital financing.

Financial Services is the secondary activity in order to improve its profitability. The financial services include fund based, fee based, project counselling issue management, loan syndication financial restructuring MEA, debenture trusteeship and equipment leasing. It provides financial assistance to private, public and joint sector. It actively participates in ***Sugar and Textiles*** to support financially. The financial assistance given to the industrial sector has in all cases been in the form of loans and the financial assistance to the cooperative sector has substantially declined over the years. It sanctioned loans to the private sector. Its assistance to the private sector projects has increased substantially over the years. It has been providing financial assistance to PSUs, Government Companies since 1969. The financial assistance have been provided for the expansion and diversification to the following.

(a) Public limited companies.

(b) Had declared a maiden dividend.

(c) Had built up sufficient internal resources.

(d) Should not have approached for budgetary support.

It provides financial assistance to a wide variety of industries. The sanctioning of loans depend upon changing conditions of national priorities. Initially it has given preference to ***Sugar and Textile projects***. It has also diversified its investment strategy and concentrated in power generation, telecom services, textiles, electronics, synthetic resims, plastics, fertilisers, basic chemicals, petroleum, refining and cement. It provides finance to industrial enterprises. This has spread over to AP, Gujarat, Maharashtra, Tamilnadu, MP and West Bengal. It has been providing assistance to enterprises in the backward regions. It has initiated measures to achieve the balanced regional development.

It activity involves in promotional activities like project identification, formulation implementation and operations. It provides consultancy fee subsidy scheme and interest subsidy scheme and assistance schemes. The consultancy fee subsidy scheme providing services to industrial units which are identified as the small, tiny and ancillary units. The scheme is applicable to small entrepreneurs in rural, cottage, tiny and small scale sector to new entrepreneurs for meeting the cost of market survey. Interest subsidy scheme is to provide encouragement to the Unemployed youth and women entrepreneurs. This scheme is implemented through SFCs. It is also providing assistance scheme to the existing industrial projects in the medium and small-scale sector.

It encourages professionalism in management to improve the quality in day to day management. The IFCI sponsored in 1973 the ***Management Development Institute*** to provide training and research in the field of banking. It established in 1977 a development banking centre as its autonomous using. The ***MDI and DBC*** have been continuously working for the development of managerial manpower in public, private joint and cooperative sectors in the industry. It diversified its business activities in the following areas.

(A) Merchant banking.

(B) Project counselling.

(C) Credit syndication.

(D) Consultancy to industrial units.

(E) Sponsoring of financial institutions.

CENTRAL BANK

Central bank controls, regulates, supervises the monetary and credit system of the country. It occupies a pivotal position in the monetary and banking structure of a nation. It is the leader of the money market. It is also empowered to handle and control the currency and credit. Central bank has been defined by various authors as presented below.

According to ***R. P. Kent*** "It may be defined as an institution charged with the responsibility of managing the expansion and contraction of the volume of money in the interest of the general public welfare."[8]

---

8. M. N. Mishra, *Money Banking and International Trade,* S. Chand and Co., p. 308.

According to the RBI "that bank as being constituted to regulate the issue of bank notes and the keeping of reserve with a view to securing monetary stability in British India and generally to operate the currency and credit system of the country to its advantage."[9]

Central banking system has played an important role in the development of countries. It plays a positive role in the development of a country. It encourages the development of integrated banking system in the country. It plays a dynamic role in the development of the country. It has facilitated the development of commercial banks as well as of industrial banks. The financial strength of a country depends upon the soundness of the policies of central banking. The objectives of the central bank are the national interest, maintenance of monetary and fiscal stability and economic development. The developing countries may be benefited by the credit and currency expansion activities. Central bank enjoys the monopoly in controlling the economic activities of the country. The aim of the credit control is to promote and maintain high levels of employment and real income. The credit control may facilitate the better environment situation for economic development.

Functions of Central Bank

The Central Bank has the authority to look after the national interest of the country. It acts as a banker to the central government. It also acts as banker's bank. It does not deal with the public deposits or loans and advances to the public. The functions of the central bank are presented below:

(a) Issue of Currency.
(b) Agent to the Central Government.
(c) Banker's Bank.
(d) Controller of Credit.
(e) Clearing Functions.
(f) Forex Management.
(g) Lender.

The Central bank's main function is to issue the required currency. The central government has the power to issue the currency. But these powers have been delegated to the central bank. The central bank is the only bank to issue the money. No other bank is authorised to issue money. The issue of currency is the most significant function of a Central bank. There are certain currencies which are still issued by the government. The main reason for the concentration of the note issue to the central bank are sumarised below.

(a) Monopoly.
(b) Delegation of authority.

The monetary management should have a uniformity in managing the issue of currency. Therefore the central bank has the capability to manage sound monetary management. The uniformity could be achieved by the state power of money. The public have gained confidence with the power of note issue by Central bank through the directions of central government. The currency circulation should operate automatically and the central bank shall have the capacity for expanding the notes circulation according to the changes in business activities. The Central bank has good contacts with the commercial banks on day to day affairs of the banking sector. There are different methods of note issues to suit the various requirements of the business and industry. Central bank have been given a wider powers to control the monetary and banking activities. The growing needs of credit are also fulfilled by the Central bank. The Central bank can manage the note issue effectively than the banks. It can exercise the proper supervision over the management of note issues.

---

9. *Ibid.* p. 309.

The Central bank is the agent of the central government. Some economists did say that the issue of notes should be vested with the state. They believed that only the government can exercise proper control over the monetary expansion. They think that the state can equitably distribute the money according to requirements. Some economists believed that the government may not as promptly as the Central bank to issue notes the government becomes powerful in issuing as much money as it can. The control of credit belongs essentially to the Central bank. The Central bank has the capacity and coordinating capability to issue the notes. Now a days it is an enlightened opinion that the note issue power should be entrusted to the Central bank. There are various methods of note issue to meet the different requirements of the nation. Money is related with a certain commodity or metal. The issue of currency, convertibility, management of money, the rules and regulations are included in monetary standard monetary standard refers to the system of money where the value of money is expressed in a particular commodity. It refers to the arrangement of money. Money standards may be categorised in two types.

(a) Metallic Standard.

(b) Paper Standard.

(a) Metallic Standard system refers to the value of money which is related with any kind of metal such as gold, silver or any other material. If the value of money is related with gold or silver, it is known as ***Monometallism.*** Under this method the money may be valued or converted or formed to gold or silver. If the money value is related with the gold, it would be ***gold standard.*** If it is related with silver it would be ***silver standard.*** The gold and silver are accepted as a legal tender and are freely minted, the standard is known as bimetallism. In this method any one can get his gold or silver minted into gold or silver coins. These coins are mutually exchangeable at a standard ratio. Multimetalism refers that the value of money is based on more than two metals. They are freely coined as an independent standard coins with unlimited legal tender. It is having a fixed ratio of exchange with each other. All the coins of different metals are freely exchangeable at a certain rate. They are freely coined and are used as a media of exchange. ***Symmetalism*** system has been suggested by ***Marshall*** in 1887. This system avoids the defects of bimetallism. The gold and silver have a separate fixed quantity to measure the value of money.

(b) Paper Standard is another tool to measure the value of money. The paper standard of money has the advancement of countries. It is useful at the time of difficulties such as war and natural calamities. The effects of the paper standard are limited to the countries of its origin. It does not adversely effect the foreign trade. It serves the political and economic purposes of the nation.

Banker's Bank is another important function of the Central Bank. The Central Bank controls the activities of the commercial bank. The Central Bank acts as the banker's bank. All the commercial banks in the country shall have deposit a certain amount of their balances with the Central Bank. It helps the commercial banks by granting loans and advances. It acts as a custodian of the reserves of other banks. It provides finance to commercial banks in various kinds. It provides the facilities of rediscounting bills of exchange. It guides and directs every organ of the banking system. It collects the amount of reserves from all commercial banks and the pooled reserves can be employed to the fullest extent possible in the most effective manner. The Central Bank's capacity will increase to create credit with the pooled amount. The pooled amount of reserves enables commercial banks to meet crisis and emergencies.

The Central Bank acts as controller of credit. The control of credit is the basic function of a Central Bank. Credit plays a predominant part in the settlement of monetary and business transactions. The quantum of credit and the creation of credit must be decided, otherwise it may dismantle the components of the economy. The unrestricted credit leads to various economic consequences. The commercial banks have been left free in expansion of credit and it may create inflationary trend for more profit. It also creates deflationary situation which tends to the fall in the prices. The aim of the credit control is presented below.

(a) Stability of exchange rate.

(b) Stability of price level.

(c) Stability of business activity.

(d) Generation of employment.

(e) Economic development.

The main objective of the credit control is to maintain the *stability of exchange* rates through the monetary standard. The exchange stability is more important for the maintenance of global confidence and the smooth functioning of the world trade. The maintenance of stable rates of exchange is based on fixed gold parities of currencies and of discipline in the interest of economic and social interests of the country.

The Central Bank is also assigned the responsibility to look after the *stability of price level* in the interest of the nation. The stabilisation of price level is preferred for the economic welfare of the country. The stable currency can eliminate disturbances and mal adjustments in the economy. The stable currency of a nation is the good health indication to the economy.

The ***stability in business activity*** is another function of the credit control. The stability in business activity leads to the elimination of business cycle and price movements. The steady growth rate in general economic activity enables the prevention of booms and slumps. The stability in business activity enhances the productivity of the nation.

The objective of the credit control is to promote and maintain high levels of employment and real income. A strong economy may create a crores of job opportunities to the unemployees. Ultimately which in turn enhance the purchasing capacity of the society. The increases in purchasing capacity leads to more demand for goods and services. The increased demand for goods and services may create profits to the manufacturers.

The most important objective of the credit control is to provide better environment for economic development. There are large amount of resources and manpower in developing countries which may be fully utilised with adequate credit and money. The developing countries should deploy the financial resources to utilise the manpower. The supply of money should be expanded and credit authorities should exercise proper control over the credit supply. In developing countries, the banking facilities should be increased. The banking sector shall concentrate on rural banking. The development of a nation depends upon the banking facilities and Rural Savings. Financial and other assistance should be provided for large, medium and small scale industries. The various methods of credit control are presented below:

(A) Quantitative Control.

(B) Selective Controls.

(A) Quantitative Controls: Quantitative controls influence the total economy of the nation. It is more effective in the developed economy and can be utilised by the government according to the situation. The quantitative control consists of the following tools to take active steps for the development of the country's economy.

(1) Bank Rate.

(2) Open Market Operations.

(3) Reserve Requirements.

The ***bank rate*** is also called as "discount rate". Bank rate is the rate at which a Central Bank accepts to advance the loans as approved securities or to rediscount the bills which are honoured by the commercial banks. If the Central Bank desires to control the volume of credit, the bank rate will be increased. The increased bank rate may discourage the quantum of loans by the commercial banks. Therefore getting of loan from banks will not be possible for a customer. The increase in bank rate shows an effect as the lending rates of the commercial banks. The Central Bank has also a right to decrease the bank rate. The lower bank rate increases the financial resources of the banks. There will be tremendous demand for loans due to low rate of interest. The credit facilities are increased and the demand for credit is also expanded. The rediscounting facilities also increased the bank rate tool will be applied by the Central Bank to control the level of prices, business activities and foreign exchange. There are also some limitations to apply the bank rate by the Central Bank.

Open Market Operations is the other tool is controlling the credit supply in the economy. The control has the right to buy and sell of securities in the market. The Central Bank can also purchase bills in the money market. The securities or bills may be government securities or other public securities. The Central Bank purchases or sells only government securities. It does not purchase private sector bills. The bills which are traded in money market should be confined to negotiable instruments. OMO show an impact on creation or cancellation of Central Bank credit. The sale and purchase of securities by the Central Bank leads to increase or decrease the quantity of money in circulation and cash reserves of the banks.

Every commercial bank should deposit certain level of cash reserves with the Central Bank. It is required by law. The reserve ratio is useful in framing the discount rate policy and activities of OMOs. An increase or decrease of minimum legal CRR will be reflected in credit supply. OMOs have shown less impact on the credit supply. But the RR will affect all parts of the credit structure, such as short and long term securities, bills and advances etc. The RR requirement has some limitations. It cannot be applied in all situations.

RR : Reserve Ratio.

(B) Selective Control: The qualitative controls will affect all the sectors of the economy. The selective control is another ***weapon*** in the hands of the Central Bank. The selective control is a credit technique which can be essential and non-essential uses of bank credit the selective control aim is to reduce the money supply for non-essential purposes and allows more credit to productive channels. These techniques enhances the production and controlling credit the selective credit controls can be applied in the form of rationing of credit, moralsuasion, margin variation and regulation of consumer credit and others.

(C) Scheduled Banks: The banks can be divided into two kinds. They are ***Scheduled and Non-scheduled*** banks. A bank which has been included in the ***Second schedule*** of the RBI act, 1934 is known as ***scheduled bank***. The bank should satisfy the following conditions.

(a) The bank should have a paid up capital and reserves of at least Rs. 5.00 lakhs.

(b) The bank should give assurance to the RBI on the depositor's welfare.

(c) The bank should be a corporation or a cooperative society.

The banks which are not included in the second schedule of the RBI act are known as ***Non-scheduled Bank***.

(D) World Bank: World Bank is a bank which function on global basis. It provides financial assistance to the member countries of the world. After the second world war two institutions were founded in 1944. They were International Monetary Fund and World Bank. The IMF was established for providing short term loans to the member countries. The world bank was formed for providing long term finance to the member countries for the purpose of reconstruction of war damaged aspects and assistance to less developed countries.

(E) Agricultural Banks: Agriculture sector needs a lot of financial assistance from banking sector. But all banks do not provide agricultural finance. Some specialised banks will provide assistance, they are known as ***"agricultural banks"***. In India agricultural finance is generally provided by cooperative institutions. The cooperative societies provide short term loans and the land development banks provide the long term credit to the agriculturists. Generally the farmers require finance for the purchase of seeds, fertilisers and other inputs. They also require long term loans for the purchase of agricultural machinery and equipment and improvement of land.

(F) Savings Bank: Savings is the most important for the development of the society. The aim of the saving bank is to encourage saving attitude among the general public and mobilised their small savings. The postal saving banks do this job. They open accounts and issue postal cash certificates to the savers. In India there is a huge availability potential savings in the society.

(G) Public Sector Banks: Public Sector Banks are owned by the central government. They are controlled by the government of India. All the Nationalised Banks and Regional Rural Banks will come under this category. These banks are regulated and directed by the RBI.

(H) Private Sector Banks: After the implementation of liberalisation, globalisation and privatisation policies. There has been a tremendous change in the banking sector. These banks are owned by the individuals or corporations. The private sector banks have been emerged after the implications of privatisation policy.

(I) Cooperative Sector Banks: The basic principle of cooperation is each for all and all for each. Cooperation means the voluntary association on the basis of equality. Cooperative bank is an institution which is established on the basis of cooperation principles. Cooperative bank deals in ordinary banking business activities. They are funded by collecting funds through shares accept deposits and grants loans. They issue shares of unlimited liability. Every shareholder in the cooperative bank will have voting right what even the number of shares he may hold. They are concerned with the rural credit and provide financial assistance for agricultural and rural activities. Cooperative banking in India has *III tier structure.* The structure is presented below.

(a) Primary credit societies at village level.

(b) Central cooperative banks at district level.

(c) State cooperative banks at the state level.

The cooperative banking started in India in 1904. The cooperative societies were established to encourage ***Thrift, self help*** and cooperation among the agriculturists, artisans and other persons.

(J) Domestic Banks: Domestic banks are registered in India and incorporated according to the banking regulation act.

(K) Foreign Banks: Foreign banks have origin in abroad and have their head office in their country. They do the banking business through their branches in India. They are regulated by the RBI, Central Government and Ministry of Finance.

(L) Exchange Banks: Exchange banks deal with the financing of foreign trade. They deal in foreign exchange and have their head offices located outside the country. The main business of these banks is exchange of currency. They also perform commercial banking activities in addition to the exchange business. The foreign banks have been enjoying the monopoly position in the foreign exchange market. The exchange banks in India are *Chartered bank, Lloyds bank, Mercantile bank, Eastern bank, Grindlays bank, Bank of America, Bank of Tokyo.*

These banks perform the following functions.

(a) Financing exports.

(b) Financing imports.

(c) Discounting bills.

(d) Financing domestic trade.

(e) Accepting deposits and granting loans.

Indian banks operate as foreign banks in other countries. At present 95 branches of 9 Indian commercial banks are operating over 25 foreign countries. These branches are located in *London, Singapore, Bahrain, and Paris*. The banks are also concentrated in the ***UK, USA, Fiji, Kenya, United Arab Emirates, Hong Kong Mauritius and Singapore***. The Bank of Baroda, State Bank of India, Bank of India Branches spread among the different countries. They are specialised in financing of foreign trade and global banking.

(M) Non–Scheduled Banks: Commercial banks have been classified into two kinds (a) scheduled bank (b) Non-scheduled bank. A bank may be categorised as a scheduled bank, if it satisfies the following conditions.

(1) The bank should be included in the second schedule of the RBI act 1934

(2) The bank has paid up capital and reserves of at least Rs. 5.00 lakhs

(3) It should ensure the RBI that its operations should be for the welfare of the depositors

(4) It must be like a corporation or a cooperative society

The banks which are not included in the second scheduled of the RBI are ***Non-scheduled banks.***

FINANCIAL PERFORMANCE OF FOREIGN BANKS IN INDIA

	Financial Ratio	*1996-97*	*1997-98*	*1998-99*	*1999-00*	*2000-01*
I.	Operating profit/loss as a percentage to Total Assets	3.62	3.91	2.32	3.24	3.05
II.	Net profit/Loss as a percentage to Total Assets	1.19	0.97	0.69	1.17	0.93
III.	Net interest income as a percentage to Total Assets	4.13	3.93	3.47	3.92	3.64
IV.	Intermediation costs as a percentage to Total Assets	3.00	2.97	3.59	3.22	(3.05)

Sources: WTO and Indian banking sector, The Road Ahead Mathew Joseph Rupa Rege Nitsure, EPW, June 15, 2002, p. 2319.

Recent Trends in Banking

The Commercial banks have drastically changed from the traditional business to innovative banking. The Indian banking aim is the upliftment of the socio-economic condition of the masses. It has changed its strategy from class banking to mass banking. Therefore there has been a remarkable change in the operations of the banks to even for non-financial areas. At present there has been a conscious reorientation of banking policy for the attainment of social goals. The reorientation of banks have been diversified towards the following areas for the fulfillment of mass banking.

(a) Traditional banking to innovative banking.

(b) Profit motive to service approach.

(c) Big customers to small customers.

(d) Class banking to mass banking king.

(e) Urban to rural approach.

(f) Short term finance to long term finance.

The banking system has faced rapid changes in ushering a new era in the nations economic development. These changes have been briefly discussed in the following sectors:

(1) Regional balance development.

(2) Deposit mobilisation.

(3) Credit deployment.

(4) New banking policy.

(5) Electronic banking.

(1) Regional Balanced Development: In India, there has been a wide gap in development of banking sector in regional disparities. There has been an uneven growth in different states of the country. The Regional imbalances of banking development have been arisen at two levels.

(a) Between Urban and rural areas.

(b) Different states of the country.

The Commercial banks were urban oriented in their business operations. The rural areas did not have any bank facilities and starved of banking facilities. The villages have been ignored by the banks. To overcome this problem the commercial banks have been taken initiative for the massive expansion of the branches in the rural areas, underdeveloped under banked and unbanked areas. In 1969, there were 8,262 total branches of the commercial banks in India. The bank branches has increased to 63,513 in June 1997. The rural areas accounted to ***52%*** in 1997 and ***22%*** in 1969.

The bank branches did not spread throughout the country and there has been an uneven growth of banking in different states of the country. Few states were fairly served and the remaining states has been neglected. According to the study made by the RBI, the All India population Bank office ratio came down to ***15,000*** in June 1997. The analysis of the relative growth of commercial banks have revealed that the states such as ***Kerala, Maharashtra, Punjab and West Bengal*** were highly developed states. The low developed states were Andhra Pradesh, Assam, Bihar, Himachal Pradesh, J & K, MP, Rajasthan and UP.

(2) Deposit Mobilisation: Deposit mobilisation is an important activity of the banking sector. The deposit collection has been regarded as the major task of banking today. The primary function of the commercial bank is to accept deposits and advancing the loans to the borrowers Deposits mobilisation is one of the basic innovation at the present situation. Collection of deposits is essentially resource mobilisation. The banks tap the savings from savers and divest them into the productive sector. This process leads to economic growth of the country. Indian banks are trying to attract more deposits by offering various saving schemes. The performance of the public sector banks in deposit mobilisation from rural areas and semi urban areas have been very commendable. The aggregate deposits of all scheduled commercial banks have increased from ***Rs. 4646 crores*** in June 1969 to ***Rs. 5,05,599*** crores in 1997.

The number of small account holders with the bank is increasing effectively. The deposits consisted of ***Time and demand deposits.*** There was a predominance of demand deposits in the past. The ratio of time deposits to total deposits have been increasing. The banks now uses credit deposit ratio as a tool of allocation of funds. The Commercial banks could extend credit in terms of any of the following:

(a) Cash credit.

(b) Overdraft.

(c) Demand and loans.

(d) Bill discounting.

(e) Hire purchase credit.

(3) Credit Deployment: Credit is the important factor of the economic development. It is the financial architecture of the economy. In the modern economy the bank credit is an important input variable in the production activities. The bank credit was largely enjoyed by big traders, industrialists and corporate sector. The sectoral allocation of bank credit has radically changed in socially desired manner. The sectoral allocation of bank credit can be analysed in pre nationalisation and post nationalisation. In pre nationalisation of banks the agriculture sector got the meagre share of bank credit. The Industry sector also got high share of bank credit in pre nationalisation period. In post nationalisation period. The bank credit has been diversified from traditional to priority sectors. The RBI and the Government of India have been formulated the guidelines for the deployment of bank credit in India.

(1) The banks should provide finance to the priority sector.

(2) The banks should advance the loans to rural and semi urban areas up to 60% of the deposits mobilised there.

(3) The banks should allocate bank credit 16% of the total credit to the agriculture sector.

(4) The banks should concentrate on development of the backward regions in the country.

(5) The banks should implement the district credit plans systematically.

(6) The priority sector is categorised in the following manner:

(a) Agriculture.

(b) SSI.

(c) Education.

(d) Consumption loans.

(e) Loans to SCs and STs.

(f) Housing loans.

(g) Small business and retail trade.

(h) Small road and water transport operators.

(i) Setting up of industrial estates.

(j) Loans to SC, ST, Corporations and Organisations.

(4) New Banking Policy: The Indian banking sector has rapidly changed to meet the growing needs of the *digital economy.* The efforts are made to strengthen the public sector banks with improved operational and technical efficiency. The Government has taken several steps to improve the quality of customers services by the banks. The banks now concentrated on mechanisation and computerisation of their branches in order to provide high quality of service to the customers. ***Electronic clearing service*** is introduced by the RBI at Mumbai and Chennai. The concept of prime lending rate is introduced in Indian banking sector. The board of Financial supervision and its advisory council were established in Nov. 1994. The Debt recovery Tribunals have been constituted at Ahmedabad, Bangalore, Kolkata, New Delhi and Jaipur. The RBI announced the Banking ombudsman scheme in 1995 under the supervision of Banking Regulation act, 1949. It is established for the speedy disposal of customer grievances. The scheme is available in Mumbai, Bhopal, New Delhi, Bangalore, Hyderabad, Chandigarh, Patna and Jaipur. The banks can now open and relocate their branches freely. The banks introduced stock investment scheme for the investors and Mutual funds. This instrument is useful in applying shares for the primary issue of the corporate sector.

The Interest rates have been rationalised deposit rates and lending rates have been freed. The bank rate is one of the active instruments in the hands of the Central Bank. The financial health of the banks has improved due to globally accepted prudential norms.

The banks at present play an important role in the settlement of the financial transactions. The liberalisation policy made the banking sector more competitive and efficient. The emergence of new private sector and foreign banks fully equipped with the latest technology. These banks have been increased more competition in the banking sector. Technology is the most important element in the banking sector. Technology makes less cost effective to the banks and provides better services to the customers. Computerisation and Mechanisation of the banks can change the future of the commercial banks. The RBI appointed a committee on Technology upgradation in banking sector. The committee submitted its report in July 1999. It recommended a new legislation on *Electronic fund transfer system* to facilitate the multiple payment systems. The committee recommended the following recommendations for smooth functioning of the banking sector.

(1) Legal framework for electronic banking.

(2) Computerisation of government transactions.

(3) Human resources development.

(4) Other issues.

(5) Electronic banking.

(1) Legal Framework for Electronic Banking: The RBI may amend its act for electronic banking. It assumes the regulatory and supervisory powers on payment and settlement systems. It may promote a new legislation on *Electronic funds Transfer system* for speedy disposal of payment settlement. This system is more useful to banks and financial institution. This system will function with the coordination of Indian Banks Association and the Department of Telecommunication. It requires encryption of data files through communication channels to the remotely located branches.

(2) Computerisation of Government Transactions: The computerisation process has made a revolutionary changes in the banking sector. The traditional banking system has been completely changed and became customer oriented approach. The banks at present think about the customer facilities due to a high competition in the market. The market is now a battlefield to the all types of banks. Therefore there is a strong need to computerise all branches of banks who are dealing with the government transaction. The government should also be computerised its departments such as *Pay & Accounts office. District Treasury offices and Drawing and Disbursing offices.* The Government departments should be computerised on priority basis.

(3) Human Resources Development: Before computerisation of bank branches, there is a strong need to provide excellent training programmes to the staff members. Education of staff on Information Technology should be given top priority. There is a need to impart necessary IT training to all levels of staff members. The training institutes of the banks should be strengthened with adequate manpower and other infrastructure facilities.

(4) Other Issues: The major other issues of the recommendations of the committee are presented below.

(a) Development of Indian Financial Network (DIFN).

(b) Management Information System (MIS).

(c) Security.

For smooth functioning of Inter bank and Intra bank application, there is a strong need for introduction of ***Very Small Aperture Terminal** (VSAT)* The operationalisation of the VSAT is expected to provide a significant thrust to the development of ***INFINET.*** The Infinet system will further facilitate connectivity within the financial sector. The VSAT network will facilitate the transactions very fast and accurately.

Management Information system will consist of Data warehousing and data Mining at individual bank level. A task force can be set up by Indian Banks association to explore the various alternatives and avenues for working out a unique indentification system for individual customer data bases at banks.

Security is the most important element in financial affairs of the transactions. The success of the technology based activities of the banking sector will depend upon the level of degree of security provided by them to the customers. The authentification and certification of the transactions are most important in the standardisation of security. The banks should adopt the standard of cryptography procedures to prevent data tamper during transmission.

(5) Electronic Banking: The Computer Revolution has made the new trend in banking sector. The common man's life style is changing very fastly and became more sophisticated. The world at large is rapidly entering into the net age the common man's life is anticipated with the extensive and intensive use of global communication networks. ***Net is an interconnection of computer communication networks covering the whole world. Internet system has crossed all geographical boundaries in the digital world.*** The Net is changing everything and anything. The emergence of *E-commerce* facilitated the growth and expansion of internet and information, technology, banking sector and financial activity remarkably. The electronic banking consists the following elements.

(a) E-Commerce.

(b) E Banking.

(c) On line banking.

(d) Offshore banking.

(e) Credit cards.

(a) E-Commerce

Electronic Commerce is one of the most common business term use in 21st century. It involves all sizes of transaction bases. It requires the digital transmission of transaction information. It can be defined as "The use of Electronic transmission mediums (Tele Communications) engage in the exchange, including buying and selling of products and services requiring transportation either physically originally from location to location."[10]

The business transaction are conducted through electronic devices. The important component of E-Com is electronic data interchange. The EDI system allow pre-established trading partners to electronically exchange business data. The EDI system Concentrated around the purchasing function. It is generally costly to implement. It is not just a technology it is a way of conducting business. It depends upon the elements (a) electronic information (b) Electronic relationship (c) Electronic transactions. The information will be spread through the computer devices such as ***Electronic data inter change, E-mail, Electronic bulletin boards.*** The tools of the e-commerce are *Internet, Intranet and extra net.* These tools are created under the network based technologies. E-commerce is an innovative approach to commercial exploitation. It is a boon to new business era to enhance the efficiency and improving productivity. It is estimated that in 1999 there are ***140 million*** internet users global basis. It is expected that the e-commerce is a growing phenomenon and 25% of business transactions is likely to be made electronically. It is expected with b2b transaction to touch ***US $ 434 billion*** by the year 2002. More and more business is looking for opportunities to operate through internet commerce. E-commerce will radically change the mode and methods of conducting business and commerce world over.

(b) Electronic Banking

Banking is the most important element in business. The growth of internet and the emergence of e-commerce are bound to change the banking business world over. E-commerce is the ability to conduct the business digitally including banking. There is a distinction between commodity transactions and financial transactions, the commodity transactions through net are called as ***E-commerce*** the financial transaction done through the Net is called as ***E-banking.*** The modern banking will tend to be more information based speedy and boundary as an impact of E-revolution. The banks should know the benefits which are available from Information Technology. They should utilise the application of the technology. The information technology, no doubt will enhance the efficiency and skills of the staff. E-banking involves ***Electronic Fund transfer*** network technologies. E-banking is knowledge based electronic device. Internet provides universal information which is required by banking sector. Most business and commercial enterprises are interested to become Internet working organisation to enhance their productivity and profitability. The first Indian bank on the internet is ***Industrial Credit and Investment Corporation of India.*** E-banking involves elimination of paper based transaction. It made a radical change in the operation of the banking services. It created a revolution in the financial sector of the country. It is the future of

10. E-Commerce, Greenstein and Fieman, TMH 2000, p. 3.

banking business in the upcoming century. The internet bank of the millennium consists of no lines, no tellers, no queues no business hours. The E-banking has the following advantages:

(a) Low cost banking.

(b) 24 x 7 days banking.

(c) Beneficial to corporate sector.

(d) Better customer retention.

The electronic banking involves four kinds of transactions. They are:

(1) C to B Customer to bank.

(2) B 2 B Bank to Bank.

(3) Electronic Central banking.

(4) Intranet procurement.

The transaction may be involved between customer and bank. These transaction are based on internet. The banking transaction will be carried on Internet. The customer can access the bank at any time for his required valuable information about his transaction. Several network innovations for e-banking can be visualised such as ***Smart card, Electronic Data interchange and electronic house.*** But all of these financial transactions should be done under the full security of the information. The E-banking operation have to be secured against unauthorised access by hackers.

The transactions between banks will be done through extranet. The extranet is restricted to banks only as well as they secured. The bulk of Intra bank transaction can be operated in the form of E-banking.

The Central bank is the supreme authority in the Indian financial system. It is the regulator of the banking sector. ***The electronic central banking*** will work under the control of the central banks. All the banks are inter connected on extranet to facilitate transactions such as cheque clearings, cash reserves management, open market operations, bills discounting etc. The Central bank is also connected with government treasury on extranet. Further the Central banks of the countries should be inter linked with the ***IMF, world bank etc.***

The transactions which are arised internal to a bank, across its subsidiaries and branches are known as intranet banking. E-banking by offering electronic funds transfer tends to minimise the circulation of currency. Thus it reduces the costs substantially. At present web based commerce on the internet is growing exponentially.

(c) On Line Banking

There is a remarkable change in the banking sector. The banking sector has been shifted from conventional banking to convenience banking. According to the traditional method of banking operations, the customer has to visit the bank in person to withdraw the cash and fund transfer. But in convenience banking system, the customer need not to go the bank. The customer is able to perform the banking operation through his office or at home through PC or LAPTOP. The online banking refers that the customers access the banks website for viewing their account details. At the same time the customer can perform the transactions through website as per their requirements. The on line banking is known as *screen banking" or "virtual banking"* The online banking is available 24 hours. Basic banking off operations can be done at any time through *ATMs.* The following functions can be done conveniently.

(a) Verifying account balance.

(b) Transfering funds.

(c) Stop payment request.

(d) Payment of utility services.

Features of E-banking: The salient features of online banking are presented below.

(1) Banking facilities are available round the clock.

(2) Banks can reduce operating costs.

(3) The cost of each transaction is reduced.

(4) Quick service is available to the customer.

(5) Customers can operate their accounts from anywhere in the world.

(6) Fast decision making.

(d) Offshore Banking

The Indian banks are carrying business operations in abroad. The Indian banks that entering into global business are known as "offshore banking". The offshore banking branches are connected to society for worldwide Inter bank Financial Telecommunication Network. *(SWIFT)* The SWIFI is used for the transmission and receipt of all international and financial messages by member banks and financial institutions.

The offshore banking provides a variety of services which are generally offered as follows:

- Issue of letter of credit and other documents.
- Participating in forward contracts and interest rate swaps.
- Issue of guarantees on behalf of customers.
- Involving in derivative products related to treasury.

CREDIT CARDS

Introduction

The economic development of society and the socio cultural changes had lead to the spectacular growth of service industry. The technological advances have increased the integration and efficiency of the financial system. After the basic needs were fulfilled, like food, shelter and clothing. There was a tremendous demand for improved satisfaction and it led to a proliferation of variation in the same product. Increasing affluence combined with increasing complexity of life has led to the phenomenon of credit cards. They provide convenience and safety in the purchasing process. It is generally known as *"Plastic Money"*. The credit cards are made of plastic. They are widely used by the consumers all around the globe. The changes in consumer behaviour and taștes led to the tremendous growth of credit cards. Credit card is a card which enables the consumers to purchase products or services without paying immediately. This credit card concept is based on the principle of "Buy now pay later". It is a document that can be used for purchase of goods and services all over the globe.

The world's first credit card was issued by Mobil oil in 1940. It was initially issued by the company to give specialised services to its regular customers. It helped to boost sales and increase the customer base. After the tremendous success of ***Mobil Card,*** various organisations began to think about the use of cards in different segments of the business. The ***Diners club, American Express and Carte Blanche Cards*** have been emerged. They were popular in USA. During the IInd world war US saw the growth of the cards. The first bank card was issued by *Franklin National bank USA* in the year 1952. In 1960 the credit card operating system was developed by Bank of America, USA. An international bank card system known as "VISA". Another international bank card system called "Master card" was established. At present the market is dominated by the VISA and Master card. In the year 1966 this system was launched by ***Barclays Bank, UK*** and they named as Barclay card. The Access card was launched in the year 1962 in UK by a consortium of banks. The *EURO CARD* was introduced in most of the west

European countries. In the year 1988, The first Woman card was launched *"My card"* by International bank of Asia in Hong Kong. There was tremendous demand for that card. Another card was introduced as *"Ladies Card"* in Malaysia. In 1990 green card was launched in UK.

The card identifies its owner. The owner of the card enjoys some privileges also. The issuer of the card issues credit cards depending on the credibility of the customers. The card issuer enters into tie up with different merchant vendors located in different geographical in various fields of business activities. The card issuer will put up a credit limit for its holders and a ceiling limit for each vendor. The card offers an opportunity to buy air, Rail ticket and stay at hotel's. The card holder need only to present the card at cash counter and has to sign some forms. The cards can be considered as a substitute for cash and cheques. The cards are not accepted by all the merchant vendors.

Process of Credit Card Business Cycle

Credit cards facilitates its holder to make purchases at various designated merchant establishment. The establishments like travel agencies, star Hotels Department stores will accept all valid cards in lieu of cash payments. The cardholder can avoid the risk of carrying cash. The following steps are involved in the process of a transaction.

Step I : A card holder purchases goods and presents the card to the designated merchant establishment.

Step II : The retail vendor verifies the number on the card against the hot list provided to him by bank

Step III : The card holder is required to sign on the voucher and the signature has to tally with the one on the credit card.

Step IV : The Retailer has to present the sales vouchers to the bank for reimbursement for the customer's purchases. The bank also charges commission from the retailer.

Step V : The bank will make payment to the retailer on behalf of the card holders.

Step VI : After completion of the process. The bank sends the bill to the cardholder and receives the money.

Benefits of Credit Card: The benefits of credit cards may be classified into two categories (a) cardholders (b) issuers.

Benefits to the Cardholders: There are so many benefits to the cardholder for using the cards.

(1) The holder need not carry cash at all times.

(2) The holder will be covered by free Insurance.

(3) It can be used as identification card.

(4) The holders are entitled to get rewards and gifts.

(5) The holders can avail special counters for Air and Travel reservations.

(6) The holders can get complimentary Magazines For ex: Diners Club provide "Signature" Magazine.

(7) Family members of the holder can avail this facility.

(8) They can enjoy free credit upto 30 to 45 days.

(9) If the card is stolen/lost the liability is limited to a maximum of Rs. 1000.

(10) Some credit cardholders will get free services such as confirmed ticket booking and Hotel reservation.

(11) Some cardholder will get benefit from the worldwide net work *ex: Master Card. visa.*

Benefits to the Issuers: There are also advantages to credit issuers such as:

(1) The business offers higher profits.

(2) The issuers can also improve their name and image by serving large number of credit holders base.

(3) This business is an additional activity to the banking sector to enhance their profitability.

Privileges

The credit cards besides providing credit facility, The issuer extends some additional facilities to attract more customers. These facilities and services are presented below:

(a) Draft on phone.

(b) Instant cash withdrawal.

(c) 24 x 7 x 365 customer service.

(d) Free Insurance.

(e) Buy anything on credit card.

(f) Joint credit card and ATM facility.

(g) Hotel discount facility.

(h) Fuel at petrol pumps at credit.

(i) Purchase protection.

(a) Draft on Phone: The credit card holders can use their cards to pay for incidental expenses what they have to do is to call the issuers bank and instruct it to make payments like telephone bills, electricity bill set.

(b) Instant Cash Withdrawal: Some issuers allow their credit cardholder to withdraw instant cash upto **60%** of his credit line from ATM in all metros. The card holders can also draw cash in case of medical emergencies for meeting with the expenses on treatment at other than their home town. This emergency medical advance facility is available with all Indian and foreign bank.

(c) Customer Service: The technology adopted by the banking sector gives more comfortable life to the customers. The revolutionary phase banking services encourages that the banks just with a phone call away assist the cardholder around the clock. Foreign banks provide a world class service to card holder. A credit card holders can call city phone banking and ask for temporary credit line any time.

(d) Free Insurance: Some of the issuers, Insure the cardholder at free of cost for a particular sum. City bank offers a complimentary personal accident insurance. The Bank of Baroda card extends insurance protection to cardholder's spouse also.

(e) Buy anything on Credit Card: The credit card are well accepted by the public. The card can be used for all occasions and seasons. It also useful for purchasing essential commodities like groceries fuel, auto accessories and cosmetic. It is useful even paying customs duties and hospital bills. We can purchase everything anywhere at any time under the sun at designated locations.

(f) ATM Facility: Indian banks and foreign banks have introduced a joint card. The joint card holders can access his accounts with the bank through ATMs.

(g) Hotels Discount Facility: The credit card holders are entitled to get discounts at all leading hotels and clubs. The card holders are eligible to avail the facilities as per the schemes which are offered by the hotels, travel agencies and on Air tickets. Even the consumer products are also available in this method.

(h) Fuel Facility: The BOB, Citi bank, Standard Chartered cards are accepted at all Bharat petroleum outlets. This is very convenient for card holders at all leading metro cities.

(i) Purchase Protection: The credit card facility protects the purchases against damage or loss due to fire and theft. For compensation the card holder can claim the value of the product damaged or lost from the ***New India Assurance company***. This protection is available for a limited period the date of purchase of the product on the credit card.

Some of these facilities are exclusive offers, Airport lounges, special hospital facilities, special travel services.

Type of Credit Cards

The credit card system is becoming very popular in India and abroad. The system facilitates a wide range of products and services. The growth of service sector depends on the pulse of the customer. The need of the customers are taken care off by different card issuers. The cards can classified into 4 basic types based on the issuers. Travel and entertainment card, bank card, retail card, fuel card. There are many types of cards which are popular in India and abroad. These cards can also be classified as follow:

(1) Based on geographical territory.

(2) Based on Franchise.

(3) Based on Status.

(4) Based on user.

(5) Based on credit recovery.

(1) Geographical Basis: Under this category, the cards can be categorised as domestic and international cards. The domestic cards are generally available from most of the banks. These cards will be valid in India and Nepal only. All these transactions will be in rupees only. International cards will be issued to persons who travel foreign countries frequently. These card holders make purchase in Dollars, these cards are subjects to the rules and regulations of the RBI. These cards will be honoured throughout the world except in India and Nepal.

(2) Based on Franchise: The cards can be classified based on the tie-up. They are *visa card, master card* Proprietary and tie up card. Visa cards can be issued by any bank which is having tie up with VISA International USA. The card holders can avail the facilities of visa net work for their transactions. Master card is a brand name for another type of card. The issuer of the card has to obtain permission from the master card corpn. USA. It will be honoured in the master card net work. Proprietary card will be issued by the issuer bank on their own brand name. These cards will be issued by banks in addition to their other tie up cards. Tie up cards are issued by a bank having a collaboration with domestic card brand. Forex: IOB has tie up with Can card. They give credit to customers on similar lines as the original card issues.

(3) Based on Status: This type of credit cards will be further classified as Standard cards, Business card and Global card. The Standard card is a normal card generally issued by all issuing banks. The card holder is offered a limited privileges when compared to other cards. These cards are issued by some banks under the brand name of classic. Business card is meant for tax consultants Chartered Accountants, small firms, solicitors and executives. These cards are very useful for their business purpose. These are more and more convenient. The business card facilitates more privileges than Standard card. Some banks are issuing these cards in the brand name of Executive. The gold card is another type of card which has got a high value for the elite. The gold card offers some additional benefits and facilities to the card holders. These cards provide more credit limits and more cash advance while comparing with other cards.

(4) Based on User: Under this category the credit cards are further classified as Individual cards and corporate cards. The Individual cards are issued to Individuals persons. Usually all brands of cards will be given to individuals. Corporate cards are issued to corporate companies and business firms only the corporate cards are issued on the name of the company. The cards will be utilised by the executives and top officials of the firms. The bills will be paid by the company to the banks.

(5) Based on the Recovery: These type of cards are again classified into two categories. They are revolving credit type card and charge card. The Revolving card is generally based on the revolving credit principle. According to this scheme, the card holder has to pay a percentage of the outstanding credit for every month. The interest is charged as the outstanding amount. The interest rate is more than 30% PA charge card is a convenient instrument. It is not a credit instrument. The issuer gives a consolidated bill for every month to the card holder. The card holder shall pay the bills on presentation of the consolidated bills. Therefore there are no interest charges on this use of cards.

Credit Cards in India

The first credit card in India was Diners Club Card in the year 1964. Andhra Bank and Central Bank were the first to launch. The Andhra Bank introduced in 1981 under the brand name of VISA classic followed by CBI in collaboration with Master Card Corporation in 1981. The other banks such as Canara bank, Bank of India, and Bank of Baroda Introduced credit cards in India. The foreign banks such as Citi Bank, Standard Chartered Bank, ANZ Grindlays Bank, Bank of America, and America express bank have also introduced cards in India through their branches in India. The cards are offered by the others banks such as Corporation bank KVB, SBI, Bank of Maharashtra, Vijaya bank and South Indian banks. In India almost all the credit cards issued by the banks are the franchises of original master card. SBI is the third largest issuer of credit cards after Citi bank and Standard bank. Standard Chartered bank has recently launched a women international card division. The card can be used but a woman to purchase tickets for movies, plays, shows and also planning for special parties. The card can also be issued for pest control, home appliance repair, gifting like cakes, and flowers, emergency services such as doctors and towing services. It offers free and comprehensive insurance package for the card holders and the family. These include accident insurance cover for self and spouse, children, education allowance, medical and purchase protection Insurance.

India has 5.3 Millions credit cards and 6.5 lakh debit cards. The average spend on a credit card at Rs. 22,000 a year. The following data will reveal the development of the credit cards in India.

THE CREDIT CARD LEDGER *(Rs. in crore)*

Year	*No. of Cards (in millions)*	*Amount spending.*
1995	1.9	17,000
1996	2.5	2,500
1997	3.1	3,650
1998	3.5	4,700
1999	4.2	6,500
2000	4.9	8,500
2001	5.3	10,500

MARKET SHARE CREDIT CARDS (UPTO 31-3-2001)

	Name of the card	*% of Market share*
(1)	Citi Bank	29#
(2)	Standard Chartered Bank	25
(3)	SBI GE	12
(4)	HSBC	10
(5)	Amex	6

Modern Trends in the Payment Business

Information technology has made decisive in roads in all walks of life. It is being used extensively for ease of operations, communications, record keeping and for obtaining the better result from the system in which it is put to use. The new technologies in the payment business resulted in shaping the future of money. As a result of this new type of cards and payment systems came into existence. The following are the latest instruments in the financial sector.

(A) Debit card

(B) Chip card

(C) Smart card

(D) Electronic commerce

(E) Co-branded card.

(a) Debit Card is the innovative instrument in the financial services sector. It is the most convenient method of payment to the merchant establishment. It needs involvement of many banks. The card holder will present the card as completion of his purchases at the merchant establishment on production of a debit card. The card details are fed through a terminal at the merchant establishment. The card holder is asked to key in his pin code which is allotted by the card issuer. On completion of the transaction. The amount is immediately debited from the card holder's account and transferred to the a/c of merchant vendor. No overdrawing is allowed.

(b) Chip Card is a plastic card with a micro chip. It can be used on existing products like debit and credit card. It is also known as stored value cards. The transactions are effected by inserting the card in a pin pad and the value of transaction amount reduces accordingly. These cards are reloadable and disposal. It avoids the trouble of carrying cash. The chip card also scores over the magnetic card and it can retain 50-60% of the latest transactions which can be produced on demand.

(c) Smart Card is in a credit card sized piece of plastic. It is a tiny integrated circuit stip card. It allows the greater amount of information than a magnetic stip card. These cards are more popular in telecom industry. The use of this card is electronic purse application. It is reloadable, high secure smart card function as a digital cash for in store and even in home or on the road transactions. It offers convenience, cost and security benefits to customers, merchants and banks. These cards reduces frauds.

(d) Electronic Commerce is popularly known as ***E-commerce.*** It is simply a term of buying, selling ordering and delivering goods over the Internet. It will provide better communication between suppliers, brokers, sub brokers, customers end users, and manufacturers. It is an inexpensive medium that reaches an attractive targeted persons. It consists of such technologies as ***E-mail, E-fund,*** Transfer, E-data interchange E-bulletin boards. The customer on the internet searches the web for a particular product of interest. The search engine contains a list with a number of potential vendors who will deal with that product. The customer selects a vendor by blowing. The customer is required to fill the order form and submits it to the vendor. The data is then transmitted to the vendor after encryption for security. The order is then processed by the vendor. The vendor sends the data to an independent authentication centre when the identities of buyer and vendor are checked. After verification of data, it is then transmitted to the vendor to despatch the goods to the buyer and settling the bill either with the bank or credit card camp.

(e) Co-branded Card: Co-branded cards are more popular in the industry. Co-branded card is the first card in the Asian sub-continent. Co-branding is an association between a well established two groups. The consumers are pragmatic and value driven. A Co-branded card of times of India with Citi bank and master card is very popular. These cards are very popular in USA.

Any Time Money (ATM)

ATM is becoming more popular in banking industry. It is known as *Any time Money*. It is also called as ***Automated Teller Machine.*** The need for increasing network capacity in banking sector requires *"A Synchronous Transfer Mode"*. The potential of ATM is its ability to carry many kinds of traffic over the same network link. ATM also provides each application with the appropriate speed and control while making the best use of network capacity. It has many benefits like increased security, better possibilities for sharing bandwidth.

Three years ago HDFC and ICICI began with rolling out their networks. ATMs were just novelty. Today the number of ATMs have swelled to 5,400. The banks prefer to share their network with competitions, rather than take in the burden of continually building their network. The banks are installing ATMs because of its cost effective. An ATM costs around Rs. 8-14 lakhs. The annual maintenance varies between Rs. 12 to 20 lakhs per year. Now an ATM is profitable if 50-100 transactions are done per day on it. If it does *260-270* the bank recovers its investment within a year. The foreign banks have used ATMs as an acquisition strategies. The public sector banks use this as retention strategy. Today the 04 private sector banks (HDFC ICICI bank, UTI bank, IDBI bank) together account for over 50% of the ATMs in India. The following table will reveal about the Network facilities of the banking sector. (during the year 2001-02).[11]

GROWTH IN ATM NETWORK (2001-02)

(1)	SBI	764
(2)	ICICI bank	495
(3)	HDFC bank	272
(4)	UTI bank	188
(5)	IDBI bank	148

ATM NETWORK (UP TO MAY 2002)

(1)	ICICI bank	1,005
(2)	IDBI bank	225
(3)	HDFC bank	479
(4)	UTI bank	491
(5)	SBI	1,070

SBI has the largest ATM network in the country covering 370 towns. UTI bank claims that over 90% of cash withdrawls now occur through ATM.

Card name	Card type	*Eligibility*			*Fee details*			*Credit details*			
		Validity	*Salaries*	*Self employed.*	*Joining*	*Add as card*	*Anl.fee.*	*Credit limits*	*Interest rate*	*Credit period*	*Revolving credit*
(1) Allahabad Bank	Master card	Global	60,000	60,000	100	0	250	NS	3%	40	10%
(2) American Express	Amex change	Global	2,00,000	2,00,000	1,500	1,500	3,100	NS	2.79%	51	2.79%
(3) American Express	Amex change	Global	1,00,000	1,00,000	NA	950	1,200	NS	NA	51	5.00%

11. Retail Banking, Business World, 27-5-2002, p. 23.

(4) American express	Amex credit	Global	1,50,000	1,50,000	0	495	995	NS	2.50%	51	5.00%
(5) American Express	Amex	Global	72,000	72,000	0	495	995	NS	2.50%	51	5.00%
(6) Andhra bank	Visa card	Indian	90,000	90,000	300	450	450	5,000	2.50%	45	NA
(7) Andhra bank	Visa card	Global	1,50,000	1,50,000	1,000	750	750	50,000	2.50%	45	NA
(8) Andhra bank	Master card	India	1,50,000	1,50,000	300	450	450	15,000	2.50%	NA	NA
(9) Bank of India	Master change	India & Nepal	1,00,000	1,00,000	250	200	400	NA	NA	45	NA
(10) Bank of India	Visa credit	India	1,00,000	1,00,000	0	175	350	NS	2.50%	NA	20.00%
(11) Bank of India	Master charge	Global	2,00,000	2,00,000	400	450	900	NA	NA	45	NA
(12) Bank of India	Visa credit	India	1,00,000	1,00,000	200	450	900	NS	2.50%	NA	20.00%
(13) Bank of India	Visa charge	Global	2,00,000	2,00,000	400	450	900	NA	NA	30	NA
(14) Bank of Maharashtra	Master credit	India	1,20,000	1,20,000	400	100	200	30,000	FD Rate	45	NA
(15) Bob card	charge	India & Nepal	75,000	75,000	0	100	100	NS	3.00%	45	10.00%
(16) Bob card	Domestic Master	India & Nepal	1,00,000	1,00,000	0	500	1,000	40,000	3.00%	45	10.00%
(17) Bob card	Master & Visa	Global	1,00,000	1,00,000	0	0	1,500	3,00,000	3.00%	45	10.00%
(18) Bob card	Vishaphoto credit	Global	1,50,000	1,50,000	0	750	1,250	75,000	2.75%	45	10.00%
(19) Bob card	Visa credit	India & Nepal	75,000	75,000	0	250	400	25,000	2.50%	45	10.00%
(20) Can card	charge	India & Nepal	60,000	60,000	250	300	400	50,000	2.50%	45	10.00%
(21) Can card	charge	India & Nepal	60,000	60,000	250	300	400	50,000	2.50%	45	10.00%
(22) Can card	Master credit	India & Nepal	60,000	60,000	250	300	400	1,00,000	2.50%	45	10%
(23) Can Card	Visa credit	India & Nepal	60,000	60,000	250	300	400	1,00,000	2.50%	45	10%
(24) CBI Int. card	Visa credit	Global	75,000	75,000	350	250%	500	30,000	2.50%	45	NA
(25) Central card	Visa card	India	75,000	75,000	350	250	500	30,000	2.50%	45	NA
(26) Citi bank	Master & Visa	Global	72,000	72,000	0	350	750	75,000	2.95%	45	5%
(27) Citi bank	Mater & Visa	Global	1,56,000	1,56,000	0	1,000	2,000	2,50,000	2.95%	50	5%
(28) Citi bank	Master & Visa	Global	96,000	96,000	0	350	750	NS	2.95%	50	5%
(29) Citi bank	Master & Visa	Global	96,000	96,000	0	350	750	75,000	2.95%	50	5%
(30) Dena card	Visa credit	India	60,000	60,000	250	300	400	25%	2.50%	50	NA
(31) HDFC	Visa credit	Global	96,000	72,000	300	250	700	NS	2.95%	50	5%
(32) HSBC	Master & Visa	Global	72,000	72,000	0	350	350	49,000	2.95%	48	2.95%
(33) HSBC	Master & Visa	Global	1,75,000	1,75,000	0	1,000	1,000	3,00,000	2.95%	48	2.95%

(34) ICICI	Visa credit	Global	1,20,000	1,20,000	300	600	1,200	3,00,000	2.50%	52	5.00%
(35) ICICI	Visa credit	Global	60,000	60,000	150	300	600	1,00,000	2.50%	50	5%
(36) ICICI	Visa credit	Global Nepal	75,000	1,00,000	100	150	300	50,000	2.95%	50	5%
(37) Indus Ind Bank	Master	Global	73,000	73,000	300	250	700	15,000	2.95%	45	5%
(38) Indusind bank	Master	Global	1,75,000	1,75,000	500	1,000	2,000	50,000	NA	45	5%
(39) PNB	Master & Visa	Global	72,000	72,000	0	0	350	49,000	2.95%	50	5%
(40) PNB	Master & Visa	Global	1,75,000	1,75,000	0	0	1,000	3,00,000	2.95%	51	5%
(41) Stanchart	Master & Visa	Global	1,00,000	1,00,000	300	500	1,200	NS	2.95%	52	5.00%
(42) Stanchart	Master & Visa	Global	60,000	72,000	100	350	700	NS	2.95%	52	5%
(43) Stanchart	Master & Visa	Global	1,50,000	1,50,000	1,000	1,000	2,000	NS	2.95%	52	5%
(44) SBI	Visa Credit	Global	75,000	60,000	250	250	500	70,000	2.75%	50	5%
(45) SBI	Visa Credit	Global	2,25,000	1,50,000	300	500	1,500	3,00,000	2.75%	50	5%
(46) SBI	Amex	Global	75,000	75,000	250	250	750	75,000	2.75%	50	5%
(47) Tata Finance	Amex Credit	Global	1,50,000	1,50,000	0	750	1,500	NA	2.50%	45	5%
(48) Tata Finance	Master credit	Global	60,000	60,000	0	250	500	NA	2.75%	45	5%

(C) INSURANCE

Introduction

Financial Services is an essential segment of financial system. Financial System in India has made commendable progress in extending its geographic spread and functional reach. The specialised financial institutions emerged in the Indian financial system to cater to the financial needs of the industrial sector. The Insurance Companies also played a prominent role in resource mobilisation and directing investments in productive areas.

Insurance Companies invest the savings of their policy holders. The policy holders will pay the amount to the insurance company in the form of premium. Insurance is just a contract between two parties. The insurance company undertakes in consideration of a sum of money to make good to the loss suffered by the party against a specified risk. There are two parties in an insurance contract (a) insurer (b) insured/beneficiary. The insurer is known as Insurance Company. The insured means a personal party who are willing to undertake an agreement with an insurer. The terms of the contract will be laid down in a document. The document is known as policy. The property which is insured is the subject matter of insurance. The property may be insured against loss arising from uncertain events.

The insurance companies collect and invest large amounts of premium. They offer financial protection to the investors, and channelising the fee to the government. They are working as long term basis. They offer policies for more than 10 years. Liquidity is not a problem to the insurance companies. They invest in the long term investment activities. The rate of returns is very low on the policies. The investments of insurance companies have been largely in government bonds, corporate bonds, mortgages and local self government bonds.

Insurance Companies are active in life, health and general. The insurance companies began to operate the pension schemes and mutual funds, pension business is a specialised form of life insurance. Life insurance covers a specified period of life of a person. General insurance covers losses caused by fire accident and marine adventures. The life insurance is different from general insurance. In life insurance the insurer has a fixed obligation to compensate the insured: In the case of general insurance the event insured against may not happen and company does not necessarily have to always compensate the party to the contract. Insurance organisations in India provide finance to the industries. The insurance organisations in India comprise two state owned monolithic institutions, namely:

(A) Life Insurance Corporation of India.

(B) General Insurance Corporation of India.

(A) Life Insurance Corporation of India (LIC)

The LIC is one of the most important financial intermediaries in India. In 1956 the LIC was set up and the insurance business has been nationalised. Till 1956 the insurance business was mixed and decentralised. There were 245 companies on the eve of nationalisation with different ages and sizes. The objectives of the LIC are

(i) To provide insurance facilities to the masses at reasonable cost.

(ii) To increase savings habits among the public.

(iii) To channelise the small savings towards industrial sector.

(iv) To maximise the benefits to the policy holders.

(v) To act as trustees of the policy holders.

(vi) To protect the policy holders individual and collective interests.

(vii) To introduce innovative schemes to meet the changing life insurance needs of the community.

(viii) To ensure efficient and courteous service to the insured public.

(ix) To provide job satisfaction to the employees.

A large number of insurance policies have been introduced by the LIC. The LIC has diversified its activities by establishing

(A) LIC Housing Finance Ltd.

(B) LIC Mutual Fund.

(C) LIC International.

(D) Jewan Bhima Sahayoga Asset Management.

LIC insurance policies make a very flexible financial instrument. The value of a policy is the present value of a lump sum or a future stream of income less than the value of future premiums. It offer various schemes, policies and plans to the investor. The following are various categories of the schemes which are offered by the LIC.

(a) Individual Insurance.

(b) Group Insurance.

(c) Group Gratuity.

(d) Group Superannuation.

(e) Non-medical insurance.

(f) Salary saving insurance.

(g) Annuities.

(h) Other Schemes.

The funds collected through the sale of various policies are invested in a variety of income generating financial assets. The fund will be built up out of the excess of premiums and investment income over claim and expenses. The life fund is evaluated from time to time. The valuation of life fund is being based on the method of discounting future income and expenditure. A life fund will be known as surplus when the value of fund is greater than the present value of future liabilities. This surplus amount will be distributed partially to all policy holders who are eligible according to the various schemes norms. The remaining surplus amount will be added to the reserve account. The LIC will distribute surplus to policy holders in three kinds (a) in the form of cash (b) as a reduction in premium (c) as an addition to the value of the policy. The LIC will distribute the surplus amount by adding the bonus to the value of policy, thus the policy is known as "Revisionary Bonus." The revisionary bonus will be calculated on the basis of original sum assured. The surplus can be categorised in two kinds (a) Revenue surplus (b) capital surplus. Revenue surplus means it is an excess of future income over future outgoings. Capital surplus means, it will be arised when the value of the fund is balanced by the values of the various assets of the life fund as recorded in the balance sheet.

The insurance policies are divided into life insurance and general insurance. The main features of the important life insurance policies are presented below.

(a) Whole life policy

(b) Endowment policy

(c) Joint life policy

(d) Annuities

(e) Sinking fund policies

(f) Janatha policy

(g) Limited payment life policy

(h) Double accident indemnity policy

(i) Convertible whole life policy

Whole life policy is the cheapest form of policy. The premium on this policy should be paid throughout the life of the assured person. The sum assured is payable only after the death of the person.

Endowment policy is the most popular form of life assurance. Under this policy, the insured amount is payable either at the end of a specified number of years or upon the death of the insured person which ever is earlier. The minimum amount for which a policy is issued under this plan is Rs. 1,000. This policy is useful for the marriage of children or for the education of children when they reach a certain age.

Joint life policy is suitable for partners firms. The policy money becomes payable either on maturity of the policy or the death of any of the persons jointly insured.

Annuities is suitable for self employed and petty businessman. The policy holder is required to pay the premium in regular instalments over a certain period or he may deposit a lump sum amount. After the assured reaches a certain age, the insurer pay back, the money by monthly, quarterly, half yearly or yearly instalments.

Sinking fund policies are more useful to the big business firms and companies. They make use of this policy for redemption of debentures, or replacement of assets or repayment of loans. The premium amount shall be paid by the companies annually. After the completion of the specified period the company gets the sum assured.

Janatha policy will be issued for a period of 10, 15 or 24 years with the condition that the policy should mature before the assured reaches 60 years of age. The policy can be taken by a person only before the age of 45. The amount of premium can be only Rs. 1,000. There is no need of formality of medical examination if the person's age is below the 3.5 years.

Limited payment life policy is similar to the whole life policy. Because the policy amount is payable only after the death of the assured. The premium amount shall be paid for a certain number of years or until the death of the person if it occurs within that period.

Double accident indemnity policy offer double amount of the policy to his survivors, if assured dies of an accident.

Convertible whole life policy facilitate the assured an option to convert the policy into an endowment policy. The rate of premium is low at initially. After sometime the assured persons have the right to convert into endowment policy.

New Jeevan Shree policy is an endowment policy with a term of minimum of 5 years and maximum of 25 years. The Jeevan Shree has undergone a sea change after it was scrapped from 31st Jan. and getting relaunched in the first week of March. With the era of guaranteed returns getting phase out, the new Jeevan Shree scheme has guaranteed additions pegged at Rs. 70 per thousand sum assured per annum at the end of each policy year again. The earlier Rs. 75 per thousand sum assured per annum. The provision for loyalty addition for policies, which were in force on the date of death or on maturity has also got scaled down and now no loyalty addition would be payable during the first four policy years. Loyalty addition is generally pegget at 5% of sum assured in the new version of Jeevan Shree.

Jeevan Surabhi is the scheme, where the premiums are payable for a limited period. It allows for a periodic increase in insurance cover basic, the free risk coverage ever during the non-premium paying period. It is available with premium payment terms of 12, 15 and 18 years, and policy terms of 15, 20 and 25 years and more back is allowed at intervals of 4 or 5 years as per the policy term.

The Money back policy with bonus 20 years, this policy provides a life cover during the term of the policy along with the maturity benefits paid in instalments by the way of survival benefits.

The Money back policy with 25 years besides providing life cover during the term of the policy, the maturity benefits are paid in instalments by way of survival benefits.

Bima Kiran is a low cost insurance policy to suit young men and women. The policy offers more privileges than other schemes. It cover risk and other attractive features are like "in-built accident" "loyalty addition" "free insurance cover after maturity". It is low cost scheme at an affordable level to enable to maximise the risk cover with a minimum amount., If the premium amounts are paid regularly the following benefits for basic sum assured of Rs. 1,000 are assured.

(a) death cover (b) accident benefit (c) on disability due to accident. On survival of the term, a minimum free cover (without accident benefit) is available for a period of 10 years at different situations.

Jeevan Kishore is a policy which provides gift to children for their secure future. Under this policy, parents or legal guardians can provide a gift to children. Children both male and female between the ages of 1 and 12 are eligible for this scheme. The risk commences either two years after the date of the commencement of the policy or after the completion of 7 years of age of the children whichever is later. However the date commencement of risk cannot in any case, go beyond the policy after the completion of 12 years of age. The policy is eligible for bonus from the waiting period also.

Children Money back policies are more useful for education, and career of children. Under this scheme, the childrens upto 10 years of age are eligible to be proposed for insurance by parents/guardians. The policy can also be gifted to the children by any person the risk commences two years from the date of the policy or from the policy immediately following the completion of 7 years of age whichever is later. In the event of death during the term of the policy before maturity assured sum becomes payable together with guaranteed addition. The policy issued only in multiples of Rs. 25,000 subject to minimum of Rs. 2,500 and maximum of Rs. 5.00 lakhs.

LIC's Investment Pattern: The Insurance Act, sec 27 laid down the investment pattern of the LIC, as follows

(a)	In Central government securities not less than	20%
(b)	In State government securities including central government securities	40%
(c)	Socially oriented sectors as indicated by GOI from time to time	50%

Forms of Financing The LIC facilitates funds to the corporate enterprises in the following kinds:

(a) Direct lending to industry.

(b) Subscription to shares and bonds of development financial institutions.

(c) Purchase of securities.

(B) General Insurance Corporation

The General Insurance Corporation was registered as a private company under the companies act 1956. It was formed as a government company under section 9 of the General Insurance (Nationalisation) Act 1972. It has four subsidiaries. The subsidiary companies have acquired considerable experience expertise and financial strength. They have established reasonable standards of conduct of business. The four subsidiary companies are:

(1) National Insurance Company, Kolkata.

(2) The New India Assurance Company, Mumbai.

(3) The Oriental Fire and Insurance Company, New Delhi.

(4) The United India Fire and General Insurance Company, Chennai.

The GIC share capital at present stands at Rs. 107.5 crore. There is a proposal to raise the capital to Rs. 200 crore. The Government of India had 50% of Share Capital and the remaining being held by public including employees. GIC holds 100% equity of its subsidiary companies. The each subsidiary company had a share capital of Rs. 40 crore. The capital of each subsidiary company should be raised to Rs. 100 crore with the central government holding 50% and the remaining proportion lies with the public and employees of the respective companies. There are at present 1124 divisional offices in the four subsidiaries throughout the country. The divisional offices supervises 3151 branches only. On an average one divisional office is looking for affairs of the three branch office. Therefore they are over staffed and need to reorganise their work in order to use the available manpower in an optimal manner. The financial authority of various branches should be reviewed in the light of the functions assigned to them.

The GIC was given charge of the overall control, superintendence and policy making for smooth operation of the general insurance business. At present the direct business is done mostly by the subsidiaries and of the GIC. The premium income of the GIC is obtained through the obligatory reinsurance premium on a sharing basis from its subsidiaries on their direct business. The GIC direct business is only in the form of aviation insurance. The general insurance business is classified as follows:

(a) Marine Insurance.

(b) Fire Insurance.

(c) Miscellaneous.

(a) Marine Insurance: Marine Insurance relates to Ships and Cargoes. A contract of marine insurance is a contract under which the insurer indemnified the insured against marine losses. The losses relates to marine adventure or to navigation or business as the sea. There are many types of policies available in India which are presented below:

(A) Voyage policy.

(B) Time policy.

(C) Mixed policy.

(D) Value policy.

(E) Floating policy.

Voyage policy is the most popular policy in marine insurance. It insures the subject "at and from" or from one place to another place. The first policy covers the subject matter both while the ship is at the port of departure and also from the time of the sailing of the ship. The next policy covers only when the ship sails from the port.

Time policy is framing the time limit for a subject matter. The subject matter is insured for a specified time not exceeding a year. Sometimes the policy period comes to an end while the ship is still away from its destination. The ship should be taken care of by a continuous clause.

Mixed policy is a combined policy of voyage and time. It covers the risk for a particular voyage to a specified period. For e.g. from Chennai to Singapore for 6 m

Valued policy specifies the accepted value of the subject matter.

Floating policy mentions the amount for which the policy is being taken out. All the particulars regarding ship, goods and destination will be specified later.

The GIC fulfils the needs of Industrial manufacturing, Commercial services, household and agricultural sectors through a wide range of Innovative products. The GIC also underwrites a very vast and diversified portfolio of general business. It has been promoting personal insurance cover in the field of livestock, poultry, horticulture, pumpsets pisiculture, sericulture and personal accidents. GIC has introduced innovative new policies like Mediclaim, Nuclear insurance pool, hut insurance, Householder's comprehensive policy, Professional Indemnity Insurance, Insurance for members of stock-exchange, etc.

(b) Fire Insurance: Fire Insurance means, it is a contract which insurer accepts in consideration of the prevention of the liability to pay the loss or damage caused by fire accident during the specified period. If in the case of loss, the assured party can claim from the company, the actual amount of loss or the maximum amount indicated in the contract, whichever is less. The following are the important fire insurance policies presented below:

(A) Floating policy.

(B) Replacement policy.

(C) Specific policy.

(D) Valued policy.

(E) Comprehensive policy.

Floating policy covers property which are lying at various locations against loss by fire. e.g., the goods placed in two godowns at various locations will be covered.

Replacement policy involves no repayment. The insurer only agrees to pay the cost of replacement of the property damaged or destroyed by the fire. It avoids the mischief made by the assured.

Specific policy covers the loss suffered by the assured. It is covered only upto a specific amount which is less than the real value of the property.

Valued policy covers to pay a fixed sum of money in respective of the amount of loss to the insured. Under this policy no profit can be made out of any loss.

Comprehensive policy covers losses arising from any type of risks such as fire, burglary, third party risks etc. It is known as all income policy. It covers loss of profit for the period during which the business are suspended due to fire occurrence.

Regulatory Framework: The GIC business is basically cyclic in nature and the investment policy of the GIC and its subsidiaries is defined in the insurance act, 1938. The Government of India has the powers to issue guidelines from time to time U/S 27 B of the insurance act, 1938 regulates the investment of the funds of the GIC and its subsidiaries. They are required to invest in the following manner.

(a) Approved securities.

(b) Approved investments.

The following financial instruments are categorised as approved securities by the insurance act 1938.

(1) Central/State government securities.

(2) Any securities guaranteed by either central or state government.

(3) Debentures or securities issued by local self government.

(4) Statutory company shares guaranteed by central/state government.

(5) Other securities (approved securities).

The following financial instruments are classified as approved investments by the act:

(1) FDRs with scheduled banks or Cooperative societies.

(2) Shares of any company which have been guaranteed by another company.

(3) Debentures issued by any Municipality.

(4) Debentures issued by a first charge on the assets of any company which have paid the interest in full or the preceding three years.

The Insurance Companies invest not more than 25% of their assets in other approved securities and investments with the consent of the board of director. The restrictions are:

(a) not to invest in the shares or debentures of a private company.

(b) not to invest in any one company more than 10% of the assets.

(c) 10% of the prescribed share capital and debentures of the company (2% in case of banking or investment company).

Objectives of the Investment Policy: The objectives of the insurance companies are presented below:

(a) to meet the needs of the national priorities.

(b) safety and security of the share capital.

(c) adequate liquidity.

(d) protection against inflation.

(e) providing better returns.

(f) marketability.

The deployment of funds in approved investments signifies the participation of GIC in national development and industrial growth. Some portion of the funds of the insurance companies have to be kept in fixed deposits. These financial instruments offer liquidity. The advantages of investment in equities are:

(a) participation in national priorities.

(b) capital appreciation.

(c) attractive net yields.

(d) protection against inflation.

(e) dividend income enjoys intercorporate tax relief.

The insurance companies also undertake the underwriting of the new issues of the existing or new companies. The process should be taken care for a maximisation of the investment income the following factors should be observed while making an investment decision.

(a) The nature of the industry.

(b) The potential growth of the industry.

(c) The history of the promotes.

(d) Gestation period of the project.

(e) Buy back period of the project.

(f) Locational advantage of the unit.

(g) Government policy.

(h) Financial feasibility of the project.

(i) Commercial viability.

The GIC and its subsidiaries invest in the following categories.

(A) The Government securities.

(B) Term loans to companies.

(C) Bill Rediscounting schemes.

(D) Others (loans to HUDCO/DDA/housing / PSUs).

It also provides financial assistance in the following ways:

(1) Direct assistance.

(2) Purposewise assistance.

(3) Sectorwise assistance.

The GIC provides financial assistance directly to the corporate sector. It finances industry by granting loans and by underwriting the shares. It has right to make direct subscription to the shares of the corporate sector.

It provides financial assistance on purpose wise basis. It renders assistance in four purposes. (1) for new projects (2) for diversification and expansion (3) for modernisation of the plant and rehabilitation (4), supplementary finance.

The GIC focus was on the financial no. of the concerns already assisted rather than going for new projects to improve its return on investment.

The GIC, is an investment institutions. Which tries to maximise its returns on investment. It provides maximum assistance to private sector. The private sector accounts for bulk of GIC's investment the share of public sector has shown wide variation the public sector is heavily funded by LIC and the private sector funded by GIC.

Malhotra Committee

As a part of reforms of the insurance sector, The Maharashtra committee has suggested a comprehensive framework covering the life and general insurance. The major elements of the recommended framework has been presented below.

(a) Insurance Intermediaries.

(b) Insurance surveyors.

(c) Product pricing.

(d) Investment issues.

(e) Restructuring.

(f) Liberalization.

(g) Rural insurance.

(h) Regulation.

(a) Insurance Intermediaries: The Malhotra committee has made the recommendations relating to the insurance intermediaries.

(a) It has been suggested that the marketing division of the insurance organisation should be thoroughly Reviewed in order to increase the marketing skills of the organisation.

(b) The development officers will play an important role in the insurance business. Therefore the role of development officers should be reviewed seriously.

(c) The development officers selection should be properly and they should be encouraged to take marketing related functions.

(d) For marketing of insurance products in rural areas a system of supervisory agents should developed. The supervisory agents. Should be posted in the villages on commission basis.

(e) The insurance organisation should concentrate on direct business without the intervention of the development officers.

(f) The insurance organisation must encourage professionalism among agents to become more competent.

(g) The system of brokers should be introduced by the insurance organisations to improve professionalism and customer service.

(h) There is a strong need to periodically review the service terms conditions and benefits of development office

(i) The incentive system should encompass the following any one incentive scheme should be followed.

   (1) Targeted portfolio as laid down by each branch

   (2) Quality of business should be judged

   (3) The amount of incentive should be reasonable

   (4) Growth of the business over the previous year of an order of 20% or Rs. 3,00,000 whicheven is lower.

(j) In backward areas the insurance policies can be sold through institutional agents such as: voluntary agencies with proven track record of social service and cooperative societies may be considered.

(b) Insurance Surveyors: The controller of Insurance has been conducting the examinations for granting the serveyorship. This system should be changed, because it has not served any useful purpose. The insurance companies should appoint a right surveyor to the right job. There is a strong need to set an institutional professional surveyors organisation the institution should be a self financed organisation the cost of establishment of the institution could be substantial and the insurance industry may provide financial and other promotional support. The Insurance industry may be represented on the governing body of the institution for the initial 5 to 7 years period. The institutions should have the overall responsibility regarding surveyor membership like code of conduct, unprofessional conduct of its members, disqualification from membership. The prospective surveyor should pass an examination to be conducted by the institution and thereafter to work as an apprentice for two years. The prospective survey or may be kept at the disposal of a senior surveyor. The Insurance companies should take some remedial actions to avoid malpractices and eventualities.

(c) Product Pricing: The LIC should publish a revised mortality table based on recent experience. The revisions should be made for every ten years. The insurance companies should provide intensive training to their workforce LIC should immediately review the system of product pricing. The renewal cost should be brought down. Therefore the insurance companies should improve the productivity of its employees and streamline its systems and procedure. The cost of production of a product share be reduced substantially by introducing computers in the organisation. Computerization of its entire range of operations is very crucial for controlling costs and improving customer service.

(d) Investment Issues: The premium amount collected by the insurance companies should invest judiciously with the combined objectivities of liquidity, maximisation of yield and safety. The insurance companies are required to generate reserves for claims that may arise in future. The return on investment from insurance funds will influence substantially on premium rates and bonuses. Therefore the insurers should maintain at all times, a prescribed minimum level of solvency as a protection to the policy holders interest. The investments of insurance fund is regulated. Investment of funds by insurance organisation are regulated in India under section 27(A) and 27(B). The Malhotra committee has recommended reductions in the extent of investments by insurance companies.

(e) Restructuring: There has been a tremendous changes in the insurance industry. A close observation reveals that the entire insurance industry must be restructured in order to meet the present situation. The restructure of the industry will definitely enhance the profitability. Therefore the following insurance institutions must be restructured to meet the market requirements.

(1) Life Insurance Industry.

(2) General Insurance.

(i) Life Insurance Industries: The life insurance industry has a vast scope for further growth of the business. According to the present situation, the entire branch operations must be revamped to meet the changing needs of the policy holders. The delegation of policy servicing responsibilities to the branches has been considerable to some extent but there is still dissatisfaction among policy holders. The delegation of authority and system of supervision are in adequate. The decision making power has slow down. The present structure of LIC does not provide sufficient assurance. In this situation the Malhotra committee has made a number of recommendations which are presented below. (a) The central office should basically work for a limited extent in order to make more effective efforts. The central office should concentrate on policy formulation, product development and pricing, personnel policies, accounts investments and systems development. The central office should be filled with highly specialised, dedicated competent personnel and professionalised. At present it has been over staffed. There should be structural changes in between zonal office and head office the committee further recommended that the delegation of financial, administrative and operational to the zonal offices should be made effectively. There should be completely restructure of the entire life insurance organisation.

(ii) General Insurance Corporation: The GIC has four subsidiary companies the subsidiaries have acquired considerable experience, expertise and financial strength established reasonable standard of conduct of business. The GIC structure should be revamped and its subsidiaries also be restructured. In a competitive environment the cost would be crucial to the success. Therefore these organisation need to reduce the cost of operating expenses substantially. There are at present 1124 divisional office to supervise 3151 branches. Therefore it is very clear that these organisations are overstaffed. It ultimately pushes the insurance product price the additional staff should be posted to branch offices to enhance the productivity per employee and reduce the cost of expenditure. Therefore the financial authority of various branches should be relieved in the changing circumstances the computerization is most important for GIC when the customer requires prompt service. All the four subsidiary companies must go for comprehensive computerization for handling the business at all levels. The provisions of the Insurance act 1938 should apply to GIC and the four subsidiary companies.

(f) Liberalization: According to the liberalization policy of the government, it is decided that the private sector may also invite to enter into the insurance segment. The entry of the private insurance companies have created a competition to the public sector institutions. The competition may offer lower prices to the policy holders. It creates efficiency and professionalism among employees. The work culture may be introduced among the workforce. It may tap the untapped new lines of business. Private insurance companies should be allowed. But mushrooming of small companies has to be avoided. No single company should be allowed to both life and general insurance business. The number of new entrants should be controlled. The rules must be rigid in case of new entrants. The minimum paid up capital should be Rs. 100 crores. But a lower amount of paid up capital may be fixed to the state level cooperative institutions which are taking up insurance business. The promoters quota should not exceed 40% of the total paid up capital. The Individuals should not be permitted to hold more than 1% of the equity. In the private insurance companies promoters should hold at all times not less than 26% of the paid up capital. The foreign companies should enter the insurance business with Indian partner as joint venture. In view of the entry of more players in the insurance business, the regulation of the industry must be strengthened. All the insurance companies must maintain adequate solvency at all times the investment norms must be followed by all insurance companies as laid down by the government from time to time. They should not invest in any affiliate of the promoters the new entrants in general insurance would have to observe the tariff regulations in force the following private sector organisations have been entered the insurance segment.

(1) ING Vyshya.
(2) Max New York life.
(3) Birla sun life.
(4) Tata AIG.
(5) ICICI prudential.
(6) SBI life insurance.
(7) HDFC standard life.
(8) OM Kotak.
(9) Alianz Bajaj.
(10) AIG.
(11) Royal Sundaram Alliance.

(g) Rural Insurance: This is the neglected segment of the insurance market. there is a strong news to concentrate in rural areas for spreading the non-traditional insurance business. For winding the network, when even possible to involve the panchayat samithis, cooperative societies and non-governmental organisation etc., in the insurance market. Special attention should be paid for self employed women. The new entrants may be required to undertake a specified proportion of their business as rural non-traditional business. Non-performance may be subjected to a penal assessment by the Insurance Regulatory Authority. The cooperative institutions may be encouraged to transact the general insurance business.

(h) Regulation: Insurance companies sell promise to indemnify the insured for a happening of specified events. Before the nationalization of LIC and GIC, they were regulated under the provisions of the Insurance act, 1938. The Insurance act was administered by the controller of Insurance.

Following the recommendations of the Malhothra committee, the government of India approved the setting up of the IRA. The Ministry of finance has the overall responsibility to regulate the insurance sector in place of the controller of Insurance. It has been assigned legal and comprehensive legislation work on the pattern of the SEBI.

Salient Features of Interim IRA

The Salient features of the interim IRA are presented below:

The IRA is headed by a chairman appointed by the government of India. The chairman was the status of an additional secretary to the central government. The chairman is the ex-officio controller of Insurance. He enjoys the powers on par with the COI. The maximum number of members in IRA are seven. From the members, three shall serve full time. They shall be nominated by the central government. The persons have experience and indepth knowledge in life insurance general insurance, finance, economic legal and other matters. The chairman and the members would hold office until the pleasure of central government. The rules and regulations may be determined by the government of India from time to time. The chairman would have appropriate powers to discharge the functions more effectively. The government would provide assistance for the smooth functioning of the IRA. The IRA is free to determine its own procedures. It has powers to call for records, returns, notes data or any other relevant material.

The government has the power to ask information on various aspects of insurance business. It is required to submit periodical reports to the government of India. The Government could assign additional Non-Statutory functions as may be considered necessary in order to promote and ensure the growth of the industry.

Insurance Regulatory and Development Authority Act, 1999 (IRDA): The IRDA was enacted in 1999 to protect the interests of the policy holders. It was enacted to regulate promote and ensure orderly growth of the insurance industry the IRA would consist of a chairperson and maximum number of members were 9. These members and chairman is to be appointed by the central government the five members of the team would be full time members. The members of the IRA shall have integrity, ability and standing with adequate knowledge, experience of life insurance, general insurance, acturial service, finance, law, accountancy, business administration etc.,

Powers and Functions: The powers and functions of the IRA are presented below:

(a) Licensing authority.

(b) Settlement machinery.

(c) Maintaining professional code of conduct.

(d) Statutory powers.

(e) Promoting and regulating the insurance organisations.

(f) Control and regulation of the terms, rates and conditions.

(g) Designing the books of accounts of the insurance industry.

(h) Supervising the functioning of tariff Advisory committee.

(i) Any other powers as may be assigned by the government.

(D) UNIT TRUST OF INDIA

Introduction

The objective of the Unit Trust is to stimulate and pool the savings of the middle and low income groups and to enable them to share the benefits and prosperity of the rapidly growing industrialisation of the nation. The UTI was set up in 1964 as a public sector financial institution by the government of India. The basic objective of the UTI is to encourage and mobilise savings of the community through the sale of units. It canalizes the savings into corporate investments with a view to maximizing yield and capital appreciation for achieving these objectives, the UTI is authorized to carry on and transact a number of business activities in the financial markets.

The initial capital of Rs. 5 crores is subscribed fully by the RBI, LIC, SBI scheduled banks and other financial institutions. The RBI, LIC and the SBI are not permitted to transfer their share capital to other institutions. The UTI was delinked from the RBI with effect from 1 2 1976. The RBI share capital was transferred to IDBI. Therefore the UTI became an associate institution of the IDBI. As per the Deepak Parekh committee recommendations, the UTI had mobilised additional permanent capital to the extent of Rs. 500 crores during the year 1999.

The UTI has empowered to carry on the following limited business activities.

(a) Sale and purchase of units as a saving instructions.

(b) Invest in securities.

(c) Deposit money with the banks.

(d) Propose and implement different types of schemes and financial plans.

The UTI act has amended in 1985 to expand its business activities and diversification to enable it to perform its basic objective more effectively. The UTI has been empowered in the following activities at present.

(a) Purchase and sale of units.

(b) Involving in the bills of exchange business segments.

(c) Grants loans and advances.

(d) Investment in the RBI issued securities or special papers.

(e) Formulation of unit schemes in collaboration with the insurance companies.

(f) Involving in immovable property transactions.

(g) Rendering financial and other assistance to any person for the acquisition of immovable property.

(h) Rendering Merchant banking and investment advisory services on fee basis.

(i) Portfolio management services to NRIs.

(j) Buy/sale of foreign exchange transactions.

(k) Entering into business as per the guidelines of the central government.

Management: The management of the business of the UTI is vested in the board of trustees. The board of trustees consists of eleven members. At present the chairman is appointed by the government of India in consultation with the IDBI. The executive trustee is appointed by the IDBI. The RBI has power to nominate one trustee and the other trustees are nominated by the IDBI.

The UTI's management pattern combines the trustees and management of the mutual fund. The custody of securities with well recognised parties for safety for the funds of the investors. The UTI constituted three AMCs in consultation with the SEBI. The AMCs were established to look after the business of US-64, equity schemes, and fixed income schemes respectively.

Tax benefits: UTI facilitates tax exceptions and concessions to its unit holders. The tax benefits are also available to the UTI itself. The UTI is exempted u/s 32 the UTI act, 1963 from the payment of taxes on its income, profit and capital gains. It is also exempted from any deduction of tax at some special benefits are offered to individuals residents and NRI. The unit holders enjoy a variety of tax benefits from their investments in units. The tax concessions to different categories of unit holders are available under the income tax act from time to time. The following exemptions are available to the unit holders.

(a) 80-L of the income tax act provides exemption to resident individuals.

(b) 88-ULIP – 20% of provident contribution rebate is available.

(c) Tax rebate is available to Equity linked savings scheme ELSS.

(d) U/S 194k from the assessment year 1995-96, a 20% deduction would be made for corporates and 15% for others.

(e) U/S 11 of the act, the income of charitable and religious trusts in any year is totally exempted from Income tax.

(f) u/s 19(21), investment by scientific research associations enjoy exemption from tax if the funds are invested in units.

(g) The tax rebate to mutual funds u/s 54 EB

(h) Investment in unit qualifies for total exemption from wealth tax both for resident and non resident individual companies.

SUMMARY

Financial institutions are the active players in the capital market. They involve in the mobilization of funds, in canalizing the savings towards the productive way they are classified into four categories, Regulatory, Intermediaries, Non-intermediaries, others. The financial institutions may further be classified as banking and Non banking. Banking institutions are based on service basis. They comprise of the commercial banks and cooperative banks. The non-banking institutions involve in the indirect finance of the corporate sector they actively participate in the capital market. The financial institutions are further classified as intermediaries and non intermediaries. All banking institutions belong to the intermediaries. All the Non-banking institutions acts as the Non-banking financial intermediaries.

The Central Bank plays an important role in the monetary and banking structure of nation. The RBI is the Central Bank of India. RBI has been occupying an important role in India financial system. The RBI is managed by a board of directors. The RBI has full authority in the aspects such as currency issuing authority, monitoring authority, banker to the union government foreign exchange control and promoting authority. The RBI treats the monetary policy as a weapon. The monetary policy is basically concerned with the regulation of money supply and interest rates.

Commercial banks are the fastest growing financial intermediaries. They provide various types of financial services to customers. They are the oldest institutions having a wide network of branches. The functions of banks are divided into primary agency and misl. The primary functions are accepting of deposits and advancing of loans. Agency functions involves many services to their customers. They act as trustees, administrators, attorneys of their customers. The misl. function will be performed by the banks to provide facilities to the customers. The evolution of Indian banking can be divided in three phases such as Ist phase (1951-64), second phase (1964-90) and IIIrd phase (1991 onwards). The banks can be categorised into various types on the basis of their ownership, functions and domiciles the various types of banks such as commercial banks, Industrial banks, Central bank, Scheduled banks, World bank. Agricultural bank, saving bank, public sector banks, private sector banks, Cooperative sector banks domestic banks foreign banks, Exchange banks, Non-schedules banks. The commercial banks have entered into Merchant banking segment through their subsidiaries. The banks provide factoring service to their customers. It is a highly specialised financial service. Venture capital is an innovative financial intermediary It provides risk capital, management and marketing expertise to highly risky and new private business. They involve in technology oriented business.

QUESTIONS

(1) "Financial Institutions are the nervous of Indian Economy". Comment it.

(2) Describe the organizational structure of the RBI and explain the functions of the RBI.

(3) What is bank rate Discuss its mechanism as a tool for credit control

(4) Discuss the Monetary policy of the RBI highlighting the new policy 2002-03 in the wake of financial liberalization.

(5) Discuss Salient features of commercial banking system in India.

(6) Discuss the courses for the low and declining profitability of commercial banks suggest measures to overcome them.

(7) Write an essay about Narasimhan committee Report I and II.

(8) Explain the different kinds of banks exists in India.

(9) What do you mean by credit card? Explain the uses of it ?

(10) Critically evaluate Insurance sector position in the era of financial liberalization.

❑ ❑ ❑

INDEX UNIT - III

FINANCIAL MARKETS

(A) Money Market : (B) Capital Market – (C) Primary Market – (D) Secondary Market

Issue Registrars to an Issue - Annexures.

D. Secondary Market: ***Introduction - Origin and Growth - Organisation of Stock Exchange - Listing of Securities - Group A Shares - Groups B Shares - Permitted Securities - Cleared Securities - Non-cleared Securities - Advantages of Listing - Trading on the Floor - Ready Delivery Contract - Forward Delivery Contract - Procedure for Dealing at Stock Exchanges - Finding a Good Broker - Placing Order - Making the Contract - Contract Note - Settlement - Type of Speculators - Bull Bear - Stag - Lame Duck - Advantages and Disadvantages of Speculation - Types of Speculative Deals - Manipulation - Rigging - Arbitrage - Kerb Deal - Cornering Wash Sales - Membership - Types of Operators - Jobbers - Brokers - Taraniwala - Budiwala - Arbitrageous - Odd Lot Dealers - Types of Orders - Net Rate Orders - Best Rate Orders - Limited Order - Stop Order - Market Rate Order - Discretionary Order - Matched Rate Order. Functions of Stock Exchanges - Stock Exchanges in India - Brokers - Indian Brokers - Foreign Brokers - Depository System - Introduction - Problems. Depositories Act - Bye Laws - SEBI Regulations - Recognition Certificate of Commencement of Business - Depository Participant - Rights of Depository - Rights of DP - Inspection Default - National Stock Exchange - Introduction - Objectives - Constitution - Wholesale Debt Market - Trading System in WDM - Settlement System in Debt Market - Capital Market Segment - Trading System in Capital Market Segment - Time Related Conditions - Price Conditions - Volume Conditions Settlement System in the Capital Market system - Institutional Market System - Bombay Stock Exchange - Introduction - Components of Sensex - OTC - Introduction.***

FINANCIAL MARKETS

The financial system of a nation works through four important elements. It refers to a set of institutional arrangement. The financial surpluses in the economy are mobilised from available surplus units and transferred to the deficit units. The important elements such as *Financial Markets, Financial Institutions, Financial services and Financial Instruments.* The financial system covers both cash and credit transactions.

Financial Assets are the claims to money and perform some functions of money. The financial assets is also known as *near money assets* They have high degree of liquidity. They are off two kinds (a). Direct assets (b) Indirect assets. Direct assets are known as primary assets The primary assets are the financial claims against real sector units. They are obligations of ultimate borrowers. Bills, Book Debts and equities are the examples of primary assets. These assets are created by the real sector units. They are issued to finance their deficit spending. Financial resource is the most important element for the smooth functioning of the corporate sector. ***Secondary assets*** are financial claims issued by the financial institutions. The FIs raise funds from the public to meet their requirements. These assets are the obligations of the financial institution. Bank deposits, LIC policies Units are the best examples of secondary assets.

Financial Markets deals with the various kinds of financial assets. Financial Markets create and allocate the credit. They play an important role in the mobilisation of savings. They are the intermediaries between lender and borrower. The economic development of a nation depends upon the capabilities of the financial market. They provide convenience and benefits to the lender and borrowers. They occupy a dominant role in the economic development of a nation. They allocate the funds to achieve the balanced regional and sectoral development. Financial markets are also known as ***credit markets.*** The credit markets cater to the credit needs of the institutions and individuals. The credit is required by both the individual and firms. The credit is meant for short and long terms. The financial market operates under perfect competition. The market will be perfect and most efficient. The ideal financial market requires the fulfillment of the following conditions.

(1) There are a large number of fund suppliers and borrowers operating in the market.

(2) The two parties in the market are rational.

(3) The two parties i.e. borrower and lenders compete for the achievements of their own interest.

(4) There are no transaction cost.

(5) There are no taxes.

(6) All the players in the market are well informed and the information is freely available to every one.

(7) The Government authority do not interfere in the working of the market.

(8) All the players in the market have same expectations.

In the perfect competition, the equilibrium in the financial markets are maintained by the demand and supply factors. The aggregate savings are the main determinant of the supply of funds. The sources of savings are ***household sector, business sector and government sector.*** The Volume of aggregate savings are influenced by the level of current income, expected income, fluctuations in income, distribution of income, degree of certainty income, amount of wealth, inflation, contingencies rate of interest etc. In addition to the above factors, another important factors is ***credit multiplier*** capacity of the banks. The development of banks and other financial institutions encourage and mobilise the savings from the community and they will deploy the fund in the market.

The demand for the funds comes from corporate sector, individual and Government. The demand for funds are investment demands. The demand for funds depends upon the many factors such as, the current level of capital stock, installed capacity utilisation, etc. These factors, are influenced by business expectations, price levels in the market, government policies, availability of funds, technological innovations, cost of funds, etc.

Efficiency

A financial market or credit market is said to be efficient when it satisfies the following.

(a) The prices of financial assets are determined by the natural forces of demand and supply of funds.

(b) Financial resources must be allocated in a proper way and in the most socially productive purposes.

(c) The market should operate at the least cost level.

(d) The market should not waste the use of resources.

There are different forms of efficiency of the financial markets which are presented below.

(a) Intrinsic valuation efficiency

(b) Rationalisation efficiency

(c) All locational efficiency

(d) Arbitrage efficiency

(e) Insurance efficiency

Intrinsic value refers to the real value of financial asset. The valuation of a financial asset is an important element in the financial market efficiency. The intrinsic value of an asset is the present value of the future stream of cash flow associated with the investment in that asset. If the market price of a financial asset is equal to its intrinsic value, then it meets the requirement of valuation efficiency. If the markets are more perfect then the valuation efficiency can be achieved.

Rationalisation efficiency refers to the operational efficiency. It can be achieved when the financial markets can minimise the administrative and transaction costs. It is possible when it provides maximum facilities and conveniences to the borrowers and lenders. The rationalisation efficiency reflects a fair return to the financial intermediaries for their valuable services. Rationalisation of all costs leads to the higher profitable position to the business community. It reduces the wasteful expenses while increasing the profitability of the business community.

The financial markets shall have allocational efficiency. They should be able to channalise their resource towards more profitable avenues. The earning is the efficiency of the market. It should allocate the resources where marginal efficiency of capital is the maximum.

Arbitrage means taking the advantage of price fluctuation in different markets at the same time. An intelligent investor can make gains by using commonly available information. If the financial market is said to be in efficient, there will be possible to gain from the use to commonly available information. If the markets are perfect such gains are not possible at all because the prices will reflect all the relevant and available information.

Insurance efficiency reflects the degree of hedging against future Uncertainties. In the perfect financial market there will be a chance to reduce the risk level of the investment.

The components of the financial market are presented below.[1]

(a) Call money market

(b) Treasury Bills market

(c) Commercial bills market

(d) Government Securities market

(e) Industrial securities market

(f) Foreign exchange market.

(g) Over the counter exchange market (OTC)

(h) Discount market

(i) Markets for Commercial paper

(j) Mortgage market

(k) Market for guarantees

(l) National Stock Exchange

(m) Derivatives market

(n) Bonds market

(o) Equities market

Financial markets are divided into two kinds.

(A) Money Market

(B) Capital Market

A. MONEY MARKET

Introduction

Money market is a market for short term credit. It refers to the institutional arrangements facilitating borrowing and lending of the short term funds. In a money market, the funds are available for a day, a week, three months, six months. These funds are available against different types of instruments such as banker's acceptances, bills of exchanges and short term securities. These all financial assets are known as "near money". The money market deals with assets of relative liquidity such as treasury bills, bills of exchange, and short term government securities.

1. I. L. M. Bhole, *Financial Institutions and Markets*, TMH, 1999.

Definition

The RBI describes the money market as "The centre for dealings, mainly of a short term character, in monetary assets; it meets the short term requirements of borrowers and provides liquidity or cash to the lenders".[2]

According to Crowther "The money market is the collective name given to the various firms and institutions that deal in the various grades of near money".[3]

Money market is like the commodity market. In money market the funds are available at a certain price. The funds are supplied by the lender and the funds are borrowed by the borrower. It refers to lending and borrowing activities of banking, financial institutions and individuals. It includes legal tender and near money. Commercial banks and Discount Houses deal in short term loans. It provides facilities for the adjustment of liquidity positions of commercial bankers. NBFIs corporate sectors and other investors. It also facilitates. The flow of funds to the most important uses in the economy. It provides funds to the finance Production and distribution. It promotes the economic growth of the Nation. It constitutes a highly efficient mechanism for credit control. The features of money market are presented below :

(1) Constituents.

(2) Dealers of money market.

(3) Near money asset.

(4) No need of personal contact.

(5) Short term funds.

(6) Heterogenous market.

(7) Fluctuations.

(8) Different from capital market.

(1) Constituents: Money market has three constituents such as (a) It has borrowers and lenders (b) It deals with short term credit instruments (c) It has a price in the form of rate of interest.

(2) Dealers of Money Market: Generally the markets are participated by lenders and borrowers. The borrowers in the money market are manufacturers traders, speculators and government institutions. Generally the lenders in the money market are commercial bank. Central bank and Non banking financial intermediaries.

(3) Near Money Asset: Money market deals in short term financial instruments which are called as "Near money asset". These assets are liquid and readily marketable. These assets are useful and against which the funds can be borrowed from the money market. These near money assets include bills of exchange, BRs, short term government securities.

(4) No Need of Personal Contact: Money market is not restricted to a particular place. It is a place where the borrowers and lenders meet each other. But in normal practice it is not necessary that the borrowers and lender should have personal contacts with each other at a specified place. The parties may carry on their deals through telephone or mail. Therefore the money market relates to arrangement for transfer of funds between lender and borrowers.

(5) Short Term Funds: Money market provides fund to the needy party for short term period. The borrowers can obtain funds for periods ranging from a day to six months.

(6) Heterogenous Market: The money market consists of several sub markets. Each market deals with a specified short term credit instrument forex, bills market, call money market.

---

2. Mithani and Gordon, *Banking and Financial System*, Himalaya Publishing House, 2002.
3. *Ibid*, p. 228.

(7) Fluctuations: Money markets change with time. The functions of money markets in different countries are broadly the same. But the financial institutions and the instruments vary considerably from country to country.

(8) Different from Capital Market: Money market is a market for short term credit and capital market is a long term market. It is different on the basis of maturity period. Money market deals with short term lending and borrowing of funds. The capital market deals with long term borrowing and lending of funds.

Functions and Importance of Money Market

Money market plays an important role in the process of industrial and commercial progress the nation. A well developed money market is essential for a modern digital economy. Money Market has important role to play in the economic development of a nation. The importance of a developed money market and its various functions are presented below:

(a) Financing Trade and Industry

(b) Profitable venture

(c) Help to Central bank

(d) Help to Government

(e) Capital formation.

(a) Financial Trade and Industry: Money market provides fund to the commercial enterprises on short term basis. It plays a crucial role in financing both domestic and international trade. Short term funds are available to the traders through bills of exchange. The bills are discounted by the bill market. In International trade the activities are carried out by the ***acceptance house.*** The money market also finances the industry by various methods. It contributes to the growth of the corporate sector. It helps the industries through the system of bills and commercial paper. It arranges loans to meet the working capital requirements of the industry. The working capital is more useful to the smooth functioning of the production schedule of the industry. The long term requirement of the fund will be supplied by the ***Capital market*** to the industry. But the capital market depends upon the nature of the money market. The interest rates of the money market influence the capital market. Therefore the money market indirectly helps the industries. Hence the short term requirements of the industrial sector may be fulfilled by the money market.

(b) Profitable Venture: The commercial banks play an important role in the money market. Generally the commercial banks function is accepting deposits from the public and advancing the loans to the borrowers. Sometimes the banks will have some idle funds at their disposal. Therefore the banks will earn profit by deploying the surplus fund into the money market. Hence the main objective of the commercial banks can be achieved. The money market provides liquidity to the investment made by the banks. Usually the excess reserves of banks are invested in near money assets. The near money assets are highly liquid and can be easily converted into cash. The commercial banks can reduce the loss by participating in money market. The money market provides a short term assignment to the commercial banks. The money market is a best place when the banks need funds in emergency. If the commercial banks have scarcity of funds they need not to approach the central bank at higher interest rate. The banks can meet their requirements by recalling their investments from the money market. Therefore the money market creates an opportunity for income generation to the commercial banks. The banks also become self sufficient with the help of the money market. The commercial banks can take the advantages of the money market according to their routine requirements.

(c) Help to Central Bank: The Central bank is the supreme authority in the banking system. The Central bank plays an important role in the economy of a nation. The existence of a developed money market smoothens the functioning of the Central bank. The money market increases the efficiency of the Central bank. The money market helps the Central bank in two methods.

(a) The indication of short run rates of interest of the money market will reflect the monetary and banking conditions in the country. This situation will guide the Central bank to adopt an appropriate banking policy.

(b) The money markets are highly sensitive and integrated, they help the Central bank to secure quick and wide spread influence on the sub markets.

(d) Helps to Government: The money market helps the government. It provides the short term funds at low cost to the government through treasury bills. The government has the borrowing capacity from other modes, which are inflationary nature. The money market helps the government in floating long term loans. The changes in the short term interest rates of the money market influence the interest rates on long term capital.

(e) Capital Formation: The money market plays a vital role in accelerating the process of capital formation. The money market tends to establish equilibrium between saving and investment. The development of the money market leads to the development of the capital market. The capital market provides a strong base for the long term nature of investments. The development of the capital market reflects the overall economy position of a nation. The capital market will be flooded with the new issues of equity. The primary market has the only one to accelerate the growth of capital formation. The New issue market depends upon the number of factors.

Characteristics of Money Market

The characteristics of the money market are presented below.

(a) In this market the short term funds are borrowed and lent.

(b) In this market the parties mutually agree on the terms and conditions of the exchange of funds.

(c) The interest rate is determined on the basis of demand and supply of money.

(d) The fund suppliers in the market are commercial banks and financial institutions.

(e) The borrowers in this markets are government, commercial banks, manufacturing concerns and firms.

Characteristics of Developed Fund Undeveloped Money Market

A strong money market is an indication to the growth of the economy. The money market influences the capital market. Ultimately the capital market accelerates the growth of the economy. Therefore the money market is the basic element for all other markets. The money market is more sensitive and integrated. The development of money market refers to a better organised and systematic market. The developed money market has greater responsibilities to change the demand and supply of short term funds in all of its segments. The extent of development of a money market is associated with the level of degree of economic development of a nation. The examples for developed money markets are ***UK and USA.*** The underdeveloped or developing countries are the examples of Underdeveloped money market. ***India*** is the best example for undeveloped money market. The following characteristics persist in the developed money market. If any of the following characteristics are not present the money market will be treated as underdeveloped.

(1) Participation of Central bank.

(2) Strong banking system.

(3) Availability of financial instruments.

(4) Active sub-markets.

(5) Structure of the market.

(6) Adequate Resources.

(7) Faith in the money market.

(1) Participation of Central Bank: A market is said to be a developed market when the Central bank involves fully which functions as monetary and banking authority in the country. The Central bank's presence is necessary to guide, control and regulate the money market. It is an essential pre-requisite for a developed money market. A powerful Central bank guides all the affairs of the money market. The ***monetary policy*** of the government will be prepared and implemented by the Central bank of the concerned nation. The Central bank formulates a suitable monetary policy to meet the needs of the money market. The Central bank assist the banking system to flourish and maintain the economic stability in the country. It enables the money market to secure adequate funds through open market operations. An efficient and experienced Central bank can properly guide, control and lead the money market towards better achievement. The Central bank is the lender of the last resort. It keeps the cash reserves of the banks and provides funds in times of emergency by granting them funds through rediscounting the eligible securities. In undeveloped money market the Central bank is unable to take effective steps to influence the money market.

(2) Strong Banking System: A developed market only exist when there is a strong infrastructural banking system in the country. However the citizens should also have the banking habits. The commercial banks are the ***oxygen*** to the developed money market. They are the basic suppliers of Short term funds. Therefore the functioning of the commercial banks will have its effect on the money market. The Commercial banks serve as a connecting link between the Central bank and various sectors of the money market. The origin of the money market is closely associated with the banking system. It the more development occur in the banking sector. The more will be the development in the money market. If the Central bank closely associates with the money market it will be easy to became a developed money market. If the commercial banks are efficiently organised. The various compartments related with them will be strongly organised. A highly organised system will enhance the level of the money market capabilities. Therefore the development of the money market is closely associated and reflected by the structure of the banking system. Any policy regarding the financing pattern of the Commercial banks have direct impact on the money market. In the underdeveloped money markets the number of developed Commercial banks are very less and their business are restricted to the urban areas the citizens of the undeveloped countries have not fully developed the banking habits.

(3) Availability of Financial Instruments: A strong money market demands a regular and adequate supply of a variety of financial instruments. The financial instruments in the money market are bills of Exchange, treasury bills. short term government bonds etc. The developed money market consist of adequate number of dealers and brokers. They actively involve in the money market. They buy and sell these assets. An underdeveloped market consists of inadequate dealers and brokers. The various types of financial instruments are not available in the undeveloped market. The various forms of securities should be available to every segment of money market in developed markets. This is possible only when the experienced dealers with such securities.

(4) Active Sub-markets: Developed money market consists of well organised sub-markets. Each and every sub-market has specialised in a particular type of financial asset. ***Forex:*** The New York money market has Commercial paper market, certificate of deposit market, treasury bills market, banker's acceptance market. Federal fund market specialised in repurchase agreement market. The money market can flourish and develop only when the sub-markets are fully developed and are associated with each other. If the sub-markets are not developed and are not coordinating to each other, the money market may not develop with full swing.

(5) Structure of the Market: The developed money market has an integrated structure. The sub-market are very closely associated with each other. The information and funds move easily and quickly from one market to another market. There will be free movement of borrowers and lenders from one segment to another. In developed money market, all the sub-markets are highly sensitive. They influence each other in all the segments of the money market. There is no inter relation between segments of the sub-markets of the undeveloped money market. There is no co-ordination between sub-markets in the undeveloped money markets.

(6) Adequate Resources: In developed markets the sub-markets have adequate resources. The undeveloped money market in unable to mobilise the required funds. If the money market is able to attract foreign funds it will be developed money market. ***New york and London money market*** are the examples of developed markets.

(7) Faith on the Capital Market: The money market can develop only with the faith in it. The dishonesty and malpractices may spoil the foundation of the money market. The political condition, viable economic growth absence of discrimination cause the up serving of the money market.

(8) Importance of Developed Money Market: The money market plays an important role in the economic development of a nation. The importance of the developed money markets are presented below:

(a) Large amount of lending.

(b) Trade and Industry.

(c) Cyclical fluctuations.

(d) Service to Government.

(a) Large amount of lending: The money market consists of borrowers and lenders. They play an important role in a developed money market. A large amount of borrowing is possible. Crores of Rupees are transferred from lender to the borrowers. The commercial banks are main suppliers of the fund. The whole economy could get a large amount of funds for development. The scarcity of funds is removed quickly. Because the commercial banks can fill the gap in shortage of funds in the money market. The banks can provide huge funds without reducing their liquidity. The money market is a suitable place for banks to **park** their idle fund in the market. The investment in financial instruments of the money market can earn certain income on the near liquid assets. The banks are able to get back the money income immediately at a short notice. The money market is useful to all the players such as Commercial banks, Financial institutions, manufacturing concerns and society.

(b) Trade and industry: The money market can provide financial assistance to trade and industry. The business concerns get their short term requirements from money market. The money market provides working capital to the corporate sector. The Individuals businessmen are mostly benefited by the acceptance house and discount house. The traders can easily get money from the bills market. The bill market is a part of money market. The discount houses or acceptance houses can discount the bills which are issued by the traders. Business men and producers get adequate funds for their purposes through the money market. The commercial banks also can benefit from the money market. Because they lend the money whenever they have surplus funds and they can procure the funds in case of scarcity of their funds. The global markets developed due to the money market.

(c) Cyclical fluctuations: The developed money market can reduce the cyclical fluctuations. The money market is highly sensitive and mechanised. The Central bank has the authority to control the economy through money market operations. The government can inject new credit to the economy in depression and siphon it off in boom. The Central bank is the supreme authority in the monetary aspects. It can control the credit through quantitative and qualitative measures. It can reduce considerably the dangerous effects of depression and crisis. The controller of the money market is ***Central bank.*** It can diffuse the effects of the cyclical fluctuations which are raised in the normal economy. These effects are possible only in a developed money market. The performance of the money market is the barometer of monetary and banking conditions in the country.

(d) ***Service to Government:*** The developed money market can service the government in every monetary aspect. The development of the economy can considerably be materialised by the government. The government can easily mobilise the funds by issuing treasury bills. The treasury bills are the most important financial instruments in the money market operations. The treasury bills can reduce additional pressure on the inflation. Because in the absence of treasury bills the government shall print the currency notes which causes the inflationary pressure on the economy.

Indian Money Market

The Financial markets are the combination of money market and capital market. Money market refers to short term finance. It deals with relatively liquid and quickly marketable assets. The money deals with the financial instruments such as ***Treasury bills, Government securities, Bills of exchange*** etc. The money market in India consists of two sectors.

(A) Organised sector.

(B) Unorganised sector.

(A) Organised Sector

The Indian Money Market originated after the establishment of the RBI in 1935. The organised sector comprises the RBI, SBI with its 7 associates, 20 nationalised banks, scheduled banks, Non-scheduled commercial banks, foreign banks and RRBs. The RBI is the apex body of the money market. The biggest lender of the money market is the RBI, which controls the entire banking sector in India. All these organisations involve in money market, which are controlled and guided by the RBI. Therefore the sector is known as ***organised sector*** of the money market. It is called organised because its parts are coordinated by the RBI. The other institutions also involve in this sector. They are LIC, GIC, UTI operate in this market indirectly. The large companies and quasi government organisations also make their surplus funds available to the organised sector through banks. The cooperative institutions also participate in the organised sector of the money market. The organised sector of Indian Money market can be further classified in the following.

1. Call Money market.
2. Treasury bill market.
3. Commercial bill market.
4. Certificate of deposits.
5. Commercial paper markets.
6. Collateral Loan market.

1. CALL MONEY MARKET

Call money deals in call loans or call money granted for one day. The important component of organised money market is the call money market. The participants in the call money market are mostly banks. It is also known as interbank call money market. The suppliers of the fund in the call money market is the banks and demand comes from the banks also. Call money market is the part of national money market. The day to day surplus funds of banks are traded in the call money market. The call money market is a short term nature. The maturity of the call market varies between one day to a ***fortnight.*** The loans of the call market are repayable on demand and at the option of either the lender or the borrower. They are highly liquid. The nature of this market in different countries varies from each other. The nature of the call market in the U.S and U.K as per their acts and regulations. Call loans and short notice in the balance sheets of banks is a highly liquid asset. They are unsecured in India. The money and credit situation in India every year is subject to seasonal fluctuations. The trading on the call market is influenced by seasonal fluctuations. The seasonal ups and downs are reflected in the volume of money at call and short notice and the rates are at different times of the year. The call money borrowings are highest around March every year. Because the withdrawals of deposits in March to meet year end tax payment. The financial institutions also withdraw the money to meet their statutory obligations. If the banks CRR increases, automatically there will be increase in call money borrowings.

Participants: The important players in the call money market are scheduled commercial banks, non-scheduled banks, foreign banks, Urban banks, Cooperative banks, Discount and Finance House of India, and securities Trading Corporation of India. The DFHI and STC borrow as well as lend like banks and primary dealers in the call market. The foreign banks borrow money from this market due to difficulties in tappings deposits and increase in the cost of servicing FCNR deposits. The large commercial banks have been regularly participating in this market excluding SBI. The SBI kept itself away from the call market till 1970. During 1970s a new development arised in the market that the direct participation in it by the term lending institutions like G, C, UTI and LIC. The indirect participation by other institutions such as IDBI, IFCI and ICICI. The continuous participation in the call market by the players would help to integrate the long term and short term money markets in the economy.

Geographical Location: Call markets are located in commercial centres like ***Mumbai, Kolkata, Chennai, Delhi and Ahmedabad.*** The stock exchanges are also located in these cities. Mumbai and Kolkata dominate call market in India. ***Mumbai*** is the financial capital of India and the head offices of RBI, LIC and UTI are located there. It also has the biggest stock exchange in Asia. The development of IT has facilitated for the flow of funds. The call rates are prevailing in different centres in different rates. There are a large number of local call markets developed and marketed by indigenous local bankers. **For e.g.:** in Gujarat the large payments or remittances are made, the local banks charge the price of overnight money is ***02 paise*** per hundred rupees per night.

Turnover of the Call Market: The turnover of the call market in India has been smaller than that of the US and UK. Because the bill market in India is underdeveloped. The call loans to bill market cannot be available. The volume of call loans depends upon the extent of trading in bills of exchange, treasury bills etc. The banks in India are not willing to offer loans to brokers and dealers in bills and securities. The another important factor is that the commercial banks can rediscount their bills from the RBI as a result of which they have much less interested towards the loans from the money market. The commercial banks holds fairly large cash reserves. Therefore there is no need to get the funds from the call market. The other factor is that the Government securities are directly sold by the RBI without much intervention by brokers and dealers. The turnover in securities traded on the stock exchanges is also relatively small. There is no scope in our financial system to extend support to the stock-Exchanges by the banks. So many regulations have been imposed by the RBI on banks in respect of loans against shares. Hence the trading activity on stock exchanges are carried out by the members using their own funds. Therefore the turnover in stock exchange has been derived by the members from private sources. There are fluctuations in the volume of demand and for supply of call loan due to various factors. The following are the causes for volatility of call market.

(1) The financial resources in the banking system depends on the extent, of deposits accruals.

(2) Any increase in deposits with banks, needs to explore possibilities of investment overseas.

(3) The bank resources flow to call market which in some of overseas for investment would increase.

(4) All the banks accrue deposits, then there will be an increase in volume of Inter bank call loan transactions.

(5) In a case such as the supply of funds to the outside of the banking system borrowers would increase.

(6) The differential growth in the deposits of different banks would lead to increase in volume of Inter bank call loans market.

(7) The demand for call loans would depend upon the stock market situation, Industrial sector needs and commercial requirements.

(8) The turnover of call market is determined by the possibility of quick investment or liquid assets.

(9) The opening of subscriptions to government loans would lead to increase for the demand to call loans.

(10) Usually the demand for call money tends to broaden in December, March, June.

(11) The velocity of the remittance and clearance system in the country leads to show an impact on the day to day volume of call loans.

(12) The policies of the RBI leads to show an impact as the volume of call market.

(13) The pressure on call money market reaches a peak towards the end of banking week. i.e. Friday.

(14) The foreign exchange market activity becomes a significant factor in the turnover of call market.

The annual statement of monetary and credit policy released on April 19, 2001 projected a GDP growth of ***6% to 6.5%*** for 2000-01 These projections are based on the assumptions of a reasonable monsoon, good performance of exports and a revival of the industrial sector. The annual policy statement also indicated that under normal circumstances and baring emergence of any adverse and unexpected developments in domestic or external sectors. The overall stance of monetary policy for 2001-02 will be as follows regarding call market.

(a) The average call money rate came down sharply from ***8.6%*** in early April to *7%* in mid Oct. 2001. During this period, The repo rate also came down from ***7%*** to *6.5%*

(b) The call market with average daily gross lending improved to Rs. 19,000 crore during May-September 01 from ***Rs. 10,900 crores*** during the corresponding period of the previous year. Therefore the Central bank feels that planned phasing out of non-banking participants from the call market has not caused any strain on the market.

STATEMENT SHOWING THE AVERAGE DAILY TURNOVER IN CALL MONEY MARKET

Fortnight ended	*Turnover per day (Rs. in crores)*	*Fortnight ended*	*Turnover per day (Rs. in crores)*
May 5, 2000	48,056	Dec. 1, 2000	47,310
May 19, 2000	39,214	Dec. 15, 2000	46,747
June 2, 2000	40,056	Dec. 29, 2000	43,568
June 16, 2000	38,300	Jan. 12, 2001	50,396
June 30, 2000	38,357	Jan. 26, 2001	49,039
July 14, 2000	42,465	Feb. 9, 2001	50,675
July 28, 2000	39 797	Feb. 23, 2001	45,987
Aug. 11, 2000	39,275	March 9, 2001	51,550
Aug. 25, 2000	35,973	March 23, 2001	50,314
Sept. 8, 2000	41,797	April 6, 2001	44,630

Sept. 22, 2000	42,933	April 20, 2001	50,957
Oct. 6, 2000	44,635	May 4, 2001	48.008
Oct. 20, 2000	45,776	May 18, 2001	41,935
Nov. 30, 2000	47,321	June 1, 2001	46,156
Nov. 17, 2000	46,805	June 15, 2001	44,790

Sources: RBI bulletin, Oct. 2001, p. S-997.

Call Rates: The call rate means, the rate of interest which will be paid on call loans. The call rates in the market are highly volatile from day to day and sometimes even from hour to hour. The rates vary from one market to another markets also. The call rates are very sensitive to changes in any demand and supply of call loans. The call rates in India are generally determined by the market forces till 1973. But in May 1973 the policy of credit squeeze introduced by the RBI leads to control the call market rates. According to the policy the RBI tightened the refinance and rediscount facilities, then the call rates have been reacts as high a level as 30% immediately. Therefore the banks defaulted in a major way in respect of cash and liquidity requirements at that time due to high cost of call money. Then it become necessary to monitor and regulate call rates within reasonable limits. Hence the Indian Banks Association fixed a ceiling of *15%* in 1973. This confirmation has no legal sanction. The IBA further reduced this ceiling to *12.5%* in March 1976. Again the IBA modified the ceiling rate *10%* in June 1977, and *8.6%* in March 1978 and *10%* in April 1980. The actual call rate level in India since 1973 had remained within the ceiling fixed by the IBA. The ceiling rates became a hurdle to many large banks. Afterwards the call rate was freed in two stages. In Oct. 88, the operations of the Discount and Finance House of India were exempted from the ceiling. From May 89 the ceilings on the call rate were withdrawn. The inter bank term money rates were also withdrawn. The 1989 onward the call rate has been frees. The call rates were determined by the market forces. In India there are now *two call rates*, one the inter bank call rate and the other DFHI lending rate. In India the call rates usually highest in Kolkata and lowest in Mumbai. In Kolkata market, there will be relatively higher demand for funds than supply in the call market. The supply of funds in call market is greater in Mumbai market due to the location of various head offices of the different financial and non-financial institutions. The demand in Kolkata, there is greater business than Mumbai. The large number of organisations concentrated in Kolkata like Jute, tea, coal absorbs a large amount of finance. Therefore usually the funds will flow from Mumbai to Kolkata. The extreme fluctuation in the call market is based on the following factors.

(1) The mechanism of CRR makes fluctuation in call market.

(2) The credit operations of some banks tend to fluctuate the market.

(3) Any disruption in the banking industry may lead to change the call market.

(4) On 31st March, most of the large business concerns withdraw the money from the banks to pay the advance tax. This volatiles the call market.

(5) The liquidity and illiquidity crisis in money markets may show an impact on call market.

(6) The mis-match between assets and liabilities of the commercial banks leads to volatility in the market.

(7) The change in Forex market also leads to volatility in the call market.

(8) The window dressing of the banks may also lead to volatility.

The present call rates are presented at the following pages.

DAILY CALL MONEY RATES FROM 1-08-2001 TO 12-08-03

As on	*Range of Borrowings*	*Rates of Lending*	*Weighted Borrowings*	*Average Rate Lending*
August 1	5.47-7.10	4.92-7.50	6.90	6.92
August 2	5.89-7.10	4.89-7.40	6.86	6.88
August 3	5.85-7.10	4.85-7.00	6.92	6.87
August 4	6.15-7.05	5.39-7.05	6.82	6.96
August 6	5.80-7.05	4.80-7.10	6.78	6.80
August 7	5.45-7.20	4.90-7.10	6.88	6.89
August 8	5.70-7.65	5.10-7.90	7.11	7.12
August 9	5.75-7.60	5.20-7.60	7.18	7.26
August 10	5.94-7.50	6.25-7.50	6.93	6.97
August 11	5.90-7.25	5.54-7.25	6.97	6.97
August 13	5.21-7.25	4.97-7.90	6.92	6.99
August 14	6.00-8.30	5.11-8.30	7.05	7.06
August 16	5.59-7.30	5.09-7.30	7.04	7.08
August 17	5.55-7.30	5.03-7.30	7.02	7.01
August 18	5.96-7.15	6.50-7.25	6.97	7.00
August 20	5.59-7.34	5.06-7.90	7.04	7.04
August 23	5.61-7.25	5.06-7.25	7.04	7.08
August 24	6.00-7.50	5.75-7.25	7.04	7.05
August 25	6.86-7.20	5.42-7.80	6.86	6.88
August 27	5.85-7.05	4.85-7.05	6.84	6.85
August 28	5.30-7.30	4.75-7.10	6.74	6.75
August 29	5.26-7.30	4.75-7.80	6.73	6.78
August 30	5.44-7.40	4.89-7.10	6.90	6.93
August 31	5.53-7.55	4.96-7.55	6.95	6.98
September 01	5.92-7.10	6.10-7.15	6.91	6.92
September 03	5.45-7.45	4.90-7.50	6.89	6.91
September 04	5.85-7.00	6.00-7.15	6.85	6.86
September 05	5.43-7.25	4.89-7.25	6.98	6.90
September 07	6.00-7.95	5.89-7.95	7.14	7.17
September 08	6.08-7.40	6.60-7.40	7.08	7.08
September 10	6.05-7.75	5.05-7.75	7.02	7.15
September 11	6.10-7.80	5.10-7.50	7.06	7.06

Sources : RBI bulletin, Oct. 2001, p. S-996.

2. TREASURY BILLS MARKET

Introduction

Treasury bills are the main financial instruments of money market. These bills are issued by the government. The borrowings of the government are monitored and controlled by the central bank. The bills are issued by the RBI on behalf of the central government. The RBI is the agent of Union Government. They are issued by tender or tap. The bills were sold to the public by tender method upto 1965. These bills were put at weekly auctions. A treasury bill is a particular kind of finance bill. It is a promissory note issued by the government. Until 1950 these bills were also issued by the state governments.

After 1950 onwards the central government has the authority to issue such bills. These bills are greater liquidity than any other kind of bills. The treasury bills are highly liquid because these bills are guaranteed by the central government. The RBI is always willing to purchase or discount them. These bills are claims against the government. They do not require any endorsement or acceptance. These bills are issued to meet the short term financial requirements of the central government. These bills have become a permanent source of funds to the government. Every year the central bank, a portion of bills are converted into long term bonds. These bills are of two kinds a) ad hoc, b) regular. Ad hoc treasury bills are issued to the state governments, semi-government departments and foreign Central banks. They are not marketable. The ad hoc bills are not sold to the banks and public.

The Regular Treasury bills are sold to the general public and banks. They are freely marketable. These bills are sold by the RBI on behalf of the Central government. The treasury bill market in India is underdeveloped. The treasury bills markets are well developed in USA and UK. In the developed market these bills occupy a key role in their economy.

The Ad hoc treasury bills were introduced in India in 1937. The government and RBI made an agreement in 1937 and 1955 between them for functioning of the treasury bills market in India. According to their agreement, the central government shall maintain with the RBI a cash balance of not less than Rs. 50 crores on Friday and Rs. 4 crores on other days. It involves free of obligation to pay interest there on and if the balance falls below these minimum levels the government account may be replenished by the creation of ad hocs in favour of the RBI. These bills are financed by the created money. But these bills are quickly replaced by borrowing against dated securities from the market. The ad hoc treasury bills became permanent sources of many for the government. These bills reduce the currency circulation in the market. These bills provide an opportunity to the state governments semi government to invest their surplus funds. These organisations helped to eliminate undesirable fluctuations in the discount rate at the treasury bills market. The ad hoc bills became the vehicle for automatic monetisation of the budget deficit. The government and RBI entered into an agreement on Sept. 9, 1994 to phase out the system of ad hoc bills.

The treasury bills are issued by the RBI on behalf of the central government at a discount. The RBI is the agent of central government. I will look after all the needs of the banking activities for the central government. The treasury bills are not a source of financing budget deficit. It is a mechanism to cover day to day mismatches in receipts and payments of the central government. It implies periodic vocation of advances made and not their accumulation year after year. The RBI introduced a system of ways and means. Advances with effect from 1-4-97 to adjust temporary mismatches in receipts and payments of the central government. The interest rate on WMA and the limit will be mutually agreed upon by the government and RBI. There is not much difference between the ad hoc treasury bills and WMA. The ad hoc treasury bills became a source of fund. The WMA became a source of funds to the state governments also. The treasury bills are sold to the public by tender or at weekly auctions. The issue of treasury bills will be announced in a press communique and tenders which quoted the lowest discount rate would be accepted. If any remaining portion was available, it was allotted to other tenders.

There were no restrictions on the class of tender. Every tender will be called for a minimum amount of Rs. 25000 or a multiple of that amount. Until 1965 these were known as intermediate treasury bills. These bills had a maturity period of 91 days and were sold at rates fixed by the RBI. With effect from 12-7-65 the treasury bills were available on tap throughout the week at rates announced from time to time accordingly. This system of selling treasury bills facilitated investment in them by the commercial banks as and when their resources increased. The ad hoc bills are issued in favour of the RBI only. The ad hoc bills not sold through the tender system. These bills purchased by the RBI on tap and are kept in its issue department the RBI may issue currency notes against these bills. These bills are nationally discharged and renewed on maturity. The government raised the funds through ad hoc bills are a short term nature but these bills well be renewed from time to time. But in practice these bills are to be treated as long term finance. These bills can be compared with the cash credit and overdraft system followed by the commercial banks at the private sector.

The treasury bills are issued in the form of promissory note. The bills can be purchased by any business concern. From August 1994. The state Governments, State pension fund, eligible provident funds have been allowed to participate in caution on a non-competitive basis. Therefore they are not allowed to bid, they should apply to the RBI and pay at the cut off rate decided by the RBI. The amount of participation may also be decided by the RBI. These parties cannot be availary rediscounting facility with the RBI for this treasury bills. There are no limits on individual bids subject to notified amount. These bills are useful as eligible security for the purpose of SLR in case of banks. Any shortfall in bids in relation to notified amount is taken up by the RBI. These bills have no automatic rediscounting facility. But the RBI may provide limited rediscounting facility to the holders of these bills.

The turnover of the treasury bills market caused changes that have occurred in it over the period. The volume of treasury bills sold every year and the amount of outstanding at the end of each year. The treasury bills market in India is limited and narrow. But this market is active in UK. In UK the banks deal in this market because they can buy or sell them to discount houses for settling their adjustments. The volume of transactions between banks and discount houses have been large the banks prefer to approach the discount houses rather than their Central bank. The discount houses themselves also involves in this market. They have ample opportunities for business in treasury bills. the discount houses also hold treasury bills because they can offer them as security for getting call loans from banks. In India the discount and finance house of India has been established for the purpose to enter in this segment as par with discount houses in UK. But the DFHI does not deal in some specific bill transactions. Now in India there is no discount house. The treasury bills market provide extremely low rate of return on this investments. The treasury bill rate in India has been the lowest rate of interest in the entire Interest rate structure. Therefore the corporate sector in India is away from this market due to low rate of return on investments. Hence the *chakravarty committee* has stated that the discount rate is too low, the general investors are not willing to hold these bills and only the banks and financial institutions purchase them. They hold these bill for short term before rediscounting them with the RBI. If the return on treasury bills increase, the banks, general investors and financial institutions will tend to be purchased. They will deploy their surplus fund temporarily in this market and this situation may leads to reduction of rediscounting pressure as the RBI. Another important factor is that, the relationship between the treasury bills market and the government securities market. The RBI put a policy that every bank should maintain SLR position. The RBI considers the government securities to fulfil the SLR situation. Hence the government securities hold a good demand among banks. It dominates the treasury bill market. The govt. securities market has reduced the importance of treasury bills as an investment medium. The RBI also encourages the government securities market by maintaining a stable prices without any risk. The LIC and other financial institutions are also required to invest a large amount of funds in this market. They have freedom to invest the remaining amount in assets which offer a better returns. The treasury bills can be categorised as follows:

(1) 14 days Treasury bills.
(2) 28 days Treasury bills.
(3) 91 days T-bills.
(4) 182 days T-bills
(5) 364 days T-bills.

(1) 14 day Treasury bills: The 14 day T-bills has been introduced from 1996-97. These bills are non-transferable. They are issued only in book entry system they would be redeemed at par. Generally the participants in this market are state government, specific bodies and foreign Central banks. The discount rate on this bills will be decided at the beginning of the year quarter. The yield on *This market is on par with the interest as ways and means*. These bills are not popular in India due to some limitations. This bills are issued every week.

(2) 28 days T-bills: These bills were introduced in 1998. The treasury bills in India issued on auction basis. The date of issue of these bills will be announced in advance to the market. The information regarding the notified amount is announced before each auction. The notified amount in respect of T-bills auction is announced in advance for the whole year separately. A uniform calendar of T-bills issuance is also announced. The state governments have been allowed to enter into this segment for investment of their surplus funds as non-competitive bidders. They are also allowed to avail the special ways and means advances against the collateral of their investment in this bills market.

(3) 91 days T-bills: The 91 days treasury bills were issued from July 1965. These were issued tap basis at a discount rate. The discount rates vary between ***2.5 to 4.6% P.A*** from July 1974 the discount rate of 4.6% remained uncharged the return on these bills were very low. However the RBI provides rediscounting facility freely for these bills. The commercial banks also invest their surplus fund into these instruments for a short term period. Generally they will park their idle funds in these instruments for ***1 or 2 days*** respectively. There will be high fluctuations in the volume of out-standing treasury bills. Therefore the RBI introduced measures. They are (a) recycling of the T-bills (b) additional early rediscounting fee. The recycling of the T-bills was introduced from Oct. 1986. Under this scheme the bills which were rediscounted by the RBI could be resold the banks. Therefore once rediscounted by the RBI can be sold to the banks. Another factor is that an additional early rediscounting fee was imposed from November 1986, in case the banks rediscounted the T-bills within 14 days of purchase. The fluctuations declined in the bills market could not become an integral part of the money market.

(4) 182 day T-bills: The 182 day treasury bills was introduced in November 1986. The Chakravarthy committee made recommendations regarding 182 day treasury bills instruments. There was a significant development in this market. These bills were sold through monthly auctions. These bills were issued without any specified amount. These bills are tailored to meet the requirements of the holders of short term liquid funds. These bills were issued at a discount. These instruments were eligible as securities for SLR purposes. These bills have rediscounting facilities. These instruments could be purchased by individuals firms, companies and corporate bodies. The bill market was not emerged as part of the money market.

(5) 364 days T-bills: The 364 treasury bills were introduced by the government in April 1992. These instruments are issued to stabilize the money market. These bills were sold on the basis of auction. The auctions for these instruments will be conducted for every fortnight. There will be no Indication when they are putting auction. Therefore the RBI does not provide rediscounting facility to these bills. These instruments have been instrumental in reducing, the net RBI credit to the government. These bills have become very popular in India. These bills provide higher yield with liquidity position. The reputed financial institutions such as IDBI, ICICI and other financial assets. These instruments have widened the money market. They provide an innovative parking place for idle funds. These bills have been to auction on monthly basis since Oct. 1988. The RBI does not purchase these bills. The response for these bills depend upon many factors such as the uncertainty in government securities market. Variations in SLR and the yield.

The treasury bills market will show an impact on the functioning of banks and monetary policy of the government. The buying of treasury bills by the banks will effect on reduction of credit creating capacity of the banks. In this situation large holding of treasury bills by banks lead to a dangerous situation. The banks always plan for the make up of loss by rediscounting bills with the Central bank. The banks participation in the treasury bills market have been increased due to the tight money policy of the RBI. There will be another dimension to study the treasury bills market is that, the banks which purchased the treasury bills will increase the power of deposit creation of banks. These bills are treated as securities for calculation of the SLR position.

3. COMMERCIAL BILL MARKET

Introduction

The Corporate sector requires two kinds of capital, they are (a) fixed capital (b) working capital. The fixed capital can be procured by the companies by issuing shares, term loans from all India financial institutions and other long term nature of the sources. The working capital of the corporate sector are mainly provided by banks through cash credit, overdrafts, and purchase or discounting of the commercial bills. In abroad the bill finance is the major source of income for the banks. But in India, the bill system is yet to became popular. The financing of bill method is flexibility to the money market. The financial instrument which is traded in the bill market is known as the bill of exchange. The bills are used for financing a deal in goods that takes some time to complete. The bill of exchange reveals that the lability to make the payment as a fixed date when the goods are bought on mercantile basis. The bill of exchange will be treated as negotiable instrument. *The Indian Negotiable Instruments Act, 1881* has defined the bill. It is a written instrument containing an unconditional order, signed by the maker, directing a certain person to pay a certain sum of money only to or to the order of a certain person or to the bearer of the instrument.

The bills of exchange are drawn by the seller *(drawer)* on the buyer ***(drawee)*** for the value of the goods delivered by him. These bills are called as trade bills. If the trade bills are accepted by the commercial banks they are known as *commercial bills*. If the seller provides some time for the payment the bill payable at a future date is known as ***usance bill.*** If the seller party is in need of finance he may approach the bank for discount of the bill. The commercial banks generally finance the business community through bill discounting method. The commercial banks can finance the seller at a negotiated discount rate therefore the bank collects the maturity proceeds of the discounted bills from the drawee. In this situation, if the bank needs emergency fund it can rediscount the bills already discounted in the commercial bill discount market. The bill is a negotiable instrument is can change ownership conveniently during its currency. It provides a clear legal safeguard. This instrument will be treated as self liquidating paper on the money market. The liquidity position of this instrument is being next only to cash, call loan, treasury bill and commercial bills. It carriers a low degree of risk of loss. It is different from other commercial loans by banks. In the U.S. the bills are known as *Banker's Acceptance.*

In the bill market, there are a number of bills available and can be categorised on the basis of their maturity. Some bills are due for payment whether the documents to title of goods accompany them or not, the type of activity they finance some bills are known as demand bills. A demand bill is payable immediately at sight or on presentment to the drawee. The bills are payable on demand and those payable on fixed date such as payable 30 days after date or on the date of the happening of a certain event, need not to be presented by the holder for acceptance. A bill which has no time for payment specified is also known as *demand bill.* The time bill is payable a specified later date. The bills also can be classified as clear bill and documentary bills. The documentary bills are accompanied by document of title to goods. The document of title are RR or bill of lading. Further the bills are also be classified as DA and DP bills. The DA bill refers to document against acceptance. The DP refers to document against payment. The DA bill becomes as a clean bill after delivery of the documents. The bills further can be classified as *Inland bills and foreign bills.* Inland bill means a bill must drawn in India and it must be payable in India. The bill must be drawn upon any person when is resident in India. The inland bill may even be endorsed in a foreign country. *Foreign bills* are drawn outside India and payable outside India by a party. The foreign bill may be payable in India or drawn on a party resident in India. The foreign bill may be drawn in India and payable outside the country. Another classification of bills can be made as *export bills and Import bills.* The export bills are drawn by the exporters on any foreign country. Import bills are drawn on importers in India by the exporters from abroad. The commercial bills can be utilised for financing the movement of goods and storage of goods. The bill of exchange was originated in UK and USA. The growth of bill financing took place mainly for international trade. The bill of exchange were used for a limited extent. The turnover of the bills market depend upon many factors such as foreign trade sector, international transactions economy of the respected country. But in India, the bill of exchange is not popular in case of the financing of agricultural operations, cottage and small scale industries etc., Agricultural bills are drawn for financing agricultural operations. The agriculture is mainly a seasonal activity and the financing to these sector for marketing of crops. The small sector industries bills are drawn for the purpose of financing the production and marketing activities. The Indian agriculture system is based on monsoon position. This sector is a highly risk area. The agricultural sector a variety of bill of exchange or promissory note known as *Hundi* The Hundi system has a long tradition of use in India. Hundi is used to raise money or to remit funds. They are used for financing inland trade by indigenous bankers. The following are the various kinds of bills of exchange.

(a) Darshini Hundi.

(b) Muddati Hundi.

(a) Darshini Hundi is also known as Bill at sight or demand. This Hundi again classified as *Shahjog, Naurjog, Dekharnar jog, Fermani jog, jokhami, and dhanjog*. This bill is used for the payment of goods originating from one country to another places. The bill payment place may be different from its place of origin.

(b) Muddati Hundi is useful for local geographical specification areas and its use is diminishing. The maturity period of this bill varies between. ***30 days to 120 days.***

The bills of exchange is also associated with indigenous bankers. The Multani Shroffs and the Chettiars have been mainly dealing in hundi. Generally the banks discount their hundis. But the SBI has stopped since 1965. The other commercial banks have been continued to extend such facilities to the Multanis. The banks involved indiscounting these hundi with reference to the personal credibility of the indigenous bankers. The authorities should make arrangements for taking advantage for the development of the bill market in the country. After the nationalization of commercial banks, they have to meet the credit requirements of the various sectors. The banks will have to provide credit to the small scale and cottage industries small borrowers and artisans. The bank shall reduce the bad debts, delays in recoveries, increasing administrative expenses. They shall have to concentrate on increasing the level of profitability. All these problems can be rectified by the banks with proper allocation of funds to all the categories of borrowers. The banks should make to efforts to improve the assessment procedure of the credit worthiness of the indigenous bankers. The commercial banks have a wide geographical locations to extend discounting facilities on the credit standing of indigenous bankers.

The bills of exchange further can be categorised as *accommodation bill and supply bills.* The accommodation bill is also known as wind bill or a kite. The accommodation bill is defined as one in which a person known as a accommodation party. The bill contains a name to accommodate another person without obtaining any consideration. *The supply bill* is a bill drawn by the suppliers or contractor on the government. These bills are issued by the parties inconcerned with the supply of goods or materials provided under contract to the concerned department. The suppliers of the goods or the materials can get advance from the banks on the basis of these bills. These bill are more useful to the suppliers and contractors. Because these parties could not get funds from the government or concerned company. Therefore the parties will make adjustments through their supply bills. These bills do not have the status of a negotiable instrument. They are not accepted by the government departments. These bills are not accompanied by documents of title to goods. The bank advances on the basis of supply bills are known as clear advance.

The Process of Bill: The bill of exchange contains an order from the creditor to the debtor in a transaction to pay a certain sum to a specified person after a certain period. The bill of exchange can be defined as. "An instrument in writing containing an unconditional order signed by the maker, directing a certain person to pay a certain sum of money only to, or to the order of a certain person or to the bearer of the instrument".[4] Therefore a bill is always drawn by the creditor on the debtor. The person who draws the bill is known as the ***drawee.*** The person on whom the bill is drawn is known as the ***drawee***. The drawee is also called as acceptor. The person drawer is called as ***Payee.*** The payee is entitled to get the bill amount on maturity date. A bill must be in writing only. A bill is always drawn on a certain person. A bill cannot be made payable to bearer on demand. A bill may be payable at sight or after the expiry of a certain specified time. There will be 3 days of grace period for a bill. The following example can reveal the process of a bill, usually in business community.

Forex: Mr. A sells goods to buyer B. The buyer will have to pay the money to the seller. But Mr. B does not have money at present and Mr. A is in need of the money. Therefore to solve this problem the bill of exchange comes into picture between these two parties, Mr. A draws a bill on B for a certain period of maturity In this situation Mr. A is known as creditor and Mr. B is called as Debtor. The creditor is known as *drawer* of the bill and the debtor is called as the ***drawee*** of the bill. Hence Mr. A sends the bill to B and in turn Mr B acknowledges his responsibility by accepting the bill. After the acceptance of the bill by Mr. B the transaction is closed for time being. In the meanwhile Mr. A can take the accepted bill to a bank for getting money by discounting it. The difference between ready money paid by the banker and the face value of the bill is called as *discount.* The discount is calculated by the bank at a rate per cent per annum on the basis of maturity value. The discounting of a bill with the bank is not a borrowing on the security of the bill and it is an act of selling the bill. Theoretically the process of bill finance is described as simple. But in practice it is quite complex. A bill has to pass through many hands before its maturity period. Acceptance is the most important element in bill financing system. The commercial banks accept these bills for earning income through commission. The discount amount on the trade bill becomes income to the commercial banks. It is an income generating activity for the banks. The acceptance business of commercial banks is very small. For development of this bill market, the banks and indigenous bankers must involve in accepting business. The RBI introduced a Bill market scheme in 1952. According to this scheme the banks are required to select the borrowers after careful examination of their credit worthiness and reputation. The dealings with these selected parties may convert their advances into bills. In India the maturity periods for bills in general are 30, or 60 or 90 or 120 days. The export bills may have a maturity period of *180 days*. Agriculture finance bills may have a maturity period of *15 months.* The bill for financing cottage industries may have a maturity period of *120 months*. The RBI has fixed a longer eligible maturity period for different bills. A bill with maturity period of *90 days* are the most popular in India. Bills are self liquidating and they promote efficient use of credit. They provide liquidity to the assets of banks.

---

4. Mithani and Gordon, Banking and Financial System, Himalaya Publishing House, p. 85.

Bill Market in India: The bill market in India is yet to be developed. The bill market depends upon the volume of credit transactions occurred in the market. The banks also should give preference to these instruments for providing credit to the business customers. The market may be developed by popularizing these instruments among the business community. The market provides rediscounting facility for these instruments. The involvement of the Central bank may develop the market. The secondary market for the bills is also quite developed. The velocity of the bill reveals the development of the market. The acceptance facility is available in India at a low cost. The participation of brokers and bankers in this market is expected for smooth functioning of the process. Therefore the bill market in India is treated as under developed. There is no real bill market in India. The following factors indicate for non development of bill market in India.

(1) The discounted bills were not actual bills.

(2) They are created by banks by converting OD/CC accounts of the customers.

(3) Bill finance is made by the banks by way of *loans* only.

(4) They are provided credit as the bills were security.

(5) The rediscounting facilities for bills market do not exist in India.

(6) The acceptance service is much restricted in India.

(7) There is no bills habit to the business community towards the bills of exchange.

Therefore the RBI has taken the innovative steps to develop this market in June 1974. It permitted the commercial banks. CIC, UTI, GIC and ICICI to rediscount the gervine trade bills. Hence this has increased the number and types of institutions taking part which play the role in this market.

The bill market in India is based on the suggestions of the *Narasimhan committee* in 1970. The RBI freed the bill rediscounting rates from *May. 1, 1989.* The specified ceiling in the rediscount rate was freed the banks and financial institutions con rediscount the bills with the discount and finance house of India *(DFHI)* The DEHI was permitted to fix its own discount rates for the bills according to the market position. The government has taken a decision for the abolition of stamp duty to activate the market. The RBI promoted a drawee bill scheme to help the small scale units. The RBI made same efforts to develop the bill market by introducing the following schemes.

(a) The scheme of 1952.

(b) The scheme of 1970.

The salient features of the 1952 scheme was presented below.

(1) All licensed schedule banks were permitted to rediscount the bill with RBI from July 1954.

(2) RBI permitted the banks for the lodgement of bill as security for loans.

(3) RBI made the funds available at concessional rate for their market.

(4) The scheme was extended to cover export bills.

The salient features of the scheme of 1970 are presented below.

(1) The rediscounting facility provided to all licensed scheduled banks.

(2) The scheme covers only genuine trade bills only.

(3) The produced bills must bear the endorsement of a licensed scheduled bank.

(4) The bill should bear at least two good signatures

(5) The refinance facility available throughout the year

(6) There is no minimum value of a single bill.

(7) The RBI excluded some of the transactions covered by selective credit controls.

The bill discounting and rediscounting system in India is yet to take root in the financial system. These schemes do not contain any concrete and direct measures to develop all the aspects of the developed bill market. The RBI has made efforts to activate the bill market and provided rediscounting facility to all the eligible banks. Generally the business customers of the banks prefer to get finance through cash credit. But the Central bank permitted all the banks to convert their CCS into bill financing system. But this situation did not help to the market. These schemes aimed primarily for providing liquidity facility for the market.

The government has also made efforts to develop this market. It appointed various committees to study the problems and for suggestion. They play a major role in development of this market.

(A) Tandon committee

(B) Chore committee

(C) Chakravarty committee

(D) Vaghul working committee.

As a result of the recommendations of these committees the RBI has taken some measures to develop this market. They are presented below:

(a) The abolition of stamp duty on bills of exchange.

(b) The setting up of DFHI as a major financial institution.

(c) The acceptance service comes under credit monitoring scheme.

(d) The procedures and documentation process shall be simplified.

(e) The RBI made access to a large number of financial institutions to develop this market.

(f) The RBI permitted the following institutions to enter into this market from May 1990:

(1) All scheduled commercial banks.

(2) ICICI.

(3) UTI.

(4) IRBI.

(5). LIC and its subsidiaries.

(6) IDBI.

(7) SIDBI.

(8) GIC.

(9) NHB.

(10) DFHI.

(11) LIC Mutual Fund.

(12) NABARD.

(13) EXIM Bank.

(14) Select Urban Cooperative Banks.

(15) IFCI.

(16) SCICI.

(17) IFCI.

(18) Can bank Mutual Fund.

(19) ECGC.

(20) SBI MF.

Reasons for Non-development of Bills Market: The Government had made all efforts to develop this market through RBI. The RBI also appointed various experts committees to develop this segment inspite of the encouraging official policy. The bill market has not developed in India. The bill market was developed in UK and the US. But in developed markets, the volume of business regarding the bill has tend to decline in the developed markets also. The following are the factors for non-development of the bills market.

(a) The government does not prefer to finance its activities through bills of exchange.

(b) The quick discounting and collection of bills by the branches of banks, quick transfer and remittances of fund have tend to narrow down the basis for using the creation of bill.

(c) The bills market were mostly established for the financing of foreign trade which were not developed.

(d) Bill discounting was a costly mode of financing system.

(e) The banks were not showing interest to finance through bill of exchange.

(f) The trade and industry have shown reluctance to the discipline of the bill finance.

(g) Bill of exchange requires the endorsement of reputed institution.

(h) The bill market has been dominated by indigenous banker, those who rely on their own sources of funds.

(i) The complicated processing loss of interest on the part of banks, absence of specialised credit information acquires, the growth of other instruments in money markets.

In order to develop a sound bill market, the RBI introduced a number of measures to strengthen the market.

4. CERTIFICATE OF DEPOSITS

Introduction

The scheme of certificate of deposits has been introduced by the RBI in June 1989. This financial instrument has been introduced in order to widen the money market and its instruments. This scheme provides greater flexibility in the parking of their idle funds. The certificate of deposits can be issued only by the scheduled commercial banks. These will be issued in multiples of Rs. 25 lakhs. The minimum size of the issue is Rs. 1 crore. The maturity period will vary between 3 months and one year. It will be issued at discount to face value. The discount rate will be freely determined according to the situation. It will be freely transferable by endorsement. They are subject to stamp duty. The RBI is the supreme authority in this segment. The RBI prescribes a limit to each bank for funds to raise under this scheme. It is a negotiable instrument. It provides maximum liquidity. The DFHI dominates the trading in CDs market. These instruments have large size of the market in primary but there is no room for the secondary market. Liquidity and marketability is the hall marks of these instruments. They are in bearer form. They are known as ***Negotiable Instrument***. They are also called as Negotiable Certificates of Deposits.

Certificate of Deposit means, an amount of money deposited in a bank for a specified period at a specified rate of interest. The concerned bank will issue a receipt which is transferable and marketable in the market. The receipts may be either in bearer form or in registered form. They are documents of title to time deposits with banks. Technically they are a part of banks time deposit. These are riskless in terms of payment of interest and principal amount.

The CDs have been introduced by many developed and developing countries. They were introduced in 1961 in the US and UK. The CDs in the form of dollars were issued in 1966 and pounds in 1968. The CDs have been emerged in many countries based on different forces and factors. They have been emerged for widening the money market in many countries. They have been introduced to restore intermediation function of banks, to strengthen the market, to innovative financial system, to mop up excess liquidity in the monetary system and as a part of financial reforms. They will be treated in global markets as ***Euro Certificates of Deposits***. They are issued in different countries to meet the competition.

They have some advantages over the time deposit. The banks issued them as a competitive tools against other financial intermediaries.

The CDs were introduced in Japan 1979, France 1985, West Germany 1986, Australia 1969, New Zealand 1971, South Korea 1974, Malaysia 1979, Indonesia 1971. Many factors have contributed to the evaluation of CDs in different countries. They are introduced as a part of marketing strategy in the financial markets by the commercial banks. In the US, the CDs are issued in any denomination from $ 1,00,000 to $ 10 millions. In UK they are not eligible collateral security for loans from the bank of England.

CDs in India: The introduction of CDs in India was being seriously assessed from the beginning of 1980s. The RBI appointed a committee to study the feasibility of CDs in India. The ***Tambe working group*** studied the market and recommended against it for the reasons. There were no secondary money markets in the country. There was the administered system of interest rates. The CDs may rise to fictitious transactions, *The Veghul committee* appointed in 1987 made recommendations for the introduction of CEs in India. They are provided short term deposit rates. The RBI formulated and launched in June 1989 a scheme permitting the banks to issue CDs with a view to widen the money market.

Original Scheme: The RBI formulated a scheme for the introduction of CDs in the form of asancve promissory notes. These notes are payable on a fixed date without any grace period. They were issued with a maturity period of 3 months to one year. These instruments would be issued at a discount, to face value. They are transferable by endorsement and can be delivered only after the *lock in period of 45 days* after the date of issue. The total outstanding of all CDs issued by bank to any point of time should not exceed *1%* of its fortnightly average deposits. All CDs are subject to the usual CRR and SLR requirements. The banks has to report about the issue of CDs to the RBI. The banks are not allowed to buy back their own CDs. The banks were not allowed to grant loans against CDs. The CDs has to bear the stamp duty at the rate *0.25 per cent* advalorem for a maturity of over *3 to 6 months of 0.375 per cent* for a maturity of over 6 months to 9 months and 0.5 per cent of a maturity of over 9 months to 12 months. They are issued to individuals corporations. Trusts companies funds and associations they are issued to NRIs also on a non-reputation basis. The discount rates may be determined by the market forces. The regional rural banks and scheduled banks were not eligible to issue CDs they are issued in multiples of Rs. 25 lakhs subject to a maximum of issue of Rs.1 crore.

Modified Scheme: The above original scheme has been modified by the RBI the rules and regulations have been framed by the RBI from time to time. These regulations are in force in 97-98 they are badly presented as follows.

(a) The minimum denomination is *Rs. 5.00 lakhs.*

(b) The minimum size of issue at a single time is *Rs. 10.00 lakhs.*

(c) The maturity period varies from *3 months to 1 year*.

(d) They are issued at a discount to face value.

(e) The discount rate of CDs are determined by the market forces.

(f) They are freely transferable after lock in period of 30 days after issue.

(g) All scheduled banks can issue them.

(h) Any one can purchase CDs.

(i) They can be issued by banks without any ceiling.

(j) They are subject to CRR and SCR requirements.

(k) Term lending institutions can also issue them with a maturity of *1 to 3 years.*

The development of CDs is based on its secondary market. The secondary market for these instruments has not developed well. Because the CDs are priced high. The holders in primary market prefer to hold them to maturity. The DFHI is key partner in the market. It quotes daily bid discount rate on CDs. Most of the CDs are said to be in replacement of the existing current account or short term deposits. In India there will be a potential for the growth of CDs in primary and secondary markets. The CDs can get support from various sources. The *demand and supply* sides of the CD market as presented below.

Large public sector undertakings and private sector corporate bodies are believed on demand side of the CDs market. UTI also has gathered huge investible funds and they do not have ready incestiment outlets. There are inter corporate funds of substantial amount to be invested in this segment. On the supply side, the banks are facing stiff competition from foreign banks and in need of exploring the use of innovative means such as CDs to occupy their share in the market. The supply and demand and favourable factors and with the support of RBI and DFHI made a good potential for growth in the coming years. The interest rates offered on CDs are high. The maturity period of 3 months at the short term end are generally popular with the investors. The organisation replace their current account with CDs. The CDs are not fresh accrual of deposits. Hence it appears to be that the banks are retaining their deposits at higher cost. This situation adversely effects the banks earnings. Because the operating expenses of the banking sector increases by the way of interest charges. Hence the banks should be allowed to buy and sell CDs in the secondary market. The rates of Interest on CDs ranges from 5.40% to 9.20%.[5]

CDs are the obligations of banks. They are issued on discount basis and similar to treasury bills or commercial bills. They are just like bonds. They may be issued directly to the investors or through the dealers. They can be issued at discount that can be freely determined the formula for the discounted value as follows:

$$D = \frac{F}{1 + \frac{(I \times N)}{(100 \times 365)}}$$

D = Discounted value of the CDs

F = Face value of the CD

I = Interest rate per annum

N = Usual period.

5. COMMERCIAL PAPER MARKET

Introduction

Money market consists many financial short term instruments. Commerlipal paper is one of the financial instruments of the money market. It provides an opportunity to well rated companies/good track record companies for raising funds on short term basis honesty is the best element to all track the funds. The Market always provides funds to sincere companies the companies which maintain *financial discipline* can procure funds from the market confidently. The investor or the fund suppliers always put. Their funds at the doors taps of the good reputed companies and sincere organisation. In the financial market credibility is the most important factor at present. The financial discipline leads to credibility. The credibility has the borrowing capacity from the market. In the recent period many good reputed companies have accursed the commercial paper market for meeting their working capital requirements.

Commercial paper is an unsecured promisor note. They are issued by well rated companies for a minimum of 3 months and maximum of *six months.* They are regulated by non banking companies directions. Those directions were issued by RBI in 1989. The directions come into force on 1-1-90.

5. EPW, August 10, 2002, p. 3311.

Salient features: The salient features of CP are presented below.

(a) They are unsecured promissory notes.

(b) The issue company shall have current ratio *1.33;1*

(c) They have maturity period from 90 days to 180 days.

(d) The minimum issue shall be *Rs. 25 lakhs*

(e) They are transferable by endorsement and delivery.

(f) The issuer company shall have tangible net wealth of Rs. 5 crores.

(g) They can be issued at discount to face value.

(h) The discount value may be decided by the issuing company

(i) They require floating expenses

(j) They may be issued to individuals, banks, companies registered, corporate bodies and union corporated bodies.

(k) They are also issued to NRIs on Non-repatriable basis.

(l) The issuer company shall get rating from CRISIL before issue as P_2 or A_2 from CRISIL or ICRA respectively.

CDs in Abroad: Commercial paper is totally new in India. They are not yet fully developed. It is quite a new instrument in the money market. The market has not developed even in the advanced nations except in the US, the CPs are known as ***Industrial paper,*** finance paper, or corporate paper. The CPs have been introduced in *UK 1986* ***France 1985***, *Spain 1982* ***Hong Kong 1982***, *Singapore 1984*. ***Netherlands 1986*** *Sweden 1980* ***Canada 1950*** respectively. They have a very flexible maturity period. In the US the maturity period shall not be more than *270 days*. Generally in the US the maturity period is 90 days or three months. In UK the maturity period will be ***7 to 364 days.*** In France 10 days to 7 years, 30 days to 365 days in Canada. In Australia they have 185 days maturity period. They are issued in domestic as well as international financial market. They are known as *Euro commercial papers.* They are normally issued in a barer form on discount to face value basis. They are issued in larger denominations. They may be issued through banks or merchant banker or dealers or brokers in the open market. Some times they may be sold through placement directly to the lenders or investors. In US they are sold through dealers who are specialised in this market. They are cheaper sources of finance than bank loans. It is at the same time a more impersonal and therefore more unreliable sources of finance. The primary market for them is active but the secondary market is yet to be developed even in advanced nations. Because the investors who purchased in the primary market will hold this instrument till maturity period. Hence there is no need of secondary market operations in the market. Another factor is that these instruments have shorter maturity period. They are issued only for short term needs of the corporate sector. The rise and popularity of CPs in abroad has been a matter of spontaneous response by the large corporations. The rising cost of the bank loans leads the large companies towards the CPs market. They found to be cheaper, simpler and flexible sources of funds the raising short term CP represents the weakening process of intermediation. It strengthen the process of *securitisation.* It brings the large borrowers and large investors together and reduces the existence of the brokers or dealers. They are primarily issued by public utilities, bank holding companies, insurance companies, transportation companies and finance companies. The buyers of the CPs are *banks, liquid business concerns, and NBFCs.*

The Industrial paper refers to the paper which is issued by a manufacturing concern or commercial or industrial concern. The finance paper means it is the lability of the finance company issued by it. Corporate paper is a wider term and reveals that it is issued by companies which may be either financial or non financial. The CPs are regarded as highly safe and liquid instruments. They are like treasury bills but unlike CDs. They are close competitors of the treasury bills. They have a buy back facility, they are issued in a bearer form. They are useful to meet the current needs of the funds for the corporate sector. They will fulfil the needs of the seasonal business.

The banks are one of the major buyers of CPs.

In India the CPs were introduced on the suggestions of the *working group* on Money market in 1987. The RBI has the supreme authority in this segment. It announced a scheme in March 1989 for the introduction of the instrument in the Indian Money Market. It issued a notification which came into effect from 1-1-90. It framed the guidelines which apply to all the NBFCs and Non financial companies. The FEMA related companies shall take the permission from the RBI to issue CPs. The CPs have the maturity period of 30 days. They may be issued on a single date or in parts. The RBI has not permitted the banks either to undertake or to co-accept the issue of CPs. The issuer of this instrument shall have to bear the stamp duty, dealers fee, rating agency fee, fee to banker, standby facility and other concerned expenses.

Guidelines Issued by the RBI: The RBI issued guidelines in respect of the sale of CPs. They are presented below.

(1) The rules come into force in 1997-98.

(2) The issuing company shall have the tangible net worth of *Rs. 4 crores.*

(3) The issuing company working capital limit should not be less than Rs. 4 crores.

(4) The company can issue CPs upto 75% of its working capital.

(5) The CP shall have a minimum denomination of Rs. ***5 lakh.***

(6) The minimum size of an issue to a single investor is Rs. ***25 lakh.***

(7) The issuing company shall have P_2 & A_2 rating from CRISIIL and ICRA.

(8) The issuing company directly issue CPs.

(9) There is no need to take RBI permission.

(10) The holder shall present the CP for payment to the issuer.

(11) There is no need of underwriting the issue of CPs.

(12) The issue of CP must be meant for working capital requirement only.

(13) There is no need for coaccepting issue of CPs.

The subscription to CPs is open to all investors. The investors in this market is consisting of large corporate bodies operating in the intercorporate funds market trusts with substantial funds and public sector corporations. Sometimes the banks also invest in this market.

Though CPs have some advantages but they have some limitations also. The intercorporate lenders and borrowers would prefer to tax free bonds rather than CPs. They have some administrative hassles. The big institutional investors like UTI, GIC and LIC are not interested towards these instruments because their investment patterns are determined by the government. They do not get any tax incentives on investment in CP. Generally the real major holders of CPs are banks. The market for CPs will grow when there exists a secondary market. The DFHI is created for the purpose of developing. The secondary market for CPs. The DFHI can acquire the CPs in primary and provide them in secondary market CP finance is not an additional finance.

CPs are likely to prove restrictive time consuming and costly. The borrower will lose the bank credit for their working capital requirement. They are unsecured instruments. It leads to a disincentive.

6. COLLATERAL LOAN MARKET

Introduction

Collateral loan market is a market where the loans are secured against collateral securities like stocks and bonds. The collateral securities are returned to the borrower when he repays the loan if the borrowers fails to pay his loan. The collateral asset becomes the property of the lender. These are mostly granted by the banks to the private parties. These are provided for a short period of a few months.

Unorganised Money Market

The unorganised sector of money market contains different agencies. These agencies have diverse policies and lack of uniformity. They are not following uniformity in lending activities. The unorganised sector of the Indian money market includes the following.

(a) Indigenous bankers

(b) Money lenders.

(c) Chit funds.

(a) Indigenous Bankers

The Indigenous bankers are the part of unorganised Indian money market. It is mostly confined to certain castes like *chatries, jains, Marwaris and chettis.* They are known as the banking cast in India. There were about 2,500 indigenous bankers in the country in 1971. They are active in commercial centres. The Indian Central Banking Enquiry committee defined the Indigenous banker as *any individual or private firm receiving deposits and dealing in Hundis or lending money.* The Indigenous bankers have concentrated mostly in the southern and western parts of India. They have been active in the rural money market. The ***Multani*** bankers play an important role in the market. They grant loans against unsecured to the traders. A Multani banker involves in business transactions with at least 300 parties every day.

They represent ancient banking system of India. They have been carrying their traditional and historical operations in different parts of the country. They spread throughout the country. They are called *chettys* in Chennai, ***sahukans, Mahajans and khatries*** in Mumbai, they are known as ***shroffs and Marwaris*** in Kolkata they are called as ***Seths and Banias***. Any individual or private firm which receives deposits, deals in hundies or engages itself in lending money business. They can be divided into three categories (a) *Multani bankers (b) Marwaris and Bengalis (c) limited business.*

The Multani bankers deal only in banking business operations. Marwaris and Bengalies involved in banking business with trade also. Some indigenous bankers deal mainly in trade and participating in limited business transactions. The indigenous banker lends and also accepts funds from the public.

Importance of Indigenous Bankers: They occupy an important place in the Indian money market. They play a vital role in financing the trade sector. They are more popular where the banks neglected certain geographical locations of the country. Some areas have not been saved properly by the banks. After nationalization, of the banks, their transactions had been declined significantly. They have control still in the market where the finance is required more demand. They become more popular due to the following reasons.

(a) They provide finance to their friends and relatives.

(b) They provide excellent service to the customers.

(c) They give loans to the persons those who neglected by banks.

(d) They have good relations with customers.

(e) They are not merely bankers to the customers.

(f) They know the customers needs and their requirements and pulse.

Functions of Indigenous Bankers: The Indigenous bankers are mixed with the society. They provide service to their customers at 24 hours. The main functions of the indigenous bankers are presented below.

(1) Accepting Deposits from the public.
(2) Providing loans to the customers.
(3) Hundi business.
(4) Other functions.

Accepting Deposits from Public: The indigenerous banker performs the same functions as performed by the commercial banks. They accept deposits from the public at a specified rate of interest. These deposits are of two kinds

(1) The demand deposits
(2) Fixed deposits.

The demand deposit means, they accept the deposits from the public and the amount will be repayable when ever the customer demands. They pay higher rate of interest than commercial banks. ***fixed deposits*** are repayable only after a fixed date. They will not be paid in advance. The depositor will have to wait till the maturity period. The collected deposit will be circulated in the market at higher interest rate.

Providing Loans to the Customers: They provide loans to customers against a security. The desired security may be in the form of *land, silver, gold and crops.* They lend the money against personal security. They sanction loans to small industrialists who ignored by the commercial banks.

Hundi Business: They deal hundies also. They buy hundies and sell them in the market. Sometimes they may also write hundies. They discount hundies. They meet the needs of small traders. They transfer the funds from are location to another location through discounting of hundies.

Other Functions: They also carry other business functions along with banking. They generally do their retail trading business. Sometimes they act as agents to large firms. They earn income in the form of commission. They are involved in speculative transactions. The following are the characteristics of the indigenous bankers.

Characteristics of Indigenous Bankers:

(1) Indigenous bankers accept deposit from the public.
(2) They their own funds in the market.
(3) They do not require any complicated formalities.
(4) They are available to the public whenever they need money.
(5) Their establishments are small and economical.
(6) They provide finance to all types of borrowers.
(7) They conduct the banking activities on the basis of their experience.
(8) They maintain simple accounts.
(9) They know about their customers thoroughly.
(10) They observe the activities of their borrowers.
(11) They have good relations among the trade community.
(12) Their presence in the rural cannot be eliminated.

Effects of Indigenous Bankers: The Indigenous banking system suffer from the following defects.

(1) Basically they are traders but a sound banking principle requires a higher specialisation skill.
(2) The indigenous banking system is entirely unorganised. They are working independently without any coordination among them.

(3) The transfer of fund is not possible in this system.

(4) Their financial capability is very low due to low resources.

(5) They do not mobilise savings on large scale from the public.

(6) They charge higher interest rate than by banks.

(7) They do not follow the sound banking principles.

(8) They grant loans even without sufficient security.

(9) They do not observe the purpose of the loan issued.

(10) They also provide loans to unproductive activities.

(11) They provide loans to speculation activities also.

(12) The do not maintain books of accounts in proper way.

(13) They will exploit the customers.

(14) Their activities cannot be regulated by the RBI.

Indigenous Bankers and Reserve Bank: The RBI is the supreme authority in the banking sector. It has been making efforts to change the unorganised system into organised system. It has been trying to bring them into its control. It has been making environment to integrate them with the modern banking system. The RBI prepared a scheme in 1937 for direct linking with indigenous bankers under certain conditions. These conditions are presented below.

(1) Every indigenous banker should have a minimum working capital of Rs. 1.00 lac.

(2) The working capital should be increased to *600 lakh*.

(3) They should concentrate on banking business only.

(4) They should leave their non banking business activities.

(5) They should maintain accounts properly.

(6) Their accounts should be audited by authorized auditors.

(7) They should submit their records to the RBI.

(8) They should submit periodical report as like scheduled banks.

(9) The Reserve Bank should have right to regulate them.

(10) The scheme was not in practice because they did not agree to accept its various conditions.

Banking Commission: The banking commission has appraised the services which rendered by the indigenous bankers. They play a very useful role in the lives of millions people. They cover all categories of the public in the society. the segments which they cover by them are ignored by the banks the commission feels that the indigenous banking system should work properly and it can be utilised for society. They should be regulated and institutionalized. The commission strongly feels that they should bring under the purview of the RBI for functioning of the banking sector more effectively the commission thought that the indigenous bankers should bring indirect control though commercial banks. The RBI should frame the rules and regulations for the commercial banks to deal with them. The banks should provide rediscounting facility to the indegeneous bankers on satisfying the following norms.

(a) They should involve fully to the banking business only.

(b) They should have own capital of not less than Rs. 1.00 lac.

(c) They should not borrow from more than a single bank.

(d) They should maintain regular books of account.

(e) They should submit annual report to the RBI.

(f) They should monitor the loans.

Reforms: In Indian economy the indigenous bankers occupy a great role in the lives of public. They should be reformed and integrated with the original system of banking. The following are the suggestions to reform them.

(a) They should be linked with the RBI.

(b) They should run the banking business separately.

(c) They should convert their business to modern banking system.

(d) They should be eliminated the competition from banks.

(e) They should maintain proper accounts and get them audited regularly.

(f) There should be convergence between banks and indigenous banks.

(g) They should stop various malpractices.

(h) The licensing system should be introduced for them.

(i) The commercial banks might discount their hundis easily.

(j) They should form association.

(k) The benefits of the bankers shall pass an on them.

(l) They should develop bill broking business.

(m) They should adopt modern accounting records.

(n) They should change their attitude in the modern world

(o) They should have a positive approach.

(p) They should become move professional and formal in their operations.

(b) Money Lenders

In the unorganised money market sector, the money lenders play an important role in the economy. Their basic activity involves money lending. The indigenous bankers also do this money lending. But their primary business is not banking. The money lenders can be classified as follows.

(a) Professional money lenders

(b) Now-professional money lenders.

Professional money lenders basic business is money lending. They are known as *"banias" "mahajans" "sowcars"* They hold licenses for money lending activities. Their main source of income is lending money.

Non-professional money lenders means occasionally they do lending business. They do not depend entirely on money lending business. They do this business in addition to their routine work. They consist of landlords, agriculturists its, traders, pensioners, rich wendors etc. They have no license to carry this business.

The money lenders can also be classified into two kinds. They are (a) Rural money lenders (b) Urban money lenders. The money lenders those who operate in villages are called as *Rural money lenders.*The lenders who operate in urban areas are known as ***urban money lenders.*** They provide loans to poor labourers, factory workers, low paid employees.

Operations: The money lenders are the part of society. They know the needs of various kinds of people. The will help the people by providing loans to meet their requirements. They possess good knowledge of the borrowers and have a minimum risk. They provide loans against security. The loans may be for the borrower's family expenditure. They have good personal contacts with their customers. They have good social contacts with their clients. In this system there is less chance for default in repayment of the loan. Because the rural system will pressure the borrowers to repay that amount. There is no uniform interest rate in this system. There are different rates of interest changed in different parts of the country. They also resort to undesirable practices.

Features of Money Lenders: The following are the salient features of money lenders.

(a) They deploy their own funds.

(b) They provide money to mainly illiterate and economically weaker sections of the society.

(c) They provide highly exploitative nature of the loans.

(d) They are unregulated.

(e) The loans may be secured or unsecured.

(f) Their operations are prompt, informal and flexible.

Effects of Money Lenders: The money lending system has the following defects.

(1) The money lenders have limited resources to meet the needs of the rural people.

(2) They charge very high interest rates.

(3) They adopt all possible types of malpractices in business.

(4) They provide unproductive purpose loans.

(5) They provide crop loans to the formers. They compel the farmers to see their produce at low prices to them.

Chit Funds

Chit Funds is one of the elements of the unorganised sector of the money market. Chit funds are recognised by law. The are required to be registered under the companies act. The central government has proposed to introduce a special legislation called chit fund Act.

Characteristics of the Unorganised Factor of Indian Money Market

The Unorganised Indian money market has the following characteristics.

(1) It consists of indigenous bankers, money lenders and chit funds.

(2) They conduct the mixed business of money lending and trading.

(3) They have good personal relations with the borrowers.

(4) They know the historical background of each and every borrower.

(5) They keep their accounts in a simple manner.

(6) They keep their business affairs very confidential.

(7) They provide loans according to the needs of the borrowers.

(8) Their operations are flexible in nature.

(9) They locate in rural and urban centres.

(10) They lend the money to all types of borrowers.

(11) They cater to the credit needs of the rural economy.

Efficiencies of the Indian Money Market: The money market is India has not developed. It suffers from a number of drawbacks. They have been presented below.

(a) The Indian money market is categorised into organised and unorganised sectors. The organised sector works under the control and guidance of the RBI. The unorganised sector locks scientific organisation. It is in unorthodox approach.

(b) There is coordination between organised and unorganised system of the Indian money market.

(c) There is wide divergence between two parts of the money market system in many factors such as structure of interest rates, lending policies.

(d) The RBI has no control over the unorganised sector of the Indian money market.

(e) In India money market, the organised sector consists of bill market. The bill market is undeveloped in India. The bill market is well developed in advance countries.

(f) The Indian banking is neglected the agriculture finance.

(g) In the unorganised sector, the financial agencies do not lend money only. They usually carry on retail trade and other activities along with lending operations.

(h) There is no coordination in unorganised money market system.

(i) The Indian money market suffers from the seasonal stringency of credit and higher interest rates during a part of the year.

(j) Indian money market suffers from the shortage of capital funds.

RBI and Money Market

The Indian Money market operates within the legal environment of the RBI. It has all the authorities regarding all the aspects of borrowing and lending of the money.

(1) The RBI introduced two schemes for the development of the bill market. They were introduced in 1952 and in 1970. It has made efforts to encourage the usage of bills in the banking system.

(2) It has taken a number of measures to improve the functioning of the indigeneous banks.

(3) The RBI has been able to reduce the differences in the interest rates between different sections as well as different centres of the money market.

(4) The RBI has taken measures to amalgamate and merge banks into few strong banks.

(5) There are certain problems faced by the RBI in controlling the money market. i.e. absence of bill market, hurdle in the way of strengthening the unorganised money market.

(6) In adequate development of call money market in India.

(7) There is no coordination among the different components of money market.

Measures for Improvement in the Money Market: The RBI and the Union government are keen on removing the deficiencies of the Indian money market. The following are the measures for improving the organisation of the money market.

(1) Money lenders required to obtain licenses for carrying lending business through an usurious loans act 1918.

(2) In order to alternative credit of the indigeneous bankers, the RBI encouraged the credit cooperative societies to provide credit facilities to the rural areas. The cooperative societies have a wide network and they spread throughout the country and covers all the needs of agriculturists, artisans and others. Cooperative banking is regarded as the only practice answer to the problem. The banking lows act was passed in 1964 for scientific banking business to regulate property.

(3) The government made efforts to meet to needs of the agriculturists more comprehensively. The government established agricultural Refinance corporation in 1963 to provide credit facilities to the agriculturists the ARC refinances the term loans which furnished by *land Mortage banks* and other institutions. The ARC was replaced by the *National Bank for agriculture and Rural development* in 1982. It is established for the purpose of providing adequate credit to the agriculture sector in India.

(4) The government established rural banks in 1970. With a view to finance primary agricultural credit societies through commercial banks. The government created a link between cooperative and joint sector banks. Therefore the banking commission proposed to establish rural banks

in India. The affairs and control of the RRBs are made responsible to the banks. RBI extended the credit guarantee scheme to coop banks.

(5) The RBI made efforts to create a link between Indigenous banks and commercial banks. As a result the indigenous bankers are entitled to get cash credit from the approved list of joint stock banks and the SBI against demand promissory notes.

(6) The RBI has taken some steps to encourage the bill market. It introduced two schemes (a) The bill market scheme 1952 (b) The new bill market scheme 1970. But they have no impact on the bill market.

(7) The government of India made efforts to strengthen the Indian money market and capital market through commercial banks. Therefore it nationalized a number of banks to provide the credit facilities in the rural areas for the priority sector.

(8) The RBI introduced a lead bank scheme in December 1969 to provide more credit facilities by eliminating banking deficiencies in rural areas. The scheme is based on area approach. The scheme entrusted the individual banks to develop a particular area in their jurisdiction.

(9) The central government has proposed to introduce a special legislation called the Nidhis and chit funds act with a view to control and regulating their activities. The banking commission has suggested uniform fund legislation for the entire country.

Vaghul Committee of Money Market

The RBI made a comprehensive review of the money market. It appointed a working group in Sept. 1986 under the chairmanship of *Shri M. Vaghul.* The group was appointed to study the money market system and recommend specific measures for their development. The group submitted its report in Jan. 13,1987. The group was appointed for the following purposes.

(a) The group was appointed to examine money market instruments and recommended specific solutions for their development.

(b) To recommend the market interest rates.

(c) To assess the impact of changes in the cash credit system.

(d) To study the possibility of increasing the players in the money market.

The group made a number of recommendations and observations for strengthening the market.

(a) Present structure of the money market.

(b) Recommendations.

Present Structure

(1) The financial markets consists of money market and capital market. The money market is a market for short term market.

(2) The short term financial assets are near to money.

(3) The instruments are liquid and can be transferable quickly.

(4) The help in equilibrating the short term surplus funds of lenders

(5) The Indian money market is narrow with a limited number of players

(6) There is also a need of new money market instruments

(7) The money market interest rates regulated by RBI and Indian Bankers Association.

(8) The interest rates of the Unorganised sector is more than the organised sector's market.

(9) In the organised sector, the volume of the business in the call money market has been increased.

(10) The RBI has taken several measures for the development of the bill scheme, there has not been satisfactory progress in this sector.

(11) The treasury bills are the part of organised money sector.

(12) The intercorporate market providing short term liquidity.

Recommendations: The Vagual group made the following recommendations for the development of the money market.

(a) The call money interest rates should be freely determined by market forces.

(b) The call market should be like an inter bank market.

(c) The government should take some steps for developing a genuine bill market.

(d) The bill discounting market should not exceed *16%* rate of interest.

(e) The rediscounting of bills should be freely allowed to all the institutions.

(f) In commercial paper market, no restrictions should be imposed on the participants.

(g) The rate of interest on commercial papers should be left to the market forces.

(h) The 182 TBs market should be developed and more players should be allowed to participate in the auctions

(i) The stamp duty involved in the bill transactions must be abolished.

(j) The government should pay all credit purchases through bills of exchange.

(k) The treasury bill refinance facility should be introduced. The refinance rate should be *1.5%* higher than the prevailing TBs rate.

(l) An autonomous body should be incorporated to deal in short term money market instruments. It should be jointly started by the RBI. The public sector banks and the financial institutions.

(m) A short term commercial paper should be introduced.

(n) The factor service should be encouraged by the banks and non bank financial institutions.

(o) Every new instrument must be approved by the RBI in money market.

Recent Measures Taken by RBI: The RBI is the supreme authority in the money market. It has the powers to regulate coordinate and guide the money market. The Vaghul committee had submitted its recommendations on 1-1-87 Based on the recommendations submitted by the group, the RBI has taken several steps to develop the money market. The following measures are recently taken by the RBI to strengthen the market.

(a) The RBI has taken steps to promote the discount and finance house of India with a view to increase the liquidity of the money market.

(b) The RBI permitted in 1991 to set up money market mutual fund by the scheduled commercial banks and their subsidiaries. This mutual funds would provide additional short term funds to the money market.

(c) In April 1987, The RBI introduced an effective interest rate on bill discounting. The ceiling rate has been raised from *11.5% to 12.5%*.

(d) The RBI has been taking several steps to increase the players in the bill rediscounting market.

(e) The RBI has been introducing several treasury bills in the money market. In 1987-182 day TBs. 1992-93-364 day TBs were introduced. These bills were taken into consideration for SCR.

(f) The RBI had been taking total deregulation of money market interest rates with effect from 1-5-89.

(g) The RBI permitted the CDs into the money market in June 1989.

(h) The RBI liberalized the credit authorisation in July 1987.

(i) The RBI promoted the DFHI with a view to increase the liquidity of the money market instrument.

(j) As a result of various measures taken by the RBI. The money market became more organised and diversified.

Discount and Finance House of India

The Vaghul group submitted its report in 1987. As per the recommendations of the group. The RBI made efforts to establish the DFHI. The DFHI was set up in April 1988. It is the apex body in the India money market. It has been set up in collaboration with the public sector banks and financial institutions. Its establishment is a major step towards developing the secondary market for Indian money market. It commenced its operations in April 25, 1988. It deals in short term money market instruments. The ultimate aim of the DFHI is increase the turnover of the money market. The Initial paid up capital is ***Rs. 150 crores.*** It has the refinance and credit facility from the RBI. It is also entitled to get support from the consortium of public sector banks. It encourages the participation of several institutions in the money market. The players in the market are scheduled commercial banks, and their subsidiaries, state and urban cooperative banks and all India financial institutions. It provides an equilibrium place for these institutions surplus and deficit position. It opened its branches at Delhi, Kolkata, Chennai Ahmedabad and Bangalore It decentralized its operations in order to provide better facilities to the Indian money market. In accordance with the announcement of the monetary policy by the RBI in April 1994, a system of primary dealers was introduced on May 14, 1994 in the money market. The RBI had also introduced the system of *Satellite Dealers* in 31-12-96. The PDs and SDs made institutional development in the money market more liquid and broaden.

Primary Dealers: The monetary policy of 1994 introduced the system of primary dealers. RBI framed the guidelines for efficient and smooth functioning of the money market.

Objectives: The primary dealers objectives are presented below.

(a) To strengthen the money market and government securities market to make more liquid and broad.

(b) To conduct open market operations more effectively.

(c) To improve the secondary market trading system in the money market.

(d) To provide the underwriting facilities to the government securities market outside the RBI.

Any subsidiary of scheduled commercial bank and all India financial institutions are eligible to apply for primary dealership. These institutions shall be related to government securities market. Any company which is incorporated under the companies act 1956 are also eligible to primary dealership. But they should be engaged in government securities market. The company institutions shall have a minimum networth of ***Rs. 50 crores.*** The net worth shall consist of paid up equity, free reserves, premium account balance, and capital reserves, If any they play an important role in the government securities market both in primary and secondary market segments. The RBI is the supreme authority and the PD is required to have a standing agreement. The PD shall bid for government dated securities and auction T-bills at a specified amount. The PDs will underwrite a portion of the issue upto a minimum fixed percentage of shortfall in subscriptions against the notified amount. A PD offers a firm two way quotation either through phone a recognised stock exchange. Every PD has to maintain the minimum capital standards at all points of time. The annual turnover of PD in a financial year should not be less than 5 times in government dated securities and 10 times in treasury bills. APD is subject to all prudential and regulation guidelines by the RBI. They should submit periodic returns as prescribed by the RBI. They should provide all rewards to the RBI. They should have a sufficient internal control system for the smooth functioning of the business. They should have physical infrastructure facilities and skilled manpower for efficient participation in primary issues.

Satellite Dealers: The RBI has introduced the satellite dealer system for the development of the supporting infrastructure for dealing and distribution arrangements in government securities and money market instruments. The subsidiaries of commercial bank/ All India financial institutions and companies are eligible to become satellite dealers. They must be predominantly in government securities market. They should have a minimum networth of *M.S crores.* They should be registered with the RBI as SD. The networth means paid up equity, free reserves, balance in share premium account and capital reserves if any. They are designed to work with the PDs in primary and secondary segment of the government securities market or money market. They would generate a turnover of Rs. 30 crores annually. The annual turnover should not be less than 5 times in the government securities market and should not be less than 3 times in respect of outright transactions. The RBI will sanction permission to the SDs in money market operations. The SD should achieve a port folio of not less than 20% in government securities in relation to the total assets. They should maintain minimum capital requirements at all times as prescribed by the RBI from time to time. The should have good infrastructure facilities.

Money Market Mutual Funds: The RBI is the supreme authority in the money market. The MMMF dealt with wholesale transactions involving large amount of transactions. They were issued to large corporates and institutional inventors. The RBI prepared a broad frame work for selling up these institutions. The RBI announced in April 1992 about the introduction of MMMFs But the scheme was finally introduced in December 1995. The scheme was introduced with a view to provide greater liquidity and depth to the market. The scheme was made more flexible and attractive to the commercial banks, financial institutions and institutional investors. The MMMF can be established by any scheduled commercial banks, public financial institutions and companies. The companies are allowed those who are defined under section *G-A* of the companies act the Mutual fund can also be eligible for setting up of MMMF. The MMMF can be operated through a trust or in the form of department. Its assets and liabilities form a part of the eligible institutions and balance sheets. It is a parking place for cash reserve. The private sector mutual funds also have been allowed to set up MMMFs with the approval of the RBI and SEBI. They can invest in any money market instruments without any ceiling. The lock in period in case of these schemes was 30 days. the RBI also allowed to set up these funds by UIT, IDBI MF, Amro bank and bank of Madurai. The first MMMF set up by Kothari pioneer in 1997. But the fund did not succeed. The UTI MMMF had mobilised Rs. 30 crores from the market in 1997. The scheme is offered to resident individuals, HUFs trusts, societies and corporates, the minimum amount of investment is Rs. 10,000. The NAV will be calculated on daily basis.

B. CAPITAL MARKET

Introduction

The Financial Markets are the centres that made provisions for buying and selling of financial claims and services. Financial Markets are classified as Money Markets and Capital Markets. Money Market deal in short term finance with a period of maturity of one year or less. ***Capital Market*** is a market for long term securities. It contains financial instruments of maturity period exceeding one year. It involves in long term nature of transactions. It is a growing element of the financial system in the Indian economy. It differs from the money market in terms of maturity period and liquidity. It is the financial pillar of Industrialised economy. The development of a nation depends upon the functions and capabilities of the Capital Market.

Capital Market is the market for long term sources of finance. It refers to meet the long term requirements of the industry. Generally the business concerns need two kinds of finance.

(a) Short term funds for working capital requirements.

(b) Long term funds for purchasing fixed assets.

Therefore the requirements of working capital of the industry are met by the money market. The long term requirements of the funds to the corporate sector are supplied by the Capital Market. It refers to the institutional arrangements which facilitates the lending and borrowing of long term funds. In this market long period maturity securities are exchanged. Generally every market is based on supply and demand forces. In Capital Market, the corporations require the funds on long term basis. They are leading borrowers of funds in the Capital Market for their business. They mobilise the funds by issuing various financial instruments. These financial instruments will have a long term maturity period. On the demand side the central government, state governments and local bodies are also included. All of these institutions need the fund to meet their development activities. The business concerns, farmers unincorporated business firms are other demanders of the Capital Market fund. On the supply side of the Capital Market, the individuals, are the bulk suppliers of fund. Their investment is done through financial intermediaries, financial institutions, banking institutions or directly. The Individuals has the largest potential savings in the country. They tend to keep their surplus funds in savings according to the prevailing interest rates. In addition to individual investors. The other suppliers in the capital market, are companies, MFs, NBFCs, financial institutions. Many organisations are both demanders and suppliers of capital Market funds in a large size. Capital markets are very dynamic. They play an important role in mobilising resources.

These mobilised resources are diverted towards productive way. Therefore it not only mobilises the savings but also helps in Industrial development of the country. The success of a country depends upon the *financial architecture* of the strong capital market. A strong capital market is required for the process of economic growth in the country. A developed and competitive capital market tends to establish equilibrium between saving and investment. The borrowers of the capital market raise funds through various instruments like ***equity, preference, bond and Mortgages.***

Functions of Capital Market

Capital Market plays a vital role in the development by mobilising the savings to the needy corporate sector. In recent years there has been a substantial growth in the Capital Market. The Capital Market involves in various functions and significance. They are presented below.

(a) Coordinator.

(b) Motivation to savings.

(c) Transformation to investment.

(d) Enhances economic growth.

(e) Stability.

(f) Advantages to investors.

(g) Barometer.

(a) Coordinator: The Capital Market functions as Coordinator between savers and investors. It mobilises the savings from those who have surplus fund and divert them to the needy persons or organisations. Therefore it acts as a facilitator of the financial resource. In this way it plays a vital role in transferring the surplus resources to deficit sectors. It increases the productivity of the industry which ultimately reflects in GDP and National income of the country. It increase the prosperity of the nation.

(b) Motivation of Savings: Capital market provides a wide range of financial instruments at all times. India has a vast number of individual savers and the crores of rupees are available with them. These resources can be attracted by the capital market with nature. The banks and Non bank financial institutions motivate the people to save more and more. In less developed countries, there are no efficient capital markets to tap the savings. In under developed countries there are very little savings due to various factors. In that countries they invest mostly in unproductive sector.

(c) Transformation of Investment: The capital market is a place where the savings are mobilised from various sources, is at the disposal of businessman and the government. It facilitates lending to the corporate sector and the government. It diverts the savings amount towards capital formation of the corporate sector. It creates assets by helping the industry. Thus it enhances the productivity and leads to industrialisation. The Industrial development of the country depends upon the dynamic nature of the capital market. It also provides facilities through banks and Non financial institutions. The development of financial institutions made the way easy to capital market. The capital has become more mobile. The Interest rate falls lead to an increase in the investment.

THE INDUSTRIAL INVESTMENT PROPOSALS (AUGUST 1991 TO MARCH 2002)

Sl. No.	*State/UTs*	*Total Investment (Rs. in crores)*	*Percentage*
(1)	Maharashtra	2,21,750	20.60
(2)	Gujarat	1,79,702	16.70
(3)	Tamil Nadu	69,012	6.41
(4)	U.P	76.081	7.07
(5)	Andhra Pradesh	1,17,310	10.90
(6)	Haryana	32,874	3.05
(7)	Rajasthan	40,278	3.74
(8)	Punjab	53,255	4.95
(9)	West Bengal	36,135	3.36
(10)	MP	43,777	4.07
(11)	Karnataka	54,490	5.06
(12)	Dadra & Nagar Haveli	19,960	1.85
(13)	Daman and Diu	4,054	0.38
(14)	Chattisgarh	26,882	2.50
(15)	Kerala	10,513	0.98
(16)	Pondicherry	7,464	0.69
(17)	Delhi	6,480	0.60
(18)	Goa	6,357	0.59
(19)	HP	9,428	0.88
(20)	Orissa	26,946	2.50
(21)	Jharkand	10,786	1.00
(22)	Uttaranchal	5,881	0.55
(23)	Assam	7,586	0.70
(24)	Bihar	4,468	0.42
(25)	Meghalaya	741	0.07
(26)	J & K	804	0.07
(27)	Chandigarh	458	0.04
(28)	Tripura	1,834	0.17
(29)	Sikkim	33	0.00
(30)	Andaman and Nicobar	332	0.03
(31)	Arunachal Pradesh	68	0.01
(32)	Nagaland	207	0.02
(33)	Lakshadeep	04	0.00
(34)	Manipur	0	0.00
(35)	Mizoram	0	0.00
(36)	More than one state	377	0.04
	Total	**10,76,327**	**100%**

Source : *EPW, 17-08-02, p. 3387.*

STATEMENT SHOWING YEAR ON YEAR GROWTH RATES OF GDP AT FACTOR COST AT CURRENT PRICES.

(per cent)

Sl. No.	*Sector*	*1998-99*	*1999-00*	*2000-01*	*2001-02*
(1)	Agriculture Forestry and Fishing	18.8	0.1	2.5	9.6
(2)	Mining and Quarrying	5.0	15.4	10.2	7.1
(3)	Manufacturing	8.5	6.0	12.3	4.7
(4)	Electricity, gas and water supply	20.4	3.3	12.9	17.6
(5)	Construction	18.1	14.7	10.4	7.4
(6)	Trade, hotels transport and communications	15.1	8.8	9.3	9.4
(7)	Financing, insurance, real estate and business services	15.8	21.5	7.3	11.6
(8)	Community social and personal services	23.6	16.0	10.0	10.0
	GDP at Factor Cost	**16.3%**	8.6%	8.0%	9.1%

Sources: *EPW, 6-7-02, p. 2671.*

STATEMENT SHOWING THE YEAR ON YEAR GROWTH RATES OF GDP AT FACTOR COST AT 1993-94 PRICES

(per cent)

Sl. No.	*Sector*	*1998-99*	*1999-00*	*2000-01*	*2001-02*
(1)	Agriculture Forestry and Fishing	7.1	0.5	–0.2	5.7
(2)	Mining and Quarrying	1.3	3.5	3.3	1.8
(3)	Manufacturing	2.5	4.4	6.7	2.8
(4)	Electricity, gas and water supply	6.4	6.7	6.2	4.6
(5)	Construction	6.1	8.2	6.8	3.6
(6)	Trade, hotels transport and communications	7.1	8.3	5.3	6.2
(7)	Financing, insurance, real estate and business services	8.4	9.6	2.9	7.8
(8)	Community, social and personal services	9.9	12.1	6.0	5.9
	GDP at Factor Cost	**6.6%**	6.0%	4.0%	5.4%

STATEMENT SHOWING THE ANNUAL GDP FROM 1998-02. AT 1993-94 PRICES

(Rs. in crores)

Sl. No.	*Sector*	*1998-99*	*1999-00*	*2000-01*	*2001-02*
(1)	Agriculture forestry and fishing	2,88,401	2,89,842	2,89,194	3,05,818
(2)	Mining and quarrying	25,996	26,908	27,796	28,306
(3)	Manufacturing	1,84,263	1,92,404	2,05,220	2,11,021
(4)	Electricity, gas and water supply	26,831	28,637	30,406	31,804
(5)	Construction	54,342	58,815	62,801	65,081
(6)	Trade, hotels transport and communications	2,34,022	2,53,506	2,66,817	2,83,369
(7)	Financing, insurance, real estate and business services	1,33,130	1,45,865	1,50,051	1,61,696
(8)	Community, social and personal services	1,36,069	1,52,523	1,61,637	1,71,137
	GDP at factor cost	**10,83,054**	11,48,500	11,93,922	12,58,232

Source : EPW, 6-7-2002, p. 2671.

STATEMENT SHOWING THE ANNUAL GDP FROM 1998-2002 AT CURRENT PRICES

(Rs. in crores)

Sl. No.	*Sector*	*1998-99*	*1999-00*	*2000-01*	*2001-02*
(1)	Agriculture forestry and fishing	4,59,899	4,60,547	4,71,981	5,17,354
(2)	Mining and quarrying	35,105	40,520	44,648	47,807
(3)	Manufacturing	2,51,793	2,66,890	2,99,753	3,13,877
(4)	Electricity, gas and water supply	42,480	43,886	49,526	58,218
(5)	Construction	91,922	1,05,440	1,16,431	1,25,014
(6)	Trade, Hotels transport and communications	3,36,038	3,65,735	3,99,623	4,37,366
(7)	Financing, Insurance, Real estate and business services	1,81,575	2,20,561	2,36,645	2,64,124
(8)	Community, social and personal services	2,17,219	2,52,059	2,77,236	3,05,050
	GDP at factor cost	**16,16,031**	17,55,638	18,95,843	20,68,810

Source : *EPW, 6-7-02, P. 2671.*

STATEMENT SHOWING STATEWISE BREAKING-UP OF FOREIGN DIRECT INVESTMENT APPROVALS DURING AUG. 1991 TO MARCH 2002.

	States	*No. of Approvals*	*Amount (Rs. in crores)*	*Percentage*
I	**Northern Region:**			
	(a) Delhi	1,857	33,470	12,1
	(b) Haryana	769	3,518	1.3
	(c) Himachal Pradesh	96	364	0.1
	(d) Punjab	181	1,968	0.7
II	**Western Region:**			
	(a) Gujarat	1,032	18,265	6.6
	(b) Maharashtra	3,854	48,409	17.4
	(c) Rajasthan	319	3,005	1.1
III	**Eastern Region:**			
	(a) Bihar	47	740	0.3
	(b) Orissa	136	8,229	3.0
	(c) West Bengal	584	8,730	3.1
IV	**North Eastern Region**	30	63	0.0
V	**Central Region:**			
	(a) Madhya Pradesh	225	9,227	3.3
	(b) U.P	730	4,790	1.7
VI	**Southern Region:**			
	(a) A.P.	975	12,753	4.6
	(b) Karnataka	1,891	21,413	7.7
	(c) Kerala	259	1,525	0.5
	(d) Tamil Nadu	2,113	23,202	8.4
	(e) Pondicherry	110	1,241	0.4
	(f) Others	6,294	76,577	27.6
		21,502	**2,77,597**	**100%**

Sources: *EPW, 31-8-02, p. 3567.*

STATEMENT SHOWING FOREIGN INVESTMENT APPROVALS AND ACTUAL SINCE 1991 AUGUST COUNTRYWISE BREAK UP

Sl. No.	*Country*	*Investment (Rs. in crores)*	*Per cent to Total*
(1)	USA	56,616	20.40
(2)	Mauritius	32,918	11.90,
(3)	UK	21,405	7.7
(4)	Japan	10,858	3.9
(5)	South Korea	9,798	3.5
(6)	Germany	8,950	3.2
(7)	Netherlands	8,636	3.1
(8)	Australia	6,734	2.4
(9)	Malaysia	5,682	2.0
(10)	France	6,234	2.2
(11)	Singapore	4,945	1.8
(12)	Italy	4,779	1.7
(13)	Israel	4,244	1.5
(14)	Belgium	4,162	1.5
(15)	Calyman Island	3,861	1.4
(16)	Switzerland	3,011	1.1
(17)	Canada	2,726	1.0
(18)	Thailand	2,726	0.98
(19)	Hongkong	2,261	0.8
(20)	South Africa	1,906	0.7
(21)	Sweden	2,039	0.7
(22)	NRIs	10,408	3.7
(23)	Euro Issues	48,447	17.4
(24)	All others	14,346	5.2
		2,77,692	100

Sources: *EPW, 31-8-2002, p. 3567.*

STATEMENT SHOWING SAVINGS AND INVESTMENT (AS A PER CENT OF GDP AT CURRENT MARKET PRICES)

Year	*Gross domestic capital formation*	*Gross domestic savings*	*Public savings*	*Private savings*	*Household savings*	*Corporate savings*
Average 1985-90	22.7	20.4	2.4	18.0	16.0	2.0
1990-91	26.3	23.1	1.1	22.0	19.3	2.7
1991-92	22.6	22.0	2.0	20.1	17.0	3.1
1992-93	23.6	21.8	1.6	20.2	17.5	2.7
1993-94	23.1	22.5	0.6	21.9	18.4	3.5
1994-95	26.0	24.8	1.7	23.2	19.7	3.5

1995-96	26.9	25.1	2.0	23.1	18.2	4.9
1996-97	24.5	23.2	1.7	21.5	17.0	4.5
1997-98	24.6	23.1	1.3	21.8	17.6	4.2
1998-99	22.7	21.7	-1.0	22.6	18.9	3.7
1999-00	24.3	23.2	-0.9	24.0	20.3	3.7
2000-01QE	24.0	23.4	-1.7	25.1	20.9	4.2

Source : EPW, 13-7-62, p. 2903.

STATEMENT SHOWING THE INDEX OF GROSS FIXED CAPITAL FORMATION (AT 1993-94 PRICES) BY INDUSTRY OF USE (BASE 1993-94) = 100)

Sl. No.	*Sector*	*1993-94*	*94-95*	*95-96*	*96-97*	*97-98*	*98-99*	*99-00*
(1)	Agriculture	100	108.3	114.1	115.3	115.6	120.2	133.6
(2)	Industry	100	116.3	158.2	159.5	152.9	143.8	139.8
(3)	Manufacturing	100	114.7	186.0	194.4	179.4	165.1	153.4
(4)	Mining & Quarry	100	193.8	123.4	76.8	77.4	70.4	79.8
(5)	Electricity water, gas	100	91.4	86.2	94.1	94.4	101.7	112.5
(6)	Construction	100	164.4	244.2	130.3	277.9	238.4	252.2
(7)	Services	100	123.5	131.2	124.2	116.0	119.2	131.0
(8)	Trade, Hotels and Restaurant	100	146.2	189.6	133.3	119.2	118.8	116.9
(9)	Transport & storage	100	123.8	131.0	131.3	106.0	101.2	118.2
(10)	Financing Insurance	100	118.7	124.6	119.4	121.1	119.8	121.6
(11)	Community Services	100	123.1	121.8	199.8	199.6	142.4	168.8
(12)	Total (1 + 2 + 3)	100	118.5	143.9	141.9	135.2	132.1	135.8

Source : EPW 13.7.02, p. 2903.

STATEMENT SHOWING INDUSTRYWISE BREAK-UP OF FDI APPROVALS SINCE AUG. 1991 TO MARCH 2002

Sl. No.	*Name of Industry*	*No. of approvals*	*Amount of approval*	*% to total*
I	Basic goods industries	3,459	1,07,576	38.8
II	Capital goods industries	6,538	25,117	9.0
III	Intermediate goods industries	811	4,993	1.8
IV	Consumer Non durable industries	4,363	27,623	10.1
V	Consumer durable industries	159	9,357	3.4
VI	Services	6,172	1.02,928	37.1
	Grand Total	21,502	2,77,597	100

Sources: EPW, 31-8-2002, p. 3567.

STATEMENT SHOWING INDUSTRYWISE FOR INVESTMENT PROPOSALS (AUGUST 1991 TO MARCH 2002)

Sl.No.	*Industry*	*Total Investment (Rs. in crores)*	*Percentage*
(1)	Textiles	1,19,464	11.10
(2)	Chemicals	1,89,036	17.56
(3)	Metallurgical	1,46,541	13.61
(4)	Miscellaneous	84,494	7.85
(5)	Electrical equipment	50,818	4.72
(6)	Food processing Industry	33,889	3.15
(7)	Veg. oil and vanaspathi	18,409	1.71
(8)	Drugs and Pharma	15,926	1.48
(9)	Sugar	43,964	4.08
(10)	Paper and Pulp	40,442	3.76
(11)	Telecommunication	30,201	2.81
(12)	Mechanical and Engg	15,853	1.47
(13)	Industrial Machinery	16,275	1.51
(14)	Cement and Gypsum	67,972	6.32
(15)	Transportation	26,098	2.42
(16)	Fermentation industries	8,819	0.82
(17)	Prime movers	6,030	0.56
(18)	Rubber goods	11,247	1.04
(19)	Fertilisers	21,688	2.02
(20)	Fuels	92,834	8.63
(21)	Leather	4,038	0.38
(22)	Ceramics	3,742	0.35
(23)	Soaps cosmetics	3,477	0.32
(24)	Scientific instruments	4,124	0.38
(25)	Office equpt.	4,149	0.39
(26)	Glass	6,448	0.60
(27)	Machine Tools	1,950	0.18
(28)	Timber products	2,629	0.24
(29)	Photographic film	1,137	0.11
(30)	Agriculture machinery	1,843	0.17
(31)	Earth moving machinery	1,074	0.10
(32)	Glue and Gelatin	353	0.03
(33)	Dyestuffs	357	0.03
(34)	Medical and Surgical	575	0.05
(35)	Industrial Instruments	134	0.01
(36)	Defence Industries	265	0.02
(37)	Map Survey and Drawings	4	0.00
(38)	Boiler and Steam Generators	28	0.00
	Total	**10,76,327**	**100.00**

Source: *EPW, 17-08-02, p. 3387.*

(d) Enhances Economic Growth: The development of the capital market is influenced by many factors like the level of savings with the public, per capital income, purchasing capacity, and the general condition of the economy. The capital market smoothens and accelerates the process of economic growth. The capital market consists of various institutions like banking and Non-banking financial institutions.

It allocates the resources very cautiously in accordance with the development needs of the country. The balanced and proper allocation of the financial resources lead to the expansion of the Industrial sector. Therefore it promotes the balances regional development. All regions should be developed in the country.

(e) Stability: The capital market provides a stable security prices in the stock market. It tends to stabilise the value of stocks and securities. It reduces the fluctuations in the prices to the minimum level. The process of stabilisation is facilitated by providing funds to the borrowers at a lower interest rates. The speculative prices in the stock market can be reduced by supply of funds. The flow of funds towards secondary market reduces the prices at certain level. Therefore the capital market provides funds to the stock market at a low rate of interest.

(f) Advantages to the Investors: The investors those who have surplus funds can invest in long term financial instruments. In capital market, a number of long term financial instruments are available to the investors at any time. Hence the investors can lend their money in the capital market at reasonable rate of interest. The capital market helps the investors in many ways. It is the coordinator to bring the buyer and seller at one place and ensures the marketability of investments. The stock market prices are published in newspapers every day which enables the investor to keep track of their investments and channalise them into most profitable way. The capital market safeguards the interest of the investors by compensating from the stock exchange compensating fund in case of fraud and default.

(g) Barometer: The development of the capital market is the indicator of the development of a nation. The prosperity and wealth of a nation depends upon the dynamic capital market. It not only reflects the general condition of the economy but also smoothens and accelerates the process of economic growth. The capital market consists a number of institutions, allocates the resources rationally in accordance with the development needs of the country. A good allocation of resources lead to expansion of trade and industry. The capital market helps both public and private sector.

The term Capital Market has been defined by different authors. According to Gitman and Joehnk, "Capital Market is the market where transactions are made in long term securities such as stocks and debentures."[6]

Capital Market has been defined "The market for relatively long term (greater than one year original maturity) financial instruments"[7]

Generally the corporate sector requires funds not only for meeting their long term requirements of funds for their new projects modernisation, expansion and diversification programmes but also for covering their operational needs. Therefore their requirement of capital is classified as given below.

(A) Long term capital.

(B) Short term capital.

(C) Venture capital.

(D) Export capital.

Long term capital represents the amount of capital invested in the form of fixed assets. Fixed assets are such as land, building, Plant and Machinery necessary for every company at the initial stage of the commencement of the production. Heavy amount of capital is required by the companies when they are going for modernisation or expansion or diversification. Therefore the requirement of long term capital is supplied by the capital market. The long term capital is also known as ***"Fixed Capital"***. Usually the corporate sector mobilises the fixed capital from the capital market through various long term maturity financial instruments. Therefore the capital market provide adequate funds to the corporate sector by offering a various financial instruments. They mobilise the funds through issue of ***Equity shares,***

6. P. Subramaniyan, *Capital Market*, Kalyani Publications.

7. Fundamentals of Financial Management.

Preference shares, Debentures, bonds etc. These financial instruments have a longer maturity period and they are treated by the companies as permanent capital. Some instruments have no maturity until the close down of a business unit.

Short term capital represents the amount of capital invested in current Assets. The Current Assets consists of cash, bank balance, Inventory, Debtors etc. The short term capital is required to meet the need of working capital of the corporate sector. Working capital is required for meeting the operating cost of the business concern. They are required to pay different amount to different parties as per their schedule. Hence they procure the working capital from the commercial banks. In India a majority of the corporate sector is funded by commercial banks for working capital needs. The working capital may be sanctioned by the banks through different modes of finance. The working capital is known as circulating capital. An adequate supply of working capital leads to smooth functioning production of the goods. There are some other avenues available to the corporate sector to meet the needs of the working capital.

Venture capital is the capital invested in highly risky ventures. It is also known as seed capital. It is a quite recent entrant in the capital market. It has great significance in helping technocrate entrepreneurs at the commencement stage of the concern. It has technical expertise. But it lacks finance.

Export capital refers for making payment in international trade. The payment of international trade involves in bills of exchange and other instruments.

Importance of Capital Market

Capital market deals with long term funds. These funds are subject to uncertainty and risk. It supplies long term funds and medium term funds to the corporate sector. It provides the mechanism for facilitating capital fund transactions. It deals in ordinary shares, bonds debentures and stocks and securities of the government. In this market the funds flow will come from savers. It converts financial assets into productive physical assets. It provides incentives to savers in the form of interest or dividend to the investors. It leads to capital formation. The following factors play an important role in the growth of the capital market.

(1) A strong and powerful Central Government.

(2) Financial dynamics.

(3) Speedy industrialisation.

(4) Attracting Foreign Investment.

(5) Investments from NRIs.

(6) Speedy implementation of policies.

(7) Regulatory changes.

(8) Globalisation.

(9) The level of savings and investment pattern of the household sectors.

(10) Development of financial theories.

(11) Sophisticated technological advances.

Players in the Capital Market

Capital Market is a market for long term funds. It requires a well structured market to enhance the financial capability of the country. The market consists a number of players. They are categorised as:

(1) Companies.

(2) Financial Intermediaries.

(3) Investors.

1. Companies: Generally every company which is a public limited company can access the capital market. The companies which are in need of finance for their projects can approach the market. The capital market provides funds from the savers of the community. The companies can mobilise the resources for their long term needs such as project cost, expansion & diversification of projects and other expenditure items. In India, the companies should get the prior permission from the securities and Exchange Board of India to raise the capital from the market. The SEBI is the most powerful organisation to monitor, control and guidance the capital market. It classifies the companies for the issue of share capital as ***New companies, existing unlisted companies and existing listed companies.*** According to its guidelines a company is a new company, if it satisfies all the following conditions.

(a) The company shall not complete ***12 months*** of commercial operations.

(b) Its audited operative results are not available.

(c) The company may set up by entrepreneurs with or without track record.

A company which can be treated as existing listed company, if its shares are listed in any recognised stock exchange in India. A company is said to be an existing unlisted company if it is a closely held or private company.

2. Financial Intermediaries: Financial intermediaries are those who assist in the process of converting savings into capital formation in the country. A strong capital formation process is the *oxygen* to the corporate sector. Therefore the intermediaries occupy a dominant role in the capital formation which ultimately lead to the growth of prosperous to the community. Their role in this situation cannot be neglected. The government should encourage these intermediaries to build a strong financial empire for the country. They are also be called as *financial architectures* of the Indian ***digital economy.*** Their network cannot be ignored. Their financial capability cannot be measured. They take active role in the capital market. The major intermediaries in the capital market are:

(a) Brokers.

(b) Stock brokers and sub brokers.

(c) Merchant bankers.

(d) Underwriters.

(e) Registrars.

(f) Mutual funds.

(g) Collecting agents.

(h) Depositories.

(i) Agents.

(j) Advertising agencies.

3. Investors: The capital market consists many number of investors. All types of investors basic objective is to get good returns on their investment. Investment means, just parking one's idle fund in a right parking place for a stipulated period of time. Every parked vehicle shall be taken away by its owners from parking place after a specific period. The same process may be applicable to the investment. Every fund owner may desire to take away the fund after a specific period. Therefore safety is the most important factor while considering the investment proposal. The investors comprise the financial and Investment companies and the general public companies. Usually the individual savers are also treated as investors. **Return** is the reward to the investors. *Risk* is the punishment to the investors for being wrong selection of their investment decision. Return is always chased by the Risk. An intelligent investor must always try to escape the risk and attract the return. All rational investors prefer return, but most investors are risk average. They attempt to get maximum capital gain. The return can be available to the investors in two types they are in the form of revenue or capital appreciation. Some investors will prefer for revenue receipt and others prefer capital appreciation. It depends upon their economic status and the effect of tax implications. The institutions and companies raise the resources from the market by designing various schemes to meet the needs and convenience of the investors. The schemes can be framed to attract all the types of investors, those who are sailing in the capital market. The main objectives of any type of investors are ***safety, profitability, liquidity and capital appreciation***.

Before Independence

The capital market in India was not scientifically developed before independence. The following are basic reasons for non-development of the capital market in India.

(a) Agriculture was the basic occupation of the people but there was no proper long term lending to this sector.

(b) The British rulers were concentrated more on London market rather than Indian capital market.

(c) The number of companies were small and the number of scrips traded on stock exchanges also were smaller.

(d) Individual investors were very few and limited.

(e) The government had imposed many restrictions on the institutional savers.

(f) The absence of specialised financial intermediaries in pre-independence period.

The capital market had not been developed properly because of the British rulers.

Indian Capital Market Post in Independence

The Indian capital market has been growing significantly after 1951. After independence many regulations have been changed for the smooth functioning of our economy. Some acts have been abolished and others have been amended according to the needs and convenience of the public. Therefore many factors have contributed to the capital market growth.

(a) Raising levels of Income and Investment.

(b) New financial Institutions.

(c) Expansion of commercial banks.

(d) Dynamic growth of specialised financial institutions.

Raising Level of Income and Investment: After 1951, there has been increase in the volume of saving and investment in the country. The capital market entirely depend upon the savings of the community. The government has taken some measures to strengthen the capital market. It provided all kinds of encouragement and tax relief to promote savings in the country. It concentrated on the investors problems and many steps have been taken to promote the welfare of the investors. After 1951, there was a spectacular growth in the joint stock companies which is an important indicator of the market there was an increase in the growth of public borrowing for investment purpose. The insurance sector also led to the promotion of savings and supply of funds in the market. The provident fund collections have been increased significantly which leads to the promotion of capital market. The increased number of financial institutions and intermediaries encouraged mobilization and channelization of country's savings.

New Financial Institutions: The financial institutions occupies an important role in the capital market. They have not only accelerated the growth but also improved its efficiency and competitiveness effectively. The following institutions provide special types of financial services:

(a) Merchant banking.

(b) Leasing and hire purchasing companies.

(c) Mutual funds.

(d) Venture capital.

(e) Other institutions.

All of the above topics will be covered in preceding chapters.

Expansion of Commercial Banks: Commercial banks are the financial nervus of the Indian economy. The Indian economy growth has been linked with the commercial bank system. They are the important constituents of the capital market. Their operations in this market are limited to purchase and sale of the government securities. Their holdings of industrial securities are very small. Recently the banks have been increasingly participating in term lending directly or indirectly through subscription of shares and debentures. Thais situation encourages investment in industrial securities.

Dynamic Growth of Specialised Financial Institutions: After independence, the government of India had been taken a number of steps to assist the private sector industries in the matter of finance. The initiative of the government lead to promote the *Industrial finance corporation of India* in 1948. It was the first financial institution, which was India's established after the independence. It was the premier financial institutions to provide the financial assistance to the corporate sector. After the formation of the IFCIs, it was followed by state finance corporations set up by state governments. These SFCs provide financial assistance to small and medium industrial units. The following institutions had been established after the independence at the initiative of the central government.

(A) Industrial credit and investment corporation of India (ICICI 1956).

(B) Industrial Development Bank of India (IDBI 1964).

(C) Unit Trust of India (1964).

(D) Life Insurance Corporation of India (1956).

These financial institutions have been rendering excellent services to the existing new and old companies. They provide finance in the form of loan assistance, underwriting new issues, and subscription to shares and debentures. These institutions are engaged in the channelizing of resources to private sector.

Distinction between Capital and Money Market

There are some differences between money market and capital market. Money market is different from the capital market on the basis of the following owing characteristics

(a) Period of time.

(b) Financial instruments.

(c) Purpose of loan.

(d) Risk.

(e) Market regulation.

(f) Liquidity.

(g) Monitoring.

(h) Players.

(a) Period of Time: The money market is a market for lending and borrowing of the short term finance. The term short term period refers to finance available for one year or less to the borrowers. Generally the borrowers will procure the fund for meeting their working capital requirements. Usually the working capital of the corporate sector is supplied by mostly commercial banks and players of the money market. While the capital market is a market where the long term funds are available at reasonable rates of interest to the borrowers. Usually the fixed capital of the corporate sector will be met by the long term nature of financial instruments. These financial instruments are available in the capital market only. The corporate sector will also be supplied the fund by the capital market for the purpose of their *project expansion, diversification* and other needs.

(b) Financial Instruments: The companies generally raise the fund from market by issuing a number of financial instruments. The money market consists of short term financial instruments such as ***call money, CDs, Bills, and collateral loans etc.,*** On the other hand the main instruments are used in the capital market for long term basis: These financial instruments such as ***shares, debentures and bonds*** are issued by the companies for their requirements.

(c) Purpose of Loans: The companies enter the money market to meet the needs of their short term finance. The money market issues different types of financial instruments for one year period to meet the needs of working capital. The working capital arrangements will be adjusted by the money market while the fixed capital by the capital market. The long term needs of finance will be adjusted by the capital market to the corporate sector.

(d) Risk: Generally the financial markets involves some degree of risk. The level of degree of risk depends upon the nature of market. The money market involves less risk level while the capital markets consists higher level of risk. The money market maturity period is one year gives little time for default to occur. On the other hand the capital market caters to the long term credit needs of the corporate sector and arrangements will be made for fixed capital to buy land or machinery.

(e) Market Regulation: In India, the market is closely observed by the prudential authorities. It is necessary to regulate the market operations for better functioning of the financial system. In the capital market the institutions are not much regulated. The money market is regulated by RBI, SEBI and Ministry of Finance.

(f) Liquidity: Liquidity is the most important factor in the money market. The role of money is creation of liquidity. The money market is a ready market for its financial assets. The basic role of capital market is providing funds to work on long term basis. The financial instruments which are available in the capital market ar productive employment and generation of assets in the economy. Asset formation is made by the capital market.

(g) Monitoring: The money market is closely associated with the Central Bank of the country. The Central Bank in India is RBI. The RBI is the supreme authority in the money market. It is directly linked with the Central Banks of India. But the capital market is regulated observed, and monitored by the SEBI. The RBI has less control on capital market.

(h) Players: The important players in the money market are Central Bank, Acceptance house, commercial banks, Non banking financial institutions, bill brokers etc., But in capital market stock exchanges, insurance companies, mortgage banks, non banking institutions are important players.

The secondary market for Money market is not active in India. But the secondary market for capital market has very active. The investment in money market is highest safety whereas the investment in capital market is not so safe. The accessibility to money market by individual is not possible but capital market provides easy accessibility to the individuals.

Structure of Capital Market in India

The structure of the capital market has undergone vast changes in recent years. The Indian capital market has transformed into a new appearance over the last four and half decades. Now it comprises an impressive network of financial institutions and financial instruments. The market for already issued securities has become more sophisticated in response to the different needs of the investors. The specialised financial institutions were involved in providing long term credit to the corporate sector. Therefore the premier financial institutions such as ICICI, IDBI, UTI, LIC and GIC constitute the largest segment. A number of new financial instruments and financial intermediaries have emerged in the capital market. Usually the capital markets are classified in two ways.

(a) On the basis of Issuer.

(b) On the basis of Instruments.

On the basis of issuer the capital markets can be classified again two types.

(a) Corporate securities market.

(b) Government securities market.

On the basis of financial instruments the capital markets are classified into two kinds.

(a) Equity market.

(b) Debt market.

Recently there has been a substantial development of the Indian capital market. It comprises various sub-markets.

Equity market is more popular in India. It refers to the market for equity shares of existing and new companies. Every company shall approach the market for raising of funds. The equity market can be divided into two categories (a) primary market (b) secondary market. Debt market represent the market for long term financial instruments such as debentures, bonds etc., The structure of Indian capital market is shown below:

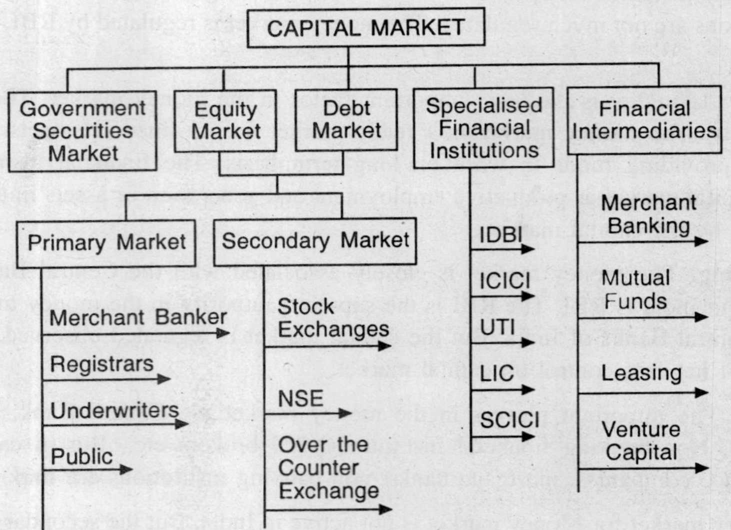

Structure of Capital Market

Components of the Capital Market

Indian capital market has a vast growth potential. It has most powerful avenue for household savings. India has a vast middle class families potential they occupy a dominant role in mobilization of resources. They play an important role in capital market. The corporate sector had been attracted 10% household savings of the community. In the developed countries more than 20 to 25 per cent of householdings are tapped by their capital markets. In the developed countries 25% of population go for shareholdings but in India such percentage is just less than 5%. The society for capital market Research and development was conducted a shareholders survey in 1990. It placed the total number of share owners at around ***90 – 100 lakh***.[8] The survey also traced the past growth of share owning population since 1955. The total number of individual share owners at the end of 1977 in India is at around 2

8. Household's Investment Preferences, SCMRD, Jan. 2001, p. 111.

crores. Most of the growth after 1990 took place during the boom years 1991-94. The analysis showed that the growth of share owners tapering of since 1995 had come to a near halt in 1997 due to persistent depression in the share market and investors bad experiences with many scrupulous company promoters and managements.

The capital market in India consist of two components.

1. New issue market or primary market
2. The secondary market.

C. PRIMARY MARKET OR NEW ISSUE MARKET

Introduction

The capital market in India consists of two kinds (a) primary market (b) secondary market Primary market is known as new issue market. The new issue market is also called as "public issue". In the primary market, new securities are sold or exchanged for cash credit or other securities. The new securities can be issued by the existing companies are newly floated companies the primary market can be defined as. "A market where new securities are bought and sold for the first time."[9]

Primary market is a new issues market. The funds are raised through the sale of new securities flow from the buyers of securities to the issuer of securities. The financial institutions play a key important role in moving funds from the savings sector to the investment sector. A large manufacturing company require bulk amount of capital for its needs. They raises funds both publicly and privately with more confident. Raising funds from the public is known as public issues. Public issue can be defined as *"Sale of bonds or stock to the general public."[10] The securities are sold to the lakhs of investors under a formal contract overseen by the government authorities. The required funds can also be raised privately to a limited number of investors. This process is known as private placement"*. The primary market creates financial claims. In this market the public can only buy the shares. Two parties are involved in this market, they are lenders and the borrowers. The funds are flown from the lenders to the borrowers.

Objectives of Capital Issues: Generally the companies requires two kinds of capital. They are (a) fixed capital (b) working capital. Fixed capital is in need of financing the capital assets. It is raised for buying of fixed assets like machinery, plant, equipment, land, building at the initial stage of a project. Sometimes existing companies can also be raised funds from the primary market. The issue of capital can be raised for any of the following purposes.

(a) Promotion of new project.
(b) Expansion of the existing capacity.
(c) Diversification.
(d) Capitalization of Reserves.
(e) Regular working capital requirement.

Sources for Raising Funds

The corporate sector usually raises funds from the market for their needs and convenience. They can procure the funds through the following sources.

(a) Issue of equity at par or premium.
(b) Issue of bonus shares.

9. C. Vanhorne, Fundamentals of Financial Management, PHI, p. 527.

10. Ibid.

(c) Issue of debentures.

(d) Issue of bonds by public sector undertakings.

(e) Issue of cumulative preference shares.

In the primary market, funds are available from lenders to park their funds on long term basis. The companies government semi government bodies PSUs and a number of other institutions borrow issue of securities by the way of shares and debentures.

Features of the NIM: The major features of the primary market are as follows:

(a) The capital market is freely accessible by any company for raising funds from the public.

(b) The corporates have freedom in fixing of issue price of a share subject to some SEBI guidelines.

(c) The companies approaches capital market rather than banks and financial institutions for rasing of funds.

(d) The mushroom growth of companies and a spate of new issue by both new companies as well as existing companies.

Classification of New Issues

The New issue market is to facilitate transfer of funds of those who have surplus income and are willing to invest to entrepreneurs. The new issues in this market may be classified as follows.

(a) First issue of new companies. (entrepreneurs without a track record).

(b) First issue of new companies (set up by existing companies with a track record).

(c) First issue by existing private/closely held company. (without 3 year track record).

(d) First issue by existing private/closely held company (with 3 year track record).

(e) First public issue by existing private/closely held/existing unlisted/without 3 year track record/but promoted by existing companies with 5 years track record).

(f) Existing private/closely held and other unlisted companies without three year track record of consistent profitability seeking disinvestment by offer to public without issuing fresh capital).

(g) Existing private closely held or other existing unlisted company with 3 years track record of consistent profitability seeking disinvestment by offer to public without issuing fresh capital.

(h) Public issue by existing listed companies.

Transactions of Primary Market

The primary market is a market, where the companies found money as per their requirements. It is to facilitate the transfer of resources from savers to entrepreneurs. The general function of NIM can be split from the operational view into three services, they are:

(a) Investigation.

(b) Underwriting.

(c) Distribution.

(a) Investigation: The new proposals of the company may be investigated by the specialised agencies. The preliminary investigations entails a careful study of investigations regarding technical economic, financial and legal aspects of the issuing companies. The specialised agency renders the following services for improving the quality of capital issues. These services include advice on such aspects of capital issues as:

(a) Determination of the class of security and the price of the issues in the light of market conditions.

(b) The timing and magnitude of issues.

(c) Methods of flotation.

(d) technique of selling.

(b) Underwriting: Underwriting is a guarantee about the success of an issue. The issuing company can eliminate the uncertainties of the public issue by making an agreement with the underwriter. The provision of underwriting is of crucial significance to the issuing company as well as investing public.

(c) Distribution: The success of a public issue depend upon many factors. The sale of securities to the ultimate investors is called as distribution. These specialise job can be handled by a highly specialised persons. These specialised persons are called as brokers and dealers in securities. They are highly specialised persons in dealing securities and debentures. They are powerful intermediaries in selling the shares to the public. They maintain regular contacts with the ultimate investors. The investors are the regular customers to the broker. They know about the buying habits and investment attitudes of the investors. They play an important role in investment decisions of the investors. They guide, direct and motivate the ultimate investors in talking a decision with regard to investment decisions.

Issue Process: The public issue is the most important event in the life of a company. The success of an issue depends upon the issue process. The issue of shares can be made by any one of the following method.

(a) Public issue through prospectus.

(b) Book building method.

(c) Private placement.

(d) Offer for sale.

(e) Rights issue.

Any one of the above methods can be adopted by the issuing company. The companies have freedom to select any one of the option to enter into the market. Let us discuss each methods advantages and their role in market.

(a) Public Issue through Prospectus: Public issue is more popular in India. It is one of the best method available to the corporate sector. Generally the corporate enterprises raise capital through the issue of securities by means of a prospectus inviting subscription from the public. In this method, the issuing company invite the public by issue of prospectus. The prospectus is a document which contains all the particulars about the issuing company. The prospectus is an evidence document to the investors. The investors can be informed about the future activities of the company and past information. The issuing company offers directly to the general public, a fixed number of shares at a stated price. The public issues are generally underwritten to ensure success without any uncertainties at the market.

The prospectus is the base for investing money into a company by the ultimate investor. Therefore the contents of the memorandum shall contain the information, according to the companies act. The disclosure of information in the prospectus shall be legal aspects of the companies act. Every care should be taken while preparing the prospectus. It also provide both civil and criminal liability for any misstatement in the prospectus. The additional information also be furnished according to the SEBI guidelines. The prospectus shall contain the following information.

(1) Company name and Registered office address.

(2) Present activities and proposed activities.

(3) Location of the industry.

(4) Particulars regarding capital such as authorized capital, subscribed and proposed issue of capital to public.

(5) Date of opening and closing of subscription list.

(6) Minimum amount of subscription.

(7) Name of broker, underwriters and others.

(8) Name of underwriters along with directors opinion regarding underwriters capabilities.

(9) A statement regarding the listing arrangements to the concerned stock exchanges.

(10) Other legal information about the company.

The public issue method has some advantages and disadvantages. This system has the advantage that the transactions are carried on in the full light of publicity. In public issues, the shares are allotted to a widerange of the investors. The share ownership is widely diffused thereby contributing to the prevention of concentration of wealth and economic power. The issues are widely distributed and the threat of an artificial restriction on the quantity of shares available is avoided. The issue of shares publicly is a highly expensive method. The cost of flotation involves underwriting expenses, brokerage, printing charges of prospectus, advertisement changes, accountancy charges, legal charges, bank charges, stamp duty, listing fee, registration charges, travelling expenses, filling of document charges, mortgage deed charges and postal charges. Therefore the public issue is suitable only to large companies for ***Mega issue.*** It cannot be useful to small issues for even large companies. It involve in preparation of prospectus printing of share application distribution of forms throughout the nation. It is a time consuming process.

(b) Book Building Method: The book building is one of the sale procedure of fresh equity. In this method, the price of the issue is left to the investors. It is also on par with the system of public issue. Public issue refers to issue of shares to the public. But in this method the issuing company incorporates all the information of the issue proposal in the offer document. The offer document will be prepared on the lines of the public issue method which includes the reserve or minimum price. The investors are required to quote the number of shares and the price at which they are willing to acquire. It is very popular method for raising finance in abroad. In India this method has not been widely accepted.

(c) Private Placement: Private placement is another method of new issue of capital. In this method the shares are offered privately to the investors or to the issue houses. Placing of securities which are unquoted is known as private placing. Generally the securities of a particular company are acquired by the issue houses and the issue houses in turn will sell to the Individual and institutional investors. The issue houses have a list of private and institutional investors who are potential to subscribe to any securities which are issued in this manner. The shares will be transferred to the individual /institutional investors with a margin by the issue houses. This method of selling new issues made by the companies are cheap. Because there is no involvement of any flotation expenses like brokerage, underwriting expenses, Advertising charges and printing and distribution of stationery.

(d) Offer for Sale: Offer for Sale means, the shares are offered through the intermediaries, i.e. Merchant, banks, Investment banks, firms stock brokers, issue houses. In this method, they will follow the process of public issue by drafting the prospectus. The prospectus contains about the prescribed minimum contents which is the basis for the sale of securities. The shares are distributed to the applicants in a non-discriminatory manner. However these issues are underwritten to avoid the possibility of the issue being left largely in the hands of financial intermediary. The offer for sale involves two stages. They are :

(a) In the first stage the issuing company sells the securities enbloc to the financial intermediary at an agreed fixed price. Therefore the shares are acquired by the financial intermediary.

(b) In the second stage the acquired financial intermediary will sell the shares to the ultimate investors. The securities which are offered to the public is generally higher than which they acquired from the issuing company. The difference between buying and selling price of equity is known as ***"turn"***. The term is known as remuneration of the issuing houses. Generally the turn, the remuneration of financial intermediary involves underwriting commission, prospectus cost, advertisement cost etc. The main advantage of this method is that the issuing company will not feel trouble in selling of the shares.

(e) Rights Issue: All of the above methods can be used by both new companies and existed companies. The existed companies shares are already listed and widely held shares can be offered to the existing shareholders. This method is known as *Rights issues.* According to this method, the existing shareholders are offered the right to subscribe to new shares in proportion to the number of shares as previously they hold. This offer will be made to existing shareholders only by a circular. The companies act sec. 81 reveals that a company shall issue right shares in the following situations.

(a) The company can issue rights offer after two years of its formation or

(b) After one year of first issue of shares.

From the above situation which ever is earlier these have to be first offered to the existing shareholders with a right to renounce them in favour of a nominee. A company can dispense with this requirement by passing a special resolution to the same effect. They are not normally underwritten. The merit of rights issue is that it is an inexpensive companies method. This method can be used only by existing companies. In this method the general investing public has no opportunity to participate in the new companies. Generally the rights issue were not underwritten. But some organisations will take care to underwrite the issue. It is only a precautionary measure. The experience of underwritten companies reveals that there is no need of the services of the underwriters in Rights issue. Therefore the company can reduce its expenses by avoiding underwriting. The other usual expenses like brokerage administrative expenses, and advertising changes are of very small extent. However it is more economical exercise for the issuing companies.

All of the above methods of flotation of new issues are suitable in different situations to different organisation.

Difference between NIM and Secondary Market

(1) The NIM deals with the fresh issue of securities to the investing public for the first time. The secondary market is a market for already issued securities. In this market the shares are moving with some velocity.

(2) The NIM provides funds directly to the Industrial projects. They are involved in capital formation but secondary market does not create any additional fund directly to the corporate sector. They provide liquidity to the market.

(3) The NIM is a market which does not have a physical existence and administrative set up. But the stock exchanges have excellent physical infrastructure and are located at various geographical Areas throughout the nation.

(4) The NIM is a market where the securities are made available the first time to the public. The secondary market serve all the sectors in India. It also makes a continuous valuation of securities traded in the market.

(5) The NIM exists in the market and it is recognised by the services that it renders services at a particular time only. But the secondary market provides all facilities in the form of a market place. It consists of dealers of security where they regularly meet at an appointed time.

Relationship between the NIM and Secondary Market

(a) The NIM is the facilitator for corporates, borrowers, and lenders. These securities are listed on a recognised stock exchange. The listing of securities creates a facility of convenience holdings of new securities which expand the initial market for them.

(b) The stock exchanges regulate the organisation of new issues for fair dealings.

(c) The NIM and secondary markets are complimentary in nature in providing capital to the industrial sector through securities.

(d) The infrastructural facilities are provided with the combination of various financial intermediaries. They provide excellent first hand information about the functioning of the corporate sector. They supply all the financial literature, information and supply of daily stock exchange lists to the investors.

(e) The response to the public issues are mainly dependent on the conditions pertaining in the stock market. If the secondary market is in active and shows a better movement then it will be reflected in the NIM. Therefore the NIM is dependent on the secondary market. If the secondary market is dull and not quite encouraging, then there is no market for new issues.

Factors to be Considered or Investment to Primary Market

Primary market is a market where the funds are available to the borrowers from savers. It is the place where the funds are at disposal of corporate sector. The market is now regulated by the SEBI. According to the SEBI guidelines the issues has the right to fix its DWN issue prices. The SEBI also issued guidelines to the corporate sector for raising of funds from the market. The SEBI guidelines reveal that the issuer companies shall disclose full information about them to the investors. The guidelines provide protection to the investors which shall be followed by the corporate sector. The investors in stock market shall behave more cautiously. They are responsible for their own decisions which are taken by them with the lack of awareness. The set of guidelines is intended to educate the investors about certain aspects which they normally should look for in the memorandum of association. They should check the contents which are disclosed by the issuing company in the memorandum of association. The memorandum shall contain all the information of prospectus accompanying all application forms before making investment in any issue. The investor may contact the company or merchant banker. If he require any additional information relating to the issue. The investors shall assess the situation and should look into the following matters.

(a) Promoter's History
(b) Objectives of the present issue
(c) Project information
(d) Product or market observation
(e) Financial information
(f) Forecasting
(g) Pricing of issue
(h) Litigations
(i) Risk factors
(j) Auditor's Report
(k) Statutory Dues
(l) Statutory clearances
(m) Careful observation
(n) Problems of New Issue Market
(o) Regulatory Framework.

(a) Promoter's History: The investors should look into the proper disclosures on all the aspects of promoters involvement in the proposed project. They should check the background of the promoters, their qualification, technical experience, past experience in the market, business capabilities, tactics, their reputation in the market etc. Therefore the investors shall make a proper assessment about the abilities of the promoters before making a investment decision. The promoters are the most important persons in running the business activities. They occupy a dominant role in the discharge of functions of the business concern. They shall procure the information with reference to the companies earlier promote by the promoters and their track record. In business sector, the past performance is the indicator to the future performance. Therefore the investors shall observe the past performance of the promoters. The investors are also required to gain some knowledge in all areas of functional management. The investors shall made independent enquiries about the promoters work culture, attitudes, philosophy and morality. They shall get the information through other sources of information such as financial magazines, business journals and media reports. The investors awareness in India is to be increased. They generally do not have any idea about the corporate sector and its structure. They burnt their fingers in the market by investing innocently. They have no minimum knowledge before taking an investment decisions. Having money with them and investing blindly in wrong companies at the wrong times at wrong prices is quiet natural in India. Some investors do not know even some simple fundamentals about the corporate sectors. Promoter's track record is the most important factor in selecting a proper portfolio by the investors. The investors in the market shall move more cautiously before taking investment decisions. The good track record of the promoters may consists the MD's background and experience in the field and composition of board of director. The board of directors are the most important members in smooth functioning of the companies. The profitability of the corporate sector depends upon the abilities of the board of Directors. The company shall have a professional management team. The management of the company shall be left to the professional managers.

(b) Objectives of the Present Issue: The investors shall check the contents of the prospectus. They shall verify that the present issue of capital may increase in profitability or not? These issue of shares may reflect in enhancement of the profitability in future or not? A close observation of the prospects content can reveal all the things about the present issue of capital. The objects of the issue of capital is more important before making investment in that company. Therefore the investors are required to check the objectives of the present issue and take the decision in this regard.

(c) Project Information: Generally the prospectus contains all the information about the proposed project/existing project. The project information is useful to the investors in evaluating their investment proposed. The projects information which is provided in the prospectus may be helpful to know about the tax incentives available or not? The location of the project also influences the profitability of the corporate sector. The investor shall observe the following aspects.

(a) Location of the project, availability of tax concessions, availability of infrastructure facilities raw materials etc.

(b) Whether the issuing company obtained appraisal of the project by financial institutions and banks? or not?

(c) Whether the appraisal agency has any financial stake in the project or not?

(d) The provisions which made to monitor the project by financial institutions and banks or any other agency.

(e) Any special advantages to that project.

(d) Product or Market Observations: Generally every investor shall aware about the companies and their activities. They should know about the demand and supply position of the product which they are producing. Whether the prospectus discloses the information about the demand and supply gap for the product or not? The investor shall observe about any marketing arrangements for the sale of the product. The investor shall also make an enquiry about the technology which the company adopted. The present technology obsolete the company product? The availability of substitutes in the market having a bearing on the demand for the product. The investors shall observe about the export potential for the product in case of an export oriented project. The arrangement which is made by the company with the foreign collaborator or agency for purchase of products.

(e) Financial Information: The investors before making investment decisions, shall observe the financial data of the issuing company. The data relating specifically to capital, Reserves and surplus, turnover, profits dividend declared and distributed, profitability ratios, book value, EPs and other information. The financial data reflects the future trend or the company.

(f) Forecasting: The guess work about the companies activities are more important while predicting a company future. The investor shall observe about the profitability projections made by the company or the appraisal agency. The investor may also be made enquiries about a particular product or a company. The past performance is the indicator of the future prospect.

(g) Pricing of Issues: The share capital can be issued to the public by offering discount or premium, or at par. A good reputed company with strong background of the experience and professionals consisting of board of directors with managerial capabilities leads to fix high premium. The price fixed by the company must be in reasonable level. The justification for pricing with reference to the past performance and future projections. It should be most important to note that these projections are based on company's own estimates or by an independent appraisal by financial institutions and banks etc. In case of existing companies movement of prices immediately before the issue to ascertain, whether prices are fair market prices or there has been rigging of the market prices.

(h) Litigations: Usually the business activities are involve without any disputes. The business operations are routine activities of the corporate sector. Any disputes with another company shall be indicated in the prospectus. The disputes in the business may not settle immediately. The conflicts between two organisations will be kept in pending under court supervision. The pending litigations having a bearings on the profitability of the company or likely to result in winding up of the company for inability to pay debts or any other costs.

(i) Risk Factors: The Risk is an important factor in the evaluation of a company. Generally every business concern face risk. There is no business without risk component. Therefore the investors shall observe the prospective of the issuing company. The prospectus indicate the risk level involved in that project. The investors shall make an enquiry about the risk component in the market from market intelligence system.

(j) Auditor's Report: Auditor's report is one of the sources of information to know about the affairs of the issuing company. The report is the part of offer document especially with reference to significant notes relating to accounting system of the issuing company. The auditor of the company could analyse all the financial data and put his remarks for better functioning of the business concern. The audited figures are the legal evidence of the financial affairs of a company. These figures are reflected in balance sheet, where the balance sheet stands for the financial status of the company as on a particular date.

(k) Statutory Dues: The offer document shall indicate, statutory dues, If any defaulted by the issuing company. The statutory dues include Bank dues and institution defaults. The document shall also indicate about payment of interest to debenture holders. Any defaults made by the company shall inform to the prospecting investors through prospectus. Any failure to show such dues, The SEBI has the authority to take action in this regard. Therefore the investors must be aware about the financial discipline of the issuing company. ***Financial Discipline*** is the most important element in the growth of a business concern. The raising of finance depends upon the financial morality of the company. **Forex:** Some companies are raising crores of rupees from the market which is based on their financial discipline. Reliance Industries Ltd., is one of the example for Mega issues.

(l) Statutory Clearances: The investor confirm himself whether the company fulfilled all the formalities for the implementation of the project or not? Sometimes the company may not be in a position to get such clearances at the time of public issue. So such information should be disclosed by the company to the public. The current status of such clearances may be indicated to the public. In our country there may be a number of clearances shall be obtained to commerce a project.

(m) Careful Observation: The investors shall make careful observation before making their investments commitment in a particular business concern. Investment means, not simply handover a cheque to the broker but they should know about the parking place of their funds. The surplus savings of the savers, park their idle fund in a safe parking place when it may be taken back by the investors. They shall take all precautions before investing the funds in the market. The management of new issues is the responsibility of merchant bankers, lead managers and co-managers.

(n) Problems of New Issue Markets: The New issue market is the important factor in capital formation of the country. The market creates financial assets in the society. This market can be defined as ***financial architure*** of the digital economy. India is a country, where the large number of individuals, available the savings at their disposal. But the NIM is unable to attract the investments from the public as less than 10% of the savings. A large portion of the capital requirements of corporate sector is placed on market privately or provided by the financial institutions. The NIM suffers from functional and institutional gaps particularly in terms of the new instruments to appeal the investing community. Therefore the wholesale for new issues is yet to develop in India and the merchant banking is in fluid stage. The merchant bankers play a leading role in the NIM. They are the pillars of the NIM. They involve in the public issue from drafting the prospectus stage to closing the public subscription time But they are presently by not playing a developmental role. They should pay proper attention towards project preparation and other allied activities. The development of the NIM in India is based on the performance of the merchant bankers, If they fail to perform effectively the small investors may be duped by the companies. Therefore they have social responsibility to the small investors. Another important factor is that, the absence of merchant bankers leads to diversions of savings towards the companies as fixed deposits. A fixed deposit with the company means a high risk comparent involved in that segment. The floating cost is very high in case of public issue. In India, the public issue means just like a social function. It requires an elaborate arrangements throughout the country participation of many players are necessary. It involves a physical strain to the small companies because the small companies generally raises a low amount of capital. Therefore the public issue is not useful to small companies. It is useful to large companies where they offer Mega issues. The new and small companies are not in a position to bear this much of flotation costs.

The public issue involves a high expensive exercise to the small investors. Because the semi-urban and rural investors has to send the application forms to the centres where the banks are authorised to accept them. Then the investor has to spend in obtaining a demand draft, postal charges for sending and suffer loss of interest and collection charges for refund orders. In public issues there are-in ordinate delays in allotment of shares, refunding of application money, posting of share certificates. All these activities will not be carried out by the companies as per schedule time. They do not pay interest for the delayed period as per the law.

All these problems may not be possible to face by the small investors. If the investors bear all these problems They are again to face some problems such as ***dividend warrants, refund orders interest payment*** not being encashable at par in all centres. Therefore they feel inconvenience in the activities which are carried out by consultants. The time taken for allotment of shares is often 2 to 3 months or even more. There is considerable loss of interest to the investors. The government issued orders in this regard that the shares allotment process shall be completed within 30 days.

In public issues, the existing companies with a good track record only receive good response from the market. The underwriters support the issue which are offered by the well known companies only. The new companies face moral support problem from the financial intermediaries. Generally the investors do prefer to debentures to equities. Therefore SEBI recently imposed new regulations on merchant banks which may improve the investment climate in the NIM.

The free pricing of issue created some problems in the market. The companies at the initial period of this implication fixed over price for their issues. Soon after few months the investors became more discrete in making investments in NIM with hefty premiums. If the premiums are unreasonable, many new issues would have become flops in raising public subscription. Thus the SEBI has imposed one condition in fixing of premiums by the companies for their issues.

(o) Regulatory Framework: The legal framework in India consist of many regulations A business concern shall fulfil all the legal formalities which framed by the government. The SEBI is the powerful organ in the primary. If has the control authority to regulate and guide the market from time to time. The corporate sector in India is regulated by ***3 organs*** of the central government, They are :

(A) Companies Act.

(B) Securities Contract Act.

(C) Securities and Exchange Board of India (SEBI).

A. COMPANIES ACT

The company law deals with the issue formalities of securities. The shares in India are issued by public limited companies. The public is generally interested in buying shares. The shares which are offered by the companies will be purchased by the investors in public issue. The issuing company shall have to fulfil some formalities before coming to the public. The following factors will reveal about the issue of shares process before approaching the public for raising finance.

(a) Issue of shares

(b) Buy back the shares *(Repurchase of shares)*

(c) Issue of shares certificates.

(a) Issue to Shares: In India every company shall be incorporated under the companies act as public limited company or company without share capital. All public limited companies have the chance to issue shares for financing their business operations. The companies while registering with the government shall submit three important documents such as ***Memorandum of Association, Articles of Association and Prospectus.*** The memorandum of association must state the amount of share capital with which it is to be registered. It is known as *"Authorised capital"* The authorised capital is an amount of shares which it can be raised at any time by issuing shares. The share capital which is issued for public offer is called as ***Issued Capital.*** The company can collect the amount by issue of shares from the subscribers. It is known as ***paid up capital.*** The share capital may be refunded by only winding up the company. A share is the right to a specified amount of the share capital a of company. It carries certain rights and liabilities which are issued to the shareholders. A share is treated as a movable property and transferable. The transfer may be effective between the transferee from the date of transfer. The transfer of share transaction must be made with the company. On transfer of the share, the transferee becomes a shareholder with the company. The shareholder has all the rights only when the transfer is registerer in the register of the members of the company. The shareholders will get a share certificate in evidence of his ownership under the company seal. The share certificate contains the name of the person in whose favour the certificate issued. A company which is incorporated as public company can issue two types of shares. They are ***equity and preference shares.*** Equity shares are the permanent capital of the company. In India equity shares are more popular, preference shares carry a preferential right to fixed dividend and the refund of the share capital when it is wound up. The preference shares are redeemable after 10 years. They can be converted into equity shares.

The authorised share capital, can be altered by the company with the acceptance of share holders at the general meeting through an ordinary resolution. The company can exercise the following changes in the capital structure, with the acceptance of shareholders.

(a) A company can increase its share capital by issuing new shares.

(b) A company can convert shares into stock and stock into shares.

(c) A company can reduce its face value of share capital.

(d) A company has the authority to cancel the shares, If the person house not been taken delivery.

(e) A company can consolidate the shares with the larger denomination.

All of these changes can be made by the company with the acceptance of shareholders at the AGM with an ordinary resolution. Any reduction in share capital is possible with special resolution and confirmation by the court.

The policy matters and business strategies are framed by the board of directors. The board of directors is the powerful organ in the corporate sector. The board has the authority to make any changes in the company subject to rules and regulations. The board of directors has the power to issue new shares to the public. The board of directors has the power to increase the share capital for the advantage of the companies with them. These chances should not be utilised by the board for their own purpose. Usually the companies can issue shares at 3 types. They are :

(A) Issue of shares at par.

(B) Issue of shares at premium.

(C) Issue of shares at discount.

The companies can issue shares at par. But some times. They offer premium. A company has the right to issue shares at premium. The share premium collected by the company shall be kept in share premium account separately. The amount of share premium can be utilised for the following purposes.

(a) Issue of fully paid bonus shares.

(b) Writing off the preliminary expenses.

(c) Writing off the floatation charges.

(d) Provision for premium which is payable on the reduction of any redeemable preference shares or debentures.

The companies can be issued shares at discount subject to the fulfillment of the following conditions.

(a) The issue of shares at discount must be authorized by the company law board.

(b) The company shall make a resolution to this effect the rate of discount shall be below *10%*. If the CLB permits, the discount rate can be beyond 10%.

(c) After completion of one year of the business, commencement them the company can issue discount.

(d) The company shall issue discount within two months of the sanctioning by the CLB. Sometimes the CLB may be specified the period of time for offering shares to the public.

(e) The prospectus shall indicate the rate of discount.

Buy back the Shares: Generally the public limited companies not permitted for purchasing their own shares. However, there are three exceptions to this permission. They are

(a) The purchase of its own shares shall be made for the benefits of its employees by the trustees of the company.

(b) The company can make advances to its employees by way of beneficial ownership. Such loans could not exceed 6 months salary of the employee.

The company shall not violate any restrictions to its officers. If it violates any restriction It will be punishable with a fine of *Rs. 1,000*. After October, 1988 the companies have been allowed to buy back their own shares or other specified securities. The companies are allow to buy back their shares from out of

(a) Its free reserves.

(b) The premium account.

(c) The proceeds of an earlier issue other than fresh issue of shares made particularly for buy back purposes.

After the liberalization policy, the government made efforts to liberalise all the earlier restrictions. The corporate sectors has been provided some extent of freedom. A company can purchase its own shares only if it satisfies the following conditions.

(a) Articles of Association shall permit for buy back of its own shares.

(b) A special resolution should be passed in general meeting to this effect.

(c) The buy back of shares should be completed within a period of *12 months* from the date of passing the special resolution.

(d) The buy back of shares do not exceed ***25%*** of the total paid up capital ***plus*** free reserves of the company.

(e) The process shall be done in accordance with the SEBI regulations.

(f) The debt equity ratio does not exceed *2:1*

The buy back of shares can be made from the following parties.

(a) The company can procure shares from the existing shareholders on proportionate basis.

(b) It can mobilise the shares from the open market

(c) From odd lots

(d) It can repurchase from its employees

The companies are required to file a declaration of solvency in a prescribed proforma before they making buy back of its shares the solvency certificate share be submitted to the Registrar of companies and SEBI. The solvency certificate in the prescribed proforma and an affidavit to that effect that, the board of directors have made a full inquiry into the affairs of the company. The inquiry shall be made to this effect and it is capable of meeting its liabilities and will not become insolvent within a period of one year of the date of declaration made by the board of directors. The statement shall be signed by at least two directors of the company, one of the person should be managing Director. The unlisted companies need not to file the declaration of solvency with the SEBI or Registrar of companies.

After completion of buy back of shares the company shall destroy physically the share certificates within 7 days of the last date of completion of buy back shares. The companies which are completed by buy back of its shares, not allowed for further issue of shares within a period of two years. However they can make banks issues or other conversion process. The companies shall record all the transactions regarding the buy back affairs. The company shall report to the ROCs and SEBI after completion of the process within 30 days. If any company violates this condition it is liable to punishment with imprisonment up to two years or with fine up to ***Rs. 50,000*** or with both. Therefore the companies shall follow all these rules and regulations strictly. The companies are not allowed to buy back securities through its subsidiaries or through its group companies etc.

Generally the companies will collect the share capital amount an instalment basis. A part of the amount will be collected as application fee while applying for shares by the investors. After the collection of application fee, the allotment fee and the remaining balance will be collected by the company on instalment basis. The balance payable on application each year cannot be less than 5% of the nominal value. The remaining will be collected by the company in kind of calls of shares. Call on shares will be made on the basis of all shares of the same class. The call must be made by the board of directors by a resolution passed at its meeting. The company shall makes calls as per the provisions laid down in Articles of Association. If any shareholder fails to pay the call amount on his shares may leads to ***forfeit the shares***. The board of directors has to serve a notice to the defaulter requiring the payment of unpaid amount together with accrued interest and a resolution of the directors to that effect. The forfeiture of shares can be done only after careful implementation of legal provisions.

Any individual can become a member of a company by the following methods.

(a) The person can subscribe its memorandum of association before its registration.

(b) Buying shares from the company and placed on the register of members.

(c) Purchasing in secondary market and placed on the register of members.

(d) Permitting his name to be on the register of members.

The member of a company can attend the meetings and cast his vote. The members of a company can have some privileges. Equity shareholders are entitled to vote on every resolution placed at any general meeting of the company.

Issue of Share Certificates: After the completion of issue process every issuing company shall issue share certificates to the shareholders. It is the prima facie evidence of the title of the members to such shares. The shareholder can use this certificate as a proof of evidence for his ownership claim. The share certificate shall contain the stamp, issued under the common seal of the company. It should be signed by the director or an authorized person. It is to be delivered within 3 months after the allotment of shares and within two months after the application for registration of transfer.

Prospectus: Prospectus is the most important document in the life of the company. There are three important documents for the formation of a company. They are *(a) Memorandum of Association (b) Articles of Association (c) Prospectus.* The Memorandum of Association is like the constitution of the company. It reveals the relationship between company and outside world. All the company affairs shall be carried out according to MA. There should not be any deviation from it. ***Articles of Association*** is related to internal management of the company. It contains all the rules and regulations of Directors, Managing Director, Managers and other. *Prospectus* is an important document while entering into the capital market. The prospectus is the basic document for the share-holders. It refers to any document by which a capital is offered to the public and on the basis of which the applicants actually subscribe. It is issued to invite the public for the subscription of any securities of a company. Every company shall draft a prospectus before approaching the public and it should be prepared according to the companies act. The companies Act framed the prescribed proforma for drafting of prospectus is a document which contains past information and credit future of the company. It provides some promises to the prospecting investor. The contents of a draft prospectus prescribed by the act are as follows.

(A) Part – I

(B) Part – II

(C) Part – III

The prescribed form of schedule must be as per IInd schedule of the companies Act.

(A) Part I

The contents of part-I shall contain the information regarding the following aspects.

(1) General Information.

(2) Capital structure of the company.

(3) Terms of the present issue.

(4) Particulars of the issue.

(5) Company management and project.

(6) Disclosure of the particulars of public issues.

(7) Disclosure of particulars of outstanding litigations.

(8) Risk factors.

(1) General Information: It should contain the information regarding the general business affairs. The company shall inform the public about the following aspects.

(a) Name and address of the Registered office of the company

(b) Consent of the SEBI for the present issue and declaration of SEBI about non-responsibility for financial soundness or correctness of statements.

(c) Letter of Intent/industrial license and declaration of the SEBI about non-responsibility for financial soundness or correctness of statements .

(d) Names of Regional stock exchanges and other stock exchanges where application made for listing of present issue.

(e) Provisions of 68 (A) of the companies act relating to punishment for the fictitious applications.

(f) Statement declaration about refund of the issue of minimum subscription of 90% is not received with 90 days of closure of the issue.

(g) Declaration about the issue of allotment letters/refunds within a period of 10 weeks and interest in case of any delay in refund at the prescribed rate under section 72 (2) (2A)

(h) Date of opening of public issue, date of closing of the issue, date of earliest closing of the issue.

(i) Name and address of auditors, and lead managers

(j) Name and address of trustee under debenture trust deed (In case of debenture issue)

(k) Whether rating from CRISIL or any rating agency has been obtained for the proposed debentures/preference shares issue.

(l) Underwriting of the issue. Name and address of the underwriters and the amount underwritten by them. Declaration by board of directors that the underwriters have sufficient resources to discharge their respective obligations.

(2) Capital Structure: The company shall indicate the following aspects

(a) Authorized, issued, subscribed and paid up capital

(b) Size of the present issue giving separately reservation of preferential allotment to promoters and others.

(c) Paid up capital

(i) after the present issue

(ii) after conversion of debentures.

(3) Term of the Issue: The term of the present issue shall be indicated as follows:

(a) Terms of payment

(b) Rights of the instrument holders.

(c) How to apply availability of forms, prospectus and mode of payment.

(d) Any special tax benefit for the company and its shareholders.

(4) Particulars of the Issue: The following aspects shall be disclosured to the public in the prospectus.

(a) objects of the issue

(b) project cost

(c) Means of financing (promoters contribution)

(5) Particulars about Company Management and Project: The following information shall be provided by the company for understanding the company activities and other aspect.

(a) History and main objects and present business of the company

(b) Particulars regarding subscriptions.

(c) Subsidiaries of the company.

(d) Promoters and their background.

(e) Names, addresses and occupations of manager, managing director and other directors including nominees.

(f) Location of project.

(g) Details about plant and machinery technology and process.

(h) Details about collaborations agreement.

(i) Particulars about the infrastructural facilities.

(j) Schedule for implementation of the project and progress so far, details for land acquisitions, civil works, installation of plant and machinery, trial production and commercial productions.

(k) Particulars of products and nature of the products consumer or Industrial and end users.

(l) Approach to marketing and proposed marketing set up.

(m) Particulars about export possibilities and export obligations If any.

(n) Details about future prospects, expected capacity utilisation during the first three years from the date of commencement of production and the expected year when the company would be able to earn cash profits and net profits.

(o) Details about the stock market data for shares debentures of the company (high low price in each of the last three years and monthly high low during the last six months.

(6) Particulars of Public Issue: The company shall disclose all the information to the public. The companies Act sec. 370 (1B) reveals about the information which is required to be given includes the year and type of issue, amount of issue, date of closure date of completion of delivery of share/debenture certificates, date of completion of project where the issue was made for financing a project and rate of dividend paid.

(7) Disclosure of Particulars of Litigations: A company which makes public issue is required to state in the prospectus outstanding litigation pertaining to matters likely to affect operation and finances of the company including disputed tax liabilities of any nature. Particulars of any criminal prosecution launched against the company and its directors for alleged offenses under the enactments, specified in Para 1 of part I of schedule XIII of the act are also required to specify particulars of default, if any, in meeting statutory dues Institutional dues and towards instrument holders like debentures fixed deposits and arrears of cumulative preference shares in relation to the company and other companies promoted by the same promoters which are listed on stock exchanges.

(8) Risk Factors: According to the SEBI guidelines every issuing company shall indicate in prospectus about the risk involved in this investment. The management should submit its views regarding its risk factors. The risk may belong to foreign exchange rate fluctuations, difficulty in availability of Raw materials or in marketing or products.

(B) Part II

The prospectus shall disclose in this part about the general information and other allied information. The company shall indicate the following aspects in the prospectus.

(a) General information.

(b) Financial information.

(c) Statutory and other information.

(a) General Information: The company should disclose the information about routine activities of the administration and other functions. The following aspects should covered in this part of the prospectus.

(a) Consent of directors, auditors, solicitors, advocates, managers, to issue, Registrar of issue, bankers to the company, bankers to the issue and experts.

(b) Expert opinion obtained if any.

(c) Changes if any in directors and auditors during the last three years and reasons thereof.

(d) Authority for the issue and details of resolution passed for the issue.

(e) Procedure and time schedule for allotment and issue of certificates.

(f) Names and addresses of the company secretary, legal advisers, lead managers co-managers, auditors, bankers to the company, bankers to the issue and brokers to the issue.

(b) Financial Information: The company should disclose the following information in the prospectus.

(i) A report by the auditors of the company with respect to the profits and losses for the five financial years preceeding the issue of prospectus. The report should also show the rates of dividend paid on each class of shares for each of the said years. If the company has been carrying on business for less than 5 years, the figures are to be given for the actual period if the five financial years immediately preceeding the issue of the prospectus cover a period of less than five years, the reports should covers as financial years as may be necessary, so that the aggregate period covered is not less than 5 years. The report should also give statement of assets and liabilities as at the last date of the latest financial year. The report should indicate the nature of any provision or adjustments made or yet to be made as respects the figure of any profits or losses and liabilities assets and liabilities of the subsidiaries as the last date to which the accounts of the company are made up must also be shown in the like manner.

(ii) If the company proposes to acquire any business, a report by a chartered accountant up on the profits and losses of the business for each of the five financial years preceeding the issue of prospectures and the assets and liabilities of business.

(c) Statutory and other Information: The following information shall disclose by the company.

(a) Minimum subscription.

(b) Expenses of the issue, payable to advisors, Registrars Managers, Trustees for the debenture holders.

(c) Underwriting commission and brokerage.

(d) Previous issue for the cash.

(e) Previous Rights issue (during last 5 years).

 (i) Date of allotment, closing date, date of refunds, date of listing of the stock exchange,

 (ii) If the issues at premium or discount and the amount thereof, and

 (iii) The amount paid or payable by way of premium.

(f) Commission paid or brokerage on previous issue.

(g) Issue of shares other than for cash.

(h) Debentures and Redeemable preference shares and other instruments issued by the company outstanding as on the date of prospectus and terms of issue.

(i) Option to subscribe.

(j) Purchase of property and its details.

(k) Details of directors proposed directors, wholetime directors, their borrowing powers and qualification shares.

(l) Full particulars about the contracts made by the company.

(m) Full particulars of the nature and interest of the promoters or every direct or in the contract.

(n) The powers and rights of members regarding voting, dividend, lien of shares and the process of modification of such rights and forfeiture of shares.

(o) The method and process of transfer of shares and transmission of shares.

(p) Revaluation of assets if any during last 5 years.

(q) Particulars about material contracts.

(C) Part III

The financial information which was submitted by the company in the prospectus, made by qualified chartered Accountant. The chartered Accountant should not be an officer or servant or a partner in the company or in employment of an officer or servant of the company or in any of its subsidiary or holding companies.

The time and place at which the copies of the balance sheets, profit and loss accounts materials, contracts and documents can be inspected.

The prospectus must end with a declaration by the directors that all the relevant provisions of the companies act, 1956 and guidelines issued by the SEBI have been complied with and that no statement made in prospectus is contrary to the provisions of the companies act 1956 and rules thereunder.

The contents of the prospectus must be true and accurate if any false statement or information contains it, the directors and promoters of the company are liable to all persons who subscribe for shares on the faith of the prospectus they are also punishable with imprisonment for a term which may extend to two years or fine which may be extended to Rs. 5,000 or both.

Prospectus and Application Form: The issuing company shall distribute application forms to the investors. Usually every company provides application forms to the investors in the new issue market. The companies act sec. 56(3) states that every application form shall be accompanied by the prospectus. The prospectus is the basic document to the investor for making investment in this company. Therefore every issuing company shall follow this rule. However there are four exceptions to this rule, they are.

(a) If the shares or debentures are not offered to the public.

(b) If the issue is Rights issue.

(c) If the shares or debentures offered are in all respects uniform with share or debentures already issued and quoted on a recognised stock exchange.

(d) If the offer is made in connection with the bona fide invitation to a person to enter into an underwriting agreement with respect to the share or debentures.

Legal Frame Work on Rights Issue

Rights issue means, the shares are offered to the existing shareholders. The companies act framed some rules and regulations for issuing of rights shares. According to the companies act, the rights issue may be offered in the following two situation, which even is earlier, must be offered at the date of the offer

(a) The company shall offer only after the expiry of two years from the incorporation of a company.

(b) A company shall issue the offer to the existing shareholders after expiry of one year from the first allotment of shares.

The rights offer must be made in the form of a notice, specifying the number of shares offered. The shareholders are provided a time less than 15 days from the date of the offer to accept. If they did not respond to the notice, it is deemed to have been declined. The shareholders has also inclusive of the option/right of renunciation. The board has the right to dispose of the shares if they think that it is advantageous to the company.

Issue of Debentures: The issue of debentures by a company vests powers with the board of directors. The board has the authority to take decision to this effect. The board should take the consent of the shareholders. The shareholders must pass an ordinary resolution. If the amount borrowed exceeds the aggregated of the paid up capital and free reserves. The debentures are of different types such as Redeemable, Mortgage convertible and Non convertible. Large companies issue Redeemable and Mortgage debenture the debentures holders are not entitled any voting rights they are not entitled to receive a copy of accounts and reports of the company. They have the right to get a copy of trust deed.

The debenture holders have the following rights which are disclosed in the prospectus.

(a) Debentures are transferable.

(b) They are transmittable on par with the same manner of equity shares.

(c) They are entitled to inspect the register of debenture holders.

(d) The rights and privileges of the debenture holders can be modified with the consent of at least *3/4th* of the amount outstanding or by a special resolution passed at the meeting of the debenture holders.

(e) The debentures are subject to other usual terms and conditions

(f) The debentures are incorporated in the trust deed between the company and the debenture trustee.

The debentures may or may not be secured. There is no provision in the act requiring the secured charge of the debentures. However, it is usual to secure the debentures by a mortgage or charge on the company's assets. The general tradition is to secure debentures by a trust deed which contains a charge. The debenture trust is created by an instrument of trust the trustees hold properties in trust for the benefit of the beneficiary. These properties will be useful in the event of default of payment of interest of the principal amount of debt advanced under terms agreed up an by selling such properties in the hands of the trustees. The mortgage to secure debentures must be registered with the Registrar of companies within 30 days of the creation of charge. Every company shall be registered with the registrar of companies for every issue of mortgage debentures. All the other provisions of the act concerning with the issues of securities, allotment and listing etc., are applicable to shares are also equally applicable to the debentures.

Legal Frame Work in Allotment of Shares: The allotment process is the most important factor in raising of funds from the market. The company shall not be made allotment. If the company is unable to raise the minimum subscription from the public. The minimum subscription amount should be stated in prospectus. The application money cannot be less than 5% of the nominal amount of each share. If the company fails to procure the minimum subscription amount within 120 days from the date of the first issue of prospectus, that collected amount must be refunded. If the company fails to refund the amount within 130 days after the issue of the prospectus, the company is liable to pay interest at the rate of **6%** the allotment should be made by the directors within a reasonable time. The company shall commence the allotment process after the completion of 5th day from the day of the opening of the such subscription list. If company violates this rule, it is liable to a fine up to Rs. 5,000.

Every issuing company shall apply to the concerned recognised stock exchange before making public issue, for permission to list these securities. The company shall also get permission for allotment of shares from the stock exchange. If it is not granted by the stock exchange, on expiry of 10 weeks from the date of the closing of the subscription list the company is required to refund that amount to the applicants. If such amount is not paid by the company within 8 days, it will have to pay interest at 4% and not more than 15%. After the completion of the allotment process the company shall file a return of allotment with the Registrar of company within 30 days from the date of allotment. The Registrar of company can grant the permission to submit the return for the extension of time.

B. SECURITIES CONTRACT ACT

The Securities contract act regulation provides the broad framework of the functioning of stock exchanges in India. The first legislative measures were enacted in 1925. This act is known as ***The Bombay Securities Contracts Control Act, 1925.*** The act was to regulate and control certain contracts for the sale and purchase of securities in the Bombay city. The government had appointed an expert committee in 1951. Under the chairmanship of A.D. Gorawala the committee had prepared a draft bill on the stock exchange regulation in India. Another committee was appointed in 1954 under the chairmanship of ***Gorawala***. The recommendations of the committee were culminated in the enactment of securities contract Regulation Act 1956. It provides the broad framework of the present scheme of the stock exchange regulation in India. Stock exchange means, it is a place where the securities are purchased and sold by the investors in a specified time. It regulates the business of buying, selling or dealing in securities.

The objectives of the SCRA is to present malpractice in securities transactions by regulating the business. The act specifies the following instruments as "securities"

(a) Shares, scrips, stocks bonds, debentures stock or other marketable securities like a nature in or of any incorporated company or other body corporate.

(b) Government securities.

(c) Rights or interests in securities.

(d) Derivatives, units or any other instrument issued by any collective investment scheme.

(e) Any other instruments such as specified by the SEBI.

A Derivative means a security derived from a debt instrument, share, loan (secured/unsecured), risk instrument or contract for differences or any other form of a security. It is contract which derives its value from the index of prices of underlying securities. Derivatives may also be regulated of outside transactions of the stock exchange through the licensing system of security dealers. The SCRA framed the general frame work of control regarding the market. It provides the government with a flexible apparatus for the regulation of stock market in India. The Securities Contract Regulation Act can be divided into the following aspects

(a) Recognised stock exchanges ***(Sec. 3-12)***

(b) Contracts and options in securities ***(Sec. 13-20)***

(c) Listing of Securities ***(Sec. 21-22A)***

(d) Penalties ***(Sec. 23 to 26)***

(e) Misl. or other matters ***(Sec. 27 to 30)***

Recognised Stock Exchanges

The stock exchanges are the most important organs in the capital market. They play a vital role in the efficient functioning of capital market. It is the place where the securities are brought and sold. It is the market place for secondhand securities. It does not help in the capital formation of the corporate sector. There is no creation of additional financial assets. It provides liquidity to the securities which are already issued. The main provisions relating to the stock exchanges for grant of recognition is based on the following factors.

(a) Applications to the SEBI
(b) Conditions
(c) Terms and period
(d) Cancellation
(e) Periodical Returns
(f) Enquiries
(g) Submission of Annual reports
(h) Amendments
(i) Bye laws of recognised exchanges
(j) Powers of the SEBI

(a) Application to the SEBI: The stock exchange authorities shall apply to the SEBI for the grant of recognition in a prescribed proforma. The application form shall be accompanied by a copy of the bye laws of the stock exchange the SEBI has the full authority to grant the recognition to the stock exchanges. The following information shall be furnished by the exchange authorities for granting of recognition to the SEBI.

(a) The full information about governing body of stock exchange.
(b) The powers and constitution of governing body.
(c) The powers and duties of the office bearers of the stock exchange.
(d) The admission process of various class members into stock exchange.
(e) The qualification required for becoming member in the stock exchange, members, suspension, expulsion and re-admission.
(f) The procedure of registration of partnership firm as members of the stock exchange.

(b) Conditions: After receipt of the applications from the stock exchange. The SEBI will scrutinising the information and may impose the following conditions for the better functioning of the stock exchange.

(a) The required qualification for the membership of stock exchange.
(b) The procedure for contracts made between members of the stock exchange.
(c) The representation of the SEBI by its nominees on the stock exchanges.
(d) The accounting procedure to be followed by the members of the stock exchanges and their periodical audit by chartered accountants.
(e) All of the rules of any stock exchange shall be amended by it with the approval of the SEBI.

(c) Terms and Period: After the receipt of application form in prescribed manner from the stock exchange. The SEBI will commence its process. The application will be closely scrutinised by the SEBI and imposes some regulations on the part of the stock exchanges. If the concerned stock exchange satisfies all the conditions, their SEBI will grant the recognition to the stock exchange. The recognition of stock exchange will be made either on permanent or temporary position. The temporary recognition is not for less than a year. The temporary recognition can be renewed further. If the stock exchange is granted the recognition, its rules can be amended with the approval of the SEBI.

(d) Cancellation: If any malpractices are made by the concerned stock exchange, the SEBI has the full authority to take any action against such institution. The SEBI is the most powerful organisation in monitoring and controlling the activities of the stock exchanges in India. It can take any action in the interest of the trade or in the public interest, after due notice, giving sufficient opportunity to show cause against withdrawal of the recognition. The SEBI may be giving notification to this affect withdraw the recognition given to a stock exchange. Therefore the stock exchanges should be more cautious because their recognition may be cancelled at any time, if they are not working properly.

(e) Periodical Returns: After getting the recognition to the stock exchanges, they have to work within the control limits of the SEBI. The SEBI is the watchdog of the stock market. It control regular monitor, guide the activities of the secondary market. Every recognised stock exchange in India shall have to furnish the periodical returns to the SEBI. The affairs of the stock exchanges shall be informed to the SEBI. In stock exchange, every member has to maintain such books of accounts and other documents as prescribed by the SEBI in the interest of trade or the public. The SEBI has the authority to inspect the books of accounts at any time without any notice. It has also powers to call for information or explanations from recognised stock exchanges or from any member of exchange. For discharging all the monitoring activities, the SEBI shall inform in writing to all the stock exchanges and members.

(f) Enquiries: The SEBI has all the powers to make an enquiry into the affairs of the governing body, of any stock exchange or any members affairs. The SEBI will appoint an enquiry committee consisting with one or more persons as it thinks fit. The appointment of inquiry committee depends upon the nature of the situation. However in case of an inquiry in concerned with the affairs of a member, the SEBI can give directions to the governing body of the stock exchange to conduct the inquiry in the manner as it is directed. The person/persons, those who are appointed for the purpose have to submit a report of the result of the inquiry to the SEBI. In such an inquiry the following persons are responsible to produce all such books accounts, documents any other information to the enquiry committee.

(a) Every director/manager/secretary/officers of the stock exchange.

(b) Every member of the stock exchange.

(c) If the member of the stock exchange is a partnership firm every partner, manager, secretary or officer.

(d) Any other person who directly or indirectly related to the above persons.

It is their duty to submit all the information whenever required by the inquiry personal committee. They shall cooperate the committee for smooth functioning of the inquiry.

(g) Submission of the Annual Reports: The recognised stock exchanges in India shall have to follow the statutory regulations. Every recognised stock exchanges in India has to furnish to the government of its annual report. Generally every stock exchange will prepare annual report. The copy of the annual report may be submitted to the SEBI for favour of kind information. These reports shall contain the information as prescribed by the SEBI.

(h) Amendments: The SEBI has the full authority on the functioning of the stock exchanges and concerned members. It can make or amend any rule or direct the recognised stock exchanges for the better functioning of the stock market. The SEBI has the authority to impose rules while granting the recognition for the stock exchanges. It has the powers to direct the stock exchanges to make or amend any rule thereof. Hence it is the duty of concerned stock exchange to make or amend the rule within two months from the date of direction. If any stock fails to comply with the guidance, the SEBI itself make or amend the rule through an order. Therefore the SEBI and the concerned stock exchanges have to approve the modification.

(i) Bye Laws of Recognised Stock Exchange: Every stock exchange in India shall get recognition from the SEBI. The SEBI is the regulatory authority in the stock exchanges affairs. The recognised stock exchange may get the prior approval from the SEBI for its bye laws. The bye law is the constitution of the stock exchange. It has the sets on conditions. Every stock exchange shall function according to its bye law. The bye law contains all the information about the better functioning of the stock market. It contains the regulation and control of contracts to provide for the activities, such as:

(a) The opening and closing time of stock exchange.

(b) The trading hours of the exchange.

(c) Periodical settlement of contracts through clearing house.

(d) The particulars about the process of delivery and payment of securities, passing of delivery orders and the regulation.

(e) Maintenance of clearing house.

(f) Periodical reports to be submitted by clearing house to the SEBI.

(g) The periodical reports shall contain the following information :

  (i) The total number of each category of security carried over from one settlement period to another.

  (ii) The total no. of each category of security contracts in respect of which have been squared up during the course of each settlement period.

  (iii) The total number of each category of security actually delivered at each clearing.

(h) The particulars about the publication by the clearing house

(i) The details regarding prohibition of blank transfers or its regulation process.

(j) The full information about the baldly or carry over settlements.

(k) The process for fixing or altering or postponing settlements.

(l) The procedure for determination and declaration of market rates.

(m) The full information about the terms, conditions and incidents of contracts.

(n) The process for regulation of the entering into making, performance, recession and termination of contracts.

(o) The particulars about the listing of securities on the stock exchange.

(p) The method and process for the settlement of disputes.

(q) The methods of levy and recovery of fees, fines and penalties.

(r) The process for fixing a scale of brokerage and other charges.

(s) Regulation of dealings by members of their own account.

(t) Separation of the function of jobbers and brokers.

(u) Any other matter in relation to emergency of trade.

(j) Powers of the SEBI: The bye laws made under this section is void and render the member concerned liable to fine, expulsion from membership for a specified period or any other penalty not involving the payment of money. The SEBI is the most powerfull organ in the capital market. It is the representative of the central government. It can make bye laws or amend all or any of the above aspects of the stock exchanges. It has the supreme authority. It can supersede the governing body of the stock exchange. It can also appoint any person to exercise and perform all the powers and duties of the governing body. It can also suspend the business of a concerned stock exchange for a period not exceeding seven days. It can also extend the period from time to time for the benefit of the general investors.

Contracts and Options in Securities

Generally the stock exchanges are the vehicles of community savings. They mobilised the funds and diverts the funds towards the productive ways. They channalise the small savings and facilitate the funds at the disposal of the corporate sector. Usually the transactions in stock exchanges can be made between two members through contracts. The legal provisions relating to contracts and options can be presented as follow:

(A) Nature of contracts.

(B) Options in securities.

The contracts in the stock market plays an important role. The major transactions are being settled in the form of contracts. Contract in securities can be done only between the members of a recognised stock exchange or through the members of a recognised stock exchange. The spot delivery contracts cannot be made between members. All other contracts are illegal. **Spot delivery contracts** They have the following characteristics

(a) Spot delivery contracts provide actual delivery of securities.

(b) The payment for these delivered securities will be made on the day of the contract or the next day.

(c) The securities will be transferred through depository system to the buyer.

The SEBI has the authority to prevent undesirable speculation in specified securities in any area. It can prohibit any contract in any specific security by any person. Any contract made after the prohibition would be illegal. The SEBI has the full authority to prohibit any contract or can permit any contract to enter into an agreement. The members of the recognised stock exchange shall get license from the SEBI. Every person doing such business has to acquire a license from the SEBI.

Options in securities were illegal and void. The enactment of securities contract Regulation Act have been permitted since Feb. 1995. The sec. 20 of the SCRA was amended for this purpose. The contract in derivatives are valid and legal since 1999 if they satisfy the following conditions.

(a) They shall be traded on a recognised stock exchange.

(b) They shall be settled on the clearing house of the recognised stock exchange in accordance with its rules and regulations.

Listing of Securities (Sec. 21-22A)

The legal provisions relating to the listing of a security with the stock exchange was stipulated in SCR Act. The ***sec. 21 and 22*** A of this act deals with the process of listing a share with the recognised stock exchange. ***Listing*** means, an admission of a scrip to trade on a stock exchange officially. It denotes like a registration of security for dealing or trading on a stock exchange. The listing is not compulsory under the companies act but it is necessary under ***section 73*** of the act. The main objective of listing a scrip with the stock exchange is to provide ready marketability and liquidity to the scrips. It ensures proper supervision and control of dealings and protect the interest of investors and general investing community. The securities contract Regulation act sec 21 empowers the SEBI to compel a company to list securities with the stock exchange in the interest of the trade or public the SEBI has the authority to impose conditions for listing of securities with the concerned stock exchanges. ***sec. 22*** of the SCRA reveals that a company has the right to appeal the SEBI, if its application for listing is refused by any recognised stock exchange in India. The ultimate decision will be taken by the SEBI and the recognised stock exchange shall obey the listing of a scrip. Further the corporate sector can appeal to the securities appellate tribunal against refusal. Therefore listing of a security with the stock exchange is the most important factor in the management of an issue. The listed securities are bought and sold through the members of recognised stock exchanges. The members of recognised stock exchanges are known as ***"Brokers"*** The prices at which the securities are bought and sold are called as ***"quotations"*** The Quotations are the official prices of the scrips on a particular stock exchange. ***sec 73*** of the companies act reveal that listing of security is compulsory if a company makes public issue of securities. The legal provisions stipulates various conditions for the listing of a security with a recognised stock exchange. The following kinds of listing is made with the recognised stock exchange.

(1) Listing of securities (first time).

(2) Offer of sale of existing issued capital.

(3) Listing of Rights Issue.

Listing of Securities

Generally the public limited companies will raise resources from the market through public issue. Public issue is becoming more popular and widely accepted process. It provide sufficient financial resources for the reputed, honest sincerity companies. Honesty is the best policy for the achievement of business goal. The public always trust the good business enterprises. The reputed business concerns mobilises funds through *Mega issues.* Therefore the companies seeking the enlistment of their securities for the first time have to apply in the prescribed form along the listing agreement and listing fee. The following documents shall submit while applying for listing.

(a) Memorandum of Association (for shares issue).

(b) The debenture trust copy (for debenture issue).

(c) Copies of all prospectuses.

(d) Copies of offers for sale.

(e) Circular for advertising offering securities for subscription or sales during last 5 years.

(f) Copies of balance sheets and audit reports for the last 5 years.

(g) In case of new companies accounts for shorter periods.

(h) Full particulars about dividends and cash bonuses paid during last 10 days.

(i) Information about dividends or interest in arrears, if any.

(j) Agreement copies with vendors/promoter, underwriters and sub-underwriters, broker and sub-brokers.

(k) Particulars about agreements made with selling agents, managing directors and technical directors.

(l) The following documents shall be submitted for the last 5 years.

  (1) Audit Report.

  (2) Balance sheet.

  (3) Valuation contract.

  (4) Court orders.

  (5) Offer for sale.

  (6) Any circular for offering securities for issue of securities.

  (7) Material contracts.

(m) Full information about the history of the company since its incorporation.

(n) All particulars regarding issue of shares and debentures for cash and other than cash. Other particulars about premium on par issue.

(o) The full information shall be submitted for any payment of commission, brokerage, discount for the present issue of shares.

(p) The following certified copies shall be submitted.

  (i) Acknowledgement from SEBI.

  (ii) Agreements made with IDBI, IFCI, ICICI If any.

(q) The full information about the company's ten highest holders of securities of each class of shares or debentures along with their addresses.

(r) Particulars about the arrangements for listing of securities with a recognised stock exchange.

In addition to the above information a company before listing its securities has to satisfy the following conditions through its articles of association.

(1) The company shall use a common form of transfer.

(2) The AGM shall permit any person that the option or the right to call off shares.

(3) The fully paid shares will be free from all lien. In case of partly paid shares, lien will be restricted to mono called.

(4) Any amount paid up in advance of calls may carry interest but shall not be eligible for dividend.

(5) There will be no forfeiture of unclaimed dividends before the claim becomes barred by law.

The following conditions shall be fulfilled by a company to become eligible for its securities for listing.

I. Minimum public offer.

II. Other conditions.

Minimum Public Offer: Every company which approaches the public for raising of finance shall satisfy the rules and regulations as per the legal provisions. Every company while making public issue, shall offer now *25%* of each class of security offered for subscription through advertisement in newspapers for at least *two days.* These conditions are not applicable to a government company and to public financial institutions. The minimum offer of *25%* do not form part of the minimum public offer from the following agencies.

(a) Subscriptions made by the central government.

(b) Subscriptions made by state governments.

(c) Subscriptions made by investment agencies of the state governments.

(d) Subscriptions made by developmental financial institutions such as *IDBI, ICICI, IFCI, UTI, & GIC*

The Minimum capital limit for listing was raised to *Rs. 10 crore* in April 1995. Usually the legal provisions will make sure about a wide distribution of shares among the general investing public. A related requirement is the minimum number of shareholders to the allotted shares in a fresh issue of capital and offer for sale of existing capital. The present legal stipulation is that there should be at least ***10 and 20** public shareholders* for every *Rs. 1.00 lakh* fresh issue of capital and offer for sale of existing capital respectively. Therefore public offer means only the offer made to the public. It the issue is offer for sale, and it is entire underwritten by PFI, banks, the conditions of minimum number of shareholders do not apply. A company may be listed after giving a six months notice. It the number of public shareholders for every ***Rs. 1.00 lakh*** of capital offered to the public is less or if the public shareholding falls below *50%* of the public offer.

Other Conditions: The legal provisions have to be fulfilled by the companies according to the rules and regulations imposed by the government from time to time. The companies having a paid up value of ***Rs. 10 crores*** and above are required to get their listed on more than one stock exchange. It is in addition to the regional stock exchange listing. Therefore all existed listing companies are required to be listed on the stock exchange, where its Registered office is located.

There is another important legal provision which is imposed by the central government, that, the company shall pay interest on excess application money for the delayed period 10 weeks from the date of closure of subscription at a specified rate. It is a pre-requisite condition for listing of securities on stock exchanges. The companies are not permitted to transfer the shares which are sold under the promoters quota. These shares will be kept in lock in period and cannot be transferred.

The company cannot advertise in the media during the period when the subscription is open. But after closing of the issue, the company can say thanks to the investors. If any violation is made by the company, listing can be refused by the concerned stock exchange.

Therefore the companies are required to fulfil the needs of statutory provisions which are imposed by the central government through its various organs in many aspects. The companies which are proposing to enlist their securities should follow some legal provisions to the stock exchange requirements relating to prospectus and public issue of share capital. The legal aspects are presented below for the clear understanding about the legal framework regarding the public issue.

(1) The company should draft the prospectus according to the companies act 1956 and it should be thoroughly scrutinised and approved by its legal advisors.

(2) The company shall appoint brokers/managers to the issue. The appointed person should not be a member of recognised stock exchange.

(3) The company should appoint an efficient, experience and capable person as underwriter. The persons must be a public financial institutions banks and approved investment bankers only. They should have a strong financial background exchange.

(4) The prospectus shall contain only the facts as highlights of the issue.

(5) The prospectus should be advertised in the media at least ***10 days*** in advance to the opening of the subscription list.

(6) The prospectus shall indicate that the subscription list may be kept for at least 3 working days.

(7) The prospectus shall also indicate that the subscription list would not be kept open for a period exceeding ***10 working days***. If the issue is underwritten by all India public financial institutions. The subscription list shall be opened for a period exceeding ***21 days*** if the issue is underwritten.

(8) Copies of all the publicity material relating to the public issue, should be filed with the stock exchange.

(9) The advertisement process for the public issue shall closely be monitored by the company, managers and advisors to the issue. Any violation of these directions will result as to be disqualified for an official quotation on the stock exchange. The company should abide the advertisement code which is issued by the SEBI.

(10) The company shall take care of about providing the prospectus copies available to all the recognised stock exchanges at least *three weeks* before the opening of the subscription list. The company should ensure strict compliance with the relevant directions.

(11) The company shall indicate in the prospectus about the application forms which have been made to the stock exchanges available at concerned places.

(12) The company should make arrangements to provide the applications at specified 30 centres if the company's issue is more than Rs. *10 crores.*

(13) The prospectus shall indicate about the mode of payment by the shareholders for subscription of share capital. It should also state that refund orders process in the prospectus for non-allottes of shares.

(14) The company shall take all precautions in printing of application forms. The application forms should bear a printed identification number of six or seven digits. It should also have all the columns for the smooth functioning of the public issue process.

(15) The application form should contain a column for showing details about the applicants tax payers *PAN* with the instructions that it should be filled up if the application is for shares/debentures of a total value of ***Rs. 20,000*** or more.

(16) If the applicant does not have any PAN, the other information about his income tax circle district/ward should be filled up for further reference.

(17) The prospectus should contain some provisions namely. An applicant should submit only one application and not more than one for the total number of shares/debentures required. Applications may be made in single or joint names or more applications in single and or joint names will be deemed to be multiple applications. If sole and/or the first applicant is one and the same. The board of directors reserves the right to reject in its absolute discretion all or any multiple applications. With a view to discourage multiple applications.

(18) The company shall make arrangements for the acceptance of allotment and call moneys through the bankers at all centres.

(19) The company shall also match arrangements for sending allotment letters or refunding orders. These activities must be completed within the stipulated time.

(20) The company shall send the share certificates/debenture certificates within *two months or 10 weeks from the date of closure of the subscription list.*

(21) The company should pay the brokerage and underwriting commission to the financial intermediaries within *70 days* from the date of closing of the subscription list.

(22) The company shall get the share certificates, which are designed by the concerned stock exchange authorities. The company should be issued a lot of *100* equity shares of Rs. 10/- each or Rs. 100 each in case of debentures. The draft format shall be sent to the stock exchange in advance to get approval.

(23) The company shall satisfy the *Sec. 73* of the companies act in the following aspects.
   (i) It should submit the letter of application before filing the prospectus with the Registrar of companies.
   (ii) It shall also submit 5 copies of the prospectus and a cutting of newspaper advertisement to the stock exchange.
   (iii) The other listing particulars should be submitted to the exchange.

(24) Generally all reputed companies will get tremendous response from the market. In the event of over subscription, the company shall made allotment of shares in consultation with the concerned stock exchange. The company should follow the directions which were issued by the SEBI. It should made allotment with the help of the SEBI nominated public representative if the company gets over subscription 5 times or more for par issues and two times for premium issues.

(25) If the company gets over subscription, the company should furnish a certificate from its auditors that the allotment process are completed as per the legal provisions to the stock exchange.

(26) The company shall inform the stock exchange about the date of completion, posting of refund orders, posting of allotment letters, certificate of shares or debentures etc.,

(27) The company shall confirm that all the activities were completed.

(28) The company should furnish a certificate from its auditors regarding the expenditure involved in the public issue. Therefore the company shall take all precautions not to involving the ceiling amount.

(29) The company should obtain a certificate from its banker regarding the number of applications received, amount collected etc.,

(30) The company should file a statement with the director of the stock exchange within 5 working days of the expiry of stipulated period containing the information that all the legal formalities have been followed as per schedule period of time.

(31) After completion of the process, the company should appoint a member of stock exchange as a market matter to look after the listed securities.

(32) Finally the company shall submit a certificate from its auditors or a practising company secretary that all legal formalities have been complied according to the law.

Public issue involves so many legal implications. The company has to comply rules and regulations at every stage. There are some fines and penalties, if the company violates any regulation. Therefore the companies shall follow all the precautions during the public issue. The issuing company shall follow the legal provisions before applying for listing of its security with the recognised stock exchange.

(a) The letters of allotment / refund letters will be issued accordingly.

(b) The letters of rights will be issued accordingly.

(c) The company will issue receipts for all securities deposited with it whether for registration or any other purpose.

(d) The share certificates will be made subdivision or consolidate through the clearing house of the stock exchange.

(e) The company will make transfer of shares on production of necessary documents by the shareholders.

(f) The transfer process will be completed within the period of ***one month*** from the date of lodgement of transfer.

(g) The information will be submitted to the stock exchange about the date board meeting, declaration or recommendation of a dividend or the issue of rights or bonus shares.

(h) The company will send the information to the stock exchange regarding dividend or cash bonuses at least 5 days before the commencement of the closure of its transfer books or the record date fixed for this purpose.

(i) The company will inform the stock exchange if there is any change in general character of the nature of business.

(j) The company will inform the stock exchange if any change arises in the board composition. The change regarding the company auditor may also be informed.

(k) The company will forward the copies of statutory and annual reports to the stock exchange.

(l) The company will inform the stock exchange authorities regarding the affairs of all kinds of meeting. Which are to be conducted in the normal duration of the business.

(m) The company will bring the following affairs to the notice of the stock exchange authorities.

- (i) Reissue of any forfeited securities.
- (ii) Any alteration of share capital.
- (iii) Book closure dates.
- (iv) Annual returns after general meeting.
- (v) Any privileges to be granted to the shareholders.
- (vi) Any change regarding securities listed on the stock exchange.

Offer of Sale of Existing Issue Capital

Generally the companies will approach the capital market for raising the finance for their long term needs of requirements. The companies can make arrangements to list their shares on a recognised stock exchange through an offer for sale of their existed issued capital. This offer for sale can also be combined with a new issue. The public offer shall comply with the provisions of governing the listing of securities on recognised stock exchanges. The following conditions shall be fulfilled by the company for an offer for sale.

(1) The net worth of the company should not be less than its existing paid up capital.

(2) While making an application for listing its securities it should not have incurred a loss in each of 3 years in preceeding time.

(3) The offer must be in a position to a wide distribution of shares among the general public.

(4) While making an offer for sale the number of public shareholders should be at least ***20*** for every ***Rs. 1.00 lakh*** worth of shares.

(5) If the share is offered at premium, it must be accepted by the SEBI.

(6) The offer should be made containing all material particulars relating to the company.

Listing of Rights Shares

A listed company can also raise the finance through the issue of right shares. ***Right share*** means offering of additional shares to the already existed shareholders in the company. Generally it is customary that, every issuing company will ask at first instance the existing shareholders to subscribe for further share capital the shareholders have also the right to get the additional shares at a specified rate fixed by the company. Rights shares are the privilege for the existed shareholders for a reputed company. The following *formalities* have to be complied with by a listed company for listing of Rights shares debentures.

(1) Section 81 (1) of the companies act reveals that A company can issue right shares in the following two situations whichever is earlier.

  (a) At any time after the expiry of two years from the formation of a company *or*

  (b) At any time after the expiry of two years from the allotment of shares in that company made for the first time after its formation.

(2) Whether the concerned stock exchanges have notified the date of rights issue of shares is to be considered.

(3) The concerned stock exchange authorities shall give a notice of at least one day in advance for transacting securities of the company by its members, before board meeting.

(4) After the approval of board meeting for issue of rights shares, the company has to intimate the stock exchange immediately by a letter or telegram.

(5) For issue of rights shares, the company has to obtain a formal consent from the. Equity shareholders in the form of a *Special Resolution* in its general meetings.

(6) The company shall announce the closure of register of members and intimate the stock exchange.

(7) The company shall issue a letter of offer to the existing shareholders. The following aspects are to be incorporated in the letter of offer.

  (a) The letter of offer should indicate the shareholders right in favour of the nominees.

  (b) The company has the right to reject any nominee of whom it does not approve.

  (c) The shareholders should be entitled to apply for additional shares.

  (d) The shareholders who have renounced their rights would not be entitled to apply for additional shares.

(e) The shares will be allotted on a fair and equitable basis.

(f) The letter of offer should provide the freedom to the directors

(8) The company will have to make arrangements for the acceptance of application forms from the centres through its bankers.

(9) If any company fails to make its arrangements, the company should borne the outstation cheque ***collection*** expenses.

(10) The company shall issue letter of offer within 6 weeks of the record date.

(11) The company shall give sufficient time not being less the ***four weeks*** to exercise their rights.

(12) The company should provide forms of renunciation to all the shareholders freely on request.

(13) The company shall provide freedom for splitting of the letter of rights.

(14) The shareholders may be provided at least ***2 to 3 weeks*** to apply for subdivision.

(15) There should not be any restriction on the number of split letters of rights.

(16) The company shall intimate the last date for submission of rights application to the concerned stock exchange.

(17) A specimen copy of the letter of offer and application form for the rights issue should be forwarded to the stock exchange.

(18) After the allotment of new shares, the company shall despatch the share certificates within ***six weeks*** of the last date.

(19) After the despatch of share certificates to the shareholders, the company should make a letter of application in the prescribed form accompanied by other related documents. At the same time a listing application in prescribed form should be submitted to the stock exchange for official quotation of the new shares issued by it.

(20) In addition to the above forms, the company has to file in duplicate with the stock exchange a distribution schedule an analysis form etc., A new issue statement form to be obtained from the stock exchange.

(21) After completion of all the legal formalities with the stock exchange, it will enlist the new shares for official dealing by its members within 3 days.

Legal Formalities after Listing of Securities: After the listing of securities with the concerned stock exchange, the company has to follow many legal provisions in smooth functioning of the stock exchanges. Every listed company is required to furnish the unaudited financial results to the stock exchange authorities on a half yearly basis in a prescribed proforma. The unaudited financial statements should be submitted within *two months* of the expiry of the period. After the listing of its security with the stock exchange, the company shall make announcement in at least in one national and one in English daily newspaper within ***48 hours*** of the conclusion of the board meetings. The board of directors must sign on unaudited half yearly results and inform the stock exchange at least 15 days in advance and issue immediately a press release in at least one national newspaper and one regional newspaper. The company shall take all precautions in preparing the unaudited financial results. It should also not substantially differ from the audited results of the company. Any deviations found in first and second half year's unaudited results of any item varies by ***20%*** compared with the audited results for the full years. Therefore the company shall give its explanation to the concerned stock exchanges.

If any violation is made by the company the concerned stock exchange can suspend or withdraw admission to dealings in securities of a company. If any company fails to comply with the above legal provisions in listing of securities. It leads to suspended the trading or withdraw the admission of the security. Any action will be taken by the concerned stock exchange after giving to the company a reasonable opportunity through a notice in writing stating the reasons to show cause against the proposed action. Therefore, if a stock exchange takes an action against a company for a continuous period not exceeding ***three months***. Then the company may appeal to the SEBI. The SEBI has the full authority in this regard. The SEBI will give sufficient time to the concerned stock exchange, it may vary or set aside the decision of the stock exchange.

Delisting of a security means withdrawal of admission to a security by the stock exchange authorities. The scrip will not be permitted to trade on the stock exchange floor. A listed company may be delisted by a recognised stock exchange in the following situations.

(a) If the number of public shareholders falls below 5 for every Rs. *1.00 lakh* share capital offered to the public.

(b) If the public shareholding falls ***below 50%*** of the public offer.

The above requirements are not applicable if the infractions are due to the holdings of development financial institutions. The stock exchanges have the authority to admit the delisted securities if they fulfil the following conditions:

(a) The company has incurred losses during the proceeding three consecutive years and its net worth has been reduced to less that its paid up capital.

(b) The security of the company has remained infrequently traded during the proceeding three years.

(c) The security of the company may remain listed at least one of the concerned exchange.

C. SECURITIES AND EXCHANGE BOARD OF INDIA (SEBI)

Introduction

The securities and exchange board of India was established in April 1988. It has been functioning under the overall administrative control of the government of India. It works under the guidance of Ministry of finance. It is the agent of the central government in capital market. It is established for the regulation and orderly functioning of the stock exchanges. It also works for protecting the investors rights, prevents malpractices in security trading and promote healthy growth of the capital markets. It was granted statutory status in 1992 under SEBI act. It has the full authority to control, regulate, monitor and direct the capital markets. It is the watch dog of the securities market. It is the most powerful organ of the central government in the capital market.

After the repeal of the capital issue control act and abolition of the CCI the SEBI was given full powers on new issue market and stock market. It has been issuing guidelines since. April 1992 for all financial intermediaries in the capital market. The guidelines have been issued with the objective of investor protection. The guidelines also include the obligations of merchant bankers in respect of free pricing, disclosure of all correct and true information and to incorporate the highlights and risk factors in investment in each issue through the prospectus. It has been established for the healthy development and regulation of the capital market.

Objectives of SEBI: The main objectives of the SEBI is to protect the interest of the investors in the securities market I has three objectives by its act

(a) to protect the interests of the investors in securities market

(b) to promote the development of securities market

(c) to regulate the securities market.

The powers of SEBI can be exercised by the way of regulations. It is an implementing agency of policy matters by the central government from time to time. It has to report every year to the central government about its activities, policies and programmes. It shall submit a report to the government which in turn will be placed before parliament.

Powers of SEBI: The following powers have been given to the SEBI with the enactment of SEBI act, 1992.

(1) Regulating the business activities in the capital market.
(2) Power to grant registration to financial intermediaries.
(3) Registering and regulating the working of the depositories, custodians, FIIs, credit rating agencies.
(4) Registering and regulating the working of venture capital funds and mutual funds.
(5) Power to grant approval to bye laws of recognised exchanges.
(6) Power to prohibit insider trading.
(7) Power to compelisting of securities by public companies.
(8) Power to control and regulate stock exchanges.
(9) Power to call for any information or explanation from recognised stock exchanges or its members.
(10) Power to levy fee.
(11) Power to regulate substantial acquisition of shares and take over of companies.
(12) Power to promote and regulate self regulatory bodies.
(13) Prohibiting fraudulent and unfair trade practices relating to the securities markets.
(14) Promoting investors, education and training of intermediaries of the securities market.
(15) Performing any other functions as may be assigned by the government from time to time.

Delegation of Powers: The Government of India has delegated some powers to the SEBI subject to such limitations. The government retains the power in relation to any matter under the act. The ***Securities Contract Regulation Act*** Sec-28 reveals that the SEBI has been authorised to exercise powers on the following aspects.

(a) It has power to call periodical returns from the exchange.
(b) It has the power to regulate and control activities in spot delivery contracts.
(c) It has the power to grant of recognition to the exchanges.
(d) It has the powers to withdraw the recognition of the exchange.
(e) It has the powers to suspend the business of a recognised exchanged.
(f) It has the powers to amend the rule with regard to ***Sec. 3(2)*** of the act.
(g) It has the powers to give directions to the recognised exchanges.
(h) It has the powers to compel a public limited company to lits show.
(i) It has the powers to grant licensing to the dealers in securities market.
(j) It has the power to hear the appeals made by companies.
(k) It has the power to exercise the legal provisions of SCRA.
(l) It has the power to make or amend rules or articles of association of a stock exchange regarding the voting rights of members of a stock exchange.

Powers to Make Rules: The central government delegated the power to the SEBI with effect from 1995. Now the SEBI is the supreme authority in the capital market. Prior to 1995 the central government had the authority to make rules for carrying out the purposes of the SEBI act. It includes the SEBI constitution maintenance of its accounts, manner of inquiry to impose penalty for defaults and constitutions of the securities appellate tribunal. Now the SEBI has the authority to make rules relating to the following intermediaries.

(a) Brokers and sub brokers.

(b) Merchant bankers.

(c) Portfolio Managers.

(d) Registrars to an Issue.

(e) Share transfer agents.

(f) Underwriters.

(g) Debentures trustees.

(h) Bankers to an issue.

Powers of Make Regulations: For the smooth functioning of the capital market the SEBI is empowered to make regulations with the approval of the government. All regulations which are made by the SEBI must be published as notification in the official gazette.

The SEBI will made the regulations which include

(a) The registration process of financial intermediaries, cancellation or suspension of registration

(b) The matters belonging to the issue of share capital and transfer of securities

(c) The powers for the regulations in respect of the registration of the following financial intermediaries

(a) Merchant bankers

(b) Lead managers

(c) Brokers and sub brokers

(d) Portfolio managers

(e) Registrars to issue

(f) Share transfer agents

(g) Bankers to the issue

(h) Underwriters

(i) Debenture trustees

Organisation of the SEBI

The SEBI is the most powerful organ in the capital market. It is the representative of the central government. It is a statutory body in the capital market. It leads, monitor, regulates controls the activities of the capital market. The organisation has divided its activities into the five operational departments. The each department will be headed by an executive director. The legal department and investigation department also are headed by the executive directors. The following are the main departments which are functioning in the organisation.

(1) Primary Market Department

(2) Issue Management and intermediaries dept.

(3) Secondary Market dept.

(4) Institutional Investment department.

(1) Primary Market Department: Primary market department is the most important division in the organisation of the SEBI. It deals with the new issue market activities. It is headed by a division chief with specific responsibilities. It relates to the policy matters of the public issues. It looks after all the regulatory issues for the primary market in India. It also involved in regulatory matters with regard to the financial intermediaries. It also looks after the investor grievances. It deals with the investor complaints for refund of application money for non allottees refund of excess money, Non receipt of dividends non receipt of share certificates etc., Therefore It has the full authority with reference to the public issues.

(2) Issue Management and Intermediaries Department: This department will take care about the scrutiny of offer document. The offer document is the most important paper in public issue. It is the tool for attracting the investors. It is the basic document which are promised by the company to the newly becoming shareholders. The offer document should contain only facts and a right projection about the future. Some companies can misguide the investors by creating a gloomy picture about their product and company. Therefore this department shall closely monitor the contents of the offer documents. This department also involved in the registration of the financial intermediary. It also monitors the activities of various financial intermediaries.

(3) Secondary Market Department: The secondary market department occupies an important role in the regulation of the capital market operations. It involves in framing the policy matters regarding stock exchange activities. It regulates the secondary market activities. It guides monitors the stock exchange administration. It continuously monitor the price movements in the stock market. It involves in the development of new investment products. It closely observes the market movements and gathers information through market surveillance It also looks about the insider trading practices. It frames the policy and regulatory matters for the secondary market in India. It also issues directions to the stock exchange administration authorities on various matters. It also looks into the affairs of stock exchanges administration inspection by making inquiry towards financial intermediaries. It also regulates the sub-brokers activities.

(4) The Institutional Investment Department: This department frames the policy matters regarding the institutional investors. The institutions investors are more important in the capital market. They will put the higher amount of investment in the stock markets. They involve in buying and selling of shares on daily basis with crores of rupees investment. The following members will be treated as institutional investors

(a) Mutual funds.

(b) Foreign institutional investors.

(c) Corporate investors

(d) Institutional investors.

It looks after mergers and acquisitions of the corporate sector. It also concentrate on Research and publications. It maintains international relations in the process of globalization. It frames the policy matters for institutional investors. The legal department will take care of all the legal matters under the supervisions of ***General counsel.*** The investigation wing is also the part of institutional investment department the investigation using carry out inspections and investigations under the supervision of the chief.

In addition to the above departments the SEBI have two advisory committees. Each committee works for primary and secondary market. These advisory committee inputs in flaming policies and regulations. These committees are constituted with market players, recognised investor associations and experts in the capital market. But these committees will have no statutory power and the SEBI may or may not bound the suggestions made by them. Further the SEBI has also expanded its activities by opening their regional offices at ***New-Delhi, Chennai, Kolkata, and Mumbai***. The regional offices shall cover all operations in northern, southern, eastern and western effectively.

Composition of the SEBI: The government proposes to make more strengthening the SEBI, it granted additional powers for the smooth functioning of the capital market operations. The SEBI act provides for the establishment of a statutory board constituted by ***6 members.*** The board will constitute with a chairman and two members who are appointed by the central government. The another are member is to be appointed by the ***RBI*** the remaining two members will be drawn from securities market with those persons having rich experience in that field. Therefore the board will maintain the best talented expertism for the better functioning of the operations of the capital market. The central government has sanctioned the SEBI as an autonomous body status with perpetual succession and common seal. The preamble of the act states that it has been established to protect the interest of the investors in securities and to promote the development and regulate the securities market. The sec. 11 of the act deals with the powers of the board. It clearly states that the board has to work to protect the interest of the investors. The statutory board was established on *21.2.92* The act further lays down that the various rules and regulations will be issued to enable the SEBI to register, regulate and monitor various financial intermediaries in the capital market.

Licensing Authority

The SEBI is the most powerful organisation in the capital market. It has the right to grant the licenses to the financial intermediaries. All financial intermediaries dealing in securities markets must compulsorily registered with the SEBI in accordance with the regulations made under the SEBI act. The financial intermediaries, without license do not have an opportunity to take up the business activities in the capital market. Therefore every financial intermediary shall get license from the SEBI. The following intermediaries are required to get license from the SEBI for commencing business activities in the capital market.

(a) Stock brokers
(b) Share transfer Agents
(c) Bankers to an Issue
(d) Registrar to an Issue
(e) Underwriters
(f) Merchant bankers
(g) Trustees of trust deed
(h) Portfolio Managers
(i) Investment Advisers
(j) Depositories
(k) Custodians
(l) FIIs
(m) Credit Rating Agencies
(n) Venture capital funds
(o) Mutual funds
(p) Other intermediaries.

On application made by the above Intermediaries in a prescribed proforma to the SEBI. SEBI will scrutiny the application form and found satisfaction, then it will grant the certificate of registration. ***The certificate of Registration*** Contains the rules and regulations for the conduct of business by the intermediaries. Every financial intermediary shall apply in a prescribed form with a fee to the SEBI. The SEBI has the right to ***cancel/suspend*** a certificate of registration issued to the financial intermediaries in accordance with rules and regulations. If an intermediary dissatisfies with the behaviour of the SEBI, can appeal to the central government. The central government issues various orders from time to time to implement the rules strictly in accordance with the provisions of the act. The central government may also issues various directions to the SEBI matters relating to the policies in writing from time to time. The SEBI has to implement the orders, which are received from the central government for the smooth functioning of the capital market. The central government has the fall authority to review the policy matters relating to the capital market.

Penalties: The central government has the authority to instruct the SEBI to follow the rules and regulations from time to time. It has provided freedom to the SEBI to implement all the directions which are issued by the government. The SEBI has been empowered to impose penalties on various Intermediaries in non-compliance with the rules and regulations which are in force from time to time. The SEBI is the supreme authority in regulating, monitoring the capital market. It has the powers to impose fines and penalties, If any intermediary do not follow the rules strictly. It has the right to call any information from any intermediary. The intermediary fails to furnish certain information to the SEBI, it can impose the following penalties below.

(a) for failure to furnish any document, return report is liable to pay ***Rs. 1,50,000.***

(b) for failure to submit the return/information or document within the specific time not exceeding ***Rs. 50,000/-*** for each day.

(c) If any intermediary fails to maintain proper books of accounts or records not exceeding ***Rs.10,000/- each*** per day.

In addition to the above failures, the intermediaries would have to pay penalty for failure to enter into agreement with the clients. A registered intermediary will have to pay a penalty not to exceed ***Rs.5 lakhs*** for every failure. If any intermediary fails to Redress the investors grievances called upon by the SEBI to pay a fine not to exceed ***Rs. 10,000*** for each such failure the SEBI has the authority to impose the fines and penalties in case of institutional investors for failure of statutory guidance. It has the right to impose the penalties for mutual funds also. The following are the different penalties if a mutual fund fails to comply with the legal provisions.

(1) If any mutual fund fails in obtaining a certificate of registration from the authorities is liable to pay the following penalty whichever is higher.

 (a) not to exceed Rs 10,000 for each day or

 (b) ***Rs. 10,00,000.***

(2) If any mutual fund default in not complying with the terms and conditions of the certificate of Registration is liable to pay the following penalty whichever is higher.

 (a) not to exceed ***Rs. 10,000*** for each day or

 (b) ***Rs. 10,00,000***

(3) If any mutual fund fails to make an application for listing of schemes with authorities is liable to pay penalty whichever is higher.

 (a) not to exceed *Rs. 5,000* per day.

 (b) ***Rs. 5,00,000*** lakhs.

(4) It any mutual fund has became default in not despatching the Unit certificates to the unit holder is liable to pay penalty not to exceed ***Rs. 5,000*** for each day default.

(5) If any mutual fund fails to refund the application money not to exceed ***Rs. 1,000*** each day of default.

(6) If any mutual fund fails to invest the collected money in portfolio, is liable to pay penalty not to exceed ***Rs. 5,00,000*** for each such default.

In addition to the above penalties, the Assets Management company of the mutual fund is also liable to pay penalty for failure of rules and regulations not to exceed ***Rs. 5,00,000*** for each failure.

Stock Brokers: The stock brokers are also important persons is the capital market. The investors are the regular customers to the brokers. They play an active role in the capital formation of the country. They are able to guide, inspire, motivate the investors. Because they are regular customer they know the pulse of the investors and guide them towards the active participation in the capital market. The stock broker is an intermediary in the capital market. He has to abide by the rules and regulations which were issued by the SEBI from time to time. The SEBI closely observes the brokers activities. It any broker involves in malpractices, he has to face severe penalties which are levied by the SEBI. The following penalties have to be paid by the brokers if they do not comply with the legal provisions.

(a) If any broker fail to issue contract notes to the client in the prescribed proforma is liable to pay not to exceed ***5 times*** the amount for which the contract note was required to be issued.

(b) If any broker fails to deliver any security or payment, the amount due to the investor in the manner and within the stipulated period of time, not to exceed ***Rs. 5,000*** for each day of default.

(c) If any broker charges excess amount of brokerage from the client prescribed by the regulation not to exceed ***Rs. 5,000*** or ***five times*** the excess charge whichever is higher is payable as fine.

Insider Trading: Insider trading is one of the method of undesirable activity. It is not permitted by the act. Insider trading is possible to carried out by the company's top level management. It is a highly specialised speculative activity. It may be defined as "sale or purchase of securities by persons who possess price sensitive information about the company". It is made possible of their status in the company. It is an unfair and unhealthy practice. It damages the integrity of the market. It is an opportunity when the companies faces the favourable and unfavourable trends. The violation of the provisions of the SEBI. Insider Regulations 1992 is treated as committing the offence of Insider trading. If an insider deals in securities on his behalf or on behalf of others on the basis of an unpublished price sensitive information or any insider communicates any unpublished price sensitive information except as required in the course of business or under any law, is liable to pay penalty upto ***Rs. 5.00 lakhs***

Takeovers: Takeover means acquiring shares in a company at a specified price by a person or another company. It implies acquisition of controlling interest in a company by another company. It simply means a change of controlling interest in a company through the acquisition of its shares by another group. The company which fails to disclose the aggregate of shareholding in a company before acquiring any shares of that company and also to make a public announcement is liable to a penalty not exceeding ***Rs. 5,00,000.***

All the above penalties will be levied by the SEBI if any one violates the legal provisions. It is empowered to conduct any inquiry into the affairs of the market.

Steps taken by SEBI: SEBI is the legal entity to look after the welfare of the common investors. The main objective of the SEBI is to provide better facilities and protection to the common investor. Therefore is has taken several steps initiated to promote, develop and regulate the capital market. These steps have been included in both the primary and secondary markets. The following steps have been taken by the SEBI to strengthen the capital market.

Primary Market

(1) Introduced a innovative product ***"Stock Invest"***.

(2) Flexibility in issue pricing.

(3) Vetting of prospectus and letter of offer by SEBI.

(4) Abridged prospectus.

(5) Fixation of promoters contribution.

(6) All financial intermediaries brought under the purview of SEBI.

(7) Public sector bonds brought under the purview of SEBI.

(8) Deployment of Issue proceeds.

(9) Guidelines for preferential allotment of shares.

(10) Risk factors shall be disclosed prominently in prospectus.

(11) Companies permitted to open private collection centres.

(12) Guidelines to develop financial institutions for disclosure and investor protection.

(13) Obligations on Merchant bankers and underwriters.

(14) Fixation of lock in period for promoters quota shares.

(15) The allotment process must be finalised in the presence of the SEBI Representative.

(16) Registration of FIIs for the development and growth of the market.

(17) In public issue, the number of minimum shares increased to **500 shares.**

(18) Code of conduct to advertisers are announced.

(19) Proportional allotment permitted in case of oversubscription.

(20) Substantial firm allotment to institutions in public issues.

(21) Shareholders to decide price and time of conversion.

(22) Underwriting for issues are made mandatory.

(23) Credit rating is made compulsory.

(24) Reduced the validity period of stock invest.

Secondary Market

(1) Registration of share shops for spot trading shares.

(2) Insider trading is declared as illegal.

(3) Forward and carryover system banned.

(4) Odd lot trading facilities provided at stock exchanges.

(5) Financial requirement and norms for corporate members.

(6) Uniform settlement system.

(7) Introduction of Jumbo transfer deeds.

(8) Regulations and transactions between brokers and clients.

(9) Introduced circuit broker system at stock exchanges to check wide fluctuations.

(10) Private mutual funds have been permitted for the welfare of the small investors.

(11) Private placement of shares banned.

(12) Capital adequacy norms are prescribed for stock brokers and other intermediaries.

(13) NSE was introduced in July 1994.

(14) Steps to ensure transparency in secondary market operations.

(15) Broker's shall keep client's money in separate account.

(16) Constitution of governing council of stock exchange.

(17) Appointment of an Executive Director.

(18) Audit inspection for members of the stock exchange.

(19) Precautions in transactions between client and brokers.

(20) Norms for multiple membership of stock exchange.

(21) Issue of contract notes is made compulsory.

Factors to be Considered for Investment in Primary Market: At present the investors must be aware that the free pricing environment makes the issuers free to fix the issue price subject to some conditions. These conditions are levied by the SEBI to regulate the primary market activities. The set of guidelines issued to educate the investors to be cautious while investing in the primary market. They are advised to check the contents of prospectus before making investment in any issue. For every details relating to the issue, They should study the detailed prospectus which is available with the company or Merchant banker. The Merchant bankers play an important role in making success of public issue by a company. They have to make more efforts about the public issue. Public issue involves so many organisation and activities. The merchant bankers are responsible for drafting a prospectus. Therefore they must take care about the disclosure of all the relevant information in the prospectus. The following factors to be examined by the investor before making investment in any public issue.

(a) Promoter's record.

(b) Professional management of the company.

(c) Objects of the present issue.

(d) Analysis of project details

(e) Product analysis.

(f) Government stability.

Therefore the investors are advised to go through the contents of the prospectus and avail the advises of the experts from media in this regard.

PRIMARY MARKET IN INDIA

Introduction

The primary market is also known as *New issue market.* It is the market where the capital formation process will take place. The huge amounts of financial resources are mobilised by the corporate sectors through public issues. A well reputed, goodwill organisation can procure the funds from the market very cheaply. The crores of funds are available at the disposal of this market. However newly established companies cannot raise sufficient resources from this market. At the same time some companies are also cheating the investors by issuing share capital with fictitious names. The new issue market faced some emerging trends in the Indian financial system, the nations development depends upon the activeness of this market. It is an asset creation market. The capital formation in the country leads to the enhancement of productivity and per capita income. It is the growth engine for other allied markets. But at present the primary market is not very active.

The organisation of the primary market earlier suffered from many problems. In earlier decade there were no separate primary Market exists. It was in Unorganised system. No one can lead this market. Therefore the study of primary market can be done through the following manner.

(A) Primary Market (structure) basis.

(B) Primary Market Activities basis.

(A) Primary Market (Structure) Basis

Primary market involves a number of financial intermediaries. The structure of the primary market a decade earlier suffered from structural lacunal. The primary market is backed by the developmental financial institutions. There were no organisational structure arrangements for the organisation of the issue of share capital. At the earlier stage the gap was filled by ICICI and a few commercial banks such as ***SBI, ANZ*** Grindlays bank. They did set up their merchant banking divisions and rendered the services to the investors. But their services had not made any significant impact due to some problems. The primary market suffered a serious drawback of the system. It was the *absence* of an in built provision for distributing the securities to the investing public. In developed countries like *USA,* The investment bankers provide a unified and comprehensive package of service. They render all the services whichever required by the issuing company during public issue time. The primary market in India has to set up merchant banking institutions with high skill and better expertise being its main sources. The primary market in India faced the organisation weakness in the following ways.

(a) Barriers to the small companies.

(b) Poor response from public.

(c) Unorganised system of market.

(d) Lack of institutional demand for industrial securities.

(e) Crowding of new issues at some times.

The liberalisation of the regulations made the new issue market more active. The abolition of the CCI in 1992, the protection of the investors in securities market and the promotion of the development and regulation of the market by the SEBI has changed the New issue market structure. The SEBI has the full authority in the new issue market to regulate, monitor and guide the market forces. To tone up the operations of the new issues in the country, The SEBI has put in place rigorous measures. The inter-mediaries have to conform to regulations designed by the SEBI. The financial intermediaries play an important role in the process of selling new issues. The legal framework for their operations has been prescribed by the SEBI. The new issue market involves many intermediaries participation. Without the cooperation of many intermediaries, it is not possible to raise finance from the market. The following intermediaries are occupy an important role in the primary market. Their legal framework, operational work and other matters will be explained in detail

1. Merchant Bankers
2. Lead Managers
3. Underwriters
4. Bankers to an Issue
5. Brokers to the Issue
6. Registrars to an Issue/STA.
7. Debenture Trustees
8. Portfolio Managers

Therefore the above intermediaries will play an important role in the primary Market. The success of the issue will depend upon the participation of the various intermediaries. The public issue depends upon the coordination activities of the issuing company. The primary market is a combination of many intermediaries.

1. Merchant Bankers

Merchant bankers play a vital role in the public issue. They work as sponsors of the capital issues. They render major services to the issuing company. They involve in determining the composition of the capital structure of the issuing company. They are able to guide the client company to give suggestions about different types of securities to be issued at a lowest cost. They involve in public issues right from drafting of prospectus and application forms, compliance with legal formalities, appointment of Registrars, Underwriters, bankers to issue, Listing of securities, selection of brokers, publicity and advertising agents printers etc. The issuing company can relay on merchant banker upto the closing of issue. Therefore the importance of the merchant bankers in the process of capital issues have been increasing day by day. It is now mandatory that all the public issues should he managed by the Merchant bankers functioning as the ***Lead Managers.*** The SEBI is the most powerful organ in the primary market. It is the controlling authority to the merchant bankers who handles the public issues on behalf of his client company. Hence the merchant banker shall follow the guidelines which are issued by the SEBI. The following condition should be fulfilled by the merchant bankers.

(1) Registration

(2) Capital adequacy requirements

(3) Obligations

1. Registration : The Registration is compulsory for every merchant banker to carry out his activities. They should register with the SEBI. SEBI is the licensing authority to the merchant bankers. According to the SEBI guidelines the merchant bankers can be classified into four categories. They are

(A)	Category I	Merchant Banker
(B)	Category II	Merchant Banker
(C)	Category III	Merchant Banker
(D)	Category IV	Merchant Banker

Category I Merchant bankers may carry any activity relating to public issue. They involve in preparation of prospectus, determining capital structure, arrangements of Intermediaries, final allotment of securities and refund of subscriptions. They will participate in all activities relating to the public issue. They also act as advisor, consultant, managers underwriters or portfolio managers. They could act as lead managers to an issue. From 9-12-97 onwards only category I merchant bankers are required to get registration with the SEBI. They should get a seperate registration of certificates for carry on the activities of underwriters and portfolio managers.

The category II merchant bankers could act as advisors, consultants, managers, Underwriters and portfolio managers. The category III merchant bankers can act as an Underwriters, adviser and consultant only.The category IV Merchant banker could act as stipulated by the law. Therefore the merchant banker has to work in public issues indifferent ways. He must coordinate all the issue related activities. The SEBI has the authority to grant a certificate of registration on consideration of all matters which are furnished by the merchant bankers. The Merchant banker shall fulfil the following conditions to get the registration of certificate from the SEBI.

(a) The merchant banker should be a body corporate.

(b) The primary dealer or satellite dealer who were register with the RBI can also carry out the activities of a merchant banker.

(c) The satellite dealer or primary dealer shall not accept deposits from the public.

(d) The merchant banker should have necessary infrastructure like adequate office staff, manpower and equipment.

(e) They should appoint at least two persons, those who are rich experience in merchant banking activities.

(f) They should have recognised professional qualification in finance, law or business management.

(g) The registration should be in the interest of the investors.

(h) The merchant bankers or their associates should not be involved in any litigation connected with the securities market.

2. Capital Adequacy Requirement: The SEBI has the authority to grant the certificate of registration to the merchant bankers. They will be granted registration by the SEBI in different categories on the basis of their capital adequacy norms. The capital adequacy consists with its net worth, paid up capital and free reserves. The SEBI has fixed the following net worth values for different categories as follows:

(a)	Category I	Rs. 5 crores.
(b)	Category II	Rs. 50,00,00
(c)	Category III	Rs. 20,00,000
(d)	Category IV	Nil.

The SEBI will monitor the activities of all the merchant bankers on half yearly basis. Every category of Registered merchant banker shall furnish to the SEBI of his half yearly unaudited financial results. They should pay the required fee to the SEBI on the basis of their status.

REGISTRATION FEE

Category of Merchant banker		*First two years*	*Third year*
I	Annually	Rs. 2,50,000	Rs. 1,00,000
II	Annually	Rs. 1,50,000	Rs. 50,000
III	Annually	Rs. 1,00,000	Rs. 25,000
IV	Annually	Rs. 5,000	Rs. 1,000
Renewal Fee			
I	Annually	Rs. 1,00,000	Rs. 20,000
II	Annually	Rs. 75,000	Rs. 10,000
III	Annually	Rs. 50,000	Rs. 5,000
IV	Annually	Rs. 5,000	Rs. 2,000

SEBI has increased the registration fee to Rs. 5,00,000 since 1999. The renewal fee shall be paid before the expiry period of three months. They shall pay the renewal fee as indicated above. If any merchant banker fails to pay renewal fee within the stipulated period of time, his registration may be suspended.

3. Obligations: The merchant bankers shall abide by the code of conduct as specified in the act. A merchant banker shall conduct his business with a high standard of integrity and fairness in his all transactions. He shall conduct his business activities in a systematic way. He shall render his services to his client at all times. He should exercise due diligence ensure proper care and exercise professional Judgement. He shall behave properly with other merchant bankers. He has to disclose all the information and the possible conflict of duties and interest when he is rendering service to his client. He should make any comment or statement against any act which is harmful to the interest of other merchant bankers while executing any assignment. He should not disclose information about his clients before other clients or press. He should not reveal his capability or influence to render certain services or his achievements before his clients. He should always render the best possible advice to his clients and ensure that all professional affairs must be dealt in very prompt, efficient and cost office way. He should deal with this client company after disclosure of the information to the SEBI. He should also inform the board of directors of the client company regarding the various assignments of the company. The merchant banker should have the following characteristics.

(1) He should provide true and adequate information without misguiding the client before taking any investment decision.

(2) He should make available the copies of prospectus memorandum of association and any other literature to the investors.

(3) He should make adequate steps for the fair allotment of shares and refund the application money without delay to the ***Non-allottees***

(4) He must pay proper attention towards investor's grievance. He shall try for settling of their problems as far as possible.

He should not involve particularly in respect of the issue of any securities, to create false market or manipulations or price rigging or spreading of price sensive information to brokers, or to other market players in the capital market. All these activities are unfair, unethical and undesirable to the investors. He is the most important person in public issue and shall be abide by all the rules and regulations framed by the SEBI.

2. Lead Managers

Lead Managers have to be associated with the issuing company till the despatch of share certificates or the refund of excess application money to the investors. They will make agreement with the issuing company for setting out their mutual rights, liabilities and obligations relating to such issues. A statement containing all these information is to be furnished to the SEBI at least one month before the opening of the issue for subscription. The lead managers have to accept a minimum underwriting obligation of 5% of the total underwriting commitment or Rs. 25 lakhs whichever is less. It the lead manager is unable to underwrite this amount, it should be assigned to the merchant banker under intimation to the SEBI. The number of lead managers will be appointed according to its issue size. The following provisions may reveal about their appointment.

Issue size		*No. of leadmers*
(a)	Less than Rs. 50 crores	2
(b)	Rs. 50 crores – 100 crores	3
(c)	Rs. 100 crores – Rs. 200 crores	4
(d)	Rs. 200 crores – Rs. 400 crores	5
(e)	Above Rs. 400 crores	5 and more

The lead managers are responsible for the verification of the contents of a prospectus or letter of offer in respect of an public issue. After the verification of content he has to submit certificate to the SEBI at least two weeks before the opening of the issue. He has to submit a due diligence certificate regarding all legal provisions have been complied by the company in connection with the public issue. The lead managers have to submit the documents to Registrar of companies and Regional stock exchange containing the following information.

(a) particulars about the public issue.

(b) contents of the offer document/prospectus

(c) Other literatures useful to the investors all of the above particulars should be submitted to the SEBI along with the prescribed fee specified below.

Issue size (Including premium)	*Fee per document*
Upto Rs. 5 crores	Rs. 10,000
Rs. 5 crores – Rs. 10 crores	Rs. 15,000
Rs. 10 crores – Rs. 50 crores	Rs. 25,000
Rs. 10 crores – Rs. 100 crores	Rs. 50,000
Rs. 100 crores – Rs. 500 crores	Rs. 2,50,000
Mote than Rs. 500 crores	Rs. 5,00,000

A lead manager/merchant banker is prohibited from acquiring securities of any company on the basis of unpublished price sensitive information during any professional assignment. He has to submit the particulars to the SEBI for any acquisition of securities of a company where the issue is being managed by him within 15 days from the date of the transaction. He has to disclose all the information to the SEBI.

(a) particulars regarding his responsibilities relating to the present issue.

(b) Any change in previously furnished information to the SEBI while granting the registration certificate

(c) The other client companies which he is involved in public issues.

(d) The full information about the capital adequacy requirements

(e) The other information relating to his professional assignments as consultent, Underwriter, managers or adviser to an issue.

The SEBI has the right to inspect the books of accounts records and documents. He has to maintain the books of account as per the legal provisions of the act. The lead Manager/Merchant banker who fails to comply with the legal provisions, the SEBI has the right to take action against them. It can levy the penalties in two kinds *(a) suspension of Registration (b) cancellation of Registration.* The suspension of the registration can be done in the following situations by the SEBI.

(a) If any violation made by the Merchant banker in relating to SEBI act, rules and regulations

(b) If the merchant banker fails to furnish any information as required by the SEBI.

(c) If he furnishes wrong information to the SEBI

(d) If he fails to submit periodical returns to the SEBI

(e) If he does not cooperate with the SEBI in any enquiry which is conducted by it.

(f) If he fails to pay the specified fee.

(g) If he involves in mal practices or in price rigging

(h) If he violates the conditions while granting registration.

(i) If he fails to maintain capital adequacy requirement as per the provisions of the act.

(j) If he violates the code of conduct of the business.

In the following situations, the SEBI has the right to *Cancel the* registration.

(1) If he is found in guilty of fraud

(2) If he is involved in conviction of a criminal offence

(3) If he is involved in deliberately at manipulation or price rigging or cornering activities.

(4) If SEBI feels that he is harmful to the investors

The SEBI is a powerful organisation in the primary market to control the activities of different kinds of intermediaries. It has the power to cancel or suspend the registration. It also imposes penalties where the merchant bankers is in non compliance of conditions for registration. The defaults made by them generally can be categorised as follows:

(a) Major defaults.

(b) Serious defaults.

(c) Minor defaults

(d) General defaulters

(e) Default in prospectus

(a) Major Defaults (3 points): The primary market consists of various financial intermediaries. The Merchant banker is one of the most important intermediary in public issues. The issuing company has a little role to play in the market. The following activities will be treated as major default by the SEBI. This kind of default attracts 3 penalty point

(a) *fails* to take up mandatory underwriting

(b) Deploying excess number of lead manager than permitted by it

(c) Involvement of unauthorised merchant banker in a public issue.

(b) Serious Defaulters: (penalty points) The SEBI is the watch dog of the capital market It observes all the intermediaries and regulates the market. If any merchant banker fails to Non-Cooperate with the SEBI in furnishing desired information or documents will be treated as serious default. This type of default attracts *4 penalty* points. If any merchant banker violates the code of conduct will be viewed as serious default. Any merchant banker who reaches cumulative penalty points of *8* leads to cancellation/suspension of registration. But there will be a chance to take corrective mistakes by them, The maximum penalty points are restricted to 4.

(c) Minor Defaults: (02 penalty points) The primary market is a combination of number of financial intermediaries. The success of the public issue depends upon many factors. But the merchant bankers will take an important role the issue process. If the following mistakes are made by the merchant bankers, It will attract two penalty points.

(a) Any advertisement material are not being prepared in compliance with rules and regulations may be treated minor default.

(b) If fails to attempt the investor's grievance promptly.

(c) If any delay made in refund of application money.

(d) If any failure provides adequate and fair disclosure to investors about the risk factors in prospectus.

(e) Failure to verify the contents of prospectus

(f) failure to non disclosure of substantial matters in highlights to the issue in prospectus.

(g) Exaggerated information incorporated in the contents of the prospectus or in any press conference, investors conference, brokers conference to market the issue of shares.

(d) General Defaults: (01 penalty point) Usually the merchant bankers dominate the public issue process. They occupy key role in the process of an issue. They should coordinate many things in post or pre issue situation. In this capital market every player shall move according to the strict rules and regulations. Every movement of the every intermediary will be observed by the market surveillance system of the SEBI. Therefore the following activities which are made by the merchant bankers will be attracted one penalty point.

(1) If the lead manager fails to submit the draft prospectus to the SEBI before filing with the Registrar of companies or stock exchanges.

(2) If the merchant bankers fails to submit the certificate of minimum subscription to the issue.

(3) Fails to despatch the share certificates, refund orders and filling listing application by the issuer.

(4) If the merchant banker fails to submit the diligence certificate in a proforma to the SEBI before opening of the public issue.

(e) Default in Prospectus: Prospectus is the constitution of public issue. It is the basic document, which the investor makes investment decision on the basis of description in the prospectus. Therefore the prospectus can be described as *"Manifesto"* of the political party. If the merchant banker fails to disclose the risk factors in the prospectus he attracts negative points. If any content disclosed in the prospectus as extraneous, and absence of listing will attract negative points. The grading points will be made as follows.

(a) Grading points of prospectus can be 10.

(b) Prospectus scoring greater than or equal to *8 points* are classified as *"A"*

(c) Prospectus scoring with *6 or* less than *8* points will be categorised as *"A"*

(d) prospectus scoring with *4 or* less than 6 points will be treated as category *"B"*.

(e) Prospectus scoring with less than *4 points* can be categorised *"C"*.

3. Underwriters

Public issue involves number of intermediaries in the primary market. Underwriter another important intermediary in the new issue market. They agree to take up securities. They provide assurance to the issuing company that the issue may be subscribed either by others or by themselves. Underwriting is not mandatory after April 1995 but its importance cannot be ignored. It is just like insurance for public issues. They are appointed by issuing in consultation with the merchant bankers to the issues. A certificate should be issued by the lead manager in relating to underwriters financial capacity this information should be disclosed in prospectus.

SEBI is the regulator of the primary market. It has the right to grant the registration to the underwriters in accordance with the provisions of the act. An Intermediary who want to act as underwriter, a certificate of registration must be obtained from the SEBI. While grating the certificate of registration, the SEBI will examine the following factors.

(a) Adequate infrastructure equipment and man power to smooth functioning of the activities.

(b) The past experience in underwriting business.

(c) Employment of at least two persons with rich experience in underwriting.

(d) The persons those who have been applied previous to the SEBI and found rejected are not eligible to grant the registration.

(e) Any person who has been previously taken disciplinary action against such person under the SEBI act or rules and regulations.

(f) The net worth should be *M. 20,00,000* (Capital + Resources).

The underwriter who has been granted registration, will have to pay a fee to the SEBI ***Rs. 2,00,000*** for the 1st and 2nd years and Rs. *1.00 lakh* for the 3rd year. A renewal fee should be paid Rs. 20,000 for every year. After 1999. The SEBI raised the *Rs. 5,00,000*. The registration will be in force, a renewal fee of ***Rs. 2,00,000*** every three year from the 4th years from the date of initial registration is payable. If any person fails to pay the required fee leads to suspension of the registration. The underwriter who has been granted registration should follow the following guidelines.

(a) General Responsibilities

(b) Code of conduct.

(a) General Responsibilities: The Underwriting is a process of insurance to the public issues. The issuing companies do not need to worry about the response for their issue because the issue is fully assured by the underwriters. Therefore they will play an important role in the capital market as per the provisions of the act, the underwriters shall get benefit from underwriting commission only. He should not be benefited either directly or indirectly. An underwriter can oblige underwriting agreements should not exceed *20 times* to his net worth. He has to subscribe for underwriting the securities within *45 days* of the receipt of intimation from the issuing company. An underwriter shall enter into an agreement with his client company. The agreement contains all the information about both parties. Full particulars should be discussed and it should be incorporated in the agreement. The SEBI has the right to inspect the books of accounts and other documents of the underwriter. An Inspection of the records if he fails to comply with the legal provisions, the SEBI has the right to take action against him. It has the right to cancel the registration or suspend the registration of any underwriter. The punishment will depend upon the situation.

(b) Code of Conduct: The person who takes the responsibility of non subscription shares by the public is known as underwriter. He is the most important intermediary in the public issue. Underwriting is an activity of profession. Therefore the underwriter shall follow the professional code of conduct. He should at all times to abide by the code of conduct. He has to maintain a high standard of integrity, dignity and fairness in his all dealings with his clients and fellow professionals. He has to ensure that all the ethical manners should be adopted in issue of capital. He has to render high standard of service and exercise due deligence and adopt independent professional Judgement. Any underwriter should not will-fully make untrue statements. He should not make any false representation in the market. He shall disclose to the issuing company about his potential areas of conflict of duties and interest of other underwriters. He should not disclose any information about the issuing to any other company. If any information came to his knowledge and deal in securities shall inform to the SEBI immediately.

4. Bankers to an Issue

The success of a public issue depends upon many factors. The primary market consists of number of intermediaries. Every intermediary has his own role in the issue process. Banker is one of the important intermediaries who collects the application money from the investors through his wide network of branches they will collect the application money along with applications and in turn it will be transmitted to the company. The SEBI is the most powerful organisation in the primary market and having the authority to grant the certificate of Registration to the bankers. Every banker must obtain a certificate from the SEBI. It grants the registration on the basis of all the activities relating to the banker for an issue with reference to the following requirements.

(a) The banker should have the necessary adequate infrastructure and manpower to effectively discharge his activities.

(b) The banker must be a scheduled bank.

(c) The grant of a certificate must be in the interest of the investors.

(d) The banker should not be involved in any litigation of any economic offence.

The Registered banker to an issue shall apply for the renewal of his registration 3 months before the expiry of the registration. The SEBI has the right to collect a fee of ***Rs. 2,50,000*** for the years two first from the date of registration and *Rs. 1,00,000* for the 3rd year to keep the registration in force. He has to pay renewal fee annually for the first two years. It is ***Rs. 1,00,000*** and ***Rs. 20,000*** for the third year. The registration fee has been changed from 1999, a fee of ***Rs. 5,00,000*** as initial registration fee and *Rs. 2,50,000* renewal fee every three years from the fourth year from the date of registration. The banker to an issue should follow guidelines in the following aspects.

(a) General Responsibilities.

(b) Code of Conduct.

(a) General Responsibilities: Usually a banker, who has been appointed as bankers to issue, shall have to follow the guidelines which are issued by the SEBI. If any violations are made against the guidelines he will be liable to pay penalty. A banker to an issue has to furnish the following information to the SEBI.

(a) His past experience as a banker to an issue.

(b) The number of public issues handled by him.

(c) The number of applications collected by him.

(d) The amount of application money collected by him

(e) The dates on which the applications are received from the investors should be forwarded to the Registrar to an issue.

(f) The particulars about the refund to the investors

The SEBI has the authority to call for any information from the bankers. The bankers to an issue are required to maintain the books of accounts, records and documents for a minimum period of 3 years after the closing of the public issue. He should maintain the books of accounts containing about the no. of applications received, amount collected, forwarded dates etc. The registered banker shall enter into an agreement with the issuing company. The agreement contains full information about the number of collection centres and the process of forwarding the same to the Registrar of issue. It also contains the full information about the daily statement during the public issue period. If any violations are made by the banker, the RBI will take disciplinary action in relation to issue payment and it should be informed to the SEBI. If the banker is prohibited from these activities, the SEBI registration is automatically deemed as cancelled or suspended according to the situation.

(b) Code of Conduct: Banking is a highly respectable profession. The banker has to follow the professional code. He should conduct his business in a dignified way. He should maintain a high standard of integrity and fairness in his all dealings. He should not do any harm to other professionals. He should not make any exaggerated statement to his clients about his capability to render the services in this aspects. He has to render best possible advice to his clients. His professional dealings must be in prompt, efficient and cost effective manner. He should not reveal the confidential information about the client to the public or others. He should follow all the legal provision, rules regulations, guidelines, resolutions and notifications. The RBI has the authority to inspect the banker on request from the SEBI. The purpose of inspection relating to books of account records, documents and investors grievances. On completion of inspection, The SEBI has the authority to take action against the banker according to the situation. Any failures made by the bankers will have to face the penalties and fines. The SEBI is empowered to suspend or cancel the registration. The following activities lead to suspend the registration of banker to issue.

(a) Fails to furnish the required information

(b) Furnishes false information

(c) Fails to resolve the investor's complaints

(d) Involved in guilty of misconduct

(e) Fails to pay required fee

(f) Fails to carry out his obligations

The following activities lead to cancellation of registration.

(1) Repeated defaults leading to suspension.

(2) Conduct of the business adversely effect the interest of the investors.

(3) Found guilty or conceited in a criminal offence.

5. Brokers to the Issue

Brokers are one of the financial intermediaries in the public issues. They are mainly concerned with the mobilisation of share capital from the investors. The brokers will be selected in consultation with the concerned stock exchanges. The inexperienced and unknown agencies into this field are discouraged. The letter consent given by the broker should be submitted to the Registrar of companies. The prospectus should disclose the names and addresses of the brokers. The brokerage is fixed at **1.5%** for all the types of public issues. The expenses for distributing the application forms should borne by the stock brokers. The company will not reimburse the expenses incurred by the brokers. The brokerage for private placement of capital is fixed at a maximum rate of **0.5%** The brokerage is not allowed in respect of promoters quota or renounced by the existing shareholders. Brokerage is not payable when the application are made by the institutions. The brokerage should be paid by the company within two months from the date of allotment to the broker. The brokerage rate should be disclosed in the prospectus.

6. Registrars to an Issue

The Registrars to an issue is one of the intermediary involved in the primary market. He carries on the activities such as collecting applications from the investors, preparing records and receiving money from the investors. He assist the issuing company for making allotment in consultation with the stock exchanges. He is involved in processing, despatching allotment letters, refund orders, certificates and other related documents related to public issue. The Registrar is also performs the function of share transfer agent. The share transfer agent is a person who maintain the records of holders of shares on behalf of the company. He deals with the matters connected with the transfer of shares. He must get the registration certificate from the SEBI. It may also be renewed every year by the SEBI on the basis of performance. He must abide the rules and regulations which are issued by the SEBI from time to time.

PRIMARY MARKET (SERVICES)

Introduction

The asset formation is the basic function of the primary market. The development of a country depends upon the activeness of this market. The SEBI is most powerful organisation to monitor the activities of the different services rendered by various intermediaries public issue involves participation of many organisations to make success the issue. Though the success of an public issue depends upon mainly on *good reputation, well known* and financial discipline of the issuing company. But we cannot ignore the services which render the services during the issue period. All formalities should be fulfilled by all participants. The public issue involves two activities. *(a) pre-issue (b) post issue*. All activities commencing with the planning of a capital issue till the opening of subscription list is classified as ***pre-issue activities.*** After the commencement of subscription list is known as *post issue services.* These services are more important and require to follow the SEBI guidelines at every moment. Every services closely monitored and reviewed by the SEBI. There will be penalties and fines. If any intermediary violates the SEBI guidelines and government regulations. The aim of the close observation by the SEBI is to protect the investors from the Indiscipline companies. At present the investors are cheated by some duped companies. The issuing companies are also required to follow the company law requirements in relation to the issue of shares. We must remember that the SEBI will control the service of the issuing company those are to be listed on the recognised stock exchanges. The company law guidelines are applicable to only unlisted company/deemed public Ltd. company/private limited company. Therefore the issuing companies have to be followed many rules and regulations as stipulated by the acts and provisions. The post issue activities will cover in detail under the unit of Financial services of this book.

Appendix

List of Annexures

Annexure 1: Back up documents from the promoters.

Annexure 2: Questionnaire to be filled by the lead manager.

Annexure 3: Application to be filed with the SEBI with draft prospectus and list of documents.

(a) Certificate of due diligence.

(b) Copy of intense allocation of responsibilities between the lead manager.

(c) Memorandum of understanding.

(d) Rights of the Lead Manager.

(e) Consequence of breach of Memorandum of Understanding.

(f) Compliance certificate.

(g) Compliance certificate by the company.

Annexure 4: Questionnaire to be filled at the site visit.

Annexure 5: Copy of prospectus.

Annexure 6: List of documents required for listing along with a copy of listing form.

Annexure 7: Application for inviting bankers to act as collecting bankers and their consent format.

Annexure 8: List of documents to be filled to Registrar of companies along with acknowledgement card.

Annexure 9: Copy of form – 2A.

Annexure 10: Copy of compliance Reports (public issue).

Annexure 11: Copy of compliance Reports (Rights issue).

Annexure–1

Back Up Documents Required from Promoters

Part I

1. Collaboration agreement, if any.
2. Appraisal note.
3. Confirmed order slip.
4. Auditors tax benefits certificate.
5. Auditors report for the last five years ending within six months from the date of opening of the issue.
6. Relevant papers of new industrial policy.
7. Memorandum in terms of new policy submit to SIA and its acknowledgement if applicable.
8. RBI approval of foreign collaboration if applicable.
9. RBI approval for issue of shares to NRIs if applicable.
10. From 5 for authorised capital.
11. Amount of shares allotted and their respective dates of allotment.
12. Auditor's certificate for the amount already brought in by the promoters.
13. Promoters' undertaking that the balance amount of promoters' contribution shall be brought in before opening of the subscription list.
14. Promoters certificate for the total number of present permanent employees of the company.
15. Promoters bio-data duly signed/certificate/mark sheet of qualifying examinations.
16. Company Secretary's certificate for other direction ships of all the directions of the company.
17. Bio-data of technical and key management personal.
18. Copy of letter of allotment/lease deed for the land covered in the project.
19. List of machineries to be procured.
20. Detail of orders placed for plant and machinery.
21. Letter with regard to sanctioned loan.
22. No Objection Certificate (NOC) from state pollution control board.
23. Schedule of implementation of the project duly signed by the architects and promoters.
24. Deployment of funds and their sources as on certified by auditor.
25. Projections as envisaged by the company, if any.
26. Promoters' certificate for outstanding litigation.
27. Promoters' certificate for litigation.
28. Promoters' certificate for defaults.
29. Promoters' certificate for material development.

Part II

30. Consent of

    (a) Lead manager(s), (b) Co-manager(s), (c) Registers, (d) bankers to the company, (e) Bankers to the issue, (f) Auditors (for inclusion of name tax report and auditors report) (g) Legal advisors, (h) company secretary (CS) (i) Directors.
31. From 32 for changes in directionship (C.S. Certificate).

32. For change in auditors since incorporation (C.S. Certificate).
33. Minutes of special resolution pursuant to section 81 (IA).
34. Working capital limits.
35. Application made to any bank for enhancement of working capital limits, if any.
36. Term loan sanction letter (S).
37. Letters of registrars regarding fees payable.
38. Letters to lead managers regarding fees payable.
39. Promoters undertaking regarding interest of the promoters and directors.
40. Copies of power of attorney for signing and corrections in the prospectus.
41. Copy of resolution under section 293 (1) (A) if any.
42. Copy of resolution under section 293 (1) (C) or (1) (d) if any.
43. Copy of board resolution authorising the register for accepting application accompanied by stock-invest.
44. Solicitors certificate to the effect that there are no statutory overdues/outstanding litigations/criminal prosecutions against the directors/company if applicable.
45. Working results of the collaborator for the last five years.
46. Names of other partnership concerns managed by the promoters.
47. Banker's report on promoters.
48. Profile/bio-data of any foreign director.

Annexure 2

Questionnaire for Walk-in Clients

(Answer Yes/No)

Q.1. Do promoters have any past experience in the same industry ? if "yes". Then please specify the number of year.

Q.2. Are the promoters new to the investing public?

Q.3. How was the response to the promoters previous issue (if any)? Rating: (Kindly rate it on a scale 1-10, 1 means excellent and 10 stands for poor).

Q.4. Where the promoters able to achieve the results as mentioned in the prospectors in the previous issue?

(a) upto 90 per cent and above

(b) 75 per cent and above

(c) Below 25 per cent.

Q.5. Are there any outstanding liabilities? if yes then please specify.

(a) contingent liabilities

(b) personal liabilities of the promoters

(c) Any other.

Q.6. What is the promoters' stake in the present project: 20-25/25-40/above 40 per cent?

Q.7. Did the promoters sell any part of their holding in the past 12 months?

Q.8. Name a few issues of similar industry, which went public recently (in the past six months) and rate them as per the investors response (Rating scale: 1-10)

Q.9. Has the project been appraised? if yes then

(a) Name the appraising agency and its take

(b) Cost of the issue

(c) Means of finance

(d) Date of commencement of operation

Q.10. At the capacity utilisation would the Break-even point (B.E.P) be achieved?

(a) 20-30 per cent

(b) 31-40 per cent

(c) above 40 per cent

Q.11. Is the project an export–oriented/import substitution one?

Q.12. What is the gestation period?

(a) 1-2 years

(b) 2-4 years

(c) 5 years and above

Q.13. What is the status of the land? owned by the company/on lease?

Q.14. What is the status of the plant and machinery?

(a) Indian/imported

(b) Already ordered to be ordered/received at the site

Q.15. Is the debt-equity ratio high? (more than 2:1)

Q.16. What is the source of raw material?

(a) Near the factory Premises

(b) Far away from the factory

(c) Imported.

Q.17. Has the company obtained the consent of the bankers with whom it is enjoying the limits?

Q.18. Has the project received all the government approvals?

Q.19. Has the company obtained the RBI's permission for NRI's participation in the issue (if any)

Q.20. Has the company got the increase in the authorised capital registered with the ROC?

Q.21. Has the company tied up for the working capital requirement?

Q.22. What kind of technology is used in the project?

(a) New

(b) Time tested

(c) Foreign collaboration

Q.23. Has the company entered into any marketing tie-up for its product? if "yes"then is it an MOV/agreement.

Q.24. Is the project liable to receive any concession benefit/incentive/from the Government? if "yes" then, please specify.

Q.25. The pricing of the issue is based on:

(a) Past EPS

(b) Net profits

(c) Corporate image

(d) Any other

Q.26. Is the pricing of the issue being done keeping mind the current trend/scenario? Rating: (kindly rate it on a scale of 1-10)

Q.27. Does the listing arrangements provide adequate liquidity? Rating: (Kindly) rate it on a scale of 1-10).

Q.28. If the company is a listed one please give

(a) The stock market data for the last 6 months.

(b) The past 3 years' financial performance

Sales Net profit EPS

Also kindly furnish the bankers confidential report.

Annexure 3

Application to the SEBI along with the List of Documents while Filling of the Draft Prospectus

SECURITIES AND EXCHANGE BOARD OF INDIA,
Kailash Building, 4th Floor,
Kasturba Gandhi Marg,
New Delhi – 110001

Reg: Public issue of (number of equity shares) equity shares of Rs (face value) each for cash at par aggregating to Rs. (amount in lakh) by (name of the company)

Dear Sir,

We forward herewith the undermentioned documents for your scrutiny and approval.

1. Draft prospectus.
2. Certificate of due diligence along with annexure.
3. Statement of inter se allocation of responsibilities.
4. Confirmation on: compliance of the SEBI guidelines.
5. Undertaking from company regarding: (a) redressal of investors' grievances, (b) provision of funds to register for despatch of refund orders/letters of allotment certificates by U.P.V/ registered post (c) getting the instruments of the proposed issue listed within the prescribed time period (d) promoters contribution will be brought in full before the subscription list opens.
6. Copy of the MOV entered into between the company and US.
7. Undertaking from lead manager (s) to get the public issue fully underwritten and to include details thereof in the final prospectus.

We shall arrange to get the issue underwritten and shall finalise the underwriters list/the banker to the issue/co-managers to the issue keeping in view the SEBI guidelines issued for this purpose.

Kindly accord your approval at an early date.

Your Faithfully,
For (Names of the merchant banker)
(Name for the person concerned and designation)

Annexure 3(A)

Copy of the Due Diligence

SECURITIES AND EXCHANGE BOARD OF INDIA,
Kailash Building, 4th Floor,
Kasturba Gandhi Marg,
New Delhi – 110001.

Dear Sirs,

Certificate of Due Diligence of Public Issue of Equity Shares of XYZ Limited.

We, the undernoted lead manager(s) to the above mentioned forthcoming issue. state as follows:

(1) We have examined various documents including those relating to litigation like commercial disputes. patent disputes, disputes with collaborations .etc.. and other materials in connection with the finalisation of the draft prospectus pertaining to the said issue.

(2) On the basis of such examination and the discussions with the company, its directions and other officers other agencies, independent verification of the statements concerning the object of the issue projected portability, price justification and the contents of the document mentioned in the annexure and other paper furnished by the company.

We confirm that:

(a) The draft prospectors forwarded to the SEBI is in conformity with the documents, materials and papers relevant to the issue.

(b) All the legal requirements connected with the said issue as also the guidelines, instructions, etc., issued by the SEBI, the Government and any other competent authority in this behalf have been complained with: and

(c) The disclosures made in the draft prospectus are true fair and adequate to enable the investors to make a well informed decision as to the investment in the proposed issue.

(3) We confirm that besides ourselves. all the intermediaries named in the prospectus are registered with the SEBI and that till date such registration is valid

(4) We have satisfied ourselves about the worth of the underwriters to fulfil their underwriting commitments

For,
Name of the Merchant Banker.
and the name of the person concerned.

Annexure to the Due Diligence Certificate

(1) Memorandum, and articles of association of the company.

(2) Letter of intent/SIA registration/foreign collaboration approval/approval for import of plant and machinery if applicable.

(3) Necessary clearances from governmental, statutory municipal authorities etc. for implementation of the project. Wherever applicable.

(4) Documents in support of the track record and experience of the promoters and their professional competence.

(5) Listing agreement of the company for existing securities on the stock exchange.

(6) Consent letter from company's auditors, bankers to the issue, bankers to the company. lead managers brokers and where applicable, proposed trustees.

(7) Application made by the company to the financial institutions/banks for financial assistance as per object of the issue and copies of relative sanction letters

(8) Underwriting letters from the proposed underwriters to the issue.

(9) Latest audited balance sheet of the company.

(10) Auditors' certificate regarding tax benefits available to the company, members and NRIs.

(11) Certificate from architects or any others competent authority on project implementation schedule furnished by the company, if applicable.

(12) Reports from government agencies/expert agencies/consultants company regarding market demand and supply for the product, industrial scenario, standing for foreign collaborators etc.

(13) Documents in support of the infrastructural facilities, raw materials availability etc.

(14) Auditors. report indicating summary of audited accounts for the period including that of subsidiaries of the company.

(15) Stock exchange quotations of the last three years duly certified by the regional stock exchange in case of an existing company.

(16) Application to the RBI and approval thereof for allotment of shares to non residents, if any as also for collaboration terms and conditions.

(17) A certificate from a director (for particular of directorship).

(18) Minutes of the meeting of board and general body of the company for matters which are in the prospectus.

(19) Revaluation certificates of company's assets given by Government valuer or any approved valuer.

(20) Environmental clearance as given by pollution control board of the state government or the central Governmental applicable

(21) Certificate from company's solicitors in regard to compliance of legal provisions of the prospectus as also applicability of FERA/MRTP provisions to the company.

(22) Other documents, reports, etc.. as are relevant, necessary for true. fair and adequate disclosures in the prospectus.

(23) The copy of the board resolution passed by the issuer authorising a representative of the registrars to act on behalf in relation to handing of stock-invests.

Place: **For ABC Merchant Banker Ltd.**

Dated:

Annexure 3 (B)

Statement of Inter se Allocation of Responsibilities between the Lead Managers

Reg: Public issue of (number of equity shares) equity shares of Rs. (face value each forcash at par aggregating to Rs. (amount in lakh) by (name of the company) we are the sole lead managers to the captioned issue. The inter se allocation responsibilities are as follows.

Activities Responsibility Coordinators

(a) Capital structuring with the relative components and formalities such as composition of debt and equity type of instruments etc.

(b) Drafting and design of prospectus and of advertisement/publicity material including news-paper advertisement and brochure. The designated lead manager shall ensure compliance with stipulated requirements and completion of prescribed formalities with stock exchange, registrar of companies and the SEBI.

(c) Marketing of the issue, which will cover, inter alia formulating marketing strategies, preparation of publicity budget, arrangement for selection of (i) ad media (ii) bankers to the issue (iii) collection centres.

(d) Tieing up underwriting arrangement and invoking under obligations.

(e) Selection of various agencies connected with the issue namely registrars to the issue printers and advertising agencies.

(f) Following up with bankers to the issue to get quick estimates of collections and advising the issuer about closure of the issue based on the correct figures.

(g) The post issue activities will involve essential follow-up stops which must include listing of certificates and refunds with the various agencies connected with the work such as registars to the issue and the bank handling refund business. Even if many of these activities would be handled by other intermediaries the designated lead manager shall be responsible for ensuring that these agencies fulfil their functions and enable him to discharge his responsibility through suitable arrangements with the issuer company.

For **ABC Merchant Bankers Ltd.**

Annexure 3(C)

Memorandum of Understanding between the Lead Manager to the Issue and the Issuer.

Whereas:

1. The company is taking steps for the issue of (number of shares) equity shares of Rs. – each for cash at par aggregating to Rs. lakh to the public the said issue of shares herein after referred to as "The Issue" and.
2. The company has approached the lead manager to manage to issue and the lead manager has accepted the engagement inter alia subject to the company entering into a memorandum of understanding for the purpose herein presented.

   Now, therefore, the company and the lead manager do hereby agree as follows:

   (i) Besides the lead managers, the co-managers/advisors to the issue if any will be appointed a later data.

   (ii) The company hereby declares that is has complied/will comply with all the statutory formalities under the companies Act. guidelines for disclosure and investor protection issued by the SEBI and other relevant statutes to enable it to make the issue and in particular in respect of the following matters:

Statutory Requirements

(a) Conversion of the company from private limited to public limited.

(b) Shareholders' resolution under section 81 (1) (A) of the companies Act, 1956.

(c) Approval of memorandum and articles of association from the stock exchange upon alteration of relevant clauses such as capital clause, names, clause, etc.

(d) SEBI acknowledgement of the draft prospectus.

(e) Compliance with the provisions of the companies Act regarding the appointment of each direction/each change in the board of directors since its incorporation.

(f) Compliance with the companies Act, regarding the appointment of auditor/each change in auditors since incorporation.

(g) Filing initial listing application with the stock exchange along with the initial listing fees.

(h) Filing the draft prospectus and a copy of all material contracts and documents as detailed in the prospectus with the ROC and obtaining an acknowledgement from ROC.

(i) Compliance with the stipulations made by stock exchanges vide announcement of issue, security deposits, stationary requirement, etc.

3. The company undertakes and declares that any information made available to the lead manager on any statement made in the offered documents would be complete in all respects and would be true and correct, and that under no circumstances it would give or withhold any information or statement which is likely to mislead the investors.
4. The company also undertakes to furnish complete audit annual report (s). other relevant documents papers information relating to pending litigations etc. to enable the lead manager to corroborate the information and statements given in the offer documents.
5. The company shall if so required, extend such facilities as may be called for by the leading manager(s) to enable to him visit the plant site, office of the company or such other place(s)

to ascertain for himself the true state of affairs of the company including the progress made in respect of project implementation status and other facts relevant to the issue.

6. The company shall extend all necessary facilities to the lead manager to interact on any matter relevant to the issue with the solicitors/legal advisors, auditors co-managers, consultants, advisors to the issue the financial institutions, banks or any other organisation and also with any other intermediaries who may be associated with the issue in any capacity whatsoever.
7. The company shall ensure that all advertisements prepared and released by the advertising agency or otherwise in connection with the issue conform to the regulations guidelines etc issued by the SEBI and instructions given by the lead managers from time to time and that it shall not make any misleading incorrect statements in the advertisement press releases or in any materials relating to the issue or at any press brokers/investors conference.
8. The company shall not, without prior approval of the lead manager appoint other intermediaries or other persons such as registers to the issue bankers to the issue, refund bankers, advertising agencies printers for printing application forms allotment advices/allotment letters, share certificates/debentures certificates refund orders or any other instrument, circulars' or advice.
9. Whenever required the company shall in consultation with the lead manager enter into a memorandum of understanding with the concerned intermedia associated with the issue. clearly setting forth their mutual rights responsibilities and obligations a certified true copy of such memorandum shall be furnished to the lead manager.
10. The company shall take such steps as are necessary to ensure the completion of allotment and despatch of letters of allotment and refund orders to the applicants including NRIs. Soon after the basis of allotment has been approved by the stock exchanges and in any case not later than the statutory time limit and in the event of failure to do so pay interest to the applicants as provide under the companies Act 1956
11. The company shall take steps to pay the underwriting commission and brokerage to the underwriters and stock brokers etc within a reasonable time.
12. The company undertakes to furnish such information and particulars regarding the issue as may be required by the lead manager to enable him to file a report with the SEBI in respect of the issue.
13. The company shall keep the lead manager informed if it encounters any problems due to dislocation of communication system or any other material adverse circumstance which is likely to prevent or which has prevented the company from complying with its obligations, whether statutory or contractual, in respect of the matters pertaining to allotment despatch of refund order/share certificates/debenture certificates, etc.
14. The company shall not resort to any legal proceeding in respect of any matter having a bearing on the issue except in consultation with and after receipt of advice from the lead managers.

Annexure 3(D)
Rights of Lead Manager(s)

(1) The lead manager reserves the right to withdraw from the issue in the capacity of lead manager if it is found at any point of time that the disclosures made by the company are not correct incomplete or involve misrepresentation of facts.

(2) The lead manager also reserves the right to withdraw from the issue if it is found that the company has intentionally or otherwise concealed information which is not in the interest of the company investors and/or the lead manager.

(3) The company will decide the issue opening date in consultation with the lead manager and will abide by the decision of the lead manager. In the event the company decided to go against such decision the lead manager reserves the right to notify all agencies connected with the issues. Underwriters and the SEBI of the breach.

(4) The fees payable to the lead manager will be Rs.— which is to be paid in the following manner.

(i) Rs... at the time of filing of prospectus with the SEBI

(ii) Rs... at the time of filing of prospectus with ROC

(iii) Rs... on closure of the issue.

Over and above the issue management fees and incidental fees. The company shall also reimburse all out of pocket expenses incurred by the lead manager. In the event of any breach by the company in the above mentioned manner of payment the lead manager reserves the right to advice the collecting banks to withhold the issue proceeds.

(5) The company will be required to obtain a written statement from the lead manager in respect of the issue. The advertising agency will release the issue closing advertisement only on the advice of the lead manager. The lead manager reserves the right to notify the SEBI of any breach on the part of the advertising agency as well as of the company. If the company proceeds with the closing of the issue at a date not agreed upon mutually with the lead manager the lead manager will not be responsible for the consequence resulting out of such a decision.

(6) The lead manager shall released of all obligations towards the company if the company acts upon a decision at any point of time in any manner contrary to the terms agreed with the lead manager.

Annexure 3(E)
Consequence of Breach

1. In the event of breach in addition to the consequences stated above the lead manager shall reserve the right to represent the case to the SEBI. The stock exchange, the ROC and other regulatory bodies against the company and /or any other agencies connected with the issue or the matter under dispute.
2. The lead manager can also represent the case to the concerned legal authorities against the company and/or any other agencies connected with the issue on the matter under dispute.
3. The lead manager if he finds it appropriate shall advise the collecting banks to withhold the issue proceeds until such time that the dispute has been clarified. The lead manager can also represent the matter to the SEBI if it feels so for an intervention from the SEBI in respect of the dispute.
4. The underwriting commitment of the lead manager shall stand withdraw if the company decides upon the issue closure date on its own and the issue is not fully subscribed.

For **ABC Co. Ltd.**

Managing Director.

Date:

Place:

For **XYZ Merchant Bankers Ltd.**

Director

Annexure 3(F)

Compliance Certificates by the Lead Manager

SECURITIES AND EXCHANGE BOARD OF INDIA
Kailash Building, 4th Floor,
Kasturba Gandhi Marg,
New Delhi – 110 001.

Dear Sirs,

Reg: Public issue of (number of equity shares) equity shares of Rs. (face value) each for cash at par aggregating to Rs. (amount in lakhs) by (name of the company)

With respect to the above. We hereby confirm that the SEBI guidelines in respect of disclosure and investor protection and all the clarifications issued by the SEBI till date have been complied with.

Your Faithfully,
For **XYZ Merchant Bankers Ltd.**

Annexure 3(G)

Compliance Certificates by the Company

To,

Name and address of the lead manager

Dear Sir,

I, _______ in my capacity as managing director of ABC Company Ltd. hereby undertake that requisite funds will be made available by the company to the registrars to the issue for the purpose of despatch of allotment letter(s)/refund order(s)/share certificate(s) by U.P.C/registered post as applicable.

For **ABC Ltd.**

(_____*Sign*______)

Managing Director

To,

Name and address of the lead Manager

Dear Sirs,

I, _______, in my capacity as managing director of M/s. ABC Ltd. do hereby undertake that all investors' grievances and complaints received in respect of the issue would be attended to expeditiously and satisfactorily.

For **ABC Ltd.**

(_____*Sign*______)

Managing Director

To,

SECURITIES AND EXCHANGE BOARD OF INDIA
Kailash Building, 4th Floor,
Kasturba Gandhi Marg,
New Delhi – 110 001.

Reg: Proposed public issue of ABC Co. Limited

I, _______, in my capacity as managing director of ABC Ltd. do hereby undertake that the equity shares of the proposed public issue shall be listed on stock exchange(s) within the prescribed time period and all necessary steps be taken and compliance be made to this effect.

For **ABC Ltd.**

(____________)

Managing Director

To,

SECURITIES AND EXCHANGE BOARD OF INDIA
Kailash Building, 4th Floor,
Kasturba Gandhi Marg,
New Delhi – 110 001.

Dear Sirs,

Reg: Public issue of (number of equity shares) equity shares of Rs (face value) each for cash at par aggregating to Rs (amount in lakhs) by (Name of the company).

With respect to the above, We hereby confirm that, the promoter's contribution will be brought in full, before the opening of the issue.

Your Faithfully

For ABC Ltd.

Managing Director

To,

Name and address of the lead manager

Dear Sir,

The Undersigned in my capacity as the promoter/director of ABC Ltd. do hereby undertake the following.

1. Once the SEBI acknowledgement card is issued no advertisement relating to the issue shall be released without giving risk factors in respects of the concerned issue.
2. Issue advertisement shall not contain any matter or matters which is/are extraneous to the contents of the offer documents.
3. In all advertisements, equal treatment in all respects shall be given to the risk factors and highlights.
4. No advertisements would include any issue slogans or brand names in the issue except the normal commercial name of the company or commercial brand names of its products already in use. The advertisements shall also not make use of models/celebrities etc.
5. In case there is a reservation for NRIs, the issue advertisement shall specify the same and indicate the source in India from where the individual NRI applicant can procure application forms.
6. We shall also strictly comply with the instructions (i) non publishing of any advertisement in newspapers to the effect/of the nature that the issue has been oversubscribed and (ii) advertisement between the date of announcement of the issue and the date of closure of the issue.
7. I shall release the following advertisements at least in two all India newspapers:
   (a) Advertisement giving full details relating to oversubscription, basis of allotment, number, value, and percentage of applications received along with stock-invest, number, value and percentage of successful allotees who have applied through stock-invest, date of completion of despatch of refund orders date of despatch of certificates and date of filing of listing application, such advertisement shall be released by us within 10 days from the date of completion of the various activities.
8. Recommendation and approval of the lead manager will be sought before releasing any issue related advertisement to the print media.

For ABC Ltd.
Managing director.

Annexure 4
Questionnaire to Get Filled by the Promoters During the Site Visit

(Yes/No)

Q.1. (a) Do the promoters have any past experience in the same line? if "Yes" then please specify the number of years

(b) What kind of product(s) would be manufactured?

(c) What is the plant capacity? (please also specify the units)

(d) Where is the plant situated?

(e) How much manpower is in use/would be there: skilled: semi killed: unskilled?

Q.2. Were there any labour problems in the past? if "yes", then are they solved now?

Q.3. How do you rate the market potential for the product? Rating: (Kindly rate it on a scale of 1-10 : 1 means excellent and 10 stands for poor)

Q.4. Funds collected by the issue would be utilised for (a) expansion (b) diversification (c) Modernisation (d) any other.

Q.5. Do you have interest in the management of any other listed/unlisted company? (If yes. please specify)

Q.6. What would be your participation in the project: 25 per cent/ 26-40 per cent/above 40 per cent?

Q.7. Has the project been appraised if "Yes" then name the appraising agency and its stake

Q.8. At the capacity utilisation is the B.E.P achieved: (a) 20-30 per cent (b) 31-40 per cent (c) above 40 per cent

Q.9. Is the project an export oriented/import substitution one?

Q.10. Did the promoters sell any part of their holding in the past 12 months?

Q.11. What is the gestation period: 1-2 year/2-4 years 5 years and above?

Q.12. What is the status of the land: owned by the company/leased?

Q.13. What is the status of the plant and machinery: (a) Indian/imported (b) already/ordered/to be ordered/received at the site

Q.14. Has the project received all the government approvals?

Q.15. Have the assets been revalued for issue of the bonus issue? if "yes", then please specify the bonus ratio

Q.16. Has any change been brought about in the accounting policies of the company? if "yes" then please specify

Q.17. What is the source of raw materials: near the factory premises/far off place/imported?

Q.18. Is the debt equity ratio high (more than 2:1)?

Q.19. Has RBI given the required permission for the foreign collaboration?

Q.20. What kind of technology is used in the project: New/time tested/foreign collaboration?

Q.21. Has the company entered into any Marketing tie-up for its product? if "yes" then is it an MOV/agreement?

Q.22. Is the project liable to receive any concession/benefit/incentive/from the government?

Q.23. What kind of instrument would you like to propose: Equity shares/preference shares/debentures? if debenture is your choice then what would you prefer FCD/PCD/NCD?
Also please specify the rate of interest?

Q.24. If the company is a listed one please give

(a) The stock market data for the last 6 months

(b) The past 3 years financial performance:

Sales newprofit EPS

* Kindly also furnish the bankers confidential report.

Annexure 6(A)

Documents and Information Required from Secretarial Department for Listing

1. Fifteen copies of memorandum and articles of association of the company.
2. Copies of statutory advertisement.
3. Copy of the statement in lieu of prospectus
4. Fifteen copies of the balance sheet with directors report for the last five years.
5. Certificate of expenses.
6. Certificate of allotment made according to the basis of allotment.
7. Certificate of defacement for non-transferable shares.

Annexure 6(B)
Application for Listing on Exchange for New Companies

Letter of Applications
(Appendix–C to Regulation–2) Regulation–1

From:

To, **Date:**

Dear Sir,

In conformity with the listing requirements of the stock exchange We hereby apply for admission of the following securities of the company to dealings on the exchange.

Annexure 7

Request and Consent of the Collecting Banker(s)

To,
Name of the banker concerned and address

Reg: *Public issue of (number of equity shares) equity shares of Rs (face value) each for cash at par aggregating to Rs (amount in lakh) by (name of the company)*

Dear Sir,

We are pleased to inform you that we are acting as sole lead managers to the captioned issue which is expected to open on the (date). We have already received the SEBI acknowledgement card for the issue.

In view of our long association with you. We will be pleased to appoint you as one of the bankers to the issue. Kindly give your acceptance at the earliest please also furnish a certificate and your consent in the enclosed formats.

Thanking you.

Yours Faithfully,

(Name of the Merchant banker)

(Name of the person concerned and designation)

To,

The lead manager,

Reg:*Public issue of (number of equity shares) equity shares of Rs (face value) each for cash of par aggregating to Rs (amount in lakh) by (Name of the company)*

Dear Sir,

With reference to the captioned subject. We hereby confirm as under

(a) We are authorised to act as bankers to an issue in accordance with the provision of sub-section (i) of section 12 of the SEBI Act, 1992.

(b) We will accept applications accompanied by stock-invest

(c) We will perform all duties connected with the work of bankers to an issue including preparation of collection statement, reconciliation and listing separately instrument wise applications.

Yours Faithfully,

(Banker)

To,
The Board of Directors
(Name of the company and address)

Reg: ***Public issue of (number of equity shares) equity shares of Rs (face value) each for cost at par aggregating to Rs (amount in lakh) by (Name of the company)***

Dear Sir,

We hereby give our consent to act as bankers to the issue for the captioned public issue and our name to be included in the prospectus as bankers to the issue.

We further authorise the company to deliver a copy of this consent to the Register of companies. Delhi and Haryana at New Delhi pursuant to section 60 of the companies act, 1956.

Thanking you,

Yours faithfully,
(Banker)

Annexure 8

Documents Required for Filing the Prospectus with ROC

1. Consent of (a) Lead manager(s), (b) Co-manager(s), (c) Registrars, (d) Bankers to the company, (e) Auditors, (f) Bankers to the issue, (g) Legal advisors, (h) Company secretary, (i) Directors, (j) Underwriters.
2. Copies of power of attorney for signing and corrections in the prospectus.
3. Copy of the board resolution authorising the registrar for accepting applications accompanied with stock-invest.
4. RBI approval for issue of shares to NRIs (if applicable)
5. Stock exchange approval of MOV and Articles of Association (AOA) and draft prospectus where the listing is proposed.

Annexure 9

Form 2A

Memorandum Containing Salient Features of the Prospectus [See Section 56(3)]

I. General information: (a) Name and address of registered office of the company (b) Issue listed at : [Name(s) stock exchange]: (c) Opening, closing and earliest closing date of the issue: (d) Name and address of lead managers: (e) Name and address of trustees under debenture trust deeds (in the case of debenture/issue): (f) Rating for the debenture/preference shares, if any obtained from crisil or any recognised rating agency.

II. Capital structure of the company: (a) Issued, subscribed and paid up capital: (b) size of present issue giving separately reservation for preferential allotment to promoters and others (c) paid up capital: (i) after the present issue, (ii) after conversion of debenture (if applicable).

III. Terms of the present Issue: (a) Authority for the issue, terms of payments and procedure and time Schedule for allotment and issue of certificates: (b) How to apply availability of forms, prospectus and mode of payment: (c) Special tax benefits to company and shareholders under the Income tax Act if any.

IV. Particulars of the Issue: (a) Objects of the issue: (b) Project cost, means of financing (including contribution of promoters).

V. Company management and project:

(a) History main objects and present business of the company:

(b) (Background of promoters, managing director/wholetime director and names of nominees of institutions if any one of the board of directions

(c) Location of the project.

(d) Plant and machinery, technology, process etc.

(e) Collaboration, performance guarantee, if any or assistance in marketing by the collaborators

(f) Infrastructure facilities for raw materials and utilities like water, electricity etc:

(g) Schedule of implementation of the project and progress made so far giving details of land acquisition, execution of civil works, Installation of plant and machinery, trial production, date of commercial production if any:

(h) The products (a) Nature of product (S): Consumer industrial and users (b) existing licensed and installed capacity of the product demand of the product - as existing, and estimated in the coming years as estimated by a Government Authority or by any other reliable institution giving sources of the information. (c) Approach of marketing and proposed marketing set up. In case of company providing services, relevant, information in regard to nature/extent of services. etc to be furnished

(i) prospectus - the expected year when the company would be able to earn net profit, declare dividend.

VI. Financial performance of the company for the last five years: (Figures to be taken from the audited annual accounts in tabular form):

(a) Balance sheet data equity capital, reserves (state revolution reserve the year of revolution and its monitory effect on assets) and borrowings:

(b) Profit and loss data: sales gross profit, net profit dividend paid if any:

(c) Any change in Accounting policies during the last three years and their effect on the profits and the reserves of the company.

(d) Stock market quotation of shares/debenture of the company: if any (high/low price in each of the last three years and monthly high/low price during the last six months).

VII. Whether all payments/refunds debenture, fixed deposits, interest on fixed deposits, debenture interest, institutional dues have been paid up to date if not details of the arrears, if any to be stated

VIII. Following particulars in Regard to the listed companies under the same management within the meaning of section 370(B) which made any capital Issue in the last three years.

(a) Name of the company:

(b) Year of issue

(c) Type of issue (public/rights/Composite):

(d) Amount of issues

(e) Date of closure of issue:

(f) Date of despatch of share/debenture certificate completed

(g) Date of completion of the project, where project of the issue was financing of a project

(h) Rate of dividend paid

IX Management perception of Risk factors: (e.g. sensitivity to foreign exchange rate fluctuations, difficulty in the availability of raw materials or in the making of products If the company does not receive application money for at least 90 per cent of the issued amount. The entire subscription will be refunded to the applicants within ninety days from the date of closure of the issue. If there is delay in the refund of application money by more than 8 days after the company becomes liable to pay the excess amount. The company will pay interest for the delayed period at prescribed rates in sub-section (2) and (2A) of section 73. No statement made in the form shall contravene any of the provisions of the companies Act. 1956 and the rules made thereunder.

Place:

Date:

Signatures of Directors

Annexure 10(A)

Public Issue: 3-Day Monitoring Report

Subscription status: (Subscribed/unsubscribed) responsibility: post-issue lead manager (to be submitted in duplicate within 3 days from closure of the public issue)

1. Name of issuer company.
2. Issue opening date
3. Earliest closing date.
4. Actual closing date
5. Date of filing prospectus with ROC
6. Issue details (as per the prospectus)
   - 6.1 Nature of instrument: (equity/FCD/PCD/NCD/others)
   - 6.2 offer price per instrument for different categories.
   - 6.3 Amount per instrument on application for different categories
   - 6.4 Issue size (Rs lakh):
     - (a) (i) Promoters contribution
       - (ii) Date of submission of auditors certificate to the SEBI for receipt of promoters contribution
     - (b) (i) Amount through offer document (including reserved categories and net public offer
       - (ii) Reserved category: Amount reserves (Rs lakh)
         - Mutual funds
         - FIS/Banks
         - FIIS
         - NRIs/OCBs
         - Employees
         - Others (please specify)
       - (iii) Net public offer
7. (a) Provisional Subscription: Details of net public offer (including unsubscribed portion of reserved categories).
   - (i) Total amount to be collected on application (Rs. lakh)
   - (ii) Amount collected on application (Rs. lakh)
   - (iii) Percentage subscribed i.e., of (ii) to (i).

   (b) Amount subscribed by the reserved categories on competitive basis (Rs. lakh)
8. Please tick mark whether 90 percentage minimum subscription of the amount through offer document is collected.

(i) Yes

(ii) No *Lead Manager(s)*

(Name signature and seal)

Date:

Place:

Note: It is the responsibility of the lead manager(s) to give correct information after verifying it from the company and the registars to the issue.

Annexure 10(B)

Public issue: 78–Day post-issue Monitoring Report

Subscription status: (subscribed/under subscribed) responsibility: post – issue lead manager(s)

(To be submitted in duplicate within 78 days from the closer of the public issue)

1. Name of the company.
2. Issue opening date
3. Actual closing date
4. 3-day report: (i) Due on, (ii) submitted on.
5. Number of collecting banks. Also specify number of bank branches.
6. Back-wise names of branches which did not submit final consolidated certificate within 21 days from closure of issue and mention the dates when they actually submitted
7. Subscription details
   (a) Public offer (net) [including unsubscribed portion of reserved category added bank to net public offer] (Rs. Lakhs)
   (1) Number of applications received
   (2) Number of instruments applied for
   (3) Amount of subscription received (Rs. lakh)
   (4) Number of times issue subscribed. Number of instruments applied for/Number of instruments under net public offer category.
   (5) Number of applications accompanied by stock inverts.
   (6) Number of instruments applied through stock inverts
   (7) Amount of subscription received through stock inverts (Rs. lakhs)
   (8) Percentage of subscription through stock-inverts in total subscription.
   (b) Information relating to reserved categories:

Reservation To	*Number of Applicants*	*Number of instruments applied for*	*Amount subscribed*
NRIs			
FIs			
FIIs			
MFs			
Employees			
Others (specify)			

8. The firm allottes who did not meet their commitments though mentioned in the prospectus (please give their names and amount and whether the promoters have subscribed to that amount before opening of the issue).
9. Actual date of finalisation on the basis of allotment (enclose copy)
10. Allotment details:
    10.1 Number of successful allottees per 1 lakh shares.
    10.2 Number of successful allottees from stock-invest applicants

10.3 Numbers of instruments allotted to stock invest applicants

10.4 Percentage stock-invest allottees in total allottes

10.5 Number of unsuccessful allottees:

(a) Refund orders

(b) Cancelled stock invests

(c) Certificate/allotment letter

(d) Certificate/allotment letter against application by stock-invest.

(e) Reason for delay in despatch, if any

(f) Whether interest paid for delayed period if so for which period

11. It there is a reservation for NRIs date(s) of completion of despatch of

11.1 Refund orders

11.2 Cancelled stock-invests

11.3 Certificate/allotment letters

11.4 Reasons for delay in despatch, if any

11.5 Whether interest paid for delayed period.

11.6 Date of submission of application to the RBI for approval for despatch of share certificates

11.7 Date of approval received from RBI.

12. Amount of refund due (Rs lakh)

13. Refund banker(s) (Name and address)

14. Date of transfer of refund amount to refund banker. if any

15. Date of completion of despatch of refund orders/cancelled stock-invests

16. Name of regional stock exchange

17. Name of other stock exchanges where listing is sought.

18. Date on which application was filled with each stock exchange (enclose copies of permission letters of stock exchanges).

19. Date when listing and trading permission given by each stock exchange (enclose copies of permission letter of stock exchanges)

20. Reasons for delay in listing for trading: if any

To be filled up in case of underwritten issues only

1. If the issue is underwritten mention the amount of issue under written

2. Extent of undersubscription on the date of closure of the issue. (a) percentage (b) Amount.

3. Total number of underwriters

4. If development notices had not been issued mention how the shortfall was met

5. Number of underwriters who development notice had been issue.

6. Date of issue of development notices

7. Number of underwriters who did not pay development (please give names, amount of underwriters and reasons for not paying).

8. In case of default from underwriters mention how the shortfall was met.

9. In case where FIs/MFs has subscribed to make up shortfall not as underwriter (a) Name of FI/MF (b) Number of instruments applied for (c) Amount received. Certified that the information given above and also in the enclosures are true to the best of our knowledge and no refund orders/allotment letters/certificates are pending for despatch in respect of the issue.

Certified that shares to be locked-in are duly inscribed with the words " share cannot be hypothecated/transferred till.....)

Date:

Place:

Lead manager(s)
(Name, signature and seal)

Note: It is the responsibility of the lead manager(s) to give correct information after verifying it from the company and the registrar to the issue.

- Please enclose: Certificate from the refund banker that the amount of refund due from the company to investors in deposited in a separate account giving details of the total amount deposited in the account and date of deposit.

Annexure 11(A)

Rights issue: 3-Day Monitoring Report

Subscription status: Subscribed/Unsubscribed

Responsibility: Post-issue lead manager.

(To be submitted in duplicate within 3 days from closure of rights issue)

1. Name of the company
2. Issue opening date
3. Actual closing date
4. Date of filing letter of offer with the stock exchange
5. Issue details (as per letter of offer):
   - 5.1 Basis of offer (ratio)
   - 5.2 Nature of instrument: (Equity/FCD/PCD/NCD/Others etc.)
   - 5.3 Offer price for instrument
   - 5.4 Amount for instrument on application
   - 5.5 Issue size (Rs. lakh)
6. Record date
7. Provisional subscription details of the issue: (i) Total amount to be collected on application (Rs lakh) (ii) Amount collected on application (Rs lakh), (iii) percentage subscribed, i.e., percentage of (ii) to (i), (iv) please tick mark whether 90 per cent minimum subscription collected:

(i) Tes
(ii) No

Date:
Place:

Lead Manager(s)

(Name, signature and seal)

Note: It is the responsibility of the lead manager(s) to give correct information after verifying it from the company and the registrar to the issue.

Annexure 11(B)

Rights issue: 50–Day post issue Monitoring Report subscription status: subscribed/unsubscribed.
Responsibility: post issue lead manager

(To be submitted in duplicate within 50 days from closure of rights issue)

1. Name of the company
2. Issue opening date
3. Actual closing date
4. Issue details (as per the letter of offer):
   - 4.1 Basis of offer
   - 4.2 Nature of instruments: (equity/FCD/PCD/NCD/etc)
   - 4.3 offer price per instrument
   - 4.4 Amount per instrument on application
   - 4.5 Issue size (Rs in lakh)
5. 3-day report (i) due on (ii) submitted on.
6. Number of collecting banks (also specify number of bank branches)
7. Bank-wise names of branches which did not submit final consolidated certificate within 21 days from closure of issue and mention the date when they actually submitted.
8. Details of subscription:
   - (i) percentage of rights taken up by
     (a) promoters (b) Other shareholders.
   - (ii) percentage of rights renounced by
     (a) promoters (b) other
   - (iii) percentage of rights taken by shareholder/renounces.
   - (iv) percentage at the disposal of the board.
   - (v) out of the unsubscribed portion as in
   - (vi) above taken by (a) promoters (b) others
9. Promoters share holding: Number of shares, percentage (a) prior to the issue (b) on expanded capital after the right issue.
10. Date of finalisation of allotment (enclose copy on the basis of allotment)
11. (a) Name and address of refund banker (b) amount of refund due (c) date of transfer of refund amount to refund banker, if any
12. Actual date (s) of completion of despatch of (a) refund orders (b) certificate/allotment letters (c) reasons for delay in despatch. if any (d) whether interest paid for delayed period, if so, for which period.
13. Name of regional stock exchange.
14. Name of other stock exchanges where listing is sought.
15. 42nd day from the date of closure of the issue.
16. Date on which application was filed with each stock exchange for listing of instruments.
17. Date when listing and trading permission given by each stock exchange (enclose copies of permission letters of stock exchanges).
18. Reason for delay in listing for trading, if any.

To be filled up in case of under subscribed Issue only.

(1) Extent of under subscription on the date of closure of the issue (a) percentage (b) amount.

(2) Details of stand-by assistance, if any (a) Number of underwriters, (b) Number of underwriters who did not pay development (please give names amount underwritten and reasons for not paying).

(3) In case where FIs/MFs has subscribed to make up shallfall not as underwriters (a) Name of the FI/MF (b) Number of instruments applied for (c) Amount received.

Certified that the information given above and also in the enclosures are true to the best of our knowledge and no refund orders/allotment letter/certificates are pending for despatch in respect of the issue.

Certified that shares to be locked in are duly inscribed with the words "share cannot be hypothecated/transferred/sold till...

Date: ***Lead manager(s)***

Place: **(Name, signature and seal)**

Note: It is responsibility of the lead manager (s) to give correct information after verifying it from the company and the registrars to the issue.

Please enclose: **Certificate from the refund banker that the amount of refund due from the company to investors is deposited in a separate account giving details of the total amount in the account and date of deposit.**

D. SECONDARY MARKET

Introduction

Secondary Market is an important component of the Capital Market. The stock exchanges are known as the Secondary Market. They play an important role in securities markets. In the stock exchanges the government securities, municipalities bonds, investment trusts debentures and other instruments are traded. It is a medium of transfer of resources for the circulated securities. In the stock exchanges, securities issued in the primary markets are bought and sold. It does not create any financial claim. Purchases and sales of the existing stocks and bonds occur in this market. Transactions in the secondary markets do not provide funds to the corporate sector. But the strong secondary market movements create a high demand for the new issue market. The NIM and the stock exchanges interlink and work together with each other. They cannot be demarked as two separate markets. It is the resale market for shares and bonds. It represents an organised market in the trading of securitics. In thc stock exchange the trading is carried on by the member of the exchange. The stock exchange is an association, or organisation of members to carry on trade in the securities. The securities are traded under certain set of rules and regulations. Some of the definitions of the stock exchanges are:

The Securities Contract Regulation Act, 1956

"Stock exchange means an association, organisation or body of individuals, whether incorporated or not, established for the purpose of assisting, regulating and controlling the business in buying, selling and dealing the securities".

According to J. F. Pyle "Security exchanges are market places where securities that have been listed thereon may be bought and sold for either investment or speculation".

Origin and Growth

The stock exchange is an organised place where the securities are bought and sold. The organised stock exchanges in India are of recent origin. They are highly specialised institutions in India. Indian stock exchanges are competing with the global stock exchanges. India is a *Sleeping Lion* and *Asia's Tiger* in the world market. Now it is in transformation stage where it enters from traditional to the *digital economy*. It has an excellent technical skill in the IT. With the help of the IT, it can become a *24 hours* stock market. It can create wonders in the market. It can teach lessons to the western markets. It has an excellent potential and talented skilled manpower to construct the technology bourses.

The first stock exchange was set up in India under the name of the ***Native share and stock brokers association of Bombay*** in 1875. At present there are *23* recognised stock exchanges under the SCRA 1956. All the stock exchanges operate under the rules, byelaws and regulations duly approved by the government. The objectives of the securities contract's act 1956 are as follows:

(1) to control the malpractices in the stock exchanges

(2) to regulate the stock markets

(3) to protect the investors interest

(4) to improve the working conditions of the exchanges

(5) to create an efficient securities market

The stock exchanges in India should work within the framework of the acts. They are involved in accordance with the following laws.

(1) Companies Act, 1956

(2) The Income Tax Act, 1961

(3) FERA, 1973

The Bombay stock exchange has been granted a permanent recognition. The other exchanges are recognised for a period of 5 years. There is no uniform structure in respect of the organisation pattern of the stock exchanges in India. There are different stock exchanges which follows different patterns. Some are public limited companies and the others are limited by guarantee or as voluntary non-profit making organisations. The organisation patterns of the recognised stock exchanges in India are presented below:

Sl. No.	*Name of the Stock Exchange*	*Year of Establishment*	*Type of Association*
1.	Bombay	1875	Voluntary
2.	Ahmedabad	1894	Voluntary
3.	Calcutta	1908	Public Ltd. Co.
4.	Madras	1908	Public Ltd. Co.
5.	Indore	1930	Voluntary
6.	Hyderabad	1943	Ltd. by guarantee
7.	Delhi	1947	Public Ltd. Co.
8.	Bangalore	1957	Public Ltd. Co.
9.	Cochin	1978	Public Ltd. Co.
10.	Kanpur	1982	Public Ltd. Co.
11.	Pune	1982	Public Ltd. Co.
12.	Ludhiana	1983	Public Ltd. Co.
13.	Guhuwathi	1983	Public Ltd. Co.
14.	Jaipur	1984	Public Ltd. Co.
15.	Kanara	1985	Public Ltd. Co.
16.	Magadh	1986	Public Ltd. Co.
17.	Bhubaneswar	1989	Ltd. by guarantee
18.	Saurashtra	1989	Ltd. by guarantee
19.	O.T.C.	1989	–
20.	Vadodara	1990	–
21.	Coimbatore	1991	–
22.	Meerut	1991	–
23.	NSE	1992	–

The stock exchanges are self regulatory organisations supervised by the Ministry of Finance under SCRA. Stock exchange regulations cover the entire operations. They are (a) enrolment of members, (b) the listing of securities, (c) the disciplinary actions.

Regulations on trading are largely confined to some specified shares. The specified shares transactions could be forwarded from one settlement period to another. Several committees examined and made recommendations to reform the organisations of the stock exchanges (1) G. S. Patel Committee (1985), (2) L. C. Gupta Committee (1991), (3) Pherwani Committee (1991), (4) Varma Committee (1997).

Organisation

A stock exchange is managed by the governing body. The governing board consists of a president, a vice-president, executive director, elected directors, public representatives and nominees of the government. The board will look after all the affairs of the stock exchange. Its affairs are monitored through various committees. They are like (a) listing committee, (b) clearing house committee, (c) defaulters committee:

Listing of Securities: Listing of shares means admitting a scrip to trade on the floor of a stock exchange. Every security issued by the companies cannot be traded at a stock exchange. The stock exchange will admit a share for the listing purpose. The following information should be submitted to the exchange for listing the security.

(a) Memorandum and Association of Articles.

(b) Prospectus.

(c) Copies of balance sheet and audited accounts.

(d) Copies of agreements with promoters, underwriters and brokers.

(e) Consent letters from SEBI.

(f) Details of Capital structure.

(g) Particulars of bonus shares and dividends declared.

(h) Agreement with MD.

(i) Compliance report regarding various provisions.

(j) A list of highest top ten holders of each class or kinds of securities of the company.

The stock exchange has the authority to withdraw or suspend the trading of a security. If the company violates any rules and regulations, the securities are classified into the following categories.

(1) Group-A shares (specified securities).

(2) Group-B shares.

(3) Permitted securities.

(4) Cleared securities.

(5) Non-cleared securities.

Listed securities are classified as cleared or specified or Group A securities and non-cleared or unspecified or Group B or cash shares.

Group A shares are allowed in forward trading. These shares are included in the cleared list of the exchange. The shares which satisfies the following conditions may be classified as "A" shares.

(a) The shares should be fully paid up equity shares.

(b) The company's paid up capital should be at least Rs. 5 crores.

(c) The company should have a growth potential.

(d) The company should be a dividend paying one.

(e) The shares should have been actively traded on the screen.

(f) The company's shares should have the market capitalisation of at least ***Rs. 10 crores.***

Group B shares are traded on cash basis. They are known as cash scrips. The carry-forward facility is not available to this group.

Permitted Securities are listed by some of the recognised stock exchanges. The recognised stock exchanges will permit the scrips even if they are not listed by them. These scrips are known as permitted securities. The permission is granted as per the rules and regulations of the stock exchange.

Cleared Securities are traded for fortnightly settlement. The payment and delivery will be completed in the third week following fortnightly clearing. The cleared securities are also known as ***specified securities.*** Speculation activity is permitted only from such shares. The concerned stock exchange has the power to pass special resolutions specifying the securities which may from time to time be included in the specified securities list.

Non-cleared Securities are traded among the brokers. These securities are not cleared through the stock exchange clearing house. These securities are not permitted to carry over facilities.

Advantages of Listing: The listing of securities has some advantages :

(1) Listing creates liquidity of the security.

(2) It enhances the marketability.

(3) It facilitates prestige to the company.

(4) It provides greater publicity for the company.

(5) Listed securities command high collateral value for the purpose of bank credit.

(6) Listed securities enjoy more public confidence.

Dealings on the stock exchange are subject to the byelaws and rules of the stock exchange. The trading floor of the exchange will carry out the operations through the authorised members. The members are permitted to enter the exchange during fixed working hours. The trading on the floor can be done in two kinds. They are Ready delivery contract and Forward delivery contract.

The Ready delivery contract is also known cash securities. They are to be settled either on the same date or within a short period of time. If the payment and delivery of securities is on same day or on the next day, it may be called as ***"spot delivery contract"***. Ready delivery contracts can be made in respect of all securities.

The Forward Delivery Contract enjoys the facility of carry over. These contracts are discharged on fixed settlement days occurring at a periodical intervals. These contracts are confined to those securities which are placed on the forward list.

Procedure for Dealing at Stock Exchanges

The investors are not allowed to enter the stock exchange for buying and selling off the securities. They have to approach the brokers. The brokers are the members of the stock exchange. The dealing in the stock exchange can only be done through them. The following procedure is followed for dealings at exchanges.

(1) Finding a good broker.

(2) Placing order.

(3) Making the contract.

(4) Contract note.

(5) Settlement.

Broker is the most important person in the stock exchange. Each and every transactions should be performed through members only. The investors should find best broker for their execution of transactions. The intending investor or seller may approach his banker for the purchase of securities. The banker can appoint own broker at the exchange and they contact for dealings on behalf of customers. Instructions from the bank will be followed by the broker and the client's account is opened by the broker. The bank assures about the financial strengtheness of the client. Therefore the broker will be introduced by the banker.

Placing Order with the broker is the second step in the process. After selecting the broker, the client places an order for purchase or sale of securities. The broker provides all the information about the corporate sector and the economy. He guides the client about the type of securities to be purchased and the proper time. If the client approaches for selling of securities, he must tell him about the favourable time for sale. However it is not advisable to depend upon the broker's advice. In India, most of the investors are buying and selling scrips only on the advice of the brokers. They, simply handover the cheque to the broker for their commitment. But the investors should know the information such as

Economy, Industry growth, Company sales, Company product, Company market share, Gross profit, Net profit, Profit before tax, Profit after tax, EPS, PE ratio, Market capitalisation etc.

Making the contract is the third step in the process. After placing an order with the broker, the broker goes to the stock exchange and fulfils the investors desire by making the deals with his counterparts. He will make enquiries and bargains on behalf of the investor.

The brokers will prepare notes after their mutual consent. The seller broker will send the selling note and the buyer will send the buying note. They provide in note about all the details of trading activities.

Settlement is the last step in the process of buying or selling of the securities in the stock exchange. Settlement is the process between two brokers. All the transactions between them will be settled in the exchange. In stock exchange contracts are categorized into two kinds. They are ready delivery contracts and forward delivery contracts. The settlement of ready delivery contracts is done between **3 to 7** days of the transactions. This contract is further classified as liquidation and square up. In liquidation settlement process, the securities will be delivered on receipt of cash. The another method is known as "squaring up", and it requires the dealings are squared by adjusting price difference only.

The settlement of Forward delivery contracts can be done through the stock exchange. These delivery contracts are done for speculative purposes. In this category, the active securities are traded. The settlement of forward contracts can be done in the following ways.

(a) Liquidation in full

(b) Liquidation by payment of differences

(c) Carry over

(a) Liquidation in Full: In this method, the securities are delivered and the payment will be received immediately the amount will be adjusted after crossing all intermediate purchases and sales.

(b) Liquidation by Payment of Differences: Under this category the purchase and sales are offset at the ruling price by paying or receiving the difference amount. Therefore the securities are not delivered. But the difference amount will be paid. The price difference will be adjusted between the two parties.

(c) Carryover: If the buyer party does not want to settle the contract but wants to carry it to a future date then, it is called as carryover. For this, the buyer party will have to pay certain amount to the seller party. The payment of consideration is called as ***Badla or Contango charges***.

Types of Speculators

The purchase of assets for profit is called as the speculation. It is a short-term activity. It is an inspiration to the stock market. It is the oxygen to the capital market. We can say that without the speculation. There is no stock market. It is different from investment. Investment is long term in nature. It creates the capital formation in the country by encouraging the savings. Investments are useful for the present and future consumption. It leads to more income and longer capital appreciation.

Speculation aims at only short term trade gains. It involves in buying and selling off the securities for the short term purpose. It is double edged sword either to get profit or loss. It may lead to profit sometimes and loss at other times. The persons who are involved in the speculation are called as the ***speculators***. They will balance the share price movements in the market. They are classified as follows:

(A) Bull.

(B) Bear.

(C) Stag.

(D) Lame Duck.

(A) Bull: A Bull is also known as Tejiwala. He is an operator who expects a rise in the prices of the securities in the future. He always thinks that the future will be very bright. He makes the purchases of shares with the intention to sell at higher prices in future. He is not interested to take the delivery of shares which he has purchased. He deals only with the differences of prices. The speculator is called a Bull because of resemblance of his behaviour with the bull. He is an optimist. He tries to raise the prices of the securities by making heavy purchases. The market is called as the Bullish market, when all the bulls enter the market at once. In this market, there will be pressure for the buying of the securities. In this market, the supply of shares are scarce and demand will be more. The scarcity of scrips may lead to arise in the share prices. They create liquidity to the market.

(B) Bear: A bear is known as ***Mondiwala.*** He expects that prices which fall in future and sells the securities at present. He purchases the securities at lower prices and sells the securities at higher prices. He is interested to purchase in the down market and sell in the up-market. He does not have securities at present. But bull sells them at in future for higher prices. When all the bears enter the market, it is known as the ***bearish market.*** A bear does not take the delivery of securities but takes the difference, if prices fall. In case the prices increases, he will have to pay the difference. If the market is dominated by bears, it is known as the bearish phase. He tends to forced down the prices of different securities. When all the bear operators start selling the securities, the pressure gradually forces down the prices. He is a pessimist. If the prices do not fall they may start spreading rumours to pull the prices down. This situation is known as the bear raid. It is quite opposite to the bull speculator.

(C) Stag: A stag is another speculator in the stock market. He is a cautious speculator. He concentrates on the primary market. He applies for the shares in the new companies and expects to sell them at a premium, if he gets an allotment. He selects only those companies whose shares are in more demand and are likely to carry a higher price. He sells the shares before being called to pay the allotment money. He does not indulge in buying and selling of the shares in the market. He depends on the securities that are allotted to him.

A stag is always expecting a rise in share prices. He behaves same as bull. According to ***Hartley Withers*** "A stag is an applicant for a need issue who applies with a view to prompt resale".

He is called "premium hunter" because he makes sale of the newly allotted shares at a profit like a genuine investor. He expect that the price of the share will soon rise and be sold for a hefty premium.

(D) Lame Duck: Lame duck is a speculator who behaves like a duck. If a bear speculator fails to fulfil his to commitments, he is called struggling like a lame duck.

The following transactions reveal the speculative natures of the affairs.

Bull Deal: For example A bull asks his broker to buy 100 shares of ABC Ltd., at *Rs. **10 each***, the broker executes the deal. At the time of settlement, the market price of shares of ABC Ltd. is Rs. 35 each. The bull would instruct his broker to sell the shares and takes the difference in prices.

(a)	Sale proceeds of 100 shares at 35/-	Rs. 3,500
(b)	Purchase consideration 100 × 10	Rs. 1,000
(c)	Bulls profit	Rs. 2,500

Bear Deal: A bear is instructured to sell 100 shares of X Ltd., at Rs. 50 each. At the time of settlement of transactions, the actual price of the share is Rs. 40 each. He would instruct the broker to purchase the shares of X Ltd., and enjoys the difference in prices.

(a)	Sale proceeds of 100 shares @ 50/-	Rs. 5,000
(b)	Purchase price 100 × 40/-	Rs. 4,000
(c)	Bears profit	Rs. 1,000

Speculation assures the risk of loss with a view to make profits. Speculation needs the full information about the capital market. It requires best expertise on the part of the speculator. The main aim of the speculation is to achieve profits through price changes. Speculation may be categorised as ***constructive speculation*** and the destructive speculation. Constructive speculation is based on predicting of future trends of prices. It requires high talent, skill foresight and intelligent analysis of the security market. Destructive speculation hardly depends on the evaluation of the security market. It has the following advantages and disadvantages.

Advantages

(1) It creates liquidity to the market.
(2) It tends stability in prices.
(3) It encourages forward trading.
(4) It peace the trading of derivative instruments.
(5) It provides continuity in the market.

Disadvantages

Speculation is an high intelligent activity. It requires a lot of skill. It needs a perfect knowledge of the capital market trends. It is useful to us but it creates problems. If the speculators skill do not match with the speculation tool, it may be a misfire. They will have to face many problems.

Types of Speculative Deals

The speculative dealings in the stock market are presented below.

(A) Manipulation.
(B) Rigging.
(C) Arbitrage.
(D) Kerb deal.
(E) Cornering.
(F) Wash sales.

Manipulation is one of the deal in the market. It is the most important activity. It involves the creation of false opinion and spreads rumours. Manipulation means the purchase and sale of the securities by a group of speculators to create an impression that such transactions are the result of the natural phenomenon. It artificially twist the prices of the securities in the market.

Rigging is another speculative dealing method. The speculator places orders to different brokers at different prices. He places orders for some buying and some selling of the securities. It is done artificially to stimulate the market. It will affect the demand and supply of the securities.

Arbitrage is a highly specialised activity. It requires a lot of skill and talent. These transactions are carried out by the speculators to earn profit at the different price in different markets. The speculator make purchases in the cheaper market and sells it in the dearer market. This situation creates artificial ups and downs in the prices of the securities.

Kerb deal means the speculators may promote the unofficial deal. For example the purchase and sale of securities before or after the official hours of business in the stock exchanges. Trading before or after the official hours is called as ***Kerb trading***. It is an unfair practice of dealing.

Cornering means the speculators some times create a scarcity of a particular scrip by purchasing a large amount of shares. They create an artificial demand for a particular scrip. The circulation will be controlled by the speculators. If the velocity of the scrip is more, it will lead to high prices. It is an unhealthy practice of trading.

Wash sales means the speculator make purchase and sale of shares at the same time. This situation may create an illusion of great activity and gives a misleading position about the worth of the security. It creates an incorrect value of a particular scrip in the market.

Membership: The stock market consists of the issuing companies, financial intermediaries and brokers. The brokers are the most important persons who match buying and selling orders from the investors. In the stock exchange only the members are allowed to trade the securities at the floor of the stock exchange. To become a member in stock exchange one has to satisfy many rules and regulations laid down by the act. The following are the important provisions as per the ***Sec. 8*** of the ***Securities Contract Act 1957***.

(1) The following conditions must be satisfied by every member of the stock exchange:

  (a) He must be 21 years of age;

  (b) He must be a citizen of India;

  (c) He must be solvent;

  (d) He should not be convicted of any offence;

  (e) He should not be expelled at any time from the exchange;

  (f) He should not be declared as defaulter by any other exchange;

  (g) He should maintain better relations with the creditor.

(2) The member is eligible for admission as a member, if he works for two years as a partner or he must be either worked as a authorised clerk or assistant.

(3) The companies are also eligible to become the members in the exchange, if they fulfil the following conditions.

  (a) The company must be established as per the sec. 322 of the companies act;

  (b) The majority of the directors are the shareholders of such company and also members of that stock exchange.

Types of Operators

The following operators are involved in the stock exchange operations. They are

(a) Jobbers.

(b) Brokers.

(c) Tarawaniwalas.

(d) Budiwalas.

(e) Arbitrageurs.

(f) Oddlot dealers.

Jobbers play an important role in the stock market operations. They are dealers in securities in the stock exchange. They buy and sell securities for themselves. They buy the securities at lower price and sell them at higher prices. The difference between the two prices is known as Jobbers turn. They cannot buy shares on behalf of public.

Brokers are the most important intermediaries in the stock exchange. They are commission agents. They work for their commission. They transact the business in the securities either for their customers or for other members. The brokers who work for their customers are called as commission brokers. The brokers who purchases for other members is known as ***floor brokers***. The brokers charge commission from both the parties for their services. The investors who do not know anything about the stock markets are greatly benefited by the expertise of the brokers.

Tarawaniwalas handle the transactions on a commission basis for other brokers. They are like tobbers. They make purchase and sale of the shares on their own account. They act as brokers on behalf of the public.

Budiwalas are the financiers in the stock exchange. They provide loans to the parties for a shorter period, i.e. 2 to 3 weeks. They charge fee, it is known as ***cantago***. The cantago may be called as ***seedbadla*** or Undabadla. They grant credit facilities to the needy parties. They act as the financiers of the market.

Arbitrageur is a dealer and enters the dealings with securities in different exchanges at the same time. It is a highly specialised activity which requires a great talent. They work for to take the advantage of the price differences in the same market or different markets.

Oddlot dealers specialises in handling the oddlots. In the stock exchanges, the prescribed round lots are traded. All of the companies have fixed market lot as ***50 or 100***. Anything less than the market lot is odd lot. The broker who specialises in oddlots is called as oddlot dealer. An oddlot arise from the issue of rights or bonus. The stock exchanges are now making the alternative arrangements for handling the oddlots.

Types of Orders

In the stock exchange the broker will buy and sell the securities on behalf of his customers. The various orders can be made by the broker for his clients. They are presented below:

(1) Net rate order.

(2) Best rate order.

(3) Limited order.

(4) Stop order.

(5) Market rate order.

(6) Discretionary order.

(7) Matched rate order.

A Net Order means the fixed rate of a particular scrip. It includes brokerage and order will be placed by the client to the broker.

The Best Rate Order means the order will be placed by a client to the broker to buy or sell at the best price immediately available in the market. If the instruction is for the purchase of the shares, the broker must try for lowest prices. If the order is placed for selling of the shares, the broker must sell highest possible price. This type of orders will be placed by the clients in the case of the actively trading shares.

Limited Order means the investor will instruct the broker to buy or sell at a stated price or better price. This order clearly indicates the maximum or minimum price that the investor is willing to accept for his trade transactions. The broker protects the customer against paying more or selling for less than the intended. In this type of order the rate depends upon the broker and client.

Stop Order means it is an order used to restrict the loss. It also protects the amount of capital gains. The order will be useful to the broker and client.

A Market Rate Order means the investor pays brokerage separately. The investor will place order for a fixed rate which is based on market conditions.

A Discretionary Order means the investor does not specify the price of securities to be bought but the transactions will be left to the broker.

A Matched Rate Order means the investor sometimes appoints two brokers. The speculator instructs one broker for buying and another for selling.

Functions of Stock Exchange

The stock exchange established for the purpose of providing a market place. The members of the stock exchange deal will the securities according to the rules and regulations laid down by the act. It protect the investors interest. The functions of the stock exchanges are as follows.

(1) It provides the liquidity to the securities.

(2) It ensures the safety and transparency.

(3) It facilitates the marketability.

(4) It brings the companies and investor together.

(5) It ensures a wider ownership securities.

(6) It provides capital to the profitable sectors.

(7) It allows the companies to float their shares on the market.

(8) It provides an orderly regulated market for the securities.

(9) If facilitates a ready market for buying and selling of the securities.

(10) It promotes savings and capital formation.

(11) It facilitates continuous market for the securities.

(12) It motivates the companies to enjoy the goodwill in the stock market.

(13) It encourages the corporate sector to improve the performance for converting various group of shares in the exchange.

Stock Exchanges India

The growth of stock exchange depends upon the growth of the corporate sector in India. In India there have been 5937 companies listed on the bourse in 2001. Every stock exchange follows its own methods of working. The stock exchange follow some important provision of the act. The provision of the act are as follows.

(A) Recognition of the stock Exchange.

(B) Control of the Government.

(C) Curbing speculation.

The securities can be traded only at the stock exchanges recognised by union government in compliance of the provisions of the securities contracts act. The recognition of the stock exchange depends on the following situation.

(1) The bye-laws of the applicant stock exchange should ensure fair dealings and must be transparent.

(2) The stock exchange should protect the interest of the genuine investors.

(3) The stock exchange should give willingness to comply the condition which may be imposed by the central government from time to time.

(4) The government should grant the recognition to the stock exchange in the interest of public and trade.

The act empowers the central government to control the working of the stock exchanges. The controlling powers of the government are presented below.

The central government controls the stock exchanges like preventing undesirable transactions in the securities. The act empowered the government relating the regulation of the procedures for recognising the stock exchanges. Their management, power, to make rules, bye-laws, or amendments, power to withdraw the recognition granted.

The central government can curb the speculative transactions of an stock exchange. The government has banned the option dealings in the securities. The government declared the kerb trading as illegal. Trading outside the stock exchange is known as kerb trading. The government reduced the life period of blank transfer to the extent of two months. The powers so far exercised by the central government have now been transferred to the SEBI. Thus the SEBI now regulates the stock market through various regulations.

Brokers

Generally every stock exchange runs through its members. The member of a stock exchange is known as the ***stock broker.*** The stock broker buys and sells the securities on behalf of his clients. The person who wants to become a stock broker, is required to get a registration certificate from the SEBI. The SEBI is the most powerful organisation to control, regulate, monitor and guide the market from time to time. It is empowered to grant the registration certificates to eligible brokers. It has the authority to impose condition before granting the certificate to a broker. A person who is granted the status of the broker by the SEBI, must abide by the rules. He is required to pay a prescribed fee to the SEBI. They are responsible for the redressal of the investor's complaint. They should bring into the notice of the SEBI regarding the nature of complaints received by them. The brokers are categorised into two.

(A) Indian Brokers

(B) Foreign Brokers

(A) Indian Brokers

The stock brokers in India should move according to the guidelines, issued by the SEBI from time to time. The SEBI has taken the monitoring function to prevent the malpractice in trading and to protect to rights of the investors. The SEBI guidelines are most important to the brokers. The broad regulatory framework of the stock exchange contain the major organisational reforms in respect of stock brokers, sub-brokers foreign brokers custodial services, depository system and stock lending scheme. The following steps are required to fulfil the legal formalities by the stock brokers.

(1) Registration.

(2) Fee.

(3) Code of conduct.

(4) Capital adequacy norms.

(5) Sub-brokers.

A stock broker in a recognised stock exchange has to get the registration with the SEBI. He should apply to the SEBI through his recognised stock exchange. The exchange may forward the application with their comments to the SEBI regarding his candidature on receipt of the application from the stock exchange the SEBI will inquire into the matters regarding stock broker. For granting of the registration, the SEBI should take consideration of many factors such as membership in recognised stock exchange, capability of the broker, his manpower and infrastructure facilities, his past experience, his discipline and suitability. After satisfying all the norms and fulfilled by the broker, then SEBI will grant the certificate of Registration to the stock broker. If he satisfies and fulfils all the norms. The selected broker should undergo some process to get the registration certificate. The function includes the submission of the report by the stock exchanges and registration of the brokers.

The selected broker has to pay the fee to the SEBI as a registration fee. The registration fee will be based on the annual turnover of the broker. The grant of ROC will be valid for 5 years. The registration fee should be paid by the broker. If his annual turnover is found to be ***Rs. 1 crore*** then ***Rs. 5000*** should be paid to the SEBI. If his turnover exceeds ***Rs. 1 crore***, Rs. 5000 + 1% of the excess of Rs. 1 crore turnover. The brokers turnover should be certified by the auditor of the concerned stock exchange. After the completion of 5 years. If the broker keep it inforce he should pay Rs. 5000 for this purpose. If a stock broker fails to pay the fee within the specified period he would be liable to pay the interest at *15%* PA for each month of delay. If the individual or firms are converted into a corporate body then the fee would be exempted for the conversion period. The corporate body should pay the fee on the basis of turnover.

Every broker who registered with the SEBI have to abide by the code of conduct. The formalities should be fulfilled by the stock broker for the smooth functioning of the stock market. The stock broker has to maintain the best relations with the investors. He should maintain high standard of integrity, promptness and fairness. He should have adequate skills, care and intelligence in discharging of his duties. He should be transparent at the price consideration in dealing with the investors. He should not involve in manipulative fraudulent transactions or spread rumour with a view to make personal gains. He should be honest while dealing with the clients. The business of the broker depends upon his degree of the level of honest nature. He must be transparent in all aspects. He should execute the orders faithfully in buying and selling of the securities.

The stock broker is required to maintain the books and records as per the legal provisions. Every registered broker should maintain, the books such as sauda book general ledger, client ledger, cash book, ledger pass book, documents register, margin register, sub-brokers accounts, member's agreement book, client consent letters register confirmation register, agreement register etc. The books and records must be preserved for 5 years.

The SEBI has the authority to suspend the registration of a broker on the following grounds.

(1) If the broker violates the SEBI provisions.

(2) Violation of the conditions for the grant of Registration.

(3) If the broker does not follow the code of conduct.

(4) If the broker involves in price rigging or cornering.

(5) If the broker is guilty of misconduct, improper business or unprofessional conduct.

(6) If the broker fails to furnish any information required by the SEBI.

(7) If the broker fails to pay the annual fee.

(8) If the broker does not cooperate during the inspection.

(9) If the broker furnishes false information to the SEBI.

(10) If the broker fails to submit the periodical returns within the stipulated period.

(11) If the broker fails to resolve the investor's complaints or to give a satisfactory explanation to the SEBI.

(12) If the membership of a broker is suspended by the stock exchange the SEBI also suspends the registrations.

The SEBI has the authority to cancel the ROC of any broker. The SEBI should indicate in writing about the defaults of the broker. It has the power to cancel the ROC in case of repeated defaults. The following situation may cause the cancellation of registration of a broker.

(1) Violation of any provisions of take over regulations and insider trading.

(2) Involves in quality offence or conviction for a criminal offence.

(3) Cancellation of membership by the stock exchange.

The suspension or cancellation of ROC can be done only after holding a thorough enquiry as laid down by the act. If the SEBI decides to cancel the registration of a broker or suspend the registration, it must be published in at least two daily newspapers. On publication of this orders, the broker is prohibited to buy and sell the securities in the market. If a broker dissatisfies with the SEBI orders he can approach the securities Appellate Tribunal for Justice.

The transactions between the client and the broker should also be regulated. Every broker should keep the clients money and his own money in separate accounts. He should not utilise the clients money for his own purpose. But however the member has the lien, set off, counter claim or otherwise against money standing to the credit of clients accounts. He should purchase the securities from the market only on receipt of 20% margin on the price of the security. The margin amount would be exempted for purchase of shares meant for ***FIIs, MFs and FIs***. The member should sell the securities on behalf of his client only on receipt of 20% of margin on the price of the securities. But MFs, FIIs and FIs are exempted from this restriction. Usually the broker must issue the contract note to a client within 24 hours for buying or selling of a scrip. He can close a transaction if the client fails to make the full payment for the execution of contract within two days of cash shares. The time limit for the specified group shares is *7 days* within the delivery of the contract note. If any loss arises it should be adjusted from the margin of the client the same process will be applied for the sale of shares by the client.

(B) Foreign Brokers

The entry of FIIs lead to emerge the foreign brokers. The SEBI has taken an initiative step to encourage the FIIs, a different set of guidelines issued by the SEBI. They are presented below :

(A) Registration.

(B) Transactions.

(C) Market operations.

Every foreign broker has to register with the SEBI. He has to disclose all the information regarding his abroad registration particulars. He should also submit an undertaking that he will operate and assist only on behalf of the registered FIIs. He should not deal the securities on his own.

DEPOSITORY SYSTEM

Introduction

The liberalised, deregulated and globalised economic environment led to the evolution of the Indian financing system. Gradually transformation shifted from the financial institutions to the Capital Market and related institutions. The gross inadequacies of the market infrastructure were revealed by the entry of the fils and capital markets growth. This was to support the volumes of securities trading in India. The existing traditional methods are time consuming. The modern techniques and state of art are to be replaced in the place of the traditional methods such as trading, clearing settlement, transfer, registration, maintenance of records, the latest technology may be helpful for the smooth functioning of the stock market. More exposure of the markets occur with the rapid changes in the investors habits. The sensex movement reflects the investors perception. It is highly influenced by the GDP. A Mathematical basis for the future expectation of the market is provided by the fast behaviour of the sensex and its link with the GDP. In 1995-96 the sensex grew 27% touching 3598.37 and the GDP at Rs. 10,73,300 crores grew 7.3% In 1995-96 the market capitalisation of the BSE was 43% of the GDP. The year also witnessed record investments of 3.05 billion by the fils. All these factors increased the systematic risks like credit risk, bad deliveries, long delayed deliveries, counterfeit scrips, forged certificates wrong signatures and stealing of shares. A new modern infrastructure has been created to over come the problems in computer recording of transaction paperless trading and depositories. The technological revolution has created waves in trading methods. Nowadays trading can be done by clicking the mouse, trading became a highly sophisticated execution in transactions. There is no need of physical presence in the stock exchange. The scenario of trading has changed with the entry of bulk buyers/FIls. The stock market reforms cleared the way for introducing depository/custody in the securities. The system of trading is based on physical transfer and efficient functioning of the markets, especially in the context of high volume transactions.

Problems: The investors face many problems regarding the buying and selling of shares in the stock market. The problems faced by the individual investors/institutional investors/foreign institutional investors are presented below:

1. Delay in the transfer of securities
2. Delay in getting the duplicate share certificate
3. Delay in getting the duplicate debenture/Bond Certificate
4. Delay in the receipt of securities allotment order for the allottees
5. Delay in the non-receipt of refund orders to the non-allottees
6. The return of share certificate is common in the following situations such as bad deliveries.
   (a) in case of forged transfer deeds
   (b) in case of false certificate
   (c) on account of forged signature
   (d) on account of mis-match of signature
7. Which of infrastructure facilities to handle a bulk volume of transactions—inadequate banking and postal facilities.

The Government of India look at initiative to Introduce the scripless trading to revamp all the problems. Through the look entry method have been taken to bring the actions in the securities without the physical delivery the ingredient of the scripless trading is the dematerialisation of the share certificates through the depositories. All the certificates are surrendered to the issues company in this method. The issuer company can cancel the share certificates after receiving them through the depository. The names of the depositors should be entered in the company Register. The name of the beneficial owner whose name is recorded with the depository should be deleted. In Sept. 1995 the government has introduced an ordinance for the depositories. This ordinance has converted into Depositories Act 1996. The depository system operates within the framework of the Depositories Act 1996 and the SEBI regulations.

Depositories Act

The objective of the Depositories Act is to provide the regulation of depositories in the securities market. The depository Act discloses the following procedure.

(a) Certificate of Commencement of business.
(b) Obligations of depositories.
(c) Enquiry and inspection.
(d) Power of the SEBI.
(e) Bye-laws.
(f) Amendments.

A certificate from the SEBI is essential for any individual/company to act as a Depository. Every company should get a registration certificate from the SEBI. Without the SEBI permission, no company is allowed to act as a depository. The SEBI is empowered to grant the certificates to the concerned parties, when they apply to the SEBI for registration. In the security it must satisfy that the depository has adequate infrastructure. He should have the technical capabilities to prevent the manipulation of records. He should also have the excellent facilities for the functioning of the trading activities.

The obligations of depository is to make an agreement with the Depository Participant (D.P) The services such as recording of allotment or transfer securities can be used by any investor. D.P should record all the transaction in a depository by surrendering the certificate to the issuer company in a prescribed manner. After receiving the certificate from the D.P the issuer company cancels the certificates and substitutes in its records the name of the depositary as a registered owner. The depository in turns records the name of the person as the beneficial owner. Generally while subscribing the shares, the investors indicate either to receive the certificate or hold with the depository. The full information about the allotment process and the names to be recorded as the beneficial owners of the financial instruments are transmitted to the depository through the public issue company. The securities which are at the disposal of the beneficial owner. The depository has the full authority to transfer the ownership. But he does not have voting rights in respect of the securities hold. Regarding the financial instrument the beneficial owner has the rights and benefits. He is also responsible for the liabilities effected from that financial instrument. The companies act indicates that every depository should maintain a register and an index of the beneficial owners. He has the right to pledge/hypothecation with the prior approval of the depository. Therefore the depository should make adjustment entries in the records accordingly. The entry made by the depository is the evidence for hypothecation. According to the bye-laws of the depository, he should inform to the issuing company about the transfer of securities. The name of the beneficial owner at regular intervals. The issuer company should also provide the necessary information in respect of the securities held by it. The beneficial has the option out of a depository. Then he has to inform the message to the depository. The depository in turn passes the message to the issues company within 30 days/ If the beneficial owner/transferee fulfils the condition and pays the fee as specified by the SEBI then the issuer issues the certificate of securities. The transactions recorded by the depository will be treated as evidence on par with sec 2 of the bankers look evidence act 1891 if any loss occurs due to the behaviour of the beneficial owner. It can be recorded by the depository from the D.P.

The SEBI monitors directs and guides all the depository transactions. It is the most powerful organisation. It controls all the activities of the depositories. The SEBI conducts the enquiry and inspection of the depositories in the interest of the public the SEBI is empowered to call for the information or make an enquiry into the affairs of the issues company/beneficial owner and D.P. It has the power to give appropriate directions for the welfare of the investors or to prevent the affairs in detrimental to the future of the investor or market. Any person can appeal to the security Appellate Tribunal if he does not satisfy with the SEBI order. Any person is liable for the punishment with imprisonment for a period of 5 years or with five or with both if he violates the rules and regulations/bye-laws. The SEBI can collect the information and asses the situation from time to time.

The SEBI has the full powers to make the regulations regarding the maintenance of records for the commencement of business. It can issue a license to the depository. If can also make regulations in the following situation:

(a) For proper maintenance of records.

(b) Prescribes the process for surrending a security certificates.

(c) Rights of depository.

(d) Obligation of the depository.

(e) The process of creating pledge.

(f) The manner of hypothecation by the beneficial owner.

(g) Fee payable for the issue of certificate of securities.

(h) Rights and obligations of the issuer company participants.

(i) The entry norms for the admission of scrips to the demat.

Bye Laws: The SEBI is empowered by the act to regulate the working affairs of the Depository. D.P and issuer company. The bye-laws are made by the depository in accordance with the provisions of the act. The SEBI should approve the bye-laws prepare by the depository. The contents of the bye-laws are presented below:

1. The entry level norms for the admission of securities in the depositories.
2. The procedure for the removal of security in the depository.

3. The condition's for dealing the securities.
4. The appointment procedure for the D.P.
5. The process of dematerialisation of securities.
6. The procedure of affairs of the transaction in a depository.
7. The system for protecting the interest of the participants.
8. The manner for protecting the interest of a beneficial owner.
9. The process of pledge in respect of the securities held with a depository.
10. The process of furnishing the information to the issuer company.
11. The process of furnishing the information to the SEBI.
12. The auditing furnishing information to the SEBI.
13. The manner of internal control standards.
14. The procedure for the settlement of any disputes between the parties.
15. The rights and obligation of the depository.
16. The rights and obligation of the D.P.
17. The procedure for the distribution of dividends to the beneficial owner.
18. The manner for the distribution of interest to the beneficial owner.
19. The procedure for transmitting the information which is received from the issuing company. To the beneficial owner regarding the dividend declaration share holders meetings and other matters.

The SEBI has the authority to direct a depository to make any bye-laws or to amend or revoke any bye-laws in writing. If any depository neglects or fails to company with the orders/direction it may make modifications or revoke the bye-laws for the welfare of the investors. The depository act can be implemented by making some amendments to the securities contract Act. Income Tax Act, The SEBI Act, Indian Stamp Acts Companies Act and Beenami Transactions Act.

SEBI: The SEBI has the authority to make regulations and control the affairs of the depository.

Regulation: The regulations of the SEBI are presented below:

(a) Registration.
(b) Certificate of Commencement of Business.
(c) Depository Participant (D.P.)
(d) Rights of depository.
(e) Rights of depository participant/Issuing Company.
(f) Inspection.
(g) Default. .

(a) Registration: Every depository must register with the SEBI. It grants the registration for the depositories for that purpose. The interested firm should apply to the SEBI in a prescribed manner along with an application fee of Rs. 50.006. The application form should be accompanied by the draft bye-laws of the proposed depository. The proposed depository may be established by an individual institutions or combination of other institutions. Generally the following institutions may think about the set up of depository services.

(a) Commercial banks.
(b) Recognised stock exchanges.
(c) Development financial institutions.
(d) Foreign banks.

(e) Body corporate (financial services orgn.)

(f) A body corporate recognised by a foreign country for providing the custodial services.

(g) A recognised financial institutions which engages in the financial services outside India.

Every proposed depository company should satisfy the following conditions:

1. Able to pay an annual fee of Rs. 10,00,000 to the SEBI.
2. Payment of registration fee of Rs. 25,00,000 within 15 days.
3. Compliance with the regulation of the SEBI bye-laws and act.
4. False information should not be furnished by the proposed depository.
5. Amendments can be made to the bye-laws from time to time as directed by the SEBI.
6. Only depository services are allowed as per the law.
7. Other than the depository services are prohibited.
8. The sponsor of the proposed depository should have at least 51% of the equity capital and the rest by the participants.
9. The depository participants are allowed to invest up to 5% of the equity.
10. No foreign entity will be allowed for more than 51% of the equity.
11. The depository should redressal the grievances within 30 days from the complaint given by participants/beneficial owners and should inform the SEBI regarding the number of complaints registered and resolved.
12. The depository should apply for the certificate of commencement of business within one year of registration.

(b) Certificate of Commencement of Business: The proposed depository will submit the application form for the registration along with other required documents and fee. One year of time will be given to the depository for getting the certificate of commencement of business from the SEBI. Before granting the certificate of commencing the business. The SEBI would scrutinise all the contents relevant to the efficient and better functioning of the depository. The SEBI may consider the following factors while granting the certificate of commencement of business.

1. The depository should have a financial soundness. It must have the net worth of more than Rs. 100 crores.
2. The bye laws of the depository must be in compliance with the provisions and it should be approved by the SEBI.
3. The depository services will depend upon the technical capability of the depository. The depository should take care of the automatic data processing system.
4. The data processing must be protested against the unauthorised access dissemination of records, alteration destruction etc.
5. The network of the depository system must be secured against any unauthorised access.
6. The depository should provide a continuous electronic means of communication among the four parties i.e. the depository. Depository participants issuer company and issuer agent.
7. The depository should provide a better quality of network services on par with the world standards.
8. The electronic access to the data storage sites and to the premisses is controlled, monitored and recorded.
9. The depository should establish adequate procedures and provide arrangements for maintaining the back up facilities.

10. The depository should provide the insurance arrangements for indemnifying the beneficial owners for any loss due to the negligence or default by him.
11. The SEBI should make a physical verification of the infrastructure facilities and systems provided by the depository.
12. The certificate of commencement of the business should be in the interest of the investors.

(c) Depository Participant: According to the SEBI regulation and depository act every depository participant should apply to the SEBI for the grant of registration. The D.P should pay a registration fee Rs. 5000 along with the application form through a depository. The depository should certify and recommend the same by forwarding the form to the SEBI within 30 days. On receipt of the application form from the depository. The SEBI considers the requirements of the D.P. The D.P. must satisfy anyone of the following categories

(a) A public financial institution (IDBI, IFCI, ICICI)
(b) A foreign bank
(c) A bank
(d) A state government sponsored financial corporation (SFC)
(e) A NBFC with some conditions.
(f) A financial consortium led by (a) to (d) orgn.
(g) A recognised stock exchange
(h) A registered custodian
(i) A clearing corporation
(j) A registered stock broker (The min. network of Rs. 50 lakhs).

On verification of the eligibility, the SEBI grants the certificate. If may be intimated through the depository the D.P should satisfy the SEBI that he has adequate infrastructure and systems. Only in the interest of investors and market. The registration will be made the SEBI permits the D.P only under the following conditions.

1. The D.P should pay the registration fee of Rs. 100 lakh within 15 days.
2. The D.P. should be in compliance with the provisions of the depository Act.
3. The D.P must comply with the bye-law agreements of the depository.
4. The depository should hold a certificate of commencement of the business while permitting the D.P
5. The D.P should inform if any wrong information is found in any manner or if there is any change in such information.
6. The D.P has to pay an annual fee of Rs. 1000 to the SEBI.
7. The grievances of the beneficial owner should be settled within thirty days.
8. The depository should inform about the nature and number of the redressal of grievances.
9. The validity period of the registration of the D.P is 5 years.
10. The registration of the D.P may be reviewed for another 5 years on payment of Rs. 10.00 lakhs.

(d) Rights of Depository: The depository should comply with the SEBI regulations depository act and bye-laws. The depository Act. Mentions the rights and obligations of the depository. The depository should state in the bye-laws. Eligible for the dematerialisation on the following elements (instruments):

(a) Scrips, bands shares debentures, or other marketable securities of any company.
(b) Units of mutual funds commercial paper, certificate of deposits. Venture capital funds. Rights issues securitised debt Unlisted securities and money market instruments.

The issuing company may make an agreement with the depository to dematerialise its securities. If the issuer company has appointed a Registrar to Issue. The agreement then it should be made among three parties i.e. The depository the D.P. and the register to the Issue. The depository should be in a capable position to coordinate and reconcile the records of ownership of the securities with the issuer and the D.P on a daily basis. The depository should have an excellent means of electronic data transfer with all the ingredients. The depository should satisfy the SEBI regarding the efficient service of the transfer of securities. The depository should allow the participant to withdraw or transfer his accounts with the compliance of the law. The depository has an obligation to arrange. The insurance facility to protect the interest of the beneficial owners. The depository has the obligation to maintain the inequity of the electronic which it holds. The depository should have the obligations to take all the precautionary approaches to secure the data safety. How even the depository should maintain the undermentioned records.

(a) The particulars about the data of transfer of the securities.

(b) The particulars of the securities dematerialised and rematerialised.

(c) The details regarding the transferors and transferee.

(d) A register and Index of the beneficial owners. The full details about their holdings at the end of every month.

(e) The correspondence made with the D.P, issuers company and beneficial owners.

(f) Other records as specified by the SEBI from time to time.

(g) All the records must be maintained for at least five years.

(h) The depository should inform the SEBI when the documents are maintained.

(i) The depository should extend the cooperation to the involved parties in dematerialisation process for the prompt and accurate clear settlement of securities transactions and conduct of business affairs.

(j) The depository should not assign any work/task to any other person without the knowledge of the SEBI.

(e) **Rights of D.P:** The depository bye-law specified that every D.P should make an agreement with the beneficial owner of the asset. The D.P should open and maintain accounts for each beneficial owner. The transfer of securities should be registered by the D.P taking the instruction from the beneficial owner. The process should be implemented in a specified manner by the bye-laws of the depository. The D.P should keep the records of instructions from the beneficial owner and make entries in his account accordingly following obligations should be fulfilled by the D.P.

1. The D.P should maintain the statement of accounts with the beneficial owner and provide the statements to him.
2. The beneficial owner will be allowed to withdraw/transfer from his account as per the agreement.
3. The D.P should provide continuous means of electronic communication to the beneficial owners.
4. The D.P should have the capabilities to review, evaluate control, systems and monitoring the internal Accounting.
5. The D.P should maintain the integrity of the data processing system.
6. The D.P should ensure that the records are to be kept safely, not destroyed or not tampered and the records are available at a particular place.
7. He should maintain his records and reconcile with every depository on a daily basis.
8. He should submit periodic returns to the SEBI and to the depository in a specified format.

9. The following records are to be maintained by the D.P.
   (a) records of transactions with depositories and beneficial owner.
   (b) The full particulars of dematerialised/rematerialised on behalf of the clients.
   (c) The register of instructions received and executed.
   (d) The records of notice, entry and approvals.
10. The records should be preserved for 5 years.
11. The D.P should not assign any work to any one without the approval of the SEBI
12. All the records should be made available to the depository

The issuing company should enter into an agreement with a depository. There is no need of agreement for the issue of Government securities. The beneficial owners are required to submit the particulars of the security certificates for dematerialisation and surrender the certificates to the D.P. The D.P in turn forwards the same to the depository along with the agreement copy of the beneficial owner. The D.P should maintain the records which contains all the information with the correspondence made to the depository on receipt of the security certificate, The issuer company immediately cancels it and further entries will be made accordingly. The issuer company would maintain a record of certificates which has been dematerialised. The issuing company should take the following steps.

(a) The issuing company should make a reconciliation of the records which are materialised by the depository on a daily basis.

(b) If the Government is a issuer. It should also reconcile the records on a daily basis of the dematerialised securities

(c) The issuer should make arrangements to continue the electronic means of communication with the depository.

(d) The issuer company must provide the information to the depository about the dematerialised securities i.e. The details of book closure, record dates annual General meetings other meetings dividends interest, conversion methods redemption of debentures warrants call money dates etc.

(e) The issuer company should provide any other information to the depository regarding the materialisation of securities.

(f) Inspection: The SEBI has the full authority to undertake the inspection of books, documents, records etc of a Depository or D.P or issuing company. The SEBI can enquire about the technical capabilities of the systems of the depository. The SEBI has the authority to investigate the affairs of the depository. D.P and beneficial owner and issuing company. The inquiry will be conducted by the SEBI for the following purposes.

(1) To ensure the smooth functioning of the affairs of specified by the law.

(2) To respond to the complaints for the investors.

(3) To look after the complains of all the provision. (SEBI Act Bye-laws depository)

(4) To take the veto powers in the interest of the investors

(g) Default: The inspection committee will submit its report after the completion of inspection to the SEBI. The SEBI may take an action in case of the default by either suspension of registration or cancellation of the depository or D.P. The SEBI may suspend the registration on the following situation.

(a) Any violation of the provisions of SEBI, Bye-laws Depository act and agreements.

(b) Any failure to furnish the full information regarding the rules and regulations.

(c) If any violation of the SEBI directions and fails to pay the annual fee.

(d) During the SEBI inspection any non-cooperation by the parties.

(e) Furnishing of false information, misleading information.

The SEBI has the authority to cancel the registration of the depository/DP/Issuing company/beneficial owner on the following grounds.

(a) Repeated defaults.

(b) If any fraud or conviction of any offence by any party.

Advantages of Depository System

(1) The ownership will bring about much needed liquidity in the capital markets and increase turnover and volumes in the markets.

(2) The ownership will be transferred to the transferee immediately on the payment by computerised book entry system.

(3) No stamp duty is required for effecting transfer of ownership.

(4) A beneficial owner would enjoy the benefits of screen based system.

NATIONAL STOCK EXCHANGE (NSE)
(India's Premier Stock Exchange)

Introduction

The Indian stock markets have come along way since the early 18th Century when securities trade was initiated under a sprawling banyan tree in front of the town hall in Mumbai the companies act that was passed in 1850, signalled the era of the joint stock companies in India. The creation of National stock exchange by the leading financial institutions in 1992 led to move the screen based trading for equities debt and hybrid instruments. The process of globalisation began with the opening up of the Indian capital markets to the foreign institutional investors in 1992. This led the foreign custodians and brokerages setting up base in India. They bought their best global practice in the Indian markets. Equity Research gained a prominence. The globalisation of markets made the Indian financial markets more vulnerable to the external events as a result of which any movement in the global market have a corresponding ripple effect in India.

The national stock exchange has been sponsored by the IDBI and co sponsored by LIC, GIC, SBI capital markets stock holding corporation, Insfrastructure Leasing and finance corporation. It emerged as a part of the capital market reform process due to the failure of the conventional stock exchange. It was established to provide transparent and efficient securities market. It was set up in Mumbai in November 1992 with a paid up equity capital of Rs. 25 crores. It was recognised by the central Government. It started its operations in June 1994 in Debt market and in equity trading in Nov 94. There was no trading floor in the stock exchange. Trading was done on the computer with the help of the PC terminals in broken offices. The NSE has a fully automated electronic screen based trading system. If was an order driven and it was not based on quote driven market. It allows two types of traded securities such as listed and permitted. It prevents the price rigging and insider trading the high powered committee (pherwari committee) recommended the establishment of the NSE with a view to provide single market.

Objectives

The objectives of the NSE are:

(a) to cover wide area geographical location.

(b) to provide an equal access and fair, efficient and transparent.

(c) to provide the shorter settlement cycles.

(d) to provide the book entry settlement system.

(e) to provide the Indian Investors with international standard service.

(f) to check the insider trading and price rigging.

(g) to protect the interest of the investors.

(h) to protect the brokers from default.

(i) to provide the listing facilities to PSUS.

(j) to spread the investment and cult to the savers in the rural and semi urban areas.

(k) to encourage the debt market.

(l) to professionalise the members to be more competent.

(m) to create more employment opportunities for the finance professionals in the orbit of the capital market.

(n) to protect the members from the default risk.

India's premier stock exchange today, NSE is evident that is has revolutionised trading in India. Through its network of 3075 VSAT exchangers across 379 cities millions of Indians who previously could not are able to trade in the stocks. The No. of companies listed the NSE and average daily turnover are presented below:

(Rs. in crores)

Year	*No. of Companies Listed*	*Average Daily Turnover*
1994-95	678	17
1995-96	1269	276
1996-97	1484	1176
1997-98	1357	1520
1998-99	1254	1651
1999-2000	1152	3303
2000-2001	1029	5337

In October 1995 the NSE became the largest exchange in India in terms of stocks transacted volumes In 2000-01 its total turnover was Rs. 17,70,457 crores.

Constitution

The NSE offers the screen based trading with National network transparency and it ensures cost effectiveness. The investment counters are spread wide in the country under the NSE electronic network. The NSE has two separate segments. (a) The wholesale Debt market segment (b) The capital market segment.

The wholesale Debt market segment WDMs deals with banks, financial institutions, other institutional participants and in PSU bonds, treasury bills, government securities, call money, commercial papers certificates of deposits etc. In this segment all are big. They are big deals, mega players, mega investors etc.

The capital market segment (CMS) deals with equities. Convertible debentures. This segment includes the securities which are traded on other stock exchanges. The CMS operates from 3-11-1994. It introduced trading in repos from 23-6-1995. The RBI has identified the NSE as the only conduit for the inter bank security deals. The NSE is free from all speculative activities, it has also become a speculators paradise banally in the speculative market separate membership is required for each segment.

The NSE has created competition to the BSE it has dominated the BSE within a short time period and exceeded the business of the 150 years old BSE NSE is set up as a cash and delivery market but it has became a circular market. In this circular market the transactions are mostly squared. The example for circular market is X selling to Y, Y selling to Z and Z selling to X.

WDM: The WDM segment consists of two parties. They are trading members and participants. The trading members are recognised the members of NSE. Generally the financial institutions, body corporate, commercial bankers are eligible to become the trading members They are selected on the basic of some selection criteria The trading member should passes at least two years experience regarding the financial services. They must posses a net worth of Rs. 2 crores. The NSE changes Rs. 30 lakh as fee from the trading members. The trading member should not withdraw his membership up to five years. The trading member must engage in securities business but not in fund based activity. The trading members can trade on their own purpose or on behalf of their clients. The participants are another party in this segment. The participants involve in buying and selling of the securities. They are responsible for the settlement of trade. The participants can be treated as the buyers of the securities for their own requirement. Their transaction are excreated through trading members. The participants can monitor all the market movements. The participants have to access the NSE trading system.

Trading System in WDM: Trading has became a sophisticated way at present the conventional system of trading has been changing with the development of information technology, trading is fully computerised. The Indian stock market has transformed the trading ways into on line trading system. The system has increased the trading velocities and reduce the time horizon. The NSE provides a facility for the screen based trading with order matching facility. The scattered trading members are connected from their respective offices to the main system at the NSE Centralised premises through a high speed efficient satellite tele communication network the trading process is an automated order matching system. It does not reveal the identify of the parties to an excreated order or a seller. It is an advantage to the members because no identity would be found. It operates on a price time priority. In screen based trading system orders are automatically matched by the computer. If an order does not find a suitable match it remains in the system and it will be displayed on the screen till a fresh order matches. The trading system facilities flexibility to the parties according to their ordering method. The process provides an excellent environment for placing an order several conditions like volume related, price related and time related can easily be placed on the system. The rapid technology development of the information system provides on line market information through various facilities in the screen based system. The entired information regarding a particular scrip or about all scrips will be available in the market. The detailed information regarding the total order in a security. The quantity traded. The high the low and the last traded prices are available through screen at any time. The debt market is easily accessible to three types of users. They are trader user privileged user and inquiry user. The trading members should keep in touch with the users. But the participant parties are allowed privileged user and inquiry by users only. the trade user is an important component in the online trading system. The trader user gives access for entering the order on the trading system. The privileged user has the right to set up a counter party. The inquiry user cannot enter orders or trade or set up exposure limits. The inquiring user can have market information and the right to set up the market watch screen. The volume of trade in the debt market segment can be executed in the negotiated or continuous market. In the continuous market the orders are automatically matched by the computer system. If the order does not find a suitable element it will be entered in the order books. The entry in the order book is known as possible order. It may be tallied later with any forthcoming order and result into a trade. The forth coming order which matches with the existing order is known as the active order. The debt market trading system facilitates trading in and other instruments as they are out right purchase and sale as Repooras non-repo traders. Repurchase agreement can be defined as "Agreements to buy securities (usually treasury bills) and to resell them at a specified higher price at a later data". The government security dealers offer the repos to the corporation.

The trading member has to indicate the trade type repo/non repo and the desired settlement term. The NSE permits the settlement term from T to T+5. The Repo term ranges from 3 to 14 days. The online trading system works on the basis of price time priority. There are two types of order which may be placed by the trading members as Repo trade and Non repo trader. In case of repo trades it facilitates the lowest buy rate in case of the buy order and in case of the sell order it arranges higher sell rate the transactions are based on passive order rate. If the buy order in case of Now-repo traders is the highest buy price and the best sell order it with the lowest price, then the orders are matched automatically by the system based on the passive or den price. All the orders are should be placed according to the specifications of the NSE. The entered transactions are beutified on the subject matter of the trade and they are divided into six parts. This classification is known as security description. All the orders are matched on the basis of the descriptors. The transaction are categorised as security type, security issue, settlement, trade type and repo term. The order transaction will be failed on the basis of security description, price volume, order type and conditions. The value of the order is indicated in "Rupees lakh" in the trading system. In the trading system every participants can set up counter party exposure limits. All the traders executed by trading members for their participant will not affect the trading members counter party exposure.

Settlement System in Debt Market

The debt market transactions are settled in Mumbai the settlement in debt market segment lies with the participants and the exchange monitors. The traders are settled as per the procedure laid down.

(a) The transactions are settled individually.

(b) Trades are settled directly between the participants.

(c) There is no settlement through the clearing house mechanism.

(d) The settlements taken place on rolling basis.

(e) Each order will be settled on the basis of specified settlement date.

(f) The NSE presently allows the settlement periods ranging from T + O to a maximum of (T + S)

(g) On the scheduled settlement date. The NSE (provide information) provides the information to the concerned numbers regarding the trades to be settled on that day.

(h) All the Government securities are settled by the participants through subsidiary General ledger account with the RBI on through exchange of physical certificates

(i) The information regarding the required settlements are reported by the member to the NSE.

(j) The other instruments are settled through the delivery to physical securities.

(k) On receipt of the information from the participants the NSE closely monitors the information.

(l) If the cancellation of trade participants are required to get it prior approved.

(m) If any disputes arises during the process one can approach the arbitration for resolving the dispute.

(n) The arbitration mechanism has been established by the NSE.

Capital Market Segment

Capital market segment course the trading in equity and retail debt. In this segment there is a strong need to up grade the professional standards of intermediaries. The intermediaries are still to develop their skills and to become more competitive. The admission standards to this segment are very rigorous. The rules and regulations are framed by the NSE. There is much stress on factors such as capital adequacies track record education and experience. Admission into this segment involves two stages. The interested person is required to go through a written examination followed by an interview.

The trading members in this segment are corporate, registered firms individuals and institutional members. The applicant should engage is fee based services only. The individual members and registered firms must have minimum net worth requirements of Rs 75.00 lakh. The corporate bodies should have Rs 1 crore. The minimum prescribe deductional qualification is graduation and two years experience in financial services/as broker/authorised assistant. The experience in any financial aspects are welcome.

Trading System in CMS

The screen based system is fully automated and works on the basis of an order driven market. The trading system provides flexibility to the members in their placement orders. Orders receives for the first time are stamped and immediately processed for a potential match. If the suitable order is not found it will be stored in different books. The orders are stored in best price and within price time sequence. The order matching rules of the NSE system reveals that the best buy order matches with the best sell order. Some time an order may match practically with another order resulting in multiple trades. The orders will match as the buy order is with the highest price and the sell order is with the lowest price members may enter orders in the system. The order will be displayed till another party puts in a counter order on the other hand the member may be reactive and put in orders that match with the existing orders on the system. The orders which are laying unmatched in the system are passive orders. The order that match with the existing orders are called active orders. The orders are always matched at the passive order price. Therefore the earlier order will get priority over the orders that come in later the trading members can enter into various types of orders depending up on their requirements there are three conditions. (a) time related conditions. (b) price related conditions (c) volume related conditions.

(a) Time Related Conditions: These transactions are executed on the basis of time conditions. In this type of order. The orders will stay in force only for a few days. The time conditions further may be classified as (a) day order (b) A good till cancelled (c) A good till days (d) An immediate or cancel. The day order is valid for the day which the order is placed. In case the order is not matched during the day it gets cancelled automatically. A good till cancelled order means. The order will remain in the trading system until it is cancelled by the member. A good till days means the order allows the thru trading members to specify the days. It will be kept in the system upto that day. Afterwords it flushes out from the system. An immediate order or cancel means it allows a trading member to sell or buy a particular security when the order is released into the market. If it fails the order will be removed from the system.

(b) Price Condition: This is the most important condition in the capital market segment. The price condition is known as "On stop". This order allows the members to place an order and gets activated only when the market price of the security exceeds a thresh old price until this situation the order does not focuses in the market. In the case of sell order, it gets triggered if the last price will be less than the sell order price.

(c) Volume Condition: The NSE may set a minimum disclosed value from time to time. In this condition the trading member may disclose only a part of the order value in the market for ex: an order of 5000 with a disclosed value condition of 500. It means that 500 is released into the market. After the order is traded another 500 will be Automatically released and so on the full order executes the quantum of disclosed value will be fixed by the NSE.

Settlement System: In the Capital Market System

The NSE operates a well defined schedule for the welfare of the investors. Trading in this segment is the short settlement cycles the following features involve in the settlement process of NSE.

(a) The settlement cycles will be announced well in advance by the NSE.
(b) The transaction will be settled through the clearing house only.
(c) There will be no settlement among the brokers.
(d) The NSE maintains the gap between in flow and out of the fund is for only one day.
(e) The NSE takes the responsibility of bad deliveries rectifying short deliveries.
(f) NSE Assures legal guarantee to the transactions and settlements.
(g) The periodic settlement is the NSE is as follows:
    (1) The trading period starts on Wednesday and ends on Tuesday of the next week.
    (2) All the transactions concluded in a particular trading period are settled during the next week.
    (3) At the end of trading period it makes delivery statements for members.
    (4) The securities are paid on every Monday following the trading period.
    (5) The pay out of the funds is on Tuesday.
    (6) The pay out day for funds and securities takes place on Wednesday.
(h) The settlement will be completed in eight days.
(i) The clearing process is automated and the NSE set up a clearing house known as National securities clearing corporation Ltd. for managing the settlement of securities.
(j) All the securities are handled by the NSECL only.
(k) The delivery members should bring the securities on the pay in day to the clearing house.
(l) The securities are distributed on the pay out day to the members.
(m) If the settlement is out of Mumbai the clearing and settlement will be done by setting up a Regional clearing house.
(n) The Canara bank is appointed as the clearing bank.
(o) All the transactions will be passed through the clearing bankerly.
(p) All the transactions are effected through the electronic fund transfer system.
(q) The clearing house makes short deliveries on Tuesday in turn they will be auctioned on Wednesday.
(r) On Thursday pay in for auction takes place and pay out on Friday.
(s) All the bad deliveries are required to be reported by Friday to the clearing house.
(t) Every Monday the delivering member is required rectify any problems.
(u) The trading system specifies turnover limits for its members in relation to their net worth.
(v) The NSE marks the market member position to maintain significant deposits on daily bases.
(w) Margins are collected from the members if they reach bey and the limits.
(x) The NSE provides prompt settlement process and assures cash settlement.

Institutional Market Segment

The NSE provides some additional facilities for its institutional investors. The institutional market segment is categorised as institutional lot segment and trade for trade segment in institutional lot segment, large volume trades take place. The trade for trade segment is meant to cater to the institutions which prefer this source as a means of minimising exposure risk. Institution lot contains in multiples of 1000 shares irrespective the securities face value institutional investors can enter into the orders separately. The institutional lot trading period commences from Wednesday to Tuesday. A trading member may enter and monitor any security in this market. All the pay in and pay out of funds are effected on the same day i.e. the subsequent Tuesday through a clearing house. All transactions and settlements of the trades will be done through clearing house only. The funds are passed to the NSE clearing house account through the clearing bank on the settlement day and will be paid by the clearing bank on the same day.

The institutional market segment consist of two conditions in the settlement of securities i.e. Institutional lots and T.T. Segment. The Securities can be delivered in institutional board lots 1000 shares and the receiving member has to accept such as good delivery on confirmation of the successful exchange of funds and securities. The custodians should report to the clearing house authorities the delivered securities should be recorded on the name of delivery member. The bank transfer forms are not allowed in the segment. The other condition is TT segment which differs in settlement the transactions are settled on a rolling basis, the transactions are required to be confirmed by T + 3 and will be settled on T + 5 the delivery of shares are to be accepted by the receiving member. The settlement of the transactions are effected between institutions and custodians and it should be reported to the NSE. The custodians are more important in the settlement cycles.

BOMBAY STOCK EXCHANGE (BSE)

Introduction

The first stock exchange was set up in India under the name of Native and Stock Brokers Association of Bombay in 1875. It was established as a voluntary non profit organisation. It is managed by an executive or the governing body. It is the premier stock exchange in India. It is the oldest market and has been recognised permanently. The other exchanges in India are reserved for every five years. Its business is not confined to Mumbai alone. There are 100 other cities in which it had set up business. It is a great surprise that the BSE membership fee in 1857 was just Re. 1 (one rupee only). Now it commands more than Rs. 2 crores. The BSE has introduced on line trading system on 19-1-1995 It provides a quote driver automated trading facility to the investors.

The market indexes have always been of great importance in security analysis, people have been observing the stock market fluctuations through market indicators. The investors use the market index as a bench mark. The economists and statisticians also use the index to study the trend of growth patterns in the economy. The investors use various indexes for their analytical purpose. They also compute and compel the index numbers. The indexes are equal weighting approach or price weighted or value weighted approaches. All these methods are used in the calculation of index. The price weighted index is a simple arithmatic average the price weighted index is the concept of indexing which involves the comparison of currently computed averages with some base value. There are two forms of Indexes. They are the paasche index and the laspeyres index. These two methods are used for determining the consumer price index. They measure the price inflation by taking the quantity as constant.

$$\text{Paasche price index} = \frac{\Sigma P_1 Q_1}{\Sigma P_o Q_1} \times 100$$

$$\text{Laspeyres index} = \frac{\Sigma P_1 Q_0}{\Sigma P_o Q_0} \times 100$$

$$\text{Fishers ideal index} = \frac{\Sigma P_1 Q_0}{\Sigma P_o Q_0} \times \frac{\Sigma P_1 Q_1}{\Sigma P_o Q_1} \times 100$$

The BSE started publishing a index number of equity prices from 2nd January 1986. With the base year 1978-79. It is known the BSE sensitive index the equity shares of 30 companies have been selected on the basis of market activity with due representation to the major industries. The shares selected and the industrial group to which they belong are presented below.

COMPONENTS OF SENSEX

Sl. No.	*Name of the Company*	*Industry group*	*Sl. No.*	*Name of the Company*	*Industry group*
1.	Hindusthan lever Ltd.	FMCG	16.	Hindalco Industries	Aluminium.
2.	Reliance Industries	Synthetic textiles	17.	ICICI	Banking
3.	Inforys technologies	Computers	18.	Bajaj Auto	Automobiles
4.	I.T.C.	Tobacco, Hotels	19.	Nestle	FMCG
5.	Reliance Petroleum	Refinery	20.	LQT	General Engineering
6.	S.B.I	Banking	21.	BHEL	Heavy Electrical
7.	H.P.C.L	Petroleum	22.	TISCO	Steel
8.	Ranbaxy	Pharmaceuticals	23.	Gujarat Ambuja Cements	Cements
9.	MTNL	Telecom	24.	TELCO	Automobiles
10.	Satyam Computers	Computers	25.	BSEC	power
11.	H.C.L. Technology	Computers	26.	A.C.C	cement
12.	Dr. Reddy lab	Pharmaceuticals	27.	Grasim Industries	Textiles
13.	Hero Honda	Automobile	28.	Glaxo Smith Kline	FMCG
14.	Zee telefilm	Entertainment	29.	Castrol	Lubricants
15.	Cipla	Pharmaceuticals	30.	Colgate Palmolive	FMCG

The method of compiliation of the sensex is based on standard and poor U.S.A. The S & P 500 is a value weighted index of 400 industrial stocks, 40 utility stocks 20 Transportation stocks and 40 financial stocks. The calculation of sensex is compute as follows.

$$P_t = \frac{\Sigma P_j\ t\ \Sigma Q_j\ t \times 0}{\Sigma P_j\ 0\ \Sigma Q_j\ 0}$$

Pit = period of stock i in period t

Qit = Number of shares outstanding for stock i in period t

Pio = price of stock i in the base period o; and

Qio = Number of shares outstanding for stock in base period o; and the base period 1978-79 has been chosen.

The sensex comparents are 30 companies from both specified and non specified groups. The BSE has launched 13 more indices and some of these have taken some shine off the sensex. But the index retains its gold standard reputation the highest is 6.150.69 An intra trading on Feb. 14, 2000 the lowest is 9.56.11 on January 25.1991 but we cannot rather dwell on that.

The BSE has seen several changes. The number of companies listed on the BSE has grown from 197 in 1946 to 5,937 today. In 2000-01 the average daily volumes were Rs. 4775. 8 crore still the exchange has lost much of its former glory with the creation of the NSE statement showing the Average daily turnover Rs in crore.

STATEMENT SHOWING THE NUMBER OF COMPANIES LISTED IN BSE

Year	*Turnover (Average daily)*	*Year*	*No. of Companies listed*
1989-90	134.80	1998-89	2275
1990-91	188.54	1989-90	2247
1991-92	332.50	1990-91	2471
1992-93	238.00	1991-92	2601
1993-94	387.78	1993-Dec.	3263
1994-95	292.02	1994-Dec.	4413
1995-96	215.79	1995-Dec.	5399
1996-97	517.85	1996-Dec.	5999
1997-98	851.00	1997-Dec.	5843
1998-99	1283.95	1998-Dec.	5860
1999-2000	2729.20	1999-Dec.	5963
2000-2001	4775.77	2000-Dec.	5937

The BSE sensex can be compared with the NYSE Dow Jones. The sensex movement is presented below.

STATEMENT SHOWING THE MOVEMENT OF SENSEX

Year	*Sensex Average*	*High for the year*
1986-87	570	659
1987-88	455	536
1988-89	613	719
1989-90	730	798
1990-91	1050	1559
1991-92	1845	4285
1992-93	2899	4286
1993-94	2895	4467
1994-95	3975	4631
1995-96	3289	3598
1996-97	3469	4069
1997-98	3812	4548
1998-99	3295	4281
1999-2000	4659	5934
2000-2001	4270	5542
2001-2002	–	3742

O.T.C.
OVER THE COUNTER EXCHANGE OF INDIA

Introduction

Over the counter exchange of India was established to fulfil the needs of the small companies. There is a strong need for the fully computerised, ringless scripless, electronic stock exchange. The trading and settlement standards are in tune with the global standards that provides capital market access to the small companies. It provides these services to the investors and to the companies. The act is known as exchange without floors and rings. It is a market place where the transaction are executed by bids and offers through the computer device.

The O.T.C was set up in 1989 as a company and registered O/S 25 of the companies act. The securities contract Regulation Act Sec. 4 recognises the OTC as a stock exchange. It is prompted by UTI, ICICI, IFCI, LIC, GIC, SBI capital markets. IDBI Can bank the financial services.

The OTC is a floor less exchange. All the activities are computerised. It allows the designated dealers to operate through their computers. All the quotations and transactions are recorded and processed in the OTC exchange. The dealers are scattered throughout the country and have the access to the central computer. The dealers are able to know the best bids and offers of the market makers in respect of each script. The interested dealer complace his order through the computer. The important documents in the OTC activities are (a) cocenter Receipt (b) sales confirmationship. If the deal is made cocenter receipt will be handed over to the buyer. The buyer should kept the CR carefully because it is a tradeable document. It is just like a share certificate. The sales confirmationship will be passed on the seller if the deal materialises. The seller should presence the certificate units the payment is made. The OTC allows only the securities of the listed companies. The listing agreement will be made on the basis of the following norms.

(a) Companies with issue capital between Rs 30 lakhs to Rs. 25 crores.

(b) Companies which have already listed their securities on the stock exchange are not eligible for listing in the OTC.

(c) Closely help companies interested in listing.

(d) Venture capital companies (20% shall be issued to the public).

(e) NBFCS with paid up capital of Rs. 1 crore are eligible for listing in the OTC.

(f) The companies which are not listed in any other stock exchanges provided.

  (1) The company should offer to the public at least 40% of the issued equity or Rs. 20 lakhs whichever is higher for companies between the ranges Rs. 30 lakh to Rs 3 crores.

  (2) For issues between Rs. 3 crore to Rs 25 crore the public offer should be 60%.

  (3) The company does not carry on the business of investment, leasing, finance hire purchase or amusement parks.

The promoters are the OTC are called as sponsor members. The sponsor members are entitled to make the listing agreements with the interested companies. They has full authority to admit a company for listing. The sponsor members will evaluate the companies performance before admitting a company. The sponsors will closely monitor the technological and financial viability of the proposed company. They also ensure that all the legal formalities have been compiled with finally they will value the shares of the company in compliance the SEBI guidelines for the issue of securities and to manage the public issue successfully. The sponsor member should act as market maker for at least 3 years and also to appoint an additional market malar for that scrip for a period of at least one year. Further the SEBI relaxed the norms for listing on the OTC. Dave committee have been appointed to review of the works of the OTC to make recommendation.

CUSTODIANS

Introduction

The evolution of the stock market lead to so many innovations. The custodial services is one of the emerging elements in the stock market. It plays a crucial role in the secondary market. The observer of the stock market, the SEBI has defined its framework and made it as the SEBI custodian of securities Regulations, 1996 for the proper conduct of the business. The custodian services relate to the safeguarding of the securities of a client. The client enters into an agreement to avail the services. The custodians offer their services to the clients on the following aspects.

(a) They provide services to maintain the accounts of the securities of a client.

(b) They collect the accruals of the benefits of the clients on behalf of him.

(c) They will equip the client about the actions taken by the issuers of securities.

(d) They reconcile the records of the clients transactions

Registration

The SEBI is the most powerful organisation in the stock market to monitor, regulate and guide the situation every custodian should register with the SEBI. They should apply for the registration to the SEBI with an application fee of ***Rs. 10,000***. On receipt of the application from the custodian, The SEBI would grant the registration if it satisfies with the particulars submitted by the custodian. The SEBI will examine whether the applicant

(a) fulfils the net worth of ***Rs. 50 crores*** (paid up capital + free reserves)

(b) has the adequate infrastructure

(c) has the best talented manpower.

(d) has the arms length relationship to be maintained in his other business affairs.

(e) the registration is in the interest of the investors.

(f) the applicant is a body corporate.

(g) his associates or employees are involved in any litigation connected with the offence.

The custodian who has been granted the registration should pay a registration fee of Rs. *15,00,000.* The SEBI after scrutinising the application, may grant the registration under certain conditions.

(a) Every custodian should fulfil the capital requirement of *Rs. 50 crore.*

(b) Every custodian has to obey the rules and regulations of the SEBI.

(c) Every custodian has to make a valid agreement with his clients for rendering services

(d) The custodian has to pay the annual fee of Rs. 5,00,000.

Any wrong information in any particular content should be informed to the custodian by the SEBI in writing.

Obligations

The custodian is an important person in the stock trading mechanism. The SEBI is the mandatory organisation to look after the interest of the general investors. The rules and regulations have been framed by the SEBI and every custodian should fulfil the Obligation

(A) Code of Conduct.

(B) Uniform norms.

(a) Code of Conduct: The custodian functions relate to the services sector. He should abide by the code of conduct. At present it become as a profession. They should maintain a high standard of integrity, transparency and maintain a professionalism manner. They must have a staff with high skill, talent and dynamism. They should be prompt in the collection of dividends from the issuer company and interest on behalf of his client. They are responsible for the movement of securities in the custody account. They should maintain the transactions of deposits and withdrawals of cash from the clients. They should be in a position of provide every thing within a short span of time. They should provide infrastructural facilities to their clients. The operating procedures and systems should be in a systematic manner. They should maintain the confidentiality of the affairs of their client. They should record the transactions in a electronically stored manner. They should take all the precautions to keep the information in storage and is not lost. They should obtain the duplicate documents to be provided in the event of loss of the original document. They should be cooperative with counterparts, depositories and clearing organisations. They should maintain an arm length relationship with other associates. They should take precautionary measures while administering the assets of their clients. They should not merge all the activities of the business. The custodian functions cannot be delegated to any other person except to the custodian. They should be in a position to monitor, review and evaluate the procedures and systems. The activities should be inspected by an expert and the report should be submitted to the SEBI within three months. The custodian should implement the internal control system in his organisation.

The custodian should maintain the records for at least five years. The SEBI has the authority to conduct the inspection under the supervision of an auditor to check the books of accounts and records. The SEBI should ensure that the accounts are being maintained properly. The SEBI has the power to investigate the complaints made by the investors. On completion of the inspection, a report should be submitted to the SEBI on the basis of the report received by the SEBI, It can call upon the custodian to take such measures as it deems fit. The registration of the custodian is liable to be suspended by the SEBI for the following reasons.

(1) Any violation of the rules and regulations of the SEBI.

(2) Failure to pay annual fee.

(3) Any breach of code of conduct.

(4) Failure to attend the complaints of the clients.

(5) Fails to submit the periodical returns to the SEBI.

(6) Non cooperation during the inspection of the SEBI.

(7) Fails to follow the guidelines of the SEBI.

(8) Furnishes false information to the SEBI.

The SEBI has the ultimate authority to punish the custodian if he fails to obey the rules and regulations of the act. It can cancel the ROC. If he involves in an offence of moral terpitude or he is guilty of repeated defaults.

(b) Uniform Norms: The SBEI controls the activities of the custodians by preparing uniforms norms. They are presented below.

(a) Custodians should work as an integral part of the system.

(b) It advice all its clients to settle their transactions through the clearing corporation.

(c) Participates in clearing and settlement process through for all the securities.

THE NATIONAL SECURITIES DEPOSITORY LTD.

Introduction

A depository is a centralised place where shares of various companies are held in Electronic form. If is basically a bank for electronic shares. In India, the *National Securities Depository Ltd.* has been set up as India's first depository. If has been promoted by three major financial institutions UTI, IDBI and NSE. it has been established with a view to provide holding of securities in the electronic form and settlement of trades done for these electronic holdings. It is responsible to every individual investors who holds electronic balances with the depository. It has designed the software for the operating systems in such a way that the software systems at the depository and the *Depository participant* office are connected. It has access to all the accounts of Individual investors maintained by the **DP** to ensure adequate control.

A DP acts as an agent of NSDL for providing its services to the investors. It has got registered with the SEBI on 7-6-1996 and has been granted the commencement of business certificate on 31-10-1996. The settlement of securities in electronic form would eliminate problems that are normally associated with the settlement of physical certificates.

(a) Mutilation of scrips due to reckless handling.

(b) Loss of certificates by postal authorities or Registrars or investors.

(c) Bad delivery of shares.

(d) Forgery of certificates.

The operating system of NSDL maintains continuous connectivity with the Registrars and transfer agents of the companies whose securities can be dematerialised in NSDL. This is done in order to perform a daily reconciliation of all account balance held with NSDL which are being admitted to the depository with securities eligible for initial dematerialisation.

Services

The NSDL offers the following services to all the investors both individual and Institutional.

(a) maintaining beneficial holding through *DPs.*

(b) providing dematerialisation

(c) providing rematerialisation of securities

(d) providing service for settlement of trades

(e) providing allotment of securities directly in the electronic form

(f) providing facilities to pledge stock dematerialised

(g) providing stock lending and borrowing facilities.

(h) providing services in issue of Right/Bonus share.

Dematerialisation

The dematerialisation process will take process as follows.

Step *I* The Investor surrenders share certificate for demat to the DP.

Step *II* The DP intimates NSDL of the request through the system.

Step *III* The DP submits the certificates to the Registrar.

Step *IV* The Registrar accepts the request from NSDL

Step *V* The Registrar informs the NSDL on completion of the dematerialisation.

Step *VI* NSDL updates its records informs the DP.

Step *VII* The DP updates its records and informs the investor. This process takes a maximum of 15 days.

Rematerialisation

Rematerialisation of share is conversion of electronic form into the physical form. The Registrar will issue a fresh certificate to this effect. The depository act provides a facility to the investor to withdraw securities from the depository to a physical form. If any investor intends to withdraw securities to physical form he approaches the depository through his *DPs.* The DP forwards the request to the

Registrar. The Registrar will verify the balances and issue fresh certificates to the investor after confirming the request with ***NSDL.*** The NSDL will reduce the balance of account to that extent. The Registrar deducts the account of NSDL as the registered owner.

Present Status of Demate Trading

At present only BSE and NSE have connections with the NSDL. A total of **8.3 crore**[11] shares have been dematerialised in the 8 scripts of the 800 odd NSE members, 729 members of BSE have opened their account for demat trading. There are another 162 companies have so for entered into an agreement for demat of their securities with the NSDL. As of today above 3,20,000 investors have switched over to this system of share trading. The first depository system was commenced on 14-1-1999. Two stocks are put under compulsory demat trading. The market capitalisation of these companies is around ***Rs. 43,732 crores.*** i.e., 11% of the total market capitalisation. Another 19 more companies have joined the demat of their stock from 15-2-1999. The market capitalisation has gone upto ***Rs. 84,464 crores.*** It is interesting to note that another 30 stocks may join the fray of E-shares by 5-4-1999 and the market capitalisation is 26%. As on there are 82 DPs registered with SEBI and 690 DP service centres across the country. The seven stock exchanges NSE, BSE, CSE, DSE, OTC, Bangalore and Ludhiana have established connectivity with NSDL. From 5-4-1999, 60 scrips comprising BSE sensex CNX and NIFTY indices will go for compulsory demat trading Mutual funds have also dematerialised more than 60% of their holdings. All Mutual funds have affirmed that by the end of Jan. 1999 around 75% of their holdings will be dematerialised.

SUMMARY

The financial system of a nation works through four important elements. They are ***Financial Markets, Financial Institutions*** *Financial Services and Financial Instruments* Financial markets deal with the various kinds of financial assets. They create and allocate credit Money Market is a market for short term credit. It deals in short term financial instruments. The commercial banks play an important role in the money market. A strong money market demands a regular and adequate supply of variety of financial instruments. It consists the borrowers and lenders. It can provide financial assistance to trade and industry. It reduces the cyclical fluctuations ***Capital Market*** is a market for long term securities. It functions as coordinator between savers and investors. It provides a wide range of financial instruments at all times. It consists many number of investors. The capital Market in India is composed of two components (a) primary Market (b) secondary market. Primary market is a new issue market. Public issue is the most important element in the life of a company. The ***stock exchanges*** are known as Secondary Market. It is a medium of transfer of resources for the circulated securities. The stock exchanges in India should work within the framework of the companies act. Income tax act, FERA 1973. They are self regulatory organisations supervised by the Ministry of Finance. Listing of shares means admitting a script on the trading floor of a stock exchange. The stock exchange has the authority to withdraw or suspend the trading of a security.

QUESTIONS

(1) What do you understand by money market? Discuss the constituents of the Indian money market.

(2) Define Money Market. What are the characteristics of a money market.

(3) Explain the structure of the Money market.

(4) Explain the various money market instruments which are available in the market.

11. Amarpreet Kaur and Padmini, **Depository System – Problems and Prospect**, Quality Publishing Company, New-Delhi 2000, p. 54.

(5) What are the various components of the Indian Money market?

(6) What is Money Market Mutual fund? Mention its salient features.

(7) What do you understand by commercial paper? Explain its features.

(8) Explain the guidelines issued by RBI on MMMF?

(9) What is capital? Explain the different categories of capital.

(10) What do you mean by Capital Market? Explain the objectives of capital market.

(11) What are the different components of Capital Market?

(12) Explain the differences between Money market and capital Market.

(13) Discuss the nature and importance of Capital Market.

(14) Write an essay on Capital Market in post liberalisation situation.

(15) Explain the various factors which affect the growth of the Capital Market.

(16) What do you understand by NIM? Explain the process for public issue by a public Ltd. Company.

(17) What do you understand by secondary Market? Distinguish between primary and secondary market.

(18) Discuss the recent trends in Indian capital Market.

(19) What do you understand by pre and post issue activities?

(20) Explain the concept of private placement? What are the benefits available under this method to the corporate sector.

(21) What are the legal requirements for listing shares?

(22) What is NSE? Describe its trading system.

❑ ❑ ❑

INDEX UNIT-IV

FINANCIAL SERVICES

Introduction – Salient Features – Constituents – Financial Instruments – Market Players – Commercial Banks – Financial Institutions – Mutual Funds – Merchant Bankers – Stock Brokers – Consultants – Underwriters – Market Makers – Specialised Institutions – Regulatory Bodies – Evolution of Financial Services in India – Initial Stage – Second Stage – Third Stage – Financial Services and Problems – Lack of Skilled Personnel – Quality of Services – Core Competence – Fee and Fund Based – Technology – Management of Risk in Financial Services – Internal Risk – Lending Institutions – Stock Broking Services – Insurance Services – Fee Based Service Companies – Leasing and Hire Purchasing Companies – External Risk – Types of Risk – Internal Rate Risk – Market Risk – Credit Risk – Currency Risk – Regulatory Risk – Capital Risk – Regulatory Framework for Financial Services – Structural Regulation – Prudential Regulation – Investor Regulation – Regulation on Banking and Financing Services – Definition of the Banking Company – Share Capital – Management – Banking Operations – Powers of the RBI – Annexures – Mutual Funds – Venture Capital – Credit Rating.

Introduction

The increasing role of private sector, market oriented economy, liberalisation globalisation, competition and efficiency have become the important elements in economic activity of the nation. The main objective of management is to increase the efficiency, productivity and lowest costs and enhancing profits. Hence the business concern is in the area of *services*. The quality and cost effectiveness will count as pre-requisite for its success. The quality of service depend upon the technology. The analysis of any firm involves the technological relationship between input and outputs. The management of a firm is to see that this relation of inputs and outputs is most upto date modern and cost effective. In ***Service*** sector, efficiency and competition are the landmarks of success, management has a role to judge. The result which will be based on cost of service quality and profits.

The banks have been forced to enter into new areas of Non-bank financial services. The *Chakravarthy and Narasimhan Committee* have recommended the need for market oriented financial system. The banks and NBFCs can function with greater autonomy, accountability and efficiency. The Narasimhan Committee has recommended that all the institutions which involve in the Capital market should work on sound guidelines within regulatory framework of the SEBI. SEBI is the most powerful organ in promoting better investor protection and widening the pool of savings and investment.

Financial deregulation, freeing of interest rates on bank's lending rates and their practices have helped the growth of financial services. The private sector was permitted to set up mutual funds, banks and financial institutions. Move recently some developments took place to expand the scope of financial services such as inviting FIIS to invest in our country and dilution of ***FERA***. The following statement reveals the importance of financial services in our economy.

SHARE OF GROSS CAPITAL FORMATION IN GDP (%)[1]

Components of GDP	*93-94*	*94-95*	*95-96*	*96-97*	*97-98*	*98-99*	*99-2000*
Agricultural, Forestry and Fisheries	1.79	1.71	1.64	1.76	1.55	1.61	1.56
Industry	10.66	12.00	16.02	14.29	12.89	11.80	10.55
Services	8.83	9.72	8.76	8.25	7.72	7.02	7.49

SHARE IN AGGREGATE NET CAPITAL STOCK (%)

	Components of GDP	*93-94*	*94-95*	*95-96*	*96-97*	*97-98*	*98-99*	*99-2000*
I	Agricultural, Forestry and Fishery	15.29	14.61	13.72	13.71	13.81	13.64	13.53
II	Industry	38.10	39.08	40.38	41.19	41.63	41.80	41.81
III	Services	46.61	46.31	45.90	45.10	44.56	44.56	44.44

Sources: Economic Times, 26-12-2001, p. 10.

A well regulated modern financial sector is essential in a globalised economy. Financial innovation contributed to the development. Market based economies have in general done better, because of the constant identification and improved satisfaction of consumer needs, including needs for financial products.

Rapid technological change creates new possibilities that make it difficult for regulators to keep up. The complexity of modern system is such that controls must give way to self regulation and revelation of information. Innovation ways have been developed to get information from markets.

Financial services is one of the element in Indian financial system. It is an important component of the financial system. It fulfils the needs of financial institution, financial markets and instruments to serve the individual and institutional investors more efficiently. The functioning of the financial system depends on the range of financial services. It include the services offered by both types of companies such as ***Asset Management Companies and Liability Management Companies.*** It not only helps to raise the adequate financial resources but also ensures their efficient deployment. The *Asset Management Company* include leasing companies, Mutual funds, Merchant bankers and portfolio Management. The ***Liability Management companies*** comprise the bill discounting houses, Acceptance houses. Financial services provide efficient management of funds services such as bill discounting, factoring, parking of short term funds in the money market. ***The LMCs*** provides specialised services such as Credit Rating, Venture Capital Financing Housing Finance etc. These services are also provided by a number of various organisations such as *NBFCs,* Insurance companies, subsidiaries of financial institutions stock exchanges specialised and general financial institutions etc. All these organisation are regulated by the *securities and Exchange Board of Ind.* RBI and the department of Banking and Insurance, Government of India through a number of legislation. It stimulates the velocity of the economic growth and development of a nation. The Indian economy has to improve the infrastructure facilities to the investors entrepreneurs, Industry and business. Financial services differ in nature from other service sector. The salient features of the financial services are discussed below.

(A) Invisible

(B) Customer Friendly

(C) Demarcation

(D) Dynamism

(E) Innovation

1. Economic Times, 26-12-2001, p. 10

The services of the finance is intangible. It smoothens the functioning of the corporate sector by providing funds within the stipulated period of time without fail. The institutions which supply them have a good image and confidence of the client but they may not succeed. The business concerns have to focus on quality and innovativeness of their services to build their credibility and gain the trust of their clients.

Financial services must be consumer friendly. They should provide according to the client needs and convenience. The provider of such services should study the requirement of the customer in detail to suggest different financial strategies which reduce the cost and stimulates the profitability of the company. The providers of such services remain in constant touch with the market. They offer new variety of products much ahead of need and impending legislation. They design innovative and universal specific projects. These services are highly skilful and they require more talent. At the present day, business concern happen to be different in terms of size, levels of production profitability and labour forces.

The basic function of business is to earn the reasonable return on their investment by producing goods and selling goods. The financial services have to be performed accordingly. Hence it needs a perfect understanding between the service providers and their clients.

Financial service is an innovative activity and requires dynamism. It has to be constantly redefined and refined on the basis of economic changes. The economic changes will depend on so many factors such as ***disposable Income, standard of living and educational changes.*** These institutions while designing new service must visualise in advance about the requirements of markets and wants of customers.

Constituents

The financial services comprise the following major constituents in the financial system. They are:

(a) Financial Instruments

(b) Market Players

(c) Specialised Institutions

(d) Regulatory Bodies

(a) Financial Instruments

Financial instrument includes equity, debt and hybrid. They are written evidences of ownership giving their holders the right to demand and receive property not in their possession. The ownership of a corporation is divided into units called share. A shareholder's interest is evidenced by a stock certificate, which status, among other things, the name of the stockholder, the class of the stock and the number of shares owned. These are written documents carrying the worth to get the future cash receipts. The securities contracts (Regulation) Act, 1956 provides that securities should include.

(i) Share, scrips, stocks, bonds, debentures stock or other marketable securities of a like nature in or of any incorporated company or other body corporates;

(ii) Government securities; and

(iii) Rights of Interest of securities.

The stocks and bonds are many particular kinds designed to meet the requirements. Government and semi government bodies also issue certificates. With the evolution of the Capital Market, new financial instruments are being introduced to suit the requirements of the companies. The Merchant Bankers and Fund managers will design new instruments to cater to the changing needs of the issuer and the investors. They will keep in view of the factors such as the yield expected by investors, price and credit risk, liquidity and quantum of funds while designing new financial instruments.

(b) Market Players

Generally money flows into various markets such as product markets, factor markets and financial market. The money which flows into financial markets reflect the investment and disinvestment process. Conversion of money into future claims of money and vice versa. The market players include the following.

(1) Commercial banks.
(2) Financing companies.
(3) Mutual funds.
(4) Merchant bankers.
(5) Stock brokers.
(6) Consultants.
(7) Underwriters.
(8) Market Makers.

1. Commercial Banks: The commercial banking has undergone a number of structural and functional changes in the developing countries. They are slowly departing from the traditional strict self financing rules by favouring risk free loans. The Commercial banking in the developed countries provide term loans to the corporate sector by participating in the capital and equipment finance. The Indian banks have recently commenced hire purchasing finance. They advance loans for purchasing consumer durable and equipment. They involve in providing loans to Agriculture sector also. Their structure has been changed from commerce to the Industries sector. The banks in the developing countries have undergone a period of significant changes. They are now playing a major role in promotion the economic growth in the development countries.

2. Financing Companies/Institutions: The importance of finance companies have been growing day by day. They play an important role in the development of a nation. They occupy a dominant role in the Indian financial system. We cannot ignore the role played by these companies in our economy. The participation of finance organisations can stimulate the economic growth. They inject a new blood to the corporate sector. All these reflections made for the evolution of a vibrant, competitive and dynamic financial system, the *NBFC* sector has recorded marked growth recently. The growth in recent years in terms of the number of ***NBFCs*** their deposits and so on. Therefore by keeping these companies in view, the *Banking Laws (Misl. provisions) act 1963* was introduced to regulate the NBFCs. The government has been taking initiative steps to frame suitable policy measures and appointed several committees from time to time to study about these institutions. The appointed committees made suitable recommendations for the healthy growth within the given a regulatory frame work. The recommendations made in this context of the contemporary financial scenario, the regulatory authorities have incorporated these factors in formulation of policy measures taken by them. The regulatory authority in this aspect is the RBI. These committees have worked in these aspects.

(A) Babathosh Datta Committee (1971)
(B) James Raj Committee (1975)
(C) Chakravarthy Committee (1985)
(D) Vaghul Committee (1987)
(E) Narasimhan Committee (1991)
(F) Shah Committee (1992)
(G) Khanna Committee (1996)

The Non-Banking Finance companies in India can be classified as follows:

(a) Residuary Non-banking Companies
(b) Investment Companies

(c) Mutual benefit Finance Companies

(d) Loan Companies

(e) Equipment Leasing Companies

(f) Hire purchase Finance Companies

(g) Housing finance companies

(h) Residuary Non-banking Companies

(i) Miscl. non-banking Companies

The NBFC is a heterogeneous group of financial institutions. They made considerable progress their growth has been much faster than of commercial banks. They pay higher interest rates to the depositors and charge lower interest rates from the borrowers. They perform various functions such as transfer of funds from the saver to the investors. They manage the funds more economical and more efficient than that by the individuals. They maintain large size of the asset portfolios. These asset portfolios enables to reap various economic of scale in portfolio management. The NBFCs reduce risk of the savers. They provide sufficient liquidity in the market. They conduct credit analysis and investigations about the credit worthiness of the borrowers. But all these activities are not possible by the Individual Lenders.

3. Mutual Funds: Mutual Funds is one of the innovative banking system. The mutual funds have been set up mainly by the subsidiaries of the public sector banks. For ex: SBI, Canara Bank, Punjab National Bank, Bank of Indian, Indian Bank, Andhra Bank, LIC, GIC also have set up mutual funds. Till 1986, UTI has a monopoly of this business in India. At present other mutual funds have also come up in the market. Mutual funds are either open ended or close ended financial intermediaries. They procure money by selling the units to the investors. They provide to obtain high return low risk combination from their indirect holding of equities and other assets. They can be classified as ***Growth oriented or Income oriented or Income and growth oriented funds.*** They offer many other financial services such as insurance share exchange housing and bank loans to their investors. They are specialised in using their funds indifferent areas. These specialised sector funds are known as ***Common stock funds, Bond funds, Money Market Funds, Municipal bond funds, Mixed funds etc.***

4. Merchant Bankers: Merchant banking is another innovative method in banking system. Commercial banks have entered into this sector. They have set up merchant banking divisions and are involved in underwriting issues. There are several financial intermediaries associated with the management of public and rights issue of capital. The intermediaries are required to register themselves with the SEBI under the relevant regulations before commencing the business operations. SEBI is the regulatory authority to control and direct the activities of the merchant bankers.

5. Stock Brokers: After the Introduction of the liberalisation policy in 1991, The entire financial sector in India has changed. The policy has registered enormous growth in terms of the number of listed companies, market capitalisation, market value of companies to *GNP (Gross national product)* and number of shareholders. The secondary market has been developed exponentially. There are *23* recognised stock exchanges in India. The *National Stock Exchange* and the ***over the Counter Stock Exchange of India*** have been established to save the investors more efficiently. The stock brokers play an important role in the stock market. They involve in buying and selling of securities in a recognised stock exchange SEBI is the most powerful organ in the stock market. It assumes the monitoring function of brokers in India. *Stock broking* has been emerging as a professional service and replacing its traditional closed character as inherited family business. If any body wants to work as a broker, a certificate of Registration from the SEBI is mandatory after satisfying all the terms and conditions. The SEBI will grant the registration to the brokers. The membership in the stock exchange can be granted as *Individual membership and corporate membership.* The Individual membership requires to fulfil the formalities of Sec. 8 of the securities contract (Regulation) Rules, 1957. Corporate membership will be granted to the companies, those who satisfy with the companies act, 1956. Further financial institutions such as ***UTI, LIC, IDBI*** and ***ICICI*** can be corporate members in the stock exchanges.

6. Consultants: Financial services are meant to provide solutions to the problems faced by the various components of the financial system. The financial innovations enable to increase the profitability of the corporate sector. The process of development and economic growth is possible only on efficient services. The consultants who are professionals in the area of ***Finance*** can provide best solutions to the problems faced by the corporate sector. They are pioneer in their field and render the quality of service with high integrity and standards. Financial consultant occupy a key role in problem solving solution like in all areas of functional management such as *production, Finance, Marketing and Human Resources.* Their services are intangible and show greater impact on the functioning of the company. They provide tailor made solution to all the problems irrespective of any area.

7. Underwriters: Underwriters occupy a dominant role in issue management of the corporate sector. They are intermediary in the primary market. They provide assurance to the companies which approach the capital market for raising the financial resources. They render valuable services to the newly promoted companies which they require believable advise. At the initial stage of formation the companies face a number of problems related to finance area. They help to the capital formation in the country. Capital formation is one of the most important factors for the economic development of a nation. Capital formation creates of strong capital asset base to the nation. This situation can stimulate the prosperity of a nation. Therefore we cannot ignore the role of the underwriters in the Capital Market. SEBI is the regulatory authority to monitor, guide, direct and review the activities of the underwriters. It issues guidelines, rules and regulations to all the intermediaries in the Capital Market from time to time.

8. Market Makers: Market Makers are associated with the stock exchanges. The market making system is very much popular in London, New York, and Chicago stock exchanges. In the New York stock exchange those who perform the basic market making function are known as ***"Specialist"***.

Their basic function is to provide the needed liquidity to a particular scrip. The specialists are known as *Market Maker*. They help in eliminating the temporary disparity between the supply and demand of a scrip. They help in maintaining a fair and orderly market. In India this function will be carried out by the over the counter Exchange of India (OTC) which has admitted dealers and has become operational. The market makers should register with the concerned stock exchange as specialist or market maker in one or more securities. They should maintain a price continuity and also to minimise the disparity between the demand and supply of a scrip. They provide other services to the investors such as Investment advice, order execution, and clearing. They also maintain strong research departments which analyse the performance of the major securities.

(c) Specialised Institutions

Financial services are meant for providing solution to various problem faced by the corporate sector. The provider of financial services remain in constant touch with the dynamic market. The financial markets are require to develop a specialised institutions to solve the financial problems of the corporate sector. These specialised institutions include *Acceptance houses, Discount Houses, Factors, Depositories, credit Rating agencies, venture capitals.* These institutions provide better solutions to the financial problems of the corporate sector. Acceptance Houses provide good solution to the corporate sector. Discount Houses is one of the financial intermediaries in the financial Markets. All the other specialised institutions render invaluable services to the corporate sector. Their presence in the market cannot be ignored.

(d) Regulatory Bodies

Regulation is the most important factor in any area of financial system. The Financial Markets are highly volatile and need a close observation by the Government. The Government of India watch the market affairs on daily basis through its nominee *SEBI*. The government regulates the financial system through various legal organs of the administration. The banking affairs are monitored by the ***RBI***. The corporate affairs are regulated by the company law board and Board for industrial and Financial Reconstruction. Therefore the regulatory authorities make the financial system to work more efficiently and perfectly.

Evolution of Financial Services in India

Financial service is one of the components of the Indian financial system. It is in the process of attaining full bloom. The financial services at present reached through a number of stages mentioned below.

(A) Initial Stage (1960-80)

(B) Second Stage (1980-90)

(C) Third stage (1990-2002)

(A) Initial Stage: Financial services at the initial stage existed between 1960 and 1980. In this period it introduced many innovative services such as Merchant banking, Insurance and leasing companies. merchant banking was unknown till 1960. The term merchant banking was used as an umbrella function. It provides a wide range of service. Its activities start from project appraisal to arranging funds from the fund suppliers. They provide service like project identifications, preparation of flexibility reports, prepares detailed project reports. It also made marketing financial, managerial and technical analyses. They also underwrote the public issues and helped in getting listed in the stock exchanges. Investment companies made their contribution in the initial stage of financial service. The UTI, LIC and GIC initiated to enter into this segment during this period. Leasing activities entered in the year of 1970. Initially leasing companies were engaged in equipment lease financing. Afterwards they have undertaken different kinds of leasing such as financial lease, operating lease and wet leasing. The No. of leasing concerns has been shot up during this period. The Initial stage of financial services was crucial period for Indian financial system.

(B) Second Stage: Financial services entered the second stage and it covered the period of *10 years approximately*. In this period it has introduced many innovative value added services such as O.T.C. share transfers, pledging of shares, mutual funds, factoring, discounting, venture capital and credit rating. These services were available in the western countries about 100 years back. Mutual funds provide major fund to the industry anywhere in the developed countries. The funds has been innovative in terms of their schemes. They provided better returns to the unit holders. Their management was transparent. The small investors welfare was secured in their hands. Their business goals were such that they created value for their investor. They have their own code of conduct. Credit rating was another important financial service which entered India during this stage. It built investor confidence in the capital market operation. It prevented mal practices in the capital market. Initially the credit rating is applied to debt instruments only. Afterwards the credit rating was applied to the commercial papers and fixed deposits. Another important financial service was introduced in this stage ***"Factoring"***. Factoring means collection of accounts receivables by a financial intermediary. A number of factoring institutions had entered into the capital market. They were Discount and Finance House of India. SBI factors, can bank factors venture capital finance entered in late 1980s. It was a highly specialised service operated by venture capital firms.

(C) Third Stage: The Third stage in financial services include the setting up of new institutions and instruments. This period started from post liberalisation. The depositories, the stock lending scheme online trading paperless trading, dematerialisation, book building aspects were introduced during this period. Depositories set up in the public sector and many financial institutions are finding this business more lucrative. The stock lending scheme approved by the Central government in 1997-98. The central government initiated steps for the setting up of a separate corporation to deal with trading of the ***Gilt bonds.*** It has also taken steps to popularise book building method to help both the investors and fund users. It had also initiated steps to introduce online trading in Bombay stock exchange and Delhi stock exchange. The computerisation in *NSE* acted as the falcrum for the development of financial services. These steps had given a fillip to paperless trading. Paperless trading saved the investors from the onslaught of brokers and jobbers. It also reduced tax evasion. SEBI had been the regulatory authority in the financial environment and issued guidelines to the Merchant bankers in relation to the capital adequacy ratio. These guidelines ensures the investor protection and created a differentiation in the market. Establishment of the SEBI was a path breaking development in terms of regulation growth and development of financial services. The efforts to revamp the companies act, Income tax act and other acts had led to the deliverance of effective financial services. The government had taken initiative steps to allow the foreign Institutional investors into the capital market. This situation had been more beneficial to the capital market. The government had also taken steps to bring down the taxes on the capital gains for the FIIs. The Mutual funds had been permitted to exercise voting power which ought to more strengthen. The Disinvestment of the public enterprises made by the central government was another realm of financial services. The financial firms has gained expertise in valuation financial and legal restructuring and making the public sector firms to be commercial in the market. Financial service firm had been mobilising resources from abroad to finance the corporate sector. They approached the *European Capital market.* The service firms learnt the expertise in raising of GDRs through global market in the digital economy. This was an excellent development in this sector. It required an understanding of raising funds abroad and also work together with world class level financial services institutions. The world standard organisations such as *Lehman brothers, Goldman Sachs, Merry Lynch and Morgan Stanley* etc., The global financial markets required a high talent excellent skill and good infrastructure to deal the affairs more effectively. It was very easy in Switzerland to approach the capital market which were more flexible in terms of procedures and expect lower interest rates. Hence the financial firms would have to change their approach from syndication to risk finance aspect. In this period new financial instruments were introduced in the market. The issue of new financial instruments related to maturity, risk and interest rate.

Financial Services and Problems

The financial services industry faces a tough competition from its global counter parts. The sector has to increase skills, to integrate itself with the rest of the world. The financial services industry faces a lot of problems constraining growth of the financial services as presented below.

(A) Lack of Skilled Personnel.

(B) Quality of service.

(C) Core competence.

(D) Fee and Fund based business.

(E) Technology.

(A) Lack of Skilled Personnel: The Indian financial services face a lot of problems. The financial service is involved with skill and talent. It is not like any other service. The availability of suitable personnel is the main constraint faced by the Indian financial system. It requires the right types of people at right place in corporate sector. The present financial service industry does not provide much salaries where the foreign financial firms offer. The public sector financial services industry is constrained by a number of restrictions imposed on salaries. Therefore, India is facing a manpower problem in finance area. But some of the organisation are making efforts to train the people in finance area specifically.

We cannot ignore the efforts made by the Hyderabad based ***Institute for certified Financial Analyst,*** *Indian Institute to Finance, New-Delhi, Institute for Financial Management Research, Chennai, National Institute of Financial Management, Faridabad.* All these institutions are conducting training programmes for Finance professionals. They conduct regular post graduate level courses in Finance area. Therefore, in future India does not face the availability of man power problem. There is a strong need to develop the Finance discipline in Academic side.

(B) Quality of Services: The survival of financial services depend upon the delivery of quality services and products at the right place, at the right price, and at the right time. The providers of financial services must use the application of the appropriate technology to process a large flow of information according to the needs of the client. The services will be provided on a fixed fee basis for various activities. The fee is decided by the regulator for rendering various services. The clients often complaints about the poor performance and high fee is charged by the service providers. The working pattern of the Merchant bankers has to be changed. The functioning of credit rating should build up the confidence in the market. The information in Finance has to be in the organised form. The data lies in crude stage, it must be gathered by taking much pains and be stratified according to the purpose. There is a strong need for conducting research in finance area. The quality of financial services will only be possible on the basis of Research activities. Research is the most important factor in developing innovative financial products and service. The financial services involves a rapid changes on day by day basis. Hence the quality of service must be improved and updated at every moment.

(C) Core Competence: Financial service is a dynamic activity and it must be provided by the providers with a great care and in depth analysis of the problem faced by the clients. They are ready to provide any service in the finance area. The providers can render the services to the needs of client companies. Some financial firms have often got involved in *Under trade practices* through giving unethical advise. The services must be in the form of cost control, cost reduction and review of process and procedures through activities.

(D) Fee and Fund Based: Financial services providers are working on the basis of either fee based or fund based activities. Some institutions provide services for fee basis. Mutual funds, credit Rating, merchant banking are the best examples for fee based services term lending, housing finance companies, venture capital, leasing companies are the examples of ***fund based services.*** They provide financial resources to their clients on interest basis. They charge the interest from their borrowers. Term lending institutions meet the long term funding needs of industries. Therefore providing funds to the corporate sector is known as *project financing*. Housing finance companies provide funds to the individuals for acquisition of house property. Venture capital provides funds to the new projects in the form of equity for innovative products. The providers of financial services either belong to fund based activities or fee based activities. Some firms involve in both the aspects.

(E) Technology: In the digital age the technology plays an important role in all aspects of the human life. Technology reduces the cost of production and stimulates the quality of the products. Technology enhances the abilities and growth of a particular sector. Lack of proper availability of technology has constrained the growth of the financial services industry in India for ex: The dealing of cheques in banks is still not developed. The physical presence is required for every transaction. The time taken to deliver the services is too long for all the transactions. The banks are now introducing **ATMs** to reduce the operating expenses and stimulating the profits.

Management of Risk in Financial Services

The financial services have introduced several new products and services. The financial markets have seen a number of bank and insurance companies failure, securities scans, and services. The industry is operating in a risky environment. The success of a financial service provides to a large extent depends on the manner which it manages the ***Risk.*** The business involves risk, without it there is no existence of business. Risk cannot be avoided. Risk is the integral part of the financial services industry. The financial services industry works with the financial claim. Financial claim is a promise to give a fixed amount under certain specified terms. All financial claims in general are risky. The financial claim affects the performance of the company that provides financial services. The risk in financial services industry is very high. The chances of default by the parties who sell the financial claims are very high. The default by the concerned parties may arise due to several reasons. The risk in financial services industry can be classified as follows:

(A) Internal Risk

(B) External Risk.

(A) Internal Risk

Internal risk means, if the finance company fails to receive the financial claim from the clients. It is also associated with changes in the interest rates in the market that reduces the value of existing financial claims. Therefore the internal risk may be described as failure of Accounts receivables by the finance company. Usually the financial companies may disburse the loans to different parties as a routine business activity, but they involve in high risk that affect the company as a whole. They often fails due to their own mistakes. There are several internal factors which contribute to the failure of the firms in the service industry. Some of the internal sources of risk faced by different financial services companies are presented below.

(1) Lending Institutions

(2) Stock broking service.

(3) Insurance service.

(4) Fee based service companies.

(5) Leasing and Hire purchase

(1) Lending Institutions: Lending institutions provide direct finance to the corporate sector for their long term nature of requirements. The lending institutions must be more careful while evaluating the loan application made by a client. A right evaluation can eliminate the half of the risk. The appraising officers of the finance company must take into all vital issues in consideration that affect the outcome of the project. The finance companies should follow a good system of appraisal and introduction of modern project appraisal techniques. The performance of finance companies depends upon the performance of a particular industry i.e. where these companies made disbursement to a specific industry, if that industry is affected or failed. Therefore a significant part of the loan portfolio turns ***bad*** and thus affects the performance.

(2) Stock Broking Services: Stock broking is one of the major financial services rendered by a specialised skilled and professional. It is a **fee** based service. This activity involves procuring the orders from the clients and delivering the documents to the clients. The brokers execute the orders which they receive from the individual investors. These transactions may raise the *bad debts.* The stock brokers have to face many problems in dealing the transactions. There are many ***fake*** documents in the market and if there is any mistake, the broker will have to take responsibility. Hence the stock broker must be in a position to take all the precautions while dealing with the various investors.

(3) Insurance Service: Insurance companies are also affected by the efficiency in evaluating the insurance proposal. The performance of insurance companies is also effected by over exposure in a particular industry or asset in a single proposal. If the Insurance company exceeds its limit to exposure. It reinsures the assets with some bigger insurance companies to share the risk the performance of the Insurance sector depends upon the efficient management of its treasury.

(4) Fee Based Service Companies: Financial services are categorised as fee based and fund based. Some institutions provide services on fee basis. They are mutual fund and merchant banking and exposed to several internal risks. The *Mutual funds* are working on the basis of mutual benefits to all the unit holders. The performance of any mutual fund directly depends on the ability of the fund manager. The fund manager should have strong base about the stock market and make investments accordingly. They are expected to study the market trend and make investment analysis exclusively for the use of his fund. *Merchant banking* is also one of the fee based service. He must handle the capital offering as per the various provisions of the ***SEBI.*** If the merchant banker fails he will attract severe punishment which includes suspension or cancellation of Registration ***credit Rating*** is also one of the fee based services. It involves in assessing the credit worthiness of the business concerns.

(5) Leasing and Hire Purchasing: The Leasing and Hire purchasing operates in a high risk segment. This business is highly competitive with too many players in the market. The corporate sector prefer lending institutions for its fund requirements because the leasing and hire purchasing companies relatively charge a high rate of interest. The cost of these sources of funding is high mainly due to their high cost borrowing and low level of leverage. The quality of the assessment of lease proposals assumes importance. The *Mismatching* of Assets and liabilities are the main problems of these companies.

(B) External Risk

External risk arises due to certain developments that take place outside the purview of the financial service company. The external sources of risk also vary for different services. The following are the external sources of risk applicable to various services.

(A) Direct financing Institutions.

(B) Fee based service companies.

(C) Leasing and Hire purchase companies.

(D) Insurance companies.

(E) Stock broking service.

The financial markets provide different types of loans. Generally commercial banks provide finance of short term nature. Term lending institutions provide finance for the long term funding needs of the industries. The performance of the direct lending institutions depend upon the quality of the credit. The evaluation of credit and investment play an important role in dealing with the external sources of risk. A bank may fail to honour the claims of the deposits holders if the ***Non-performing Assets*** of the bank are above its net worth. All these institutions risk depend upon their disbursed loan portfolios. Some financial service companies provide *fee based services* to the clients. They provide only a service and advice the clients regarding various financial problems. They find considerably reduces their risk of operations. The performance of these companies depend upon the quality of service offered by them to the customers. Merchant banking, mutual funds, credit Rating, securitisation, Merger and Acquisition corporate Restructuring are the best examples of fee based services. A change in the regulation of these companies will have impact on their operational performance ***Leasing and Hire purchase*** companies raise financial resources from the market through deposits and other means. They involve in lending to the industrial sector in the form of providing assets. They do not lend money directly to the industries. Their service is very close to the banking sector. The performance of these organisations depend upon the quality of the portfolio of leased assets. The ***Leasing company*** can technically take back the asset in the event of non-receipt of the lease rental but the resale value is quite very low when compared to the outstanding obligation. Another important external factor for risk associated with these companies are, that they invest their surplus money in stock market operations. As the security prices are affected by so many factors, so the security market prices have become the external risk to these companies. They are also affected by the frequent changes in the regulation. The RBI is the regulatory authority and has put rigid norms in raising the deposits from the public the performance of these companies also depend on their ability to attract the deposits from the public. *Insurance companies* are associated with risk regarding the assets of their clients. They collect the premium amount from the insurer in turn invest this amount in securities or lend to outsiders. Therefore they deal with the external environment. The insurance company may fail to honour its obligation if its investments have made turned useless. They are exposed to external problems such as *moral hazard and adverse selection* Moral hazard is the tendency of the insurer, because the party may use the asset in a proper way when they did not made insurance, otherwise if they got insurance of the asset, they will run that asset without any proper care. The adverse selection is the tendency of insuring the low quality asset. The price of insurance is same for all the assets but the owner of the assets that are in bad shape will find insurance more attractive and are more likely to insure the poor assets rather than *sound assets* stock broking service is one of the important financial services. They buy and sell securities on behalf of the clients. They work for a small amount of brokerage. They render the services for commission. Though their activity appears very simple but the risk from the external sources are very high. Their external source of risk is associated with two factors.

They are:

(a) Failure of other brokers in the market

(b) Failure to honour the commitment by the client.

Hence any change in the attitude of the above two parties will adversely effect the performance of stock broking service.

Types of Risk

Financial service is one of the element in the financial system. It is a highly skilled and talented assignment. It should be handled by a trained people only. It is not an ordinary service like others. It is associated with many risk factors. They face both Internal and external risks. The *Risk* always chased these services the providers of financial services must be always in proper way to reduce their level of risk. They must always take the steps for precautions otherwise they have to face the consequences. They are doing these assignments with the public money they may face various kinds of risks while they discharging their duties. The following different kinds of Risks are associated with them.

(a) Interest Rate Risk

(b) Market Risk

(c) Credit Risk

(d) Currency Risk

(e) Regulatory Risk

(f) Gap Risk.

(a) Interest Rate Risk: Interest rate risk is associated with the changes in market interest rates. It affects the firms which involve in fund based activities. The Interest rates are volatile and the financial service industry has to face the situation. The service providers are exposed to risk in their treasury operations, lending and mobilisation of financial resources the loan portfolio of banking and leasing companies is highly influenced by market interest rates. The fluctuations in the interest rates affects the profitability of the financial services companies by way of resource mobilisation. Therefore changes in the market interest rate is difficult to forecast. These firms have to face and manage the interest rate risk. The interest rates play a major role in the financial markets. It affects the different segments like *stock market, money market and foreign exchange market.* It is unavoidable and have to be managed accordingly. There are two ways involved in the management of interest rate risk. The interest rate risk can be done for each asset and liability exposed to interest rate risk. The second way is to select appropriate instrument to manage it.

(b) Market Risk: Financial services companies generally invest a part of the funds in securities. The investment is exposed to the market risk. The risk occurs on account of changes in the economy. The investment made in securities are also affected. But the firms can develop an efficient portfolio to reduce the risk arise. It could help them to reduce the unsystematic risk. The market risk is also known as *systematic risk.* It cannot be eliminated. It can be reduced only through derivative products. The investment companies, mutual funds and others offering the portfolio management services are mostly affected by this risk. The impact of this risk is limited to other financial service companies. It is the minimum risk which is exposed. It can be managed by the financial services company by switch over the funds from one market to another market to reduce the risk **For ex:** A mutual fund may shift some part of their investment from the stock market to debt market when they expect that the economy will under perform in a specified period.

(c) Credit Risk: Risk is an integral part of any business. The reward is directly proportional to the risk undertaken. The financial services firms such as banking leasing and hire purchasing etc., are involved in fund based activities. The credit risk is associated with fund based activities. It arises in evaluating the proposals for lending. The bad debts that arise during the recovery of loan are called as *credit risk.* The NPAs in banking sector are to be treated as credit risk. The credit rating institutions help to quantify the risk. There are several options in quantifying the risk. The firms can adopt any option to manage this risk. They allocate the fund according to the clients financial discipline. After disbursing the loan to the client, the finance company must get the information from the borrowers regarding NPAs: Non-performing Assets business affairs. It should also collect the information from the market intelligence system. The continuous observation make the way more sophistication in assessing the financial worthiness of a borrower the observation raises some doubts about the loan account and the action to be taken accordingly.

(d) Currency Risk: Currency risk is associated with **forex** market. Banks, financial institutions and money changers are generally affected by these sources of risk. The financial companies which deal in foreign exchange are exposed to this kind of risk. It arises because of changes in the currency value. The changes in currency value arise due to the fundamental economic growth of the two nations. The economic strength of the two countries depend upon the short run demand and supply gap. These firms usually hold foreign currencies and the *forex market* is volatile which will affect the profitability. It can be managed by selecting an appropriate hedging instrument.

(e) Regulatory Risk: The financial companies which have been categorised as fee and fund based concerns are required to work under various legal provisions. The Merchant banking companies and other service providers have to exercise due diligence in their business operations. These formalities may have to be submitted to the regulatory bodies such as *SEBI, RBI and CLB etc.,* For ex: Merchant bankers are required to submit the reports to the SEBI. The lead managers have to submit an application form is prescribed before the public or rights issue opens for subscription. Any failure by the financial service companies lead to cancellation or suspension of their registration this risk can be managed by bringing in more efficient professionals.

(f) Gap Risk: The gap risk is also known as *Asset liability gap risk.* It applies to fund based service companies. Usually the finance companies may procure the funds from the market. The external sources of finance play a major role in the fund based concerns. The duration of liability is an important factor which cannot be neglected while lending the money. If a finance concern gives a *5 year loan* against a deposit for two years. Therefore there will be a mismatch between asset and liability. If this situation exceeds a predetermined level it may lead to insolvency. This risk can be managed by coordinating approach which is known as ***Asset liability Management.*** It can also be managed by predicting interest rates.

Regulatory Framework for Financial Services

The economy will grow with a better financial system of a nation. The financial system should work on the basis of asset creation better credit flow to all the sectors and stimulating the per capita income of a nation. The asset creation is possible only with the efficient primary market the credit flow to all sectors in the function of banking institutions. The banking institutions allow the economy to expand more and more. The financial services industry channels the savings into productive way. It helps the economic activities to grow without any handles the importance of the financial services cannot be ignored in the ***digital economy.*** This sector is governed by strict rules and regulations. In a competitive market the services are required more efficiently and effectively. The financial firms often take high risk to maximise the return and thus susceptible to default. There will be a scope that can imperil the interest of the investors in this sector there will be a lot of scope for frauds mismanagement of funds, and scams. Therefore the regulations are in place to protect the Investor's rights. The regulatory frame work to this sector can be categorised in three forms.

(A) Structural Regulations

(B) Prudential Norms

(C) Investor Protection Regulations

(A) Structural Regulations: Financial service companies provide fee and fund based services to the clients. The regulations are meant for proper working environment by the companies. They control the activities, monitor and review the affairs of a concern. They impose strict rules and regulations to move in a right direction. The objective of these regulations is to provide and protect safety to the innocent investors. The regulation demarcs the lines between activities of financial institutions. The security and exchange Board of India *(SEBI)* insists that the merchant bankers and stock brokers to separate all their fund based activities. The regulations cover the internal management of financial institutions and other concerns in relation to capital adequacy, liquidity and solvency. The RBI is the regulatory authority in the banking sector.

(B) Prudential Norms: The development of an economy depend upon the efficient financial system. The efficiency of the financial system depends upon the strict rules and regulations imposed by the regulatory bodies. The objective of the prudential norm is to restrict the firms without adequate resources entering into a particular field. These norms could be framed for the smooth functioning of the industry.

(C) Investor's Protection Regulations: The main objective of all the regulatory agencies in the financial sector is to protect the interest of the investors. The innocent investor will be duped by inefficient financial companies. In India the investors are mostly cheated by the finance companies. *CRB capital, pennar paterson,* and other finance companies duped the investors. Crores of rupees are deposited by middle class families, low income group levels but their dreams are burnt by the ***financial parasites.*** Therefore the investors are the weakest participants of the financial markets, and need a strong protection from malpractice, fraud and scams. The regulatory agencies should step in to protect the interest of the investors. These regulations need larger disclosure of information.

The rules and regulations ensure the financial soundness and safety of the financial institutions. They maintain the integrity of the transmission mechanism and protection of clients of the financial services. They ensure to improve the efficiency of the financial companies and provide benefits to the investors and borrowers. At the same time the regulations should not block the development of the financial services industry. The financial services regulations can be divided into four categories.

(1) Regulations on Banking and financing services.

(2) Regulations on Insurance services.

(3) Regulations on Investment services.

(4) Regulations on Merchant banking and other services.

Regulation on Banking and Financing Services

Financial companies mobilised savings and lend the money to various clients. Accepting deposits and lending money are the two important activities of these kind of companies they help the capital formation in the nation. *Asset* creation is the most important element in the financial system. The government frames the policy matters relating to savings and lending but entrust the responsibility of monitoring them to the central bank. The central bank is the nerve centre of the Indian financial system. The ***RBI*** is the central bank and it is the nerve centre of the economy. It regulates all the Institutions which are associated with savings and lending. The role of RBI is to frame regulations for the smooth functioning of the financial institutions. It regulates commercial banks and *NBFCs.* Banking institutions in India are regulated by the RBI and the policy matters are framed by the central government. The ***RBI*** is empowered to develop a sound banking system in the country. It is the supreme authority in this sector. It is the licensing authority to permit the establishment of new bank or branch.

The banking regulation act was passed in *Feb. 1949.* The act was applicable to all the banking companies except to the cooperative banks. The objectives of this act was to develop a healthy and sound banking system in India. The important provisions of the banking regulation act were as follows:

(A) Definition of banking company

(B) Share capital

(C) Management

(D) Banking operations

(E) Powers of the RBI.

(A) Definition of Banking Company: The act defined banking company as one which is engaged in the accepting for the purpose of lending or investment of deposits of money from the public, repayable on demand or otherwise and withdrawal by cheque, draft, order or otherwise". The firms or companies or group of Individuals are banned to use the words *"bank" or "banking company".* The banks are empowered to undertake other banking activities like bill discounting.

(B) Share Capital: The banking regulation act lays down important provisions regarding the share capital of the banks. As per act the minimum paid up capital for an Indian banking company is ***Rs. 5 lakhs.*** The minimum paid up is Rs. *10 lakhs* where the bank has places of business in more than one state and situated in Bombay or Calcutta. They should maintain a reserve fund of not less than 20% of its profits. The subscribed share capital of the bank should not be less than **50%** of the authorised capital. The paid up capital should not be less than 50% of subscribed capital.

(C) Management: As per the banking regulation act, a bank cannot be run by a managing agent or by an insolvent person or who takes commission in the profits of the company or who is convicted of moral turpitude. The voting rights should be in proportion to the contribution of the paid up capital. A single shareholder has the maximum voting rights up to 5% of the total voting rights.

(D) Banking Operations: The act protects the interest of the depositors. It imposes certain regulations as the business operations of the banks.

(1) A bank cannot grant loans on the basis of security provided by its own shares.

(2) It cannot grant unsecured loans to any of its directors or to firms or private concern

(3) It cannot undertake direct or indirect trading

(4) It cannot form a subsidiary company.

(E) Powers of the RBI: The act provides adequate powers to the RBI for the smooth functioning of the banking sector in India. It controls and regulates the banks. It lays down that every bank should keep cash reserves at rate of **5%** of its demand deposits and 2% of its total deposits. Every bank should deposit with it not less than 20% of its total demand in the kind of cash, gold or in approved securities. It has the powers to make rules and regulations regarding the management affairs of the banks. The banking regulation act of 1949 and its subsequent amendments have to play an important role in ensuring the development of banking system in the country. The various provisions of the act is to protect the interest of the depositor.

The RBI effectively regulates the credit flow through monetary policy. It controls the amount available for credit by prescribing CRR and SLRs. The list of credit control techniques have been already discussed. The banking act covers all aspects of the banking business operations such as definition of banking, licensing, functioning capital and Reserve requirements and liquidity provision.

Non-Banking financial companies plays a significant role in the Indian financial system they broaden the range of financial services the efficiency of the emerging financial system basically based on the quality and range of the package of financial services which are largely provided by the ***NBFCs.*** They have recorded market growth in recent years. The mushroom growth of the NBFCs had caused many unhealthy developments in this segment of the financial system. After considering these moments, the government has taken steps to regulate this segment through the ***Banking Law Act 1963*** has been introduced to regulate the NBFCs. The RBI is the regulatory authority to this segment.

There are different kinds of NBFCs. They have recorded marked growth in terms of number of firms and their deposits. Therefore various number of firms and deposits. There are various categ... of such firms which are as follow

(A) Investment companies.

(B) Mutual benefit finance companies.

(C) Hire purchase finance companies.

(D) Loan companies.

(E) Equipment leasing companies.

(F) Residuary Non-banking finance company.

(G) Housing finance company.

(H) Misl. finance and Non-banking company.

The regulatory authorities have been assigned to frame the suitable policy measures to strengthen this segment, they are more competent and efficient to meet the growing competition on global basis. Hence the authorities have taken steps to appoint several committees from time to time to study an indepth study of these institutions and made suitable recommendations for the healthy growth of this segment. The suggestions and recommendations have been made by them in view of the present scenario. On the basis of these suggestions the regulatory authority framed the policy measures to strengthen this sector.

The RBI has the full control on this segment and involved in the policy framing and implementation of various schemes. The banking act delegates the powers to the RBI on the following affairs of the NBFCs.

(a) RBI has the powers of granting licenses to NBFCs.

(b) The NBFCs are required to submit their periodical statements to the RBI

(c) RBI has the authority to classify these companies which are eligible to mobilised funds from the public.

(d) It prescribes the horizons of the capital limits.

(e) NBFCs are required to maintain statutory reserve levels.

(f) It has the powers to determine the capital adequacy norms, accounting standards, provision for bad and doubtful debts.

(g) It has the powers to collect any information from the NBFCs relating to the working affairs.

(h) It has the powers to punish the NBFCs, if they fail to oblige the legal formalities.

(i) It has the power to cancel or suspend the registration of NBFCs.

The RBI act regulates various kinds of NBFCs under the provisions of ***Chapter III-B and Chapter III-C*** which are presented below.

Annexure

Chapter III B: The RBI act, 1934 empowers to regulate all the NBFCs in India. In this act chapter III B and III C dealt with entire gamut of operations of the NBFCs. The salient features of this chapter is presented for a thorough understanding of the legal provisions. The chapter contains the following provisions regarding NBFCs and financial institutions.

(A) Deposits.

(B) Financial Institutions.

(C) Non-Banking Financial Company.

(D) Repayment of Deposits.

A. Deposits

The term deposit has been defined to include any receipt of money by way of deposit or loan or in any other form. The following items such as certain receipts are excluded.

(i) amount received from a bank.

(ii) amount received from SFCs or any other FIs.

(iii) amount received in course of business by the way of security deposit, dealership deposit, earnest money deposit, advance against order for goods/properties/services.

(iv) Amount received from an individual/firm association relating to money lending.

(v) Amount received by way of subscription in respect of a chit.

B. Financial Institutions

Financial institutions means any non-banking/financial companies engaged in any of the following activities.

(i) Financial by way of loans, advances any activity except its own

(ii) Acquisition of shares/bonds/debentures/securities.

(iii) Hire purchase

(iv) Any class of Insurance. Stock broking and chits.

(v) Collection of money by way of subscriptions/sale of units/any other manner and their disbursement.

C. Non-Banking Financial Company (NBFC)

Means (i) a financial institution which is a company, (ii) a non-banking institution which is a company and which has its principle business the receiving of deposits under any scheme/arrangement/in any other manner or lending in any manner and (iii) such other non-banking institutions/class of institutions as the RBI with the prior approval of the Government and by notification in the official gazette may specify.

Registration and Net Owned Funds (NOFCs): With effect from January 1997, in order to commence (new company) carry on (existing company) the business of a Non-banking financial institution (NBFI), a NBFC must obtain a certificate of registration from the RBI. Moreover its minimum NOF (net owned funds) must be Rs 50 lakh/such other amount not exceeding Rs 200 lakh specified by the RBI. The NOFs means (a) paid-up capital and free reserves as per the latest balance sheet minus accumulated losses, if any, deferred revenue expenditure and other intangible assets (b) (i) less investments in share of subsidiaries/ companies in the same group/all other NBFCs and (ii) the book value of debentures/bonds/ outstanding loans and advances including hire – purchase and lease finance made to an deposits with. Subsidiaries/companies in the same group in excess of 10 per cent of (a) above.

An existing NBFC has to apply for registration within six months but it may continue to carry on business until a certificate is issued to it or rejection of application is communicated. Moreover such a company is allowed to attain the level of the minimum NOF within three years which may be extended by the RBI by another three years. Within 3 months of fulfilling the requirements of the minimum NOF, the NBFC must inform the RBI.

While considering an application for registration the RBI would consider that the NBFC fulfils the following conditions.

The NBFC is/would be in a position to pay its present/future depositors in full as and when their claims accrue:

Its affairs are not being/likely to be conducted in a manner detrimental to the interests of its present/future depositors:

The general character of the management/proposed management would not be prejudicial to the public interest/interest of the depositors:

It has adequate capital structure and earning prospects:

The public interest would be served by the grant of the certificate to commence/carry on business in India:

The grant of certificate would not be prejudicial to the operation/consolidation of the financial sector consistent with the monetary stability and economic growth considering such other relevant factors specified by the RBI.

Any other condition, fulfilment of which in the opinion of the RBI. Would be necessary to ensure that the commencement / carrying on business in India would not be prejudicial to the public interest / in interest of the depositors.

The RBI may impose conditions while granting registration. It may cancel a certificate of registration, of the NBFC.

(i) Ceases to carry on the business in India;

(ii) Has failed to comply with any condition subject to which the certificate was issued:

(iii) At any time fails to fulfil any of the above conditions which RBI considered while granting registration:

(iv) Fails to (a) comply with any directions issued by the RBI under the provisions relating to registration. (b) maintain accounts in accordance with the requirements of any law / direction / order issued by the RBI under these provisions and (c) submit / offer for inspection its books of accounts / other relevant documents when so demanded by an inspecting authority of the RBI:

(v) Has been prohibited from accepting deposits by an order of the RBI under those provisions which have been in force for a period of at least 3 months.

Maintenance of Assets: The NBFCs are required to invest in India in unencumbered approved securities at least 5 per cent or higher percentage as specified by the RBI from time to time, of the outstanding deposits at the close of business on the last working day of the second preceding quarter. The RBI may however. Specify different percentages of investment in respect of different classes of NBFCs. The approved securities mean securities of any state government/central government and bonds unconditionally guaranteed by them as regards the payment of interest as well as the repayment of principal. Included in unencumbered approved securities are approved securities lodged by the NBFCs with another institution for an advance / any other arrangement to the extent to which such securities have not been drawn against/ availed of/ encumbered in any manner. The basis of valuation of such securities would be cost or current market price. To ensure compliance of the maintenance of the percentage of assets, the NBFCs may be required to furnish a return in such form/ manner and for such periods as specified by the RBI.

In case the amount invested at the close of business on any day falls below the specified rate. The NBFC would have to pay to the RBI on the shortfall a penal interest at a rate of 3 per cent per annum above the bank rate, if the shortfall continues in the subsequent quarters, the rate of panel interest would be five per cent per annum above the bank rate. The penal interest must be paid within 14 days from the date of the issue/ serving of the notice by the RBI for the payment. Failing which the RBI can approach an appropriate court for a direction for payment. The certificate/ direction issued by the court would be enforceable like a decree in a suit. However, if the RBI is satisfied that the defaulting NBFC had sufficient cause for its failure. It may not demand the payment of the penal interest.

Reserve Fund: Every NBFC must create a reserve fund to which at least 20 per cent of its net profit must be transferred before the declaration of any dividend. The reserve fund can be used/ appropriated only for purpose specified by the RBI from time to time. Every appropriation should be reported to it within 21 days from the date of withdrawal. The RBI for sufficient cause in any particular case may extend the period or condone any delay. The central government may, on the recommendation of the RBI, exempt by an order in writing any NBFC for a specified period from the above requirements, having regard to the adequacy of the paid-up capital and reserves in relation to deposit liabilities. But such exemption can be granted only if the reserve fund together with the share premium account of the NBFC is not less than its paid-up capital.

Power of Regulation/Prohibitions: The RBI can by general/ special order regulate of prohibit the issue by any non-Banking institutions (NBI) the issue of any prospectus or advertisement soliciting deposits of money from the public and specify conditions subject to which they can be issued.

With effect from January 1997, in public interest or to regulate the financial system/ to prevent the affairs of a NBFC being conducted in a manner detrimental to the interests of the depositors/ prejudicial to the interest of the company. The RBI can determine policy and give directions to all/ any or NBFCs relating to (a) income recognition, accounting standards, provisioning for bad and doubtful debts, capital adequency based on risk weights for assets and credit conversion factors for off balance sheet items (b) deployments of funds the NBFCs would be bound to follow the policy determined/ directions issued. In addition the RBI may give directions to NBFC(s) in particular so as to ;

The purpose for which advances/ other fund based/ non-based accommodation may not be made:

The maximum amount of advances/ other financial accommodation/ investment in shares/ other securities having regard to the paid-up capital, reserves and deposits of the NBFC and other relevant considerations may be made by the NBFC(s).

Power to Collect Information from NBIs: The RBI can issue direction to NBIs to furnish information relating to/ connected with deposits. The information may relate to aspects such as amount of deposits. Its period and purpose, rates of interest and other terms and conditions on which deposits are received. It may also issue directions to NBIs in respect on these matters. Non compliance of these directions may lead to the prohibition of acceptance of deposits by the NBI. Any NBI can also be required to furnish to depositors a copy of its balance sheet profit and loss account or other annual accounts.

Power to Call for Information from FIs and Issue Directions: To regulate the credit system. The RBI can ask for information from FIs relating to their business as well as issue directions for the conduct of their business. The information sought may cover matters such a paid-up capital, reserves or other liabilities. Investments persons to/ purpose and periods for which finance provided terms and conditions including rate of interest etc while issuing direction RBI has to give due regard to the conditions in which and the objects for which the FI has been established. Its statutory responsibilities and the effect its business would have on trends in the money and capital market.

Duties of Auditors (NBI): It is mandatory for every NBI to furnish the statements/ information/ particulars called for and comply with any direction given by the RBI. The auditors of a NBI have an obligation to inquire into the status of compliance with these requirements relating to deposits and report to the RBI. With effect from January 1997, in public interest/ in the interest of the depositors or for the purpose of proper assessment of the books of accounts, the RBI may issue directions to NBFC(s)/their auditors relating to balance sheet. Profit and loss accounts, disclosure of liabilities in the books of accounts and any related matter. The auditors should include in his statutory report under the companies Act, the contents of the report submitted to the RBI regarding the compliance status. With effect from January 1997, the RBI can, in public interest/ in the interest of the NBFC(s)/depositors. Order for a special audit of the accounts in relation to any specified transactions/ period(s). It can also appoint an auditor(s) to conduct the special audit who would report to it. The remuneration of the auditors fixed by the RBI having regard to the nature and volume of work involved and the expenses of incidental to the audit would be done by the concerned NBFC. An NBFC which isolates any of the provisions/ fails to comply with any directions(s) may be prohibited from accepting any deposit. If necessary in public interest/ in the interest of the depositors the RBI may further direct such a company not be sell/ transfer/ create charge or mortgage or deal in any manner with its properties/ assets for a period not exceeding 6 months from the date of the order without its prior written permission.

On being satisfied that the NBFC (a) is unable to pay its debt, i.e., has refused failed to meet within 5 days any lawful demand, (b) has been disqualified to carry on business, (c) has been prohibited from receiving any deposit by order in force for not less than 3 months. (d) its continuance is detrimental to public interest/ in the interest of the deposition the RBI may file an application under the companies Act for its winding-up, a copy of which must be sent to the Registrar of companies. All the provisions of the companies Act would be applicable to the winding up process.

Inspection: The RBI has powers of inspection by its officers/ employees or any other person (inspecting authority) of any NBI/FI (a) for purpose of verifying the correctness/completeness of any statement/information/particular furnished to it or obtaining any information/particulars which the NBI/FI has failed to furnished and (b) if it is necessary or expedient to inspect that NBI/FI. The management/directors/officers/employees of the NBI/FI have to produce all books of accounts/documents and furnish all information/statements relating to its business to the inspection authority which may also examine them on oath.

Soliciting Deposits, Disclosure of Information and Exemption: Any person is not allowed to solicit deposit on behalf of NBFC by publishing a prospectus or advertisement or in any other manner unless he is authorised in writing and the advertisement/prospectus conforms to the RBI stipulations and other provisions of law.

With effect from January 1977, any information relating to a NBFC contained in any statement/return submitted by it/obtained through audit/inspection by the RBI would be treated confidential and would not be disclosed. This restriction, however, does not apply to:

Disclosure of information submitted by a NBFC with the previous permission of the RBI publication by RBI in public interest of any information collected by it in a consolidated form without disclosing the name of the NBFC or its borrowers;

Disclosure/publication by a NBFC/RBI of any such information to another NBFC or in accordance with practice and usage customary amongst such companies or as permitted/required under any other law.

However, in public interest, in the interest of the depositors/NBFC, or to prevent the affairs of the NBFC being conducted in a manner detrimental to the interest of the depositors. The RBI may on its own or on request furnishes/communicates any information relating to the conduct of business of a

NBFC to authority can compel it to produce/give inspection of any statement/other material obtained by it from the NBFCs.

The RBI is empowered to exempt NBIs/NBFCs, from the application of any/all provision(s) either generally on for specified period subject to any condition/limitations/restrictions imposed by it.

D. Repayment of Deposit

These provisions override all other laws in force. With effect from January, 1977, deposits accepted by NBFCs should be repaid in accordance with the relevant terms and conditions or renewed. If a NBFC fails to repay any deposit the company law board (CLB) is empowered to order repayment of deposit immediately/within a specified time and subject to the specified conditions. The CLB would have to satisfy itself either on its own motion or an application of the depositor(s) that it is necessary to do so to safeguard the interests of the company/depositors or in public interest.

The depositor(s) can nominate one person to whom in the event of his/their death, the deposit money would be returned by the NBFI. The nominee depositor would become entitled to all the rights of the depositor(s) unless the nomination is varied/cancelled in the prescribed manner, if the nominee is a minor, the depositor(s) can appoint any person to receive the amount of deposit in the event of his death during the monitarily of the nominee the payment to the nominee would constitute a full discharged to the NBFI of its liability in respect of the deposit. The NBFI would neither receive any notice of claim of any person other than those in whose name(s) a deposit is held nor would it be bound by any such notice even though expressly given to it. However, it would have to take note of any decree/order/certificate/other authority from a court of competent Jurisdiction relating to such deposit produced before it.

Penalties: If in any prospectus/advertisement inviting deposit from the public whoever wilfully makes a false statement in any material particular knowing it to be false or wilfully omits to make a material statement, would be punishable with imprisonment for a term up to three years and would also be liable to a fine, failure by a person to produce any book/account/other document or to furnish any statement/information/particulars is punishable with fine up to Rs. 2000 in respect of cash offence and persistence in such failure or refusal with further fine extending to Rs. 100 for every day after the first during which the offence continues.

With effect from January 1977. The penalties for contravention of the provisions of the RBI Act are as listed below.

Relating to the requirement of registration and net owned funds of NBF(s) (Section 451 A). Imprisonment for a term of not less than one year but may extend up to five years, and fine of not less than Rs. one lakh which may extend to Rs. 5 lakh.

Failure of auditors to comply with any direction/order of the RBI (Section 45 MA) a fine not exceeding Rs. 5,000.

Non-compliance with any order of the company law board relating to repayment of deposit (Section 45 QA) imprisonment for a term of up to three years and a fine of not less than Rs. 50 for every day during which non-compliance conditions, if any person. Other than an auditor, receives any deposit in contravention of, or fails to comply with any direction given/order made by RBI under chapter III B he can be punished with imprisonment up to three years and a fine up to a maximum of twice the amount of deposit received.

In case of issue of any prospectus/advertisement by an unauthorised person or violation of orders pertaining to condition subject to which any prospectus/advertisement can be issued, the penalty. Would be imprisonment extending to three years and a fine which may extend to twice the amount of deposit called for.

Power of RBI to Impose Fine: Where the above contravention/defaults are committed by a NBFC, the RBI is authorised with effect from January 1997, to impose.

A penalty not exceeding Rs. 5,000, where the contravention relates to the requirement of registration and net owned funds or receipt of any deposit/compliance with any direction given/order made a penalty of Rs 5 lakh or twice the amount involved in such contravention/default in case of continuation of the violation, a further penalty up to Rs. 25,000 for every day, after the first during which the default continues the penalty imposed by the RBI is payable within 30 days from the date on which the notice demanding payment is served on the NBFC. In the event of non payment, the RBI may obtain a direction from a court specifying in a certificate the sum payable by the NBFC. The certificate would be enforceable in the same manner as if it were a decree made by the court in a civil suit.

Provisions of Chapter III-C

Subject to the provisions of chapter III-B, non-corporate are not permitted to accept deposits after April 1, 1997. However individual can accept deposits from (1) relatives (2) any other individual for his personal use but not for lending or business purposes. The non-corporate entities which hold deposits should repay it immediately after such deposit becomes due for repayment or within two years from the date of such commencement whichever is earlier. The non corporate entities are prohibited from issuing/causing to be issued any advertisement in any form for soliciting deposit.

If certain documents relating to acceptance of deposits in contravention of the requirements are secreted in any place, a court on application by an authorised officer of RBI/state government may issue a warrant to search for such documents. Such warrants would have the same effect as one issued under the code of criminal procedure.

If a person contravances any of the above provisions he would be punishable with imprisonment for a term which may extend to two years or with a fine up to twice the amount of deposit received or Rs. 2,000 whichever is more or with both. Generally, the imprisonment and the fine would not be less than one year and Rs. 1,000 respectively. A fine exceeding Rs. 2,000 may be imposed in special circumstances.

RBI Acceptance of Public Deposits Directions. In pursuance of its power under the provisions of chapters III B and C, the RBI has issued directions to regulate NBIs/FIs. These directions contain provisions regulating amount/period of deposit, rates of interest, brokerage and so on. They also exempt from their purview certain types of borrowing/amounts received by these entities. The direction issued by the RBI so far are; (i) NBFC, directions 1997. (ii) MNBCs Directions, 1977 and (iii) BNBCs directions 1987. They also pertain to advertisement namely, NBFCs/MNBCs/RNBCs advertisement Rules 1977. In public interest and the regulate credit system to the advantage of the country, in exercise of the powers conferred by section 4SJ/K/L/MA of the amended RBI Act, the RBI issued in place of NBFC Directions, 1977 NBFCs acceptance of public deposits (RBI) Directions, 1998.

Scope and Meaning of NBFCs/MNBCs/RNBCs Meaning of NBFCs

The direction apply to a NBFC which is define to include only the non-banking institution which is any hire purchase finance. Investment loan or mutual benefit financial company and an equipment leasing company but excludes an insurance/stock exchange stock broking company/merchant banking company. They are also not applicable to such NBFCs which do not accept/hold public deposits. They have to pass a resolution in a meeting of the board of Directors within 30 days of the commencement of the financial year to the effect that they have neither accepted nor would accept any public deposit during the year. Investment companies which have a required shares/securities of their own group/holding/subsidiary companies only of not less than 90 per cent of their total assets. Do not trade in these shares/securities and do not accept/hold public deposits are also exempt from these directions.

For this purpose their Board of Directors have to pass a resolution within 30 days of the commencement of each financial year to this effect.

The RBI can grant, to avoid any hardship/for any just and sufficient reason extension of time to comply with or exempt any NBFC/class of NBFCs from all or any these directions either generally or for any specified period subject to such conditions as it may impose.

The term company refers to public/private Indian/foreign company. The NBFCs for the purpose of these directions, are classified into five categories.

Equipment Leasing Company (ELC) Hire-Purchase Finance Company (HPFC): Means any company which is a financial institution carrying on as its principal business the activity of leasing of equipment.

Is a company which is financial institutions carrying on its principal business hire-purchase transactions.

Investment Company (IC): Means a company which is a financial institution carrying on as its principal business the acquisition of securities.

Loan Company (LC): Means any company which is a financial institutions carrying on as its principal business the providing of finance whether by making loans or advance of otherwise for any activity other than its own.

Mutual Benefits Financial Company (MBFC) is a company which is a financial institution and which is notified by the central Government under section 620-A of the companies Act, 1956.

The question as to whether a company is a financial institution or not would be decided by the RBI in consultation with the government. Moreover, the question as to whether a financial institution is a company in any of the foregoing five categories would be decided by the RBI having regard to the principal business of the company and other relevant factors. The principal business of a financial company engaged both in hire-purchase financing and equipment leasing activities will be decided by the RBI after taking together the volume of both types of business and other related factors. In order to be classified as ELC/HPFC, a NBFC should have not less than 60 per cent of its assets and derive not less than 60 per cent of its income from equipment leasing and hire purchase activities taken together. The audited balance sheet at the NBFCs as on reclassification, of an NBFC in to appropriate category till then the norm of 51 per cent lease and hire-purchase assets and one-third of the income out of the two activities would continue.

All new NBFCs incorporated after January 9, 1977 will be provisionally classified as loan or investment companies for a period of one year. The classification will be reviewed on the basis of their asset/income pattern as disclosed in their balance sheet/profit and loss accounts and other related aspects. The existing NBFCs/those which remain unclassified will be classified on the basis of their principal activity as evidenced from their financial statements into various categories such as leasing/hire-purchase/loan/investment/MNBCs/RNBCs. Only such companies as have been specifically notified under section 620-A of the companies Act by the government will be classified as nidhi companies. The NBFCs which have been incorporated with the intention of function as Nidhi will be classified as loan companies and the directions applicable to loan companies will be made applicable to them till such modification.

Meaning of MBFCs: A MBFC means a company or a financial institutions carrying on all or any of the following types of business.

(a) Collection of money in one lump sum/instalments by way of (i) contribution/subscription (ii) sale of units/certificates/other instruments. (iii) in any other manner, (iv) as membership/admission fee, (v) service charges to/or in respect of any saving, mutual benefits, thrift or any other scheme/arrangement and utilization of the collected money or the income accruing from investment for all/any of the following purposes;

(b) Manage/conduct/supervise transaction/arrangement relating to an agreement with subscribers, every one of whom subscribes a certain sum in instalments over a definite period and is entitled to prize amount on the basis of draw of lots or by auction/tender etc.

(c) Conduct any other form of chit/kuri.

(d) Undertake/carry on/engage in/execute any other business similar to those referred to above.

Residuary Non-Banking Finance Companies (RNBCs): The RBI directions, 1987 define RBNCs as companies which are non banking institutions receiving deposits under any scheme/arrangement in one lump sum/instalments by way of contribution/subscriptions or by sale of units/certificate/other instruments or in any other manner. The NBFCs and MNBCs are excluded from the category of RNBCs. In other words, all non-banking companies other than NBFCs and MNBCs fall into the category of RNBCs.

Acceptance of Public Deposits

The directions regulate acceptance of public deposits as defined under section 451 (bb) of the RBI Act excluding the following:

Received from or guaranteed by central/state government, local authority, foreign government/citizen, authority, person;

Received from IDBI/LIC/GIC/SIDBI/UTI/NABARD/electricity Boards/TITC/NIDC/ICICI/IFCI /IIBI/STC/REC/MMTC/SIDCs/ADB/IFC any institution specified by the RBI. Received from any other company.

Received by way of subscription of shares/stocks/bonds/debentures, or by way of calls advance of shares;

Received from directors/sharesholders provided the amount is not given out of borrowed/acquired funds from others;

Raised by issue of convertible bonds/secured debentures not exceeding the market value of the security; and

Brought by way of unsecured loan in pursuance of stipulations of lending public financial institutions such as SFCs, banks, GIC, those specified by the companies Act (section 4-A) by promoters or their relatives but not from friends/business associates till the repayment of the institutional loans.

Restrictions on Mutual Benefit Financial Companies (MBFC)

Such companies can accept/renew deposits only from their share holders provided they are not in the nature of current account deposits. However, they cannot issue advertisement in any form and in any media for inviting deposits from them. They are also not permitted to pay any brokerage/commission/incentive or any other benefit to any person for collecting deposits. The other provision of these directions are not applicable to MBFCs with the exception of the ceiling on the rate of interest on deposits (specified subsequently).

Restrictions on Non-Banking Financial Companies (NBFCs)

Minimum credit rating the NBFCs which have a minimum net owned funds (NOF) of Rupees twenty five lakh can accept public deposits, provided they obtain minimum investment grade on other specified credit rating for their fixed deposits from one of the approved rating agencies at least once a year. A copy of the rating must be sent to the RBI along with the return a prudential norms. The RBI must also be inform in writing within 15 days of the up grading/downgrading of the ratings, if any. The stipulated minimum credit rating from the various credit rating agencies: with effect from January 31, 1998 are as specified below.

	Credit Rating Agency	*Minimum Rating*
1.	Credit rating information services of India Ltd. (CRISIL)	FA-(FA Minus)
2.	Investment Information and credit Rating Agency of India Ltd. (ICRA)	MA-(MA Minus)
3.	Credit Analysis & Research Ltd. (CARE)	CARE BBB (FD)
4.	Duffs phelps credit Rating India (p) Ltd. (DCR India)	Ind BBB-(BBB Minus)

Period of Deposits: The NBFCs cannot accept deposits payable on demand they can accept/renew deposits for a minimum period of 12 months to a maximum period of 60 months.

Ceiling on Quantum of Deposits: ELCs/HPFCs with a minimum of Rs. 25 lakh having a rating of 'A' and above but less than "AA" and complying with the prescribed prudential norms can accept /renew deposits up to a maximum of 1.5 times of their NOFs. Net owned funds mean (a) paid-up capital and free reserves as per the latest balance sheet including the paid-up reference shares which are compulsorily converted into equity minus accumulated losses. If any deferred revenue expenditure and other intangible assets (b) (i) less investments in shares of subsidiary/group companies/all other NBFCs and (ii) the book value of outstanding loans and advance including hire-purchase/base finance made to, and deposits with, subsidiaries/group companies in excess of 10 per cent of (a) above. Free reserves are the aggregate of balance in the share premium account. Capital and debenture redemption reserves and any other reserves shown/published in the balance sheet and created through an allocation of profiles not being a reserve created for repayment of any future liability or for depreciation in any asset or for bad debts or reserves created by revaluation of assets. The ceilings on such companies having a rating of AA and above but less than AAA and AAA respectively are 2.5 times and four times their NOFs. The ElCs and HPFC having rating of minimum investment grade, i.e. below A can also access public deposits up to a maximum of one-half of their NOF.

ICs and LCs the restrictions on the maximum amount deposits for those complying with prudential norms are:

Having a rating of A and above but less than AA, one half of NOFs:

Having a rating of AA and above but less than AAA, equal to NOFs: and

Having a rating of not less than AAA twice the NOFs.

In case of downgrading of the credit rating to any lower level all NBFCs must immediately stop accepting deposit/renewing existing deposits report the portion within 15 days to RBI and must reduce the amount of excess public deposits within a period of one year or such further period as may be extended by the RBI. Similarly, all NBFCs which hold deposits in excess of the appropriate level/unwarranted by the credit rating as on January 1998 cannot accept deposits/renew existing deposits and have to repay one-third of the excess public deposit by the end of December every year so that the entire excess deposit is repaid/regularised in three years till December 31, 2000. During the 3-year period, the ELCs/HPFCs which are rated investment grade or above and LCs/ ICs which have rating of A and above are allowed to accept/renew deposits subject to the stipulation of excess deposit by one-third each year. The ELCs/HPFCs which are unrated or rated below minimum investment grade and LCs/ICs which are unrated or rated below the specified grade of A however are allowed only to renew the maturing public deposits and not to accept fresh public deposits.

Ceiling on the Rate of Investments: There is a ceiling of 16 per cent per annum on the rate of interest on deposits with effect from January 2, 1998. It may be paid on compounded at rests not shorter than monthly rests.

Payment of Brokerage: The permissible brokerage commission, incentive or any other benefit on deposits with all NBFCs is two per cent of the deposit. The expenses by way of reimbursement on the basis of related vouchers/bills produced up to 0.5 per cent of the deposits are also permitted.

Renewal of Deposits: The NBFCs can permit existing depositors to renew their deposits before maturity to avail of the benefit of higher rate of interest provided.

(1) The deposit is renewed in accordance with other provisions of these directions and for a longer duration than the remaining period of the original contract and

(2) The interest on the expired period of the deposit is reduced by one per cent from the rate which the NBFC would have ordinarily paid had the deposit been accepted for the period for which it has run, any interest paid earlier in excess of such reduced rate is recovered/adjusted. In this context, depositor means any person who has made a deposit with a company or a heir. Legal representative administrator or assignee of the depositor.

Payment of Interest on Overdue Deposits

The directions permit the NBFCs to pay interest at their discretion, on overdue public deposits/or a portion of a from the date of maturity if:

The total amount/part of the over due deposit is renewed from the date of maturity till some future date according to other provisions of these directions and

The interest should be at appropriate rate operative on the date of maturity of such overdue deposits which would be payable only on the amount of the renewed deposits.

If the NBFC fails to repay the deposit along with interest on maturity on the claim made by the depositor. It would be liable to pay interest from the date of claim till the date of repayment at the rate as applicable to the deposit.

Joint Deposits: Deposits may be accepted by the NBFCs in joint names with/without any of the classes, i.e., either on survivor number one or survivor(s), any one or survivor(s).

Particulars in Application Forms: All NBFCs are required to accept/renew deposits only on a written application form to be supplied by them to the depositors. The form should contain all particulars specified in the NBFCs/MNBCs advertisement Rules, 1977 which are summarised in Appendix 1-B. After January 2 1998 the application form should also contain the specific category of the deposits, i.e. share-holder/director/promoter/member of public with effect from the same date, the directions specify the inclusion of the following additional information in them:

(1) The credit rating assigned for the fixed deposits and the name of the credit rating agency.

(2) In case of non-repayment of the deposit/a part as per the terms and condition of such deposit, the depositor may approach the Eastern/Western/Northern/Southern Bench of the Company Law Board (specify full address) under whose Jurisdiction the registered office of the NBFC is located.

(3) In case of any deficiency of the NBFC is servicing its deposits, the depositor may approach the national/state/District Level Consumer Research forum for relief.

(4) A statement that the financial position of the NBFC as disclosed and the declarations made in the application form are true and correct and the NBFC and its board of directors are responsible for their correctness and veracity.

(5) The financial activities of the NBFC are regulated by the RBI. It must however be distinctly understood that the RBI does not undertake any responsibility for the financial soundness or for the

correctness of any of the statements or the representations made or opinions expressed and for repayment of deposit/discharge of liabilities by the NBFC.

(6) At the end of application form but before the signature of the depositor, the following verification clause by the depositor should be appended "I have gone through the financial and other statements/particulars/declarations made/furnished by the NBFC and after careful consideration I am making the deposit with the NBFC at my own risk and volition."

Advertisement and Statement in Lieu of Advertisement

All NBFCs have to mandatorily comply with the provisions of the NBFCs/MNBCs Advertisement Rules, 1977. A specimen of these is given in Appendix 1-B. They also should specify in every advertisement the following.

(i) Actual rate of return by way of interest premium bonus, other advantages to the depositors.

(ii) Mode of repayment of deposit.

(iii) Maturity period of deposit.

(iv) Interest payable on deposit.

(v) Rate of interest payable on pre-mature withdrawal of the deposit.

(vi) Terms and conditions for renewal of deposits; and

(vii) Any other special features relating to the terms and conditions for acceptance/renewal of deposits.

Where a NBFC intends to accept deposits without inviting such deposits. It has to file a statement in lieu of advertisement with the RBI containing all the particulars specified above and duly signed in the specified manner. Such a statement is valid for six months. Fresh statements would have to be delivered in each succeeding year before accepting public deposit in that financial year.

Repayment of Deposits: The directions do not permit premature withdrawal of deposits within three months from the date of acceptance. The NBFCs are required to pay interest on withdrawal before maturity at the request of the depositors at specified rates, namely, **(i)** no interest on withdrawals between three and six months **(ii)** not more than 10 per cent per annum between 6 and 12 months and **(iii)** one per cent less than the contracted rate on withdrawals after 12 months but before maturity. In the case of MNBCs the interest on such withdrawals is nil between 3-6 months and 1 per cent less than the contracted rate after six months but before maturity. The RNBCs can deduct 2 per cent from the rate which they would have normally paid to the depositors up on maturity, on withdrawal after one year but before the expiry of the period of deposit. However, in the event of death of a depositor, the deposit can be repaid prematurely to the surviving depositor (s) in the case of joint holding with survivor clause, or to the nominee or to legal heirs with interest at the contracted rate up to the date of repayment, Moreover loan can be granted to a depositor after the expiry of three months from the date of deposit at a rate of interest 2 per cent above the contracted rate in the deposit by a NBFC up to 75 per cent of the amount of deposit and up to 70 per cent by a MNBC.

Deposit Receipts: All NBFCs/MNBCs/RNBCs have to furnish to the depositors/Joint depositors or their agents a receipt of the deposit stating the date of deposit, name of the depositor (s) the amount of deposit (in words and figures) rate of interest and date of Maturity. It must be signed by an officer who can act on behalf of the company in this regard.

Register of Deposits: All NBFCs/MNBCs/RNBCs have to keep register (s) of deposits containing cash depositor's particulars detailed of follows:

(a) Name and address.

(b) Date and amount of each deposit.

(c) Duration and due date of each deposit.

(d) Date and amount of accrued interest/premium on each deposit.

(e) Date of claim made by the depositor.

(f) Date and amount of each repayment of principal/interest/premium.

(g) Reasons for delay in repayment beyond five working days.

(h) Any other particulars relating to the deposit.

The register must be preserved in good order for least eight years following the financial year in which the latest entry is made of the repayment/renewal of any deposit of which particulars are contained in the register.

Special Provisions

Information to be Included in the Board's Report: In every report of the board of directors under section 217 of the Companies Act the following particulars or information must be included.

(i) The total number of accounts of public deposit of the NBFC which have not been claimed by the depositors or not paid by the NBFC after the date on which the deposit became due for repayment; and

(ii) The total amounts due to such accounts remaining unclaimed or unpaid beyond the due dates.

These particulars or information should be furnished with reference to the position as on the last day of the financial year to which the report relates and if the amounts remaining unclaimed or undisbursed exceed in the aggregate a sum of rupees five lakh. The report should also contain a statement on the steps taken or proposed to be taken by the Board of Directors for the repayment of the remaining unclaimed or undisbursed amounts due to the depositors.

Safe Custody of Approved Securities: All NBFCs have to designate one of the scheduled commercial banks as its designated banker in the place where their registered offices are situated intimate in writing to the Regional office of the RBI under whose Jurisdiction the registered office is situated, and entrust to such bank the unencumbered approved securities required to be maintained by it in pursuance to section 451 B of the RBI Act. However a NBFC can entrust these securities to its designated banker at a place other than the place at which it registered office is located or keep in the form of constituent's Subsidiary General Account which its designated scheduled commercial Bank with the prior approval in writing of Regional office to the RBI under whose Jurisdiction its registered office is situated.

The securities should contain to be entrusted to such designated bank for the benefit of the depositors and cannot be withdrawn or encashed or otherwise dealt with by the NBFC except for repayment of the depositors. But it may withdraw a portion of such securities proportionate to the reduction of its public deposits duly certified to that effect by its auditor, it may substitute securities by entrusting substitute securities of equal value to the designated bank before such withdrawal.

Maintenance of Liquid Assets: Under section 451 B, the RBI has specified that NBFCs holding public deposits should maintain minimum liquid assets in the form of unencumbered approved securities at 12.5 per cent and 15 per cent of public deposits with effect from April 1, 1998 and April 1, 1999 respectively.

In the case of RNBCs, a sum not less than the aggregate amount of their liabilities to the depositors is to be held by them as specified investment. The RNBC are required to submit a certificate from an auditor to this effect every six months, i.e., on June 30 and December 31. The aggregate amount of liabilities mean total deposits received together with interest/premium/bonus, etc., accrued on the amount of deposits according to the terms of the contract. The directions stipulate the RNBCs should deploy their funds in such a way that of their aggregate liabilities.

(i) Not less than 10 per cent is in fixed deposits in public sector bank which can be withdrawn only for repayment of deposits.

(ii) Not less than 70 per cent is held in the form of unencumbered approved securities valued at market value, of which not less than 10 per cent is in securities of Central/State Government/Government guaranteed bonds and

(iii) Not more than 20 per cent or ten times the net owned funds of the RNBC, whichever is lower, is in other safe investments approved by the Board of Directors.

Employees Security Deposit: All NBFCs receiving any amount in the ordinary course of their business security deposit from any of their employees for due performance of their duties should keep such amount in an account with a scheduled commercial bank or in the post office in the joint names of the employee and the NBFC on the conditions that the amount would not be withdrawn without the consent in writing of the employee, and it is repayable to the employee along with interest payable on such deposit account unless such amount or any part is liable to be appropriated by the NBFC for the failure on the part of the employee for due performance of his duties.

Submission of Accounts: All NBFCs accepting/holding public deposits have to deliver to the RBI at the regional office of the Department of non-banking supervision within whose Jurisdiction their registered office are located, an audited balance sheet as on the last date of each financial year and an audited profit and loss account in respect of that year as passed by the company in general meeting, together with a copy of the report of the Board of Directors within fifteen days of such meeting as also a copy of the report and the notes on accounts furnished by its auditor.

Provisions of Submitting Auditor's Certificate: All NBFCs holding accepting public deposits are required to furnish to the RBI along with a copy of the audited balance sheet a copy of the auditor's report to the Board of Directors and a certificate from its auditor, to the effect that the full liabilities to the depositors of the company, including interest payable are properly reflected in the balance sheet, and that the company is in a position to meet the amount of such liabilities to the depositors.

Returns to be Submitted to the RBI: The NBFCs holding/accepting public deposits much submit to the RBI a return furnishing the information specified in the first schedule with reference to its financial position as on the specified date. They should also within one month from the occurrence of any change in the following matters intimate to the RBI.

(i) The complete postal address, telephone number(s) and fax number(s) of the registered/corporate office.

(ii) The names and residential address of the directors of the company.

(iii) The names and the official designations of its principal officers.

(iv) The specimen signatures of the officers authorised to sign on behalf of the company and

(v) The names and office addresses of the auditors of the company

Prudential Norms

Pursuant to the recommendations of the Narsimhan Committee and Shah Committee, the RBI had prescribed with effect from April 1993, prudential norms for all types of financial companies with net owned funds of Rs. 50 lakh and above which had to be compulsorily, registered with it. These were in conformity with the standards and disclose norms applicable to banks and development/public financial institutions. In public interest and to regulate the credit system to the advantage of the country, in exercise of the powers conferred by section 46 JA of the amended RBI Act. The RBI Issued directions with effect from January 2, 1998: NBFCs prudential Norms Directions, 1998. The prudential norms described in this section relate to:

(1) Income recognition
(2) Accounting standards
(3) Asset clarification
(4) Provisioning for loans and advances (bad and doubtful debts)
(5) Capital adequacy and
(6) Concentration of credit/investments.

The provisions of the directions apply to all NBFCs excluding MBFCs with a NOF of Rs. 25 lakh and above and accepting/holding public securities of group/holding/subsidiary companies the book value of which being not less than 90 per cent of their total assets and do not trade in such securities and not accepting public deposits are outside the scope of these directions, similarly the provisions of the directions pertaining to capital adequacy requirements and concentration of credit/investment are not applicable Co LCs/ICs/HPFCs/ELCs which have NOF of Rs. 25 lakh and above but do not accept public deposits.

1. Income Recognition

The policy of income recognition is based on record of recovery according to recognised accounting principles. Income on non-performing assets (NPAs) should be recognised only when it is actually realised. Interest on NPAs should not be booked as income if such interest has remained past due for more than six months on and from March 31, 1998, past due means an amount of income/interest which remains unpaid for a period of 30 days beyond the due date. The lease rentals/hire purchase instalments in respect of non-performing lease/hire purchase assets should not be given credit in the profit and loss account.

Income from Investments: Income from dividend on shares of companies/units of mutual funds have to be credited on cash basis if, however, the company has declared the dividend in its annual general meeting and the NBFCs right an accrual basis. Interest income from bonds/debentures of companies and Government securities/bonds if the interest rate is predetermined, serviced regularly and is not in arrears may be taken credit on accrual basis. Similarly accrual basis may be used in regard to income on securities of companies/public sector undertakings, the payment of interest and repayment of principal of which have been guaranteed by the central/State Government.

The basis of treating a credit facility as NPA is as detailed below.

Asset: In respect of which interest has remained past due for six months.

Term Loan: inclusive of unpaid interest when the instalment is overdue for more than six months/on which interest amount remained past due for six months.

Bill: which remains overdue for six months.

Other Current Assets: The interest in respect of a debt/income on a receivable in the nature of short-term loans/advances, which facility remained overdue for a period of six months.

Sale of Assets/Services Rendered: Any dues on account of these/reimbursement of expenses rendered which remained overdue for a period of six months.

Lease Rentals/Hire Purchase Instalments: which has become overdue for a period of more than twelve months.

Other Credit Facilities: Balance outstanding including interest accrued made available to the borrower/beneficiary in the same capacity when any of the credit facilities become NPA.

2. Accounting Standards

All accounting standards and guidance notes issued by the Institute of Chartered Accounts of India (ICAI) must be followed in so far as they are not inconsistent with any of the provisions of these directions.

Accounting for Investments: All investments in securities should be classified into current and long term investments. A current investment means an investment which is by its nature readily realisable and is intended to be held for not more than one year from the date of investment. Current investment should be valued at cost or market value whichever is lower:

Each category of such investments should be valued scrip-wise and depreciation/appreciation be aggregated under each category net depreciation, if any for each category of investment should be provided for/charged to profit and loss account. Net appreciation, if any, should be ignored. The appreciation in one category of investments cannot be set-off against appreciation in another category.

A Long-term Investment: is any investment other than current investments. It should be valued in accordance with the ICAI's accounting standards.

Unquoted Equity Shares: These equity shares should be valued at cost or break-up value whichever is lower. In necessary, break-up value may be substituted by fair value. In case of non availability of balance sheets for two years they should be valued at one rupee only. The break-up value is defined as the equity capital plus reserves minus intangible assets and revaluation reserves divided by the number of equity shares of investee company while fair value refers to the mean of the break-up value and the earning value in terms of the value of an equity share computed by taking the average of profits after tax as reduced by the preference dividend and adjusted for extraordinary and non recurring items for the immediately preceding three years and further divided by the number of equity shares of the investee company and capitalised in case of predominately manufacturing company trading company and any other company including NBFC at eighteen and twelve per cents respectively if the investee company is a loss making company, the earning value would be zero.

Unquoted Preference: The shares are not be valued at the lower of the cost and face value. The basis to value investments in unquoted Government securities/guaranteed bonds, commercial papers and treasury bills should be carrying cost i.e. book value of the assets and interest accrued but not received. The valuation of investment in units of mutual funds should be based on market price/rate in the absence of availability of which, the latest declared net asset value in respect of each particular scheme should be used.

Unquoted Debentures: Depending on the terms should be treated as long-term loans/other type of credit facilities for the purpose of income recognition and asset classification.

3. Asset Classification

NBFCs are required to classify their loans and advances. lease/hire purchase assets and any other forms of credit into four broad groups, viz., (i) standard assets (ii) substandard assets (iii) doubtful assets and (iv) loss assets, Broadly speaking classification of credit into the above categories is to be done taking into account the degree of well-defined credit weakness and extent of dependence on collateral security for realisation of dues. The class of assets cannot be upgraded merely as a result of rescheduling unless it satisfies the conditions for the upgradation. The NBFC must keep the following definition in mind while classifying the assets.

Standard Assets: Standard assets is one in respect of which no default in repayment of principal or payment of interest is perceived and which does not disclose any problems, not carry more than the normal risk attached to the business.

Sub Standard Assets: Sub standard assets are (i) which has been classified as NPA for a period not exceeding two years (ii) where the terms of the agreement regarding interest and/or principal have been renegotiated or rescheduled after commencement of operations until the expiry of one year of satisfactory performance under the renegotiated/rescheduled terms.

Doubtful Assets: A doubtful assets means term loan/lease asset/hire purchase assets/any other asset which remains substandard asset for a period exceeding two years.

Loss Assets: A loss asset is one where loss has been identified by the NBFC, or internal or external auditors, or the RBI inspection to the extent the amounts has not been written off, wholly. Alternatively, it may be an asset which is adversely affected by a potential threat of non recoverability due to either erosion in the value of the security/non availability of security or due to any fraudulent act/omission on the part of the borrower.

4. Provisioning Requirements

Taking into account the time lag between an account becoming non-performing, its recognition as such, the realisation of the security and the erosion over time in the value of security charged. NBFC have to make provisions against sub standard assets, doubtful assets and loss assets detailed as follows:

Loans, Advances and Other Credit Facilities Including Bills Purchases and Discounted: Loss Assets the entire asset is to be written off if the assets are permitted to remain in the books for any reason, 100 per cent of the outstanding should be provided for.

Doubtful Assets: (a) 100 per cent provision to the extend to which the advance is not covered by the realisable value of the security to which the NBFC has a valid recourse, should be made. The realisable value is to be estimated on a realistic basis: (b) In addition, depending upon the period for which the asset has remained doubtful. provision to the extend of 20 per cent to 50 per cent of the secured portion (i.e. estimated realisable value of the outstanding) made on the following basis.

Period for which the asset has been considered as doubtful	*Per cent of provision*
upto one year	20
one to three years	30
more than three years	50

Sub Standard Assets: A general provision of 10 per cent of total outstanding is to be made.

Lease and Hire-purchase Assets: The provisioning requirements are on detailed below:

(i) Where the amount of lease rental/the charges are overdue up to 12 months nil.

(ii) Where any amount is overdue (a) in respect of hire-purchase for more than 12 months, but contracts, overdue instalments up to 24 months (as reduced by the applicable finance charges not credited to the profit and loss account and being carried forward as unmatured finance charges) and in respect of lease contracts overdues lease rentals taken to the credit of profit and loss account in the previous 12 months, entire amount (b) An additional of not less than 10 per cent of the net book value.

(iii) Where the amount is overdue between 24 and 36 months as in (ii) (a) plus not less than 50 per cent of the net book value: and

(iv) In case of the overdue being more than 36 months as in (ii) (a) plus at least 100 per cent of the net book value.

The net book value means: (a) the depreciated book value of the leased assets plus/minus, the balance in the lease adjustment account, and (b) in case of hire-purchase asset, the amount of future instalments receivable as reduced by the balance of the unmatured financial charge.

The amount of caution/margin money or value of any other security to which the NBFC has valid recourse may however, be deducted against the additional provisions necessary (but not against the provision made for overdues) and only the balance additional provision should be made for the above mentioned amount.

The income recognition of NPAs and provisioning against NPA, as two different aspects of prudential norms and provisions as per the norms are required to be made on NPAS by the NBFCs on total outstanding balance including the depreciated book value of the leased asset under reference and after adjusting the balance, if any in the lease adjustment account. The fact that income on an NPA has not been recognised cannot be taken as a reason for not making provisions.

Discloser in Balance Sheet: All NBFCs, accepting/holding public deposits must separately disclose in their balance sheets the provisioning in respect of NPAs without netting them from the income/against the value of the assets. They should be distinctly indicated under separate heads as (i) provision for bad and doubtful debts and (ii) provision for depreciation in investments. Moreover they should not be appropriated from the general provision and loss reserves if any by the NBFCs. The provision for each year should be debited to the profit and loss account. The excess, if any held under the heads general provision and loss reserves may be written back without making adjustment against them.

5. Capital Adequacy Requirements

All NBFCs are required to maintain a minimum Capital ratio of Tier I and Tier II Capital of 10 per cent on/before March 31, 1998 and 12 per cent on/before March 31, 1998 of the aggregate risk weighted assets and risk adjusted value of off-balance sheet items. The total of Tier II capital at any point of time should not exceed 100 per cent of Tier I capital. The Tier I capital means owned funds (i.e. paid-up equity capital preference shares which are compulsorily convertible into equity, free reserves, balance is share premium account and capital reserves representing surplus arising out of sale proceeds of assets, excluding reserves created by revaluation of assets as reduced by accumulated losses book value of intangible assets and deferred revenues expenditure, if any) less investment in shares of other NBFCs and shares/debentures/bonds/outstanding loans and advances including hire-purchase and lease finance made to and deposits with subsidiaries and companies in the same groups in excess in aggregate of 10 per cent of owned funds. Tire II capital consists of

(i) Preference Shares: other than those which are compulsorily convertible into equity.

(ii) Revaluation Reserves: These reserves arise from revaluation of assets that are undervalued in the books, typically premises and marketable securities. The extent to which the revaluation reserves can be relied upon as a cushion for unexpected losses depends mainly upon the level of certainly that can be placed on estimates of the market values of the relevant assets, the subsequent deterioration in values under difficult market conditions or in a forced sale potential for actual liquidation at those values tax consequences of revaluation etc. Therefore it is prudent to consider revaluation reserves at a discount of 55 per cent when determining their value for inclusion in Tier- II capital.

(iii) General Provisioning and Loss Reserves: To the extent these are not attributable to the actual diminution in value or identifiable potential loss in any specific asset and are available to meet unexpected losses. They are included in Tier-II Capital. Adequate care is to be taken to see that sufficient provisions have been made to meet all known losses and forseeable potential losses before considering general provisions and loss reserves to be part of Tier-II capital. General provision/loss reserves provisions can be admitted up to a maximum of 1.25 per cent of weighted risk assets.

(iv) Hybrid Debt: In this category, fall a number of capital instruments which combine certain characteristics of equity and certain characteristics of debt. Each has a particular feature which can be considered to affect its quality as capital.

(v) Subordinated Debt: To be eligible for inclusion in Tier-II capital, the instrument should be fully paid, unsecured, subordinated to the claims of other creditors free of restrictive clauses and should not be redeemable at the initiative of the holder or without the consent of the NBFCs supervisory authorities. These instruments after carry a fixed maturity and as they approach maturity. They have to be subjected to progressive discount for inclusion in Tier-II capital. The rates of discounting are as under.

(i)	where are date of maturity is beyond 4 years but does not exceed 5 years	20 per cent
(ii)	where the date of maturity is beyond 3 year but does not exceed 4 years	40 per cent
(iii)	where the date of maturity is beyond 2 year but does not exceed 3 years	60 per cent
(iv)	where the date of maturity is beyond 1 year but does not exceed 2 years	80 per cent
(v)	where the date of maturity does not exceed on year	100 per cent

The discounted value of subordinated debt should not exceed 50 per cent of Tier-I capital.

Risk Weighted Assets: Risk weighted assets means the weighted aggregate of funded and non-funded items detailed as follows: Degree of credit risks expressed as percentage weightings have been assigned to balance sheet assets and conversion factors to off-balance sheet items. The value of each asset/item is to be multiplied by the revelent weights to produce risk adjusted values of assets and off-balance sheet items. The aggregate should be taken into account for reckoning the minimum capital ratio. The weights allotted to each of items of assets and off-balance sheet items are listed as follows:

	Weighted risk assets: On-Balance sheet items	*Percentage Weights*
(i)	**Cash and bank balance** including fixed deposits and certificates of deposits with banks	0
(ii)	**Investments**	
	(a) Government and approved securities	0
	(b) Shares/debentures/bonds/units of mutual funds/CPs	100
(iii)	**Current assets**	
	(a) Stock on hire (net book value) (see note 2)	100
	(b) Inter-corporate loans/deposits	100
	(c) Loans and advances fully secured by company's own deposits	0
	(d) Loans to staff	0
	(e) Other secured loans and advances considered good	100
	(f) Bills purchased/ discounted	100
	(g) Others (to be specified)	100
(iv)	**Fixed assets (net of depreciation)**	
	(a) Asset leased out (net book value)	100
	(b) premises	100
	(c) Furniture and fixture	
(v)	**Other assets**	
	(a) Income tax deducted at source (net of provisions)	0
	(b) Advance tax paid (net of provisions)	0
	(c) Interest due on Government securities	0
	(d) others (to be specified)	100

Notes: 1. Netting may be done only in respect of assets where provisions for depreciation or for bad and doubtful debts have been made.

2. Assets which have been deducted from owned fund to arrive at net owned fund have a weightage of 'O' Zero.

Off-balance Sheet Items: The credit risk exposure attached to off-balance sheet items should be first calculated by multiplying the face amount of each of the off-balance sheet items by the "credit conversion factor" as indicated in the table below. This has to be again multiplied by the risk weight of 100.

	Nature of item	*Capital conversion factors (per cent)*
(i)	Financial & other guarantees	100
(ii)	Shares/debentures underwriting obligations	50
(iii)	Partly-paid shares/debentures	100
(iv)	Bills discounted/rediscounted	100
(v)	Lease contracts entered into but yet to be executed	100
(vi)	Other contingent liabilities (to be specified)	50

Note: Cash margins/depositors are deducted before applying the conversion factor.

Loans against Own Shares: All NBFCs having a NOF of Rs. 25 lakh and above and accepting/holding public deposits are prohibited from lending against their own shares. Any outstanding loan granted by a NBFC against its own shares on the date of commencement of these directions (January 2, 1998) should be recovered as per the repayment schedule.

6. Concentration of Credit/Investment

The NBFCs accepting/holding public deposits cannot lend to any single borrowers and single group of borrowers in excess of 15 and 25 per cent of their owned funds respectively. The ceiling on investment in shares of another company and a single group of companies in the same. The permissible ceiling on loans and investments taken together is 25 per cent to a single party and 40 per cent to single group of parties. Any excess on the date of commencement of these directions must be brought down as per the repayment schedule in due course for determining these limits, off-balance sheet exposures should be converted into credit risk by applying the appropriate conversion factors. The investments in debentures should be treated as credit and not investment for purposes of determining the concentration of credit. Moreover, the ceilings on credit/investment would be applicable to the own group of the NBFCs as well as to the other group of borrowers/invested companies.

Submission of Half-yearly Return: The NBFCs including the NBFCs have to submit a half-yearly return on prudential norms within three months as on September and March every year in the prescribed format to the RBI.

Exemption: To avoid any hardship/for any other just and sufficient reason, The RBI may grant extension of time to comply with/exempt any NBFC/class of NBFCs from all/any of the provisions of these direction either generally or for any specified period subject to such conditions as it may impose.

NBFCs Auditors Report (RBI) Direction, 1998

In exercise of the powers conferred by sub-section (IA) of section US MA of the amended RBI Act, the RBI has given directions to statutory auditors of the NBFCs with effect from January 2, 1998. They are applicable to all auditors of NBFCs as defined in section 451(F) of RBI Act. The main contents/ requirements of the directions are briefly discussed in this section.

Matters included in Auditors Reports: In addition the normal auditor's report under section 227 of the Companies Act on the financial statements of NBFCs to the shareholders, the auditors should also make a separate report to the Board of Directors of the NBFCs containing statements on matters of supervisory concern to the RBI detailed below.

In case of all NBFCs: The auditors have to report whether the NBFC.

Has applied for registration with the RBI:

Is incorporated before January 9, 1997:

Has received any communication about grant/refusal of certificate of registration: and has obtained a certificate of registration of incorporation on/after January 9 1997.

In case of NBFCs, Accepting/Holding Public Deposits: The auditors are directed to include a statement on the following additional matters

(1) Whether the public deposits accepted by the NBFC together with other borrowings, namely issue of unsecured non-convertible debentures/bonds to public from shareholders and any other deposit not excluded from the definition of the NBFCs Direction, 1998 are within the limits admissible under the provisions of these directions.

(2) Whether the credit rating for fixed deposits assigned by the rating agency on the specified date is in force and the aggregate amount of the outstanding deposits at any point of time during the year has exceeded the limit specified by the rating agency.

(3) Whether the NBFC has complied with the prudential norms on income recognition accounting standards asset classification, provisioning for bad and doubtful debts and concentration of credit/investment as specified by the NBFCs prudential norms Directions 1998.

(4) Whether the NBFC has defaulted in paying to its depositors the interest and/or principal amount of the deposits after such interest and/or principal became due.

(5) Whether the capital adequacy ratio as disclosed in the return submitted to the RBI in terms of the RBI prudential Norms Directions, 1998 has been correctly determined and whether such ratio is in conformity/compliance with the minimum capital to risk asset ratio prescribed by the RBI.

(6) Whether the NBFC has complied with the liquidity requirements and kept the approved securities with a designated bank.

(7) Whether the NBFC has furnished to the RBI within the stipulated period the half yearly return on the specified prudential norms and.

(8) Whether the NBFC has furnished to the RBI within the stipulated period the return on deposits as specified in the first schedule to the NBFC Directions, 1998.

In case of NBFCs Not Accepting Public Deposits: The auditors report should also include a statement as to whether (1) The Board of Directors of the NBFC has passed a resolution for non-acceptance of any public deposits (2) the NBFC has accepted any public deposits during the period and (3) the NBFC has complied with the prudential norms relating to income recognition, accounting standards, asset classification and provisioning for bad and doubtful debts as applicable to it.

As regards investment company (IC) type of NBFCs which do not accept public deposits and has invested at least 90 per cent of its assets in the securities of its group/holding/subsidiary companies as long-term investment. The statement in the auditor's report should mention whether.

The Board of directors has passed a resolution for the non-acceptance of public deposits:

The IC has accepted any public deposits during the relevant period/year:

The NBFC has through a resolution of the Board of Directors identified the group/holding/subsidiary companies.

The cost of investments in group/holding/subsidiary companies is not less than 90 per cent of the cost of the total assets of the NBFC/IC at any point of time throughout the accounting period: and the IC has continued to hold securities of group/holding/subsidiary companies as long term investments and has not traded in those investments during the accounting period/year.

Unfavourable/Qualified Statements

In case the statements in the auditors report relating to the above matters are unfavourable/qualified, the reasons for the same should also be stated, if the auditor is unable to express any opinion on any of the above items/statements, such fact together with reason (s) has also be to included in the auditors report.

Obligation of the Auditors to RBI: The auditors of the NBFCs have an obligation to submit a report to the regional office of the Department of Non-Banking supervision of the RBI under whose jurisdiction the registered office of the NBFC is located in regard to the following directly:

(i) Any of the statement by the auditors under these directions are unfavourable/qualified.

(ii) In the opinion of the auditors, the NBFC has not complied with the provisions of the NBFC Directions 1998/NBFC prudential norms directions, 1998 to the extent applicable to it!

(iii) The NBFC has not in his opinion, complied with the provisions of chapter III-B of the amended RBI Act.

The RBI has also written to the institute of Chartered Accountants of India (ICAI) stressing the importance to the auditors compliance with these directions. It has drawn attention the penal provisions under the RBI Act which will be applicable to the earning auditors. They will not be considered for appointment/approval as auditors of commercial banks and their cases will be referred to ICAI for disciplinary action.

Summary of Recommendations of the Vasudev Task Force on NBFCs

1. Diversification of financial markets is an important component of financial sector reforms. In this environment. The NBFCs have flourished and have become prominent in a wide range of activities like hire purchase finance housing finance equipment leasing finance loans and investments.
2. It is recognised that the existing legislative and regulatory frame work requires further retirement and improvement because of the rising number of defaulting NBFCs and the need for an efficient and quick system for the redressal of grievances of individual depositors. The procedure for taking over the assets and liquidation of defaulting and insolvent NBFCs remains deficient and is neither able to effectively prevent assets stripping nor does it enable quick disposal of assets for the benefit of all creditors whether secured or unsecured. There is also the perception that the regulatory regime in some respects is over restrictive and has constrained the growth of well performing healthy NBFCs.
3. The three-year period for attaining minimum NOF of Rs. 25 lakh would expire in January, 2000. Any extension granted by the RBI should be made conditional up on the concerned NBFC having taken adequate steps to increases NOF in the initial three year period and satisfactory arrangements to attain the minimum capital requirement as may be applicable at that point of time within the extended period further, the present minimum capital requirement of Rs. 25 lakh itself may have to be reviewed upward keeping in view the need to import greater financial soundness and achieve economic of scale in terms of efficiency of operations and higher managerial skills.
4. It would be necessary for the RBI to draw up a time bound programme for the disposal of applications for registration as on NBFC. Given the fact that the operations of NBFCs are often concentrated in the farflung areas, the RBI may apprise the state Government of the companies which have been granted registration as well as the companies whose applications have been rejected.

5. Given the relatively risk involved in NBFCs operations a higher level of CRAR (Capital to Risk Assets Ratio) compared to banks is essential. While the present stipulations of 12 per cent of CRAR for all rated NBFCs may continue. The RBI may prescribe a higher CRAR of say 15 per cent for those NBFCs which seek public deposit without credit rating.
6. It is also necessary that the prudential norms be reviewed by RBI taking into account the international norms and the norms applicable to the commercial banks in India as also the general economic climate in the country. The RBI should prescribe ceiling for exposure to the real estate sector and also investment in capital markets specially unquoted shares. The norms for exposures to connected companies in high risk and speculative avenues. The RBI may stipulate that the NBFCs should invest at least 25 per cent of their reserves in marketable securities apart from the SLR securities already held by the NBFCs.
7. The need for regulations on the deposit taking activities of NBFCs has basically arisen because of the information asymmetry that exists between an uninformed depositor and the NBFC. Further, the deposits raised from the public are more likely to be of short term duration resulting in maturity mismatches between asset and liability and the attendant risk. Linking of the quantum of public deposits with credit rating. However, presents a different set of issues. A part from having the effect of conferring regulatory functions on the rating agencies, it also exposes the NBFCs to frequent asset liability mismatched arising out of changes in credit rating. In view of the additional level of comfort provided by a credit rating. It is appropriate for the RBI to stipulate a higher ceiling for public deposit for those companies which have obtained rating for their instrument. However, for reasons mentioned above, it may not be necessary to link the quantum of deposit to the rating per-se provided the rating is above the minimum investment grade. In summary, the proposed ceiling could be as under.

Type of company		*Limit of public deposits*
NBFC with not less than Rs. 25 lakh	:	No access to public deposits
Equipment leasing/Hire purchase (EL/HP) company without credit rating	:	1.5 times of NOF or Rs. 10 crore, whichever is lower (higher CRAR of 1.5%)
EL/HP Company with investment grade credit rating or above	:	4 times of NOF
Loan/investment companies with investment grade rating or above	:	1.5 times NOF (higher CRAR of 1.5%)

8. The RBI should consider measures for easing the flow of credit from banks to NBFCs and then consider prescribing a suitable ratio as between secured and unsecured deposits of NBFCs.
9. The liquid asset ratio should be increased to 25 per cent of public deposit from the present level in a phased manner. By a suitable statutory provision The Unsecured depositors may be given a first charge on these liquid assets so that an unsecured depositor is at least assured of a return of one out-of-every-four rupees deposited by him.
10. The RBI can be statutorily empowered to appoint depositors' grievance redressal authorities with specified territorial jurisdiction. The office of the Banking ombudsman, could be a viable option for such appointment. This will also entail amendments in the RBI Act.
11. If the depositor's grievances is a one off problem, a fraction of the deposit equivalent to ratio of the liquid asset to the total public deposits may be paid to the depositor directly under the orders of this authority. As regards the balance payment, this authority may pass a suitable order.
12. To provide legal strength to the order of such authority. The order could be transmitted by this authority to the principal civil court of the district in which the registered office of the

company is situated or to such competent principal civil court as desired by the depositor and such an order would be enforceable as a decree of such principal court.

13. Till such time as the amendments for setting up depositors' grievance redressal authorities are carried out it is essential that the Company Law Board (CLB) tightens its procedures for dealing with the complaints of deposits and puts in place a mechanism for the speedy disposal of these complaints. This regional offices of the RBI and the regional offices of the CLB should set up a coordination mechanism to ensure that the defaulting companies are speedily dealt with for violation of any regulatory/statutory requirements.

14. State Governments may set up cells at the state and district level to help disseminate information relating to procedure for the redressal of depositor's grievance.

15. The procedure for the liquidation of NBFCs should be substantially online with those available for banks. So that these proceedings can quickly be brought to completion and the claims of various depositors and other creditors are settled as early as possible.

16. There is an imperative need for reviewing the particulars given in advertisements. Dues from the group companies, the business ventures in which the directors are interested and the amount of exposure including the non-fund based facilities provided to such entitles should also be included in the advertisement.

17. There is a need for the RBI to continue to take more intensive measures for a sustained depositors' awareness campaign. These publicity campaigns should be through print and electronic media, seminars conference, etc. Associations of NBFCs and various investors for a such as consumers' Education Research Centre, Investors' Grievances Forum, Depositors' Association, etc. should also be actively involved in these campaigns.

18. It would not be judicious to introduce a deposit insurance scheme for the depositors in NBFCs because of the moral hazard issues likelihood of asset stripping and the likely negative impact on the growth of a healthy NBFC sector.

19. A separate instrumentality for the regulation and supervision of NBFCs under the aegis of the RBI should be set up. It should have the representation of experts and other professionals and should help the overall supervisory policies of the RBI. Rules and regulation for the new instrumentality should provide enough flexibility for induction of specialists and experts with requisite supervisory skills. The RBI should have a separate executive Director for this purpose, supervised by a Deputy Governor, so that there is a greater focus on regulation and supervision of the NBFC sector.

20. The RBI could use the services of chartered accountants with suitable experience of capabilities to carry out inspection of the smaller NBFCs.

21. The offsite surveillance mechanism should pick up any significant spurt in NPAs and any bunching of repayment of deposits.

22. It is important to have a very sensitive market intelligence system which could trigger on site inspection followed by appropriate regulatory responses.

23. The RBI should be vested with powers to direct a particular NBFC or a class of NBFCs to seek prior approval of the RBI before appointing its statutory auditors.

24. Wherever the RBI has reasons to believe that the management of an NBFC is likely to indulge in fraudulent activities to the detriment of the company or its depositors, the RBI may notify such company and on notification. The assets of the company shall stand attached and the management of the assets be vested with a custodian to be appointed by the RBI. The assets may then be disposed of under of a special court or of a High court to be notified as a special

court for this purpose suitable amendments may be made in the RBI Act to put in place such an arrangement.

Regulations on Insurance Services

After the introduction of liberalisation policy the government dismantle several restrictions in financial and insurance services. The government has made in union budget 1997-98, a small beginning to allow private parties in the health insurance sector. This sector expected to see major changes in the forthcoming years. The government of India has appointed a committee to improve the efficiency of insurance services in India. The committee headed by ***Sri R. N. Malhotra***, The former Governor of RBI in April 1993. The committee has submitted its report to the government in Jan. 1994. It suggested a comprehensive framework covering the entire gamut of life and general insurance. It recommended to allow the private and foreign companies into this sector. It also recommended that, the government should reduce its holding from LIC and GIC. The committee had also recommended to appoint a Insurance Regulatory Authority in the form of statutory body like **SEBI**. Therefore the Government of India approved the setting up of Interim *IRA* on the basis of committee recommendations. On 6-9-95 the government replaced the controller of Insurance and appointed *Insurance Regulatory Authority*. This sector was in overall the control, under the Ministry of Finance. It has been entrusted with the task of preparing a comprehensive legislation. It has full authority in all aspects of the insurance sector. It is the regulatory authority in its sector. It has the chairman with ex-officio status of an additional secretary to the government. It has not exceeding 7 members in its board, 3 shall serve full time and shall be nominated by the union government. These nominated members shall be amongst persons having experience and knowledge in life and general insurance, finance and economic matters.

Regulations on Investment Services

Investment is the accumulation of savings. The savings may be channalised towards productive way. The Investment services are primarily fund based activities. Investment service play an important role in capital market operations. The mutual fund and venture capital requires investment services. The portfolio management service is in advisory nature. Stock broking is also come under this category. The regulatory bodies in this sector are presented below.

(A) Securities Contract Regulation Act, 1956

(B) SEBI Regulations

(C) RBI

The Securities Contract Regulation Act, 1956 deals with the secondary market operations. It is administered by the Department of Economic Affairs in the Ministry of Finance. The act lay down the rules and regulations about stock exchange functions sec 3 of the act deal with the Recognition of stock exchanges. Every recognised stock exchange shall submit annual reports to the central government. It also lay down rules regarding the listing of securities.

The Securities and Exchange Board of India was set up as an administrative body in April 1988. It control and regulate securities market. It also regulate all financial intermediaries. It has the full authority in all aspects of the capital market.

The Reserve Bank of India is the regulatory authority in the case of Banking and Non-Banking financial companies. It has the full powers in all aspects of these sectors.

The following financial services will cover in this chapter.

(A) Mutual Funds

(B) Venture Capital

(C) Credit Rating

A. MUTUAL FUNDS IN INDIA

Introduction

The investment preferences of householders have changed dramatically. In India, the household sector accounts for over 8% of the GDP which plays a significant change in their investment preferences. The investors investment preference may shown an impact on the economy. In the enverging economic environment of competes live markets. The investment pattern has been changed all over the financial landscape as a result of financial liberalisation. The household sector is the main provider of savings in the economy. Hence, the direction into which such savings are channelled determines the direction of growth of the financial sector. The financial development occurred because of the technical invention and through the mode of popular joint stock company. The joint stock form made the large scale industry possible by collecting large amounts of capital. Subsequent financial innovations have carried the process further the risk reduction and liquidity. The capital is generated out of savings leading to investment which is a part of the financial system. The organised financial comprises of money market, capital market, new issue market, stock market etc led by RBI, DFHI, banks, financial institutions mutual funds merchant banks and all other intermediaries regulated by the SEBI and the RBI. There are specialised, investment institutions which help those savers who do not understand the functioning of the capital market and remain away from the capital market because of the complicated procedure involved in analysing and interpreting the investment opportunities. These institution which acts as investment, conduits, pool the savings of many individual investors and combine them into a fairly large and well diversified portfolio investments. All these features are available in mutual fund. Mutual funds are an investment vehicle for the investors to enjoy the expert management skills of professional and maximine the return with an accepted risk. These are the trusts for the public savers to pool their savings. In the entire globe, the trend has been for the individual investor shifting from the direct investment in equities to the mutual fund rate.

Definition: Mutual fund can be defined as "is a form of collective investment that is useful in spreading risks and optimising returns" A mutual fund offers safety, it provides the services to the investors and offers a wide variety securities within the reach of the most modern investors. Mutual funds are fast developing into magic wands for the retail investor. Mutual funds has been defined "Mutual fund is a non depository non banking financial intermediary which acts as an important vehicle for bringing wealth holders and deficit units together indirectly." *Pierce James*

According to Weston I Fred & Brigham "Mutual fund is a corporation which accepts money from the investors and user. The some way to buy stocks, long term bonds, short term debt instruments issues by the issuer".

The SEBI has defined mutual funds as sec-2(m). "Mutual funds means of fund established in the form of a trust by a sponsor to raise money by the trustees through the sale of units to the public under one or more schemes for investing insecurities in accordance with these regulations".

A mutual fund is an investment company or a trust that pools the resources of thousands of units holders and invests on behalf of them in security markets. The mutual funds have been functioning as an agent to mobilise that sources from various investor, the unit trust, Investment trusts, mutual funds banks. Investment Companies, real estate. Investment trusts trust companies and personal trust funds etc. All these names contain some common characteristics the Investment trust is an investment holding company and very popular in U.K. This investment trust will be incorporated under the companies act. It has the same type of the capital structure like the Industrial company. The unit trust is established and is obliged to buy back units whenever an investors wants to sell them. But investment trust cannot buy back its shares and the investor has to sell his shares on the stock market. Investment trust can raise long term debt and can retain a part of its income. The unit trust always maintains a direct relation between the value of the unit and the value of the fund. Mutual savings banks are popular in USA. They offer professional fund management entrusted to them by pension plans of business and institutions. Mutual funds are very popular in USA, Canada and India. Mutual fund is a trust at law. A mutual fund performs the basic function of buying and selling securities on behalf of its unit holders. Mutual funds provide opportunity to the investors to secure a better rate of return on their savings by utilising the benefit of professional management of portfolios. Mutual funds helps the small investors to obtain high return, low risk combinations from their scientifically managed portfolios. Mutual funds are convenient and efficient investment vehicles. They can take a portfolio of securities including the blue chip companies. The mutual fund welt has spread much faster and over a wider area than the equity cult within a very short period. The society for Capital Market Research and Development conducted a study regarding the investors preference towards the mutual funds. The study finally concluded that there are 2/3 rd of middle class households in India. The study further reveals that the shift towards mutual funds has resulted in the declining popularity of certain other financial assets like LIC policies, Bank Fixed Deposits, National Savings Certificates and company deposits. The Unit Trust is basically a pure intermediary which involves the capital appreciation. The small investors cannot directly invest in the instruments such as certificate of Deposit Commercial paper and treasury bills because they require heavy amount of investment mutual funds provide continuous supervision, analysis, investment consultancy. Judicious investment decision expert, experienced, professional management at low costs. The investors have to pay expenses like administrative fees, management expenses and transaction costs for getting these services.

Advantages: The advantages of the mutual funds relative to the stock market are as follows:

(1) Low transaction costs.

(2) Benefits of high talent and expertism.

(3) Diversification.

(4) Tax deductions.

(5) Low, risk and better return.

(6) Investors protection.

(1) Low Transaction Costs: The Mutual fund is a specialised institution which acts as investment intermediary and channelises the savings of a large number of people. The mutual funds are able to get the economies of large scale because pooling of the large amount at their disposal for investment in the market. This reduces the costs in the form of brokerage fee, commission, etc. Thus a small investor gets the benefits of economies.

(2) Benefits of High Talent Expertism: The investors in India have no knowledge about the stock market operations. They are unable to know the position of market situation. They do not know about the economy, per capital income, demand consumption, companies operations, efficiency, their earning capability, profit booking etc. The stock market is a highly volatile and even sometimes the experts may feel in confession. The entire stock market depends upon many factors. The common investor has no observation about all these movements. The stock market is a heaven for those with high expertism, indepth knowledge, scientific analysis. Through understanding about the industry, company and pulse of the customer, dynamism, courage, mental stability, financial muscle etc. The Indian investors are highly influenced by the brokers decision. They do not take any investment decisions regarding a particular scrip. They simply handover the cheque to the broker on their recommendations. They do not know when to buy, when to sell, what price, at what price the scrip should be sold etc. The buying price of a particular scrip in the stock market is the most important factor in determining the profits. The sale price / disposal of a financial asset in the market is also a very important element in designing and constructing a portfolio. The portfolio a management is a highly specialised skillful activity. It requires a continuous monitoring and evolution. A small investor cannot be an expert in the portfolio management.

If the investor invests in mutual funds, he gets all the benefits of the above said factors. All these activities are performed by the mutual funds. They will appoint a high talented, specially trained experts in the portfolio management, equity analysts, fund managers etc. To achieve the targeted return assured by the fund to the investors. The funds can be professionally employed through the mutual fund ensuring good returns. The fund managers have extensive research facilities at their disposal. They are able to analyse the performance and prospectus of various companies and take good decisions in making the investments fruitful.

(3) Diversification: In mutual funds a large number of investors small savings can be pooled. The investor can also buy shares of one or two companies. Therefore the mutual funds can be used to buy shares of many different companies. Diversification reduces the risk of a portfolio. Diversification requires an additional amount of investment. In diversification sometimes more risk may be evolved. Thus the portfolios constructions, expansion and diversification is very easy in the mutual funds.

(4) Tax Deduction: The income tax act of 1961 provides some tax deductions and exemptions to the mutual funds. The mutual funds can be designed to suit the tax payers needs. A large number of mutual funds have come up with the schemes ensuring tax benefits to the subscribers. Generally the tax payers contribute in these funds. According to these schemes, the investors are required to keep the money in the fund for a certain period called "lock up" with at present is 3 years. These funds distribute the profits among the unit holders. The units will be repurchased by the fund at current NAV. The pooled amount is used to acquire shares and debt instruments. The NAV of the units varies with values of the financial assets held by the mutual funds.

(5) Low Risk and Better Returns: A mutual fund will be operated by the efficient fund managers. The fund managers have basic and extraordinary skills in their areas. They are well versed with the market movement. They know how to move in a highly volatile market. They are able to reduce the risk factor and increase high return to the unit fund. A small investor on the other hand, may not be in a position to minimise such risks. Therefore the mutual funds can reduce risk and maximise return to the holders.

(6) Investors Protection: Mutual funds in India are regulated by the SEBI. The SEBI regulations of 1996 provide better protection to the investors. The mutual funds activities are also monitored by the SEBI (mutual funds) regulations. The SEBI regulations impart a great degree of flexibility and facilitate competition.

Mutual Funds in India

The first mutual funds in India was started in 1964. The Unit Trust of India was set up under a special UTI act in 1963. All mutual funds have to be registered with the SEBI. The UTI is involved in mobilising small savings and channelising them into productive averages. The Government of India permitted the commercial banks to launch mutual funds in India by amending the banking regulation act in 1987. A number of commercial banks have started mutual funds to mop up savings in the society. The SEBI has launched a mutual fund called the SBI mutual fund in 1987. The first scheme launched was known as "Magnum Regular Income Scheme" and another scheme was "Magnum Monthly Income Scheme" with a tax benefit U/S 80 cc and "Magnum Regular Income" with 12% minimum assured rate of return per annum. The Canara Bank formed. The Canara Bank mutual fund with the objective of housing investment expertise for the benefit of investors. It had also started two schemes Canstock and Canshare in 1987. The object of these schemes was a long term capital appreciation by adopting strategies. The objective was to secure a regular income and growth. The Indian Bank had also established a mutual fund called the Indian Bank Mutual and in 1990, it floated schemes such as "Swarna Pushpa and Ratna Ind 88A, Ind Jyothi, Swarna Jyothi". Ind 88A was a tax saving growth scheme. The Punjab National Bank set up a mutual fund called the PNB Mutual Fund in 1990. It had floated a PNB Regular Income plus scheme. It had way back facility after one year. The Bank of India introduced rising monthly income scheme schedule with an objective of a doubling the amount after 5 years period. The LIC mutual fund was set up in 1989 by the LIC. It had introduced open schemes such as "Dhana Raksha 1989".

Dhana Sahayog and Dhana Vidya, Dhana Shree Dhan 80 CCB. Dhan Tax saver Dhana Samirdhi etc. The GIC Mutual fund was set up in 1990. It had launched schemes like GIC SAFE, GIC Rise. The government of India allowed the private sector corporates to join the mutual fund sector on 14-2-1992. Afterwards a number of private sector companies had approached the SEBI for permission to set up private mutual fund. The Alliance capital had set up the Alliance equity(D)(G). The Birla mutual fund had introduced, Birla Advantage, Birla MNC (D)(G). The INC Mutual fund had set up IG portfolio (D)(G) ING Income portfolio. The fenpellon mutual fund had introduced Tempceton India Income. Templet on MIP. The Tata mutual fund had set up Tata income (D)(G). The Sun mutual fund had set up Sun F and C money value. Kotak Mahindra mutual fund had set up K-30, K-Tech, K gilt, K liquid, Chola Mutual Fund had introduced Cholagilt saving, Cholagilt investments. The pioneer mutual fund had set up pioneer ITI Blueship (D)(G) pioneer ITI primaplus (D) pioneer (IT index) The DSP mutual fund had set up DSP ML balanced (D)(G). The T.M. Mutual Fund had introduced T.M. India Bond (D)(G). J M Income Bond (D)(G) Reliance Mutual Fund introduced Reliance Income (DH) (DY) Sundaram Mutual Fund had set up Sundaram Bond Savers (D)(G) Scheves, Zurich Mutual Fund introduced Zurich India prudence D Zurich India prudence – G scheme prudential ICICI Mutual Fund has set up prudential ICICI MP prudential ICICI MP(G) prudential liquid plan. The IDBI Mutual Fund introduced IDBI principal, IDBI Income scheme. Grindlays bank has set up Grindlays SSI. Grindlays SSIDQ schemes HDFC introduced HDFC Income (D)(G) HDEC (Liquid) schemes etc. All of these mutual funds has entered the market with the liberalisation of rules and regulations by the government. In November 1995, the government has been permitted private sector mutual funds to set up money market mutual funds. The IDBI mutual fund regulations of 1996 provides registration, constitution, management and schemes of mutual funds in India. Money market mutual fund averaged in the U.S. in 1972 and is now coming up in many countries. MMF are established for the purpose to purchase large pools of short term financial instruments. In a board the average maturity period of investments is about 40 days. The investors will use the MMMF with the prior approval of the RBI and SEBI. Since 1-4-96 the MMME has available to only corporates and mutual funds. The maturity period of MMME has also been reduced. Bank of Madurai, Amro Bank, UTI, IDBI, MF were given clearance to set up MMMIFS. The first MMMF established by the Kothari pioneer in 1997 did not succeed. The UTI started its MMMF on 23-4-97 and collected about Rs. 30 crore. The scheme has offered to resident individuals, HUFs, trusts, societies and corporates. The MMMF is involved in buying and selling of money market instruments only. They will construct the portfolio with treasury bills, government securities call money. Commercial paper, commercial bills, certificates of deposits etc.

The period 1996-98 was the worst in the history of the mutual funds. But several AMCs used the opportunity to restructure their portfolios and were ready for the 1999 boom in equities. In the year 1999-2000. The value of assets under the management swelled to Rs. 10,746 crores. Then the equity melt down happened. At present there are 34 mutual fund houses managing 614 schemes and Rs. 94,571 crores in asset. All of them will not survive, but performance and transparency will prove in the long run.

(Rs. in crores)

Year	*Corpus fund (AMC)*	*Year*	*Corpus fund (AMC)*
1964-69	65	1993-94	46,988
1969-74	172	1994-95	61,301
1974-79	402	1995-96	75,050
1979-84	1261	1996-97	80,539
1986-87	4563	1997-98	68,984
1987-88	6739	1998-99	68,472
1989-90	13,456	1999-2000	1,07,946
1990-91	19,111	2000-01	90,587
1991-92	23,060	2001-02	94,571
1992-93	37,480		

Private Sector funds recorded higher fresh sales as compared from May 2000 – July 2001. Redemptions were also higher than in June. It resulted in a net inflow of Rs. 2,430 crore. Private sector funds utilised this period to increase their product offering Taxes Mutual Fund launched a debt and gilt fund. Bank sponsored funds a net inflow of Rs. 61 crore. Institutions backed funds also saw a sharp full in net inflows. Mutual funds can be classified as "by category" or based on functioning of schemes. The relevant data for the period may 2000 to July 2001 for mutual funds (category) was presented in below:

Mutual Funds by Category

(a) UTI mutual fund;

(b) Private sector mutual funds (excluding UTI Banks Sponsore and Institute);

(c) Banks sponsored mutual funds (BOB, BOI, Can bank PNB, SBI);

(d) Institutions backed mutual funds (Rs. in crores).

UTI Particulars	*May 2000*	*June 2000*	*July 2000*	*May 2001*	*June 2001*	*July 2001*
Sales	1,224	1,410	774	376	1,858	23
Redemption	1,100	557	134	2,302	2,265	83
Net Sales	124	853	640	–1,926	–407	–63
Private Sector Mutual Funds (excluding UTI banks sponsored institutions)						
Sales	5,015	3,931	4,208	6,815	9,886	112
Redemption	4,034	3,528	3,580	4,030	6,787	88
Net Sales	981	403	628	2,785	3,099	243
Banks Sponsored Mutual Funds						
Sales	95	101	373	389	835	337
Redemption	161	92	90	196	187	27
Net Sales	–66	9	283	253	648	6
Institutions Backed Mutual Funds						
Sales	95	105	66	357	561	531

Redemption	216	91	117	245	225	397
Net Sales	–121	14	–51	112	336	134

Particulars	*May 2000*	*June 2000*	*July 2000*	*May 2001*	*June 2001*	*July 2001*
All Mutual Funds (Including UTI)						
(a) Sales	6,429	5,547	5,421	7,937	13,140	1,235
(b) Redemption	5,511	4,268	3,921	6,713	9,464	1,037
(c) Net Sales	918	1,279	1,500	1,204	3,676	198

Mutual Funds by Schemes

The Mutual Funds can also be classified according to the scheme:

(a) Growth Schemes
(b) Income Funds
(c) Balanced Funds
(d) Liquid and Money Market Funds
(e) Gilt Funds
(f) Equity Linked Sallings Schemes

(A) Growth Schemes

Particulars	*May 2000*	*June 2000*	*July 2000*	*May 2001*	*June 2001*	*July 2001*
(a) Sales	1,018	741	1,325	87	112	59
(b) Redemption	482	481	960	190	80	135
(c) Net Sales	532	260	365	–103	32	–76

(B) Income Funds

Particulars	*May 2000*	*June 2000*	*July 2000*	*May 2001*	*June 2001*	*July 2001*
(a) Sales	2,043	2,068	1,423	2,909	6,297	375
(b) Redemption	1,962	1,400	1,003	1,074	496	368
(c) Net Sales	80	688	420	1,835	4,801	78

(C) Balanced Funds

Particulars	*May 2000*	*June 2000*	*July 2000*	*May 2001*	*June 2001*	*July 2001*
(a) Sales	698	517	499	64	43	9
(b) Redemption	285	290	98	1,725	2,105	115
(c) Net Sales	413	227	401	1,661	–2,062	–10

(D) Liquid and Money Market Funds

Particulars	*May 2000*	*June 2000*	*July 2000*	*May 2001*	*June 2001*	*July 2001*
(a) Sales	2,147	1,847	1,850	4,348	5,991	8,074

(b) Redemption	2,247	1,573	1,387	3,378	5,550	6,038
(c) Net Sales	–100	274	463	970	491	2,036

(E) Gilt Funds

Particulars	*May 2000*	*June 2000*	*July 2000*	*May 2001*	*June 2001*	*July 2001*
(a) Sales	481	363	318	526	695	489
(b) Redemption	522	513	466	152	258	390
(c) Net Sales	–41	–150	–148	374	437	99

(F) Equity Linked Savings Scheme

Particulars	*May 2000*	*June 2000*	*July 2000*	*May 2001*	*June 2001*	*July 2001*
(a) Sales	42	11	6	3	2	3
(b) Redemption	12	11	7	194	25	11
(c) Net Sales	30	0	–1	–191	–23	–8

Funds Flows by Category: All Mutual Funds taken together recorded a net inflow of Rs. 1,989 crores. While fresh sales fell to Rs. 12,359 crores redemption increased to Rs. 10,370 crore.

The Unit Trust of India saw another month of mat outflow. The redemptions also fell subsequently to Rs. 873 crore. There was a net out go of Rs. 636 crore. The private sector mutual funds, recorded higher fresh sales as compared to June. Redemptions were also higher than in June and this resulted in a net inflow of Rs. 2,430 crore. Private sector funds utilised this period to increase their product offerings. Tarus mutual fund launched a debt and gilt fund. Banks sponsored funds saw a net inflow of Rs. 61 crore. Institution backed funds also saw a sharp fall in a net inflows. The amount in this case was Rs. 134 crores.

Funds Flow by Type: The mutual funds can be classified as growth the schemes income funds, balanced funds, liquid funds, and equity linked saving funds. All of these schemes are to be discussed in proceeding pager Debt funds saw fresh sales fall by 40% redemptions on the other hand were higher by 467. The net result was that not sales fell to double digit levels. The fresh sales were dismally low, reaching single digit levels. In US-64 had fully closed. The exit route in July there were no redemptions from this fund liquid and money market funds were the winners during the period May 2000 – July 2001. The fresh sales increased by Rs. 200 crore over June. Redemptions increased by a little over Rs. 500 crore on the whole, this type of fund received a net inflow of Rs. 2,036 crore. This is a record for the analysis period. The strong inflows into liquid and money market funds could also be an indicator of investors perception that the rally in bond markets is coming to an end. Gilt funds saw fresh sales of Rs. 489 crore. The redemption stood at Rs. 390 crore and net result was an inflow of Rs. 99 crore. Most funds were moving into medium tenure paper and gilt funds can also expect returns to show down tax saving funds continued to remain due. Inflows were minimal and there was a net flow of Rs. 8 crore.

Investment Trust: The Investment Trust is a financial institution. It collects a small amount of investible funds from a large number of investors. The trust pools the amount of savings and invest them in stock market by constructing a suitable portfolio. A small investor may not have large funds to purchase the securities in many companies. It is fully authorised to deploy the funds as it likes. It is very usual in the stock market. The prices are highly volatile. Then there is a danger of loss due to fluctuations. Diversification is the process of risk reduction. The portfolio risk can be reduced by diversification. The investment trust collects the funds from the public by selling the shares of trusts.

The trusts deploys the funds in the market as it desires. The selection of securities are decided by the trustees. The trust distributes the income among its members in the form of dividend. The trust will make investments from the consolidated fund created from the subscriptions of various members of the trust. The first investment trust was established by the Royal family of Belgium. Scothish American Investment Trust was established in 1873. In USA the investment trust was established during 1925-1927. The investment trust were established due to the substantial expansion of finance area and speculative spirit in that period.

Investment Trust in India: The first Industrial Investment Trust was established in 1933 by M/s Premchand, Roychand in Mumbai. After the establishment of this fund. The member of other trusts were formed such as investment and financed company Kolkata. General investment and trust company, Kolkata. Tata investment trust, Mumbai. Most of the investment trusts are established by the industrial groups. These trusts try to make managerial central of the companies whose securities they are going to purchase. The trusts are organised as private companies. The investment trusts are used as a tool to control more and more units by owning and controlling the shares. The investment trusts are categorised into two types. (a) Management Investment Trust (b) Fixed Investment Trusts. The management investment trusts have full freedom over the funds which they collect the fixed Investment trust is confined to a fixed list of securities. The management of the fund is not empowered to change. The portfolio except in unforeseen situation. The fixed investment trust is better than the trust. Fixed investment trust is also known as unit trust. The objective of the fund is to protect the investors from managerial manipulations. These trusts suffer from a number of drawbacks. There is no opportunity for diversification of investments. All of these funds are kept in few companies scrips only. The expenses for running the trust is very high. At present there is no existence of fixed investment trusts. These trusts are almost absolute in these days. The trusts in India can play an important role in the economy. The trust should be regulated properly for better management.

Organisation

The mutual funds in India are regulated by SEBI. The SEBI has authority to register both public and private sectors mutual fund. The mutual funds set up by LIC and GIC are regulated by the investment division, ministry of finance. All intermediaries and players in the capital mutual are brought under the SEBI authorisation and regulation. If the mutual funds are started by the commercial banks. They should get the RBI permission also. The SEBI has taken over the responsibility of regulating inspecting and controlling. The activities of all the mutual funds except MME. The mutual funds in India have five key parties involved.

(a) The Sponsors.

(b) The Board of Trustees.

(c) The Asset Management Company.

(d) The Custodian.

(e) The Chitholders.

The sponsors are the important party in establishing a mutual fund. Every mutual fund is formed by a sponsor. According to the SEBI guidelines. Sponsors can be defined as "sponsor means anybody corporate who acting alone or in combination with another body corporate, establishes a mutual fund after completing formalities thereof the sponsors could be a registered company or a scheduled bank or all India or state level financial institution. The sponsors must have a good track record a positive networth and consistent record of profitability and a good financial standing during the last 5 years. The board of trustees is another party which plays an important role in the formation and management of the mutual fund. According to the guidelines issued by SEBI, it has defined as "trustee is a person who holds the property of mutual fund in trust for the benefit of the unit holders" The trustee eligibility is determined on the basis of eligibility and suitability will be examined from the composition of the board of directors. The SEBI will examine and approve the memorandum of Association "of the trustee company SEBI has the authority to examine and approve the draft of the trust deed. Asset management company means a company formed and registered under the companies act 1956 and was approved by the board under regulations 20. The approval of the AMC was based on good track record professional experience net worth etc. Custodian means a person carrying on the activity of safe keeping of the securities or participating in any clearing system on behalf of the clients to effect deliveries of the securities. The custodian is an independent organisation delinked with the sponsors, the trustees and AMC. The SEBI would approve the custodian when granting the authorisation for setting up mutual fund as a part of the composite authorisation. The custodian is responsible for the coordination with the brokers, the actual transfer and storage of stocks and handling the property of the trust. The custodian is answerable to the AMC. The AMC conducts the research and based on it manager. The fund or portfolio the AMC is responsible for floating and managing, the schemes etc. It receives the fee for the securities readers by it. The guidelines of SEBI should be implemented by the trust board. The AMC has to report on a quaterly basis its activities, investments and operations through AMC. It should report to the trustees and to the SEBI separately in respect to their operations and results. The ME should prepare an annual report and submit to the investors of the fund and to the SEBI. The board of trustees is governed by the deed and the policy in respect of each scheme should be laid down for getting the approval from SEBI. The management of ME is a top decision making function rests with the board of trustees as per the latest guidelines of the SEBI. The brain of the mutual fund is the trustees and it is governed by a trust deed. The experts and specialists will be on the board of trustees. The AMC will look after the routine functions of fund. All MFs should be managed by the experts high talented skill fund managers and professionals. The experts in this area are finance professionals. The AMC will manage the fund by making investment decisions. The fund be converted in major categories which are regular income investments growth oriented and money market instruments. The MF should concentrate before taking decisions about the fundamental analysis of the economy, industry and company. The fund can invest towards research and appoint experts investment analysts portfolio managers and a host of other specialists.

Organisation Structure of MF

The mutual funds in India are regulated by SEBI. The SEBI has the authority to register both public and private sectors MF. The MF set up should be done according to the norms of the SEBI. The SEBI has provided "Fourtier" system for managing the affairs of the fund. The MFs are designed to suit the needs and preferences of the investors. The choice of the fund will be determined by the investor himself. The investor should frame his investment objectives regarding whether he expects a regular income or capital appreciation or high earnings or low risk etc. Then the objective will help to choose the best fund among different alternatives. The MFs will adopt different strategies to meet the investors objectives. In India the MFs can be classified into five categories. The classification of funds can be based on various factors.

(1) based on ownership status.

(2) based on schemes of operation.

(3) based on portfolio objectives.

(4) based on location.

(5) others.

1. Ownership Status: The MFs in India can be established by either public sector or private sector. The public sector mutual funds has been functioning since 63-64 the UTI has been functioning since 1964. In 1987 the second public sector MF was launched by SBI. SBI MF was the first among all the commercial banks. The government has given the permission to PSBS for entering the MF sector to curb. The monopoly of the UTI, Can bank, BOI, PNB, GTC, LIC, mutual funds have joined operations in the business at a short span of time private sector corporates have been permitted by the government on Feb. 14, 1992. Since then a no. of private companies have approached SEBI for the approval of mutual fund. The SEBI has provided the guidelines for registration constitution & management of the funds.

2. Scheme of Operations: Mutual funds can be classified on the basis of their operations. The MFs can be divided into 3 categories. i.e. open ended, close ended and open can close ended schemes.

Open Ended Schemes: A much fund which offers units for sale without specifying and duration for redemption. An investor can subscribe it at any time. The scheme will be opened throughout the year and investor can redeem his holding at any time. The enter and exit of the scheme is very easy. The MF repurchases the units at periodically announced rates. The repurchase prices are based upon the Net Asset Value. The NAV of the scheme will depend upon the stock market prices. The open ended funds provide high liquidity to the investors. The sale price of units are also announced by the fund from time to time for subscription. For ex. US 64, ULIP of UTI Dhanavridhi, Dhanaraksha, Magnum balance fund, Magnum Instant cash fund of the SBI.

Close Ended Scheme: A mutual fund which offer units for sale to the public only at the time of initial issue. The scheme is also offered to the investors at a specified period of time after closing the time, the investor cannot subscribe to the scheme. A close ordered scheme of MF. The period of maturity will be announced in advance. The investor can buy or sell the units of the scheme in secondary market. The price in the secondary market is determined on the basis of demand and supply. The close ended scheme can be easily managed by the fund managers. The fund manager can evolve long term investment strategies depending upon the life of the scheme Master gain – 92. Grand master of UTI Dhana. Sainridhi, Dhanasree of CICMF can double Canstar, Cangrowth of Canara Bank. Ind Jyothi Swarna Jyothi of Indian Bank are some of the examples of close ended schemes. Open cum close ended scheme. The scheme is offered by the MF is kept open for a specific interval and it runs the scheme as a close scheme. The scheme is a combination of both open and close ended funds. The kind of schemes are permitted by SEBI in recent years only. In offer document, the scheme rules and regulations will be announced. The units of the scheme may be listed in stock exchange. These may be traded in the stock exchange regularly.

3. Portfolio Basis: MFs can be classified on the basis of portfolio. The schemes are classified as follows:

(a) Balanced funds
(b) Equity funds
(c) Bond funds
(d) Growth funds
(e) Tax benefit funds
(f) Specialised funds
(g) MMMF
(h) Leveraged funds

(a) Balanced funds: Balanced funds means the amount collected from this scheme is deployed in the market by purchasing equity and fixed income bearing securities. The combination of both the financial assets will be fixed MF. Some MFs spent some amount on the equity preference and debentures. Therefore the situation may ensure certain amount of interest and dividend. Some MFs maintain a ratio between equity and preference share in 50:50. The balanced fund ensures both the capital appreciation and regular return in the form of dividend and interest. The investors have advantage both in return and interest. The investors capital appreciation. It is also known as income and growth funds. Examples of balanced fund schemes can triple of commercial bank, Canara bank, Dhanaraksha 1989 of LIC, ULIP 1971, Unit scheme 95(D), HDFC Balanced fund, Tata balanced fund, Prudential ICICI balanced, Alliance 1995 etc.

(b) Equity funds: Equity fund scheme units will be offered to the investors by the MFs. This scheme proceeds will deploy for purchase of shares. The fund undertakes risks associated with the investment in equity of the reputed companies. This scheme is also further classified as income fund and growth funds. Examples of equity fund schemes. UGC 10,000, UTI Pharma and Health Care, UTI Service Sector, UTI Software, K-Tech Alliance Millennium, Magnum IT, Prudential ICICI Mec. etc.

(c) Bond funds: Bond funds proceeds will be spent for acquiring bonds. The bonds ensure fixed regular income. It ensures regular income to the investors. The bonds are available in the market at lower prices in some situations. Therefore, the net income on these funds will go higher. Some companies offer non-convertible bonds including shares. Any investor who subscribes for the share will have to take up bonds also. Ex. UTI bond, UTI Mahila Unit Scheme, UTI NRI, Tata income, Alliance Income fund, 54 FAD, IDBI principal, K-bond deposit, K-bond, wholesale, Sundaram bond saver. Templet on income builder, LIC bond-G, sunpec money value bond, Zurich India high interest-D, ILEFS bond.

(d) Growth funds: Growth fund objective is to provide capital appreciation for the value of investments. The scheme concentrates on value appreciation of securities. The risk involved in this scheme is very high. The scheme will not give preference for regularity of income. Growth fund is also called as long hawl investments. The scheme is a long term based fund.

(e) Tax benefit funds: Perhaps Tax Schemes are designed to meet the tax payers needs. The investor who contribute the scheme is entitled to get the tax concession in Income-Tax.

The lock in period is 3 years. The scheme distributes the profits among the unit holders. A large number of MES have come up with many schemes. These schemes provides benefits like income, capital appreciation and tax concessions. The proceeds of these shares would be deployed to acquire equity and debentures. Usually all the tax payers will contribute for these funds. For Ex. Magnum tax gain, Pioneer ITI tax shield.

(f) Specialised funds/sector funds: Sector funds invests in a particular type of securities. The scheme objective is to make investments in a particular area or industry. If any investor wants to invest in a particular security he will perform a fund which deals in such securities. Ex. Birla MNC, UTI Pharma K-Tech, Magnum IT, UTI Software, Pioneer ITI.

(g) Money Market Mutual Funds: MMMF is a scheme which has been set up with the objective of investing in money market investments. The fund involves in buying of instruments from the money market like treasury bills, call money, commercial paper, commercial bill, certificate of deposits, government securities. The maturity period will be less than 1 year for all these investments. The MMMF contribute the only portfolio of MMMF. Ex. UTI MMMF, IDBI principal, Money Market fund.

(h) Leveraged funds: The aim of leveraged funds portfolio is to maximise the capital appreciation to the investors. In this type of schemes, the financial assets will be purchased by borrowing the fund at the cost of interest and the gain from holding shares is the profit of the leveraged fund. Leveraged funds involves in speculative activities to earn more and more profit.

4. Based on Location: Mutual funds may be categorised on the basis of location where they mobilise funds as domestic fund and off share funds. Domestic funds mobilise savings from public within the country offshore mutual funds are the mobilise funds from abroad for investment in India.

5. Others: Other types of mutual funds such as loan funds and non-loan funds. These funds are not very popular in the country.

Objectives of a Mutual Funds

The objectives of mutual funds are presented below:

(a) To provide a better opportunity to low income group investors.

(b) To provide a better expertism, talent, selectful, scientific approach towards stock-market activities.

(c) To manage small investors portfolios that provides regular Income growth, safety, liquidity and diversification.

Importance of Mutual Funds

The mutual funds mobilises a large amount of savings from the small investors savings. The funds attracts resources mainly from middle class families. Their savings potential is very high in India. The pooling of large amount of resources operating economies and the ability to commit the large secure of money for long periods the mutual funds will enjoy ample resources at their disposal by mobilising from various investors. The mutual funds gain a lot of significance from the investors. It has been proved in the case of master gain. (a) scheme of unit trust. The scheme has mobilised Rs. 4,500 crores from the market and created history in the market. But the Unit Trust failed to manage that scheme. In India the investors do not have any basic knowledge about the portfolio management therefore the investors are investing in mutual funds they are important due to the following reasons.

(a) The mutual funds have been functioning like financial intermediaries in mobilising the savings of the public.

(b) The mutual fund invest in a variety of securities where there is a demand.

(c) Mutual funds appoint experts to get the benefits of speculation activities.

(d) Mutual funds will handle the investors fund with utmost care and try to fulfil the needs of unit holders.

(e) Mutual funds leads to a general prosperity to the investors.

(f) The fund managers will apply all the stock market technicians to enhance the fund of the NAV.

(g) The mutual funds will attract foreign investments by offering off share funds.

(h) Per capita income of rural and urban middle class people are increasing and their savings are channalised towards mutual funds sector. The fund diverts the resources towards industrial undertaking units acquiring the financial assets of various companies.

(i) The mutual funds have tremendous scope for growth in the country.

(j) The liberalisation and industrial policies gave a scope for the growth of the country. The government should prepare an agenda about the utilising of the vast resources available with the mutual funds. There are certain areas to be developed such as water resources, road, agriculture etc. The Government of India can divert the resources towards construction of dams, water sheds and creation of irrigation facilities, development of agriculture sector, development of co-operative service, sector, benefits will pass to the farmers. The mutual funds may also enter into power sector to improve the production of power by providing large amount of savings. In future the mutual funds may be like UTI (agri.), UTI (power), UTI (roads), UTI (housing) etc.

Regulatory Framework

The mutual funds in India are governed by the UTI act of 1963, Indian trust act of 1882, companies act of 1956, securities act of 1956 and the other tax laws the overall monitoring and supervising are done by the Ministry of Finance. The RBI and the SEBI. The RBI had issued guidelines for the bank sponsored mutual funds in 1987. Afterwards it also received the guidelines from the Minister of Finance in 1991. The SEBI also issued guidelines in 1991 and comprehensive set of regulations in 1993. After the successful growth of mutual funds industry, it became necessary that all mutual funds in India should follow uniform norms for the valuation of investments and accounting practices. This leads to better comparison for the evaluation of the evaluation of fund industry, it became performance the SEBI issued new mutual fund regulations in December 1996 based on the recommendations of the mutual fund 2000 report. All mutual funds in India including the UTI is regulated by the SEBI. The off share funds are governed by the Ministry of Finance, the government of India, and the RBI, MMMFs are governed by the RBI. The SEBI regulations aim at facilitating competition, transparency, investor's protection etc.

Registration of Mutual Funds

According to SEBI guidelines the following process is involved for the registration of a mutual fund.

(1) Every mutual fund should be registered with the SEBI under registration.

(2) An application for registration should be made in form by the fund sponsor and shall be addressed to the SEBI.

(3) Not withstanding anything contained in sub-registration. (1) Any application made by a sponsor prior coming into force of these regulations containing such particulars are mentioned in the form shall be treated as an application made in pursuance of the sub-regulation. (1) and should be dealt with accordingly provided that the fee payable in respect of the application made under such regulation shall be the same as is referred to in the sub-regulation of regulation.

(4) Every application for registration under the regulation shall be accompanied with an application fee as specified in schedule II by means of a cheque or bank draft in favour of the SEBI payable at Mumbai.

Regulation (5): The SEBI regulation indicates that subject to the provisions that under sub-regulation (3) of regulation 3, any application which is not complete in all aspects and does not confirm to the particulars specified in the form, shall be rejected provided that before rejecting any such application, the applicant shall be given an opportunity to remove within the time specified such objections as may be indicated by the board.

Regulation (6); (1): The regulation 6 deals with the furnishing information clarification and personal representation. The SEBI may require the sponsor to furnish such further information or clarification as may be considered necessary for the grant of registration the sponsor should appear before the SEBI.

Regulation (7): This regulation indicates the consideration of application and after obtaining such further information as may be required should decide on the application and for registration not more than 3 months from the date of receipt.

Regulation (8): This regulation deals with the conditions for the registration of a mutual fund. For the purpose of granting the registration the board should take into the Account all the matters which are relevant to efficient and ordinary conduct of the affairs of a mutual funds and in a particular the following:

(a) The sponsor must possess a sound track record and experience in the relevant field of financial services for a period of 5 years. He should possess professional competence financial soundness and general reputation of affairness and integrity in his business transactions "sound track record means net worth dividend paying capacity and the profitability of the sponsor".

(b) Mutual fund is in the form of a trust and the trust deed has been approved by the board.

(c) An Asset management company who holds an approval of the board has been appointed to manage the affairs of the mutual fund and operates the schemes of such funds.

(d) The sponsor contributes at least 40% to the net worth of the AMC.

(e) The sponsor or any of its director or the principal officer employed by the mutual fund. The management looks after the affairs involving moral turpitude or gravity of any economic offence.

Regulation 9: It deals with the grant of the registration. The board on being satisfied that the application is complete in all respects and all particulars. Sought have been furnished and that the mutual fund is eligible for registration may register with fund subject to;

(a) Receipt of registration fee indicated in Schedule II of the act in a manner specified by the board.

(b) The terms of and conditions specified in regulations 12.

Where a mutual fund is found to be eligible for grant of registration, the board shall grant a certificate in Form B.

Regulation 10: (a) According to the regulation every mutual fund registered under these regulations, should pay annual fee, for every financial year, from the year following the year registration as specified in Schedule II. (b) The annual fee should be remitted to the board in the manner specified in such regulation (1) of regulation 4 before the beginning of each financial year.

Regulation 11: The regulation deals with the failure of the payment of fee by the mutual fund. If any fund fails to remit annual fee as provided in sub-regulation (2) of regulation 10. The board may prohibit the mutual fund from the launching any new schemes till the fee has been remitted.

(2) Without prejudice to these regulations, the board may be on being satisfied with the reasons for the delay and subject to such conditions as it may be deems fit permit the sponsor to pay the annual fee at any time within 2 months from the commencement of the financial year to which such further.

Regulation 12: According to the regulation every fund which is granted registration is subject to fulfil the following terms and conditions.

(a) Complying with the provisions of these regulation.

(b) Informing forth with the board as soon as it comes to the knowledge of the sponsor or the trusters that any information or particulars previously submitted to the board where either considering or false in any material respect.

(c) Informing forthwith the board of any material change in the information or particulars previously furnished which have a bearing on the registration granted by it.

(d) The sponsor the AMC trustees and the custodiance should comply with the provisions of the regulations.

(e) Allowing examination of the directors, officers and the other employees in the course of inspection and extending full co-operation on its behalf.

(f) Agreeing the produce books of accounts, documents and such other information as sought for the board in the course of inspection.

Regulation 13: It deals with the situation procedure where registration is not granted by the SEBI. The following process involved while denying registration.

(i) Where an application does not satisfy the requirements mentioned in regulation & the board shall reject the application.

(ii) The information about the rejection of application will be communicated to the application has been rejected.

(iii) The applicant who is aggrieved by the decision of the board under the sub-regulation (2) may within the period of 30 days from the date of receipt of such intimation can apply to the board for reconsideration of its decision.

(iv) The board shall as soon as possible in the light of the submissions made in the application and wherever necessary, after giving an opportunity for personal hearing, convey its decision in writing to the applicant.

Regulation 14: According to this regulation, it deals with the constitution and management of the mutual fund. The mutual fund shall be constituted in the form of a trust in accordance with the provisions of the Indian trust act 1882 (of 1882).

Regulation 15: The regulations informs about the appointment procedure of the trust the process for the appointment of the trust is as follows:

(1) A company shall be appointed as a trustee to manage the mutual fund provided that the board may regarding the special circumstances can permit the appointment of a board of trustees, as trustees of a mutual fund.

(2) The appointment of trustees should be subjected inter alia to the following conditions mainly.

(a) The trustees are persons who have experience in financial services and are not found guilty of any economic offence.

(b) The names of the trustees should be forwarded to the board.

(c) Any change in the appointment of the trustee's should be subjected to the approval of the board.

(d) No trustee should retire unless another person is appointed in the place of retired trustee.

(e) No person should be a trustee or a director of a trustee company in more than one mutual fund.

(f) Atleast 50% of the trustees should be independent members and no such trustee should be an affiliate or subsidiary of the sponsor.

(g) An AMC, any of its directors, officers or employee's should not act as a trustee of any mutual fund.

Regulation 16: The regulation deals with the process of registration under the registration act. The investment of the trust shall be of the Indian Registration act of 1908 executed by the sponsor in favour of the trustees named in such instruments and shall contain such clauses as maintained in schedule III and such clauses which are necessary for safeguarding the interests of the unit holders.

(2) No trust deed shall contain a clause which has the effect of

(a) Limiting or extinguishing the obligations and liability of the trust in relation to any mutual fund or the unit holders or

(b) Indemnifying of the trustees or the Assets management company for the loss of damage caused to the unit holders by their acts of negligence or acts of commissions or omissions.

(c) The trust deed should be made available for the inspection by any member from the public at the registered office or the principal place of business of the mutual fund and if so desired a copy of the same should be made available to any person on payment of a normal fee as decided by the mutual fund.

Regulation 17:

(1) The section deals with the obligations of the trustee as per the law. The trustees shall have a right to obtain from the AMC such information as relevant to the management of the affairs concerning the operations of the trust and may also call for periodical reports from the AMC.

(2) Where the trustees have reason to believe that the conduct of the business of the mutual fund is not in conformity with these regulations. They should forthwith take such remedial steps as necessary to rectify the situation and keep the board informed of the same with full particulars.

(3) The trustees should take the steps to execute all the documents, which are necessary to secure the acquisition disposal. It also assures the transactions that are entered into by the AMC are properly made in accordance with these regulations.

(4) The trustees should be responsible for ensuring that the AMC complies with these regulations.

(5) The trustee should enter into an agreement with the AMC which contains the clauses as specified in such Schedule IV and such other clauses which are necessary for the purpose of investment of the funds of the mutual fund then such agreement will be approved by the board.

(6) The trustees should be accountable for and be the custodian of the prosperity of the respective schemes and should hold the same interest for the benefit of the unit holders in accordance with these regulations and the instruments of the trust.

(7) The trustees should take steps to ensure that the transactions concerning mutual funds are in accordance with the provisions of the trust deed and Schedule III of these regulations.

(8) The trustees should be responsible for the calculation of any income due to be paid to the fund and also of any income received in the mutual fund for the holders of the Units of any Schedule in accordance these regulations and the trust deed.

(9) The trustees should receive a quarterly report from the AMC and submit a 6 monthly report to the board on the activities of the fund.

(10) The trustees should call for the meeting of the unit holders.

  (a) on a re-acquisition of 3/4th of the unit holders of any scheme or of all the schemes together or

  (b) When the majority of the trustees decide to and up or prematurally redeem the units or modify any scheme.

  (c) Whenever required to do so by the board in the interest of unit holders.

Regulation 18: The regulation deals with the process of setting up of the AMC according to the rules and regulations the following steps required for the approval of the AMC.

(i) The application for the approval of the AMC shall be made in form A.

(ii) The memorandum and articles of association of the AMC shall be submitted to the board along with the Application for approval under sub-regulation (i).

(iii) The provisions of regulations 5, 6 and 7 should apply to the applications made under sub-regulation (1) of this regulation as they apply to the application for registration of a mutual fund.

Regulation 19:

(1) The regulation explains the process of getting of an appointment of the AMC. The act indicates that the sponsor, the trustee should appoint an AMC who is approved by the board to manage the affairs of the mutual fund and operate the schemes of the such fund.

(2) The appointment of an AMC can be terminated by majority of the trustees or by 75% of the unit holders of the scheme.

(3) Any change in the appointment of the AMC should be subjected to prior approval of the board.

Regulation 20: The regulation deals with the approval of the AMC. For the grant of approval from the AMC the board may take into account all the matters which are relevant to efficient and orderly conduct of the affairs of the AMC and in particular the following namely.

(a) The existing AMC has a sound track record general reputation fairness interaction.

(b) The directors of AMC are persons of high fame and stand having atleast 5 years of professional experience in the relevant fields such as portfolio management, instrument analysis, financial administration.

(c) The board of directors of the AMC has least 50% directors who are not affiliate or associated in any manner with the sponsor or any of its subsidiaries or the trustees.

(d) The chairman of the AMC should not be the director of the trustee company or truster of the board of trustees.

(e) The AMC shall have a minimum net worth of Rupees Five Crores.

Regulation 21: The regulation explains about the terms and conditions of approval of the AMC the grant of approval of the AMC under regulation 20 shall be subject to the following terms and conditions namely.

(a) The AMC has professionals with adequate experience in the management of mutual funds.

(b) Any director of AMC shall not hold the position of a director in another AMC or of a trustee in any mutual fund.

(c) The AMC shall forthwith inform the board of any material change a bearing on the approval granted by it.

(d) No change in the management of the AMC shall be made without prior approval of the board.

(e) The AMC undertakes to comply with these regulations.

Regulation 22: This section deals about situation, if the approval is not granted to an AMC.

(1) When an application made under regulation 18 for grant of approval does not satisfy the requirements laid down in regulation 21, the board may reject the application.

(2) The decision to reject the application shall be communicated to the applicant in writing stating the grounds on which the application has been rejected.

(3) The AMC which is aggrieved by the decision of the board under sub regulation (1) may within a period of 30 days from the date of receipt of such intimation apply to the board for reconsideration of its decission.

(4) The board shall as soon as possible in the light of the submission made in the application under regulation (3) and whenever necessary after giving an opportunity for personal hearing communicate its decision in writing to the applicant.

Regulation 23: The regulation inform about the retrictions on business activities of the AMC. No asset management company shall

(a) act as trustee of any mutual fund.

(b) undertake any other business activities except activities like financial services consultancy exchange of research on commercial basis as long as any such activities of one not in conflict with the activities of the mutual fund.

(c) act as an AMC for any other mutual fund to hold the position of trustee in a trust or act as a director in another AMC.

(d) permit any director of the AMC.

Regulation 24: The regulation defines the role and obligations of an AMC. The following process tells us about the rule position regarding the obligations of the AMC.

(i) The AMC shall take all responsible steps and exercise all due negligence and assure that the investment of funds pertaining to any scheme is not contrary to the provisionals of these regulations and the trust deed.

(ii) The AMC shall be responsible for the acts of commission and a missions by the employees or the person whose services have been obtained by the company.

(iii) The AMC shall submit to the trustee, quarterly reports on March 31, June 30, September 30 and December 31 on its activities and the compliance with these regulations.

(iv) The AMC shall be expected to meet all its expenses and make provisions for

(a) office space, personal including security analysts and portfolio managers.

(b) regulatory compliance and reporting sources.

(c) preparation and distribution of the funds prospectus, annual periodic reports and other investors communications.

(d) according to services and preparation of tax returns.

(e) advertising and other sales materials.

(f) inservance courage and other services.

(v) The trustees of the mutual fund may terminate the assignment of the AMC at any time after receiving a reasonable notice in writing from the AMC.

(vi) Notwithstanding anything contained in any contract or agreement. The AMC or its directors or the officers shall not be any civil liability to the mutual fund for the acts of commissions and omissions while holding such position or office.

Regulation 25: The mutual fund shall have custodian. He is not having associated with AMC is in any way.

Regulation 26: The regulation explains about the process of approval of custodian.

(i) The custodian shall make in application inform A for registration.

(ii) The provisions of 5, 6 and 7 shall so far as may be apply to the application made under sub-regulation (1) of this regulation.

(iii) For grant of approval of the custodian, the board may take into account all matters which are relevant to efficient and orderly conduct of the affairs of the custodian and in particular the following namely.

(a) The existing custodian has a sound track record, general regulation and fairness in transactions.

(b) The applicant himself or the employee or the persons who have experience in proceeding custodian services.

(c) The applicant has the infrastructure, office space and personal to provide custodian services.

(d) The applicant or the director or the parties are not found guilty of any economic offence.

(e) The applicant is not the sponsor or trustee of any mutual fund.

(iv) The grant of approval to the custodian shall be subject to the following terms and conditions namely;

(a) The custodian or its directors, partners will not in any way be directly or indirectly affiliated or associated with any AMC.

(b) The custodian will not act as sponsor or the trustee of any fund.

(c) The custodian will not act as a custodian of more than one mutual fund without the approval of the SEBI.

The rules and regulations framed by the SEBI. Every mutual fund in India has to follow the rules and the regulations from 27 to 39 which indicates about the schemes of mutual funds.

Regulation 27: It deals with the procedure for the announcement of schemes.

Regulation 28: It reveals the contents of public-city material.

Regulation 29: It means the rules regarding misleading statement.

Regulation 30: It indicates about the steps involved enlisting of the schemes with the concerned stock exchange.

Regulation 31: This clause explains about the minimum amount to be raised from the market through various schemes closed ended Rs. 20 crores open ended as fifty crores.

Regulation 32: This section tell us about that the schemes should be kept open for the public subscription for a period of 45 days.

Regulation 33: It indicates about the process of refund to an investor when the mutual fund scheme fails.

Regulation 34: It reveals that the allotted applicant should receive the unit certificates from the fund within 10 weeks in case of close ended schemes and 6 weeks in case of an open ended scheme.

Regulation 35: This provision deals with the transfer process of Unit Scheme Certificates.

Regulation 36: It indicates the winding up process of a mutual fund.

Regulation 37: It tells the effect of winding up of the schemes.

Regulation 38: It explains the procedure and manner of winding up of schemes.

Regulation 39: This provision deals with the declaration of winding up of schemes.

The regulations from 40 to 46 indicates about the investment objectives and valuation policies of the mutual fund the rules from 47 to 65 tells about the general obligations of the mutual funds on various aspects. Regulations 65 to 75 informs about the procedure for an action in case of default regarding various conditions.

RBI Guidelines

The Commercial banks are considered to follow the guidelines which are issued by the RBI on certain aspects as indicated below.

- Every mutual fund should be constituted as a trust under the Indian trust act and the sponsoring bank should appoint board of trustee.
- The trustees in addition to ability and integrity should have the power capacity to deal the investment decisions and investors protection.
- The overall direction, control, super intendence and management of the affairs and business should vest in the board of trustees.
- The routine functions of the schemes should be looked after by a full pledged executive trustee.
- The executive trustee should not discharge any other discharge responsibility in the concerned bank.
- An healthy relationship should be maintained between the sponsor and the board of trustees.
- Care should be taken so that there will be no clash interest between the trustee board and the concerned bank.
- The sponsor bank should contribute the corpus fund as specified by the RBI no additional contribution should be made by the sponsor bank to the corpus without the prior approval of the RBI.
- The sponsor Bank should contribute the corpus bank fund as specified and maintain in each of the funds schemes by the way of its stake, an amount equivalent to 1% of the amount outstanding.

- The banks should obtain the RBI's prior approval before announcing any scheme of mutual funds.
- The investment objectives and policies of the mutual fund should be laid down in the trust dead and every scheme launched by the fund must be in accordance with such board objectives and policies.
- The MF should make a clear statement while inviting the public about the investment objectives of the fund and its policies.
- The subscription amounts collected by the mutual funds are primarily intended to be channelised in the capital market investments.
- The MFs should not undertake director in direct lending portfolio funds management under writing bill discounting, money operations etc. which are essentially banks/merchant banking functions etc.
- There is no objection to the mutual funds in investing the initially collected amount for a scheme in the money market instruments radius counting of bills or bank deposits for a period of not exceeding 6 months.
- The mutual funds may also invest their temporary surplus fund in similar instruments upto not more than 25% of their total investible funds. Such short term/temporary investments can however be made only if they are permissible under the character of the funds.
- The mutual funds should take delivery of scrips purchased and in the case of scrips sold, give delivery there of the purchases. The scrips purchased should be transferred in the funds name.
- A mutual fund should not make short sale/purchase of securities or carry over the transactions from the settlement period to the next settlement period.
- The mutual fund should not make investments in any other mutual funds similar collective investment schemes. The funds should not also invest in the shares of the investment companies/corporations.
- The mutual funds should not hold under any one scheme more than 5% of issued share capital of debenture stock of any company.
- In case the mutual fund operate more than one scheme more than 5% of issued share capital or debenture. The holding in respect of all its schemes put together should not exceed 15% of the paid up capital or debenture stock of a company.
- The total amount invested by a fund from any of its schemes in the shares, debentures of any specific industry should not exceed 15% of schemes fund. This provision will not however apply to a scheme which has been floated for investments in one or more specified industries and a declaration has been made to that effect.
- The maximum spread between the purchase and selling prices of units/shares of any scheme should not be more than 5%.
- The total cost of managing any scheme under a fund should be kept more than 5% of the total income of the scheme.
- Income distribution by the way of dividend or capitalisation of gains should not be made on the basis of revaluation of the stockholders or unrealised capital appreciation.
- The fund should create depreciation on investments to held and provision for bad or doubtful debts, the auditors should satisfy before declaring any dividend.

- Further the fund should create a dividend equalisation fund for each scheme by appropriating a part of its surplus income.
- A mutual fund should maintain to create separate accounts of each scheme, launched by it, segregating the assets under each scheme. No Utilising of assets between the schemes should take place, except with the prior approval of the board of trustees and at the prevailing market rates.
- The board of trustees of mutual funds should prepare an annual statements of accounts in respect of each of the schemes which should contain, statements of assets and liabilities and income and expenditure accounts, duly audited by the qualified auditors further an abridged version of the annual accounts together with the reports of auditors and the board of trustees, should be published for the information of subscribers to the concerned scheme.
- The board of trustees of mutual funds should disclose the NAV of each of the schemes and the method of valuation for the benefit of the concerned subscribers.
- The sponsors bank should furnish to the RBI in duplicate the following reports on a regular basis.
- A half-yearly report indicating the performance of the reports of auditors and the report of the board of trustees.
- A half-yearly report indicating the performance of the mutual fund as a whole as well as each scheme.
- Audital annual statement of accounts together with the reports of auditors and the report of the board of trustees.
- Schemewise details of investment portfolio of the funds, value of such investments, changes in the portfolio since the previous annual report and industry wise exposure.

Company's Guidelines

Mutual funds generally invest in shares, debentures and other securities of the blue chip companies and in the money market investments the guidelines issued by the government indicates that a mutual fund in a private sector can be sponsored by one or more limited companies having a sound track record. The company or companies which wants to establish a mutual fund should establish the fund as a trust under the Indian Trust Act of 1882. The sponsoring company should incorporate an AMC. The AMC should have a net worth prescribed by the government the sponsoring company should have at least a 40% stake in the paid up capital of the AMC. In order to meet this requirement of 40% stake, the sponsoring company or companies have to subscribe to the shares of the AMC by complying with the provisions of sec 372 of the companies act (rule 11). According to the rule 11(c) the sponsoring company can invest only upto 25% of the subscribed equity capital since the sponsoring company has to get the approval of its shareholders in a general meeting and the central meeting and the central government as required by the sub-section (4) of section 372 of the act for investing in the shares of the AMC. As stated above, the mutual fund is required to be established as a trust Indian trust act section (3) define the term test has "an obligation annexed to the ownership of property and arising out of a confidence reposed in and accepted by the owner or declared and accepted by him for the benefit of another and the owner". Sec 41 (2) of the act provides that a person who has agreed in writing to become a member and whose name's entered in the registered of members shall be a member of a company. A person means a natural person or a corporation. A trust is not a legal unity. It is only a legal arrangement, it is not a person. According to Sec 153 of the act, no notice of trust shall be entered on the register of members. To overcome the section 41 and 153 of the act, in practice mutual funds gets the shares registered with either in the name of the sponsoring company or in the name of asset management company or in the name of custodian company. According to the company the government rules and regulations every mutual fund should avail the services of the custodian. According to the government regulations every mutual fund should get the shares purchased and transferred to the funds name and scheme also.

If the shares are not registered in the name of the mutual fund, the mutual fund should comply with section 187-C of the act by giving the declaration inform II as prescribed by the companies rules of 1975 as contemplated in subsection (2) of section 187 C of the act within 30 days from the date of registration of transfer of shares should be some is concerned company. Consequently the company whose name the mutual funds shares are registered has to file form no. This prescribed by the companies within 30 days from the date of registration of transfer of shares as required by sub-section (1) of sec 187 C of the act when forms I & II prescribed under section 187 C are filed with the company, the company is required to the file form No III prescribed under the companies rules, 1975, with the register of companies within 30 days from the date of receipt forms I & II from the shareholding company and of the mutual fund by paying the appropriate filing fees as prescribed in schedule X of the act. Section 187-C of the act does not apply to the shares purchased or acquired by the mutual fund since the shares are registered in the company's name and to the account of mutual fund.

Sec. 153-3 of the act provides that where any shares or debenture exceeding a certain value are held in trust by any person, such person has to make a declaration to the public trustee appointed by the central government under section 153-A of the act within 60 days inform No. 1 annexed to trustees Rules, 1964 and send a copy of the declaration to the company concerned within 21 days after the declaration in Form I shall be made in respect of the shares or debentures held by it as such on or before 31st March, company wise by the end of May of May every year. If there is any change in the shareholding or debentures holding given in the declaration in Form I the person who has given the declaration has to send a report in form II appended to the trustees rules 1964, to the public trustee notifying such change within 30 days from the date of such change.

According to the companies act 187-B section indicates that the public trustee all the powers and rights exercisable by mutual funds. The mutual fund and the sponsoring companies are required to comply with some of the number same provision of the companies act 1956.

Risk Factors of a Mutual Fund

Risk is the essence of the valuation of the financial investment. The value of a financial asset depends upon many factors. Risk means a chance the expected gain profit or return may not materialise. The actual outcome of the investment may be less than the expected outcome. If the certainty of outcomes expected variance is zero it is called a risk free. Risk can be defined as "The variability of returns from those that are expected" the actual.

On the investment may determing the value and making the investment choices. Risk and Return are the foundations for maximising the shareholders wealth. The return can be defined as "Income received on an investment plus any change in market price, usually expressed as a percentage of beginning market price of the investment." The return comes from two sources income plus any price appreciation for common stock the one-period return can be computed with the following formula.

$R = \frac{Dt + (P_t - p_t - 1)}{P_t - 1}$ Dt = cash dividend at the end of the time period t

Pt = stock price at the time period t

R = Actual return

t = A particular time period in the past/future

(pt - 1) = stock price at time period t - 1

The return which we expect is different from the return which we receive for highly risky securities the actual rate of return can be viewed as a random variable subject to a "probability distribution. It can be defined as A set of possible values that random variable can assume and their associated probabilities of occurrence. The probability distribution is based on two factor of the distribution.

a) The expected return b) the standard duration. The expected return is a weighted average of the possible returns with the weights being the probabilities of occurrence". The expected return can be defined as "the weighted average of possible returns, with the weights being the probabilities of occurrence". The expected return can be calculated by the following formula.

$\overline{R} = \Sigma (R_i) (P_i)$

$\overline{R}$ = Expected return

R_i = Return for the ith possibility

P_i = The probability of a return occurring

n = The total number of possibilities.

The another factor which influences the probable distribution is the standard deviation. The expected return is based around the dispersion or variability of a financial asset. The conventional measure of dispersion is the standard deviation. Standard deviation can be defined as "A statistical measure of the variability of a distribution around its mean it is the source root of the variance". The standard deviation of returns depends upon the variability of returns. The standard deviation of return depends upon the variability of returns. The standard deviation can be expressed mathematically as

$$\sqrt{\Sigma(R_i - \overline{R})^2 (P_i)}$$

θ = standard deviation

R_i = return an investment

$\overline{R}$ = The expected return on investment

P_i = probability occurrence of the financial asset.

The standard deviation sometimes confuses and sometimes makes to fall in dilemma when compared with the risk of a financial assets. To overcome the limitations of the standard deviation it can be better to find out its co-efficient of variation the co-efficient of variation can be found by dividing the standard deviation with the expected return. The co-efficient of variation can be defined as "The ratio of the deviation of a distribution to the measure of the distr ution of the deviation. It is a measure of relative risk". The co-efficient of variation can be calculated by the following formula.

$$CV = \frac{\sigma}{\overline{R}}$$

$\overline{\sigma}$ = standard deviation

$\overline{R}$ = expected returns

Thus co-efficient of variation is a measure of the risk permit of expected return. The larger CV. The larger the relative risk of the financial assets the average investor is a wise to risk. The risky investments should offer higher expected returns then less risky investments in order to make the people and hold it. Therefore the risk average can be defined as "Term applied to an investor who demands a higher expected return the higher risk". The low risk investments some times produce at rate higher returns. Investors usually make their investments in a single financial asset or they deploy their wealth in a combination of two or more investments. There is combination of investments are called as "portfolio" portfolio can be defined as "A combination of two or more securities or assets" mutual fund performance depends upon the management of portfolio. The NAV is the barometer of performance of any type of mutual fund. The reflection of better management of portfolio is an indication of the high NAV of the units. The expected returns of a portfolio is a weighted average of the expected returns of the securities comprising that portfolio. The weights are equal to the proportion of total funds in vested in each security the formula for the expected return of a portfolio can be as follows:

$\overline{R}_j = \Sigma W_j R_j$

$j = 1$

$\overline{R}_p$ = the expected return on portfolio.

W_j = The proportion of the investments in security j.

$\overline{R}_p$ = The expected return for security j

m = The total number of different securities in the portfolio.

The fund managers of the mutual fund will have to concentrate on many factors like portfolio standard deviation, co-variance, correlation, co-efficient etc. The portfolio management also concentrates on the diversification. The concept of diversification is to spread the risk across a number of assets or investments. The meaningful diversification reduces the risk. The portfolio risk comprises two components.

Total Risk = Systematic risk + unsystematic Risk.

The systematic risk means the overall movements of the general market or economy. It is caused by a number of factors. This type of risk is inescapable. The systematic risk is also called market risk or non-diversifiable risk. The systematic risk can be defined as "The variability of return on stocks or portfolios associated with changes in return on the market as a whole". The diversification cannot reduce this risk another risk element is unsystematic risk. The unsystematic risk also called as "Non – market risk" or diversifiable risk" The non-systematic risk can be reduced by the diversification the securities total return is not related to the overall market variability. The unsystematic risk can be defined as the "variability return of stocks or portfolios not explained by general market movements. It is avoidable through diversification". The unsystematic risk is violated to a particular company or industry. Unsystematic risk is independent of economic, political and other factors that affect all the assets in a systematic manner. All the risk associated with the market portfolio theories have developed a critical important concept "Beta" Beta is a measure of relative risk of security. Beta is coefficient measuring securities of a stock's returns to changes in returns on the market portfolio. The Beta of portfolio is simply a weighted average of the individual stock betas in the portfolio. The security with a higher (than 1) beta is more volatile than the market, and the net asset with a lower (than 1) beta would rise or fall slowly than the market for ex: β = lis for every one percentage change in the market return, on an average the security return also will changes by one per cent.

To understand the financial market in a better way it is necessary to know the value of financial asset. The value of (a) financial assets are highly influenced by the return and risk. The fund managers should keep in mind about these components in their portfolios. These two elements can be ignored under any circumstances The fund manager skill reflects in the risk reduction of portfolio and enhance the return to an efficient portfolio. The risks may be classified in a number of ways.

The following are said to be the major types of risks which a mutual fund should not be ignored while designing the innovative schemes to meet the needs of the unit holders. They are default risk liquidity risk, financial risk, maturity risk, inflation risk, currency risk, country risk business risk, Interest risk, rate risk. Default risk, means the failure of repayment on the part of the debtor. The debtor fails to pay the capital and income risk. It has the capital risk and income risk. It effects the fund based activities Liquidity risk means a situation where the assets will be sold in the market after a great inconvenience which costs in terms of money and time. It can be bought and sold quickly without any price concessions and transactions costs it is called as liquid risk. Financial risk is concerned with the debt equity ratio of the company. The higher debt equity ratio, the higher the financial risk. The more debt component of the capital structure leads to financial risk. Maturity risk means the risk will arises when the financial assets maturity happens to be longer. The time factor leads the risk. The long term debt involve greater risk. Inflation risk is closely associated with the fixed income security. It is the risk that the real income on a financial asset is less than the nominal income. It is also known as purchasing power risk purchasing power risk is associated with a chance of the purchasing power of the invested money declines due to inflation. (that the firms which are involved). The inflation is actually the risk of uncertain inflation currency risk refers that the firm which are involved in the global transaction affects the variability in cash flow according to the fluctuations of Forex market. It arises mainly when the demand and supply for the foreign currency changes. It is also known as "Exchange risk" banks and EIS are also normally affected by these sources of risk. Country risk means the uncertainty in respect of an investment in a particular country. The country risk has many elements. The political risk and economic stability are the other important elements. Business risk arises due to the nature of a firms business. The business risk has two elements i.e controllable. The controllable risk means the firm can control that component by the efficient operating conditions are beyond its control. Business risk can be measured by the analysis of the earning capability of a firm over a time. Interest rate risk refers that the variability in income of financial asset due to changes in the level of market interest rated. It exists all types securities.

Unforeseen risk proves that every long term stock investors too dump a fund at the worst time. A fund past performance tends to be an unreliable guide except for the worst funds. Volatility in the market is a row line consistent. The funds managers have much more control over the risks than returns, the investor may expect ups and downs in the market and can use the risk indicators to choose a relatively well placed fund speculators can bear higher risk for higher returns the technique reveals the risks that are likely to be most rewarding.

Risk indicators involve mathematics Beta is the most common measure of the risk. A beta of 1, matches market risk, less than 1 a fund is calmer than the market Alpha is a performance measure adjusted for the risk. A fund that responds more to the markets advances than the deadlines has a positive Alpha.

Growth funds concentrates on the companies which have rapidly increasing earnings and riskier than the values funds which hunts for those stocks at low multiples of earnings or book value. To reduce the over all risk a balanced portfolio of funds should be placed across the spectrum with perhaps a slight till towards small stocks and value for the term in.

Performance Valuation of Mutual Funds

The SEBI has come out with a standard format of the balance sheet for mutual funds in India. The mutual funds industry does not have a standard accounting policy and comparison may be done after the adjustments the mutual fund performance is based on the Net Asset value. The NAV of the unit is an important concept and it is the basis for the unit pricing. In the case of open ended and closed end schemes the NAV can be calculated as follows :

$$\text{NAV} = \frac{\text{Total market value of the Assets in the portfolio of the fund–liabilities}}{\text{Number of funds units out standing}}$$

The NAV is determined by the stock market prices. The stock market prices are influenced by the supply the demand and the other factors the units are discounted to the extent value of the net asset value, and the average discount have been about 25% and in certain cases the discounts are as high as 30 to 50% the following factors may give rise to discounts.

(i) The close ended fund units are very limited trading in value and volume.

(ii) The close ended scheme units floating is very small.

(iii) high administrative expenses and management fees causes low dividend which in turn low the prices

(iv) The units prices are very low because the brokers offers low prices which they have to hold them for a more time.

(v) On overall the market for these units is limited while comparing with the cooperate shares.

The NAV includes dividends, interest accruals and reduction of liabilities, expenses besides market value of investments the causes for the non-satisfactory performance of the mutual funds are as follows:

(a) poor investment planning.

(b) too much diversification of portfolio.

(c) blue chip scrips do not yield more than average return.

(d) high turn over of portfolio leads to huge payment of brokerage.

(e) wrong prediction about income, profitability, interpretation of government policies.

Sufficiency of Mutual Fund

A good mutual fund always works for the satisfaction of the unit holders. The elevation of a mutual fund can be done by taking the following factors into consideration.

Liquidity: A good mutual fund should create liquidity to its unit holders in the form of limiting on a stock exchange.

Stability: A mutual fund should be stable and offer a wide range of schemes for a long term period.

Growth: The fund must concentrate on increasing the NAV's consistent growth in dividend and capital appreciation.

Returns: A fund should assure better returns to its unit holders and try to achieve the goal.

Credibility: Previous track record of issuer and investor before investing should decide and verify the track record

Management Approach

Manage: The management of a fund depends upon many factors i.e. diversification, risk bearing, return maximisation.

Method of Valuation of the Investments: Every mutual fund in India should value investments according to the following valuation norms.

(a) Traded securities

(b) Non-traded securities

(c) Rights shares

While valuing the traded securities the following factors should be taken into consideration.

(i) The securities should be valued at the least quoted closing price on the bourse

(ii) If the scrips are traded on more than one stock exchange, generally the AMC is left to select the appropriate stock exchange the reasons selection should be recorded in writing. Usually all the scrips can be valued at the prices quoted on the stock exchange where a majority in value of the securities are principally treated.

(iii) In a particular valuation day, if a security has not be treated on the selected stock exchange may be taken.

(iv) In some situations, when a scrip is not traded in any stock exchange on a specific valuation day. The earliest previous day quotation may be used for consideration. But such date should not be more than 60 days prior to the valuation date.

The non-traded securities will be valued in the following manner.

(a) A scrip may be treated as a non-traded scrip, if it is not traded on any stock exchange for a period of 30 days prior to the valuation date.

(b) The asset management company has the authority to value. The non-traded securities in the following procedure.

 (i) The board of directors of the AMC should prescribe the norms for valuation of non traded securities.

 (ii) The decision of the board of directors of the AMC must be documented in the minutes and the supporting data in respect of each security. So valued must be preserved.

 (iii) The methods used to find out the value of non traded security should be periodically review by the trustees of the mutual funds.

 (iv) The auditors of the MFS should be reported as fair and reasonable in their report on the value accounts of the mutual fund.

 (v) The equity instruments should be reported valued on the basis of capitalisation of earnings or NAV method.

 (vi) The debt instruments should be valued on the yield to maturity fund basis.

 (vii) The value of investments like call money, short term deposits, re-discounted bills should be valued at the cost plus accrual.

 (viii) The value of other money market instruments should be valued at the yield for which they are currently traded.

 (ix) The government securities should be valued at yield to maturity based on the current market rates.

 (x) For the valuation of the non traded instruments would be valued as follows. Cost of the non traded instrument accrued at the beginning of the day + Redemption value – the cost (spread to the remaining maturity prior of the investment)

 (xi) For the valuation of non-convertable debenture, it will be treated as debt instrument and valued accordingly.

 (xii) In case of convertible debentures, the convertible component should be valued as an equity instrument.

 (xiii) If the financial instruments have been brought on repo basis, the instrument must be valued as:
 The resale price – interest upto the date of resales.

 (xiv) If the financial instrument has been sold on repo basis.
 Repurchase price – Interest (upto the date of repurchase price) – The value of the instrument. If the repurchase price exceeds the investment value of the depreciation should be provided if the repurchase price is lower than the value of the instrument, adjustment must be taken into consideration.

 (xv) In case of valuation of equity, the warrants to subscribe for shares attached to instruments can be valued at the value of the share minus the cost of warrant.

The value of rights shares should be calculated as: The price of the rights share may either cum right price or an ex right price. "The cum right price gives the buyer, besides the ownership of shares already held, the right to apply for new shares offered by the company, while the existing shares held by the seller and not the right to apply for additional shares offered by the company. Ex-right price is quoted either after the rights shares have already been allotted by the companies or the time to apply for right shares has already expired the value of the right can be calculated by the following formula.

$$R = \frac{M - S}{N + 1}$$

R = Value of one right

M = Cum-right market price of a share

S = Subscription price for a new share

N = No. of shares held required to purchase one new share.

The valuation of a share ex-right can be obtained by the following formula.

$$P = \frac{MN + S}{N + 1}$$

P = Theoretical market value of share ex-right

M = cum-right market price

N = Number of old shares entitling to purchase one new share

S = Subscription price for a new share

After nativity the value of a right can also be calculated by the following formula.

$$R = \frac{P - S}{N}$$

R = Value of one right

P = Ex-right market price of share

N = Number of old shares utilising to new one share

S = Subscription price for one new share

Alternatively, until they are traded, the value of the right shares can also be calculated by applying the following formula.

$$V = \frac{N}{M} \times (P_{ex} - P_o)$$

V = Value of Right's share

N = No. of Right's offered

M = No. of original shares hold

P_{ex} = Ex-rights price

P_o = Rights offer price

While calculating the NAV of the MFS all expenses and incomes accrued upto the valuation date should be taken into consideration. The management expenses, and other expenses should be accrued on daily basis shall be adjusted. Any changes in portfolio of the mutual fund are to be recorded in the books upto a period of seven days following the date of the transaction the NAV calculation should not be effected by more than two per cent.

The price of the units must be determined with reference to the last determined NAV unless

(a) The sale price is determined with or without fixed premium added to the future NAV which declared in advance.

(b) While determining the prices of the Units, it must be assured that the repurchase price is not lower than 93% and the sale price is not higher than 107% of the NAV.

General Obligations: Every mutual fund in India should work according to the general obligations which were imposed by the act. Generally the mutual funds should fulfil the following obligations.

(1) Maintenance of proper books of Accounts.

(2) Accounting policies and standards.

(3) Financial year.

(4) Initial expenses treatment/issue expenses.

(5) Issue of warrants.

(6) Annual report.

(7) Auditor's report.

(8) Disclosure norms.

(9) Procedure for action in case of default.

The important obligation of a mutual fund in the maintenance the proper books of accounts according to the sub-regulation (2) of the sub regulations 1993. The mutual funds should keep the books or accounts to explain its transactions and to disclose it any point of time the financial position of the fund in particular give a true and fair view of the state of the affairs of the fund. The mutual fund shall inform to SEBI the place where the books, records and documents are maintained and available.

The mutual fund shall follow the accounting policies and standards to provide appropriate details in the following manner.

(a) The mutual funds should present all investments in the balancesheet at market value.

(b) The mutual fund while determining the holding cost of investment and the gain or loss on sale of investments, the average cost procedure should be followed.

(c) The income of a scheme is generally earned by the mutual fund is in the form of dividend. Income should be recognised by the fund on the date the share is quoted on an ex-dividend basis.

(d) If the shares are not quoted on the stock exchange. The dividend income should be recognised on the date of declaration by the concerned company.

(e) In case of debt instruments income must be calculated on a daily basis for the concerned period of the time.

(f) The financial statement of the mutual fund should reflect the transactions for the purchase or sale of investments for a particular trade date but not as of the settlement date.

(g) While evaluating the income of a scheme, bonus shares are also to be taken into consideration. The original shares are valued on ex-bonus basis.

(h) In case of rights entitlements, it should be recognised only when the original shares on which the rights entitlement accrues are traded on stock exchange on an ex-right basis.

(i) If the accrued income has not been received for a beyond due date, the provision should be made in revenue account of the scheme.

(j) In case of open ended scheme units are sold if any positive amount is arised it should be credited to reserves, and if negative amount fund it should be debited to reserves the face value will be created to capital account.

(k) If units are repurchased of an open ended scheme, if any positive amount is arised it should be debited to reserve and if negative should be credited to reserves the face value being debited to the capital account.

(l) Every mutual fund should maintain an equalisation for open ended scheme, on sale of the units an appropriate part of the proceeds should be credited to it. When the units repurchased by the MF an appropriate amount should be debited to equalisation account. The net balance of this account should be adjusted in revenue amount.

(m) Every mutual fund should maintain capital account for each close ended scheme. In this scheme, if the mutual fund repurchase its units, the per value of the unit should be debited to capital account. If any positive amount is available, it should be credited to reserves and if any negative, it should be debited to reserves.

(n) A proportionate initial expenses should also be transferred to the reserves.

(o) The investment in different financial instruments should include stamp charges, brokerage charges etc.

(p) In case of debt instruments, if any discount is found in purchasing moment, it should be reduced from the cost of investment.

(q) If any under writing commission received by the mutual fund, it should be treated as revenue only when there is no development on the scheme. If there is development, the under writing commission should be adjusted according to the proportion.

Financial Year: Accounting year for all to schemes shall end on the same end on the same date which shall be March 31. In case of a new scheme which is commenced the accounting year, the discourage and reporting requirement would apply for the period beginning from the date of its commenced and ending on the last date of the relevant accounting year of the mutual fund.

Treatment of Issue Expenses: Every mutual fund should identify all expenses clearly and must be appropriate for each scheme. The asset management company (AMC) is important organ in mutual fund. It will undertake the functions of buying and selling securities of the each scheme. The AMC renders the investment advisory services on turnover basis of the schemes. It will charge the fee to mutual fund which is fully disclosed in the offer document subject to the following.

(a) If the net assets do not exceeds Rs. 100 crores, the commissioner fee is one and a quarter of one per cent of the weekly average net assets in each accounting year for each scheme.

(b) If the net assets exceeds Rs. 100 crores, one per cent of the excess amount over Rs. 100 crores will be charged.

(c) In addition to the above fee the AMC may change the MF with the following expenses.

   (a) Initial issue cost sponsoring the fund and its schemes.

   (b) Recurring expenses such as brokerage marketing and selling expenses, registrar's services for transfer of shares agents commissions all of these initial expenses in respect of any one scheme shall not exceed 6% of the fund raised under that scheme in addition to the above expenses, the following expenses may also be changed to the mutual fund.

      (i) Fee and expenses of trustee
      (ii) audit fee
      (iii) custodian fee
      (iv) cost of funds from location to location.
      (v) winding up costs for terminating a mutual fund/scheme.
      (vi) cost of statutory advertisements.
      (vii) cost regarding to investor communication
      (viii) any such other costs may be approved by the SEBI.

Treatment of Initial Expenses: The initial expenses must be accounted in the books of account of each scheme specified as below.

(i) The issue of the scheme can be classified into two categories.

   (a) load

   (b) no load basis or sometimes it may issue as mixed basis the type of issue should be clearly explained to the investors in the other document in the case of a close ended scheme floated on a load basis the initial issue expenses should be amortised on a weekly basis over the period of the scheme.

(ii) In the case of open ended schemes, the unamortized portion of the expenses are to be

(iii) In case of open ended schemes, floated on the load basis. The initial expenses may be amortised over a period not exceeding 5 years. The expenses incurred during the life of an open ended scheme cannot be amortised.

(iv) In case of load basis open end and close end schemes. The unamortised portion of the expenses are to be included in the calculation of net asset value. But such portion should not be included for calculation of the advisory service to the AMC.

(v) If the schemes floated on a no load basis the AMC can lay on an additional management for not exceeding 1% of the NAV. The AMC is entitled to levy a contingent charges as follow.
   (a) It may be entitled to levy a contingent deferred sales charge for redemption during the first four years after purchase should not exceed 4% of the reduce redemption proceeds in the first year.
   (b) It is 3% in the second year.
   (c) It is 2% in the third year.
   (d) It is 1% in the fourth year.

(vi) The distribution charges, in case of load schemes should be borned by the Scheme of the mutual fund.

(vii) The distribution charges in case of load schemes should be borne by the asset management company.

All the initial expenses together should not exceed to 6%. If any amount exceed it should be borne by the AMC, the total expenses of the scheme excluding issue/redemption expenses but including the investment management and advisory fee are subject to the following limits.

(a) On the first Rs. 100 crores of the average weekly net assets 2.5%.

(b) On the next Rs. 300 crores of the average weekly net assets 2.25%.

(c) On the next Rs. 300 crores of the average weekly net assets 2%.

(d) On the balance of the assets 1.75%

Any expenditure exceeding limits should be borne by the AMC/Trustee/Sponsor. The SEBI cannot be approved the expenses beyond the certain level of percentage.

Issue of Warrants: The issue of warrants or dividends to the unit holders must be dispatch within 42 days of the declaration of the dividend, repurchase proceeds must be paid to unit holder within 10 days from the date of repurchase/redemption.

Annual Report: Every mutual fund should prepare annual report on scheme wise basis or an abridged summary. It shall be published through an advertisement within 6 months from the date of the relevant financial year. The Annual report abridged summary shall contain details as specified in Schedules VII and VIII of the act.

The annual report of the every mutual fund shall be made available for inspection at the head office of the mutual fund. If any number so required, a copy thereof shall be made available on payment of nominal fee as specified by the mutual fund.

Auditor's Report: The books of accounts of the every mutual funds should be audited by an auditor. The auditor shall be different from the auditor of the AMC. According to the Sabli regulation 65, the auditor may be defined as "Auditor means a person who is qualified to audit the accounts of a company U/C 224 of the companies Act 1956". An auditor of the mutual fund should be appointed by the trustees. The audit report shall form a part of the annual report of the mutual fund. The auditors should comprise of a certificate to the effect of that

(a) he has obtained all informations and explanations which to the best of his knowledge and belief were necessary for the purpose of his audit.

(b) The statements of accounts has been prepared in accordance with accounting policies and standards as specified by the SEBI.

(c) The balance sheet and the revenue account give a fair and true view of the scheme, state of affairs and surplus or deficit in the fund for the accounting period to which the balance sheet or as the case may be the revenue account relates.

Disclosure Norms: The scheme wise annual report of the mutual fund or its abridged summary thereof should be published through an "advertisement" and an abridged scheme wise annual report shall be mailed to all the unit holders within six months from the date of closure of the relevant accounting year. The report shall contain all the information as specified by the SEBI. The report should reflect a true and fair view of the operations of the mutual fund. But the abridged information shall not contain full portfolio disclosure but must contain details regarding fund activities according to the SEBI norms. If any mutual fund publish full accounts in newspapers, the full portfolio disclosure is not required. Every mutual fund should submit all the information to the SEBI within 6 months from the date of closure of each financial year. The mutual fund, AMC, trustees, custodian, sponsor of the mutual fund should make such disclosure or submits such documents as they may be called upon to do so by SEBI. The MF should furnish the periodical reports to the SEBI as follows:

(a) Copies of the duly audited annual statements of accounts including the balance sheet for the mutual fund and in respect of each scheme once a year.

(b) A company of six monthly unaudited accounts.

(c) A quarterly statements of movements in net assets for each of the schemes of the fund.

(d) A quarterly portfolio statement including changes from the previous periods for each scheme.

The sale of units should be done by the trustees or the AMC after providing sufficient information made available for the investors to take a informed decision. The trustees of the mutual funds are bound to make disclosures to the unit holders. It is response of the trustees to keep the investors informed about all the available information. SEBI is the most powerful organisation in the financial sector of the nation. It has the full authority in the Primary market, Secondary market, Money market and Mutual fund industry. All the mutual funds in India shall act as per the guidelines norms issued by the SEBI from time to time in force. SEBI is the watch dog of the stock market and mutual fund sector. The SEBI is empowered to suspend registration of a mutual fund. If a mutual fund fails in the following situations.

(a) Fails to furnish any information.

(b) Fails to furnish wrong information to relating to its activities.

(c) Fails to submit periodical returns.

(d) Fails to comply with directions.

(e) Fails to resolve investor complaint.

(f) In guilty of misconduct/unprofessional ethics.

(g) Fails to pay any fee.

(h) Fails to maintain net worth of the Asset management company.

The SEBI has the authority to cancel the registration of a mutual fund or impose a penalty on the following grounds.

(a) If the mutual fund asset management company trustees of the mutual fund involved in price rigging or manipulation or concerning activities affecting the securities market and the investor interest.

(b) The mutual fund or AMC or trustees or custodian is guilty of fraud or is convicted of a criminal offence.

(c) The mutual fund has been guilty or repeated defaults which result in suspension of the registration.

(d) The financial position of the mutual fund deteriorates to such an extent that the board is of the opinion. That its continuance is not in the interest of investors and other mutual funds.

Therefore, the SEBI has the full authority in either cancellation of a registration of a mutual fund or suspension of registration of the license of the fund/AMC/trustee. The suspension/cancellation of a certificate of the mutual fund should be preceded by an inquiry by enquiry officers. The SEBI has the authority to appoint an enquiry officer. The enquiry officer shall issue a notice of the MF/AMC/Trustee/Custodian as the case may be at the registered office or the principal place of business of the concerned. The MF/AMC/Trustee/custodian may within 30 days from the date of receipt of such notice furnish to the enquiry officer a reply together with copies of documentary or other evidence relied on by him or sought by the board from him.

The enquiry officer shall give to the concerned person a reasonable opportunity of being heard to enable him to make submissions in support of his reply under the sub regulation (3). The alleged person of his reply under or any other person as behalf of him should be presented before the enquiry officer. But no advocate is permitted on behalf of the person. But in some time the SEBI will give permission to attend the advocate on behalf of the MF/AMC/Trustee. The enquiry officer shall after taking into account all relevant facts and submissions made by the party submit a report to the board and recommended the penalty to be awarded as also the grounds on the basis of which the penalty proposed in the notice is justified on the basis of the report the SEBI would issue a show cause notice which the mutual fund must replay within 14 days. After hearing the reply, it would approve the action for default. Every order passed under sub-regulation (3) shall be self contained and give reasons for the conclusion stated than including justification of the penalty imposed by that order. The board shall send a copy of the order under sub regulation (3) to the MF and central government on and from the date of suspension. The MF shall cease to carry on any activity related to MF during the period of suspension on and from the date of cancellation the MF shall cease to carry on any activity related to that MF. The order of suspension of cancellation of registration passed under sub regulation (3) of regulation 71, shall be published in atleast two daily newspapers by the board. Any person aggrieved by an order of the board may prefer an appeal to the central government.

Winding Up of Schemes: In mutual fund, there are basically two kinds of schemes available to the investors. They are categorised as (i) open ended scheme (ii) close ended scheme.

An open ended scheme shall be wind up if the total number of units outstanding after repurchases at any point of time follows below 50% of the originally issued number of units. A close ended schemes of a mutual fund may be wound up.

(a) On the expiry of the period of time if any, fixed for the duration of the scheme by that scheme or

(b) On the happening of any event which in the opinion of trustees, requires the scheme to be wound up or

(c) If 70% of the unit holders of a scheme pass a resolution that the scheme be wound up; or

(d) If the board so directs in the interest of the unit holders.

If a scheme is to be wound up in pursuance to sub-regulation of the act, the trustees shall give notice of the circumstances leading to the winding up of the scheme on and from the date of advertisement of the winding up the trustees or the AMC as the case may be shall:

(a) cease to carry on any business activities.

(b) cease to create and cancel units in the scheme.

(c) cease to issue and redeem units in the schemes.

Procedure and Manner of Winding Up: The mutual fund of the trustee shall call a meeting of the unit holders to consider and pass necessary resolutions by simple majority of the unit holders present and voting at the meeting for authorising the trustees or any other persons to take steps for winding up of the scheme.

(a) The trustee or the person authorised under the act shall dispose of the assets of the scheme concerned in the best interest of the unit holders of that scheme.
The trustee or the person authorised under the act (delete) shall dispose of the assets of the scheme concerned in the best interest of unit holders of that scheme.

(b) The proceeds of sale made in pursuance of clause (a) above shall in the first instance be utilised towards discharge of such liabilities as are properly due under the scheme and after making appropriate provisions for meeting the expenses connected with such winding up the balance shall be paid to the unit holders in proportion to their respective interest in the assets of the schemes as on the date when the decision for winding up trustees was taken.

On the completion of the winding up the trustees shall forward to the SEBI and after the receipt of the report, if the board is satisfied that all measures for winding up of the scheme have been completed, the scheme shall cease to exist.

DISCLOSING THROUGH THE WEB MUTUAL FUNDS STYLE

Recent Developments: Over the course of the past year, the returns many equity mutual funds remained in negative territory. This has been largely due to the direction taken by the markets, the fund managers could not give returns due to market situation. The mutual funds now issued as investments which empower investors to participate in the growth of financial market fund investments are transparent as investors are regularly informed about their portfolio. The latest development in the market is mutual funds are also providing information on websites. The websites of different funds focus on the information required by the investors. Daily disclosures of the NAV, regular monthly updates and information on dividends and changes in the load structure are the things which all the investors should below are before investing.

www. alliance capital india.com

The site provides the first hand information about the net asset value of the fund. The previous days NAV of all the schemes is provided in an easily accessible manner on the site and is updated regularly. The site contains the information such as news about dividend declaration funds holding in its different schemes etc. The quarterly reports also contains the same information. The information about the portfolio usually contains only the top ten holdings of the particular scheme. The website provide the financial data about the funds returns over different time periods as well as the benchmark of the sector.

The site provides offer document for all the funds schemes. These can be down loaded in a format. There can also be requested through — e-mail as well as post. A facility for receiving the NAV the funds schemes as well as news up dates through e-mail is also provided on the site.

The site also provides information about the funds as well as its key personnel along with the directors and the trustees details about the qualification and the experience of the key personnel also provided telephone numbers and addresses of the funds offices in different cities as well as their of its transfer agents are provided the funds site has a learning centre which has a section of frequently asked question and an archieve of useful articals from the investment manager. Here also some of the information is out dated. A glossary and simple savings calculator are also present on the site.

www.pioneeriti.com:

The PIONEER ITI can breached through above address. The fund is upto the mark by presenting the latest information on NAVs of its different schemes. A facility for the daily receipt of NAV through e-mail is also provided.

The portfolio of the funds and different schemes are presented under the heading of the monthly performance reports. Pioneer ITI is among few funds which provides full disclosure of the portfolios for each month of the year. The information about returns will be provided and is also to be updated on a weekly basis.

The funds site provides a number of tools for the financial planning these include savings, networth and inflation calculator. The savings and newworth calculator are require detailed inputs and one's financial position. These concerned para metres provides a realistic time frame for developing a saving plan. The inflation calculator is a simple tool to demonstrate the effect of inflation on the current prices.

Forms required for marketing the investments, redemptions or switches are provided in a down loaded format these also includes the slips for the information about the change of address. Change of account number and other routine communication between investor and the fund.

The funds CEO communicates with the investors on a monthly basis through the site. This is usually as some as the communication as that provided in the monthly fact sheet. This is based on the issues faced by the investor and provides inputs for targets oriented investing. As the proliferation of ranking surveys are being carried out the funds are eager to impress the investors about their performance. This information is also provided by the fund and usually shows the results of the latest ranking exercises. The fund also provided the data of different volatility measures of its different schemes. The significance of these also communicated the fund provides the detailed information, about itself and its sponsors. Information about the funds key personnels and trustees is also not present. The sites section on the EAQ's provides a series of questions which take investors through the entire process of investing and the possible questions which arises in an investors mind. These also indicates general questions on mutual funds and the concept of fund investing reports about the funds in different sanctions of the press are included in the site. The site provides the address and telephone numbers of its offices in different cities.

BASICS OF FUNDS MANAGEMENT

The key objective behind every investment is to get better return out of the same, with a moderate degree of risk associated with it. But, in order to reep the benefits from an investment, be it equity and should be in a bonds, MFs, FDs. The investor should be better informed and should be in a position to take a call based on certain analysis, and not just be a layman putting the hard earned money on rumours and information floating around in the market place.

In case of the assets of mutual fund which is pool of assets from the individual investors, the most significant risk is the pool fund performance. While analysing the performance of a fund, crisil in its research tries to address only portfolio (market) risk and not the credit, counter party, operation and risks. In case of pension funds and insurance companies, sufficient research has taken place on asset liability management. In the Banking sector, already there exist sophisticated models to measure and manage the risk. In case of a funds operations fund advisors demands are increasing to understood how performance has been achieved for the risk assumed.

For a majority of funds performance is assessed against the prescribed bench marks for the some. A number of methods to assess portfolio risk do exist and many of the funds adopt standard deviations as a measure of risk along with a few others for the. simple fact that no single modes can predict risk accurately. The basic idea of evaluation of a mutual fund can be implemental more accurately by taking into account the whole organisation. Also, once the risk management process is put in place in a fund.

House, it would prove better for key people chief investment officers (CIO) fund managers, research analysts, dealers to take cautious decisions based on the set of defined parameters.

In the context of a funds performance diversification is in inverse proportion with the risk, within certain limits. The market linked risk from economy-related factors like fiscal policy industrial policy, money supply inflation. etc.. cannot be eliminated. Thus, the risk that can be explained by the market conditions is called, systematic risk and the unexplained residual risk (which could be company or industry or instrument specific) is called unsystematic risks..

Top of the Pops: These are a Few of their Favourite Sectors

The scores have changed, so has the popularity. The pharmacubical sector –riding high on expanding global demand for generic drugs has emerged as the most popular sector among mutual funds for the quarter ended September 2001. However, even after having its seen during these three months, Infosys technologies still tops the funds popularity index chart.

In spite of the ET-crisil fund popularity index chart, for the September quarter, indicating a 44.8% fall in proporsity to invest in infosys technologies by mutual funds. It still ruled as the most popular stock hold by funds.

The proporsity to invest by funds in pharmaceutical stocks rose sharply by 37.76%. However, the proporsity to invest fell to 55-62 per cent in case of information technology stocks for the quarter ended September, 2001.

During the same period, most funds pared their holdings in Infoseys technologies by 23 per cent. The total percentage to net asset value (NAV) of the scrip in funds slipped .42 per cent to 4.97 per cent even the price of the scrip fell 26 per cent to 2.400.

For the some period, stock performances of the private sector mutual funds (excluding UTI) indicator four of the top 20 stocks in their portfolio are pharmaceutical stocks. Two information technology stocks are not a single one from the media and telecom sector.

THE VALUE – WEIGHTED HOLDINGS

Scrips	*Sept 29, 2001*	*Jun 30, 2001*	*Chg (%)*
Ranbaxy labs	2.96	0.96	208.84
ACC	2.63	1.32	99.54
Dr. Reddy's labs	4.93	2.84	73.68
Hero Honda Motors	3.61	2.13	69.55
Cipla	5.79	4.23	36.76
HCL	3.57	2.64	34.97
Reliance Ind	4.74	3.85	23.12
ITC	3.6	3.01	19.74
Grasim Industries	3.19	2.82	13.02
Satyam Computers	2.65	2.47	7.41
MTNL	1.05	0.98	7.06
AVANTIS pharma	2.07	2.03	1.86
VSNL	2.16	2.12	1.68
HPCL	1.87	1.82	–0.13
BHEL	2.57	2.66	–3.68
BPCL	2.57	1.99	–5.23
SBI	1.81	2.05	–11.88

Sources: The Economic Times, 9-11-2001, CRISL Fund Tracker, p. 7.

On the other hand, the remaining 14 of these top 20, stocks, belonging to core sector like capital good, engineering, cement, steel, petroleum products and petro chemicals.

Diversification is clearly the new months in the mutual funds industry, as is evident from the ET-crisil analysis of the changing proformance of fund managers. The study excludes all the overseas registered foreign industritional investor (FII) without portolio details as well as domestic mutual funds monalith Unit Trust of India due to non-availability of its portfolio for the period ended September 2001.

Hindalco industries	1.81	2.05	–11.88
L & T	3.66	4.22	–13.33
Infosys technologies	4.92	8.49	–42.04

Analysis of the top equity holding are based on 2 factors the number of schemes. Comprising a particular stock and the simple average of the percentage holdings of each scheme in the particular stock (without considering the absolute value of the holdings) It is therefore an amalgamation of how commonly owned. The scrip is and the extent to which the funds are willing to allocate their portfolios (irrespective of the size of at portfolio) to that scrip we call this popularity index.

The sample size includes 98 equity and balanced schemes which account for over 70 per cent of the total assets of the private sector domestic mutual funds in these two categories (please see accompanying tables)

THE VALUE, VOLUME, PRICE GAMES

	Value (Rs. M)			***Volume (100's)***			***Price (R)***		
	Sep-2001	*Jun-2001*	*chg(%)*	*Sep 2001*	*June-2001*	*chg(%)*	*Sep-2001*	*June-2001*	*chg(%)*
Infosys Tech	746.74	1543.46	-51.62	311.14	406.18	–23.40	2400.00	3794.95	–36.8
Cipla	883.86	5901.40	–1.95	792.70	789.32	0.43	1115.00	1142.00	–2.3
HLL	547.77	537.19	1.97	2646.23	2632.66	0.53	207.00	204.05	1.4
L & T	554.56	801.27	–30.79	2705.72	3647.11	–3.15	157.00	219.70	–28.5
Reliance Indus	719.45	921.36	–21.91	949.78	2481.11	9.05	265.90	317.35	–28.1
ITC Ltd.	550.59	558.91	–1.49	3221.45	741.3	28.12	579.70	754.00	–23.1
ACC	398.98	308.37	29.38	3984.03	2259.95	42.55	123.85	136.45	–9.2
BHEL	474.10	685.84	–30.87	2256.20	3853.02	3.40	119.00	178.00	–33.1
HDCL	275.59	297.74	–7.44	3151.41	1878.48	20.11	122.15	158.50	–22.8
Satyam Computers	400.23	590.51	-32.22	1557.73	3485.91	-9.60	127.00	169.40	-25.00
VSNL	328.60	322.79	1.80	1681.10	1010.46	54.16	210.95	319.45	–33
SBI	277.38	399.34	–30.54	2935.30	1827.67	–8.02	165.00	218.50	24
Hero Honda Motors	548.75	411.42	33.38	2935.30	2837.08	3.45	186.95	145.00	2.8
Hindalco Ind.	276.15	406.65	–31.92	542.17	472.78	14.68	509.35	853.00	–40.0
MTNL	160.47	196.15	–18.19	1263.57	1556.16	–18.80	127.00	126.05	0.75

So, which stocks pre in and which ones are out of favour will find managers? The popularity index of September 2001 has many as eight new extracts. These includes three pharmaceuticals stocks, to telecommunications stocks and one each from automobiles cement and steel industry. The eight new entrants comprise of Grasim industries in the (9th position) Dr. Reddy's (10th position), Avanth's Pharma (11th position) VSNL (16th position) Hero Honda (18th position) Hindalco Industries and MNTL taking the last two position respectively.

Information technology stocks such as digital global software HCL technologies. Wipro and Hughes, software all of which were among the most sought after stocks by funds for the quarter ended June 2001 have dropped out of the top 20. Stocks held by funds during the following quarter. Pharmaceuticals ranked 11th in June quarter moved out of the top 20 holdings of funds in the September.

Lets take a closer look at the most popular stocks. At the top Infosys remains the most preferred stock yet, however, the extent of its popularity has been eroding since December 2000. That's evident from the intensity of preference of propensity of invest which is measured by the percentage change in the combined score of how commonly owned. The stocks is and the simple average portfolio allocated to it between two periods.

The propensity to invest in Infosys technologies dropped by nearly 44.87 per cent for the quarter ended September 2001. In fact the intensity of preference for just three stocks of the top ten in the popularity index dipped dramatically for the September quarter Satyam computers slipped 60.18 per cent between June-September, while HCL Technologies fell 63.77 per cent.

Reliance Industries dipped 26.95 per cent and Bharat Heavy electricals fell by 14.87 per cent. A look at the value volume, the private sector mutual fund. A look at the volume, value figures will corroborate this third. In the case of Infosys the private sector mutual funds shed as much as 23 per cent of their volume holding in the stock.

This coupled with nearly 36 per cent Exosin the price of stock between June-September 2001 has resulted in a 51.62 per cent decline in the actual value of the funds Infosys holding, which came down to Rs. 746.74 millions on September 30, 2001.

On the other hand, Cipla, the second most popular stock witnessed a 14.8 per cent increase in the property to invest by funds in September 2001 over June 2001. Funds shed 0.43 per cent of the volume of them Cipla holdings even as price, dipped 2 per cent in the same period.

THE POPULARITY INDEX

Base ; Sep = 100	*Sep'01*		*June'01*		*Index chg(%)*
Company	*Index*	*Rank*	*Index*	*Rank*	
Infosys Techonogies	55.13	1	100	1	–44.87
Cipla	49.98	2	43.53	4	14.8
Hindustan Lever	40.55	3	32.11	7	26.29
Larsen & Toubro	38.5	4	34.65	5	11.13
Reliance Industries	37.90	5	52.01	2	–26.95
LTC	37.92	6	16.05	14	105.34
Bharat Heavy Electricals	31.37	8	36.85	9	–14.87
Grasim Industries	29.3	9	27.05	NA	8.35
Dr. Reddy Laboratories	27.62	10	10.38	NA	106.12
Bombay Laboratories	26.82	11	5.11	NA	424.89
Avantis Pharma	24.03	12	17.52	NA	37.2
Bharat Petrolium Corp.	17	13	16.93	NA	0.38
Hindustan Petro Corp.	16.08	14	13.86	17	15.95
Satyam Computure Services	14.2	15	35.66	18	–60.18
Videsh Sanchar Nigam	13.18	16	7.18	3	83.56
State Bank of India	13.13	17	10.47	NA	25.39

Hero Honda Motors	12.	18	9.49	19	30.68
Hindalco Industries	9.09	19	8.53	NA	6.50
Mahanagar Telephone Nigam	8.99	20	5.9	NA	52.2

Source: Economic Times, dt. 9.11.02, p. 7.

So the pure value of the funds holdings in Cipla, came down by nearly 1.0 per cent to Rs. 883.8 bm other pharmaceutical stocks like Dr. Reedy's Laboratories and Ranbaxy Laboratories entered the popularity index chart in September 2001. The sharpest Jump in popularity is seen in new extrant Ranbaxy Laboratories. It is the only stock in top 20 list in which funds value holding jumped a whooping 229 per cent to Rs 453. million. The same can be attributed to a 147 per cent increase in the volume holding, of the scrip in funds. The share price of the stock rose 33 per cent to Rs. 645 in September 2001.

REVISED METHODOLOGY

The redefined new methodology user superior returns score criteria instead of the sharp ratio, which was used for previous five quarters, the new CPR methodology is based on the following criteria — superior return score, concentration of the scheme portfolio liquidity and asset size of the scheme.

Final performance score is computed over four half year periods with the time weighing of 20 per cent 24 per cent, 26 per cent and 30 per cent. This is dawn so that the latest performance gets higher weightage.

Since hegetime sharpe ratio does not have theoretical significance it has been discontinual. Within a category, average daily/weekly returns of all schemes convened is obtained. Over the two-year period using this a benchmark, daily/weekly differential returns series is calculated. The superiors returns score takes into account market volatility in deciding realistic performance arising out of valuation anamalies, noticed especially in debt funds. The same is used globally by S & P for mutual fund evaluation.

The superior return score is forward. Looking in comparison to the historical shape ratio used earlier. The use of this new methodology is expected anomatics if any.

The industry concentration measures the exposure of mutual fund schemes (if equity and balance categories) in various industries over and above the industry distribution partners in the S & P.

CNX Nifty equity Index. In case of company concentration, the ranking makes use of the nifty index as a benchmark. It measures that part of the concentration risk that arises from deviating from the benchmark for deciding over-exposure on/nifty stocks, individual nifty stocks limits are considered. The liquidity criterian captures internal and external liquidity.

The Internal liquidity risk is computed by comparing the investment in each security against the depth of the market turnover for that security. This address the issue of impact cast inquired stocks or problems associated with non-sychorised trading arising out of infrequent trading. In debt finals the earlier CRP methodology made use of credit ratings of debt instruments to prove liquidity. But now debt portfolio asset quality is a factor of default or migration statistics arising out of credit risk history maintain by crisil to the various securities. This new parameter has replaced the liquidity parameter used in the earlier CPR ranking procedure for debt.

External liquidity risk refers to the influence on price that other funds or investors holding similar securities would face if they were to move is or out stocks. This calculated by comparing the average market capitalization (both turnover and market capitalization have quarterly weights as explained in internal liquidity ratio).

Liquidity of gifts funds is captured in the same manner in which the internal liquidity of the liquidity fund is captured. The assert site refers to the net investable funds of the mutual funds schemes.

This criticism is chosen as the complexity of fund management increases with an increase in the assets managed by these funds.

Accordingly higher score is assigned to larger schemes.

The ET- crisil composite performance ranking (CRISIL- CPR) for mutual funds covers all open – ended schemes, which have disclosed, their net asset values (NAV) for at least two years and make a 100 per cents disclosure of their portfolio composition. Crisil has undertaken to rank the various mutual fund schemes on a quarterly basis. A new category – Gifts- has been added in the CPR, for the quarter ended. September '01. The minimum cut off site of funds to be included in the CRP universe has been fixed at Rs. 10 crore for equity and balance funds, Rs. 40 crore for debt and required funds and Rs. 20 crore for gift funds. The earlier ranking methodology used to enplay percentile method to rank funds.

SURVIVING THE MELT DOWN

For analysis of Information Technology (IT) funds, ET and crisil studied the performance of the top ten information technology funds and tracked their returns over a one-year period ended September 2001. To track the changing performances of funds, the study tracked the composition of the portfolio of technology funds over a one-year period. We also analysed fund holding and like value of these holdings in information technology stocks for this period.

The average point-to-point return of these funds for a one-year period ended September 2001 was a negative 64 per cent. For the same period, Tata IT sector, fund came across as the best performer with a negative returns of 43.21 per cent whore as chola freedom technology cumulative fund, the second best performer, gave a negative returns of 52 per cent. Allience New millenium fund and the Kotak Mahindra, K-tech fund gave negative returns of 10 per cent and 72 per cent respectively.

Funds that used call money as a hedging mechanism have been able to draw some satisfaction in find sight for the period under consideration. Tata IT sector fund and chola freedom Technology have been able to out perform all their peers with their high exposure to call money.

Tata IT sector fund had over 36 per cent of its total assets invested in call money where as chola freedom, Technology had over 42 per cent of its assets invested in call and cash. Meanwhile worse performers like alliance new millenium fund and Kotex Mahendra. K-Tech find that gave negative returns of 70 per cent and 72 per cent of their total assets invested in call money, respectively.

Funds that gave higher negative returns were not better if in terms of stock selection in comparisons to fund that gave lower negative returns.

SLIP SLIDING RETURNS

Schemes	*Sep. 2001*	*Oct. 2000*	*% chg*
Tata IT Sector Fund Growth	6.13	10.80	–43.21
Chola freedom Technology-cumulative	7.07	14.85	–53.39
Prudential ICICI Technology Fund Growth	2.08	5.51	62.66
Birldit fund-Plan B-growth	5.97	17.35	–65.59
D S P Mesrall Lynch Technology fund	2.68	7.94	–66.25
1L & FSE Comfund-growth	1.91	5.73	–66.67
SBI Magnum Sector Umbrella-Infotech	4.60	15.03	–69.39
Alliance New Millennium fund-growth	2.48	8.28	–70.05
Pioneer ITI Infotech fund-growth	7.92	27.69	–71.40
Kotak Mahindra K-tech-fund	1.96	7.07	–72.27

Ergo, which technology stocks have been the hot favourite with funds. As per our analysis for the one-year period ended September 2001, most technology funds off loaded blue chip technology stocks and bought a few bank stocks. Infosys technologies which was the top holding of information technology funds in October 2000 at Rs. 16 bn fell to Rs. 7.21 bn in September 2001 fund's shed their holdings in SSI from Rs. 10.07 bn in October 2000 to Rs. 0.65 bn in September 2001. In case of NIIT, funds have recommended their holding from Rs. 7.30 bn to Rs. 6.01 bn exposure in HCL technology fell from Rs. 3.54 bn to Rs. 9.88 bn and in case of Wipro Technologies, the holding fell from Rs. 1.13 bn to Rs. 4.81 bn. So was the value change triggered by a variation in the volume of stocks hold by funds or was it due to an erosin or appreciation in the prices of these stocks to answer these questions we looked at the stock holdings of fund holding in polaries software shot up the highest between October 2000 and September 2000 and September 2001. Close on the heels of polaries were others like VSNL, Zee Telefilms, Sonata software and HCL Technologies.

FUNDS AND THEIR HOLDINGS

Stocks	*Sept. 2001*	*Oct. 2000*	*%chg*
Bharat Electronics	10.17	6.72	52.32
Citi Comp. Securities & Investments	31.57	22.46	40.56
Polaris Software	105.08	86.82	21.03
HDFL Bank	71.27	62.37	14.27
MTNL	60.71	64.52	–5.90
ICICI	19.95	21.35	–6.56
Digital Global Software	341.72	397.95	–14.13
Moser Baer India	70.37	91.43	–23.03
Hughes Software Systems	184.92	384.63	–51.92
Infosys Technologies	721.83	1,610.05	–55.17
Mphasis BPL	354,48	988.07	–64.12
Mastek	10.68	112.27	–90.49
Aptech	21.08	236.52	–91.19
NIIT	5.54	730.10	–99.24
HCL Technologies	1.18	6.63	–82.20
			Rs.(BN)

Clearly, fund holdings in stocks like Satyam Computers, Wipro Technologies, NIIT, and Mphasis fail substantially during the period. Meanwhile fund holding in stocks Zee Telefilms, VSNL, Sonata Software, Higher software, HCL technologies, HDFS bank, Citicop securities and investments and Bharat Electronics increased during this one year period ended September '01 increased during this period.

In spite of all this, like information technology, story is not yet over for most of these technology funds. According to Samir Arora, fund manager emerging markets, alliance capital mutual fund, the fundamental story of the Indian software. Sector is still very strong and good results from a few leading IT companies highlight that there is a strong value proposition offered by these companies.

Surely funds would have their own set of reasons for changing investment preferences considering their choice for stocks at very high valuation. May be it is time for information technology funds to realign their portfolio so as to keep them in tune with the valuation of some of these blue chip companies that are currently available at attractive rates.

Here is making some sense out of the jumble, ET and Crisil can have introduced a comprehensive revised methodology of ranking open end mutual fund schemes, as of September 30 '2001. For the first time gift funds (long term) have been included for the CPR oversize.

Sixty-four open-ended schemes across 20 funds ranked for the quarter-ended September 30, 2001, Fifteen out of 19 schemes have changed their ranks and few changes have occurred. In liquid funds tops CPRI. As many as 14 out of 18 schemes in the general debt fund category have changed their ranks. Sundown Bond sever regains CPRI in the debt category quarter ended Sep. 30, 2001, moves a notch we from CPR 2 to CPRI Pioneer ITI Income builder account moves to CPRI from CPRs. Alliance 95 fails retain its lead among balanced funds, falls to CPR 3, while other 6 funds, ranked in the past change ranks. There is a new entrant in this category.

Templet as India liquid fund averages as the CPR 1 in the liquid fund category, pushes down prudential ICICI liquid plan, a notch to CPR 2.

Focused investment strategy, active fund management and the ability to head the markets are the main characteristics of the top performance of the Composite Performance Ranking (CPR) of mutual funds. For the quarter ended September 01, Sundaram Bond saves has regained CPRI in debt category while Templeton India growth fund has retained its CPR-1 ranking among general equity funds.

JM Balance fund – Growth has emerged as CPRI among the balanced fund schemes and Templeton India Liquid Fund – Growth has done the same in the liquidity fund category Templeton. India gsec fund. Growth has emerged as the topper among gift funds, included for the first time in CPR. The CPR erense covered 64 open ended schemes as against 58 in the previous period, across 20 houses for the quarter ended September 2001.

OPEN-ENDED GENERAL DEBT FUND

Schemes	June 2001	Superior returns	Asset site	Company concore	Asset quality	Sep.20
Pioneer ITI income bolder Account plora growth	3	1	3	5	9	1↑
Sundaram Bond Saver Growth	2	2	10	2	7	1↑
Birla Income Plusplan B-Growth	3	5	7	8	14	2↑
DSP Merrill Lynch Bonafide	4	6	1	7	3	2↑
JM Income Fund Growth	1	3	11	9	11	2
Prudential ICICI Income Plan Growth	3	4	9	4	6	2
Alliance Income Fund Growth	3	8	4	12	16	3↔
Chola Triple Ace-cumulative	1	11	13	16	4	↓
LIC Mutual Bond Fund-Growths	N/A	7	2	1	13	3
Son & Money Value Fund-Bond	3	12	16	13	15	3↔
Templeton India Income Fund-Growth	2	9	5	3	1	3↓
Zurich India high interest fund growth	3	10	8	14	5	3↔
L&FS Bond Fund Growth	N/A	15	18	10	12	4
Reliance Income Fund-Growth	3	14	12	6	17	4
SBI Magnum Liquifund Growth	4	16	6	15	8	4←
Tata Income Fund Application	5	13	17	18	18	4↑

Schemes	Sep 2000	June 2001	Superior return	Asset site	Company Securities	Assent quality
ING income portfolio-Growth	5↓	4	18	15	17	2
Jardine Fleming India Bond fund Growth	5↔	5	17	14	11	1

Source: *Denotes CPR methodology has been different in June 2001, as its revamp has come in Sept. 2001.*

Open Ended Equity Funds

Some impleasant facts about the Indian bonuses first! After all, the BSE sensex was a down by 19 per cent for the quarter under review and down by 37 per cent for the two year period ended September '01. No wonder, even equity funds too were in the red during this period. Hence majority of equity funds saw their net assets shrink. Although all 19 funds ranks in this category have given negative returns for the 2 years period ended September 2001. Though in September in relative terms Templeton India growth fund and Zurich India equity fund, both have given the least negative returns.

Templeton India Growth fund has managed to retain CPRI in their quarter too. Sharing the honour along with Zurich India Equity Fund, which has horned up as notch. The farmer managed to retain its top trank due to its low validity score, its focus on value investing and diversified nature of its portfolio. The latter do so the strengths of its returns by being selective and achieving the right mix of new and old economy stocks in its portfolio. Even when the technology media telecom sector come under pressure, the multi sector focussed investments made by these funds helped them to impart stability to their net asset value.

OPEN ENDED GENERAL EQUITY FUNDS

	CDR Rank Quality END				Score (As of Sept 2000)			
	Sep 2001	*June 2001*	*Superior returns*	*Asset site*	*Industry*	*Company*	*Liquid Extance*	*All on*
Templeton India Growth Fund	1↔	1	1	6	6	11	14	16
Zurich India Growth Fund	1↑	2	2	10	18	17	5	12
Pioneer ITI Prima Fund Growth	2↑	3	5	7	15	10	12	14
Prudential ICICI Growth Plan Growth	2↔	2	4	3	13	8	6	13
Sundaram Growth Fund	2↑	3	3	13	5	1	19	4
Zurich India Top 200 Fund Growth	2↑	4	6	14	8	2	18	9
Alliance Equity Fund-Growth	3↓	2	12	2	7	14	2	17
DSP Merill Lynch Equity Fund	3↑	4	11	12	11	3	13	2
JM Equity Fund Growth	3↑	5	9	19	4	7	8	1
K30	3↔	3	13	15	1	5	9	7
Pioneer ITI Blue Chip fund Growth	3↓	1	8	4	2	15	10	18
Sun F&C Value Fund Growth	3↔	3	10	16	14	4	11	3
Tata Pure Equity Fund Growth	3↓	2	7	11	10	12	15	6
Birla Advantage Fund	4↓	3	14	1	17	9	17	19
Can Bonus	4↑	5	17	13	3	6	16	8
ING Growth Portfolio Growth	4↔	4	16	9	19	19	1	5
Pioneer ITI Prima-Fund-Growth	4↓	3	15	18	16	18	3	11
SBI Magnum Equity Fund	5↓	3	18	8	9	13	9	10
SBI Magnum Multi Lerphum scheme 1993	5↓	4	19	5	12	16	7	18

Note: For instant in September'01 TIGF had 14 per cent exposure in TMT, 18 per cent in PMCG. 7 per cent in pharmaceuticals and diversified 5 per cent.

Source: *Denotes CPR methodology has been different in June 2001 as its revamp has come in Sept. 2001.*

Likewise, Zurich, India growth fund had 12 per cent exposure in the TMT sector, 13 per cent to much, and 14 per cent to pharmaceuticals. The high exposure of the fund to sectors like fund and pharmaceuticals helped if to move up on the CPR list.

For the three months to September, the led exposure to highly liquid stocks such as Infosys Technologies, Satyam computers and Reliance Industries.

Other like Sundaram Growth fund, Pioneer ITI Prima plus and Zurich India Top 200 have moved up the ladder by performing better on CPR scores.

On the other end of the scale, pioneer ITI Blue Chip fund slipped from CPRI in June to CPR 3 in the latest quarter.

The key reason is sharp fall to funds performance in September could have been clue to its concentrated holdings in technology media telecom (TMT) stocks. During September 2001, the funds exposure to new economy sectors declined and that of the old economy increased.

In June 2000, Pioneer ITI Blue chip fund had the highest exposure of the 38 per cent of its assets in the technology. Media telecom sector, in fast moving consumer goods if hand the 13 per cent in pharmaceuticals it has 9 per cent. Pharma in old economy sector, it had over 21 per cent.

The funds exposure to telecom-media technology declined to 13 per cent of its total assets, in FMch and pharmaceuticals its holding increased to 10 per cent and 12 per cent K30, Can bonus and Sundaram Growth were some of the well diversified funds in the quarter ended September 2001. ING Growth fund was the least diversified fund as its five stocks from sectors like information technology and media contribution 80 per cent of its total assets.

On the other hand, Zurich India Top 200 and Sundaram Growth funds fared badly as they had investments in illiquid companies like Oil & Natural Gas Corporation (ONGC), IDC, Smithkline Beecham consumes, Gas Authority of India (GAIL) contains cooperation of India and ingersoll Rand (India)

Some equity funds also saw their net assets shrink considerably while other actually garnered more funds despite the volatile markets and high redemption pressures.

Ten of the 19 equity schemes in the category saw a growth in their asset site. These were Zurich India equity fund. Alliance equity fund DSP Merrisll Lynch Equity fund ING Growth portfolio K30, Prudential ICICI Growth Funds SBI Magnum Equity fund, SBI Magnum Malliplier 1993, Sun F&C value fund, Tata pure equity fund and Pioneer ITI, Blue chip fund.

Zurich India equity fund experienced meagre compus decline (3 per cent) between June 2001, to Sept. 2001. The funds whose corpses experienced, deadlines included, Alliance equity fund (behind by 25 per cent) DSP Merrill Lynch Equity Fund, ING Growth portfolio (down by 27 per cent) Rs. 30 Prudential ICICI Growth SBI Magnum equity SBI Magnum multiplier 1993, Sun F&C value fund (down by over 24 per cent), Tata pure equity fund and Pioneer the Blue chip (down by over the per cent)

Open-end General Debt Funds

The Salegory saw the largest churn in the ranks. As many as fourteen out of the 18 funds moved places. Two new funds have entered this category. These are LIC Mutual fund and Zurich India High Inter Fund, Pioneer ITI income Builder Account (IBA), plant and Sundaram Bond Silver movea up from their 3rd and 2nd rank to CPR-1 this quarter.

It is notable that Sundaram Bond scres has been the best performer in all their quarters except in june 2001 meanwhile in income fund-growth, consultant CPR-1 performer since the last four quarter scipped to CPR-2 in the September ended quarter.

OPEN ENDED LIQUID FUNDS

	CPR Rank for the quarter ended		*Scores as on the Sept. 2001*		
	Sept.2001	*June 2001*	*Superior returns*	*Assets site*	*company concert*
Templeton India liquid Fund-Growth	1↑	2	1	1	2
Pioneer ITI treasury Mgmt. A/c Growth	2↑	3	2	5	4
Prudential ICI liquid Plan-Growth	2↓	1	3	4	7
Alliance cash Manager-Growth	3↓	2	7	3	1
Birla cash Plus-Growth	3↓	2	5	2	5
Dundee liquidity Fund-Appreciation	3↔	3	6	12	10
IDBI principal-Money Market Fund	3↑	4	8	10	12
JM High liquidity Fund-Growth	3↔	3	4	8	6
Reliance Liquid Fund-Treasury Plan-Growth	3↔	3	9	6	3
DSP Marill Lynch liquidity Fund Growth	4↓	3	10	7	11
SBI Magnum Insta cash-cash	4↔	4	11	9	9
Tata liquidity Fund-Growth	5↔	5	12	11	8

Source: Denot CPR methodology has been different in June 2001, its revamp has come in Sept. 2001.

It is notable that Sundaram bond, saver has been the best performs in all these quarters expert in June 2001. Meanwhile, JM income Fund-Growth consistent CPR-1 performes since the last four quarter seipped to CPR-2 in the September ended quarter.

Chola Triple Ace, the top performer in the previous quarter has slipped to CPR-3

The fund moved up from CPR-5 in June 2000, consistently, one notch upper very quarter to CPR-1 in June 2001. Chola freedom income has not been considered for ranking in the quarter as it did not meet the asset site criteria under the revised CPR methodology.

OPEN ENDED – BALANCED FUNDS

Schemes	*Sep 2001*	*June 2001*	*Concentration*				*Liquidity*	
			Superior returns	*Assets sites*	*Industry*	*Debt Assets*	*External*	*Total*
JM Balance Fund-Growth	1↑	2	1	9	8	1	8	4
Tata Balance Fund-Growth	2↑	3	3	5	2	6	7	5
Zurich India Prudential Fund-Growth	2↑	3	2	6	9	3	4	8
Alliance 95 Fund-Growth	3↓	1	4	2	2	7	1	6
Birla Balance Fund-Growth	3	N/A	6	1	4	8	9	9
Can Triple	3↔	3	5	3	1	4	3	3
DSP Merill Lynch balance fund-Growth	4↔	4	7	7	3	2	5	1
SBI Magnum balance fund	4↓	2	8	4	5	5	6	7
Cangage	5↔	5	9	8	7	9	2	2

\# *Asset site here is in relation to optimum fund category gifts. Funds falling aboves below the optimum site are penalised for the new CPR methodology please send the separate story.*

* *Denotes CPR methodology has been different in Lune 2001, as its revamp has come in Sept. 2001.*

Birla Income Plus bond DSP Merill Lynch Bond fund. Both moved upto CPR-2 from CPR-3 and CPR-4 in June ended quarter, similarly, Templeton India Income fund moved up one notch 15 CPR 2, up from CPR-3 in the last quarter Reliance Income Fund also moved down one notch to CPR-4 from CPR-3, ING Income, fund supped one month to CPR-5, down from CPR-4 in the last quarter.

As of September 2001, the fund had an exposure of the per cent in 'AA+' Paper, 45 per cent in 'AAA' papers and 30 per cent in government securities.

The superlative performance of Sundaram Bond saver was mainly due to its highly liquidity portfolio. As of September 2001, Sundaram Bond saver had an exposure of 45 per cent in call and money market instruments. In 'AAA' rated paper 38 per cent and in 'AA' rated one's 1% per cent. The minds medium risk portfolio profile its investment strategy of having a lower exposure to gifts and higher exposure to 'AAA' rated paper and 'AA' rated paper having a medium maturity profile of 3.5 years contributed to its superior performance in the September ended quarter.

OPEN-ENDED LONG GIFT FUNDS

Name of Scheme	*CPR Ranks*	*Score can on Sept. 30*		
	Sept. 1	*Superior returns*	*Asset site*	*Gift liquid*
Templeton India Gesec Fund-Growth	1	1	1	3
Tata Gift Securities Fund-Appreciation	2	2	5	6
DSP Merrill Lynch Govt sec fund (p) Growth	3	3	4	5
Prudential ICICI gift-investment-Growth	3	4	2	4
Birla Gift plus plan B (Investment) Growth	4	5	6	2
Gift-Investment-Growth	5	6	3	1

* Introduced CPR ranking of funds for the first time this quarter.

DSP Merrill Lynch Bond Fund which moved up CPR-2 From CPR 4 had an exposure of 38 per cent in money market instruments, in 'AAA' rated paper 53 per cent and 'AA' rated paper 9 per cent. The fund had average maturity duration of 4.29 years.

Lower exposure to gifts and higher exposure corporate paper with medium maturity profile helped the fund to move two notches upto CPR-2 in September.

On the other hand, chola triple all slipped two notches in the September ended quarter. This could have been due to erosion in its corpus by 38 per cent between June 30, 2001 and September 29, 2001. The fund also slipped on the company concentration parameter. This could have been due to the funds relatively higher exposure to IDBI paper which was down graded in July 2001. The funds exposure to government securities fell from 35 per cent in june to 21 per cent to September. A detailed analysis also shows that the debt schemes in general massive erosion in the corpuses between June and September. For instance corpus of alliance. Income fund declined 26 per cent, Jardine Flaming (JF) bond fund fell 47 per cent, Sun P&C value bond corpus fell 34 per cent ING Income funds eroded 29 per cent and Tata income funds declined, 44 per cent. Only the corpus of three funds LIC Mutual Bond fund, IL&FS send fund and SBI Magnum Ligibond moved up by 22 per cent 4 per cent and 3 per cent.

Rider: An extity wishing to use their rankings in its prospectus/offer document/ advertisement/ promotion/sales literature, or wisning to disseminate these rankings may do so only with the written permission of ET and crisil.

A CASE STUDY OF MORGAN STANLEY

Morgan Stanley (Growth fund) quarterly news letter.

Dear Unit Holder

For the half year ended December 31, 2001, the net asset value ("Nav") of the Morgan Stanley. Growth fund ("FUND") rose by 54% while the bench mark indus. BSF 200 and S&P CNX 500 fell by 4.5% and 3.5% respectively. For the one year ended December 31, 2001 the funds NAV fell by 16.2% while the BSE 200 fell by 21.9% (see table 1 for details)

In the immediate after month as September 11, several extra arguments were put forth on how the world had changed following the tragedy, instead as reflected in the stinging rally global financial markets have staged over the past 4 months, September 11 made for a significant from information. The global economy was in trouble prior to September 11 but following that event economic policy makers across the world went into stimulus over-economic policy then prevent any growth collapse. The policy efforts appear to have succeded and most investors are now looking at 2002 as a year prospector gains.

The year 2001 was otherwise one of the most difficult years. For equity investors in recent history with global markets going through their worst phase. Since 1973-74, the severity of deadlines was such that it was virtually impossible for any equality mutual fund to generate positive returns. Our strategies bench and management quality that in turn would fit in with our global sector falls. The important of the letters in the over all investment process cannot be exaggerated as the past few years have dramatically changed the characteristics of the Indian market.

The Indian market now looks and behaves like other major global markets. The correlation between India's and the rest of the world's equity markets (led by the US) is also longer restricted to sectors like technology. This co-relation is also selected telecom, financial and industrial sectors. Even the largely domestic oriented consumer sector in the Indian market makers measure line with global trends. A major reason for the strong orient correlation is that the Indian markets can past santage centre wise basis) is quite similar to the major global ineffential relative weights of technology pharmaceuticals efforts the overall consumer sector in the Indian market into the world index. There are glaring exceptions like financial the sike weight in India to half that asset of sinerging market inses. But if the fast is any deposit, adds are the weights will get more alligned in carrying the coming with the financials in the Indian market appreciatively be on the site.

Another sector in which we have invited to an overweight position in waste materials. It indeed among ball market its underway preserved on a global economic recovery. Then the commodity sector its ability the place to be commeditive have seen the maximum capital dis over the past decade and gave the greatest operating loving leverage and so a revival in growth will mean disproportionate mention for commodity sector, of course of expectations of a 2002 recently are dashed, and so for it is not done deal. This commodities will suffer but then so will the entire equity mertial universe.

RANDHIR SHARMA, PORTFOLIO MANAGER

Calculations PHGF NAV Performance	*NAV*	*BSE 200*	*Sunsex 5*
Returns designed a half year [(+) (-)]	5.4%	– 4.5%	– 3.5%
Compound usualised Growth Rate			
last 1 year	–16.2%	–21.9%	–23.3%
last 3 years	11.8%	4.0%	6.1%
last 4 years	11.8%	2.2%	3.4%
Since the return of the scheme (1st Jan, 94)	3.5%	–3.7%	–4.4%

Key Notes: Top 25 securities of MSHF accounts for 77.85 of total portfolio approximately 96% of the portfolio is held in dematerialised form the total cost of investments and market value as at December 31, 2001 in ADR/GDR's of Indian companies amounted to approx. Rs. 38.51 crores Rs. 36.05 crores respectively against the approved limit of Rs. 101.85 crores. Further RBI has extended the approval to invest in ADR/GDR's up to September 17, 2002. Approximately 95% of the dividend declared in July 2001 encashed by the MSGF investors. MSIS are taking continuous steps to encourage remaining investors to claim unpaid dividends. Further to the approval of the board of trustees in their meeting held on August 18, 2000. We have to inform you that Morgan Stanley and operation modalities to enable MSGF to invest in derivative products.

In order to expedite speedier credit of the dividend proceeds. We request the unit holders to furnish the Bank A/c details to Karly Consultants at the below mentioned address. We like to remind you that MSGF has paid 30 dividends of Rs. 0.75 per unit on 24/7/1999 Rs. 0.75 on 19/05/2000 and 1.00 Re. 02/07/2001. Unit holders who have either not received or encashed their dividend warrants are requested to forward a duly signed written request to highly Consultants Ltd. at the below mentioned address indicating the details of their investment in the fund.

Kavery Consultations Limited

Unit: Morgan Stanely Growth Fund.

4b, Avenue 4, Street No.1.

Banara Hill, Hyderabad 500034.

MORGAN STANLEY GROWTH FUND
TOP 25 HOLDINGS AS ON DEC. 31, 2001

Sr.No.	*Name of Security*	*% of Total Net*
1.	Hero Honda	8.55%
2.	Infosys Technologies	6.83%
3.	Wipro*	5.82%
4.	State Bank of India*	5.47%
5.	HDFC	5.02%
6.	HDFC Bank*	4.23%
7.	Container Corporation	3.93%
8.	MTNL*	3.09%
9.	Dr. Reedy's Laboratory*	3.03%
10.	ITC	3.02%
11.	Hindustan Level Convert	2.98%
12.	Gujarat Ambuja*	2.94%
13.	Cipla	2.68%
14.	Bharat Heavy Electronics	2.20%
15.	Smithkline Beecham consumer	2.20%
16.	Reliance Petroleum	1.89%
17.	Dabur	1.84%
18.	Tata Power	1.70%
19.	Colgate Palmolive	1.68%
20.	Hindalco	1.64%
21.	Hindu Petroleum	1.61%

22.	HCL Technologies	1.47%
23.	Reliance Industries	1.45%
24.	Cummins	1.44%
25.	Telco	1.40%
	Total	77.85%

* Includes local shares and ADR's/GDR's.
Unaudited financial results for the quarter ended December 30, 2001.

ABEL PGEO BALANCE SHEET AS AT DECEMBER 31, 2001 *(Rs. in Lacs)*

	Liabilities	*as on 31.12.2001.*	
1	Unit Capital		
1.1	Initial contribution by sector	5	
1.2	Unit Capital	65,429	65,434
2	Reserves & Surplus		
2.1	Unit Premium Reserve	3,808	
2.2	Revenue Reserves	2,504	6,312
3	Loans & Borrowings		
3.1	From Banks		
3.2	From others		
4	Current Liabilities & Provisions		
4.1	Provisions for loss/depreciation in value of investments		
4.2	Provision for doubful income/deposit		
4.3	Proposed Income Distribution		
4.4	Other Current Liabilities & Provisions	1502	1502
	Total		73,248

	Assets		
1	Investments		
1.1	Equity & Preference shares	67,698	
1.2	Privately placed documents/bonds		
1.3	Debenture & Bond listed awaiting listing on recognised stock exchange	15	
1.4	Term loan		
1.5	Government Securities		
1.6	Others	5	67,718
2	Deposits		
2.1	With Schedule Banks	4,350	
2.2	With others		4,350
3	Other Current Assets		
3.1	Cash & Bank Balance	1	

3.2	Others	1,179	1,180
4	Fixed Assets (at depreciation value)		
5	Deferred Revenues Expenditure (to the extent not written off)		
	Total		73,248

RE-CONCILIATION TO NET ASSET VALUE PER UNIT

Net assets as per Balance sheet (Total Assets less current Liabilities & Provisions and settler's contribution)	71,741
No. of units in issue (in lacs)	6,543
Net Asset value per unit (in Rs.)	10.93

ABRIDGED REVENUE ACCOUNT FOR THE PERIOD APRIL 01, 2001 TO DECEMBER 31, 2001

		01.04.2001 to 31.12.2001 (in Lacs)
I.	Income	
1.1	Dividend	1,587
1.2	Interest	292
1.3	Net profit on sales (redemption of investment other than inter-scheme transfer/sale)	
1.4	Net profit on inter scheme transfer/sale of investment	
1.5	Other Income	
1.6	Realised Gains on foreign currency Transaction	9
	Total	1,888

		01.04.2001 to 31.12.2001 (in Lacs)
II.	Expenses & Losses	
2.1	Management, Trusteeship, administrative & other operating expenses	1,014
2.2	Provisions for doubtful Income	
2.3	Provisions for doubtful deposits/current assets	
2.4	Net loss on sale/redemption of investments (other than inter-scheme transfer/scale	14,403
2.5	Net loss on inter-scheme transfer/sale	
2.6	Realised loss on foreign currency transaction	
	Total	15,417

Excess of Income over Expenses & Losses	13,529
Net change in unrealised depreciation appreciation of investments	15,547
Net Surplus (deficit) transferred to Revenue Reserve	2018

Note: The prices and redemption value of the units and income from the carriage well as down with the fluctuational in the market value of its investments. The information is not necessarily indicative of further results and may not necessarily provide basis for comparison with other investments.

STRONG PERFORMANCE ON THE DOWN SIDE BY TEMPLETON INDIA GROWTH (A CASE STUDY OF TEMPLETON INDIA MUTUAL FUND)

The past two years have seen equity markets deliver negative returns in succession in the bear market. TIGF has managed to hold on the returns and in the process beat the index. The fund with its value investment philosophy also ranks against the top funds in the medium terms of 3 years.

Backgrounds: TIGF was launched in August 1996. During its IPO the scheme garnered Rs. 50.15 crore the funds investment objective is to achieve long term growth of capital through value investing in order to control risk the fund does not allocate more than 30% of the portfolio to any single sector.

Performance: Though the fund has beaten its benchmark. The sensex its returns since its inception and over the past five years are not very attractive. It is the returns over the three year period and in the last year which make the fund a top performance both against the benchmark as well as its peer group. This performance has been based on the funds ability to preserve value in the falling markets of the past two years. In fact the scheme has been in the top quartile of its peer group. This performance has been based on the funds ability. The fund did not fare too well compared to competition in 1999 and was in the 3rd quartile of its peer group.

RETURNS PROFILE

Period	*TIGF*	*Sensex*
Since inception	7.1	0.25
Last year	6.9	2.75
Last 3 years	24.14	2.16
Last 1 year	0.75	17.1

BULL PHASE RETURNS

20/10/98 – 11/02/2000	144.14	113.09
22/5/2000 – 5/7/2000	13.61	25.30
23/10/2000 – 12/02/2001	24.77	21.73
21/09/2001 – 21/02/2002	41.83	37.32

* Returns are annualised

* Amit Kumar, The Economic Times Monday 25, Feb. 2002, p. 2.

BEAR PHASE RETURNS

11/2/2000 – 21/9/2001	– 39.15	– 56.17
11/2/2000 – 22/5/2000	– 21.16	– 33.93
12/2/2001 – 12/4/2001	– 22.34	– 27.74
29/5/2001 – 21/9/2001	– 25.54	– 43.19

VOLATILITY STATISTICS

		TIGF	*Sensex*
a	Standard deviation	3.6	4.43
b	Co-efficient variation	– 17.14	12.30
c	Beta	0.71	–

Calculated an early average returns for tracking year.

In 1997, the first full calendar year for the year for the scheme it lost 123 as against again of 18.6% by the benchmark the next year was no better as the fund returned a negative 21.71% as compared to – 16.55% by the sensex. These were the early years of growth for IT sector scrips. In addition to these FMCG and pharma stocks were also doing well. The fund was however loaded with value oriented cyclical and commodity stocks. According to the fund management much of the under performance in these years can be traced to the effect the south East Asian Economic crisis had on the economically linked commodity stocks in the portfolio. The fund was also hurt by the absence of large – capital stocks such as HLL, which the fund management felt were overvalued. Valuation concerns also recited in the scheme avoiding MNC pharma stocks. In the case of IT the AMC loose the view that stocks in the market were not sufficiently large in terms of market cap to be considered for the portfolio.

In 1999, the stock markets boomed the Pharma FMCG and technology were the out performing sectors in the early part of the year. These were replaced by technology media and telecom, towards the latter half of the year. This year saw the fund generate a return of 87.65%. This the way beneath the triple digit returns generated by the peer groups.

Fund Features

Fund type	:	Open ended equity diversified scheme.
Investment Options	:	Growth dividend payout dividend reinvestment.
Entry load	:	2%
Exit load	:	nil
Min. Investment	:	Mutual fund in multiple of 500 thereafter.
Dividend history	:	15% in April 2000.
Website	:	www.Templeton India.com

The fund however out performed the sensex which returned 63.83%. The fund management feels that internal restructures which prevent a greater than exposure to any single sector kept a cap on its returns. Thus even by December, 1999 its IT exposure was 25.56%. This was only 6% greater than the benchmark.

While the fund restricted exposure to IT stocks because of internal guidelines. The absence and under exposure to other sector remains difficult to fathom thus the media sector, another performer of the year was given the miss, media stocks such as Zee which had run up significantly were no where to be seen in telecom stocks. Thus though the fund had a 3.11% telecom sector exposure against 4.33% in the benchmark, stock as Global Tele systems and HFCL were absent from the portfolio.

The very things which kept the funds NAV from rising in 1999 stopped it from collapsing in 2000. This was the year, when the longest bull run in the Indian markets came to an end. Markets ended the year down 20.65%. The fund on the other hand lost only 3.84% IT exposure at 31.24% in March end was 7.76% more than that of the benchmark. By the year end, this gap had fallen to 3.78% consistent over exposure to capital goods, strong investments in chemicals and petro-chemicals along with other Non-TMT sectors kept the NAV stable.

Towards the end of the year. PSU stocks were on the up move. In the run up to budget 2001. The fund gained significantly compared to gain of 21.73% by the sensex the funds returned 24.77%. The post budget crash saw the fund hold its own. A loss of 22.34% was amongst the lowest in the peer group and significantly less than the 27.74% of the benchmark year 2001 also saw it switch from being over weight in IT to being under weight even the run up in IT scrips post Sept. 21 did not see it reverse position, though significant qualities of Satyam were added to the portfolio.

PORTFOLIO COMPOSITION VS BENCHMARK

	Sector	Sensex	TIGE
(a)	Capital goods	1.38	4.47
(b)	Chemical & petro chemical	12.03	6.82
(c)	Construction	2.31	1.08
(d)	Consumer durables	0.00	0.37
(e)	Diversified	2.82	2.78
(f)	Finance	5.73	6.63
(g)	FMCG	27.64	11.50
(h)	Health care	9.35	10.14
(i)	IT	15.75	10.64
(j)	Media & Publishing	1.93	3.32
(k)	Metal and Mining	3.45	3.84
(l)	Oil & Gas	8.55	2.91
(m)	Power	1.07	2.2
(n)	Telecom	2.76	4.51
(o)	Tourism	0.00	0.91
(p)	Transport & Equipment and services	5.22	21.75
	Total	100%	100%
	As on 31-1-2002		

Outlook: The fund is now over exposed to auto shares. The fund management how ever feels that this exposure is a stock specific play thus while Hero Honda can be considered a growth play in Telco revamping is the diving force. This is also the situation in IT, where the fund is currently under exposed. Having reposed faith in the outsourling model, it feels that bottom up stock picking will define the funds investments here. Though PSU stocks are booming, the fund has indicated it will not be very aggressive on the disinvestment trail. Rather the AMC feels it prudent to assign a value to the earning power of individual companies as this has come down considerably the fund has proved its ability to conserve value in a falling market. Its performance in bull phase and the recent rally has also been superior to that of the benchmark. These returns have however been lower than that of other long term performers in the poor group.

Inspite of this, investment in the fund can be made on defensive considerations. The funds beta of less than one standard testament to this.

In view of these factors, the scheme can form between 25 to 35% of an equity fund portfolio.

Service and Disclosure Standards

The fund endeavours to dispatch dividend warrants within a turn around of 7+7 days. A lacunae in the funds disclosure is that it does not give full portfolio disclosure in terms of the number of shares of individual stocks on a monthly basis though this practice is within the ambit of regulation an investor cannot at a glance figure out changes in the portfolio. While the funds quarterly news letters contains this information. They do not discuss changes in the portfolio or comment much on the funds strategies.

Portfolio – TIGE

1	Hero Honda Motors	7.66
2	Bajaj Auto	6.19
3	Infosys	5.76
4	ITC	5.27
5	Reliance Industries	5.04
6	Rambaxy Laboratories	4.97
7	TELCO	4.21
8	Smithkline Beecham	4.18
9	Cipla	3.92
10	Satyam Computer Services	3.70
11	Motor Industries Co.	3.69
12	ICICI Bank	3.35
13	Zee Telefilms	3.32
14	Bharat Petroleum Corpn	2.91
15	Grasim Industries	2.78
16	Hindalco	2.67
17	MTNL	2.32
18	Tata Power	2.20
19	VSNL	2.19
20	Nestle India	2.19
21	Cummins India	1.89
22	Asian Paints	1.78
23	BHEL	1.49
24	HDFC	1.28
25	Dr. Reddy's Lab	1.25
26	NALCO	1.18
27	Hughes Software	1.18
28	ABB	1.09
29	Gujarat Ambuja	1.08
30	Indian Hotels	0.91
31	Titan Industries	0.37
32	Indian Aluminium	0.00
33	Cash	8.11
	Total	100%

B. VENTURE CAPITAL

Introduction

Venture capital is a type of financial intermediary emerged in USA. It is a financial intermediary very popular during 1978. In America, early 1980 in Britain in the mid 1980 Singapore and Canada. It has become popular in 1987 in India. It is a long term investment which involves in high risk industrial projects with reward possibilities. It is involved in financing the new business and professional activities carrying higher expectation to come up with the success. It is a source of long term finance for innovative projects. It plays a vital role in providing the long term capital to a vide variety of enterprises.

Venture capital provides finance on risk capital to little known unregistered high risky. Technology oriented knowledge based activities or industries which have long development cycles small private business etc. It also renders the management and marketing expertise to the units. It is an organised financing with relatively new enterprises to achieve substantial benefits. The venture capital is the part of the primary market. It is an important source of funds for technology based industries. It helps the commercial enterprises where conventional financing agencies cannot reach. The business concern requires a sizeable equity contribution to the project cost where securities and technocrats cannot always provide. The venture capital provides the equity to help the projects to get out of research laboratory and into the market. Financial resources will be provided not as a loan but as an investment in the venture. It is regarded as "pre-public" financing. Venture capital companies generally support the management as a minority partner. The venture capital financial assistance is made available in 3 kinds. They are equity conditional loan and income notes. The V.C. firm contributes in the form of equity which does not exceed 49% of the total equity. Another type of assistance is available in the form of conditional loan ranging between 2% and 15% of the required. It is repayable in the form of Royalty between 2% and 15%. The income notes has combining features of conventional and conditional loans. The rate of royalty is based on the profitability of the business. All these type of assistance are tailored to meet the investment needs of entrepreneurs at different phases. Development start up launching the financing for meeting the growth of expansion are the 3 phases. The development start is the risk less and requires almost attention.

Features: Venture Capital fund has the following features.

(a) Venture capitalists assume risk.

(b) It is a long term financial instrument with capital appreciation.

(c) Venture capitalists provide – technical commercial, managerial, financial and entrepreneurial services.

(d) It involves investment in small industries with high risk and assures a better return in future.

Financial Support: Venture Capital companies has to appoint marketing specialists in product launching to capture the market. The V.C. board should consist of private business executives academic scientists engineers patent attorneys, bankers and brokers.

The various kinds of financial requirement involves the following.

(a) Seed capital to bring a research idea to the development stage.

(b) Financial requirement to set up initial infrastructure on manufacturing, distribution sourcing and marketing without any cash inflows from sales.

(c) This stage of financing is to add to their range of products or switch over from unsuccessful product range.

(d) This is the final stage of capital requirement for expansion or diversification.

Whether to finance these projects in order to finance. It is based on the information available research and selection etc. Venture Capital research team will evaluate the investment proposals based on the factors like ROI. Track record of entrepreneurs, market consideration exit routes. The success of the venture capital depends upon the business environment, statutory regulations, taxation levels future, revenue costs, capacity utilisation and sales levels, investors of venture capital have no liquidity for a period of time. Venture Capital proposals are attractive in high technology area. The VC funds require professionals. The preferred form of organisation for the VC is the limited company. VC firms are not permitted to money market operation. Portfolio investments, brokers, fundamental management and financial services.

Instruments: The methods of financing are practiced by the VC companies.

(A) Shares (B) Debt

Shares: The following types of shares are available for investment in the venture capital firms.

(1) Equity shares (2) Preference shares (3) Convertable preference shares

The equity shares are usually issued by the companies. They are a good growth of the unit. There is an anticipation that there would be a significant growth in the value of equity over a period of time in the form of equity the contribution does not exceed 49% of the total equity ranging between 2% and 15% of the investment. The other instruments are in general nature the types of assistance are tailored to meet the investment needs of entrepreneurs of different stages.

Technological Revolution

The present technological revolution has witnessed the re-emergence of small and medium firms. These firms play an important role in the development of technology. The introduction of computer aided design/computer aided management (CAD/CAM) flexible manufacturing system Bio-Technology. These developments have increased the global competitiveness of small and medium hi-tech firms. There is a tremendous scope of development in agriculture. The role of small and medium technology firms can easily spread into the entire country in agriculture sector. The venture capital firms can also concentrate on farm management, development of seed capital with quality, low duration, period of cultivation development of water resources, land development, soil technology, agro based industries like food processing etc.

The introduction of appropriate changes in the company law and banking law are considered advisable to enable their successful participation in the current technological revolution, certain positive policies should be formulated for sustainable development.

The investments of VCFs differs from organisation to organisation. The VCFs are usually characterised by substantial control over management decisions and protection against downside risk some VCFs have a set on the companies board of directors VC is a high risk – high return business because these projects are untested and are undertaken by new persons without experience. The expected returns from VC investment are very high. The funds are usually expected to be tied up for three to ten years. Usually VCFs in addition to using their own funds are banking upon the sources to get funds in the form of equity through All India Financial Institutions. FIIs, Private Sector, Nationalised banks, Private Sector, Public Sector and NRIs.

Venture Capital firms can recover their investments if the organisation has a commercial run. There are various alternatives are available for the venture capitalists are presented below.

(a) Initial public offering.

(b) Buyback of the shares.

(c) Sale of the firm to another company.

(d) Sale to new investors.

Initial public offering is the opportunity for a venture capitalist to offer their holdings for public sale and liquidate the investment. Buyback of shares means the promoters of the investee company buy the shares by the venture capital companies as investment. It provides liquidity to VCFs by encashing their holdings. Sometimes the venture capitalists can recover their investments by selling the holdings of their investments to outsider who is invested in purchasing the whole enterprise. Sale to investor is the final alternative to the venture capitalist. Venture Capitalist can sell its equity holding to a new venture capital company who is invested in buying the ownership position of the venture capitalist.

The union finance ministry has issued guidelines for the establishment and functioning of the venture capital activities

(1) Any company can undertake the finance activities by agreeing to abide by these guidelines.

(2) Interested companies can put an application and details of the proposals to SEBI with a suitable explanatory note.

(3) Application for the issue of share capital by the companies should be made to the SEBI under capital issues act.

(4) In case of all India Public sector financial instructions the SBI and other scheduled banks. If they want to establish a venture capital firms, they should get the approval from the RBI.

(5) VCFs are managed by the professionals with an advocate experience in industry finance and accounts etc.

(6) If the VCFs are established by the Subsidiaries of banks/instructions or in house schemes. They should maintain their independence and an arm length relationship. However, they would be free to draw the professional expertise and infrastructure of the parent organisation with the interests of their shareholders and clients minimising costs.

(7) The full time Chairman/President/Chief Executive/Executive Directors/whole time director should not hold any position in any other company.

(8) VC assistance should go basically to high risk involved and high technology based concerns.

(9) The financial assistance mainly be equity support through loan support to supplement this may also be done.

(10) VC assistance should cover those enterprises which fulfil the following parameters.

   (a) The total investment of the concerns should not exceed Rs. 10 crores.

   (b) The concern should be in the new technology development concept and it must be like a pilot project.

   (c) The project should be in a position from pilot to commercial stage which is an innovative technology.

   (d) The project promoters/entrepreneurs should be relatively new or professionally or technically qualified with sufficient financial resources.

   (e) Investments in the firms engaged in trading broking, investment or financial services agency or liaison work should not be permitted.

   (f) Investments in assisted units for their expansion or strengthening or investments for the revival of the risk units would be permitted.

   (g) The assisted company should be in the form of a limited company and it must employ professionally qualified to maintain its accounts.

   (h) The VCF should invest at least 60% of its funds into VCF activities.

   (i) The VC investment during the first 12 months permissible investment is a level of 30% should be reached for VC financing activity by the end of second year 60% by the end of third year 15% by the end of the fifth year of its operations. The balance may be invested in any new issue or existing company of equity, debentures, bonds ceps or other securities approved for these purposes by the SEBI.

(j) Investment in leasing sector should not exceed 5% of the total funds deployed, including the first year.

(k) The VC firms can raise funds through public issues or private placements.

(l) Foreign equity upto 25% would be permitted in the venture capital firms.

(m) NRI investment would be permitted upto 74% in venture capital concerns (on non-repartition basis)

(n) The NRI investment would be permitted 25% per cent on a repatriable basis.

(o) For NRI investment an application should be submitted to the ministry of finance with a copy to the chairman, SEBI.

(p) The maximum debt equity ratio will be permitted 1:1:5.

(q) The VCFs can be listed according to the prescribed norms.

(r) The V/C issue may be underwritten at the discretion of the promoters.

(s) The pricing of shares at the time of disinvestment by a public issue of general, offer for sale by the V/Cs may be done then.

(t) The pricing of shares will be based on the factors like book value profit earning capacity. All these factors should be disclosed to the public.

(u) The Tax exemption treatment would be available to the approved capital firms only.

(v) The venture capital firms which want to enjoy these tax benefits should obtain a letter of eligibility from IDBI/ICICI or any nominated agency of the government.

Tax on Concession: According to the Income-Tax Act 1961 sec 10 deals with tax concessions to the VCFs. The VCFs are exempted from the payment of capital gains tax and income tax. For preferential tax treatment under the capital gains, the VCF should follow the guidelines issues by the central government. The VCF should operate like the mutual funds. According to the guidelines mutual funds are not allowed to invest more than 5% in the equity of a single company and 15% in a particular industry. If the investments are made in sick units and export oriented units then the exemptions will be provided export oriented units. Various liberalisation measures have been taken deep roots in the economy. The government is in favour of effective steps to boost the VC outfits. In the present environment, many path breaking technologies, in the field of micro-electronics, bio-technology computers have raised small units with the support of venture capital. The dynamism, the thrust of innovations and entrepreneur cannot be ignored. The globally reputed firms like Microsoft, Genteh, Apple, DEC, MICRO, Intel, Lotus and Federal Express backed venture capital support. They emerged industry standard in their fields. After implementation of liberalisation and globalisation policies more steps are required by the government, financial institution, private sector and other agencies are subjected to a tax of 25%. There are some distinctions between public sector VCFs and private sector venture capital firms. Tax concessions are discretionary in case of public sector. The long term prospects of the industry remains high, high tech, projects should be encouraged by various methods.

Entrepreneurship introduces a critical element of dynamism into an economic system. It is not a coincidence that the worlds leading economy. The United States is believed to be the most entrepreneurial society in the world. In USA, 4 Indian American venture capitalists creating wonders in the industry. According to portfolio, the following ranks were found.

1.	Vinod Khosla	7	94	2
2.	Havaue	72	51	26
3.	Yogen Dala	68	48	58
4.	Atiq Raja	94	14	100

Venture Capital in India: In India, venture capital industry is located in four centers Mumbai, Delhi, Kolkatta and Bangalore. The venture capital in India can be classified into four categories.

(a) Companies set up by financial institution.

(b) Companies set up in the private sector.

(c) Companies set up by commercial banks and

(d) Companies set up by state level financial institutions.

In India, if any person wants to establish venture capital, he has to get approval from the ministry of finance. Now the SEBI has the power to grant licenses for the venture capital firms. The venture capital firms have been established in India in the form of a limited company. The firm should invest atleast 60% of its funds in venture proposals. The remaining amount may be in its funds in venture proposals. The remaining amount may be invested in the form of new issue of equity, debenture and bonds. The venture capital firms can invest upto 15% of the total employed in the leasing sector. The venture capital firms in India are not permitted to enter into the money market operations, broking, portfolio investments fund management and financial services. Funds may be raised through public issue/private placement.

Today India has over 50 VC funds and equity funds operating in the country. The estimated investment of risk capital in 2001 is Rs. 7200 crores against just over Rs. 4800 crores in 2000. To get world class entrepreneurs from India, the role of risk capital needs are to be emphasised. The IT and non-both fields must be mustered. India's top venture capital funds and their business turnover is presented below.

		(Rs.in crores) 2001-02
(a)	Warburg pincus	Rs. 3360 crores
(b)	ICICI venture funds management company	Rs. 1200 crores
(c)	Chrysalis	
(d)	Indoceam chase at	
(e)	Citi bank equity	480
(f)	Hongkong Sanghai Banking Corporation	336
(g)	Bank of America	312
(h)	Walden International	264
(i)	Baring private equity partners	248
(j)	GE capital services	240
(k)	Global Technology	190
(l)	Infinity Technology Investments	160

Venture capital Investment trends are estimated by venture capital association sector wise and year wise particulars are presented below.

Year	*Figures in Million*
1997	20
1998	80
1999	250
2000	500
2001	1200
2002	1100*
2003	1500*

* The opportunity areas for venture capital are software services, software products, Internet based services, Infotech bio-tech, wireless agri products and processed foods. The following are some of the institutions which offering venture capital finance.

(1) IDBI venture capital funds.

(2) Technology development and information company of India.

(3) Risk Capital and Technology Finance Corporation Ltd.

(4) Can Bank venture capital fund.

(5) 20th century venture capital fund.

(6) Indus Venture capital fund.

(7) APIDC venture capital Ltd.

(8) India Investment Fund.

(9) Credit Capital Venture Ltd.

(10) Gujarat Venture Finance Ltd.

LEASING

Introduction

The important function of finance is to provide the funds required by the firm for capital investment. The capital investment includes investment in fixed assets. The fixed assets such as land, building, plant, machinery and other properties which are necessary for long term use in the business activities. For all the requirements, the company has to meet the funds either through internal financing or through the external borrowings. The heavy amount of expenditure in the capital assets is a sunk investment. The leased assets will be utilised as per the terms and conditions of the leasing agreement. Leasing has emerged as a source of long term financing of the corporate sector. A lease represents a contractual agreement between two parties.

A lease is an arrangement under which a lease acquires the right to use the asset without ownership title of it in return for a series of produce lease rentals to the lessor (owner). The lease has been defined by equipment leasing association of UK as "A lease as a contract between the leaser and lessor for the hire of a specified asset selected for a manufacturer or vendor of such assets by the lease".

The International Accounting standard defines lease as "an agreement where by the lessor conveys to the lessee in return for rent the right to use an asset for an agreed period of time".

Lease is a written agreement allowing the economic use of the assets for a stipulated period of time. The lease agreement takes between both the parties the lessor and the "lessee" The owner of the asset lessor and the user is known as "lessee". Leasing represents an alternative sources to ownership. A lease can be treated as the functional equipment of debt. Lease is a form of hire for which rent is paid. The total amount of rental collected from the leased asset is treated as income in the books of the lessee. Any type of fixed assets can be leased, for ex: construction equipments plant and machinery, aircraft, ships, computers, office machines motor transport, agriculture equipment, heavy industrial equipments etc.

Objectives of Leasing

Lease financing may enhance the growth of industries and services. The main objects of leasing are presented below.

(a) To carry on the business of buying selling, leasing, letting on easy payment system.

(b) To promote industrial finance in the form of advance, deposits or lend money, securities and properties to or with any company, body corporate firm, person or association falling under the same management.

(c) To manage the funds of investors by investing in various avenues.

(d) To carry on and undertake the business of portfolio investment in equity shares, preference shares, stocks and debentures.

(e) To provide a package of investment/merchant banking services by acting as managers to public issues by underwriting securities.

Steps Involved in Leasing: A contract of lease provides a person an opportunity to use an asset which belongs to another person (lessor). The following steps involved in a leasing transaction may be summarised as follows:

(1) At the first instance the lessee has to take a decision regarding the required asset. Then he has to select the manufacture or the Supplier before Selecting the type of machine he takes. If he considers various factors.

(2) In the second stage the lesser enters into a lease agreements with the lessor, the lease agreement contains some obligations return the lessor and lessee.

  (a) during the lease period, the lease is irrevocable

  (b) The quantum amount of periodical rental during the lease period.

  (c) details of any option to renew the related to purchase the asset at the end of the basic lease period. If there is no indication about the option to the lessee, the lessor takes possession of the asset and is entitled to any residual value.

  (d) The details regarding the responsibility for the payment of cost, maintenance and repairs taxes, insurance and other expenses.

  (e) The payment of expenses in lease transactions depend up on types of lease agreement.

(3) After fulfilling the formalities like signing of lease agreements, the lessor approach the manufacturer or supplier to supply the asset.

(4) On receipt of the order from the lesser, the lessor makes payment to the supplier after the asset has been delivered, tested and accepted by the lesseer.

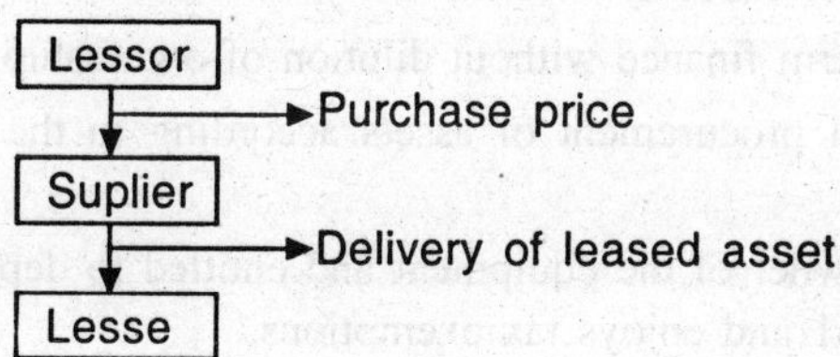

The above chart explains the relationship between supplier, lessor and lessee.

The following factors give more meaningful explanation for thorough understanding about the lease finance.

(a) Fair market value.

(b) Residual value.

(c) Net lease.

(d) Operating lease.

(e) Financial lease.

The fair market value can be defined as "The price at which property can be sold in an arms length transaction".

The Residual value may be defined as the value of a leased asset at the end of the lease period.

The operating lease is relatively short term phenomenon. It is often cancellable at the option of the Lessee with proper notice. It does not give lessee all the benefits and risks that are associated with the asset. The lessor is responsible for the maintenance of asset, insurance and all other relevant expenditure. The operating lease is shorter than the assets economic life. The lessor does not recover its investment during the first lease period. It includes the leaving of copying machines, computers hardware, word processors and automobiles.

Financial lease can be defined as "A long term lease that is not cancellable. It is long term in nature and a sources of financing. It is also known as capital clause" It may be leveraged or non-leveraged. It is non-cancellable and requires maintenance, property taxes and insurance which it to be provided by the lessee. Financial lease is availed in connection with leasing of land, buildings, Industrial plants and warehouses.

In this lease, all the risks incidental to the ownership of the asset and the benefits which arise will be transferred to the lessee except the legal title. The lease should bear cost of insurance, repairs and maintenance of the end lease. The financial lease is also known as "Close end lease" The rental payments are fixed and that it also ensures return of the total investment at a predetermined rate of return. Financial lease is one which satisfies one or more of the following conditions.

(a) The owner of the assets transfer title to the user at the end of the lease period.

(b) The lease facilities on option to buy the asset at a bargain price.

(c) The lease period shall be equal or greater that 75% of the estimated economic life of the asset.

(d) At the commencement of the lease the present value of the minimum lease payments equal or exceeds 90% of the fair value of the property.

Factors Influencing Leasing: Now a days lease financing very popular boost the productivity of industry. It is more helpful in implementation of expansion modernisation and diversification. A number of factors account for the lesser preferring arrangements. These factors account for the lessers preferring arrangements. These are:

(a) The user is willing to pay more to reduce his debt.

(b) It provides 100% deductibility of cost.

(c) It facilitates long term finance without dilution of ownership.

(d) It allows piecemeal procurement of assets according to the needs and convenience of the user.

(e) The lessor is the owner of the equipment and entitled to depreciate on lease rates under the Income tax act 1961 and enjoys tax exemptions.

(f) It facilitates after tax cost of leasing could be less than the after tax cost of equity financing.

(g) The lease is self liquidating position.

(h) There is no interruption in the utilisation of machines and equipment except in case of default by the lessee.

(i) The use/lessee need not make heavy investment in the asset on lease and it utilises this margin for working capital of the firm.

Types of Lease Financing

The following are the financial lease arrangements:

(A) Sale and lease back.

(B) Direct leasing.

(C) Leveraged leasing.

A. Sale and Lease Back: Under this method, a business concern sells an asset to one of their party, and this party leases it back to the firm. The equipment/asset sold at its market value. This method is very popular with the firms which facing short term liquidity crunch. The firm receives the sale price in cash and gets the right to use the asset during the basic lease period. The firm makes regular rental payments to the owner/lessor. The title of the asset lies with the lessor. He is also naturally entitled to any residual value of the asset might have at the end of the lease period. This method is beneficial both for the user and owner. The owner gets the benefit in terms of tax credit due to depreciation. The sale and lease back can be defined as "The sale of an asset with the agreement to immediately lease it back for an extended period of time".

B. Direct Leasing: According to this method, the vendor sells the asset to the lessor who in turn leases it to the lessee. The lessee/user use the asset along with a contractual obligation to make lease payments to the lessor. The major types of lessors are manufactures, financial companies, banks, Independent leasing companies and firms. In this type of leasing, a company acquires the use of asset which unable to own previously. A wide variety of direct leasing arrangements meet various needs of firms.

C. Leveraged Leasing: Leveraged leasing is popular in financing big assets such as aircrafts, heavy machinery equipment. These assets require large capital outlays. Such a type of lease arrangement involves three parties. The lessee, the lessor and the lender. The lesser contracts to make periodic payment over the basic lease period and in return, is entitled to the use of the asset over that period of time. The lessor procures the asset according to the terms of the lease and finances the acquisition in part by an equity investment the remaining is provided by lender The Lessor is entitled to deduct all depreciation charges associated with the asset. Leveraged leasing can be defined as " A lease arrangement in which the lessor provides an equity portion consusally to 40% of the leased assets cost and third party lenders provide the balance of the followings.

Advantages of Leasing: Investing in capital assets generally needs substantial cash outlay. It is not possible always to incur the heavy expenditure of amount in cash.

Therefore the leasing is the best alternative source of financing. Leasing facilitates as a source of long term funds that can be used for acquisition of capital assets. The advantages of leasing can be presented as follows:

1. Leasing facilitates a firm without heavy amount of investment to utilise the asset. The firm is only to make periodical rental payments. Leasing saves considerable funds for alternative uses.
2. Leasing provides assets in cheaper and faster sources. Leasing organisations are providing finance faster than the bankers. The rental payments are fixed according to the expected profits.
3. The Lessee role is limited to utilise the assets for a fixed period of time and he does not bare the risk of absolesence of the asset
4. Leasing arrangement is more beneficial to small firms because they are unable to raise the funds on account of paucity of financial resources.
5. Leasing facilitates lower rental charges to the lessees, because of the tax advantages
6. According to the lease agreement, the lessee gets a right to use the asset without title. The asset acquired on lease basis does not become a part of the property of the lessee. The rental payments are revenue nature, the lessee can be avail the change of several government incentives.

Disadvantages: Acquisition of assets through lease finance result the same disadvantages which are presented in below.

(a) In lease financing the lessee never gets the ownership of the asset. He gets only a right use there is no change for the sale of the asset.

(b) In the lease agreement, if the lessee is in default position in rental payments the lessor will take over the asset and the lesser has no right to prevent him from doing so.

(c) In the lease financing system the lessees has no right and no power in possession of the asset

CREDIT RATING

Introduction

The Debt Market in India has been increasing. The number of companies that have been borrowing directly from the capital market also create a healthy situation. The industrial environment has become more and more competitive demanding for the supply of funds The investors have been increasing towards the capital market and they find a borrowers assurance in the timely payment of interest and principal. At the present situation, the investors need an independent and credible agency which judges impartially and gives a better direction in this regard. The quality of debt obligation depends upon many factors. The companies needs are different, the investors expectations are different; the financial institutions environment is different for making the investment decisions. For a thorough understanding of the concept of credit rating, it is necessary to know the definitions given by some authorities in this field. It is a process of evaluating the risk associated with the credit instrument.

Definition: Credit rating can be defined as "Credit Rating is designed exclusively for the purpose of grading bonds according to their investment quality.

According to Moody's Investor Service: Ratings are designed exclusively for the purpose of grading according to their investment qualities."

S&P defined the Credit Rating as: "A S&P's corporate or municipal debt ranging is a current assessment of the credit worthiness of on obligator with respect to specific obligation."

The CRISIL has defined the Credit Rating as: 'The crisil rating symbols indicate in a summarized manner crisil's current opinion as to the relative safety of timely payment of interest and principle or a debenture, preference share, fixed deposit or short term instruments".

Credit rating is not a recommendation to the investors/buyers of a financial product. It is not a method of evaluation of the company. It is not a one time evaluation of risk. It has to be done by specialised, expert, reputed, accredited institutions. The rating process is meant for the debt instruments. It do not grade the whole organisation. It is only confined to the financial affairs of the concern. It reflects the issuers financial strength, the soundness of operations, efficiency of top-level management and overall performance of the organisation. Generally the rating firms undertake the task of rating the financial instruments on a request by the organisation issuing that instrument. It is an act of assigning values to the financial instruments by estimating the solvency. The rating reflects the financial status of the company in the market. Credit Rating is just like getting of the ISI Mark to a commodity. It is an observation made by the outside concern regarding the financial capabilities of a firm. Equity shares cannot be rated like bonds, debentures or any debt instrument.

The first credit rating services emerged in U.S.A. in 1909. It was first introduced by John Moody. His ratings become popular with the investors. In U.S.A, the S & P ratings become very popular in 1920. They began to rate the companies and governing bodies issuing bonds to the public. The first credit rating was done by the CRISIL in 1988 in India. The ratings have been the indicators of the current opinion of the relative capability of timely servicing the debts and obligations. Different instruments of the same company may carry different credit rating. The credit rating is highly beneficial to both the investors and the borrowing companies.

The benefits to various parties concerned with the rating are listed below:

(A) To the Investors.

(B) To the Borrowers.

(C) To the Government.

(D) To the Credit Rating Companies.

(A) To the Investors: The following are the advantages to the investors due to the credit rating services.

(1) The investors will get the best quality of information at low cost.

(2) The investor can take the calculated risk in their investments.

(3) The credit rating services encourage the common man to invest his savings in the capital market for getting the higher returns.

(4) CR will provide safeguard against the bankruptcy and other malpracticies by the corporate sector.

(5) CR will guide the investors by rating the instruments to various companies for the investment making decision.

(B) To The Borrowers:

(1) Companies with good rating can enter the capital market confidently.

(2) For sincere and honest corporate buyers, they can raise large resources of funds from the market at cheaper rates.

(3) It can be used as a marketing tool.

(4) The good rating can attract the foreign collaborators.

(5) It is the barometer of financial discipline among the corporate borrowers.

(6) These is no scope for propaganda among the companies during the rise of resources from the market.

(C) To The Government:

(1) Fair and good ratings motivate the investors towards the investment. Therefore the idle fund will be channelized for the productive uses.

(2) Mega issues can enhance the employment opportunities which will be attractted by the credit rating.

(3) It provides protection to the investors without any burden on the part of the government.

(4) It facilitates the formulation of public policy guidelines on institutional investments.

(D) To the Credit Rating Companies:

(1) Honest and impartial credit rating agencies would definitely survive in the market.

(2) The existence and development of the credit rating companies largely depend upon their performance.

(3) The credibility is the life of the rating companies.

(4) There will be tremendous scope for other allied financial services.

Types of Credit Rating

Credit Ratings are of various types, depending upon the needs of the rates. The following are the common types of the credit Rating:

(a) Debentures/Bond Rating.

(b) Commercial Paper Rating.

(c) Equity Ratings.

Debentures/Bond rating is the major business of the credit rating agencies. Rating the debentures/bonds or debt securities issued by a company or semi-government is called Bond rating. Commercial paper means a short term, unsecured promissory note. These papers are generally issued by the large companies. They are very popular in U.S.A. It is mandatory on the part of a company to obtain the rating approved by the rating agency to issue the commercial paper. In USA, there is much demand for rating of these papers. The rating of equity capital is called equity rating. For corporates Debt is Jam, equity is Giner.

According to the Economic Times Reports, the corporate sector raised debt and equity just Rs. 1101 crores, and Rs. 6 crores respectively in the first half of the fiscal year 2001-2002. The debt private placement Market managed more than Rs. 22,500 crores.

Significantly, a total of Rs. 12,272 crores were raised by the AAA rated paper. On the other hand, Rs. 2025 crores of paper was the rated paper. The Corporate Debt Issues became very popular in the, last 3 years. To put the things in perspective Rs. 1,60,000 crores corporate debt was issued in the public issues/structured private placements in the last 3 years. In the first 6 months of the financial years, Rs. 45,00,000 crores worth corporate debt is raised in the global markets. This provides the big picture of the funds availability and potential to grow. Corporate debt issues are preferred to bank borrowing because of flexible structuring with multiple options, floating or indexed interest coupons, better pricing, debenture trustee supervision, credit rating, credit enhancement facilitates the decision-making by the issues and the investors. It provides a better fit on the expectations. Corporate debt issues also help in reaching the retail investors who get a better yield.

Limitations to Ratings: The credit ratings are important to the investment activity in the capital market. But the ratings have the following limitations:

(a) Ratings of the financial debt instruments are only the indicators of risk.

(b) Ratings are only a time-bound gradings of quality of a financial product.

(c) Ratings carry some weight because opinions are made by the experts in the field and poor grade instruments will get flop in the market.

(d) If the rating agencies are not retaining the best talented expert professionals, then the ratings will become undependable.

(e) Rating agencies do not give the ratings of equity.

Credit rating provides a relative ranking of the credit quality of the debt instruments. It does not evaluate about the reasonableness of issue price, possibility of capital gains, liquidity in the secondary market, risk of pre-payment by issue or interest or exchange risks. It is an opinion expressed by an independent professional organisation. It helps the issuer of debt instruments to price their issue correctly and to reach out the potential investors. The credit rating is compulsory for the following cases:

(a) All Non-banking financial companies that have net owned funds of more than Rs. 5 lakhs are required to register with the RBI and get themselves compulsorily credit rated every year.

(b) In case of finance companies which have net-owned funds of less than Rs. 2 crores should get their first credit rating done.

(c) Credit rating is compulsory for issuing the FCDs which have a conversion period of more than 18 months.

(d) Credit rating is compulsory in case of non-convertible debentures whose maturity period exceeds 18 months.

(e) All commercial paper issues will have to be credit rated and the rating should be a minimum of P2/A2/PR2 as the case may be. The rating should not be more than 2 months between the date of rating and the date of issue.

Scope of Credit Rating: The scope of the credit rating in India is restricted the debt instruments. The financial instruments such as debentures, bonds, fixed deposits and commercial papers are rated. But in the developed countries like U.S.A and U.K, the equity shares are also rated. In the present environment, the CR has become an obligation. There is a strong need of the CR in the market. The lack of the information in the market about the issuer and the instrument led to the need for the CR. The corporate sector entirely depends upon the public for the project finance. This has resulted in the issuance of a number of debt instruments. The capital market is dominated by the share brokers and the other intermediaries. Sometimes they canvas for themselves. They motivate the investors in favour of a particular financial instrument. Therefore to overcome this problem, it is necessary for the safety of the investors to rate the debt instruments in the market. If the CR does not exist in the market, the investors may fall in dilemma and there will be chance to cheat the innocent investors. After the introduction of free pricing of securities by the companies, the CR has become a weapon in the hands of the investors to analyse the financial instruments floated by the issuing company.

Objectives of the Credit Rating

The basic objective of the credit rating is to provide the best and low cost information to the investors to take the investment decision, in a particular instrument. The following are the objectives of the credit rating system.

(a) It imposes a financial discipline on the borrowers.

(b) It helps the financial intermediary in discharging the functions relating to the debt issues.

(c) It guides the investor regarding his commitment towards a particular debt instrument for his better returns.

(d) It facilitates the formulation of the public guidelines on the institutional investment.

(e) It may provide adequate funds for the high-rated companies at a low rate of interest.

(f) It lends greater credibility to the financial and other representations.

(g) It encourages transparency of information and better accounting standard.

Credit Rating Process: The credit rating process involves the following procedure:

(1) The issuing company approaches the rating agencies.

(2) On the basis of client needs, rating agency appoints a team of experts to appraise the financial position of the company.

(3) The experts team makes report to the agency after evaluating the clients financial positions.

(4) Credit rating agency submits, its observation about the quality of debt instrument through symbols.

Credit Rating Agencies in India: The credit rating is a specific evaluation about the credit quality of the issuer of securities. It is done for a particular financial instrument. It has assumed great importance for the individual investors, brokers and financial advisers with the expansion of the capital market. The credit rating agencies not only rate the instruments of the private corporate sector but also rate the public sector units debt instruments. The proposed bond issued by the PSUs should be evaluated by the SEBI and the credit Rating Agencies. The permission has been granted with a view of making the PSU bonds more attractive in the market. The credit rating agency does not create a fiduciary relationship between the credit rating agency and the rating users. Unsolicited credit rating exists in abroad. It is based on the information provided by the issuing company. Credit Rating Agencies consider various factors such as risk composition, market situation, operating efficiency, track record, accounting quality, planning and control systems, financial flexibility, profitability, liquidity and asset quality of the issuer company. It completes its task and assigns the grades. The ratings are continuously monitored by the agency and the grades are changed, suspended or withdrawn by it at any time according to the new information. It is not only to guide the investors, fund managers, brokers, financial analysts, but it is also used to misguide them which depend on the sincerity and honesty of the agency.

In India, the following agencies are fully involving in the credit Rating activities.

(1) Credit Rating and Information Services of India (Crisil).

(2) Investment Information and Credit Rating Agency of India Limited (ICRA).

(3) Credit Analysis and Research Limited (Care).

(4) Onida Individual Credit Rating Agency of India Limited (ONICRA).

CRISIL

Credit Rating and Information Services of India (CRISIL) was established in January 1988. It was floated by ICICI, UTI, LIC, GIC, Asian development Bank and SEBI. The other shareholders include the Housing Development Finance Corporation, General Insurance Corporation, Bank of India, Bank of Baroda, Allahabad Bank, Indian Overseas Bank, Canara Bank, UCO Bank, Standard Chartered Bank, Vyshya Bank, Bank of Madura, Bank of Tokyo, Grindlays Bank, Hongkong and Shangai Banking Corporation, Deutsche Bank and ICICI Bank.

Its objective is to undertake the assignments of the credit rating based on the proposal made by the issuer companies for their financial products. They are debentures, fixed deposit programmes, commercial paper programmes, short term borrowing instruments and preference shares The CRISIL rating is necessary for the authorities and banks. The CRISIL provides not only the credit rating but also renders services to the corporate sector covering the topics like structure of the industry, degree of competition and business situations.

The CRISIL entered a stategic alliance with the Standard and Poor's in 1995. Its services include information services, infrastructure services and consultancy. Its information services offer the corporate research reports. It also prepares CRISIL 500 Index which will be very useful to the corporate sector. Its consultancy working render assistance to power, telecom and infrastructure financing. It rates the rupee dominated debt instruments. The CRISIL informs its current opinion about the relative safety of timely payment of interest and principal on the rated financial instruments. It assigns rating after considering all the factors of the borrowing company; and also about the issuer company. It reviews the principal business fundamentals like competitive position, interest burden and tax aspects. The CRISIL's investment grade rating symbols are categorised into "Highest safety" "High safety" and "Adequate safety".

CRISIL's Rating Process: The CRISIL takes the assignment from the issuer company for a fixed rate of charges for rendering the services. It appoints highly skilled and talented experts, equity analyst, market specialists, the evaluation of a particular financial instrument is carried out by professionally qualified persons. The evaluation includes data collection, financial analysis and discussions with key personnel in the company. The company should render all the latest information to the CRISIL on the desired aspects at the time of requesting for a rating. The CRISIL assigns the work to a team of experts which will be responsible for carryingout the rating assignment. The team obtains all the information and interacts with the company officials. The findings of the team are presented to an internal committee of the CRISIL. Thereafter the findings will be transmited to the rating committee. It consists of some directors (outside persons) to take a decision on the rating. The ratings assigned by the rating committee will be informed to the issuing company. In this juncture, if the company wants to submit any information, it can do so. The rating process involves a careful analysis and strict confidentiality of the clients information. The directors of the issuing company do not get involved in the rating process. Once the confirmation of rating is made by the CRISIL, it is obligated to monitor the rating over the life of the debt instrument.

The CRISIL also undertakes the ratings of the mutual funds. The company offers a package to the corporate customers. Credit rating has a much broader connotation than the financial analysis. The crisil card which is a corporate data based on 500 companies with individual cards on each company. It also runs the CRISIL BANK CARD which is a data base on 30 public and private sector banks. The CRISIL ECOSCAN is a data base providing the data on major sectors of the Indians economy. It also published the CRISIL VIEW, which publishes its opinion on the credit quality of a company and provides indepth analysis of published information. This bulletin is meant for institutional investors and brokers. The CRISIL has also established Advisory services division to provide more services to the needs of the corporate sector and investor community. The division offers the following services.

(a) Funds mobilization for the public sector undertakings.

(b) Evaluation of privatization/disinvestment to PSUs.

(c) Upgrading of credit evaluation for banks and other lending institutions and also monitoring system.

The CRISIL has carried out evaluation for a few state governments and state electricity boards for the use of private investors planning infrastructure projects. State governments and municipal bodies seek to raise funds from the debt market. These issuers are expected to use the ratings in future.

CRISIL's Rating Process: The credit ratings are based on the latest information which are provided by the issuer company to the rating agency. In evaluation of credit worthiness of a issuer company's financial product, it will analyse all the factors regarding the business analysis and financial analysis for manufacturing concern. It also undertakes the credit rating to the assessment of financial companies.

The CRISIL generally rates the following concerns:

(A) Evaluation of Manufacturing companies.

(B) Evaluation of financial companies.

A. Evaluation of Manufacturing Companies:

The credit rating process involves a detailed exercise regarding the financial data or the company. The evaluation also includes visits to factories and offices of the company for holding discussions with the company officials, bankers, creditors, auditors for clarity of information. The evaluation process requires the desk work, out door work and other allied works. The key factors usually considered in the evaluation of a manufacturing concern are:

1. Business analysis.
2. Financial analysis.

1. Business Analysis: It is the most important factor in the evaluation of a manufacturing concern. Under this analysis, it will examine about the risks involved in the operation of the smooth functioning of the company. The Risk is the essence of the valuation of a firm. The value of a financial asset depends upon their return and risk. The risk is measurable. The risk can be defined as "the variability of returns from those that are expected. The total risk of a firm consists of two components which are presented below:

Total risk = systematic risk + unsystematic risk.

The systematic risk means, it effects the overall market of the nation such as the changes in the economy, tax reforms introduced by the government, or a change in the world environment. The systematic risk is inescapable. It is caused by a wide rage of factors like recession, war, and structural changes in the economy. It is also known as "Market Risk or Non-diversifiable Risk". It can be defined as" the variability of return on stocks or portfolios associated with the changes in return on the market as a whole". Another risk component is unsystematic risk which is unique to a particular company or industry. The unsystematic risk is independent of economic, political and other factors. It accounts between 60 to 75% of the total risk involved in a company. It can be defined as the variability of return on stocks or portfolios not explained by general market movements. It is avoidable through diversification. It can be reduced or ever eliminated through diversification. It is also known as "Non-market risk or diversifiable risk". ***Industry risk*** means the level of competition from others in the market. It also includes the market factors such as demand and supply position of a particular product, the government policies regarding the industry position. ***Marketing risk*** means the association of competitive advantages or disadvantages, market share, selling and distribution channels. The review also includes the quality of customer service rendered by the client. The customer service is the highly influential factor in enhancing the sales volume of a commercial enterprise. The review also focuses on the operating efficiency of the firm. The volume of profitability will depend upon the utilisation of the capacity installed. The mass production of the commodities will boost up the gross marginal profit. The CRISIL team will steady about the locational advantages, raw material availability, prices, labour relationship and product cost structure. The industrial peace is the other important element in the evaluation of a firm. The better industrial relationship between the management and labour definitely enhances the production level of a manufacturing concern which reflects in the profitability of a company. The team also studies, the cost reduction control system which is followed by the issuer company. They undertake the close study about the legal position of the company. The position includes the terms and conditions of the prospectus, the trustees and their duties and responsibilities and the system of timely payment. It also observes the protection against forgery and frauds. The experts will also evaluate the management and promoters position. It examines the selectors of the track record of manager, top level executives and promoters.

They also study about their qualifications and experience regarding the business capabilities. The team also observes the planning and control system adopted and implemented by the company. They study about the business capacity to adjust with the flexibility of latest environment. The CRISIL team examines the fundamental analysis. Under this analysis the crisil will examine the liquidity, profitability and solvency position of the rating company.

2. Financial Analysis: Under this, the CRISIL examines the earning capability, accounting quality, financial status and cash flows. The factors which reflect the financial analysis are presented below:

(a) Earning capability.

(b) Accounting standards.

(c) Financial status.

(d) Analysis of cash inflows.

(e) Management evaluation.

(a) Earning Capability: The team examines the earning capability of the issuer company. They will also assess about the future earnings and earning protection. Earning protection is the most important element in the growth of a company. Retaining the present earnings is the most problematic aspect in the business environment. Business is uncertain and no one knows what happens tomorrow. Though the present earning is low, the future capabilities may turn the status of the company. It is based on the general economy of the state. It is also based on the quantum level of production.

(b) Accounting Standards: The profits of the corporate sector are declared by the Accounting Department. It fully involves in book-keeping and maintenance of records. After completion of the routine process of the accounting, the company submits its reports to the shareholders in the AGM. The over-statement/understatement of profit depends on the maintenance of the accuracy of accounts. The team verifies the auditors qualification and experience they also examine the method of income recognition. The team also scrutinises the method of inventory valuation and depreciation policies and thorough check will be done on all the items of the balance sheet on both sides.

(c) Financial Status: The team analyses the financial plans of the company and their implementations. The procurement of funds and disbursing of funds are the important tasks of the finance department. The team also examines the efficiency of the finance wing in all aspects. They verify profitability ratios, proportion of interest and net profit.

(d) Analysis of Cash Inflows: The CRISIL team investigates the debt equity mix and variability of future cash flows. They assess the requirement of the fixed capital and working capital. The adequacy of cash flows reflect in working capital management, current ratio, inventory to sales etc. The financial flexibility is also examined in terms of capital financing plans, flexibility in financing through alternate method etc.

(e) Management Evaluation: The experts examine the relation of track records with promoters, managers and top-level executives. The experts also examine the abilities, skill, talent, dynamism, managerial skill, problem solving capacity, implementation of the plans, decision making capacity etc. They evaluate the targets, company philosophy, and financial strategies. They also check the capacity of adjust with flexibility. Foresight is the most important element to a commercial enterprise. The top-level management should have a top-level foresight about the company's future that enables the company to move in a right direction.

B. Evaluation of Financial Companies

The following aspects are covered by the CRISIL experts while evaluating the financial companies.

(a) Regulatory and structural environment.

(b) Fundamental analysis.

They closely examine the structure and regulatory framework of the financial system. The rules and regulations are to be followed by the finance companies. SEBI, RBI, MOF, ROC and department of Company Affairs are the statutory concerns with reference to finance companies. The RBI issues guidelines to the finance companies & the SEBI gives direction to the finance companies in regard to the mobilization of resources. The trends in regulation/deregulation and their impact on the company will be examined.

The fundamental analysis will be done by the CRISIL's group of experts. They will analyse the liquidity position of the company, asset quality, profitability and financial sound etc. The team also checks the interest and the tax sensitivity of the company. The analysis of the liquidity position includes capital structure, matching of assets and liabilities, the top level management policy on liquid assets in relation to financing commitments and refunding of deposits. The capital structure refers to the make up of a firms capitalization. It represents the mix of different sources of long term funds in the total capitalization of the company. The term capital structure is used for the mix of capitalization. The experts should undertake the pattern of capital structure in case of the newly established companies. The company can undertake any of the following methods.

(a) Capital structure with equity shares only.

(b) Capital structure with both equity and preference shares.

(c) Capital structure with equity shares and debentures.

(d) Capital structure with debentures, equity and preference shares.

The choice of an appropriate capital structure depends on a number of factors such as nature of the company's business, regularity of earnings, conditions of the market, attitude of the investor. The other factor in the fundamental analysis is the asset quality. The asset quality depends on the company's credit risk management. The committee undertakes a system for monitoring the credit affairs of the company. They also examine the sectors risk involved in a particular position. The exposure to the individual borrowers and management of credit will be studied in depth. The profitability analysis is the other factor in the valuation of the finance companies. The team also examines the historic profits and fund deployment. The quantum of revenues arose on the non-fund based services. The team observes the financial position of the company. It closely observes the financial average of the company. They examine the exposure of interest rate changes. They observe the hedge against the interest rate and tax law changes.

The valuation is carried out by the CRISIL team which effects the credit evaluation of the company. The companies will present information to the crisil on the areas which are discussed above at the time of requesting for a rating. The credit rating process generally involves a period of 4 to 6 weeks. The ratings of the company deposits are made compulsory under the new companies bill of 1993. The RBI also made it compulsory for all the NBFCs registered with it to get themselves rated before they approach the public. The crisil adopted the conventional rating system which is available in the advanced countries. The symbols are assigned by the CRISIL for different financial instruments in different ways. The CRISIL undertakes the ratings of various financial instruments as follows:

(a) Rating of debentures.

(b) Rating of fixed deposit schemes.

(c) Rating for short term instruments.

(a) Rating of Debentures

	SYMBOLS	*MEANING*
I	AAA (Triple A) Highest Safety	The Debentures which are rated AAA are judged as the highest debt instrument in timely payment of interest and principal. This ratings reflect that the issue is fundamentally very strong.
II	AA (Double A) High Safety	The Debentures which are rated AA are judged as high safety of timely payment of interest and principal amount. They differ slightly from AAA issues.
III	A Adequate Safety	The debentures which are rated A are judged as adequate safety of timely payment of interest and principal amount. But any change in circumstances adversely affects such issues more than the above graded categories.
IV	BBB Triple B Moderate Safety	The debentures which are rated BBB are judged to provide adequate safety of timely payment of interest and principal amount of present. But changes in circumstances are likely to lead to a weakened capacity to pay interest and repay the principal than higher rated categories.
V	BB Double B Inadequate safety	The debentures which are rated BB are judged to carry inadequate safety of timely payment of interest and principal amount. The uncertainties will lead the issuer to inadequate capacity to make timely interest and principal payments.
VI	B High Risk	The debentures which are rated as B category are treated as greater susceptibility to default. Though currently interest and principal payments are met any adverse situation would lead to lack of ability or willingness to pay interest or principal amount.
VII	C Substituted Risk	The debentures which are rated "C" category reveals that the investment made in this instrument make it to default. Therefore the investor should think twice before investing in this category of debt instruments. The timely payment of interest and principal is possible only if favourable situations continue.
VIII	D Default	The debentures which are rated "D" are in defaults. If the company is in areas of interest or principal payments. It is doubtful on maturity. These debentures are more speculative and the interest may be received only on liquidation or reorganization.

(b) Rating of Fixed Deposits Schemes: The fixed ratings made by the crisis carry the symbol 'F'. The ratings are classified as follows:

	Symbol	*Meaning*
I	FAAA Triple A Highest Safety	The fixed deposits which carries "FAAA" reveals the degree of safety regarding the prompt payment of interest and principal amount.
II	FAA F Double A High Safety	This rating reveals that the amount of interest and principal will be paid within a stipulated period of time.
III	FA Adequate Safety	This rating carries the degree of safety regarding the timely payment of interest and principal amount. The financial position of the company is satisfactory.
IV	FB Inadequate Safety	This rating reveals that the company is not in a position to pay the interest and principal amount within a stipulated period of time.
V	FC High Risk	This rating indicates the payment of interest and principal amount is doubtful.
VI	FD Default	This rating indicates that the issue is either in default or expected to be in default and there is no assurance for the payment.

(c) Rating of Short Term Instruments: The short term instruments are also rated by the CRISIL. The ratings of the short term instruments commence from the letter "P". The ratings have been presented below:

	Symbol	*Meaning*
I	P_1 Highest safety	The ratings reveal that the interests payment will be made according to the time and the principal amount will be paid in time. The investment in this instrument is very safe.
II	P_2 High safety	This rating indicates that the payment of interest within a stipulated time and the principal amount will be paid on maturity.
III	P_3 Adequate safety	This rating reveals the degree of safety for the timely payment of interest and principal amount.
IV	P_4 Inadequate safety	This rating reveals that the timely payment of interest on the instrument is minimal.
V	P_5 Default	This rating indicates that the company is unable to refund the amount on maturity.

The overall ratings of the CRISIL to various debt instruments is as follows:

	Debentures	*Fixed Deposits*	*Short term instruments*
AAA	Highest safety	FAAA Highest safety	P_1 Highest safety
AA	High safety	FAA High safety	P_2 High safety
A	Adequate safety	FA Adequate safety	P_3 Adequate safety
BBB	Moderate safety	FB Inadequate safety	P_4 Inadequate safety
BB	Inadequate safety	FC High risk	P_5 Default
B	High risk	FC Default	
C	Substantial risk		
D	Default		

The investors must decide themselves how much of their portfolio would like to invest either in fixed deposits or debentures of a company. After taking the decision, he must identify what risk he is willing to take. The above ratings indicate the degree of risk level in various instruments for rating the debt instruments, the CRISIL charges the fee as follows:

Fee Structure for Fixed Deposits: The fee charged by the CRISIL is of two kinds:

1. Initial Rating Fee.
2. Annual Surveillance Fee.

The Initial rating fee will be charged by the CRISIL as 0.05% of the outstanding amount of the fixed deposits subjected to a minimum of Rs. 40,000/-. The minimum fee for the initial rating will depend on the nature and size of the operations of the company. The Annual Surveillance fee is 0.03% of the outstanding amount of the fixed deposits subjected to a minimum of Rs. 25,000 per annum. The charges are subjected to change. But it will not exceed 0.05% of the outstanding amount of the fixed deposits. In addition to the above charges, any additional expenses incurred (if any) will be charged to the client by the CRISIL.

Fee Structure for Debentures Programme: The fee charged by the CRISIL in case of debentures are as follows:

(a) Initial rating fee will be charged as 0.10% of the amount of debenture issue size and it is subjected to a minimum of Rs. 40,000/-. The minimum fee for initial rating depends on the nature and size of the company.

(b) The Annual Surveillance fee will be charged as 0.03% of the amount of debenture issue size and it is subjected to a minimum of 25,000 per annum. The charges are subject to change.

(c) Any other expenses incurred by the CRISIL will be charged to the client company.

Fee Structure for Commercial Paper Programme: The fee charged by the CRISIL in case of commercial paper programme is presented below:

(a) Initial rating fee will be charged by the CRISIL as 0.10% of the amount of the commercial paper permissible under the RBI guidelines. The minimum fee for the initial rating will depend on the nature of the business and the size of the operations.

(b) Surveillance fee should be charged as 0.03% of the amount of the commercial paper permissible by the RBI. It is subjected to a minimum of Rs. 25,000 per annum. The rates are subject to change. All other expenses will be charged if any incurred by the CRISIL.

The CRISIL offers services to the clients and the evaluation of information will be kept under confidential until the announcement of rating officially.

INVESTMENT INFORMATION AND CREDIT RATING AGENCY OF INDIA [ICRA]

The ICRA was promoted by the Industrial Finance Corporation of India. It has come into existence in August 1991. It has its headquarters at Delhi. It was an independent company limited by shares with an authorised share capital of Rs. 10 crores. The paid up share capital of the agency is Rs. 5 crores. The IFCI has contributed 26% of the share capital and the balance is contributed by UTI, GIC, PNB, Central bank of India, Bank of Baroda, UCO Bank etc. The ICRA is the second rating agency in India. It is established as a competitor to the CRISIL. The shareholders of the agency are as follows:

IFCI, UTI, SBI, PNB, LIC, GIC, EXIM, Allahabad Bank, Canara Bank, Central Bank of India, Citi Bank, Indian Bank, Indian Overseas Bank, Oriental Bank of Commerce, UCO bank, UBI, United Bank of India, Vyshya Bank Ltd, Housing Development Finance Corporation Ltd., Infrastructure Leasing and Finance Service Ltd., and 20th Century Finance Corporation Ltd., It is managed by a board of directors. The board consists of seasoned professionals with finance and economic background. The board includes nominees from the government and the RBI.

The main objective is to assess the credit instruments and assign a grade constant to the risk associated with such instrument. The rating is based on an objective analysis of the information provided by the client company. The objectives of the ICRA are as follows:

(a) To guide the investors in making well-informed investing dicisions

(b) To assist the issuer company in raising funds from wider investors.

(c) It acts as a marketing tool.

(d) To create a healthy competitive environment in the capital market.

Services: The ICRA provides services in credit assessment and general assessment. The credit assessment involves in taking up of assignments for the credit assessment of the companies intending to use the same for obtaining the financial assistance from commercial banks, Financial Investment Institutions, Factoring companies and Financial service companies. The assessment reveals the opinion of the ICRA. The General assessment provides services. If any banker approaches, it prepares as per the requirements of the general assessment report. The service is also likely to be useful to the NBFC's for the purpose of merger, amalgamation, acquisition, joint venture, collaboration and factoring of debt. It does not specify any symbol in respect of general assessment. It provides a report on various aspects of the companies.

The Rating Process in ICRA: The Rating process will commence when the issuer company approaches the ICRA for rating the issue. Then the ICRA informs to the issuer company about the required data. Therefore the desired data will be procured by the client. A group of annalists takes up the work of collection of data and procures information from the books and records of the concerns. The rating agency also interacts with the executives. For the purpose of rating the issuer, the ICRA will utilise the service of Inhouse research and data base as well as Industry studies of reputable agencies. It ensures the confidentiality of all the information collected during the rating process. Once the Rating Agency assigns a symbol, the agency should monitor the rating till redemption/repayment of the debt obligation. The following are the various steps involved in the Rating process of the debt instrument.

(a) The rating process is not restricted to any examination of the financial measures.

(b) The analytical framework is divided into several categories.

(c) The analysis indicates the financial discipline of the issuer company.

The ICRA undertakes a close observation of various parameters. They are presented below.

1. Industry Risk.
2. Market Position.
3. Operating Efficiency.
4. Evaluation of Management.
5. Accounting Standards.
6. Financial Capacity.
7. Cash flow Adequacy.

1. Industry Risk: The experts team examines the Industry growth. It also observes the evaluation of strength and weakness of the unit. They also gather information about the intensity of competition to the issuing company. The volume of the market, the No. of players in the market, the market share of each company, threat from the new entrants, technology used by the competitors/new entrants. The risk means the chance of occurring a future loss.

2. Market Position: The experts team assesses the market situation. They examine the abilities which would increase the market share of the company. They will assure the future estimation of the sales while meeting the market players. The competition from the existing and the new companies will be taken into consideration. They study about the brand-strengths and also the position of the issuer company in the market. The team examines the price variability of different brands which are available in the market. The experts should analyse the distribution and marketing strengths of the issuer company. They also examine the weakness of the marketing/distributional channel. A detailed study will be done by the experts to strengthen the effective channel of distribution.

3. Operating Efficiency: The group of experts analyse the production schedules of the issuer company. They examine the abilities which are going to reduce the cost. They procure and compare the data regarding the installed capacity and produced units. A high level of production capacity utilisation enhances the level of production and reduces the cost of production per unit. They compare the issuer company data with the competitors data. Then they draw a conclusion about the efficiency of the issuing company. The team examines the labour relationship in the issuer company. Industrial peace is the most important factor to achieve the substantial target. The access to raw material also shows substantial cost savings in the form of transportation charges. The latest sophisticated technology also saves the time and the cost more effectively.

4. Evaluation of Management: The experts closely evaluate the track record of the issuer company management. They check the capabilities of the top-level management, their qualifications and experience. Their technical, financial and managerial capabilities are closely monitored and evaluated by the team of experts. They may check the process of the systems for financial and strategic planning. They will review about the control process and budgeting of the issuer organisation. The team also examines the credibility of the management plans and the extent of commitment towards achieving the organisational goals. They also study about the organisational structure and layers in the management with the operating environment and management strategy. They focus on the skill and quality at different levels of workers and managerial capacities. The team checks the process of delegation of authority and succession about the planning.

5. Accounting Standards: The team thoroughly checks the accounts which are maintained by the Accounts Department of the company. Financial statements are the most important factors. They decide the results of the issuer company. The profits that are declared by the company depends on the accuracy of the accounts. The quality of the accounts depends on the Accounting standards.

6. Financial Capabilities: The team focuses on the financial strength of the issuer company. They evaluate the financial position of the company by observing the parameters like EPS, PE Ratio, Gross Profit Ratio, Earnings before Depreciation and Tax, Profit before Tax, Profit after Tax, Capital structure, cost of capital, Management of working capital, the Ratio between the current Assets and Fixed Asset, the Return on the capital employed, the Financial Leverage, Liquidity Ratio, cash flows, the Balance between the Accounts receivable and payable and the other areas.

7. Cash Flow Analysis: The information required for evaluating the cash flow analysis is the magnitude and variability of future cash flows relative to the credit affairs. The experts also examine the cash flows from the group companies.

All the above parameters will be closely monitored by the team of experts. The required information will be submitted by the issuer company to the rating agency. Sometimes, the rating agency can procure the data from its own sources. However, the following parameters may be gathered through visits (a) Internal Sources and (b) External Sources.

The information from the ***Internal Sources*** is the most important element in the assessment of a firm. The team visits the plant and discussions are made with the factory officials regarding the type of technology they adopted. They examine the records of all the departments like Production, Finance, Accounts, Marketing and Personnel. The internal sources are procured from operating personnel, top management and business unit heads.

The information which is available from the outside perview of the company is known as ***External Sources.*** The information can be procured from the bankers of the issuing company. They provide all the financial aspects of the issuing company on request. The Auditors of the issuing company provides a valuable information and guides the rating firm. The competitors are also one of the important external sources of the information. The competitor reveals all the facts regarding the strength and weakness of the issuing company. The Industry expert is another source of information. Their suggestions and criticism play an important role in the evaluation of a firm. They judge the position of the issuing company in the market. The Industry experts know all the aspects of the market players and their comments will influence the image of the company. The suppliers can have the first hand information about the issuing company. They tell about the utilisation capacity and technical details of the issuing company. The Dealers/Distributors of the issuing company can have the first-hand information about the market position. They are able to know the pulse of the customers and their behaviour. The dealers can suggest about the production modification, if necessary. The customers have the final authority to comment about the product, its quality, price and availability etc. The consumer is the king in the market.

Rating Scale: The primary objective of the ICRA is to provide guidance to the investors and creditors in determining the credit risk associated with the debt securities. The rating reflects an independent, professional and impartial assessment of such credit risk. The ratings are not the recommendations to buy/sell/hold securities. It is a symbolic indicator of the current opinion/comment about the capability of the issuer company. It is an objective analysis of the information and classification obtained from the concerns. The ICRA rates Long term, Medium Term and Short Term Debt Instruments. The rating symbols and their implications are as follows:

1. Long Term Instruments Rating Scale
2. Medium Term Instruments Rating Scale
3. Short Term Instruments Rating Scale

1. LONG TERM INSTRUMENT RATING SCALE [DEBENTURES, BONDS, PREFERENCE SHARES]

Symbol		*Description*
LAAA	Highest Safety	The Debentures/Bonds/PS which are rated as "LAAA" Indicates fundamentally very strong position. There is no risk factor involved in this issue of debt instrument. In any adverse situation also, the degree of safety does not affect the timely payment of principal and interest as per the terms and conditions of the issue.
LAA	High Safety	The debt instruments which are rated as "LAA" reveals the risk position of the issue. In this category, the risk factors are moderate and may vary slightly. The fundamentals are very strong that the perspect of the timely payment of principal and interest will be paid even in an adverse situation.
LA	Adequate Safety	The financial instruments which are rated as "LA" reveals that the risk factors are more variable and greater in periods of economic stress. The protective factors are very average. If any adverse situation arises, it may effect the timely payment of principal and interest as per terms of the issue.
LBBB	Moderate Safety	The debt instruments which are rated as "LBBB" indicates considerable variability in the risk factors. The protected factors are below average. Any adverse changes in business/economic circumstances are likely to affect the payment of principal and interest as per the terms of the issue.
LBB	Inadequate Safety	This symbol reveals the payment of principal plus interest on an adequate safety. The timely payment of interest and principal are more likely to affect the present or prospective changes in business or economic circumstances. The protective factors fluctuate in case of changes in the economic conditions.

LB	Risk Prone	The debt instruments which are rated as "LB" indicates that the protective factors are narrow. Obligations may not be fulfilled. Any adverse changes in the business or economic conditions results in inability to redeem the debt as per the terms and conditions of the issue.
LC	Substantial risk	The rating symbol "LC" reveals that the investment in this issue involves risk and timely servicing of debts is possible only in case of continuous existence of favourable circumstances.
LD	Default	The rating reveals that it is an extremely speculative instrument. It is already in default in the payment of principal and interest. As per the terms, it is expected to default. The refund is possible only on liquidation or reorganisation.

2. MEDIUM TERM RATING SCALE [FIXED DEPOSIT]

MAAA	Highest Safety	The instruments which are rated as "MAAA" indicates the highest safety. It is the best one as per the terms in the timely payment of principal and interest.
MAA	High Safety	Investment in this category of instrument is very safe. The prospect of timely servicing the interest and principal as per the terms is high but not as high as in the above category.
MA	Adequate Safety	The rating reveals the timely servicing of the interest and principal is adequate. Debt servicing may be affected by the adverse changes in the business or economic conditions
MB	Inadequate Safety	The timely payment of interest and principal are more likely to be affected by the future uncertainties.
MC	Risk Prone	The rating reveals that the susceptibility to default is high. Any adverse changes in the business or economic condition result in inability to service the debts on time as per the terms and condition of the issue.

3. SHORT TERM INSTRUMENT RATING SCALE [COMMERCIAL PAPER]

A_1	Highest Safety	The rating indicates that the prospect of timely payment of debt/obligation is the best.
A_2	High Safety	The relative safety is lower than A_1 rating
A_3	Adequate Safety	The prospect of timely payment of interest instalment is adequate. The fundamental strength may affect any adverse change in the business or economic conditions.
A_4	Risk Prone	The rating indicates that the degree of safety is low. Any adverse change in business or economic conditions results in default.
A_5	Default	The rating indicates the default position or the position which is expected to default.

SCHEDULE OF FEE:

I.	Initial Rating Fee:	a. Fixed Deposits – 0.05% of the outstanding amount of the fixed deposit. b. Debentures – 0.10% of the issue size. c. Commercial Paper – 0.10% of the issue size.
II.	Annual Surveillance Fee:	0.03% of the outstanding amount.
III.	Credit Assessment Fee:	0.05% of all the outstanding debts as on the last balance sheet. It is subjected to a minimum of Rs. 25,000 and maximum of Rs. 5 lakhs.
IV.	General Assessment Fee:	A flat fee of Rs. 50,000 for each company is to be assessed. It is subjected to a maximum of Rs. 10.00 lakhs. This however does not apply to the general assessment of overal portfolio fees for which would be decided. According to the nature and volume of the work involved.

Note: 1. All fees are non-refundable.

2. The minimum and maximum fee rating should be Rs. 50,000 and Rs. 20.00 lakhs respectively.
3. The minimum and maximum Surveillance fee should be Rs. 30,000 and Rs. 10.00 lakhs respectively.
4. In case of convertible debenture, no rating fee should be payable for a part of the debenture if they are convertible within a period of 12 months.
5. All other pocket expenses are to be charged to the issuing company on actual basis.
6. The fee for other rating instruments/services would be decided on the basis of financial instruments.
7. A separate fee should be charged for involving in the preparation of the project appraisal.

The ICRA ratings are helpful to the borrowing companies to access the capital market and money market for raising a larger volume of resources from a large investor's base. If the ratings are done by the ICRA, the less known companies are also able to access the capital market and money market.

CREDIT ANALYSIS AND RESEARCH LTD. [CARE]

Introduction

The Care is the third credit rating agency in India. These ratings are accepted by the SEBI, the RBI and the Government of India. It is promoted by the IDBI and other institutions. The regulatory authorities have made rating a necessary grading for entering into the market. It is incorporated as a Public Limited Company under the Indian Companies Act. It has commenced its operations in Oct. 1993. The Care is run by the Board of Directors. It consists of eminent persons with a varied experience in financial services and allied areas. The company is an autonomous body and enjoys full freedom in its operations and the ratings are also accepted by the market. It maintains its integrity, independence and credibility. It offers a wide range of products and services in the field of credit information and equity research. It has had the benefit of close relations with the reputed credit rating agencies in the world.

The shareholders of the CARE includes IDBI, UTI, Canara Bank, Credit Capital Venture Fund India Ltd., Sundaram Finance Ltd., The Federal Bank Ltd., The Vyshya Bank Ltd., First Leasing Company of India Ltd., ITC Classic Finance Ltd., Kalimatta Investment Company Ltd., The Investment Corporation of India Ltd., Varuna Investment Ltd., 20th Century Finance Corporation Ltd.

The CARE fully involves in rating all types of Debt Instruments such as:

1. Fixed Deposits
2. Certificate of Deposits [CDs]
3. Commercial Paper [CP]
4. Debentures
5. Structured Obligations.

It also undertakes general credit analysis rating of the corporate sector for the use of lenders, bankers and other institutions. The ratings and symbols are presented below for a detailed discussion.

LONG TERM AND MEDIUM TERM INSTRUMENTS

Symbol	*Explanation*
CARE AAA CARE AAA FD/CD/SO	The debt instruments which carries "CARE AAA" ratings are considered to be the best quality, carrying no investments risk. This category of debt instruments are protected by the stable cash flows with good margin. This is a strong payment signal even in an adverse situation.
CARE AA CARE AA FD/CD/SO	The debt instruments carrying this grading are judged to be of high quality by all standards. These are also categorised as high investment grades. They are rated lower than securities. Any change in the assumption may have a greater impact. The risk involved in this category of securities are quite different from "CARE AAA" instruments.

CARE A CARE A FD/CD/SO	The debt instruments which are classified as "CARE A" ratings are considered as Upper medium grade instruments. It has many favourable investment attributes. Adequate safety is available for principal and interest amount of the debt instrument. Adverse situation of the business/economic conditions may not show an impact on this issue.
CARE BBB CARE BBB FD/CD/SO	The debt instruments which are classified as "CARE BBB" ratings are considered as investment grade. It indicates the adequate safety for the payment of interest and principal amount at the time of rating. Any adverse situation in business or economic conditions may more likely to weaker the debt servicing capability compared to the high rated instruments.
CASE BB CARE BB FD/CD/SO	This category of debt instruments are considered to be speculative within adequate protection for interest and principal payments.
CARE B CARE B FD/CD/SO	The debt instruments are classified as susceptible to default. The adverse situation in business or economic conditions lead to default.
CARE C CARE C FD/CD/SO	These debt instruments carry high investment risk. This may lead to default in the payment of interest and principal.
CARE D CARE D FD/CD/SO	These categories of investments are in the least safety position. They are either in default or likely to be in default.

Short Term Instruments

The debt instruments rated by the CARE for Short Term Instruments are presented below:

(a) PR – 1

(b) PR – 2

(c) PR – 3

(d) PR – 4

(e) PR – 5

(a) PR – 1: The Short Term Instruments which are rated as "PR – 1" reveals that the issuing company has superior capacity for the repayment of short term promissory obligations. Issuers of such type of instrument will normally be characterised by the leading market positions in established industries. High rates of returns on funds are possible.

(b) PR – 2: The issue of these categorised instruments have strong capacity for the repayment of short term promissory obligations. These issuers have the characteristics which resemble the PR – 1 Instruments but to a lessor degree.

(c) PR – 3: The instrument have an adequate capacity for the repayment of short term obligations. The variability in earnings and profitability results in changes in the level of debt protection.

(d) PR – 4: These category instruments have minimal degree of safety regarding the timely payment of short term promissory obligations and the safety is likely to be adversely affected by the short term in less favourable conditions.

(e) PR – 5: This category of instrument is in default or it is likely to default on maturity.

Credit Analysis Rating

CARE – 1: This rating reveals the excellent capability in debt management. The management of debt can be done more effectively. Such business concerns will be normally market leaders in the respective sector.

CARE – 2: This rating indicates a very good debt management capability. These companies are normally regarded as close to those rated as CARE – 1, but with a lower capability to withstand the changes in assumptions.

CARE – 3: This rating reveals that the company has good capability for debt management. These companies are regarded as minimum grade. The assumptions that do not materialise may impair debt management capability in future.

CARE – 4: The rating indicates the satisfactory capability for debt management. The capacity to meet the obligations is likely to affect the short term adversity or in less favourable conditions.

CARE – 5: The rating deals with the poor capability of the debt management. These companies are in default or likely to default in meeting their debt obligations.

CARE – 6: The debt management capability covers a wide range of services. The ratings are expressed only in limited number of symbols. It assigns + or - signs to be shown after the assign rating to indicate the relative position within the brand covered by the rating symbol.

Sources: Information Pamphlet issued by the CARE.

SUMMARY

The investment preferences of households have changed dramatically. In India, the household sector accounts over 80% of the GDP which plays a significant change in their investment preferences. The financial development occurred because of the technical invention and through the mode of popular joint stock company. The joint stock form made the large scale industry possible by collecting large amounts of capital. The capital is generated out of savings leading to investment which is apart of the financial system.

In the entire globe, the trend has been for the individual investor shifting from the direct investment in equities to the mutual fund route. The mutual fund offers safety and it provides services to the investors. The Unit Trust is established and obliged to buy-back units whenever and investor wants to sell them. Mutual savings banks are popular in U.S.A. They help the small investors to obtain high return low risk contributions from their scientifically managed portfolios. The small investors cannot directly invest in the instruments such as certificate of deposits, commercial paper and treasury bills. The Mutual funds facilitated advantages to the unit holders. In India all the funds have to be registered with the SEBI. The government of India permitted the commercial banks to enter into this segment. It also permitted the private sector to set up Money Market Mutual Funds. Mutual funds can be classified as by category and by scheme wise. The investment trust is a financial institution. If collects a small amount of investible funds from a large number of investors. The Mutual funds have five key parties. They are the sponsors, the board of trustees, the AMC, the custodian and the unit holders. They can be classified into 5 categories. They are based on the ownership status, schemes of operating, portfolio objectives and location. The mutual funds should be registered with the SEBI. The SEBI regulations from 1 to 75 informs about various rules and regulations to be followed by the Mutual funds. The RBI issued guidelines for the commercial to enter into the mutual fund sector. The Mutual funds should also follow the guidelines issued by the company law. Risk is the essence of the valuation of a financial instrument. The return which we select is different from the return which we receive. The total risk consists of systematic risk and unsystematic risk. The risk can be classified into several ways like Default risk, Liquidity risk, Maturity risk, Inflation risk, purchasing power risk, currency risk, exchange risk, Business risk. The Risk indicators involve Mathematics. Beta is the most common measure of the risk. Alpha is a performance measure adjusted for the risk. The Net Asset value is determined by the stock market prices. The stock markets are influenced by the supply, demand and other factors. A good Mutual fund always works for the satisfaction of the unit holders. The Mutual funds in India should be evaluated on the valuation norms, traded securities, non-traded securities and Rights shares. Every Mutual fund in India should work according to the general obligations like maintenance of proper books of accounts, audit, annual report, disclosure norms, procedure for action in case of default. The winding up of the mutual fund can be done by the trustee. The trustee of the mutual fund should call a meeting of the unit holders to consider and pass necessary resolutions by the simple majority of the unit holders present. On the completion of the winding up, the trustees should forward to the SEBI.

Venture capital is a type of financial intermediary emerged in U.S.A. It provides finance or risk capital to unregistered, high risky technology oriented units. The VC contributes in the form of equity upto 49% of the total equity. The V.C firms have to appoint Marketing specialists in Product launching to capture the market. The methods of financing are practiced by the V.C.F. shares and debts. The present technological revolution has witnessed the re-emergence of small and medium firms. The introduction of appropriate changes in the company law and Banking law are considered available to enable their successful participation in the current technological revolution. The union finance Ministry has issued guidelines for the establishment and functioning of the venture capital activities. Income tax Act 1961 deals with the tax concessions to the VCFs. Entrepreneurship introduces a critical element of dynamics into an economic system. In India, the VCFs are located in Mumbai, Delhi, Kolcutta and Bangalore. Leasing has emerged as a source of long term financing of the corporate sector. A lease represents contractual agreement between 2 parties.

Footnotes:

1. Van Horne Fundamentals of Financial Managements, P.No. 91, 1997 PHI.
2. IBID 95.
3. Van Horne Fundamentals of Financial Managements, P No. 95, 1997 PHI.
4. Van Horne Fundamentals of Financial Managements, P.No. 100, 1997.
5. Ibid., p. 100.
6. Ibid., p. 109.
7. N. Gopal Swamy, *Inside Capital Market*, Deecan Publication, P.No. III-166.
8. Amit Kumar, *The Economic Times*, Dt. 7/2001.

❑ ❑ ❑